HANDBOOK OF RESEARCH METHODS IN BEHAVIOURAL ECONOMICS

This book is dedicated to the late John Tomer, my good friend and fellow traveller on the journey towards developing a more pluralistic, open-minded and empathetic economics and academic community. John passed on 7 December 2019. You'll be sorely missed.

Handbook of Research Methods in Behavioural Economics

An Interdisciplinary Approach

Edited by

Morris Altman

Dean, University of Dundee School of Business, and Chair Professor of Behavioural and Institutional Economics and Co-operatives, University of Dundee, Scotland, UK

Cheltenham, UK • Northampton, MA, USA

© Morris Altman 2023

Cover image: Chris Yang on Unsplash

All rights reserved. No part of this publication may be reproduced, stored in a retrieval system or transmitted in any form or by any means, electronic, mechanical or photocopying, recording, or otherwise without the prior permission of the publisher.

Published by
Edward Elgar Publishing Limited
The Lypiatts
15 Lansdown Road
Cheltenham
Glos GL50 2JA
UK

Edward Elgar Publishing, Inc.
William Pratt House
9 Dewey Court
Northampton
Massachusetts 01060
USA

A catalogue record for this book
is available from the British Library

Library of Congress Control Number: 2022952293

This book is available electronically in the **Elgar**online
Economics subject collection
http://dx.doi.org/10.4337/9781839107948

Printed on elemental chlorine free (ECF)
recycled paper containing 30% Post-Consumer Waste

ISBN 978 1 83910 793 1 (cased)
ISBN 978 1 83910 794 8 (eBook)

Printed and bound in the USA

Contents

List of contributors		viii
1	Introduction to the *Handbook of Research Methods in Behavioural Economics* *Morris Altman*	1

PART I BEHAVIOURAL ECONOMICS METHODS IN GENERAL

2	Behavioural economic methods *Gerrit Antonides*	14
3	Behavioural economics: What have we missed? Exploring 'classical' behavioural economics roots in AI, cognitive psychology and complexity theory *Steve J. Bickley and Benno Torgler*	32
4	Assumptions in economic modelling: How behavioural economics can enlighten *Beryl Y. Chang*	60

PART II REAL-WORLD ECONOMICS

5	Realeconomik: Using the messy human experience to drive clean theoretical advance in economics *Gigi Foster and Paul Frijters*	80
6	The common-sense economy *Pascal Moliner and Patrick Rateau*	104

PART III BEHAVIOURAL MACROECONOMICS

7	Behavioural methods for macroeconomics: Modelling investment *Michelle Baddeley*	120
8	The business cycle and the cycles of behavioural economics *Tobias F. Rötheli*	137

PART IV BEHAVIOURAL LABOUR ECONOMICS AND THE THEORY OF THE FIRM

9	Behavioural labour economics *Morris Altman*	153
10	Some implications of x-efficiency theory for the role of managerial quality as a key determinant of firm performance and productivity *Sodany Tong*	172

| 11 | Behavioural theories of the firm with a focus on x-efficiency and effort discretion: Implications for analysis
Morris Altman | 190 |

PART V MONEY AND BEHAVIOURAL ECONOMICS

| 12 | The psychology of money
Agata Gasiorowska and Tomasz Zaleskiewicz | 209 |
| 13 | Taking financial advice: Going beyond making good decisions
Tomasz Zaleskiewicz and Agata Gasiorowska | 226 |

PART VI BEHAVIOURAL APPROACHES TO HEALTH ECONOMICS

14	Bounded rationality, imperfect and costly information and sub-optimal outcomes in the sports and health and fitness industries *Hannah Rachel Josepha Altman and Morris Altman*	243
15	Empirical methods and methodological developments in economics of health and health behaviour: A discussion of theory and applications *Nazmi Sari*	268
16	The behavioural impact of pandemics: Incomplete markets and the supply chain *David A. Savage and Derek Friday*	285

PART VII 'EMOTIONS', MORALS AND BEHAVIOURAL ECONOMICS

17	Economics of trust: Its nature, measures, determinants and application *Jefferson Arapoc*	307
18	Intuition and behavioural economics: A very brief history *Roger Frantz*	321
19	Conserve the planet, not empathy! Revising the empathy conservation framework *Natalia V. Czap and Hans J. Czap*	332
20	Behavioural economics of morality and sustainability *Shinji Teraji*	353
21	Antisocial punishment *Alexis V. Belianin*	369

PART VIII EVALUATION AND FORMATION OF BELIEFS AND PREFERENCES

| 22 | Auction methods of valuation and the endowment effect
Fang-Fang Tang | 377 |

23	Statistical approaches to the analysis of belief patterns *David Leiser*	400
24	Motivated preferences *Matthew G. Nagler*	412
25	Might ambiguity exist when none seems to exist? *Mina Mahmoudi, Mark Pingle and Rattaphon Wuthisatian*	428

PART IX BEHAVIOURAL APPROACHES TO POLICY

26	Norms, networks, nudges: Non-traditional approaches to improve healthy behaviours *Irene Mussio and Angela C.M. De Oliveira*	444
27	Bridging psychology and sociology: Towards a socio-ecological perspective in behavioural economics and policy *Noah V. Peters and Lucia A. Reisch*	473

Index 493

Contributors

Hannah Rachel Josepha Altman holds a BCOM BHS MPhil and is in the final stages of her PhD in behavioural sports economics at the Queensland University of Technology Business School (QUT) in Brisbane, Australia, under the supervision of Benno Torgler and Rob Robergs. Her external supervisor is Brad Humphreys of West Virginia University. She prides herself on real-world motivated research that stems from ten years of international fitness industry experience. She has co-edited a pioneering book in behavioural sports economics and a number of peer-reviewed book chapters on behavioural sports, decision-making and supply and demand determinants in the health and fitness industry given imperfect information.

Morris Altman is a Chair Professor of Behavioural and Institutional Economics and Cooperatives and Dean of the University of Dundee School of Business, University of Dundee, United Kingdom. He is also an Emeritus Professor at the University of Saskatchewan, Canada. Morris earned his PhD in 1984 from McGill University in Montreal, Canada. He is widely published in behavioural and institutional economics, theories of the firm, cooperative organisations and economic history. He is former President of the Society for the Advancement of Behavioral Economics (SABE), former editor of the Journal of Socio-Economics and co-founder of the Review of Behavioral Economics.

Gerrit Antonides is an Emeritus Professor of Economics of Consumers and Households at Wageningen University, the Netherlands. He has published research papers and textbooks in the areas of economic psychology, consumer behaviour and behavioural economics, particularly about the financial behaviour of consumers and households, food consumption, environmental behaviour, mental accounting and time preference.

Jefferson Arapoc is an Assistant Professor in Economics at the University of the Philippines Los Baños. He is also a research fellow in the Centre for Behavioural Economics, Society and Technology (BEST) at the Queensland University of Technology (QUT), Australia. His research interests include topics on behavioural economics such as nudging and prosocial behaviour. In addition, he has engaged in both academic research and consultancy projects for both government and multilateral organisations. Lastly, he is a co-founder and the managing editor of Usapang Econ, an advocacy project in the Philippines that aims to make economics fun and relatable to the general public.

Michelle Baddeley is a behavioural economist interested in themes of behavioural macroeconomics, behavioural finance, labour economics and social influences on household decision-making. She has a Bachelor of Economics and a BA (Psychology) from the University of Queensland, Australia and a Master's/PhD in Economics from the University of Cambridge, UK. Her recent books include *Behavioural Economics – A Very Short Introduction* (Oxford University Press, 2016), *Behavioural Economics and Finance* (Routledge, 2nd edition in 2018) and *Copycats and Contrarians – Why We Follow Others and When We Don't* (Yale University Press, 2017).

Alexis V. Belianin is a Laboratory Head and Senior Research Fellow at the International Laboratory for Experimental and Behavioural Economics, Higher School of Economics University, Moscow, Russia.

Steve J. Bickley is a PhD researcher in the School of Economics and Finance and the Centre for Behavioural Economics, Society and Technology (BEST), Queensland University of Technology, Australia. He also holds an engineering honours degree (electrical) from the Queensland University of Technology. His primary research interest lies in complexity economics, artificial intelligence and quantitative social science.

Beryl Y. Chang is an award-winning author in economics and finance. She has been a published author and referee for numerous journals in areas of applied micro- and macroeconomics, interdisciplinary and behavioural economics, international and financial economics, industrial organisation and risk management. Ms Chang has given courses in financial economics, corporate finance, behavioural economics and international financial markets, among others, at New York University and Columbia University. Her recent lectures and research interests include quantum economics, applied micro-macroeconomics, behavioural economics, international/financial economics, industrial organisation and risk management. At the industry level, Ms. Chang served as an economist and senior officer at the US Trust, Bank of America NA, JPMorgan Chase & Co. and Citigroup Inc., while successfully managing the risk performance of large credit and investment portfolios during her tenure for over a decade. She also served as a credit risk consultant for international institutions.

Hans J. Czap is an Associate Professor of Economics at the University of Michigan-Dearborn and an Associate Director of the Behavioral and Experimental Economics and Policy (BEEP) Lab. He has a PhD in economics from the University of Nebraska-Lincoln. His research interests include finding new ways to increase environmental protection using behavioural economics, identifying determinants of corruption and its impact on society, and the effect of practice-based approaches to teaching on trust and cooperation.

Natalia V. Czap is a Professor of Economics at the University of Michigan-Dearborn and the Director of the Behavioral and Experimental Economics and Policy (BEEP) Lab. She has a PhD in economics from the University of Nebraska-Lincoln and a PhD in mathematical economics from Moscow State University, Russia. Her research focuses on empathy conservation, the effect of empathy nudging on pro-environmental behaviour, gender differences in environmental decisions, as well as the impact of practice-based learning on cooperation, trust, perception of effort and happiness. She serves as a treasurer and member of the executive committee of the Society for the Advancement of Behavioral Economics.

Roger Frantz is an Emeritus Professor of Economics at San Diego State University, USA.

Derek Friday holds a PhD from the University of Newcastle, Australia, and has over ten years of experience in supply chain management and project management as an academic and practitioner. Derek is a chartered member of the Chartered Institute of Logistics and Transport Australia, where he volunteers on various management committees. He has worked as a consultant and project manager for Inland Transportation and Related Services projects with the United Nations missions in Africa. Derek's interdisciplinary research focuses on issues of uncertainty and risk in supply chain management. Specific issues of interest include how interfirm collaboration capabilities reinforce the resilience of supply chain ecosystems under multiple and simultaneous stressors: cybersecurity, climate change, geo-political tensions, consumer behaviour, pandemics and natural disasters.

Gigi Foster holds a PhD in Economics from the University of Maryland and a BA in Ethics, Politics and Economics from Yale University, CT. She researches education, social influence, corruption, lab experiments, time use, behavioural economics and Australian policy, publishing in specialised, cross-disciplinary and lay outlets. Named 2019 Young Economist of the Year by the Economic Society of Australia, Gigi engages regularly outside the academy as one of Australia's leading economics communicators, including via co-hosting *The Economists* on ABC Radio National. She is also a nationally awarded tertiary educator.

Paul Frijters holds a PhD in Economics from the University of Amsterdam, Netherlands, and a Master's in Econometrics from the University of Groningen, Netherlands. He contributes to many areas of social scientific inquiry and is in the top 1 per cent of cited economists. Paul worked in Australia for 15 years and was the Research Director of the RUMiCI Project, a collaborative international investigation of rural-to-urban migration in China and Indonesia tracking 20,000 individuals for many years. In 2009 he was voted Australia's best young economist by the Economic Society of Australia. His recent work includes developing the WELLBY, a new tool for wellbeing policymaking that has been adopted by the UK bureaucracy.

Agata Gasiorowska is an Associate Professor affiliated with the Center for Research in Economic Behavior at the Faculty of Psychology in Wroclaw of SWPS University, Poland. She received a PhD in Management from the Wroclaw University of Technology in 2003, a PhD in Psychology from the University of Wroclaw in 2009, and a Habilitation in Psychology from SWPS University in 2014. She has undertaken research on the psychology of money and consumer behaviour and is interested primarily in money attitudes, financial literacy and market mentality.

David Leiser is a Full Professor of Economic and Social Psychology in the Department of Psychology at Ben-Gurion University, Israel, and Dean of the School of Behavioral Sciences at Netanya Academic College, Israel. He was educated in mathematics (Hebrew University of Jerusalem, BSc), adult education (University of Illinois at Urbana Champaign, MSc) and psychology (Université de Genève, Switzerland, PhD). He is Co-Founder and Deputy Director of the Centre for Research on Pension, Insurance and Financial Literacy at Ben-Gurion University. He is a former President of the International Association for Research in Economic Psychology, and of the Economic Psychology Division of the International Association for Applied Psychology. His current work centres on the analysis of lay understanding in the economic domain and on its significance for public policy.

Mina Mahmoudi is a Lecturer at Rensselaer Polytechnic Institute, Troy, New York, USA.

Pascal Moliner is a Full Professor of Social Psychology at the University Paul Valéry-Montpellier 3 (Epsylon Lab.), France. He has directed the Laboratory of Social Psychology and the Doctoral School (Territories, Time, Societies and Development) of this university. He currently directs the master's degree in Cognitive and Socio-Cognitive Dynamics. He is the author of numerous books and articles on social representation theory, social cognition and identity.

Irene Mussio has a PhD in Resource Economics from the University of Massachusetts Amherst and is a Postdoctoral Research Associate at the Newcastle University Business School (Economics) and the UKRI GCRF Living Deltas Research Hub, UK. Her work lies in the intersection between environmental, health and behavioural economics. Her research topics involve mental health, individual preferences and the experience of risk, including risk trade-offs and the impact of climate change on risky behaviours and mortality. More specifically, Irene focuses on the relationship between risk and behaviour using different tools and methods, including economic experiments and economic valuation.

Matthew G. Nagler is a Professor of Economics at the City College of New York and the Graduate Center at the City University of New York. His research encompasses behavioural economics, social economics and applied microeconomics with a recent focus on individual decision-making and the formation of preferences. He has served on the Social and Behavioral Sciences Team in the Obama White House, and prior to academia served as a staff economist at the US Federal Communications Commission and as an antitrust consultant.

Angela C.M. de Oliveira had a PhD in Economics from the University of Texas at Dallas and is a Professor of Resource Economics at the University of Massachusetts Amherst. Her research examines what makes decision-makers different from each other and how this can be accounted for by policy. She uses controlled laboratory techniques to determine the robustness of how individual and societal differences affect behaviour.

Noah V. Peters is a PhD Researcher at the University of Cambridge, UK. With a background in sociology, politics and economics, his research fuses insights from all areas of the social sciences. He is particularly interested in the effects of social stratification on economic decision-making and the distributional impacts of behavioural public policy. Noah advocates mixed-methods research and applies both quantitative and qualitative research techniques.

Mark Pingle is a Professor of Economics at the University of Nevada, Reno. His research in behavioural economics has focused on understanding how different bounds to rationality influence the decisions people make and how they make decisions differently in different situations. He has also focused on exploring how boundedly rational people cope with uncertainty, especially ambiguity. He is a past president of the Society for the Advancement of Behavioral Economics. He is a current or past associate editor for the *Journal of Economics Behaviour and Organization*, the *Journal of Behavioral and Experimental Economics* and the *Review of Behavioral Economics*.

Patrick Rateau is a Full Professor of Social Psychology at the University Paul Valéry-Montpellier 3 (Epsylon Lab.), France. He is the author of numerous books and articles on social representation theory and methods, social memory and environmental psychology.

Lucia A. Reisch is the El-Erian Professor for Behavioural Economics and Public Policy at the University of Cambridge, UK. She is a behavioural economist with a PhD in economics and social sciences and one of Europe's leading academic experts in behavioural insights-based policies. She has published widely cited papers on sustainable consumer behaviour, behavioural insights and consumer policy.

Tobias F. Rötheli is a Professor of Macroeconomics at the University of Erfurt, Germany. His research focuses on the bounded rationality of decision-makers, particularly regarding the formation of expectations and combines experimental and econometric analyses.

Nazmi Sari earned his PhD in Economics at Boston University, MA. Currently, he is a Professor of Economics at the University of Saskatchewan, Canada, and a faculty associate at the Canadian Center for Health Economics, University of Toronto. Dr Sari's research programmes have focused on provider reimbursements and healthcare financing reforms; economics of sports and exercise; quality and efficiency issues in hospital markets; economics of smoking; and economic evaluation of specific healthcare interventions and programmes. His research has been published in economics, health economics, health policy and health sciences journals and has been supported by several funding agencies including the Canadian Institute of Health Research, Saskatchewan Health Research Foundation and the US Centers for Medicare and Medicaid Services.

David A. Savage was an Associate Professor of Behavioural Economics at the University of Newcastle, Australia, until his sudden death in June 2021. His research focused on decision-making in disasters, extreme environments, life-and-death situations, and high-stress work or play environments. While this stems from a behavioural economics viewpoint, it extends into the broader social sciences, seeking to marry behavioural aspects of the social sciences, including supply chain management, to the empirical rigour of economics.

Fang-Fang Tang has a PhD in Quantitative Economics and Informatics from the University of Bonn, Germany (under the supervision of Reinhard Selten) and is a Professor of Economics, Finance and Marketing at the National School of Development and BiMBA, Peking University, China. Tang is among the 'Most-Cited Chinese Researchers', ranked by Elsevier, in the category of 'Business, Management and Accounting' (2014–2020, one of the only two from Peking University ranked in this category all these years) and 'Theoretical Economics' (2021) – the only one in Mainland China who has been cited most in both the categories of 'Business, Management and Accounting' and 'Theoretical Economics'.

Shinji Teraji is a Professor of Economics at Yamaguchi University, Japan. He holds a PhD degree in Economics from Kobe University. His research interests include behavioural economics, institutional economics, economic methodology and post-Keynesian economics. He has published peer-reviewed articles in the *Review of Political Economy*, *International Review of Economics*, *Mind and Society*, *Journal of Socio-Economics* and *Research in Economics*, among others. His latest books are *Evolving Norms: Cognitive Perspectives in Economics* (Palgrave Macmillan, 2016), *The Cognitive Basis of Institutions: A Synthesis of Behavioral and Institutional Economics* (Academic Press, 2018) and *Behavioral Public Economics: Social Incentives and Social Preferences* (Routledge, 2021).

Sodany Tong is an economist trained in New Zealand and Australia. She is a PhD graduate in Economics from the University of Newcastle, Australia. Since 2014, her work has focused on the implications of managerial quality in firm performance and productivity. Her main research focus is on x-efficiency theory and productivity determination. She has worked collaboratively with various government departments in New Zealand and is an active Western Economic Association International member.

Benno Torgler is a Professor of Economics in the School of Economics and Finance and the Centre for Behavioural Economics, Society and Technology (BEST), Queensland University of Technology, Australia. His primary research interest lies in the area of behavioural economics, but he has also published in journals with a political science, social psychology, sociology and biology focus.

Rattaphon Wuthisatian is an Associate Professor in the School of Business at Southern Oregon University, USA.

Cameron Xu is entering Cornell University, NY, where he will major in Statistics. He has a strong interest in behavioural economics, data science and economic modelling. In particular, he is interested in the use of agent-based economic modelling to predict economic events, and he is interested in the intersection of big data with economics.

Tomasz Zaleskiewicz is a Professor of Psychology at the SWPS University of Social Sciences and Humanities, Wroclaw, Poland. His research interests include decision-making under risk and uncertainty, risk perception and the psychological aspects of financial decision-making. His current research projects concern the psychological consequences of people's engagement in market relationships and the role of mental imagery in decision-making under risk. He is a co-editor of the book *Psychological Perspectives on Financial Decision Making* (Springer, 2020) and a co-author of the book *Human Behaviour in Pandemics: Social and Psychological Determinants in a Global Health Crisis* (Routledge, 2022).

1. Introduction to the *Handbook of Research Methods in Behavioural Economics*
Morris Altman

INTRODUCTION

This book comprises 27 original chapters that exemplify behavioural economics methodology in many of its dimensions. They demonstrate how behavioural economics can provide insights on a variety of economic issues and inform policy as well as contributing to an enriched and nuanced understanding of human behaviour in an economic context. These chapters take us well beyond the narrow focus of traditional economics on prices and incomes as the core determinants of economic behaviour and outcomes in the economic realm, but also with regards to the strictly non-economic realm. The approach in this book is to incorporate chapters that take different behaviouralist approaches and or methodologies – a pluralistic approach to behavioural economics (see also Tomer 2007). This includes analytical narratives provided by economic psychologists who engage important economic questions from the perspective of various tools afforded to us in the psychology analytical toolbox (Lewis, Webley and Furnham 1995). However, most chapters in the book have been crafted by economists. Overall, I've taken an agnostic approach in constructing this book, which provides readers with a broader perspective on possible methodologies one can adopt to address an array of economic and related questions.

Herbert Simon (1959, 1978, 1986, 1987), was one of the first scholars to challenge conventional neoclassical or mainstream economics from a robust methodological perspective. For Simon, what was of vital importance was the extent to which economic models are built on realistic behavioural assumptions (Altman 2006). By realistic, Simon refers to whether the model's simplifying assumptions are reality-based. Simon argued that conventional economics paid little if any heed to the realism of its modelling assumptions. And, it is important to note that by behavioural Simon refers to limitations of humans' computational capabilities as well as limitations or opportunities created by an individual's decision-making environment. This environment can incorporate imperfect, asymmetric and costly information as well as transaction costs, for example, where the latter is a significant component of North's (1990) new institutional economics as well as of Williamson's (1975) (a colleague of Simon) and of Coase's (1937) theory of the firm. The decision-making environment can also incorporate differences in bargaining power across decision-makers (critical to the 'old' institutional economics (Commons 1931) championed by Galbraith (1952, 1973)).

These realities can result in sub-optimal outcomes, not predicted by conventional economics. And choices made by individuals can even persistently deviate from conventional economic predictions. In addition, individuals might be motivated by preferences not typically incorporated by conventional economics into the preference function of individuals such as fairness, relative positioning, altruism, peer pressure and interest in firm survival or relative success as opposed to profit maximisation.[1] These differences can also generate deviations from conventional economic predictions. Hence the importance of non-economic variables in determining choice behaviour.

Also, of considerable importance to behavioural economics is that modelling that bears the realism of one's modelling assumptions in mind can ultimately provide one with a more robust *causal* model. Even if the conventional model generates a 'good' or 'excellent' analytical prediction (a high correlation coefficient often being an excellent proxy), this good fit may simply represent a spurious correlation and will, therefore, be a highly misleading representation of reality. Such a spurious correlation can, therefore, also generate serious errors in policy, having detrimental real-world effects. A behavioural model with more robust assumptions, tested against reality, not only yields good or excellent predictions but also yields a much more robust causal analysis than the conventional methodological approach. For Simon, economic analysis is not about good predictions, rather it is fundamentally about robust causal analysis. Also, one might argue that if one structures one's analysis using a conventional model without considering alternative models with more realistic underpinning modelling assumptions, one's modelling can be completely undermined by severe omitted variable bias. The conventional methodological results in one constructing a highly misleading descriptive and causal analytical narrative.

AS-IF BEHAVIOURAL ECONOMICS METHODOLOGY

Not all behavioural economists abide by this reality-matters-for-assumptions methodological perspective. There are behavioural economists who add non-economic independent variables to determine if the revised model provides a better fit or a higher correlation. If it does, then this more pluralistically attuned model is proffered as a substitute for the conventional price-focused model. The same could be done if the revised model has the same fit as the conventional model. One could then assume that individuals behave in a manner consistent with more behaviouralist-attuned assumptions.

This type of as-if modelling in some ways follows the methodological leanings of Friedman (1953) wherein one searches for the best fit, the best analytical prediction, not necessarily paying keen attention to the realism of one's modelling assumptions (Berg and Gigerenzer 2010). However, this approach can represent an important first step in helping to identify alternative variables that are not purely economic in nature that can contribute to explaining human behaviour. They can also help filter out or in behavioural and non-behavioural variables that are unlikely to be a good fit.

ASSUMPTIONS, PREDICTIONS AND CAUSALITY

This is a methodological approach that builds on some of Friedman's methodological contributions but breaks with his approach by explicitly considering and modelling non-economic variables, which can be a critical building block of a behavioural economics–informed analytical narrative. A next step would be testing the simplifying assumptions against reality. Even at the first step, which is what most of contemporary economics focuses upon, the pluralist behavioural methodological twist marks an important advance in economic modelling because it considers non-economic causal variables as potentially important causal determinants of choice behaviour.

This focus on analytical prediction irrespective of the model's simplifying assumptions realism is well rooted and articulated by Friedman's (1953) paper on economic methodology. The main point made by Friedman is that being concerned about the assumption one makes should be beside the point, as long as the model predicts well. If it does not, then the model needs to be refined, which might require revising the modelling assumptions. But this in no way implies, for Friedman, that these assumptions should be more realistic. If the prediction is strong, one should assume that individual behaves as if they are acting in accordance with the model's modelling assumptions. For example, Friedman maintains that if one can empirically demonstrate that a firm is maximising profit, then one can assume that decision-makers and, indeed, all firm members, are behaving in a manner consistent with the microeconomic principles of profit maximisation: marginal costs equal marginal benefits. This would be the case even if the firm manager, for example, never ever heard of these concepts.

Practically speaking, what follows logically from this narrative is that if a firm is maximising profit one assumes that economic agents, firm decision-makers, should actually adopt these simple rules of thumb for their firms to be a success. Following the marginal costs, equal marginal benefit should be the *se qua non* for firm success. These theoretical principles also become optimal and rational behavioural norms. However, from the perspective of Simon's methodological perspective on behavioural economics, the question becomes: is this actually how decision-makers behave in successful firms and should these neoclassical theoretical norms be the signpost by which rational agents should behave to garner optimal outcomes (in terms of maximising profits)? Behavioural economics attempts to determine how individuals make successful choices and unsuccessful choices and what are the key determinants of these choices. These analyses help to inform the benchmarks for best practice behaviour given humans' decision-making capabilities and their decision-making environment. Behavioural economics also delves into how capabilities and environments can be reconfigured to improve the choices individuals make given the objectives that they have.[2]

BOUNDED RATIONALITY VS HEURISTICS AND BIASES MODELLING

This brings us to two important specific methodological contributions by Simon (1987): bounded rationality and satisficing. Related to this there is Simon's critique of the neoclassical or conventional economics narrative of rationality. These directly speak to what are the benchmarks for 'best practice' behaviour and the determinants of such behaviour. Simon argues that even with the best of intentions individual *can't* behave in a neoclassically rational manner. The best that they can do is to behave in a boundedly rational manner. This does not mean that individuals are irrational. People are simply not neoclassically rational. Boundedly rational individuals are, in fact, smart (Altman 2020; March 1978) decision-makers.

Bounded rationality refers to best practice behaviour given their limited decision-making capabilities and their decision-making environment, which is typically sub-optimal. These two constraints or parameters are assumed away in conventional economics. Satisficing is Simon's substitute for maximising or minimising such as abiding by a precise marginal benefit equals marginal cost rule in real-world choice behaviour. Satisficing is doing the best that one can, given one's limited decision-making capabilities and one's decision-making environment. Satisficing can involve decision rules that make sense given these real-world parameters. This can involve the use of decision-making heuristics or shortcuts that can significantly deviate from neoclassical norms but are rational or smart given an individual's limited decision-making capabilities and this person's decision-making environment. Neoclassical behavioural norms can even result in sub-optimal outcomes and, in this sense, adopting such norms would be irrational.[3] In behavioural economics, following in the methodological tradition of Simon, what rational behavioural norms are is determined by the context within which one makes decisions. This is a point also reiterated more recently by Vernon Smith (2003). Optimal norms are context determined. They cannot be stipulated in a context-independent manner irrespective of how logically robust such norms might be from a modelling, mathematical or logical perspective.

This early debate on neoclassical rationality still has resonance, especially with regard to the norms that are considered to be both realisable and optimal. And this, in turn, has implications for the type of public policy behavioural economists might recommend which is differentiated from conventional or neoclassical public policy narratives. There are largely two different approaches that evolved in contemporary behavioural economics, with one point of methodological convergence. This is that behavioural economics models or narratives should be a reasonable reflection of how the real world works and that contemporary neoclassical economics is seriously lacking in its relationship with real-world behaviour. The most dominant point of reference stems from the early contributions of Kahneman and Tversky (1979; see also Kahneman 2003, 2011) where they developed their *heuristics and biases* methodological approach. From this perspective, the fact, the reality, that individuals aren't neoclassically rational means that individuals' behaviours are biased and result in their behaviours tending to deviate from neoclassical norms. The baseline for optimality remains neoclassical norms. These biases are to a certain extent due to humans using decision-making shortcuts or heuristics to make their decisions. Furthermore, for the most part, these biases are not correctible and are, rather, bred in the bone. They also present what they consider to be descriptive theories, explaining how people behave, albeit sub-optimally.

This heuristics and biases methodological narrative has given rise to the nudging narrative pioneered by Thaler and Sunstein (2008) wherein individuals should be nudged towards behaving optimally even if and when individuals have a preference for their current modes of behaviour. In the nudging approach, one has choice architects who design the nudges to yield what approaches optimality in outcomes.

FAST AND FRUGAL HEURISTICS

Another approach to behavioural economics relates to the research of Gerd Gigerenzer (2007; Todd and Gigerenzer 2003) and associate researchers who advocated for a fast and frugal modelling of decision-making. This approach overlaps with the research of Vernon Smith (2003) who pioneered the field of contemporary 'experimental economics'. They both agree that neoclassical theory does not offer a robust explanation of human behaviour, but they both concur that, for the most part, human behaviour is effective, efficient, rational and unbiased, even if it deviates from neoclassical norms. Moreover, such non-neoclassical behaviour is, more often than not, normatively *superior* to conventional economic or neoclassical behavioural norms. In other words, heuristics can generate outcomes that are superior to what would be obtained if individuals somehow adhered to neoclassical behavioural norms.

This methodological approach is very much in line with the principle of ecological rationality (Hayek 1952) where current practices should be optimal because individuals adopted these practices in practice, in a specific context, given their knowledge base. Optimal norms are determined exogenously in a context-independent manner. This is a similar methodological approach taken by Smith (2003) wherein, for example, one can locate firms (in an experimental environment) which perform well *because* they have not adopted neoclassical norms whereas firms that behave more or less neoclassically fail. From this perspective, individuals are assumed to be rational (and unbiased) and evolutionary learners (Bayesian updaters) whose choices yield optimal outcomes. This methodological perspective is also consistent with the conventional economic view that inefficiency can't be tolerated on the market. If there are sub-optimal outcomes, then this can be attributed to unnecessary interferences with the market mechanism (apart from market failures) as opposed to any inherent biases on the part of decision-makers.

SMART DECISION-MAKING IN THE REAL WORLD

More in line with Simon's methodological narrative is that individuals are rational (but not neoclassically so), in the sense of being smart or intelligent (see also Altman 2020; March 1978). But this does not imply that their decisions are optimal from a social perspective or even from an individual's perspective (private rationality). Rational individuals can make bad decisions from their own perspective if they don't have the appropriate information and decision-making capabilities. An additional determinant of poor decisions can be the lack of power in the decision-making process.

A further complication would be sociological variables such as peer pressure and 'environmental' factors (Akerlof and Kranton 2010; Becker 1996). Moreover, the mental model that individuals use can affect the decisions they make (Altman 2014; Denzau and North 1994). An inappropriate mental model can yield sub-optimal outcomes. This is particularly important when a mental model provides an inaccurate understanding of how to achieve preferred goals or objectives and the implications of one's decisions. In other words, individuals can end up adopting 'bad' heuristics – not all fast and frugal heuristics need be optimal. However, change these decision-making parameters, and the individual's actual decisions and choices can approach her or his preferred decisions and choices. There is no irrationality here.

From this perspective, one can have rational errors in decision-making. Also, introducing technical changes in the decision-making toolbox, such as calculators and then computers, can dramatically improve individuals' decision-making capabilities as long as individuals are provided with the skill sets to appropriately use the new technologies. Given that real humans are not robotic decision-makers, technology can and has improved our decision-making capabilities. But this factor can be overlooked if one uses a model which assumes that decision-making is optimal from the get-go.

Apart from this, the preferred choices of individuals (their 'utility-maximising' choices) can result in outcomes which are sub-optimal from a social perspective. Here too there need not be any biased decision-making. An important example of this is at the level of the firm where members of the firm hierarchy can maximise their utility in a manner that results in firms operating at a much lower level of productivity than they can given their factor inputs, what Leibenstein (1966) refers to as x-inefficiency. Managers and owners can meet their income targets, their share value targets and their non-monetary targets without their firm being as productive as possible.

The firm can survive and even prosper in protected markets or by cutting costs, such as labour benefits, inside of the firm. Here too one has an example of rational inefficiency. Note that in this narrative the problem is not that members of the firm hierarchy are not employing conventional economic or neoclassical behaviour norms. Rather, it is a function of organising the firm in a manner consistent with their rational preferences which, in turn, are inconsistent with the firm being as efficient as it can be (Altman 1990, 2006).

BEHAVIOURAL ECONOMICS METHODOLOGIES AND POLICY OPTIONS

The different approaches to behavioural economics suggest different sets of policies to generate decisions that will yield relatively optimal outcomes. Over the past decade or so the nudging approach derived from the Kahneman and Tversky methodological platform has become preeminent. A central thread running through this approach is the assumption that individuals are inherently biased and, therefore, require experts (choice architects) to nudge them towards choices that the experts deem to be in the best interest of the individual (these would be considered optimal choices).

This approach to policy is very much albeit not solely oriented towards getting individuals to make choices that are determined by experts. This requires determining which choices are optimal and determining the best, most efficient and effective means of getting individuals to make choices consistent with the experts' preferred choices. There is a bias in the literature towards soft or non-coercive nudging. There is some overlap here with the literature on institutional design.

A focus on institutional design (which refers to the decision-making environment) and on decision-making capabilities is most specific to the bounded rationality approach to behavioural economics, pioneered by Simon. From this methodological perspective, individuals are smart (non-neoclassically rational) but are susceptible to errors in decision-making, even if individuals are not systemically biased. Errors are a function of a sub-optimal decision-making environment and decision-making capabilities that are sub-par. Errors can also be a function of the adoption of incorrect mental models which, in itself, relate to a sub-optimal decision-making environment. In this case, the policy focus is on improving the decision-making environment and individuals' decision-making capabilities. What becomes of vital analytical importance is identifying those specific factors that must be changed in these domains, to reduce the extent of rational errors in decision-making.

In the extreme, the ecological rationality methodological approach is much less interventionist in terms of policy implications. If one assumes that decisions and choices are optimal resulting in optimal outcomes, there is no need for policy intervention. There are no biases that require correcting, decision-making environments do not require any adjustments, and individuals' decision-making capabilities require no improvements.

EXPERIMENTAL AND BEHAVIOURAL ECONOMICS

Academics and policymakers often convolute behavioural and experimental economics. There is also a methodological perspective adhered to by many economists that there is only one way to conduct economic experiments. The correct methodology is typically identified with classroom-type experiments following the protocols developed by Vernon Smith who pioneered contemporary experimental economics (Smith 1962, 1976). What's important to note from a methodological perspective is that experimental economics, whichever methodology one adopts, is only one tool amongst an arsenal of tools in the economics toolbox, that can be used to empirically test various hypotheses and also to develop models and theories that require further development and testing.

Behavioural economists have long made use of traditional data sets, case studies, economic history narratives, anthropological inquiries, field studies, surveys and interviews, for example, to develop models and to test hypotheses. It would be an analytical and methodological misadventure for behavioural economists to simply focus on experimental economics. What experimental economics has provided is an important additional tool in the behavioural economists' analytical toolbox (Charness and Pingle 2022; Schram and Ule 2019).

CONCLUSION

What links the different methodological approaches to behavioural economics is the empirically based rejection of the view that conventional neoclassical economics provides a robust explanation for choice behaviour. Also rejected is the view that conventional economics provides a robust descriptive model of human behaviour. There is also general agreement that it is critically important to incorporate non-economic variables in one's models. Methodologies diverge, however, when it comes to how one models human behaviour. In particular, there are different approaches to:

- What rational behaviour is;
- The importance of reality-informed simplifying assumptions;
- The use of as-if methodology to construct and revise models;
- Whether or not individuals are smart or boundedly rational or systemically biased;
- Whether there can be sub-optimal choices;
- If sub-optimal choices exist, whether they are biased-driven or a function of the decision-making environment and individuals' decision-making capabilities;
- Policies to improve decision-making if, indeed, initial decision-making processes and resulting choices are sub-optimal.

CONTRIBUTIONS TO THIS VOLUME

Part I of this book is 'Behavioural economics methods in general'. In his chapter, 'Behavioural economics methods', Gerrit Antonides describes how psychological concepts and measurements have been applied in behavioural economics and integrated into economic models. In their 'Behavioural economics: what have we missed? Exploring "classical" behavioural economics roots in AI, cognitive psychology and complexity theory', Steve J. Bickley and Benno Torgler address the question of what behavioural economics is and what its roots are and in so doing provide insight into the methodological benefits of the behavioural economics approach for analysis and policy. Beryl Y. Chang, in her 'Assumptions in economic modelling: how behavioural economics can enlighten', demonstrates the essential significance of assumptions for economic modelling. The use value of specific assumptions can't simply be taken at face value.

In Part II, 'Real-world economics', Gigi Foster and Paul Frijters, in their 'Realeconomik: using the messy human experience to drive clean theoretical advance in economics', argue that incrementally building upon accepted conventional assumptions, such as selfishness, by introducing altruism and more specifically love, can advance our understanding of human behaviour. Pascal Moliner and Patrick Rateau, in 'The common-sense economy', present the theory of social representation and its implication for the study of economic phenomena. They describe how social representation (especially by non-expert individuals) can lead individuals to make decisions that significantly deviate from economic or neoclassical rationality.

In Part III, 'Behavioural macroeconomics', Michelle Baddeley in 'Behavioural methods for macroeconomics: modelling investment' analysis some of the pitfalls associated with aggregation in macroeconomic models generally and in behavioural macroeconomic investment models in particular. She also explores the implications of building behavioural macroeconomic models founded on more realistic assumptions about how people think, decide and interact. Tobias F. Rötheli in, 'The business cycle and the cycles of behavioural economics', presents a historical overview of business cycle modelling from the perspective of the different analytical narratives developed by behavioural economists. He makes the point that in times of deep recessions and crises, economists become receptive to psychological views on human decision-making, which is critically important for the robust modelling of business cycles.

In Part IV, 'Behavioural labour economics and the theory of the firm', Morris Altman in 'Behavioural labour economics' presents an alternative model of labour supply based on an individual's target income and target nonmarket time. He also discusses how information asymmetries, limited information processing capabilities and job search constraints and social norms are also core determinants of labour supply. Sodany Tong in 'Some implications of x-efficiency theory for the role of managerial quality as a key determinant of firm performance and productivity' applies Leibenstein's x-efficiency theory to analyse empirically the effect of managerial quality on the level of x-efficiency across firms and countries. She finds that managerial quality and managers' choices affect both employees' effort inputs and, thereby, overall firm performance. Finally, Morris Altman in 'Behavioural theories of the firm with a focus on x-efficiency and effort discretion: implications for analysis' presents a behavioural model of the firm building on x-efficiency and efficiency wage theory. In this model, effort is variable in the production function and technical change can be induced by changing cost variables inside the firm. Key causal variables include labour costs, fairness, power and the quality and quantity of quality management.

Part V, 'Money and behavioural economics', comprises two chapters by Agata Gasiorowska and Tomasz Zaleskiewicz. In 'The psychology of money', they argue, based on a review of the literature, that people's beliefs and behaviours regarding money's purchasing power and its symbolic meanings go far beyond money understood as an economic force and diverge from assumptions underlying economic models. They offer potential new directions for investigating the psychology of money and suggest practical implications derived from their findings. In, 'Taking financial advice: going beyond making good decisions', Gasiorowska and Zaleskiewicz argue that when individuals turn to experts for financial advice, they often use their own beliefs as a reference point and tend to depreciate recommendations which are at odds with those beliefs. This represents a form of the psychological confirmation effect which detracts from making optimal financial decisions.

In Part VI, 'Behavioural approaches to health economics', Hannah Rachel Josepha Altman and Morris Altman in 'Bounded rationality, imperfect and costly information and sub-optimal outcomes in the sports and health and fitness industries' showcase behavioural economics methodological approaches to decision-making and policy using the example of the health and fitness industry, choices made that affect the level of obesity, and athletes and trainers' and coaches' choices with regards to realising targeted levels of performance. They draw attention to the significance of individuals' decision-making capabilities and the decision-making environment, which have critical social and institutional determinants, to better understand why sub-optimal choices are made by rational agents. Nazmi Sari, in 'Empirical methods and methodological developments in economics of health and health behavior', explores and reviews methodological developments relevant to economics of health and health behaviour with specific examples derived from related literature on smoking, diet, obesity, and physical activity. After discussing randomised control trials based on experimental data, alternative methods based on observational data are presented with specific examples derived from empirical literature. David A. Savage and Derek Friday in 'The behavioural impact of pandemics: incomplete markets and the supply chain' explore the conceptual relationship between human behaviour and the market/supply chain problems exposed by the COVID-19 pandemic around the world. This is done using the lens of complex systems linking individuals and group behaviours to demand, supply and the supply chain side problems caused by the COVID-19 pandemic.

In the first chapter of Part VII, '"Emotions", morals and behavioural economics', Jefferson Arapoc in, 'Economics of trust: its nature, measures, determinants, and application' presents reviews the literature on how trust is defined, categorised and measured with a specific focus on economics. He also surveys the determinants of trust ranging from age and sex to income class and institutions. He also discusses why trust, which is a heuristic, is desirable for any kind of social interaction. In, 'Intuition and behavioural economics', Roger Frantz argues that intuition is a heuristic that can possibly improve decision-making by real-world humans. Whether or not intuition plays a positive role depends on the circumstance and how it is employed. This is a contract to contemporary economics that regards intuition as a form of irrational or biased behaviour. Natalia V. Czap and Hans J. Czap in, 'Conserve the planet, *not* empathy! Revising the empathy conservation framework', discuss the four main areas of environmental economics – air, energy, waste and water – with a focus on conservation. They summarise the key insights learned for conservation behaviour from studies on behavioural biases, social norms and other-regarding preferences. They then revise their empathy conservation framework to include biases, reputation and signalling, with significant policy implications. Shinji Teraji in 'Behavioral economics of morality and sustainability' argues that conventional economics focuses on external incentives to encourage cooperative behaviour with regards to governing common-pool resources. However, since people exhibit prosocial behaviour, external incentives can sometimes crowd the intrinsic motivation to act prosocially. Teraji argues that resource conservation policy would be more effective by incorporating and further enhancing social incentives into policy design. Alexis V. Belianin, in his 'Antisocial punishment', reviews findings on antisocial punishment (sanctioning), or situations when less cooperative people sanction more cooperative ones. He attempts to explain this puzzling but quite pervasive behaviour because it is costly to the punisher and explicitly harmful to society, including the punisher himself.

In Part VIII, 'Evaluation and formation of beliefs and preferences', Fang-Fang Tang, in 'Auction methods of valuation and the endowment effect', reviews the literature which demonstrates through experiments the significant difference between people's valuation of gains and losses (the endowment effect), which tends to increase with the number of trials. This chapter explores the recent finding that this gap tends to stabilise at about the ninth round of experiments in the context of a pilot set of experiments. David Leiser in 'Statistical approaches to the analysis of belief patterns' reviews the statistics-based (derived from surveys) literature on lay beliefs and understanding given that they are important determinants of expectations and behaviour and shape the acceptance of public policy. He further examines the statistical techniques used to analyse the data. This overview is conducted through the prism of studies on the meaning of inflation, the good-begets-good heuristic in macroeconomics, the perceived causes of the financial crisis and the nature of capitalism. In 'Motivated preferences', Matthew G. Nagler explores the role of focusing effort directed at improving one's attitude towards an object. He considers applicable theoretical methodology for analysing key cases involving such adjustments in effort, as well as several empirically relevant applications. This is significant since discretionary cognitive focusing effort can influence perceived preferences given individuals' limited cognitive resources. In 'Might ambiguity exist when none seems to exist?' Mina Mahmoudi, Mark Pingle and Rattaphon Wuthisatian argue that bounded rationality may effectively create ambiguity which goes against the conventional economic worldview. This chapter examines data from an experiment that allows one to compare decisionmaking behaviour under total ambiguity with that under 'no ambiguity'. The evidence indicates that people experience ambiguity even when none seems to be present and that ambiguity biases decision behaviour in a systematic way.

In the last part of this book, 'Behavioural approaches to policy', Irene Mussio and Angela C.M. De Oliveira in 'Norms, networks, nudges: non-traditional approaches to improve healthy behaviours' argue that health costs, mortality risk and the benefits of healthy choices are frequently misestimated and undervalued by individuals, resulting in too many health risks relative to the social (and sometimes individual) optimal and increasing pressure on the health system. They argue that researchers and health policy advocates may need to examine non-regulatory, low-cost behavioural interventions, such as peer effects and networks in preference formation and diffusion, in order to improve health and welfare as opposed to more explicit interventionist approaches. Noah V. Peters and Lucia A. Reisch in 'Bridging psychology and sociology: towards a socio-ecological perspective in behavioural economics and policy' contribute to interdisciplinary approaches in behavioural economics by offering a theoretically rigorous yet applied perspective, thereby sketching core components of a 'behavioural public policy of practice'. They outline new methodological pathways associated with their propositions and debate how this extended interdisciplinary purview can facilitate a balance between undue complexity and over-simplification.

NOTES

1. It should be noted, however, that one of pioneers of contemporary economic theory or neoclassical theory, Gary Becker, was highly critical of his colleagues' ignoring sociological variables in modelling choice behaviour.
2. This involves carefully examining how individuals behave within real firms. The behavioural methodological approach leads one to derive and model optimal norms from real-world behaviour within successful firms (Cyert and March 1963; Hirschman 1970; Schwartz 2018).
3. According to the Collins English Language Dictionary, irrationality is defined as: 'If you describe someone's feelings and behavior as irrational, you mean they are not based on logical reasons or clear thinking'.

REFERENCES

Akerlof, G. (1970). "The Market for Lemons: Quality Uncertainty and the Market Mechanism," *Quarterly Journal of Economics,* 84(3): 488–500.

Akerlof, George A. and Rachel E. Kranton (2010). *Identity Economics: How Our Identities Shape Our Work, Wages, and Well-Being.* Princeton: Princeton University Press.

Altman, M. (1990). "Interfirm, Interregional, and International Differences in Labor Productivity: Variations in the Levels of 'X-Inefficiency' as a Function of Differential Labor Costs," in M. Perlman and K. Weiermair, eds., *Studies in Economic Rationality: X- Efficiency Examined and Extolled.* Ann Arbor: University of Michigan Press: 323–350.

Altman, M. (1999). "The Methodology of Economics and the Survivor Principle Revisited and Revised: Some Welfare and Public Policy Implications of Modeling the Economic Agent," *Review of Social Economics*, 57: 427–449.

Altman, M. (2006). "What a Difference an Assumption Makes: Effort Discretion, Economic Theory, and Public Policy," in M. Altman, ed., *Handbook of Contemporary Behavioral Economics: Foundations and Developments.* London: Routledge: 125–164.

Altman, M. (2014). "Mental Models, Bargaining Power, and Institutional Change," World Interdisciplinary Network for Institutional Research, Old Royal Naval College, Greenwich University. London, UK, September 11–14.

Altman, M. (2020). *Smart Economic Decision-Making in a Complex World.* London/Cambridge: Academic Press/Elsevier Science.

Becker, G.S. (1996). *Accounting for Tastes.* Cambridge and London: Harvard University Press.

Berg, N. and G. Gigerenzer (2010). "As-If Behavioral Economics: Neoclassical Economics in Disguise?" *History of Economic Ideas*, 18: 133–166.

Charness, G. and M. Pingle, eds. (2022). *The Art of Experimental Economics: Twenty Top Papers Reviewed.* New York: Routledge.

Coase, R.H. (1937). "The Nature of the Firm," *Economica*, 4: 386–405.

Commons, J.R. (1931). "Institutional Economics," *American Economic Review*, 21: 648–657.

Cyert, R.M. and J.C. March (1963). *A Behavioral Theory of the Firm.* Englewood Cliffs: Prentice-Hall.

Denzau, A. and D.C. North (1994). "Shared Mental Models: Ideologies and Institutions," *Kyklos* Fasc. 1: 3–31.

Friedman, M. (1953). "The Methodology of Positive Economics," in M. Friedman, *Essays in Positive Economics.* Chicago: University of Chicago Press: 3–43.

Galbraith, J.K. (1952). *American Capitalism.* Boston: Houghton-Mifflin.

Galbraith, J.K. (1973). "Power and the Useful Economist," *American Economic Review*, 63: 1–11.

Gigerenzer, G. (2007). *Gut Feelings: The Intelligence of the Unconscious.* New York: Viking.

Hayek, F.A. (1952). *The Sensory Order.* Chicago: University of Chicago Press.

Hirschman, Albert O. (1970). *Exit, Voice, and Loyalty: Responses to Decline in Firms, Organizations, and States.* Cambridge: Harvard University Press.

Kahneman, D. and A. Tversky (1979). "Prospect Theory: An Analysis of Decisions under Risk, *Econometrica*, 47: 313–327.

Kahneman, D., J.L. Knetsch and R.H. Thaler (1990). "Experimental Tests of the Endowment Effect and the Coase Theorem," *Journal of Political Economy*, 98: 1325–1348.

Kahneman, D. (2003). "Maps of Bounded Rationality: Psychology for Behavioral Economics," *American Economic Review,* 93: 1449–1475.

Kahneman, D. (2011). *Thinking, Fast and Slow.* New York: Farrar, Straus and Giroux.

Keynes, J.M. (1936) [2007]. *The General Theory of Employment, Interest and Money.* London: Macmillan.

Leibenstein, H. (1966). "Allocative Efficiency vs. X-efficiency," *American Economic Review*, 56: 392–415.

Lewis, A., P. Webley and A. Furnham (1995). *The New Economic Mind: The Social Psychology of Economic Behaviour.* Brighton: Harvester Wheatsheaf.

March, J.G. (1978). "Bounded Rationality, Ambiguity, and the Engineering of Choice," *Bell Journal of Economics*, 9: 587–608.

North, D.C. (1990). *Institutions, Institutional Change and Economic Performance.* Cambridge: Cambridge University Press.

Schram, A. and A. Ule, eds. (2019). *Handbook of Research Methods and Applications in Experimental Economics.* Cheltenham: Edward Elgar.

Schwartz, H. (2018). *Producer and Organizational Decision-Making: Is Behavioral Economics Losing Its Way?* New York: Archway Publishing, Simon and Schuster.

Shiller, R. and G. Akerlof (2015). *Phishing for Phools: The Economics of Manipulation and Deception.* Princeton: Princeton University Press.

Simon, H.A. (1959). "Theories of Decision Making in Economics and Behavioral Science." *American Economic Review,* 49: 252–283.

Simon, H.A. (1978). "Rationality as a Process and as a Product of Thought," *American Economic Review,* 70: 1–16.

Simon, H.A. (1986). "Rationality in Psychology and Economics." *Journal of Business,* 59: S209–224.

Simon, H.A. (1987). "Behavioral Economics," in J. Eatwell, M. Millgate and P. Newman, eds., *The New Palgrave: A Dictionary of Economics.* London: Macmillan: 221–225.

Smith, V.L. (1962). "An Experimental Study of Competitive Market Behavior," *Journal of Political Economy,* 70: 111–137.

Smith, V.L. (1976). "Experimental Economics: Induced Value Theory," *American Economic Review,* 66: 274–279.

Smith, V.L. (2003). "Constructivist and Ecological Rationality in Economics," *American Economic Review,* 93: 465–508.

Thaler, R.H. and C.R. Sunstein (2008). *Nudge: Improving Decisions about Health, Wealth, and Happiness.* New York: Penguin Books.

Todd, P.M. and G. Gigerenzer (2003). "Bounding Rationality to the World," *Journal of Economic Psychology,* 24: 143–165.

Tomer, J. (2007). "What Is Behavioral Economics?" *Journal of Behavioral and Experimental Economics (formerly Journal of Socio-Economics),* 36: 463–479.

Williamson, O.E. (1975). *Markets and Hierarchies: Analysis and Antitrust Implications.* New York: Free Press.

PART I

BEHAVIOURAL ECONOMICS METHODS IN GENERAL

2. Behavioural economic methods
Gerrit Antonides

INTRODUCTION

Behavioural economics has been defined as 'the combination of psychology and economics that investigates what happens in markets in which some of the agents display human limitations and complications' (Mullainathan and Thaler, 2001, p. 1094). This definition focuses on the contribution of psychology to the economic analysis of human behaviour, thus excluding socioeconomics, economic anthropology and neuroeconomics as possibly relevant disciplines, overviews of which can be found in Hellmich (2017), Carrier (2012) and Glimcher and Fehr (2013), respectively. The main human limitations distinguished in Mullainathan and Thaler (2001) are bounded rationality, bounded willpower and bounded self-interest – factors causing deviations from predictions of the standard economic model of behaviour. Although such human characteristics of economic agents are not recognised in the current standard economic model, this has not always been the case in economic theory. For example, Adam Smith and Jeremy Bentham referred to human emotions (see Kahneman, Wakker and Sarin, 1997; Ashraf, Camerer and Loewenstein, 2005), which were later abandoned in neoclassical economic theory (see Angner and Loewenstein, 2012).

The development of economic theory roughly followed similar developments in psychology, i.e., introspection (e.g., Wilhelm Wundt) and psychoanalysis (e.g., Freud) at the turn of the 19th century, then behaviourism in the early 20th century and the cognitive revolution in the 1950s and 1960s. Economic theory paralleled these developments with the emergence of postwar neoclassical theory (or ordinalism), followed by some early behavioural economic insights in the 1960s (e.g., Herbert Simon, George Katona) and the onset of contemporary behavioural economics (e.g., Daniel Kahneman, Amos Tversky). Angner and Loewenstein (2012) provide a more detailed overview of the history of behavioural economics.

Together with the rise of contemporary behavioural economics, the discipline of economic psychology emerged, in which psychological theory was applied to economic behaviour (Van Raaij, 1999). Although behavioural economics frequently uses experimental methods in research, the field of experimental economics is generally associated with testing the standard economic model rather than the application of psychological insights in economic theory (Antonides, Bolger and Trip, 2006; Angner and Loewenstein, 2012).

Here, we aim at describing the methods used in behavioural economics and distinguishing these methods from those used in standard economic practice. We also describe the contributions of psychological insights to economics. Since behavioural economics has started by showing a number of anomalies – essentially deviations from standard economic predictions – we will first explain these results in the second section. In the third section, we deal with different types of utility than are usually defined in economics. The fourth section deals with measures of economically relevant concepts – utility, well-being, preferences and the different methodologies used. The fifth section shows a number of ways in which psychological insights have been integrated into economic theory. The sixth section concludes.

ANOMALIES

The standard economic model assumes rationality as observed by revealed preferences, resulting in some weird types of decision-making as in Frank and Cartwright's crank oil example (2015). The example describes a man who drinks crank oil and then dies in agony. The conclusion from the standard model would be that the man must have liked the crank oil very much, otherwise, he would not have preferred drinking it to living. Rationality also assumes optimal thought processes in which actors obtain their best possible outcomes, given their preferences and opportunities. The assumption of optimal thought processes can be disconfirmed easily, for example by letting people either choose between two different lotteries or make a bid for each lottery, one with high probability and low prize, and one with low probability and high prize, both with an equal expected outcome (Lichtenstein and Slovic, 1971). In choosing, the high probability lottery is preferred, whereas, in bidding, the high prize lottery is preferred. The results hold up under a variety of conditions (Grether and Plott, 1979), thus violating procedure invariance (Tversky and Thaler, 1990), according to which different procedures (i.e., choosing or bidding) should lead to similar outcomes.

The standard model assumes stable preferences, which also has been found not to hold true in a number of experiments on dynamic choices, offering people exactly the same choices at different points in time. Thaler (1981, p. 202) offered the following thought experiment: 'Choose between one apple today or two apples tomorrow', then 'Choose between one apple in one year or two apples in one year plus one day'. Some people would choose one apple today, but everyone offered the option would wait one more day to obtain the two apples in one year plus one day. This result reflects the dynamic inconsistency of preferences. In a similar way, actual choices involving real money show a higher preference to forego the receipt of a certain amount of money in favour of a higher future amount if the choices are offered in the distant future rather than in the near future (e.g., Antonides and Wunderink, 2001). For an overview of research on dynamic inconsistency, see Frederick, Loewenstein and O'Donoghue (2002).

Another assumption concerns intransitive preferences, i.e., the violation of the preference ordering A > B > C in making pairwise choices. Tversky (1969) identifies intransitive choices between lotteries varying in probabilities, prize amounts and expected values, and between college applicants varying in intellectual ability, emotional stability and social facility. Guadalupe-Lanas et al. (2020) describe substantial intransitivity of consumer preferences for edible goods.

The aforementioned violations of important economic assumptions have become known as anomalies.[1] Often, such anomalies indicate the construction of preference (Slovic, 1995), either caused by external influences from the environment or by the calculation of preferences in the decision process (Warren, McGraw and Van Boven, 2011). Such anomalies have also been characterised as heuristics and biases, a large number of which have been catalogued.[2] A large volume of research projects has been devoted to the discovery and validation of anomalies in the economic model, thus casting doubt on the realism of economic theory. In fact, behavioural economics has often given the impression of being a science of anomalies. We argue that the discovery of anomalies has only been the first step in the process. Further steps include showing the occurrence of such anomalies in daily life and business practices, and the integration of these discoveries into economic theory.

In order to show the existence of anomalies in daily life, behavioural economics has made efforts to facilitate the study of psychological factors in economic behaviour. These efforts include a distinction between different types of utility and the development of direct measures of economic concepts, to be considered next.

DIFFERENT TYPES OF UTILITY

The standard economic model appears to be concerned with decision utility only, capturing the utility inferred from choices (as in the crank oil example earlier). But other measures of utility are arguably important both to well-being and to an accurate understanding of decisions. Decision utility is possibly influenced by both remembered utility and predicted utility (Kahneman, Wakker and Sarin, 1997). Remembered utility captures the memories related to some experience, e.g., consumption. Obviously, nice memories may lead to decisions to repeat experiences. Alternatively, predicted utility consists of perceptions or expectations about experiences. Kahneman and Snell (1992) showed that people generally predicted a declining satisfaction with repeated experiences (e.g., enjoyment of consuming ice cream or listening to short music pieces), whereas their actual satisfaction did not decline with repetitions. Furthermore, Read and Loewenstein (1995) showed that people's simultaneous choices (in advance of their experiences) yielded more variety than their sequential choices (after experiencing them consecutively), indicating another difference between predicted utility and experienced utility (see also Read et al., 2001). Differences between predicted and experienced utility may be explained by projection bias – the inability to empathise with experiences different from the here and now (Loewenstein, O'Donoghue and Rabin, 2003). Alternatively, predicted satisfaction may be instigated by other consumers' experiences, as frequently reported on hotel or restaurant websites (Mauri and Minazza, 2013).

Experienced utility consists of instantaneous utility – a flow of immediate hedonic and affective experiences over time. One might conceive of temporally integrating the instantaneous utility flow to obtain the total utility of an episode (Kahneman, Wakker and Sarin, 1997). But it does not appear to be the case that such a temporally integrated total utility is what people recall in daily life. Rather, recollections are explained better by the so-called peak-and-end rule, i.e., by both the most extreme and the final instant utility of an experience, and duration neglect, indicating that the duration of the experience does not matter in conceiving one's total utility. Kahneman et al. (1993) showed that the total utility for patients undergoing a painful colonoscopy procedure was explained by both the most extreme pain during the procedure and the pain experienced at the end of the procedure. By adding a little less painful experience at the end, the global evaluation of the entire procedure was improved, thus demonstrating duration neglect. Ross and Simonson (1991) showed that the total utility of playing two computer games – one interesting game and one boring game – was reported higher if the interesting game was played last than if it was played first, thus demonstrating the end effect. Verhoef, Antonides and De Hoog (2004) found both pead-and-end effects in the evaluation of agent–client conversations at a call centre.

A different dimension of distinction in utility relative to those referenced earlier is between outcome utility and procedural utility. The term procedural utility refers to the non-instrumental pleasures and displeasures of processes. Frey, Benz and Stutzer (2004) contend that people frequently prefer fair procedures to beneficial outcomes because they contribute to a positive sense of self, autonomy, relatedness and competence. Examples include tax compliance being correlated with respectful treatment of taxpayers, democratic participation being correlated with life satisfaction and higher job satisfaction for self-employed people than employees (ceteris paribus), among others. Kahneman, Knetsch and Thaler (1986a, 1986b) provide evidence of procedural fairness affecting people's preferences for the allocation of football match tickets, generally showing preference for standing in a queue rather than selling the tickets to the highest bidder. Other evidence is related to transaction costs in purchasing the same beer at the grocery store or at a fancy resort (Thaler, 1985). People appear to find a high price at the resort fairer than a high price at the grocery store. Another famous example comes from experimental studies of the ultimatum game (Güth, Schmittberger and Schwartz, 1982), in which player A distributes a sum of money, say $10, between themself and player B. If player B agrees with the offer the sum will be allocated as player A proposed, otherwise both get nothing. In contrast with the game-theoretic prediction – A leaving the smallest possible amount to B – many offers are of the 60–40 per cent type. In all these examples, procedural fairness turns out more important than economic benefits (i.e., outcomes) in people's decision-making.

A somewhat different process than described earlier is adaptive preference formation, holding that preferences for goods may be adapted to the possibilities of obtaining those goods, resulting in sour grapes (Elster, 1982).[3] For example, a consumer with a small budget may prefer a small car to a large car, reasoning that a large car is environmentally unfriendly, rather than admitting that the budget is too small to obtain the large car. Such a process may be explained by a motivation to reduce cognitive dissonance (Festinger, 1957), caused by the incompatibility of wanting the large car and the impossibility to buy it. Elster (1982) also gives an example of maladaptive preference formation, characterised by 'forbidden fruit is sweet', which is caused by the instantaneous infeasibility to obtain a certain good.

So far, we have considered relatively short-term preference changes, but what can behavioural economics contribute to explaining long-term changes? In one view, preference changes may be non-existent because preferences are demonstrably stable and similar across people (Stigler and Becker, 1977). Instead, long-term changes in behaviour may be explained from different Z-production technologies, based on time and human capital inputs. An example of a Z-commodity is the appreciation of music, which can be more efficiently produced and consumed by previous time spent on listening and musical education while doing so, leaving the actual utility of musical appreciation unchanged. This view of stable and uniform preferences has been challenged on the basis of parsimony, in that behaviours can often be explained more directly as involving changes in utility (Hirschman, 1984) on the basis that changes in personality over time justify the use of different utility functions (Caplan, 2003) and on the basis that variations in the demand for Z-commodities lack explanation (Cowen, 1989). The fifth section includes several ways in which economic theory may explain preference changes, e.g., with respect to the influence of personal identity and income evaluation.

MEASURES OF ECONOMICALLY RELEVANT CONCEPTS

In addition to showing the existence of anomalies in the standard economic model, frequently in laboratory experiments, other attempts at gaining more insight into human decision-making have been based on measuring economically relevant concepts directly, including well-being and preferences. Such measures then may be related to a broad range of economic behaviours outside of the laboratory. Such endeavour contributes to the scaling-up of small-scale laboratory findings to larger markets and settings, as advocated in List (2021). We include measures that are either based on laboratory tasks or verbal questionnaires. We focus on the most frequently used concepts in economic research.

Loss Aversion

Loss aversion implies that a loss is evaluated as more unpleasurable than a commensurate gain is evaluated as pleasurable (Kahneman and Tversky, 1979). An indication of loss aversion is the endowment effect, holding that preventing the loss of an object in possession is worth more than the acquisition of that object not in possession (Kahneman, Knetsch and Thaler, 1990, 1991). Loss aversion has been shown to be related to selling stock (Shefrin and Statman, 1985), default options in organ donations (Johnson and Goldstein, 2003), brand switching (Hartman, Doane and Woo, 1991) and spending income framed as either a bonus or a rebate (Epley, Mak and Idson, 2006), among many other applications.

Gächter, Johnson and Herrmann (2007) have developed a measure of loss aversion in both riskless and risky choices, based on monetary values of willingness to accept the loss of an object in possession (WTA) and willingness to pay to acquire the object (WTP), as previously used in laboratory experiments. The riskless choices comprised WTP and WTA for a miniature car; the risky choices comprised choices to play lotteries with a fixed gain (6 euros) and various amounts of losses (2–7 euros). The ratio of WTA and WTP in the riskless choices, and the lottery which was just acceptable, served as the measures of loss aversion. All choices were made 'for real', using the mechanism described in Becker, De Groot and Marschak (1964). Significantly more loss aversion was observed at higher ages, lower levels of schooling and higher levels of income and wealth. Loss aversion measures for riskless and risky choices were highly correlated (Spearman's rho = 0.635).

De Baets and Buelens (2012) developed an 18-item verbal questionnaire (Cronbach's alpha = 0.82) to measure loss aversion, including items such as 'I would feel very emotional if my car (bike) would be stolen' and 'I get easily attached to material things (my car, my furniture)'. Significantly higher loss aversion was associated with lower education, younger age and higher measured anxiety. The education effect is consistent with Gächter, Johnson and Herrmann (2007), but the age effect is not.

Risk

Holt and Laury (2002) measured risk aversion on the basis of lottery choices with either low (up to $3.85) or high monetary stakes (up to $346.50, i.e., 90 times the low stakes). Using responses from university student and staff samples, they made estimates of the Pratt-Arrow measure of relative risk aversion. They observed significantly more risk aversion at higher stakes. They ran similar lotteries both hypothetical and 'for real' and observed significantly lower risk aversion in the hypothetical case relative to the 'real' case. Using this same lottery procedure with a sample of farmers, Vollmer, Hermann and Musshof (2017) showed that farmers who took less production risk in their regular work exhibited higher risk aversion in the lotteries.

In their seminal paper introducing prospect theory, Kahneman and Tversky (1979) made the case that risk preferences differ between positive and negative outcomes under uncertainty, reflecting a value function that takes a different shape in the domain of losses relative to the domain of gains. Typically, people tend to be risk averse with respect to positive changes relative to their reference point and risk-seeking with respect to negative changes.

Kahneman and Tversky (1979) also showed overweighting of small probabilities and underweighting of moderate probabilities. More evidence for this phenomenon was obtained by Van de Stadt, Antonides and Van Praag (1984), who offered people a survey question involving an income gamble with equal chances of losing and winning (50 per cent). If their income would fall by 5 per cent, they had to state what percentage increase would lead them to just accept the game (similar questions were asked with 10 per cent, 20 per cent and 30 per cent of loss). They estimated people's perceived probability of 50 per cent that best explained their answers at 45 per cent (for a logarithmic function), resp. 47 per cent (for a lognormal function). Note that the lognormal utility function is convex for small incomes and concave for larger incomes.

Falk et al. (2016) adapted the lottery task for use in large surveys, presenting respondents with only five questions organised progressively – each successive question adapted based upon responses to the previous one – their risk aversion measure derived based on the response at which the respondent changed from preferring the lottery to the safe alternative. In addition, they asked: 'In general, how willing are you to take risks?', providing an 11-point scale for the response. Then, the answers to the two categories of questions were averaged with roughly equal weights, with the weights determined based on their effectiveness in explaining different types of behaviour. A small subsample answered the same questions one week later, showing a test–retest correlation of 0.35. Falk et al. (2018) reported the results of the questions in 76 countries with over 80,000 respondents, showing higher risk aversion for women than men, for those with lower mathematical skills and for elderly people. Low risk aversion, or risk-taking, was associated with smoking behaviour and being self-employed. Also, controlling for other factors, risk-taking was associated with respondents in countries with higher GDP.

The risk measures described here were conceived as being applicable to a large range of behaviours, although they were based mainly on financial risks. Weber, Blais and Betz (2002) showed that both risk perceptions and risk preferences are domain-specific: they tend to differ across financial, health/safety, social, ethical and recreational risks. They developed a 40-item domain-specific risk-attitude scale (DOSPERT), consisting of verbal items with respect to both the likelihood of engagement in different behaviours and how risky each behaviour was perceived. For example, they asked respondents to indicate on a seven-point scale the likelihood that they would engage in 'investing 10 per cent of your annual income in a moderate growth mutual fund' (financial domain) and 'taking some questionable deductions on your income tax return' (ethical domain). Cronbach's alphas were 0.88 for the risk-behaviour scale and 0.89 for the risk-perception scale. Despite the high internal consistency, the correlations of the risk-behaviour scales across domains were moderate, and in some instances even negative. Correlations indicating one-month test–retest reliabilities varied between 0.44 and 0.80 for the risk behaviour scales and between 0.42 and 0.67 for the risk-perception scales. Men and women differed both in their perceptions and likelihood to engage in different behaviours. Men had lower risk perceptions than women in all domains except for gambling and social risk, where differences were not significant. Men were also more likely to engage in risky behaviours than women, except for the social domain, in which women were more likely to take risks. Blais and Weber (2006) refined DOSPERT and reduced it to 30 items, showing Cronbach's alphas ranging from 0.71 to 0.86 for risk behaviours and from 0.74 to 0.83 for risk perceptions. Most individuals showed negative correlations between risk perceptions and risk behaviours, suggesting that they were perceived-risk averse.

Time

The economic concept of time preference indicates how future outcomes are valued in the present and has implications for saving and borrowing behaviour. Standard economic models typically use the interest rate to calculate present values of future outcomes. However, much larger subjective discount rates have been found in consumer decision-making, indicating high impatience (Hausman, 1979; Gately, 1980). Moreover, subjective discount rates have been found to be higher in the near than in the far future, for smaller as opposed to larger outcomes and for losses as distinct from gains (Thaler, 1981). Time preference has been measured by so-called time-tradeoff questions of the type 'Do you prefer $100 today or $150 in a year?' (Harrison, Lau and Williams, 2002) and appears to be higher for older individuals and for individuals with lower levels of education and income.

To measure time preference, Falk et al. (2016) adapted their risk preference measurement approach of asking five questions organised progressively, in addition to one verbal question: 'In comparison to others, are you a person who is generally willing to give up something today in order to benefit from that in the future?' The two categories of questions were averaged using weights of 0.71 and 0.29, respectively (Falk et al., 2018). The one-month test–retest correlation was 0.67. Impatience appeared to be somewhat higher for women than for men, and lower for those with better math skills. Both the young and old people were more impatient than the middle-aged, in line with Read and Read (2004).

Time preference can be related to the psychological concept of willingness to delay gratification (Mischel, 1974). It has been observed in experiments that children vary with respect to their willingness to defer a reward (e.g., a certain amount of candy) in order to receive a larger reward (e.g., a larger amount of candy) at some later point in time. Delay of gratification has a very pervasive and stable effect on behaviour. It was observed, for example, that a preschool child's ability to delay gratification for pretzels or marshmallows is related to her socially competent behaviour some 12 years later (Mischel, 1984). Since delay of gratification can be a highly consequential personal trait, in psychology this concept has been measured by means of a verbal scale indicating the respondent's level of consideration of future consequences (Strathman et al., 1994).[4] Twelve survey questions were initially employed, such as: 'I consider how things might be in the future and try to influence those things with my day-to-day behaviour' (Strathman et al., 1994, p. 752); later, the survey battery was reduced to eight questions (Petrocelli, 2003). Typically, the answers to the scale items are factor-analysed, then used to explain behaviour. The time orientation scale has been shown to vary with different types of behaviour. Future time orientation was related to less smoking, drinking and gambling behaviour; more environmental preservation (Joireman et al., 2001); higher academic achievement and cooperation (Wolf et al., 2009); fewer bank account overdrafts (Gattig, 2002); less saving and credit card debt (Joireman, Sprott and Spangenberg, 2005); and more pension saving (Howlett, Kees and Kemp, 2008).

Several authors have used the consideration of future consequences scale to categorise responses into short-term and long-term time orientations (Joireman et al., 2008; Crockett et al., 2009; Hevey et al., 2010; Toepoel, 2010). This distinction may be relevant in explaining the dynamic inconsistency indicated earlier. Van Beek, Antonides and Handgraaf (2013) showed that time orientation may also be domain-specific, meaning that the general version of the questionnaire does not explain differences in behaviour across different domains.

Social Preference

In many situations, cooperative behaviour is more efficacious or otherwise appropriate than the pursuit of immediate advantage for oneself. In social relationships, such as the family, individuals benefit from a range of interpersonal influences. In many instances, such as blood donation, people behave selflessly in the interest of others. These modes of behaviour are examples of altruistic behaviours the strength of which may vary across people and across situations. In economics, social preferences have been formally accounted for by including the utility of others in the utility function of an individual (Becker, 1991).

Murphy and Ackermann (2014) provide an overview of measurement methods for social preferences, based on a task in which (mostly) two-person outcome distributions are presented to participants. The most popular type of task is the nine-item triple-dominance measure (Van Lange et al., 1997) which presents nine triples of outcome distributions between the participant and an arbitrary other person, e.g., 480–480, 540–280 and 480–80. A participant's preference for the first distribution would indicate a cooperative motivation (joint outcome is the highest), preference for the second an individualistic motivation (own outcome is the highest), and preference for the third a competitive motivation (difference between own and other's outcome is the highest). An individual's motivational type is assessed by counting the choices of each type. An even simpler procedure allowing a continuous measure of social preference is the circle-test (Sonnemans, Van Dijk and Van Winden, 2006), which asks an individual to point somewhere on the circle presented on a computer screen. The screen then shows a vector running from the origin of the circle to the corresponding outcome distribution on the arc of the circle and the individual can then adjust the vector angle. Murphy, Ackermann and Handgraaf (2011) developed yet another continuous measurement method, a slider, for assessing social preferences. By adjusting the slider, individuals choose a point on a continuous outcome distribution lying on a straight line running from one ideal type (e.g., altruistic) to another (e.g., competition). Since there are four economically relevant types, the slider measure contains six slider items (connecting outcomes for all ideal types), resulting in a point estimate for social preference.

Charness and Rabin (2002) have studied a number of individual choices with respect to outcome distributions and developed a social preference model in which the parameters (weights given to own and other's outcomes) are different in situations where the own outcome is higher or lower than the other's outcome, and whether the other person has behaved unfairly (i.e., not choosing a mutually beneficial division hoping to receive a higher outcome herself). Analysing a large number of different outcome distribution choices, a model of 'reciprocal charity' performed best. This model yielded a weight of 0.425 for the other's outcome (on the [0, 1] scale) if the other person's outcome was low compared to the individual, and a weight of −0.089 if the other person had acted unfairly (indicating negative reciprocity). The weight for the other's outcome, if the other's outcome was relatively high, was not significant, indicating no concern for the other if the other was ahead.

In economics and psychology, altruism has been related to public good contributions (Offerman, Sonnemans and Schram, 1996), helping behaviour (Fischer et al., 2011), voluntarism (Unger, 1991), gifts and charitable donations and behaviour in social dilemma situations and negotiations.

Falk et al. (2016) measured altruistic preferences by both asking respondents to make a donation to charity and asking: 'How willing are you to give to good causes without expecting anything in return?' The answers were weighted by 0.64 and 0.36, respectively. The one-month test–retest correlation of the weighted average measure was 0.42. The altruism measure, together with measures of reciprocity, correlated significantly with the dollar value of a country's donations and volunteering activities as a share of GDP. Furthermore, altruism was significantly related to helping strangers and sending money or goods to other people in need (Falk et al., 2016).

Well-being

Since the standard economic model essentially centres on the concept of revealed preference, it tends to be agnostic to the direct measurement of utility. However, in behavioural economics, numerous revelatory findings, often deviating from standard economic predictions, have emerged from direct measures of utility and well-being. Easterlin (1974), using repeated cross-section data from the US on simple happiness questions, discovered a remarkably stable across-cross-section level of happiness, despite substantial increases in real income. However, he found within-cross-section significantly positive relationships between income and happiness. The paradoxical findings were explained from rising aspiration levels over time, due to increased possibilities of spending (Easterlin, 2001). The global happiness question 'Taken all together, how would you say things are these days – would you say that you are very happy, pretty happy, or not too happy?' typically indicates remembered utility, as described earlier. Despite the general finding of a marginally decreasing level of happiness with higher income (Stevenson and Wolfers, 2013), not all happiness measures have yielded the same result. Kahneman and Deaton (2010) have showed a generally positive relationship between income and scores on a (global) happiness ladder question. However, for several measures of emotional well-being (positive affect, feeling blue and stress), the positive relationship only held up to a certain income level, then became insignificant. Emotional well-being referred to 'experiences of yesterday', suggesting more relationship with experienced utility of today than remembered utility from global happiness ratings, possibly influencing the differences in results. An attempt at measuring experience utility has been made by Kahneman et al. (2004) using the Day Reconstruction Method (DRM). The DRM asks people to report what they did during the previous day and how they felt during different episodes. Surprisingly, individuals reported the most positive and least negative feelings during episodes spent with intimate relations, socialising and relaxing – activities on which they spent the least amount of time.

(Remembered) subjective well-being – global happiness – has been positively related to people's income in relation to the average income in their social reference group (Ferrer-i-Carbonell, 2005), having sought information and taken precautionary measures in case of an income decline (Antonides, 2007), green consumption and conservation (Welsch and Kühling, 2010), and negatively with experiencing airport noise (Van Praag and Baarsma, 2005) and nitrogen dioxide air pollution (Welsch, 2007), for example.

There has been some discussion about the extent to which people may adapt to life events influencing their well-being (Lucas, 2007). Brickman, Coates and Janoff-Bulman (1978) found evidence of surprising adaptation in quadriplegics, but their results have been challenged by Mehnert et al. (1990). Easterlin (2003) agrees that happiness may recover after life events but states that setpoint theory – assuming a rather constant level of happiness over one's lifetime – makes too strong assumptions of full adaptation. Yet, it may be useful to investigate more objective indicators of well-being based on experienced utility, as proposed by Kahneman (1999).

An especially economically relevant measure of happiness is income evaluation, in which people report how good or bad they evaluate each of a number of incomes, including their own. On the basis of the answers, Van Praag and Frijters (1999) estimated a lognormal income evaluation function, the location of which was found to depend on respondents' own income (poor people being happier with the same income than rich people), family size (smaller families being happier with the same income than larger families) and the average income of the respondent's social reference group (Kapteyn, Van Praag and Van Herwaarden, 1978). Yet, income evaluation is not fully adjusted after changes in these factors, indicating incomplete adaptation – consistent with findings in the well-being literature.

Other Behavioural Economic Measures

A number of other scales have been developed in behavioural economics, including positive and negative reciprocity and trust (Falk et al., 2016, 2018), mental accounting (Soman, 2001; Antonides, De Groot and Van Raaij, 2011; Olsen et al., 2019), scarcity (Van Dijk, Van der Werf and Van Dillen, 2020) and financial stress (De Bruijn and Antonides, 2020).

INTEGRATION OF ECONOMIC AND PSYCHOLOGICAL MODELS AND INSIGHTS

In addition to showing anomalies of the standard economic model in both experiments and surveys and developing measurement scales, economic theory has made several adaptations in order to accommodate behavioural insights. These adaptations focus on the main deviations from the standard economic model, as described earlier, in addition to utility based on characteristics of goods and technical efficiency models.

Loss Aversion

The idea of asymmetric utilities for gains and losses has been applied in economic demand theory in different ways. Putler (1992) showed loss aversion by adding differences between (logarithmic) purchase prices and reference prices for eggs, separately for positive and negative differences. Prices of the previous week served as reference prices. If the purchase price was higher than the reference price, demand tended to decrease more than it tended to increase if the purchase price was lower than the reference price, indicating loss aversion caused by price increases. Similar results with different specifications of demand equations were found in Talukdar and Lindsey (2013) for broccoli, grapes and raisins and Yan et al. (2016) for low-sugar biscuits and low-fat cream. In contrast to findings for healthy food, reverse loss aversion effects have been found in Talukdar and Lindsey (2013) for relatively unhealthy foods such as beef, soft drinks and potato chips; in Krisnamurthi, Mazumdar and Raj (1992) for coffee when it was out of stock; and in Maynard and Subramaniam (2015) for cheese, butter and margarine. The difference in findings may be due to different perceptions of palatability for healthy and unhealthy food (Raghunathan, Maylor and Hoyer, 2006) and to stockpiling behaviour for goods that can keep fresh for several weeks (Maynard and Subramaniam, 2015).

Time Preference

In order to accommodate dynamic inconsistency, Laibson (1997) proposed a quasi-hyperbolic discount function capturing the consumer's impatience in the short run. The function equals the standard exponential discount rate δ for later periods, multiplied by a constant for the immediate future, i.e., $\beta^{\delta t}$, with $\beta = 1$ in the first period.

Angeletos et al. (2001) showed that US consumers' financial data concerning saving and borrowing are more consistent with hyperbolic than exponential discount rates. Laibson, Repetto and Tobacman (2007) estimate the short-run discount rate at 39.5 per cent and a long-run discount rate at 4.3 per cent. The estimated short-run discount rate is of similar magnitude as estimated discount rates in explaining consumer investments in energy-efficient equipment (Hausman, 1979; Gately, 1980). The evidence of separate short-run and long-run discount rates is consistent with the short-term and long-term time orientation scales in Joireman et al. (2008) although they have never been related empirically.

Risk Preference

The standard economic model already captures risk preferences by means of concave utility functions exhibiting diminishing marginal utility, on the basis of which relative risk aversion can be assessed. Gandelman and Hernández-Murillo (2015) estimate risk aversion from income (as a proxy for consumption) and well-being measures (as a proxy for utility) in the World Gallup Poll for 75 countries. They find an average value close to 1, associated with a logarithmic utility function of consumption.

O'Donoghue and Somerville (2018) argue that concave utility functions cannot explain the phenomenon of risk aversion for small stakes, as contrasted with risk acceptance in gambles in which the individual may lose a small amount but win an extremely large amount. They state that the asymmetric value function is better able to explain individuals' preferences in this respect.

Social Preference

Charness and Rabin (2002) developed a utility function of two-player outcomes in a two-person distribution game. Utility was based on the outcomes of each player, moderated by whether the outcome of one player was higher or lower than the outcome of the other player, and whether the other player had behaved unfairly. They then observed whether the players' actual behaviours were in agreement with strategies of narrow self-interest, competitiveness, difference aversion or social welfare, and estimated the utility parameters from these observations. Their model of simple-altruism model successfully explained most of the variation in the players' choices.

The household economic model (Becker, 1991) assumes a household utility function based on the outcomes of both household partners, thus capturing social preferences. Later, household bargaining models were developed incorporating altruistic preferences in the utility function of each household partner by assuming that one household partner valued the other partner's outcomes (Manser and Brown, 1980; McElroy and Horney, 1981; Lundberg and Pollak, 1993). Finally, the collective household model assumes that the household maximises the weighted sum of the partners' utility functions, each of which partially depends on their own and the other's outcomes, subject to constraints (Apps and Rees, 1997; Chiappori, 1997).

Characteristics

A popular psychological model explaining behaviour is the theory of planned behaviour (Ajzen, 1991, 2012). The theory explains behavioural intentions from attitudes, social norms and perceived behavioural control. Attitudes consist of the weighted sum of beliefs (b) about the relevant attributes of an object, weighted by the perceived importance of the attributes (e), i.e., $\sum b_i e_i / I$ ($i=1, ..., I$), with I the number of relevant attributes. The concept of psychological attitude is similar to the economic concept of utility (Antonides, 1989). Lancaster (1979) defines utility on the basis of objective characteristics of goods, in a similar way as in the theory of planned behaviour, although the importance weights usually are replaced by estimated parameters in empirical models. Ratchford (1979) defines utility as $U = \sum z_i w_i + w_{i+1} y$ with z characteristics, w weights and y the quantity of a composite of other goods. Although utility may be defined on a good's characteristics, the latter may also be transformed into subjective values, more efficiently capturing the carriers of utility. A common transformation of objective into subjective values is the power function, called the power law in Stevens (1957), i.e., $c\varphi^b$ with φ the objective value of the characteristic, b and c the coefficients of transformation. The power function resembles the well-known Cobb-Douglas function in economics. The characteristics model has been applied in consumer choice models (Deaton and Muellbauer, 1980; McFadden, 1973) and marketing (Wierenga, 1984).

Other Applications

Several other applications of integrating psychological factors into economic models exist, notably Akerlof and Kranton's (2000) identity or self-image factor as an argument in the utility function; Nagler's theory of motivated preference (2021), showing how preferences are adapted due to cognitive effort spent on reconciling attitudes which are discrepant with current outcomes or behaviours; and Ali (2020) and Qian, Antonides and Heerink (2021), who considered unfavourable personality characteristics as causing deviations from optimal economic behaviour in technical efficiency models.

CONCLUSION

Behavioural economics has developed from its initial efforts in showing anomalies of the standard economic model into a behavioural science measuring psychological phenomena and incorporating psychological insights into economic models. However, much effort still has to be done in order to better explain economic behaviour and in reconciling economic anomalies with standard economic models.

The measurement scales based on both economic and psychological research show the existence of anomalies in the economic model and offer opportunities to apply the resulting insights to a much wider range of behaviours than usually studied in the laboratory. They also are feasible for use in surveys, and in this sense are complementary to field experiments. Most measurement scales are quite general, thus neglecting domain specificity, except for some specific time preference and risk preference scales. In this respect, the verbal scales seem to have better external validity than the more specific economic questionnaires, at the expense of the precise economic interpretation, for example with respect to the magnitude of discounting or risk aversion. Ideally, the verbal scales could be calibrated with the more quantitative scales in order to clarify their economic meaning.

With respect to the integration of psychological insights in economic models, it appears that this development is still in its infancy stage. Several theoretical attempts have been made to model psychological factors or processes in the utility function but still lack empirical support. Promising exceptions are the theories on good characteristics and loss aversion in the theory of consumer demand, the household economic model dealing with altruism and the technical efficiency model capturing non-economic factors.

NOTES

1. 'Anomalies' refers to a series of articles (co-)edited by Richard Thaler in the *Journal of Economic Perspectives*.
2. See the Cognitive Bias Index (2016).
3. According to Aesop's fable of the fox and the grapes, a fox that cannot reach grapes from a vine subsequently states that they are undesirable.
4. The term 'time orientation' is typically used in psychology in lieu of 'time preference', the preferred term in economics. The concepts have somewhat different interpretations in the two disciplines (cf. Nyhus and Webley, 2006).

REFERENCES

Ajzen, Icek 1991. "The theory of planned behavior." *Organizational Behavior and Human Decision Processes* **50**: 179–211.
Ajzen, Icek 2012. "The theory of planned behavior." *Handbook of Theories of Social Psychology* **1**: 438–459.
Akerlof, George A. and Rachel E. Kranton 2000. "Economics and identity." *Quarterly Journal of Economics* **65**(3): 715–753.
Ali, Daniel A., Derick Bowen and Klaus Deininger 2020. "Personality traits, technology adoption, and technical efficiency: Evidence from smallholder rice farms in Ghana." *The Journal of Development Studies* **56**(7): 1330–1348.
Angeletos, George-Marios, David Laibson, Andrea Repetto, Jeremy Tobacman and Stephen Weinberg 2001. "The hyperbolic consumption model: Calibration, simulation, and empirical evaluation." *Journal of Economic Perspectives* **15**(3): 47–68.
Antonides, Gerrit 2007. "Income evaluation and happiness in the case of an income decline." *Kyklos* **60**(4): 467–484.
Antonides, Gerrit, Fergus Bolger and Ger Trip 2006. "Classroom experiments in behavioral economics." In Morris Altman (ed), *Handbook of Contemporary Behavioral Economics: Foundations and Developments* (pp. 379–404). Armonk, NY: M.E. Sharpe.
Antonides, Gerrit, I. Manon de Groot and W. Fred van Raaij 2011. "Mental budgeting and the management of household finance." *Journal of Economic Psychology* **32**(4): 546–555.
Antonides, Gerrit and Sophia R. Wunderink 2001. "Subjective time preference and willingness to pay for an energy-saving durable good." *Zeitschrift für Sozialpsychologie* **32**(3): 133–141.
Apps, Patricia F. and Ray Rees 1997. "Collective labor supply and household production." *Journal of Political Economy* **105**: 178–190.
Ashraf, Nava, Colin F. Camerer and George Loewenstein 2005. "Adam Smith, behavioral Economist." *Journal of Economic Perspectives* **19**: 131–145.
Becker, Gary S. 1991. *A Treatise on the Family*. Cambridge: Cambridge University Press.
Becker, Gordon M., Morris H. DeGroot and Jacob Marschak 1964. "Measuring utility by a single-response sequential method." *Behavioral Science* **9**(3): 226–232.
Blais, Ann-Renée and Elke U. Weber 2006. "A domain-specific risk-taking (DOSPERT) scale for adult populations." *Judgment and Decision Making* **1**(1): 33–47.
Brickman, Philip, Dan Coates and Ronnie Janoff-Bulman 1978. "Lottery winners and accident victims: Is happiness relative?" *Journal of Personality and Social Psychology* **36**: 917–927.
Caplan, Bryan 2003. "Stigler–Becker versus Myers–Briggs: Why preference-based explanations are scientifically meaningful and empirically important." *Journal of Economic Behavior and Organization* **50**: 391–405.
Carrier, James G. 2012. *A Handbook of Economic Anthropology*. Northampton, MA: Edward Elgar.
Charness, Gary and Matthew Rabin 2002. "Understanding social preferences with simple tests." *The Quarterly Journal of Economics* **117**(3): 817v869.

Chiappori, Pierre-André 1997. "Introducing household production in collective models of labor supply." *Journal of Political Economy* **105**: 191–209.
Cognitive Bias Codex 2016. Retrieved 1 April 2021 at https://dailynous.com/2016/09/14/cognitive-bias-codex/
Cowen, Tyler 1989. "Are all tastes constant and identical? A critique of Stigler and Becker." *Journal of Economic Behavior and Organization* **11**: 127–135.
Crockett, Rachel A., John Weinman, Matthew Hankins and Theresa Marteau 2009. "Time orientation and health related behavior: Measurement in general population samples." *Psychology and Health* **24**(3): 333–350.
Deaton, Angus and John Muellbauer 1980. *Economics and Consumer Behavior*. Cambridge: Cambridge University Press.
De Baets, Shari and Marc Buelens 2012. "Development of the loss aversion questionnaire." Gent: Vlerick Business School, Report 2012/09. Accessed 15 April 2021 at https://public.vlerick.com/Publications/3120e52a-f011-e211-96a6-005056a635ed.pdf.
De Bruijn, Ernst-Jan and Gerrit Antonides 2020. "Determinants of financial worry and rumination." *Journal of Economic Psychology* **76**: 102233.
Easterlin, Richard A. 1974. "Does economic growth improve the human lot?" In Paul A. David and Melvin W. Reder (eds), *Nations and Households in Economic Growth: Essays in Honour of Moses Abramovitz* (pp. 98–125). New York: Academic Press Inc.
Easterlin, Richard A. 2001. "Income and happiness: Towards a unified theory." *The Economic Journal* **111**, 465–484.
Easterlin, Richard A. 2003. "Explaining happiness." *Proceedings of the National Academy of Sciences* **100**(19): 11176–11183.
Elster, John 1982. "Sour grapes—utilitarianism and the genesis of wants." In Amartya Sen and Bernard Williams (eds), *Utilitarianism and Beyond* (pp. 219–238). Cambridge: Cambridge University Press.
Epley, Nicholas, Dennis Mak and Lorraine C. Idson 2006. "Rebate or bonus? The impact of income framing on spending and saving." *Journal of Behavioral Decision Making* **19**(4): 213–227.
Falk, Armin, Anke Becker, Thomas Dohmen, Benjamin Enke, David Huffman and Uwe Sunde 2018. "Global evidence on economic preferences." *The Quarterly Journal of Economics* **133**(4): 1645–1692.
Falk, Armin, Anke Becker, Thomas Dohmen, David Huffman and Uwe Sunde 2016. "The preference survey module: A validated instrument for measuring risk, time, and social preferences." Bonn: IZA Discussion Paper No. 9674.
Ferrer-i-Carbonell, Ada 2005. "Income and well-being: An empirical analysis of the comparison income effect." *Journal of Public Economics* **89**: 997–1019.
Festinger, Leon (1957). *A Theory of Cognitive Dissonance*. Stanford, CA: Stanford University Press.
Fischer, Peter, Jochim I. Krueger, Tobias Greitemeyer, Claudia Vogrincic, Andreas Kastenmüller, Dieter Frey, Moritz Heene, Magdalena Wicher and Martina Kainbacher 2011. "The bystander-effect: A meta-analytic review on bystander intervention in dangerous and non-dangerous emergencies." *Psychological Bulletin* **137**(4): 517–537.
Frank, Robert and Edward Cartwright 2015. *Microeconomics and Behavior*. London: McGraw-Hill.
Frederick, Shane, George Loewenstein and Ted O'Donoghue 2002. "Time discounting and time preference: A critical review." *Journal of Economic Literature* **40**: 351–401.
Gächter, Simon, Eric J. Johnson and Andreas Herrmann 2007. "Individual-level loss aversion in riskless and risky choices." Bonn: IZA Discussion paper No. 2961.
Gandelman, Nestor and Ruben Hernández-Murillo 2015. "Risk aversion at the country level." Federal Reserve Bank of St. Louis *Review* **97**(1): 53v66.
Gately, Dermot 1980. "Individual discount rates and the purchase and utilization of energy-using durables: Comment." *Bell Journal of Economics* **11**(1): 373–374.
Gattig, Alexander 2002. *Intertemporal Decision Making*. Groningen: Interuniversity Center for Social Science Theory and Methodology.
Glimcher, Paul W. and Ernst Fehr 2013. *Neuroeconomics. Decision Making and the Brain*. Amsterdam: Elsevier.
Grether, David M. and Charles R. Plott 1979. "Economic theory of choice and the preference reversal phenomenon." *American Economic Review* **69**(4): 623–638.

Guadalupe-Lanas, Jorge, Jorge Cruz-Cárdenas, Verónica Artola-Jarrín and Andrés Palacio-Fierro 2020. "Empirical evidence for intransitivity in consumer preferences." *Helyon* **6**: e03459.
Guth,Werner, Rolf Schmittberger and Bernd Schwarz 1982. "An experimental analysis of ultimatum bargaining." *Journal of Economic Behavior and Organization* **3**: 367–388.
Harrison, Glenn W., Morton I. Lau and Melonie B. Williams 2002. "Estimating individual discount rates in Denmark: A field experiment." *American Economic Review* **92**(5): 1606–1617.
Hartman, Raymond S., Michael J. Doane and Chi-Keung Woo 1991. "Consumer rationality and the status quo." *Quarterly Journal of Economics* **106**: 141–162.
Hausman, Jerry A. 1979. "Individual discount rates and the purchase and utilization of energy-using durables." *Bell Journal of Economic* **10**(1): 33–54.
Hellmich, Simon N. 2017. "What is socioeconomics? An overview of theories, methods, and themes in the field." *Forum for Social Economics* **46**(1): 3–25.
Hevey, David, Maria M. Pertl, Kevin Thomas, Laura Maher, A. Craig and S. Ni Chuinneagain 2010. "Consideration of future consequences scale: Confirmatory Factor Analysis." *Personality and Individual Differences* **48**: 654–657.
Hirschman, Albert O. 1984. "Against parsimony: Three easy ways of complicating some categories of economic discourse." *American Economic Review* **74**: 89–96.
Howlett, Elizabeth, Jeremy Kees and Elyria Kemp 2008. "The role of self-regulation. Future orientation, and financial knowledge in long-term financial decisions." *Journal of Consumer Affairs* **42**: 223–242.
Johnson, Eric J. and Daniel G. Goldstein 2003. "Do defaults save lives?" *Science* **302**: 1338–1339.
Joireman, Jeffrey, Jeremy Kees and David E. Sprott 2010. "Concern with immediate consequences magnifies the impact of compulsive buying on credit card debt within college students." *Journal Consumer Affairs* **44**(1): 155–178.
Joireman, Jeffrey A., Daniel Balliet, David Sprott, Eric Spangenberg and Jenifer Schultz 2008. "Consideration of future consequences, ego-depletion, and self-control: Support for distinguishing between CFC-immediate and CFC-future sub-scales." *Personality and Individual Differences* **48**: 15–21.
Joireman, Jeffrey A., Terell P. Lasane, Jennifer Bennett, Diana Richards and Salma Solaimani 2001. "Integrating social value orientation and the consideration of future consequences within the extended norm activation model of proenvironmental behavior." *British Journal of Social Psychology* **40**: 133–155.
Joireman, Jeffrey A., David E. Sprott and Eric Spangenberg 2005. "Fiscal responsibility and the consideration of future consequences." *Personality and Individual Differences* **39**: 1159–1168.
Kahneman, Daniel 1999. "Objective happiness." In Daniel Kahneman, Ed Diener and Norbert Schwarz (eds), *Well-Being: The Foundations of Hedonic Psychology* (pp. 3–25). New York: Russell Sage Foundation.
Kahneman, Daniel and Angus Deaton 2010. "High income improves evaluation of life but not emotional well-being." *Proceedings of the National Academy of Sciences* **107**(38): 16489–16493.
Kahneman, Daniel, Barbara L. Fredrickson, Charles A. Schreiber and Donald A. Redelmeier 1993. "When more pain is preferred to less: Adding a better end." *Psychological Science* **4**: 401–405.
Kahneman, Daniel, Jack L. Knetsch and Richard H. Thaler 1986a. "Fairness as a constraint on profit seeking: Entitlements in the market." *American Economic Review* **76**(4): 728–741.
Kahneman, Daniel, Jack L. Knetsch and Richard H. Thaler 1986b. "Fairness and the assumptions of economics." *Journal of Business* **59**(4): S285–S300.
Kahneman, Daniel, Jack L. Knetsch and Richard H. Thaler 1990. "Experimental tests of the endowment effect and the Coase theorem." *Journal of Political Economy* **98**(6): 1325–1347.
Kahneman, Daniel, Jack L. Knetsch and Richard H. Thaler 1991. "The endowment effect, loss aversion, and the status quo bias." *Journal of Economic Perspectives* **5**: 193–206.
Kahneman, Daniel, Alan B. Krueger, David A. Schkade, Norbert Schwarz and Arthur A. Stone 2004. "A survey method for characterizing daily life experience: The day reconstruction method." *Science* **306**: 1776–1780.
Kahneman, Daniel and Jackie S. Snell 1992. "Predicting a changing taste: Do people know what they will like?" *Journal of Behavioral Decision Making* **5**(3): 187–200.
Kahneman, Daniel, Peter Wakker and Rakesh Sarin 1997. "Back to Bentham. Explorations of experienced utility." *Quarterly Journal of Economics* **112**: 375–406.

Kapteyn, Arie, Bernard M.S. van Praag and Floor G. van Herwaarden 1978. "Individual welfare functions and social reference spaces." *Economics Letters* **1**: 173–177.

Krishnamurthi, Lakshman, Tridib Mazumdar and S.P. Raj 1992. "Asymmetric response to price in consumer brand choice and purchase quantity decisions." *Journal of Consumer Research* **19**(3): 387–400.

Laibson, David 1997. "Golden eggs and hyperbolic discounting." *Quarterly Journal of Economics* **112**(2): 443–477.

Laibson, David, Andrea Repetto and Jeremy Tobacman 2007. "Estimating discount functions with consumption choices over the lifecycle." NBER Working Paper No. 13314.

Lancaster, Kelvin J. 1979. *Variety, Equity and Efficiency*. New York: Columbia University Press.

Lichtenstein, Sarah and Paul Slovic 1971. "Reversal of preferences between bids and choices in gambling decisions." *Journal of Experimental Psychology* **89**: 46–55.

List, J. 2021. *The Voltage Effect*. Toronto: Penguin Random House Canada.

Loewenstein, Gerorge, Ted O'Donoghue and Matthew Rabin 2003. "Projection bias in predicting future utility." *The Quarterly Journal of Economics* **118**(4): 1209–1248.

Lucas, Richard E. 2007. "Adaptation and the set-point model of subjective well-being: Does happiness change after major life events?" *Current Directions in Psychological Science* **16**(2): 75–79.

Lundberg, Shelly and Robert Pollak 1993. "Separate spheres bargaining and the marriage market." *Journal of Political Economy* **101**(6): 988–1010.

Manser, Marilyn and Murray Brown 1980. "Marriage household decision-making: A bargaining analysis." *International Economic Review* **21**: 31–44.

Mauria, Aurelio G. and Roberta Minazzi 2013. "Web reviews influence on expectations and purchasing intentions of hotel potential customers." *International Journal of Hospitality Management* **34**: 99–107.

Maynard, Leigh and Vijay Subramaniam 2015. "Testing for sources of irreversible consumer demand." *Economics World* **3**(1): 1–17.

McElroy Marjorie B. and Mary J. Horney 1981. "Nash-bargained household decisions: Toward a generalization of the theory of demand." *International Economic Review* **22**: 333–349.

McFadden, Daniel 1973. "Conditional logit analysis of qualitative choice behavior." In Paul Zarembka (ed), *Frontiers in Econometrics*, (pp. 105–142). New York: Academic Press.

Mehnert, Thoman, Herbert H. Kraus, Rosemary Nadler and Mary Boyd 1990. "Correlates of life satisfaction in those with disabling conditions." *Rehabilitation Psychology* **35**: 3–17.

Mischel, Walter 1974. "Processes in delay of gratification." In Leonard Berkowitz (ed), *Advances in Experimental Social Psychology*, Vol. 7 (pp. 249–292). New York: Academic Press.

Mischel, Walter 1984. "Convergences and challenges in the search for consistency." *American Psychologist* **39**: 351–364.

Mullainathan, Sendhil and Richard H. Thaler 2001. "Behavioral economics." In Neil Smelser and Paul Baltes (eds), *International Encyclopedia of the Social and Behavioral Sciences,* Vol. 20 (pp. 1094–1100). Oxford: Oxford University Press.

Murphy, Ryan O. and Kurt A. Ackermann 2014. "Social Value Orientation: Theoretical and measurement issues in the study of social preferences." *Personality and Social Psychology Review* **18**(1): 13–41.

Murphy, Ryan O., Kurt A. Ackermann and Michel J.J. Handgraaf 2011. "Measuring social value orientation." *Judgment and Decision Making* **6**(8): 771–781.

Nagler, Matthew G. 2021. "Thoughts matter: A theory of motivated preference." Working paper, City University of New York.

Nyhus, Ellen K. and Paul Webley 2006. "Discounting, self-control, and saving." In Morris Altman (ed), *Handbook of Contemporary Behavioral Economics* (pp. 297–325). New York: M.E. Sharpe.

O'Donoghue, Ted and Jason Somerville 2018. "Modeling risk aversion in economics." *Journal of Economic Perspectives* **32**(2): 91–114.

Olsen, Jerome, Matthias Kasper, Christoph Kogler, Stephan Muehlbacher and Erich Kirchler 2019. "Mental accounting of income tax and value added tax among self-employed business owners." *Journal of Economic Psychology* **70**: 125–139.

Petrocelli, John V. 2003. "Factor validation of the consideration of future consequences scale." *Journal of Social Psychology* **143**: 404–413.

Putler, Daniel S. 1992. "Incorporating reference price effects into a theory of consumer choice." *Marketing Science* **11**(3): 287–309.

Qian, Chen, Gerrit Antonides and Nico Heerink 2021. "Do farmers' personalities matter for how well they perform? The impact of personality traits on technical efficiency of Chinese rice farmers." Working paper, Wageningen University.

Raghunathan, Rajagopal, Rebecca W. Naylor and Wayne D. Hoyer 2006. "The unhealthy = tasty intuition and its effects on taste inferences, enjoyment, and choice of food products." *Journal of Marketing* **70**(4): 170–184.

Ratchford, Brian T. 1979. "Operationalizing economic models of demand for product characteristics." *Journal of Consumer Research* **6**: 76v85.

Read, Daniel, Gerrit Antonides, Laura van den Ouden and Harry Trienekens 2001. "Which is better: Simultaneous or sequential choice?" *Organizational Behavior and Human Decision Processes* **84**(1): 54–70.

Read, Daniel and N. Liliana Read 2004. "Time discounting over the life span." *Organization Behavior and Human Decision Processes* **94**(1): 22–32.

Ross, William T. and Itamar Simonson 1991. "Evaluations of pairs of experiences: A preference for happy endings." *Journal of Behavioral Decision Making* **4**: 273–282.

Shefrin, Hersh and Meir Statman 1985. "The disposition to sell winners too early and ride losers too long: Theory and evidence." *Journal of Finance* **40**(3): 777–790.

Slovic, Paul 1995. "The construction of preference." *American Psychologist* **50**(5): 364–371.

Soman, Dilip 2001. "The mental accounting of sunk time costs: Why time is not like money." *Journal of Behavioral Decision Making* **14**: 169–185.

Sonnemans, Joep, Frans van Dijk and Frans van Winden 2006. "On the dynamics of social ties structures in groups." *Journal of Economic Psychology* **27**(2): 187–204.

Stevenson, Betsey and Justin Wolfers 2013. "Subjective well-being and income: Is there any evidence of satiation?" *American Economic Review: Papers and Proceedings* **103**(3): 598–604.

Stigler, George and Gary Becker 1977. "De gustibus non est disputandum." *American Economic Review* **67**: 76–90.

Strathman, Alan, Faith Gleicher, David S. Boninger and C. Scott Edwards 1994. "The consideration of future consequences: Weighing immediate and distant outcomes of behavior." *Journal of Personality and Social Psychology* **66**: 742–752.

Talukdar, Debabrata and Charles Lindsey 2013. "To buy or not to buy: Consumers' demand response patterns for healthy versus unhealthy food." *Journal of Marketing* **77**(2): 124–138.

Thaler, Richard H. 1981. "Some empirical evidence on dynamic inconsistency." *Economics Letters* **8**: 201–207.

Thaler, Richard H. 1985. "Mental accounting and consumer choice." *Marketing Science* **4**: 199–214.

Toepoel, Vera 2010. "Is consideration of future consequences a changeable construct?" *Personality and Individual Differences* **48**: 951–956.

Tversky, Amos 1969. "Intransitivity of preferences." *Psychological Review* **76**(1): 31–48.

Tversky, Amos and Richard Thaler 1990. "Anomalies. Preference reversals." *Journal of Economic Perspectives* **4**(2): 201–211.

Unger, Lynette S. 1991. "Altruism as a motivation to volunteer." *Journal of Economic Psychology* **12**: 71–100.

Van Beek, Jannette, Gerrit Antonides and Michel J.J. Handgraaf 2013. "Eat now, exercise later: The relation between consideration of immediate and future consequences and healthy behavior." *Personality and Individual Differences* **54**: 785–791.

Van de Stadt, Huib, Gerrit Antonides and Bernard M.S. van Praag 1984. "Empirical testing of the expected utility model." *Journal of Economic Psychology* **5**: 17–29.

Van Dijk, Wilco W., Minou M.B. van der Werf and Lotte F. van Dillen 2020. "The Psychological Inventory of Financial Scarcity (PIFS): A Psychometric Evaluation." Working paper, Leyden University.

Van Lange, Paul A.M., Wilma Otten, Ellen M.M. de Bruin and Jeffrey A. Joireman 1997. "Development of prosocial, individualistic, and competitive orientations: Theory and preliminary evidence." *Journal of Personality and Social Psychology* **73**(4): 733–746.

Van Praag, Bernard M.S. and Barbara E. Baarsma 2005. Using happiness surveys to value intangibles: The case of airport noise." *Economic Journal* **115**(500): 224–246.
Van Praag, Bernard M.S. and Paul Frijters 1999. "The measurement of welfare and well-being: The Leyden approach." In Daniel Kahneman, Ed Diener and Norbert Schwarz (eds), *Well-Being: The Foundations of Hedonic Psychology* (pp. 413–433). New York: Russell Sage Foundation.
Van Raaij, W. Fred 1999. "History of economic psychology." In Peter Earl and Simon Kemp (eds), *The Elgar Companion to Consumer Research and Economic Psychology* (pp. 289–296). Aldershot: Edward Elgar.
Verhoef, Peter C., Gerrit Antonides and Arnoud N. de Hoog 2004. "Service encounters as a sequence of events: The importance of peak experiences." *Journal of Service Research* **7**: 53–64.
Vollmer, Elisabeth, Daniel Hermann and Oliver Musshof 2017. "Is the risk attitude measured with the Holt and Laury task reflected in farmers' production risk?" *European Review of Agricultural Economics* **44**(3): 399–424.
Warren, Caleb, A. Peter McGraw and Leaf van Boven 2011. "Values and preferences: Defining preference construction." *Cognitive Science* **2**(2): 193–205.
Weber, Elke U., Ann-Renée Blais and Nany E. Betz 2002. "A domain-specific risk-attitude scale: Measuring risk perceptions and risk behaviors." *Journal of Behavioral Decision Making* **15**: 263–290.
Welsch, Heinz 2007. "Environmental welfare analysis: A life satisfaction approach." *Ecological Economics* **62**: 544–551.
Welsch, Heinz and Jan Kühling. 2010. "Pro-environmental behavior and rational consumer choice: Evidence from surveys of life satisfaction." *Journal of Economic Psychology* **31**: 405–420.
Wierenga, Berend 1984. "Empirical test of the Lancaster characteristics model." *International Journal of Research in Marketing* **1**: 263–293.
Wolf, Scott T., Taya R. Cohen, Jeffrey L. Kirchner, Andrew Rea, R.M. Montoya and Chester A. Insko 2009. "Reducing intergroup conflict through the consideration of future consequences." *European Journal of Social Psychology* **39**: 831–841.
Yan, Ji, Kun Tian, Saeed Heravi and Peter Morgan 2016. "Asymmetric demand patterns for products with added nutritional benefits and products without nutritional benefits." *European Journal of Marketing* **50**(9/10): 1672–1702.

3. Behavioural economics: What have we missed? Exploring 'classical' behavioural economics roots in AI, cognitive psychology and complexity theory

Steve J. Bickley and Benno Torgler

INTRODUCTION

Behavioural economics (BE) 'tries to explain (and ultimately, to apply these findings into practice) why individuals frequently make [*seemingly*] irrational choices, and why and how their behaviour does not match the patterns predicted by neoclassical models' (Diacon et al. 2013, p. 29). While BE's value in explaining individual behaviours is clear, it is less clear whether and how it contributes to any greater understanding of the associated social phenomena that may emerge (Heap 2013):

> Quite a few economists identify themselves as behavioural economists these days. Although they share common characteristics, they do behavioural economics (BE) in significantly different ways. Many of them would be hard pressed to articulate exactly what it is that makes them behavioural economists.
>
> (Tomer 2007, p. 463)

So, in this chapter, we ask (conceptually and methodologically): what exactly is BE and what are its roots? And further, what may we have missed along the way?

Kao and Velupillai (2015) make a clear distinction between modern behavioural economics (MBE) and classical behavioural economics (CBE) distinguished by their methodological, epistemological and philosophical approaches, norms and ideals. Sent (2004) made a somewhat similar observation, referring to CBE and MBE as 'old' and 'new' BE, respectively. MBE remains largely within the orthodox neoclassical framework of 'optimisation under constraints', attempting to improve the realism of its mathematical modelling by 'providing it with more realistic psychological foundations' (Camerer & Loewenstein 2004, p. 1). Hence, MBE is to some degree 'stuck' within the concepts and methods typical of neoclassical economics. In contrast, CBE questions whether BE should break free entirely from the incumbent neoclassical paradigm, questioning both its ontology (i.e., the complex and interconnected nature of dynamic networks of historically and context-defined agents as opposed to representative agents in idealised, axiomatic worlds) and epistemology (i.e., algorithmic, adaptive, rationally bounded agents as opposed to those which demonstrate 'Olympian rationality and optimisation', within some perfectly specified task environment). See Simon (1990) for discussion. Ultimately, MBE is the dominant (and lasting) form of BE evident in the literature today. As Sent (2004) describes, '[t]he transition period ended in favour of efforts to strengthen mainstream economics by taking rationality as the yardstick as opposed to ones to develop an alternative squarely based on bounded rationality' (p. 747).

We argue that revisiting CBE concepts and methods will benefit the wider BE research program by questioning its yardstick approach to 'Olympian' rationality and optimisation and in doing so, exploring the 'how' and 'why' of economic behaviours (micro, meso and macro) in greater detail and clarity. We will then do the same for fields which share similar ontological and epistemological roots with CBE and BE more generally, in particular, cognitive psychology, complexity theory and artificial intelligence (AI). By revisiting CBE (and related fields) we look to engage in 'deeper' (and potentially more profound) scientific discussions of ontological and epistemological importance (Spiegler & Milberg 2014), as opposed to the seemingly more method-focused contributions of MBE. Although the latter are undoubtedly important in their own right, they may not allow BE to live up to its full potential in improving the predictive power of contextualised and boundedly rational economics. To compare and guide the combination of methods typical of each field, we present a conceptual framework we call 'CMM' (constrained methods matrix), extending the impact and relevance of Minsky's (1992) causal diversity matrix (CDM) to BE and the social sciences more generally by incorporating measures of informational complexity and uncertainty. Behavioural economists and social scientists can use CMM to guide their selection of tools and methods of investigation with respect to the *problem faced* (i.e., number of potential causal factors and the scale of their effects) and the *complexity* (i.e., volume, variety and velocity – three of the four Vs of big data) and *uncertainty* (i.e., information that is partial or not representative, not fully reliable and/or inherently imprecise and/or conflicting evidence [Bhatnagar & Kanal 1986] – i.e., veracity, the last of the four Vs of big data) of the information, data and knowledge available at hand to solve the problem. Together – with both concepts *and* methods – we argue this will overcome the current awkward phase in which BE finds itself (somewhat neoclassical, somewhat behavioural) and enable a more contextualised and boundedly rational economics with greater predictive power and real-world relevance.

In the next section, we introduce and detail the common ground between concepts in MBE and CBE, as well as the major departures between the two streams of BE. We then extend this exploration to the fields of cognitive psychology, complexity theory and AI. In the third section, we do the same for methods as opposed to concepts, leveraging the aforementioned CMM methods framework (see Figure 3.3) as a guiding hand. In the fourth section, we identify future research directions for concepts and methods (respectively) that we deem as promising research avenues for the continued advancement of BE towards real-world relevance and practicality. In particular, we discuss cognitive models, micro, meso and macro foundations and big data for concepts and neuroscience, agent-based models (ABM) and AI for methods. We then provide concluding remarks to summarise our primary theses; we as a discipline (BE) must look back *and* side to side for insights and methods from other research paradigms, practice academic bravery and resilience, and widen the scope of BE policy and practice by learning to compare and combine a more diverse suite of conceptual foundations and methodological toolkits.

CONCEPTS

Methods can become somewhat of a means to an end, heavily influenced by the deeper levels that define key aspects of research investigations: *which phenomena are worthwhile to study? What can be (practically) measured? What assumptions can we make? What defines successful scientific knowledge generation?* Whilst we do not suggest that methods are defined wholly and completely by the deeper levels of scientific knowledge, we recognise the influence of conceptual thinking on the creation and adaptation of methods to test (confirm or reject) more 'foundational' scientific speculations and hence, explore which concepts BE may embrace from CBE and its related fields. Doing so will provide context to the methods explored in the third section.

CBE and MBE

CBE takes the view of agents and institutions as information processing systems (Simon 1979), underpinned by algorithmic and computational resources and procedures and engaging with complex decision problems. Under this lens, agents and institutions receive information from their (local) surrounding environment as inputs to internal decision-making processes and procedures, which they modify and adapt to suit the specific needs of the current context (i.e., task environment). CBE, in contrast to MBE, assumes no underlying preference order (utility curve) and postulates that agent decision-making, at any level and against any institutional setting, is subject to bounded rationality and emulates satisficing behaviours. CBE also focuses on the behaviour of agents and institutions in disequilibrium or non-equilibrium situations, as opposed to focusing on behaviours in or near equilibrium (a special case of collective behaviour) as is the case with MBE – which, in doing so, 'accepts mathematical analysis of (uncountably) infinite events or iterations, infinite horizon optimisation problems and probabilities defined over s-algebras and arbitrary measure spaces', whereas 'CBE only exemplifies cases which contain finitely large search spaces and [are] constrained by finite-time horizon' (Kao & Velupillai 2015, p. 240). Adaptive and satisficing economic behaviour seems natural (and intuitive) within ever-evolving, time-space constrained and history-dependent (socio)economic systems where turbulence – due to both endogenous *and* exogenous activity and events – keeps the system in a non-equilibrium or disequilibrium state. Hence, it justifies the requirement for agents to constantly assess and re-assess the performance and efficiency of their decision-making heuristics and behaviours; or in other words, to think about their thinking and adjust themselves accordingly. Lo (2017) offers fruitful insights into the area of financial markets, using the idea of adaptive agents[1] who are boundedly rational and therefore make suboptimal decisions, but also learn from past experience and revise their heuristics via negative feedback. Lo uses the term 'approximately rational' (p. 188) as individuals adapt to their environment. Maladaptation, for example, emerges when heuristics are taken out of the environmental context in which they emerged.

Essentially, CBE focuses on 'discovering the empirical laws that describe behaviour correctly and as accurately as possible' (Sent 2004, p. 742), as opposed to focusing only on empirical laws that satisfy mathematical axioms and strong assumptions for optimising behaviours. Under a framework of bounded rationality and satisficing, agents and institutions are only able to make use of information which is readily accessible to them (information that is often inherently incomplete and approximate, see e.g., McCarthy [2000] for further discussion) and only to the extent that their available cognitive and computational resources enable. In other words, one cannot make use of information which is not made available either by perception on the part of the individual or deception by others, and one is not able to perform computations which require greater computational resources than those presently available or for which one has the capacity to employ. Intelligent decision-makers (whether human, animal or artificial) are dealing with computationally complex problems and hence, navigating through 'deep', complex and less-structured search spaces. Often they make use of heuristics (i.e., decision rules) and perform satisficing behaviours (e.g., 'close enough is good enough' behaviour) to reduce complexity and achieve something which is at least satisfactory to their needs, wants, desires or goals (Simon 1996). Their behaviours may turn out to be some best approximate of the optimising behaviours exhibited by 'Olympian' rationalists in certain situations and contexts, but more often than not, they do not reach such 'Olympian' status. This 'deeper' interpretation or understanding of bounded rationality (as opposed to the MBE interpretation which stops at the boundedly rational decision-making capabilities of computationally constrained agents) necessitates and encourages an accurate and computational approximation of both the agent *and* the environment to which they contribute, shape and adapt in order to become algorithmically implementable.

Cognitive Psychology

In building a more accurate picture of the *individual* in economics, cognitive psychology takes the view of humans as *information processing systems* (Simon 1979), similar to CBE. Sternberg and Sternberg (2016) define cognitive psychology as the 'study of how people perceive, learn, remember, and think about information [. . .] [and relatedly,] learn, structure, store, and use knowledge. This makes possible the algorithmic representation of decision-making procedures and processes that are used when agents face complex (socio)economic problems' (pp. 3–16). Herb Simon (1996b) points out in his autobiography *Models of My Life* that his most important years of life as a scientist were 1955 and 1956. In the last months of 1955, he focused his attention and efforts on the psychology of human problem-solving – or to the more precise, on discovering the symbolic processes that humans use in thinking. Simon, together with Al Newell (whom he first met in 1952 at RAND) and Cliff Shaw (who was an outstanding systems programmer) saw the use of the computer as a general processor for symbols and therefore, thoughts. They invented list-processing languages to create the Logic Theorist (LT), which was the first computer program able to solve non-numerical problems via selective search, therefore pioneering AI. Herb Simon and Allen Newell presented their Logic Theorist at the 1956 symposium on information theory at MIT, a moment George Miller described as the birthday of cognitive science, as well as his own rejection of behaviouralism and cognitive awakening (Gazzaniga et al. 2014; Hunt 2007).

Computer science had the largest impact on cognitive psychology relative to other influences such as neuroscience or the study of language (Hunt 2007). Newell, Simon and Shaw's General Problem Solver (GPS) (1959) was a program developed around the agenda of understanding information processing and human problem solving (for a detailed discussion, see Torgler 2021b) and brought 'a metamorphosis in cognitive psychology by giving psychologists a more detailed and workable conception of mental processes than any they had previously had, plus a practical way to investigate them' (Hunt 2007, p. 595). For Simon, the importance of the computer was comparable to the microscope for biology: 'It provided a way to set up experiments in such a manner as to test constructs which had been formulated for psychological processes in a sharp and unequivocal manner' (Crosson 1992, p. 440).

Decision problems (particularly those which are vague, uncertain, ambiguous and ill-structured) characterise much of everyday human and (socio)economic life. Owing to this complexity, humans (limited in their ability to optimise 'rationally') instead satisfice and use decision rules based on the often incomplete and approximate information currently available at hand. Indeed, in facing such complex decision problems, 'deductive means are of limited value due to undecidabilities and unsolvabilities, [so] agents consciously resort to non-deductive means for solving decision problems' (Al-Suwailem 2011, p. 485). In other words, they rely on heuristics, decision rules, rules of thumb and biases to reduce cognitive loading and effort and achieve (subjectively) satisfactory outcomes rather than the 'best' or 'optimal' ones. Many such heuristics and biases have been identified in the BE, psychology and social science literature (Benartzi & Thaler 2007; Gilovich et al. 2002; Tversky & Kahneman 1974).

Under the humans as *information processing systems* framework, it is important to understand how humans perceive and make sense of approximate concepts (McCarthy 2000) and also ill-structured problems. It is also important to understand how humans generate, represent, accumulate and adapt their knowledge from experience, learning, culture and genetics alike. Minsky (1988) derived the idea of a K-line to explore agent learning and knowledge generation, representation, adaptation and evolution. A K-line is a snapshot of a mental state (or sequence of mental states) that when later activated will put you into a similar state and hence, can be used to guide decision-making and behaviours. This concept of a K-line could be used to help model and understand knowledge acquisition, accumulation, storage, retrieval and adaptation in human, animal and artificial agents alike and equally, in networks (societies) of agents. For example, when an agent successfully solves a complex decision problem, a new K-line could be initiated and its relation to other K-lines established. When facing the same (or a similar problem), the new K-line can be activated and hence, emotions and mental processes similar to those activated during the initial problem-solving event can be aroused to help guide the search for a suitable solution in the current problem. In doing so, they prompt to ask crucial questions such as: *how was the problem solved previously? What were the failed attempts and why did they fail? How should a similar failure be avoided in the future?* When faced with a novel decision problem, similarities and differences to problems faced previously can be identified and their associated K-lines activated (and adapted) for use in light of the current problem and task environment. In a sense, we engage counterfactual thinking (Costello & McCarthy 1999) in exploring the various possible *what-ifs* and learning from these non-experiences before we engage physically in the real world. The malleability (i.e., adaptivity) of individual K-lines – in other words, their *elaboration tolerance* (McCarthy 1998) – determines the ability to incorporate new experiences, knowledge and information into existing knowledge structures and cognitive frameworks which may simultaneously operate (or self-organise) on more than one (hierarchical) level of cognition.

This – we would say – is a slightly more ambitious (and comprehensive) programme in comparison to Kahneman's (2011) 'thinking fast and slow' with only two levels (i.e., the fast system 1 and the slow system 2). Such 'dumbbell' mentalities can be a useful nicety (simplification) for empirical analyses but can lead to false analogies and constrained thinking (Minsky 1988). With only two systems we aggregate all kinds of 'slow' thinking together as one; as if to say that planning, optimisation and resourcefulness are of the same nature. For example, Sloman (2001) presents H-Cogaff, a three-level architecture which supports simultaneous, interdependent, adaptive reactive, deliberative and reflective processes and thinking. This allows two levels of 'system 2' thinking: one which thinks about issues and problems at hand and one that performs meta-cognition (i.e., thinking about thinking), but Sloman does not reject the idea of more levels of cognition. Minsky's (2007) *Emotion Machine* offers another such multi-level (six levels) cognitive architecture, including instinctive, learned, deliberative, reflective, self-reflective and self-conscious processes and thinking, further unravelling the full gamut of potential human (and animal) cognition, and leaving room for future discoveries and breakthroughs via a flexible, multi-level framework.[2] Whilst originating in the field of AI, these conceptual frameworks can provide useful ways to think about cognition in human, animal and artificial agents alike. Surprisingly, there has been some reluctance among cognitive psychologists to invest more efforts into such multi-level frameworks or unified theories of cognition as suggested by Newell in his 1987 William James Lectures at Harvard University (Newell 1994). Psychology gravitates towards small and easily testable micro-theories (for a discussion see Bach 2009, p. 7). In contrast, the work on cognitive architectures is driven by understanding cognition through construction and design. See Sloman and Chrisley (2005) for discussion on such 'higher-order design of bootstrapping mechanisms' (p. 154).

Complexity Theory

Complexity theory is a collection of concepts and methods used to identify, characterise, analyse and manage[3] complex systems, studying emergent and adaptive agent behaviours in such systems and settings defined by time-space and historical-time constraints and characteristics. Complex systems are themselves made up of a large number of interacting parts which interact in non-simple and complex ways (Simon 1962); furthermore, they are typically dissipative, open structures (Foster 2005) that exchange energy and information with their surrounding environment. The emergent phenomena and behaviours of such systems which evolve over time are often highly unpredictable from observation of the constituent parts alone. As summarised nicely by Gomes and Gubareva (2021):

> Complexity emerges because of the heterogeneous nature of agents. Agents are not alike; they differ in their preferences, endowments, expectations, hierarchical position, degree of connectivity, and ability to engage in successful interactions, among other features. Furthermore, as the interaction takes place, agents learn, adapt, and mutate, leading to a systematic and never-ending evolutionary process where both the individual agents and the whole socioeconomic structure are subject to constant and perpetual change. Out-of-equilibrium dynamics are the rule and not the exception. [. . .] The behaviour of humans coevolve with the environment; cooperation and competition, the formation and dissolution of alliances, the establishment of new relations and loss of others, introduce systematic changes in the intended goals and in the strategies followed to attain them. The changing nature of agents in a complex system preserves the micro-diversity and generates emergent phenomena that fuels the evolutionary dynamics of the ecosystem as a whole. Stability is not an inherent characteristic of the economy or any of its constituent parts; on the contrary, [socio]economic ecosystems are unstable, evolutionary and complex.
>
> (p. 316)

Human systems (e.g., social, industrial, economic, cultural or artificial) regularly involve a large number of heterogeneous human agents who act and react almost simultaneously (i.e., in real time) and may be spread across varied geographical proximities when they do so. Such systems often exhibit complexity as they behave qualitatively different from the random Brownian motion assumed in conventional econometric theories (Mandelbrot & Hudson 2004). Human systems often exhibit complex behaviours such as non-linearity, sharp discontinuities and highly unpredictable collective properties which are not attributable merely to the aggregate sum of individual agents' behaviour (Holling 2001). Thus, the complexity approach in economics is essential to enable greater realism in theory and modelling and to shed light on the intra- and inter-systemic causal relations between variables which help fuel the self-organisation, non-linearity and endogenous feedback mechanisms evident in most 'real-world' data of complex human systems (Choudhury 2013).[4]

Most complex systems, whether human, natural or artificial, are dynamic and hierarchical in structure with each level serving two functions: to conserve and stabilise conditions for faster and smaller levels and to generate and test novelty/innovations and survival/optimisation strategies for slower and larger levels (Simon 2001). Prigogine (1980) observed that each level of a hierarchical system operates on a different spatio-temporal scale and constantly evolves in function and form over time. Rather than a reference to top-down authoritative control, hierarchical in the sense conveyed here refers to semi-autonomous and interacting levels (subsystems and agents) which communicate a small set of local information or resource constraints to the next higher (slower and coarser) level in the system. The formation of hierarchical structures is not uncommon in human social and societal systems: individuals form groups, and groups form organisations and markets that make up cities, societies, nations and global sub-regions (Helbing 2009). Such hierarchical structures exhibit near decomposability, meaning approximately independent short-run behaviours of individual agents and long-run dependence of individual agents' behaviour on collective behaviours (Simon 1962). Ceddia et al. (2013), drawing on Ulanowicz (1997), generalise such hierarchical systems by approximating to three nested levels of hierarchy, each of which operates on a comparatively different but related spatio-temporal scale, with feedback loops as depicted in Figure 3.1. However, there is no specific limit as to the configuration of feedback and feedforward loops between hierarchical levels, and contextual information often enters into the picture at every level as depicted by the dotted and dashed lines, respectively. The focal level is the level of focus for the main phenomena of interest by the research team (e.g., monthly indicators of economic growth of a certain local government county). The upper level corresponds to the level immediately 'above' the focal level (e.g., the state or nation in which the local government county resides) in which the system and focal level is embedded and reflects the macro influences on focal level dynamics. The lower level corresponds to the level immediately 'below' the focal level (e.g., the decision-making processes of households, businesses, individuals and institutions which co-exist and interact within the local government county) containing the constituent parts or components of the focal level.

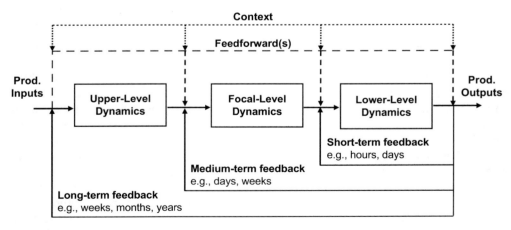

Figure 3.1 Nested feedback loops of a hierarchical system composed of three levels: the upper level, the focal level and the lower level

As Simon (1962) suggests, for 'most systems in nature, it is somewhat arbitrary as to where we leave off the partitioning, and what subsystems we take as elementary' (p. 468). Thus, the model depicted in Figure 3.1 provides a flexible conceptual framework for the modelling of complex human socioeconomic systems which can be adapted for micro-, meso- *and* macroeconomic analyses. Coupled with a varied and wide analytical toolkit, complexity theory can redefine how evolutionary and adaptive economics processes and procedures rise and fall over time-space constrained, historically dependent contexts and environments. Fascinating opportunities are available for behavioural economists to think about how such a perspective feeds back into the public policy area and policy solutions in general. Colander and Kupers (2014) provide wonderful insights with respect to a complexity policy frame that creates government solutions allowing an eco-structure conducive to giving people the institutional space to self-organise in ways that solve social problems. Complexity does not necessarily mean that the social system becomes unpredictable and uncontrollable; we simply need the proper concepts, methods and building blocks to better explore complexity. Behavioural economics can contribute to the derivation of such solutions, as they will require a good understanding of how people make choices and how people influence each other in the decision-making process.

Artificial Intelligence

Not all approaches in AI are created (or dreamed) equal, nor do they focus on the same aspects or measures of intelligence, as demonstrated by the varied design of intelligent agents. Indeed the road to 'true' AI has been long, winding and bumpy, and our final destination still remains out of reach. Russell and Norvig (2010) identify and cluster the four main approaches to AI: *thinking humanly, thinking rationally, acting humanly* and *acting rationally*. As depicted in Figure 3.2, these clusters are defined by their focus (thought processes/procedures or

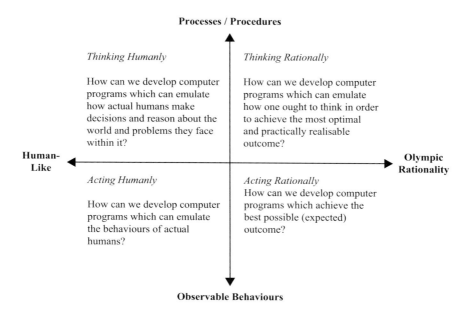

Figure 3.2   Approaches to artificial intelligence studies

observable behavioural phenomenon) and measure of humanness (rationally bounded and human-like or 'Olympian' rationality). Such clusters have led to a vast and varied literature.

For the most part, the rational-agent or *acting rationally* approach has dominated AI research owing to its generality and strong mathematical foundations. In particular, AI methods such as machine learning (ML) and deep learning (DL) – iterative methods of learning based on probability theory and statistics – have helped humans achieve great engineering feats, even under circumstances where there remain large uncertainties in current states, observations and future predictions. These approaches, classed 'narrow' AI, are typically domain- and problem-specific and hence, lack the breadth of knowledge and adaptability to new situations that are expected of 'true' or general AI systems (Baum et al. 2011; Goertzel & Pennachin 2007), particularly when operating in complex decision environments where perfect rationality (i.e., perfect knowledge of the problem space, unlimited cognitive capabilities and hence consistency in observed behaviours) is infeasible or unlikely to be attained. In the long run, these 'narrow' approaches to AI will need to be replaced with more realistic models which can operate within and across the realms of pre-defined (user-specified) objective functions without requiring that these functions be completely and correctly specified (i.e., can deal with uncertainty) (Russell & Norvig 2010). A mixed and integrated approach to the various AI methods (i.e., ways of thinking) may prove to be what is needed to advance AI technologies to the human level (Minsky 1992).

The procedural-behavioural and rational-descriptive debates in AI are somewhat akin to debates in CBE and MBE. The former looks to 'describe[s] behaviour correctly and as accurately as possible' (Sent 2004, p. 742) and does not shy away from the unobservability of mental procedures and processes. Hence, CBE aligns more closely with the human-centred approaches to AI. MBE, in contrast, takes 'Olympian' rationality as a basis from which to measure the efficacy of decision-making and hence, appeals to the 'narrow' AI approaches mentioned previously. Some have argued (Beal & Winston 2009; McCarthy 2007; Minsky 2007; Nilsson 1995) that a return to the original aims and goals of 'classical' AI – being the understanding, modelling and replication of human mental processes, decision-making and reasoning – will be what ultimately catapults the field of AI towards human-level AI and in doing so, meet the high expectations of industry, government and the general public alike. Along the same line of thinking, a mutual enrichment of knowledge, concepts and methods between AI and behavioural economics will be of great benefit to both fields.

METHODS

As our econometric and statistical methods have become stronger (and equally, our focus on specialising and mastering these methods), we tend to lose sight of the bigger picture and of the alternative methods available for solving real-world problems. Rather than celebrating and welcoming diversity of approach and process, silos of accepted methods begin to form in academic fields wherein norms support the incumbent approach – and perhaps if lucky, the gradual incorporation of alternative (yet often similar) methods into practice. Bach (2009) points out that a field's credibility

> may be due to their focus on an area that allows a homogenous methodology and thus, the growth and establishment of scientific routines, communities, and rules of advancement. But this strictness comes at a price: the individual fields tend to diverge, not just in the content that they capture, but

also in the ways they produce and compare results. Thus, it not only becomes difficult to bridge the terminological gaps and methodological differences in order to gain an integrative understanding of an individual phenomenon – the results from different disciplines might completely resist attempts at translation beyond a shallow and superficial level.

(pp. 7–8)

Rather than engage in the never-ending debate on which methods, representations or algorithms may be (subjectively) 'best', Minsky (1992) offers what we think is a very powerful and intuitive conceptual tool to encourage diversity in AI problem-solving methods – the causal diversity matrix (CDM). The CDM captures nicely the diversity in approaches required to reach human-level AI, arguing that to attain *true* 'expert' status, AI systems of the future will need versatility in their *ways to think* as 'no single method works well for all problems' and 'different kinds of problems need different kinds of reasoning' (Minsky 1992, p. 1). As Sloman (2008) stresses, '[t]here usually is no "best" alternative' (p. 4).

Given the current (and narrow) method-focused contributions of MBE, we see that a conceptual framework such as the CDM could provide the impetus (and starting point) for behavioural economists (and social scientists more generally) to look beyond what is mainstream and common practice and, further, allow us to engage more deeply with a wider suite of concepts, tools, methods, representations and algorithms than currently available within the bounds of MBE. Similar calls have been made for methodological diversity with the idea of triangulation (Ramsay 1998) or parallel non-equivalent descriptions (Giampietro & Mayumi 2000) and mixed methods more generally (Cronin 2016), providing further support for the use of such a visual tool in the CDM methods matrix.

Here, we extend Minsky's (1992) CDM by incorporating measures of informational complexity (i.e., volume, variety and velocity) and uncertainty (i.e., veracity). We do this because we can only solve a problem with the data (i.e., stimuli with no meaning and perhaps not yet registered), information (i.e., interpreted data) and knowledge (i.e., learned information incorporated into the agent's current and future reasoning resources)[5] that we currently have available (see Figure 3.3). This includes information from both our own previous experiences and existing knowledge, and also the data and information we can extract from our environment and the specific task at hand. Hence, we propose to name this matrix the constrained methods matrix (CMM) owing to the restricted nature of the rationally bounded agents that we are and the boundedly rational environments in which we are embedded. The CMM can guide one's choice of method and in particular, for the problems (often 'wicked') faced by behavioural economists (and social scientists more generally) which we believe require a more diverse approach than we have currently seen within the literature. We also believe that CMM can make more tractable those problems which were previously intractable, by way of manipulating informational uncertainty and complexity. For example, we may try to increase the volume and variety of data available in the current problem we face to increase informational complexity and move us towards methods like analogy-based reasoning, fuzzy logic and neural networks. It is important to remember that the matrix partitions are not hard lines and hence, overlap of methods (similarity across method classes) and shared empirical/conceptual roots is not uncommon.

In the following subsections, we use the CMM to situate each of CBE, MBE, cognitive psychology, complexity theory and AI with respect to the typical methods of choice employed by the researchers in each (sub-)field. We by no means suggest that these are the only methods employed in these fields; however, we see the value in this exercise comes from looking

42   *Handbook of research methods in behavioural economics*

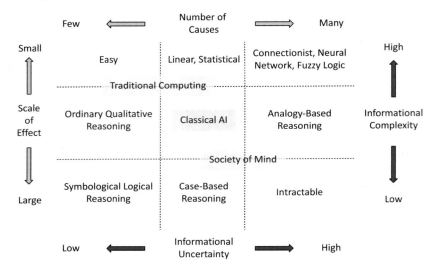

Figure 3.3   *The constrained methods matrix (CMM)*

outside standard practice. By typifying (albeit somewhat crudely) each field, we can then begin to contrast and compare them in a more structured way. For each method, once we commit to the method *and* to the way it should be used, we can make predictions that can be scientifically tested on the basis of assumptions (and hypotheses) embedded within the specific method. We can then go on to seek out differences, synergies, combinations and transformations between the insights offered by each method and hence, approach the same problem or phenomena from multiple perspectives. Whenever a problem presents difficulties, we can 'start to switch among different *Ways to Think* – by selecting different sets of resources that can help you to divide the problem into smaller parts, or find suggestive analogies, or retrieve solutions from memories – or even ask some other person for help' (Minsky 2007, p. 4). This concept of multiple *Ways of Think* can equip BE (and social science) researchers, practitioners and proponents with the tools and mindset to approach a problem from many perspectives and hence, gain some deeper appreciation for the mechanisms, relationships and context at play.

CBE and MBE

Kao and Velupillai (2015, p. 249) stress that:

> MBE is fostered by Orthodox Economic Theory, Game Theory, Mathematical Finance Theory and Recursive Methods, Experimental Economics and Neuroeconomics, Computational Economics and Subjective Probability Theory. CBE [. . . on the other hand,] is based fundamentally on a model of computation – hence, Computable Economics – computational complexity theory, nonlinear dynamics and algorithmic probability theory.

By and large, behavioural economists in general 'draw on evidence of many kinds and are comfortable using different methods to generate such evidence' (Angner & Loewenstein 2007, p. 688), suggesting that behavioural economists may be somewhat comfortable with CMM to begin with. However, MBE (and economics in general) has generally tended towards the heavy use of mathematical axioms, formal logic and statistical methods for prediction and modelling, and are increasingly turning to/accepting of neural network AI methods (hybrid or not) such as ML and DL, algorithms capable of self-learning from large stores of structured and unstructured data. CBE, on the other hand, is interested in evolution and the processes of becoming and structural change, and hence suits more the use of 'softer' empirical approaches, using narratives to describe events with specific attention to context (spatial and temporal), particularly in situations where the behaviours and systems in question are complex and mostly unpredictable (Ramos-Martin 2003). Hence, CBE perches itself more towards the middle-left of CMM. However, its major proponents did not shy away from venturing across its fuzzy methodological boundary lines, retaining a flexible approach to problem solving. Whilst there is nothing wrong with either positioning, some mutual enrichment may breathe new life into otherwise spice-less (or spice-low) fields of research.

Narratives focus on a qualitative/quantitative understanding which describes:
- the human context for the narrative; the hierarchical nature of the system;
- the attractors which may be accessible to the system;
- how the system behaves in the neighbourhood of each attractor, potentially in terms of a quantitative simulation model;
- the positive and negative feedbacks and autocatalytic loops and associated gradients which organize the system about an attractor;
- what might enable and disable these loops and hence might promote or discourage the system from being in the neighbourhood of an attractor; and
- what might be likely to precipitate flips between attractors.

(Kay et al. 1999, pp. 728–729)

Hence, narratives can inform policymakers and the community about:
- possible future states of organization of the system;
- understanding of conditions under which these states might occur;
- understanding of the trade-offs which the different states represent;
- appropriate schemes for ensuring the ability to adapt to different situations;
- and perhaps most importantly, the appropriate level of confidence that the narrative deserves; that is our degree of uncertainty.

(Kay et al. 1999, pp. 728–729)

BE (and economics in general) tends to still focus on statistical aggregation of behaviours (individual, firms, organisations) – albeit with improved psychological foundations. However, what we are missing is a specific focus on the outliers (e.g., entrepreneurs, innovators) (Schwartz 2019) which typically fall outside or are omitted from the 'average' populations of interest. In other words, those that violate the three typical 'degrees of deviation' from perfect rationality observed in real humans (Rabin 1998): sensitive to reference levels, loss aversion and other-regarding preferences; naïve inference/extrapolation and confirmation bias; and framing effects, preference reversals and unclear self-goals and preferences. More importantly, we are missing the individual 'micro' in our microeconomic foundations, especially when then aggregating up to the macro level, owing in part to the complexity of non-linear and dynamic systems. Such studies could expand on the work by Schelling (2006) on how the behavioural characteristics of individuals lead to social aggregates and shape the characteristics of their aggregates also. The computational foundations of CBE lend themselves nicely to this gap and it is popular to use ABM to implement such (see the fourth section for a more detailed discussion of ABM). Individuals (and their differences – outliers and all) can be algorithmically implemented and hence, their behaviours, interactions and self-organising structures can be examined with greater clarity. We can then choose whether to aggregate individual behaviours for macro-analyses or to hone in on individual (sub)populations for more targeted analyses. Heterogeneity can be modelled much better in an ABM framework compared to mathematical models that rely mostly on a limited number of different types. For example, when Shiller (1984) explored stock prices and social dynamics, he relied only on two types: smart-money investors and ordinary investors who are faced with uncertainty and act as noise traders, which means that the estimated value is based at least in part on noise; therefore, decisions are too optimistic or too pessimistic. Stuart Kauffman (2016) shows that we cannot mathematise much of economic life or the evolution of the economy. Together with narratives, the computational modelling of CBE can be equipped by behavioural economists (and social scientists more generally) to improve the tractability and real-world applicability of their models and forecasts, and at the same time, ease the barriers to effective communication and understanding in policymakers, researchers and the general public.

Cognitive Psychology

McBride and Cutting (2017) classify the approaches in cognitive psychology into three broad streams: case studies (for theory generation), correlational studies (for theory testing) and experimental studies (for prediction from theory). Its diverse methodological toolkit includes lab, field and natural experiments (with defined treatment and control groups and sufficient control of salient dependent and independent variables); psychobiological research, e.g., measuring brain activity during the completion of a cognitive task using functional magnetic resonance imaging (fMRI) technology or electroencephalogram (EEG); self-reports; case studies; naturalistic observation; and computer simulations and artificial intelligence (Sternberg & Sternberg 2016). Thus, as a diverse and interdisciplinary field, cognitive psychology (and its various sub-branches, e.g., social psychology, developmental psychology) methods expand through the middle-left to the top-right of CMM. The early ambitions of cognitive psychology researchers may have been greater with the generation(s) of researchers – such as Herbert Simon, Allan Newell, Marvin Minsky, Margaret Boden and Aaron Sloman – focused on applying cognitive psychology to 'classical AI' (or general AI). The 'Mind as Machine' approach (Boden 2008) has been mutually beneficial for the fields of cognitive psychology (by way of allowing simulation and testing of theories) and AI (by way of inspiring forms, processes and structures for models) alike. Bach (2009) stresses that

> [t]he goal of building cognitive architectures is to achieve an understanding of mental processes by constructing testable information processing models [. . .] The integration of regularities obtained in experimental psychology into the architecture is not just a re-formulation of what is already known but requires an additional commitment to a way this regularity is realized, and thus a more refined hypothesis, which in turn makes further predictions that can be taken into the lab of the experimental psychologist [. . .] the path of designing, implementing, and experimentally testing cognitive architectures seems to be the only productive way to extend philosophy of mind beyond its given bi-millennial heritage.
>
> (pp. 13, 16)

Of particular interest to BE is the increasing use of neuroscience techniques to explore the neurophysiological underpinnings of human behaviour, and economic decision-making more specifically (Camerer et al. 2005; Loewenstein et al. 2008). Historically, behavioural neuroscience has been at the core of the cognitive revolution. However, the interest shifted away from thought processes towards physical events but retained a natural interest in identifying how and where memory works at the cellular level (Hunt 2007, p. 600). However, neuroscience has been limited by the physically available measures:

> We can tell from physical measures that the left temporal region of the brain is active when we read, but we cannot discriminate the activity induced by reading Shakespeare from that induced by reading Agatha Christie. Therefore, in order to explain representational-level thought, we must introduce a detailed theory of the functions required to produce such thinking. This is the point at which a computational theory of information processing, in the abstract, becomes essential.
> (Hunt 1989, p. 605)

The problem is that neuroscientists have biased towards focusing on what they could observe. Thus far, they have failed to progress substantially in the *ways to think* – and therefore in areas such as knowledge representation; features that provide human thinking with its resourcefulness; or how our brains construct new mental objects and process. Fascinating AI theories were neglected; hence, we could begin to find ways of testing theories of human cognition such as K-lines, with the goal of determining whether this explains how humans actually learn and represent knowledge. Network science is another interesting research avenue gaining increasing popularity in cognitive psychology, cognitive science (Vitevitch 2020) and economics alike. But connectionists have emphasised that thinking does not proceed in a computer-like serial manner, but rather as a parallel processing system (Rumelhart & McClelland 1987; McClelland et al. 1987). This has not advanced attempts to find new avenues for improving on the pioneering cognitive architectures, despite the fact that parallel elements are also included in systems such as Soar. However, progress among more intelligent computation systems such as quantum computing is providing new interesting avenues for merging those insights and expanding theoretical and practical boundaries (Bickley et al. 2021). Adding these to complexity theory is a natural progression towards more structure in the methodological approaches.

Complexity Theory

Manson (2001) clusters complexity theory by three major research directions and their associated concepts and methods: *algorithmic complexity*, focused on the difficulty faced in describing system characteristics and closely linked to mathematical complexity and information processing theories; *deterministic complexity*, dealing with largely stable systems prone to sudden discontinuities via the interaction of few key variables and closely linked to chaos, contagion and catastrophe theories; and *aggregate complexity*, concerning how individual elements work in parallel to create systems which exhibit complex and varied behaviours and linked closely to self-organisation and emergent behaviour theories. Concepts and methods from non-linear dynamic systems theory, non-equilibrium thermodynamics, dissipative structures, self-organisation theory, catastrophe theory, self-organised criticality, anti-chaos and chaos theory are some of those included under the 'complexity' banner (Mathews et al. 1999), all looking to help explain and characterise different aspects of complex system behaviour. For example, catastrophe theory focuses on discontinuous and out-of-equilibrium system states, attempting to mathematically describe sharp discontinuities in agent behaviours and (r) evolutionary change over time and hence, can be useful in studies of innovation and organisational change.

Complexity theory can be traced back to similar conceptual frameworks in the study of neural networks (McCulloch & Pitts 1990), cybernetics (Wiener 1961) and cellular automata (von Neumann 1966), thus situating itself from the left-middle across to the top-right of the CMM matrix.[6] Complexity theory also owes a large portion of its theory and methodological toolkit to general systems theory and shares a similar sentiment of anti-reductionism and holism by acknowledging the complex, indivisible interactions between sub-systems and agents (Von Bertalanffy 1972), thus demonstrating some focus on methods of analogy-based reasoning also. Simon (1962) argued that in contrast to general systems theory, complexity science should not try to attribute standard properties which are applicable across all physical, biological and social systems. Rather, complexity science should search for common properties among diverse kinds of complex systems. Despite the promising nature of complexity science, the acceptance and application of complexity theories to the social sciences (outside the use of non-linear modelling methods) are still in their early stages (Elsner 2017; Mathews et al. 1999). Perhaps this is due to a lack of general consensus on what exactly constitutes a complex system in the first place and how it can be quantitatively determined in a robust and reliable manner (Mitchell 2009). Nonetheless, complexity theory offers a useful conceptual and methodological toolkit for the study and understanding of multi-scale, hierarchical systems – human, animal, natural, artificial and ecosystem alike.

Artificial Intelligence

Adapted from Minsky's (1992) CDM, the CMM matrix can be used fluently within the AI problem-solving domain. As discussed previously in the second section, the *acting rationally* approach in AI has led the field for the last few decades, situated more firmly towards the top-right of the CMM matrix. Logical reasoning algorithms dominated the AI landscape in the 1950s before more data-driven approaches (of today's primary focus) came to rule, but there are efforts to combine the two approaches (unified or hybrid) in what is being dubbed neuro-symbolic AI (Alexandre 1997; De Raedt et al. 2020). Hilario (1997) provides an overview of strategies for such integration of symbolic and neural AI methods. Russell and Norvig (2010) offer a descriptive account of the various methods used in AI, aligned to each of the four approaches discussed in the second section. The *acting humanly* approach in AI combines six disciplines: natural language processing, knowledge representation, automated reasoning, ML, computer vision and robotics; thus, they are AI-as-engineering as well as AI-as-science problems. The *thinking humanly* approach relies heavily on cognitive science, with new knowledge typically generated in three ways: introspection, psychological experiments and brain imaging. Hence, concepts and methods overlap strongly with works in cognitive psychology. The *thinking rationally* approach is built firmly on logic (formal and symbolic) with probability theory enabling reasoning with uncertainty. Finally, the *acting rationally* approach in AI encourages a somewhat more mixed approach with a mix of inference and deduction. The same disciplines mentioned in the *acting humanly* approach also apply here in the *acting rationally* approach; however, most algorithms are still considered 'narrow' AI for their heavy domain-focus and lack of generalisability/diversity in ways to think.

Advances in text/semantic analysis using AI methods (Benlahbib & Nfaoui 2020) would be of great interest to BE in exploring the role and dynamics of narratives, for example, in exploring the shifts in media sentiment and public opinion. Perspectives such as narrative economics (Shiller 2017, 2019), the formation of public opinions as a complex adaptive system (Ginneken 2003; Mehdi et al. 2013), and storied spaces as the human equivalent of complex adaptive systems (Baskin 2008) could inform such efforts. AI methods such as ML and DL are proven in economics and finance for predicting observation values and movements, classifying and/or clustering observations, and forecasting observations (Gogas & Papadimitriou 2021). Other notable ML methods applied in economics-related fields include anomaly detection, credit card fraud detection, aquatic product export volume prediction, stock price prediction, mobile social commerce, e-banking failures, customer behaviour and recommender systems (Nosratabadi et al. 2020). Further, the design of an AI agent forces one to consider how such an artificial system or entity should think and behave, and how this can be done ethically (Bickley & Torgler 2022). To do so, we may look to something more familiar, i.e., human thinking and behaviours. Thus, AI can help us in the attempt to design human-like agents, or in situations where it is desired to be more rational than the typical human might be.

AI is intrinsically reliant on the computational infrastructure it uses to undertake its mission(s), so further advancements are enabled by technological innovations relating to computational hardware, cloud computing architectures, and more recently, quantum computing (Dunjko & Briegel 2018), as well as other enabling technologies such as big data, IoT and distributed ledger technologies (Rabah 2018). The overlap between AI and quantum computing methods and technologies allows revisiting what one may learn from expert systems (Bickley et al. 2021), vastly popular during the earlier days of practical applications of AI in research and industry. Further, AI could also be used in the data generation process. Costello and McCarthy (1999) explain 'useful counterfactuals', detailing a possible method of increasing the size of training datasets, stressing '[o]ften it is better to imagine a data point than to experience it' (p. 4).

FUTURE DIRECTIONS

Although promoting the link between sciences and humanities has been called the greatest enterprise of the mind (Wilson 1998), the analytical techniques developed in the classical Newtonian framework may not be able to successfully explain human behaviour (Bouchard 2008). Indeed, as this deterministic framework was developed to model mechanical systems (Boulding 1956), there is reason to suppose that humans do not follow the requisite assumptions of Newtonian-style mathematics (Kitto & Kortschak 2013). Hence, new methods are needed to develop more sophisticated models that can handle the complex interdependencies between underlying assumptions, observed communications and the resulting individual behaviours. But how can such an advance be achieved? How do social systems emerge from the interactions of their constituent individuals (Torgler 2019)? Do they exhibit *downward causation* (Campbell 1990) or is a bottom-up model still possible? These questions, which have preoccupied many fields, including sociology, anthropology, psychology and economics, are not unique to the social sciences. Similar questions were asked in the hard sciences throughout the last century in fields such as cybernetics, nonlinear science and systems theory, and have produced myriad models of complex behaviour (Holland 1995; Mitchell 2009; Page 2011; Miller & Page 2007).

In the following sections, we first highlight research directions in light of the aforementioned questions for the conceptual advancement of BE, with a particular focus on cognitive models, *micro*, *meso* and *macro* foundations and big data. We then do the same for methodological advancement in the areas of neuroscience, ABM and AI in particular.

Concepts

Cognitive models and architectures

> We need to open the black box of decision making, and come up with some completely new and fresh modelling devices.
>
> (Rubinstein 2003, p. 1215)

Minsky et al. (2004) – speaking specifically of AI agents, but no less applicable to the study of human agents – propose eight types of reasoning: spatial, physical, bodily, visual, psychological, reflective, conversational and educational.[7] We can think of these types of reasoning as methods between which agents (human or artificial) can choose (and/or use in parallel) to explore their world, gather information, interact with others and navigate their many problems, opportunities and dilemmas – and ultimately, to enact their goals and visions through action. In tandem with the hierarchical cognitive models discussed first in the second section, we can then begin to construct more sophisticated agents to test our theories and intuitions, using the multiple *ways to think* in CMM (see Figure 3.3) to facilitate such artificial thinking and reasoning processes. We must not only focus on goals as 'it is not enough to know its goals. We must know also a great deal about its internal structure and particularly its mechanisms of adaptation' (Simon 1959, p. 255).

Cognitive models based on massive parallel information integration could be explored *within* a bounded rationality framework of satisficing rather than as an extension to neoclassical utility maximisation. Kunda and Thagard (1996), for example, developed a parallel processing model of impression formation which considers the joint and independent influence of stereotypes and individuating information. Sloman (2001) and Minsky (2007) both call for considerations of different hierarchical levels of cognition, distinguishing between different forms of reactive, deliberate and reflective thinking in their three- and six-level cognitive models, respectively. The importance of this distinction has still not yet been made in BE and in the social sciences more generally. Kahneman's (2011) schema of systems 1 and 2 is an encouraging first step but such 'dumbbell' thinking can constrain thinking and lead us down the path of oversimplifications and false analogies (Minsky 1988). Somewhat of a paradigm shift in cognitive psychology is situated, distributed and embodied (SDE) cognition (Petracca 2017). Cognition in the SDE framework is *situated* (contextualised and linked with action), *distributed* (using the resources of social and technological institutions and their environment in order to succeed) and *embodied* (indivisible from an evolutionarily formed, physical and dependent time-space path) (Hommel 2015). Despite the fact that some consider SDE a departure from bounded rationality, we contend that they do not need to be mutually exclusive theories; SDE can sit firmly within the bounded rationality framework, as can bounded rationality in SDE. To us, both research campaigns offer elements which the other may not and hence, we contend a 'best of both worlds' approach may be more suitable than the use of either in isolation.

Thus, further exploration of cognitive models, architectures, mechanisms and structures is warranted alongside further advancement of goal-oriented behaviour and decision models. For example, one could equip an AI agent with CMM to find multiple ways to help solve problems and represent situations, (non)experiences and problem-specific task environments for future recall, reasoning and learning. Like CDM, CMM is a useful preliminary tool to enable/assist such thinking processes, but further work can be done to identify other salient dimensions to compare and combine the methods of CMM. For example, methods of CMM can be aligned to the independence of causal factors, similarity to previous problems, expressivity of the representation/explanation, tractability (speed/efficiency) of the inference, ease of representation and robustness/reliability.

Micro, meso and macro foundations

The fact that complex emergent patterns are notoriously difficult to identify (Kitto 2008) and even more difficult to simulate mathematically presents a major challenge: how to model the ways in which a set of individuals form an emergent society that in turn affects them – in other words, treating groups, organisations and societies as if they were organisms or open complex living systems (Torgler 2019).[8] Because the new economy is organic – that is, always discovering, creating and in process (Arthur 2006) – knowledge, information and insights are key resources in a constantly changing world where possibilities and problems are created, as ongoing ecological interactions call for additional responses (Torgler 2019):

> In such an environment, entities are not always stable and events not always repeatable, presenting significant challenges for the empiricist. Hence, understanding change in these settings requires comprehending the dynamic communication and feedback channels within the system, as well as the architecture and design of social institutions.
>
> (p. 215)

Equally, a varied set of representations and methods is required for handling, sorting and adapting this knowledge for use in everyday life. Conventional economic and financial modelling methods have placed strict (often unrealistic) assumptions on human decision-making processes to help control for this complexity and non-linearity, ease the computational requirements and appease long-standing mathematical methods of optimisation and equilibrium (Foster & Metcalfe 2012). However, these methods have trouble accounting for rare yet significant events such as stock market crashes, bank runs, large-scale industrial safety incidents, radical shifts in public opinion and (social) media hysteria events. Further, the conventional macroeconomic methods for aggregate summation of individual agents' behaviour do not hold for complex systems, as the fundamental assumption that agents are homogeneous and rational clearly no longer holds when looking at 'real-world' data (Kirman 2010). Nowadays, it is more widely accepted that humans (and the systems they form) are boundedly rational and rely on behavioural (biases) and decision-making rules (heuristics) to govern their everyday decision-making (Castelfranchi 2000), and

> what is urgently needed is the development of new theories concerning the emergence, maintenance and decline of meso rules since it is these that stand between the macro and the micro and provide the order and continuity in the economic system that allow us to consider it a "system" rather than some kind of statistical "random walk".
>
> (Foster 2004, p. 32)

This is different from the *quasi*-micro foundations of mainstream macroeconomics, 'a microfoundation based on assumptions of no heterogeneous agent interaction', thus allowing limited room for communication, even 'when, for many people, it is precisely the heterogenous agent interaction that leads to central characteristics of the macro economy' (Holt et al. 2011, p. 365). Complexity theory can provide the foundation from which to explore the process and issues of (socio)economic system formation, as opposed to resource allocation alone (Tabb 1999). That is, how an economy merges, grows, reacts and adapts in structure and dynamics over time can be used to shed new light on classic economics problems by developing models which can account for complex economic phenomena not just at equilibrium but in out-of-equilibrium states as well (Arthur 2014).

Big Data
As the rise of big data has profound implications for the way science is done, it is pertinent to think about what impact this may have on the study and practice of behavioural economics. Big data is already pervasive and '[s]ince computers are now involved in many economic transactions, Big Data will only get bigger' (Varian 2014, p. 24). One such promising area for the application of big data is in understanding patterns of human mobility and interaction, the antecedent of most economic activity. In general, human mobility data have some deep-rooted regularities (Song et al. 2010). Identifying these offers ways of developing accurate predictive models that are scientifically grounded, can help in understanding and improving our societal well-being and public health, and inform how we might cope with crises such as pandemics, climate/weather disasters and other nasty and often unexpected events. Big data provides new opportunities in understanding the dynamics of social interactions by observing actual behaviour rather than just beliefs (Pentland 2014; Torgler 2019). Mobility data allow us to harness human digital footprints or 'digital bread-crumbs' of our daily activities (Almaatouq et al. 2016, p. 407). Mobility data can include origin-destination pairs, travel modes (e.g., roads, rail, walking, cycling), places of visits, duration of visits and number/diversity of human interactions, to name a few, and such data can also be associated with demographic information including age, gender, race and nationality. This provides a richness of information and context on individual patterns of movement and social behaviour not formerly possible with more rigid and traditional policy instruments (Bickley et al. 2021). Such data also contribute to a better understanding of the social context and social fabric, and how they influence human behaviour and interactions. If we can observe some of the things an individual does, then we can infer (most of) the rest by comparing them to the people with whom they regularly hang out and interact, and in this sense, begin to understand (and intervene) in the formation and persistence of complex social phenomena and emergent outcomes based on individual patterns of behaviour and mobility. The analysis of human mobility data is the basis of understanding how people and groups are connected together and mingle (mix) over time. Alex 'Sandy' Pentland notes the importance of this, as for a long time big data left humans out of the equation. Equally, we can leverage AI and big data to further progress on our commitments to Sustainable Development Goals (Vinuesa et al. 2020) by helping to interpret and monitor the environment, guide our problem-solving process, design strategies and action plans, and decide when/if to carry them out. We can also leverage this to encourage, support and carry out sustainability innovation and entrepreneurship (Bickley et al. 2021) and adapt business models in light of findings (Di Vaio et al. 2020).

Methods

Neuroscience
Neuroscience is expected to provide important insights into human cognition and behaviour 'either directly or because neuro-science will reshape what is believed about psychology which in turn informs economics' by allowing one to 'infer details about how the brain works' (Camerer et al. 2005, p. 9). Thus, neuroscience is not just important for setting the stage for research in cognition, but it also lays the foundation upon which higher-order thinking and

reasoning processes take place, like those required for representing and solving problems faced by agents (human, animal or artificial) in their everyday lives. In principle, all neuroscientific tools can be used to investigate (socio)economic decision-making. Essentially, the *where* of cognition is more precisely answered by the methods for measuring changes in cerebral blood flow or metabolism (fMRI and PET), whereas the *when* is better assessed by EEG and MEG, so a combination/hybrid of both approaches would deliver the best results. Insights from neuroscience can offer both incremental and more radical contributions to economics (Camerer et al. 2005): incremental by adding variables to or modifications of conventional models of decision-making based on empirical evidence, radical by questioning the implicit assumptions of conventional decision-making models and potentially redefining them in alignment with real-world observations. Unfortunately, such neuroscientific methods are often unviable in natural environments due to the restrictive nature of technologies underlying the data capture process, and hence, ecological validity is sometimes called into question. Fortunately, as the story has been told in experimental economics, as long as decisions are related to real consequences then ecological validity can hold (Reuter & Montag 2016) provided that the researchers' implicit and explicit assumptions are not violated. Regardless, neuroscientific methods can help in both informing and clarifying our models of human cognition and allows us to test the various theories and models of human cognition and help to determine, for example, the neurobiological bases of pro-social behaviours (Harbecke & Herrmann-Pillath 2020). Technological advances in neuroscience around wearable, non-intrusive and non-invasive instruments provide new avenues in the area of behavioural economics by studying the human mind and human behaviour in the real world rather than the laboratory (for a detailed discussion, see Torgler 2019).

Agent-based Models (ABM)

In ABM, a system is modelled as a collection of autonomous decision-making units called agents, wherein each agent assesses its situation and makes decisions based on a set of rules that allows to track individuals and their interactions in networks (of networks) of agents over time and space (Bonabeau 2002), hence enabling fine-grained analyses of individual behaviours and emergent phenomena in networks and systems of agents. In other words, 'ABM allows the disaggregation of systems into individual components that can potentially have their own characteristics and rule sets' (Crooks & Heppenstall 2012, p. 85). ABMs have demonstrated clear potential in helping to analyse, characterise and define complex systems of many agents through the evolution and application of simple agent rules over time (Yang 2020) and are heavily used in complexity science analyses. ABMs enable a direct representation of layered and hierarchical systems and their upward and downward effects on a particular observed phenomenon (Gräbner 2017). However, ABMs suffer several issues, including agent granularity (i.e., corresponding to some level of lumpiness and a 'small numbers' effect), non-linear dynamics that present difficulties in parameter estimation, and difficulties with model replication and comparison (LeBaron 2016). Model development should focus heavily on building comprehensive models that operate in the context of the observed reality and can deliver testable predictions about agents' behaviours within such a context to support empirical testing. The strength of such agent-based models is their ability to visualise system dynamics that are otherwise difficult to solve mathematically (Reilsback & Grimm 2012). In particular, one such approach may use a micro-specification to explore the evolution of norms and conflict dynamics based on predefined (local) communication channels or rules (bottom-up approach) while still observing the macro-structure (societal implications) and the time required for the system to attain equilibrium or observe out-of-equilibrium dynamics (e.g., the long-lived transient behaviours suggested by Epstein 2006, p. 23). There are many ABM tools and software programs; Abar et al. (2017) provide a comprehensive account of the state of the art. Advanced AI techniques such as goal-oriented action planning (GOAP) may also enrich the practice and design of ABMs (Zhang et al. 2009), initialising agents with goals (and sub-goals) from which agents can choose to realise desired outcomes through actions and sub-actions aligned to each goal and its sub-goals. Action logics (e.g., event calculus) are also worth considering (see Bickley & Torgler 2022 for further discussion).

Artificial Intelligence

Comparisons and combinations of different 'ways of thinking' (see e.g., Figure 3.3) are important; the methods through which data are collected, curated and integrated into scientific modelling are essential in understanding our world (Coveney et al. 2016). Varian (2014) stresses that '[d]ata manipulation tools and techniques developed for small datasets will become increasingly inadequate to deal with new problems. Researchers in ML have developed ways to deal with large datasets and economists interested in dealing with such data would be well advised to invest in learning these techniques' (pp. 24–25). As ML is predictive while econometrics is explanatory and historically based on economic theory, a combination of both tools is fascinating but also challenging. In general, data analysis in statistics and econometrics can be classified into four groups: 1) prediction, 2) summarisation, 3) estimation and 4) hypothesis testing (Varian 2014). Using different methods provides the ability to use both AI and econometric methods to explain the same phenomenon from different perspectives. Further, traditional data analytics techniques struggle to deal with big data – big data are often noisy and, unlike survey data, not collected to answer specific questions. AI can therefore help overcome these deficiencies and barriers. In addition, AI methods can be implemented first, followed by attempts to explain what is going on to better understand the underlying correlations and co-occurrences, hence, moving towards a causal relationship and a situation where one (or both) method(s) inform each other. Thus, a combination of cross-validation and trying to reveal fundamental processes can be beneficial in the decision-making process or in generating meta-knowledge (knowledge about knowledge) (Zheng et al. 2017). Mullainathan and Spiess (2017) stress that

> [f]or empiricists, these theory- and data-driven modes of analysis have always coexisted. Many estimation approaches have been (often by necessity) based on top-down, theory-driven, deductive reasoning. At the same time, other approaches have aimed to simply let the data speak. ML provides a powerful tool to hear, more clearly than ever, what the data have to say.
>
> (pp. 103–104)

Thus, these approaches are not in conflict *per se*, and both approaches may be important when trying to understand human behaviour, interactions and networks (and networks of networks), with the aim being to predict human responses to future events and novel circumstances. Exploring such a relationship is particularly important when working with new data that are subject to high dimensionality and when predictions are an input to an important policy problem and/or objective. AI offers the chance to take further leaps and bounds in practice and policy with advances in the hardware side of computation – namely, cloud computing and quantum computing (Dunjko & Briegel 2018) among other enabling technologies such as big data, IoT and distributed ledger technologies (Rabah 2018). These technological advances allow us to revisit what one may learn from expert systems (Bickley et al. 2021), for example.

CONCLUSION

In summarising this chapter, we now return to the two questions posed in the introductory section: *what exactly is BE?* and *what may we have missed along the way?* By revisiting BE's conceptual and methodological roots, we aimed to shed light on these questions and point our readers towards potentially fruitful avenues of research and exploration. Equally, we hope that we have enriched our readers with a refreshing array of diverse conceptual and methodological topics covered and that our readers see the importance and validity of incorporating such topics into their own (socio)economic policy and practice.

In exploring the first question, we see that BE is a diverse and interdisciplinary field. Its proponents and subscribers are comfortable with wielding a diverse range of methods and instruments and making use of evidence from outside of economics. The distinction between old (classical) and new (modern) BE has also been made: the former (CBE) sought to depart more drastically from the standard neoclassical paradigm, questioning its relevance and real-world applicability; the latter (MBE) remained within the neoclassical optimisation framework, seeking instead to improve (or repair) the psychological underpinnings of neoclassical methods and models. There is a general appreciation for the diversity in approaches that BE maintains; however, as discussed in the third section, further work can be done to foster multiple *ways to think* about a problem, much in the spirit of triangulation, parallel non-equivalent descriptions and mixed methods more generally.

In exploring the second question, we see that the MBE interpretation of bounded rationality is narrow, omitting the bounded nature of the environment itself (i.e., context) and focusing only on the limited information processing capabilities of the decision-maker. We have also conveyed an (increasing) appreciation for the true complexity of human systems where aggregates cannot be reduced to the sum of individual constituents, particularly in a constantly changing world where possibilities and problems are created, as ongoing ecological interactions call for additional responses. Complexity theory approaches provide a useful conceptual framework and methodological toolkit to explore and characterise such problems. Last but not least, we contend that behavioural economics and the social sciences more generally will benefit greatly from paying closer attention to the design and application of cognitive models in various intelligent agents (human, animal, artificial). To gain a deeper appreciation for the procedures, mechanisms and thought processes which underlie (socio)economic decision-making, we must venture further into the individual and seek to shed light on the 'black box' of human decision-making. Only then can we build, from the ground up, more contextualised and rationally bounded economics with greater predictive power and real-world relevance.

NOTES

1. Scholars such as Vernon Smith and Gerd Gigerenzer built their arguments around adaptability, survival and ecological rationality. They clashed with the more static perspective of a reference frame paradigm around the work of Amos Tversky and Daniel Kahneman (see Smith 1989, 2005; Gigerenzer 2004; Kahneman and Tversky 1996; Gigerenzer 1996). For a discussion, see also Lewis (2017) and Torgler (2021a). Eric Wanner attempted to assemble a working group on experimental economics at the Russell Sage Foundation, including Vernon Smith or Charles Plott together with

Kahneman or associates; however, it did not work out due to such fundamental different theoretical interests (Heukelom 2014).
2. For a discussion on the importance of cognitive architectures for economics, see Torgler (2021b).
3. Manage, in our use here, is the use of 'control' measures (e.g., policy interventions, regulation, stimulus packages and incentive schemes) to keep complex systems within desirable or specified bounds.
4. For a discussion of complexity in psychology with a focus on the theory of nonlinear dynamical systems, see the edited volume by Guastello, Koopmans and Pincus (2009).
5. See Aamodt and Nygard (1995) for an AI perspective on data, information and knowledge, and Boisot and Canals (2004) for an (evolutionary) economics perspective.
6. For an excellent overview on complexity theory, see Mitchell (2009).
7. See also the work of Howard Gardner (1993, 2006) who has pioneered the idea of multiple intelligences.
8. For a discussion how economics and social science questions can be explored and modelled in a manner similar to a living or biological system, see Torgler (2016).

REFERENCES

Aamodt, A., & Nygård, M. (1995). Different roles and mutual dependencies of data, information, and knowledge—an AI perspective on their integration. *Data & Knowledge Engineering, 16*(3), 191–222.

Abar, S., Theodoropoulos, G. K., Lemarinier, P., & O'Hare, G. M. (2017). Agent based modelling and simulation tools: A review of the state-of-art software. *Computer Science Review, 24*, 13–33.

Alexandre, F. (1997). Tools and experiments for hybrid neuro-symbolic processing. In *Proceedings Ninth IEEE International Conference on Tools with Artificial Intelligence* (pp. 338–345). New Jersey, USA: IEEE.

Almaatouq, A., Radaelli, L., Pentland, A., & Shmueli, E. (2016). Are you your friends' friend? Poor perception of friendship ties limits the ability to promote behavioral change. *PloS One, 11*(3), e0151588.

Al-Suwailem, S. (2011). Behavioural complexity. *Journal of Economic Surveys, 25*(3), 481–506.

Angner, E., & Loewenstein, G. (2007). Behavioral economics. In U. Mäki, D. Gabbay, P. Thagard & J. Woods (Eds.), *Handbook of the philosophy of science: Philosophy of economics* (pp. 641–690). Amsterdam, NL: Elsevier Science.

Arthur, W. B. (2006). *The Nature of Technology: What It Is and How It Evolves*. New York, USA: Free Press.

Arthur, W. B. (2014). Complexity economics: A different framework for economic thought. In W. B. Arthur (Ed.), *Complexity Economics* (pp. 1–29). Oxford, UK: Oxford University Press.

Bach, J. (2009). *Principles of synthetic intelligence Psi: An architecture of motivated cognition*. Oxford, UK: Oxford University Press.

Baskin, K. (2008). Storied spaces: The human equivalent of complex adaptive systems. *Emergence: Complexity and Organization, 10*(2), 1–12.

Baum, S. D., Goertzel, B., & Goertzel, T. G. (2011). How long until human-level AI? Results from an expert assessment. *Technological Forecasting and Social Change, 78*(1), 185–195.

Beal, J., & Winston, P. H. (2009). Guest editors' introduction: The new frontier of human-level artificial intelligence. *Intelligent Systems, 24*(4), 21–23.

Benartzi, S., & Thaler, R. (2007). Heuristics and biases in retirement savings behavior. *Journal of Economic Perspectives, 21*(3), 81–104.

Benlahbib, A., & Nfaoui, E. H. (2020). A hybrid approach for generating reputation based on opinions fusion and sentiment analysis. *Journal of Organizational Computing and Electronic Commerce, 30*(1), 9–27.

Bhatnagar, R. K., & Kanal, L. N. (1986). Handling uncertain information: A review of numeric and non-numeric methods. *Machine Intelligence and Pattern Recognition, 4*, 3–26.

Bickley, S. J., Chan, H. F., Schmidt, S. L., & Torgler, B. (2021). Quantum-sapiens: The quantum bases for human expertise, knowledge, and problem-solving. *Technology Analysis & Strategic Management*, 1–13. DOI: 10.1080/09537325.2021.1921137. For an Extended Version with Applications, see

CREMA Working Paper Series 2021-14, Centre for Research in Economics, Management, and the Arts (CREMA), Zurich, Switzerland, http://www.crema-research.ch/papers/2021-14.pdf.

Bickley, S. J., Macintyre, A., & Torgler, B. (2021). Artificial Intelligence and Big Data in Sustainable Entrepreneurship. CREMA Working Paper Series 2021-11, Centre for Research in Economics, Management, and the Arts (CREMA), Zurich, Switzerland.

Bickley, S. J., & Torgler, B. (2022). Cognitive architectures for artificial intelligence ethics. AI & SOCIETY, 1-19. DOI: 10.1007/s00146-022-01452-9.

Boden, M. A. (2008). *Mind as machine: A history of cognitive science*. Oxford, UK: Oxford University Press.

Boisot, M., & Canals, A. (2004). Data, information and knowledge: Have we got it right? *Journal of Evolutionary Economics*, *14*(1), 43–67.

Bonabeau, E. (2002). Agent-based modeling: Methods and techniques for simulating human systems. *Proceedings of the National Academy of Sciences*, *99*(suppl. 3), 7280–7287.

Bouchaud, J. P. (2008). Economics needs a scientific revolution. *Nature*, *455*(7217), 1181–1181.

Boulding, K. E. (1956). General systems theory—the skeleton of science. *Management Science*, *2*(3), 197–208.

Camerer, C., Loewenstein, G., & Prelec, D. (2005). Neuroeconomics: How neuroscience can inform economics. *Journal of Economic Literature*, *43*(1), 9–64.

Camerer, C. F., & Loewenstein, G. (2004). Behavioral economics: Past, present, future. In C. Camerer, G. Loewenstein & M. Rabin (Eds.), *Advances in Behavioral Economics* (pp. 1–52). Princeton, NJ, USA: Princeton University Press.

Campbell, D. T. (1990). Levels of organization, downward causation, and the selection-theory approach to evolutionary epistemology. In E. Tobach & G. Greenberg (Eds.), *Scientific methodology in the study of mind: Evolutionary epistemology* (pp. 1–17). Hillsdale, NJ: Erlbaum.

Castelfranchi, C. (2000). Through the agents' minds: Cognititve meaditors of social action. *Mind & Society*, *1*(1), 109–140.

Ceddia, M. G., Bardsley, N. O., Goodwin, R., Holloway, G. J., Nocella, G., & Stasi, A. (2013). A complex system perspective on the emergence and spread of infectious diseases: Integrating economic and ecological aspects. *Ecological Economics*, *90*(C), 124–131. DOI: 10.1016/j.ecolecon.2013.03.013.

Choudhury, M. A. (2013). Complexity and endogeneity in economic modelling. *Kybernetes*, *42*(2), 226–240.

Churchland, P. M., & Churchland, P. S. (1990). Could a machine think? *Scientific American*, *262*(1), 32–39.

Cohen-Cole, J. (2007). Instituting the science of mind: Intellectual economies and disciplinary exchange at Harvard's Center for cognitive studies. *The British Journal for the History of Science*, *40*(4), 567–597.

Colander, D., & Kupers, R. (2014). *Complexity and the art of public policy: Solving society's problems from the bottom up*. Princeton, NJ, USA: Princeton University Press.

Costello, T., & McCarthy, J. (1999). Useful counterfactuals. *Linköping Electronic Articles in Computer and Information Science*, *3*(2), 1–28.

Coveney, P. V., Dougherty, E. R., & Highfield, R. R. (2016). Big Data need big theory too. *Philosophical Transactions of the Royal Society A: Mathematical, Physical and Engineering Sciences*, *374*(2080), 20160153.

Cronin, B. (2016). Multiple and mixed methods research for economics. In F. S. Lee & B. Cronin (Eds.), *Handbook of research methods and applications in heterodox economics*. Cheltenham, UK: Edward Elgar Publishing.

Crooks, A. T., & Heppenstall, A. J. (2012). Introduction to agent-based modelling. In A. Heppenstall, A. Crooks, M. L. Lee & M. Batty (Eds.), *Agent-based models of geographical systems* (pp. 85–105). Dordrecht, NL: Springer.

Crosson, F. J. (1992). Psyche and the computer: Integrating the shadow. In S. Koch & D. E. Leary (Eds.), *A century of psychology as science* (pp. 437–451). Washington, USA: APA Publishing.

De Raedt, L., Dumančić, S., Manhaeve, R., & Marra, G. (2020). From statistical relational to neuro-symbolic artificial intelligence. *arXiv preprint*, arXiv:2003.08316.

Diacon, P.-E., Donici, G.-A., & Maha, L.-G. (2013). Perspectives of economics–Behavioural economics. *Theoretical and Applied Economics*, *20*(7), 27–32.

Di Vaio, A., Palladino, R., Hassan, R., & Escobar, O. (2020). Artificial intelligence and business models in the sustainable development goals perspective: A systematic literature review. *Journal of Business Research*, *121*, 283–314.

Dunjko, V., & Briegel, H. J. (2018). Machine learning & artificial intelligence in the quantum domain: A review of recent progress. *Reports on Progress in Physics*, *81*(7), 074001.

Eagle, N., & Greene, K. (2014). *Reality mining: Using Big Data to engineer a better world*. Cambridge, MA, USA: MIT Press.

Elsner, W. (2017). Complexity economics as heterodoxy: Theory and policy. *Journal of Economic Issues*, *51*(4), 939–978.

Epstein, J. M. (2006). *Generative social science: Studies in agent-based computational modelling*, Vol. 13. Princeton, NJ, USA: Princeton University Press.

Foster, J. (2005). From simplistic to complex systems in economics. *Cambridge Journal of Economics*, *29*(6), 873–892.

Foster, J., & Metcalfe, J. S. (2012). Economic emergence: An evolutionary economic perspective. *Journal of Economic Behavior and Organization*, *82*(2–3), 420–432.

Gardner, H. E. (1993). *Frames of mind: The theory of multiple intelligences*. New York, USA: Basic Books.

Gardner, H. E. (2006). *Multiple intelligences: New Horizons*. New York, USA: Basic Books.

Gazzaniga, M., Ivry, R., & Mangun, G. (2014). *Cognitive neuroscience: The biology of the mind* (Fourth edition.). New York, USA: W.W. Norton & Company.

Giampietro, M., & Mayumi, K. (2000). Multiple-scale integrated assessment of societal metabolism: Introducing the approach. *Population and Environment*, *22*(2), 109–153.

Gigerenzer, G. (1996). On narrow norms and vague heuristics: A reply to Kahneman and Tversky. *Psychological Review*, *100*, 592–596.

Gigerenzer, G. (2004). Striking a blow for sanity in theories of rationality. In M. Augier & J. G. March (Eds.), *Models of a man: Essays in memory of Herbert A. Simon* (pp. 389–409). Cambridge, MA, USA: MIT Press.

Gilovich, T., Griffin, D., & Kahneman, D. (2002). *Heuristics and biases: The psychology of intuitive judgment*. Cambridge, UK: Cambridge University Press.

Ginneken, J. V. (2003). *Collective behavior and public opinion: Rapid shifts in opinion and communication*. New Jersey, USA: Lawrence Erlbaum.

Goertzel, B., & Pennachin, C. (2007). *Artificial general intelligence* (Vol. 2). Dordrecht, NL: Springer.

Gogas, P., & Papadimitriou, T. (2021). Machine learning in economics and finance. *Computational Economics*, *57*(1), 1–4.

Gomes, O., & Gubareva, M. (2021). Complex systems in economics and where to find them. *Journal of Systems Science and Complexity*, *34*(1), 314–338. DOI: 10.1007/s11424-020-9149-1.

Gräbner, C. (2017). The complementary relationship between institutional and complexity economics: The example of deep mechanismic explanations. *Journal of Economic Issues*, *51*(2), 392–400.

Guastello, S. J., Koopmans, M., & Pincus, D. (Eds.). (2009). *Chaos and complexity in psychology: The theory of nonlinear dynamical systems*. Cambridge, UK: Cambridge University Press.

Harbecke, J., & Herrmann-Pillath, C. (Eds.). (2020). *Social neuroeconomics: Mechanistic integration of the neurosciences and the social sciences*. London, UK: Routledge.

Heap, S. P. H. (2013). What is the meaning of behavioural economics? *Cambridge Journal of Economics*, *37*(5), 985–1000.

Helbing, D. (2009). Managing complexity in socio-economic systems. *European Review*, *17*(2), 423–438.

Heukelom, F. (2014). *Behavioral economics: A history*. Cambridge, UK: Cambridge University Press.

Hilario, M. (1997). An overview of strategies for neurosymbolic integration. In R. Sun & F. Alexandre (Eds.), *Connectionist-symbolic integration: From unified to hybrid approaches* (pp. 13–36). New Jersey, USA: Lawrence Erlbaum Associates.

Holland, J. H. (1995). *Hidden order: How adaptation builds complexity*. New York, USA: Basic Books.

Holling, C. S. (2001). Understanding the complexity of economic, ecological, and social systems. *Ecosystems*, *4*(5), 390–405.

Holt, R. P., Rosser Jr, J. B., & Colander, D. (2011). The complexity era in economics. *Review of Political Economy*, *23*(3), 357–369.

Hommel, B. (2015). The theory of event coding (TEC) as embodied-cognition framework. *Frontiers in Psychology*, *6*, 1318–1318.
Hunt, M. (2007). *The Story of Psychology*. Victoria, AUS: Anchor Books.
Kahneman, D. (2011). *Thinking, fast and slow*. New York, USA: Macmillan.
Kahneman, D., & Tversky, A. (1996). On the reality of cognitive illusions. *Psychological Review*, *103*, 582–591.
Kao, Y.-F., & Velupillai, K. V. (2015). Behavioural economics: Classical and modern. *The European Journal of the History of Economic Thought*, *22*(2), 236–271.
Kauffman, S. A. (2016). *Humanity in a creative universe*. Oxford, UK: Oxford University Press.
Kay, J. J., Regier, H. A., Boyle, M., & Francis, G. (1999). An ecosystem approach for sustainability: Addressing the challenge of complexity. *Futures*, *31*(7), 721–742.
Kenning, P., & Plassmann, H. (2005). NeuroEconomics: An overview from an economic perspective. *Brain Research Bulletin*, *67*(5), 343–354.
Kirman, A. (2010). The economic crisis is a crisis for economic theory. *CESifo Economic Studies*, *56*(4), 498–535.
Kitto, K. (2008). High end complexity. *International Journal of General Systems*, *37*(6), 689–714.
Kitto, K., & Kortschak, R. D. (2013). Contextual models and the non-Newtonian paradigm. *Progress in Biophysics and Molecular Biology*, *113*(1), 97–107.
Kunda, Z., & Thagard, P. (1996). Forming impressions from stereotypes, traits, and behaviors: A parallel-constraint-satisfaction theory. *Psychological Review*, *103*(2), 284.
LeBaron, B. (2016). Financial price dynamics and agent-based models as inspired by Benoit Mandelbrot. *The European Physical Journal Special Topics*, *225*(17), 3243–3254.
Lewis, M. (2017). *The undoing project: A friendship that changed the world*. New York, USA: Penguin Books.
Lo, A. W. (2017). *Adaptive markets: Financial evolution at the speed of thought*. Princeton, USA: Princeton University Press.
Loewenstein, G., Rick, S., & Cohen, J. D. (2008). Neuroeconomics. *Annual Review of Psychology*, *59*, 647–672.
Mandelbrot, B. B., & Hudson, R. L. (2004). *The (Mis)Behavior of markets: A fractal view of risk, ruin, and reward*. New York, USA: Basic Books.
Manson, S. M. (2001). Simplifying complexity: A review of complexity theory. *Geoforum*, *32*(3), 405–414.
Mathews, K. M., White, M. C., & Long, R. G. (1999). Why study the complexity sciences in the social sciences? *Human Relations*, *52*(4), 439–462.
McBride, D. M., & Cutting, J. C. (2017). *Cognitive psychology: Theory, process, and methodology*. New York, USA: SAGE Publications.
McCarthy, J. (1998). Elaboration tolerance. In R. Miller & M. Shanahan (Eds.), *Fourth symposium on logical formalizations of commonsense reasoning* (pp. 198–216), London, UK.
McCarthy, J. (2000). *Approximate objects and approximate theories*. Palo Alto, USA: Stanford University Press.
McCarthy, J. (2007). From here to human-level AI. *Artificial Intelligence*, *171*(18), 1174–1182.
McClelland, J. L., Feldman, J., Hayes, P., & Rumelhart, D. E. (1987). *Parallel distributed processing, Vol 2: Psychological and Biological Models*. A Bradford Book. Cambridge, MA, USA: MIT Press.
McCulloch, W. S., & Pitts, W. (1990). A logical calculus of the ideas immanent in nervous activity. *Bulletin of Mathematical Biology*, *52*(1–2), 99–115.
Mehdi, M., Juliane, E. K., Pantelis, P. A., & Hansjörg, N. (2013). Social influence and the collective dynamics of opinion formation. *PLoS ONE*, *8*(11), e78433.
Miller, J. H., & Page, S. E. (2007). *Complex adaptive systems: An introduction to computational models of social life*. Princeton, NJ, USA: Princeton University Press.
Minsky, M. (1988). *The society of mind*. London, UK: Pan Books.
Minsky, M. (1992). Future of AI technology. *Toshiba Review*, *47*(7), 1–3.
Minsky, M. (2007). *The emotion machine: Commonsense thinking, artificial intelligence, and the future of the human mind*. New York, USA: Simon and Schuster.
Minsky, M. L., Singh, P., & Sloman, A. (2004). The St. Thomas common sense symposium: designing architectures for human-level intelligence. *AI Magazine*, *25*(2), 113–113.

Mitchell, M. (2009). *Complexity: A guided tour.* Oxford, UK: Oxford University Press.
Mullainathan, S., & Spiess, J. (2017). Machine learning: An applied econometric approach. *Journal of Economic Perspectives, 31*(2), 87–106.
Newell, A. (1994). *Unified theories of cognition.* Cambridge, MA, USA: Harvard University Press.
Newell, A., Shaw, J. C., & Simon, H. A. (1959). Report on a general problem solving program. In *IFIP congress* (vol. 256, p. 64).
Nilsson, N. J. (1995). Eye on the prize. *AI Magazine, 16*(2), 9–9.
Nilsson, N. J. (2009). *The quest for artificial intelligence.* Cambridge, UK: Cambridge University Press.
Nosratabadi, S., Mosavi, A., Duan, P., Ghamisi, P., Filip, F., Band, S., Reuter, U., Gama, J., & Gandomi, A. (2020). Data science in economics: Comprehensive review of advanced machine learning and deep learning methods. *Mathematics, 8*(10), 1–25. DOI: 10.3390/math8101799.
Page, S. E. (2011). *Diversity and complexity.* Princeton, NJ, USA: Princeton University Press.
Pentland, A. (2014). *Social physics: How good ideas spread-the lessons from a new science.* London, UK: Penguin Books.
Petracca, E. (2017). A cognition paradigm clash: Simon, situated cognition and the interpretation of bounded rationality. *Journal of Economic Methodology, 24*(1), 20–40.
Prigogine, I. (1980). *From being to becoming: Time and complexity in the physical sciences.* New York, USA: W.H. Freeman.
Rabah, K. (2018). Convergence of AI, IoT, big data and blockchain: A review. *The Lake Institute Journal, 1*(1), 1–18.
Rabin, M. (1998). Psychology and economics. *Journal of Economic Literature, 36*(1), 11–46.
Ramos-Martin, J. (2003). Empiricism in ecological economics: A perspective from complex systems theory. *Ecological Economics, 46*(3), 387–398.
Ramsay, J. (1998). Problems with empiricism and the philosophy of science: Implications for purchasing research. *European Journal of Purchasing and Supply Management, 4,* 163–173.
Reilsback, S. F., and Grimm, V. (2012). *Agent-based and individual-based modelling.* Princeton, NJ, USA: Princeton University Press.
Reuter, M., & Montag, C. (2016). Neuroeconomics—An introduction. In M. Reuter & C. Montag, *Neuroeconomics* (pp. 1–10). Berlin, Heidelberg: Springer.
Riecken, D. (1994). M: An architecture of integrated agents. *Communications of the ACM, 37*(7), 106–146.
Rubinstein, A. (2003). "Economics and psychology"? The case of hyperbolic discounting. *International Economic Review, 44*(4), 1207–1216.
Rumelhart, D. E., & McClelland, J. L. (1987). *Parallel distributed processing: Explorations in the Microstructures of Cognition, Volume 1: Foundations.* A Bradford Book. Cambridge, MA, USA: MIT Press.
Russell, S. J., & Norvig, P. (2010). *Artificial intelligence-A modern approach, third international edition.* London, UK: Pearson Education London.
Schelling, T. C. (2006). *Micromotives and macrobehavior.* New York, USA: W.W. Norton & Company.
Schwartz, H. (2019). Is behavioral economics losing its way? Available at SSRN 3354835.
Sent, E.-M. (2004). Behavioral economics: How psychology made its (limited) way back into economics. *History of Political Economy, 36*(4), 735–760.
Shiller, R. (2017). Narrative economics. *The American Economic Review, 107*(4), 967–1004.
Shiller, R. (2019). *Narrative economics: How stories go viral & drive major economic events.* Princeton, NJ, USA: Princeton University Press.
Shiller, R. J., Fischer, S., & Friedman, B. M. (1984). Stock prices and social dynamics. *Brookings Papers on Economic Activity, 1984*(2), 457–510.
Simon, H. A. (1959). Theories of decision-making in economics and behavioral science. *The American Economic Review, 49*(3), 253–283.
Simon, H. (1962). The architecture of complexity. *Proceedings of the American Philosophical Society, 106*(6), 467–482.
Simon, H. (1990). *Reason in human affairs.* Palo Alto, USA: Stanford University Press.
Simon, H. (2001). Complex systems: The interplay of organisations and markets in contemporary society. *Computational & Mathematical Organisation Theory, 7*(1), 79–85.
Simon, H. A. (1979). Information processing models of cognition. *Annual Review of Psychology, 30*(1), 363–396.

Simon, H. A. (1983). *Reason in human affairs*. Palo Alto, USA: Stanford University Press.
Simon, H. A. (1996a). *The sciences of the artificial*. Cambridge, MA, USA: MIT Press.
Simon, H. A. (1996b). *Models of my life*. Cambridge, MA, USA: MIT Press.
Singh, P. (2003). The panalogy architecture for commonsense computing brief description.
Sloman, A. (2001). Beyond shallow models of emotion. *Cognitive Processing*, *2*(1), 177–198.
Sloman, A. (2008). Putting the pieces together again. In R. Sun (Ed.), *Cambridge handbook on computational psychology* (pp. 684–709). Cambridge, UK: Cambridge University Press.
Sloman, A., & Chrisley, R. L. (2005). More things than are dreamt of in your biology: Information-processing in biologically inspired robots. *Cognitive Systems Research*, *6*(2), 145–174.
Smith, V. L. (1989). Theory, experiment and economics. *Journal of Economic Perspectives*, *3*(1), 151–169.
Smith, V. L. (2005). Behavioral economics research and the foundations of economics. *The Journal of Socio-Economics*, *34*(2), 135–150.
Song, C., Qu, Z., Blumm, N., & Barabási, A. L. (2010). Limits of predictability in human mobility. *Science*, *327*(5968), 1018–1021.
Spiegler, P. M., & Milberg, W. (2014). Methodenstreit 2013? Historical perspective on the contemporary debate over how to reform economics. *The Forum for Social Economics*, *43*(1), 7–7.
Sternberg, R. J., & Sternberg, K. (2016). *Cognitive psychology*. Toronto, CAN: Nelson Education.
Tabb, W. K. (1999). *Reconstructing political economy: The great divide in economic thought*. London, UK: Routledge.
Tomer, J. F. (2007). What is behavioral economics? *Journal of Socio-Economics*, *36*(3), 463–479.
Torgler, B. (2016). Can tax compliance research profit from biology? *Review of Behavioural Economics*, *3*, 113–144.
Torgler, B. (2019). Opportunities and challenges of portable biological, social, and behavioral sensing systems for the social sciences. In G. Foster (Ed.), *Biophysical measurement in experimental social science research* (pp. 197–224). Cambridge, MA, USA: Academic Press.
Torgler, B. (2021a). The Power of Public Choice in Law and Economics, Center for Research in Economics, Management and the Arts (CREMA). Working Paper No. 2021-04, Zurich.
Torgler, B. (2021b). Symbiotics> Economics?. Center for Research in Economics, Management and the Arts (CREMA). Working Paper No. 2021-15, Zurich.
Tversky, A., & Kahneman, D. (1974). Judgment under uncertainty: Heuristics and biases. *Science*, *185*(4157), 1124–1131.
Ulanowicz, R. E. (1997). *Ecology, the ascendent perspective*. New York, USA: Columbia University Press.
Varian, H. R. (2014). Big data: New tricks for econometrics. *Journal of Economic Perspectives*, *28*(2), 3–28.
Vinuesa, R., Azizpour, H., Leite, I., Balaam, M., Dignum, V., Domisch, S., Felländer, A., Langhans, S. D., Tegmark, M., & Nerini, F. F. (2020). The role of artificial intelligence in achieving the Sustainable Development Goals. *Nature Communications*, *11*(1), 1–10.
Vitevitch, M. (2020). *Network science in cognitive psychology*. London, UK: Routledge.
von Bertalanffy, L. (1972). The history and status of general systems theory. *Academy of Management Journal*, *15*(4), 407–426.
von Neumann, J. (1966). *Theory of self-reproducing automata*. Urbana, IL, USA: University of Illinois Press.
Wiener, N. (1961). *Cybernetics: Or control and communication in the animal and the machine* (2nd ed.). Cambridge, MA, USA: MIT Press.
Wilson, E. O. (1998). *Consilience: The unity of knowledge*. New York, USA: Vintage Books.
Yang, J. (2020). Two tales of complex system analysis: MaxEnt and agent-based modeling. *The European Physical Journal Special Topics*, *229*(9), 1623–1643.
Zhang, H., Shen, Z., & Miao, C. (2009). Enabling goal oriented action planning with goal net. In *2009 IEEE/WIC/ACM International Joint Conference on Web Intelligence and Intelligent Agent Technology* (vol. 2) (pp. 271–274), Washington, USA.
Zheng, E., Tan, Y., Goes, P., Chellappa, R., Wu, D., Shaw, M., Sheng, O., & Gupta, A. (2017). When econometrics meets machine learning. *Data and Information Management*, *1*(2), 75–83. DOI: 10.1515/dim-2017-0012.

4. Assumptions in economic modelling: How behavioural economics can enlighten
Beryl Y. Chang

INTRODUCTION

> Unreality of premises is not a virtue in scientific theory; it is a necessary evil – a concession to the finite computing capacity of the scientist that is made tolerable by the principle of continuity of approximation.
>
> (Herbert Simon, qtd. in Hausman 1994)

What exactly is the principle of continuity of approximation? In Simon's words: 'if the conditions of the real world approximate sufficiently well the assumptions of an ideal type, the derivations from these assumptions will be approximately correct' (qtd. in Hausman 1994). The 2008 global financial crisis (GFC) originated in the US certainly revealed whether the conditions of the real world approximate well the assumptions of the market ideal type – those in the innovative financial products after the deregulation, the quantitatively hard-wired risk modelling looking primarily in regressive terms and the behaviours of all economic actors and institutions in the midst of the subprime mortgage lending – the derivations from the assumptions shocked most, including the chairman of the central bank in the US.

Assumptions, explicitly or implicitly made in economic modelling given unobservable future events, are critical components leading to theoretical conclusions and decision-making at a particular moment in the effort to maintain a nation's economic conditions. They are indispensable guiding mechanisms in policy-making at both the federal and corporate levels from modelling to execution and therefore vital to generating economic outcomes. Considering numerous market failures around the world, however, issues regarding the realism of assumptions in modelling are the subject of debate and are challenging the foundations of conventional economic theories, aka neoclassical economics. And in more recent decades, the topic of assumptions in modelling became a cornerstone in behavioural economics.

What and how can behavioural economics contribute to the improvements while addressing the issue of realism of assumptions in economic modelling that dominated in the past century and is considered inadequate, too simplistic and detached from today's world in terms of its explanatory and predictive powers? Given its development in recent years, the study of behavioural economics is not only about understandings of human psychology and behaviour in economic exchanges in a particular market structure, but also about realism in market terms so economic events, developments and outcomes can be understood and explained for policy-making, crisis prevention or market sustainability and the overall improvements of life qualities in society. In the former, it is about the awareness of the intrinsic nature of humans such as behaviour under fear or fundamental uncertainties in the environment and various incentives or lack thereof among multiple market participants. In the latter, it is about how economic agents interact among themselves given the existing as well as changing dynamics of a capitalist economy. These investigations and inclusions of human and market behaviour in the assumptions of economic modelling are expected to outperform those of the conventional methods that disregard both human characteristics as well as market realism in today's complex economic system with interactive mechanisms.

In conventional theories, economic models focus almost exclusively on quantitative measures and regressive correlations for quick and elegant tractability without paying attention to underlying human and social psychology in the real-world context, which is a huge and important part of economic activities and events with *Homo sapiens*. The inclusion of these human and social mechanisms as assumptions in economic modelling improves not only predictions beyond the 'as-if' scenarios in pseudo form but also the understanding and explanations of economic behaviour on an ongoing basis: how individuals and firms form beliefs or make economic decisions and whether they should accept or promote a particular product given existing market and institutional structures and interactions in an evolving horizon. To put it simply, the study of economics is more about explanations of market phenomena and the behavioural approach is a step closer to expectations of market outcomes with more understanding in place of the usual 'random' variables. This is especially the case when there are various shades of human intentions that do not always generate positive outcomes assumed in conventional theories in an uncoordinated capitalist market with unquantifiable forces. As one prominent economist put it: 'math is secondary; it is simply one of the tools in the behavioral economics' toolbox as high correlations are often spurious – they are only suggestive of causation and getting assumptions right helps distinguishing between spurious correlations, and actual causation' (Altman 2012).

In the following, I focus the discussion surrounding the issues of realism in assumptions of economic modelling on: i) the research methods that are explored, adopted and debated in the past century and ii) the applications in economic modelling with behavioural implications. In the first part, I present the origins and sources of beliefs in the non-realist approach to economic modelling with different schools of thought, their shortcomings and root causes in the absence of realism in assumptions of economic modelling and how they become less relevant to prediction as they claim to achieve. Then I introduce the emergence of behavioural economics as a significant contributor to causal factors in search of explanations for economic events and outcomes. In the second part, I show how decision-making leading to real economic behaviours, given simultaneous constraints such as time, information and knowledge in changing form, at both individual and institutional levels of various economic aspects, misaligns with assumptions in the conventional methods as illustrations of inadequacies in economic modelling.

ASSUMPTIONS IN ECONOMIC METHODS WITH PHILOSOPHICAL FOUNDATIONS

> When a theory fails to explain and predict well because its underlying assumptions are unrealistic, then it is time to reject or revise the theory by constructing it on a sounder base of assumptions.
> (Wilkinson 2008)

But how do we give a sounder base or define the realism of economic assumptions? In philosophical terms, realism is defined somewhat differently from realisticness. The former relates to scientific or methodological doctrines, often in physical sciences, to include some eternal truth and the latter is about various attributes of representations of some phenomenon such as practical usefulness, observability and empiricism (Maki 2002). In the real world, realisticness and realism are related referentially as well as in representations at times while realisticness may be considered a variable that is subject to change given survival instinct (Boylan and O'Gorman 1995). In the context of assumptions in economic modelling, realism shall include intrinsic (though maybe less observable) characteristics of *Homo sapiens* that intersect with or transcend realisticness and set constraints in achieving certain tasks. These constraints (or potentials given human will) are largely determined by circumstantial, purposive, judgemental, knowable or unknowable horizons in time in a particular market environment in terms of feasibility and possibility of solving an economic problem in question.

With *Homo sapiens* in the context of economic modelling or potentially as a critical factor to the cause of economic outcomes, the human variable is therefore indispensable in establishing economic theory and methods, the purpose of which is to understand, explain and possibly anticipate economic events for market order and conditions that affect human lives. However, in the pursuit of economic science, many had mistaken a methodological science such as mathematics and statistics for a substantive science such as economics in making assumptions as well as estimations of economic events while ignoring the fundamental purpose of understanding and explanations for the discipline.[1] In the following, I discuss issues surrounding methodologies in economics that have been practised and taught widely in the past century as well as proposals in more recent decades: 1) instrumentalism and logical positivism, 2) constructive empiricism and scientific realism and 3) behaviouralism as part of causal holism.

Instrumentalism and Logical Positivism

What is an instrument in scientific inquiries? A tool such as an engine can be considered an instrument moving from A to B. It neither sums up nor explains (Boylan and O'Gorman 1995). In economics, instrumentalism often refers to methods in the forms of mathematics as tools in the attempt to analyse, predict or formulate laws, but they do not necessarily explain and reveal the hidden aspects of the phenomenon under study. The tools therefore serve as intellectual instruments with a non-realistic approach to efficiency, human cognition and understanding within the limit of the tool.

In the pursuit of economic science and in conjunction with mathematical instruments and tools, conventional theorists adopted a set of rules that consider only the observables in the past that are verifiable in looking backwards as true science and cognitively meaningful. This set of rules, which is regarded as logical positivism, considers that mathematics and logic are the only valid forms of knowledge that can be obtained through natural science while rejecting human opinions and value judgements as part of scientific study.[2] These methods of instrumentalism and logical positivism sought in the understanding of economic events and market behaviour set foundations for an array of assumptions made in economic modelling that dominated conventional theories for decades if not centuries. The best illustration of the assumptions associated with these methods can be found in the famous F-twist ('Essay on the methodology of positive economics') by the known economist Milton Friedman, who is only interested in models pertaining to the domain of mathematics and logic, the 'observable phenomena' and the logical tool of axiomatisation in approaching scientific theory (Boylan and O'Gorman 1995).

What are the implications for assumptions made in the F-twist, explicitly or implicitly? Friedman says that 'assumptions are "largely" irrelevant to the validation of theories, which ought to be judged "almost" solely in terms of their instrumental value in generating accurate predictions' (qtd. in Blaug 1992). But what is the theoretical underpinning for the claim that assumptions do not matter or are mostly irrelevant? Did a real-world case such as the 2008 GFC show the instrumental value in generating accurate predictions? Or are economic events almost always guaranteed to succeed with positive outcomes due to optimisation as a result of human survival mechanisms and competitive market forces?

To answer the question of the claim that assumptions do not matter, and as economists theorise on concepts such as people's expectations of some future events in the real world, it becomes clear that most of these expectations are not observable or precisely measurable. For an instrumentalist, though perhaps not an absolute unrealist, with the realisation that people's intentions or motivations in reality are not always observable, as future events cannot be observed or precisely measured now, assumptions made in economic models therefore do not matter or are irrelevant, especially as the purpose of modelling is to predict – so the tool is all that counts in a model! Apparently, it never occurred to an instrumentalist that 'unobservables' in hard data do not mean inaccessible by intuitions or other senses in humans. They are often 'common sensibles' or can be explained by human and social psychologies. So instead, what has been developed in the conventional practice in economics is the presumption that what is real is observable. But as Maki argued, being real by no means implies being observable: much or most of the world is unobservable (Maki 2002). Assumptions have significant roles in economic modelling because they have direct linkages to the make-up of a theory, whether they are relevant, misleading or spot on. Furthermore, economic policies that are derived from these economic theories and modelling will have a direct impact on the performance of a market in the creation of values or mishaps.

Now since an accurate prediction of a model is the most important for an instrumentalist, what are the necessary assumptions implied in generating such a model, with the aim for a positive outcome? The most well-known assumption made in the F-twist is the 'as-if' statement, which says that a good theory that makes accurate predictions means that individuals behave 'as if' they follow the behavioural assumptions (Blaug 1992). But what are these behavioural assumptions and implications that would generate positive economic outcomes as prescribed in the model prediction?

First, it assumes rationality with the logic positivist method and no complications, or the behaviour of an omniscient *Homo economicus* with boundary conditions equivalent to an isolated system so an instrument or the theory can be held to apply. This is shown in the 'as-if' method which restricts a range of variables to be taken into account or that 'bodies in the atmosphere behave as if they were falling in a vacuum' (Boylan and O'Gorman 1995). Second, the method assumes the survival principle with positive outcomes through calculating optimisation or that the behaviour actor will achieve what s/he intends to accomplish with guaranteed success due to the urge to survive and as it is impossible for a modeller to know the process and steps s/he takes to be included in the model. So implicitly, the motivations and capabilities of an economic actor to maximise or optimise certain utility and profit leading to positive outcomes are all given, and only the optimal behaviour and results are consistent with survival (Altman 2008). In other words, what is expected to come out is what one puts in. Or to make accurate predictions, one will need to follow these specific behavioural assumptions for the pre-specified outcome. This is vivid evidence of circular reasoning, making the drawing after the arrow is shot at the tree as the target of a prediction: 'first I fire the arrow at the tree, and then I paint the target around it', as the boy archer explained to the duke in his hunting trip (Cohen and Stewart 1995).

So lastly and to the aforementioned assumptions, since the instrument, which is often represented by mathematics in order to optimise, does not solve for conflicts that are regarded as externalities, a prescriptive monist system is assumed with no countervailing forces, or processes in between these forces do not matter. There is no consideration of the constraints of time, of the ecological, circumstantial surprising factors and obstacles to the possibilities of unsuccessful efforts in the attempt to survive. Consequently, the market is assumed to be stable as regulations are assumed to be effective with certain functional relationships and essentially a closed system. Is this how the real-world economy works in an advanced capitalist market?

But what is the real-world economy we are speaking of? Is it some desired economic outcome with prescribed and assumed behaviour by the instrumentalists or the realities of the limits and asymmetries of knowledge, changes in certain market structures due to innovations, counter-party and non-coordinated acts with conflict of interests and all human factors in an interactive market along with the processes or procedural steps in achieving certain objectives? In today's complex market, as Altman put it, 'the survival principle cannot be interpreted to predict that only optimal outcomes survive or the notion of multiple equilibria – that the survival principle is no guarantee of optimal decisions yielding optimal results' (Altman 2008).

According to Melitz (Blaug 1992), assumptions are differentiated between 'auxiliary' and 'generative' forms. The former is used to set certain theoretical conditions such as ceteris paribus to illustrate logical consequences; the latter, such as profit maximisation, is to derive the hypothesis for a particular goal in prediction. Melitz also considers that assumptions used in economics usually function in either capacity but the discrepancy between the auxiliary assumptions with a predetermined condition and reality is a more serious problem for testing a theory than the lack of realism in the generative assumptions, which are intentions or motivations with less fixed terms. In the case of an instrumentalist, if the generative and auxiliary assumptions intersect with each other, discrepancies between the assumptions and the reality can be even more severe a problem than in the former case due to the overlap. In the F-twist, the auxiliary assumptions are the rational *Homo economicus* in 'as-if' conditions with a somewhat closed system while the generative assumption is the logical positivist outcome of economic events given the survival urge of man. These assumptions of narrowly defined rationality and logic positivism can be seriously challenged or truly irrelevant when the reality is *Homo sapiens* in search of survival in complex pluralistic and uncertain market conditions. To refute the claim that assumptions do not matter, Simon argued that: 'Our predictions of the operations of markets and of the economy are sensitive to our assumptions about mechanisms at the level of decision processes' (qtd. in Altman 2008). In other words, our predictions are likely dependent on the assumptions we make.

Constructive Empiricism and Realism

Sharing some characteristics of the conventional theory and an alternative to realism as defined earlier, there is the school of constructive empiricism or veristic realism represented by Bas van Fraassen. It follows logical positivism in that its theory is constructed on empirical evidence with a focus on the observables and considerations of necessary logic only. In other words, constructive empiricists pay no attention to the unobservables or reject any metaphysical existence and possibilities. Apparently, believers of constructive empiricism are unaware that future events may not be like the known past or a specific kind of empirical evidence, and that the causal discourse is epistemically limited to an individual for an outcome that is contingent on the acts of the aggregate.

A constructive empiricist would adopt an extreme case such as the approach in Terence Hutchison (qtd. in Blaug 1992), who insists on 'independent verification of all assumptions by objective data obtained through sense observation' and propose 'a program that begins with facts rather than assumptions'. This approach, however, had met fierce rejection by the British economist Franck Knight, who concluded that 'It is not possible to "verify" any proposition about "economics" behavior by any "empirical" procedure' and stressed that economic behaviour is goal-directed and depends on the meaning of one's intuitive knowledge in terms of its purposive character (qtd. in Blaug 1992).

Given the human urge to know and to look forward, the verification of assumptions with historical and retroactive data or basing judgements on facts in static form without regarding a specific environment following either the logical positivist or constructive empiricist methods for future events is problematic. In response to these non-realist approaches taking into account only the observable factors and excluding multiple criteria in human intentions, there is the scientific realism led by Tony Lawson. It claims that knowledge is progressive, which involves time and change, while the unobservational aspects of knowledge, though with anticipatory cause, are how reasons and predictions are formed (Lawson 1997).

What sets scientific realism apart from other ideals is the inclusion of the existence of the unobservables as in Lawson's transcendental realism. It posits that the 'central aim of economic theory is to provide explanations in terms of hidden generative structures' and mechanisms, which are non-empirical. These mechanisms can produce enduring intrinsic structures but go unnoticed in the observable world. Nonetheless, these generative non-empirical mechanisms need to be inferred from empirical evidence known as abduction or retroduction (Boylan and O'Gorman 1995). From the ontological and epistemological perspective, the observable and unobservable aspects of a theory are on equal footing. In other words, ontological commitments or the admission of the existence of some knowledge should not be determined by the constructive empiricist's arbitrary division between the observable and the unobservable (Boylan and O'Gorman 1995). The empirical feature of a statement or a theory in this case is only one part of the existence of some phenomenon.

Maki has categorised three kinds of realism: ontological, representational and veristic, which concern what the world is. For Boylan, however, these semantic realisms do not capture what is distinctive of Lawson's scientific realism, say from an empiricist/positivist perspective, while Friedman is considered both a semantic realist and a methodological instrumentalist. It is the failure in recognising this distinction that made Friedman's thesis hopelessly ambiguous (Boylan and O'Gorman 1995). On the relation between realism and isolation, such as ceteris paribus, which does not give the entire truth about reality, Maki remarked that it is unrealistic in that it has to isolate certain factors and ignore others and therefore does not present the whole truth (Maki 2002). One example of this type of isolation is the maximisation hypothesis or an assumption in conventional theory. It is unrealistic in that it does not tell 'the whole truth' because maximisation is a hypothesis that refers to a motive not modelled after human behaviour in business or a particular working environment and therefore involves isolation: it isolates the maximisation motive from other factors, such as employee morale and changes in the market conditions, so the hypothesis is veristically unrealistic. This is also the case when there are deterministic obstacles in the environment that prevent the intention of maximising due to time, information and other constraints. Friedman failed to keep these distinctions and opted for an unqualified veristic unrealism (Boylan and O'Gorman 1995).

Causal Holism and Behavioural Economics

While economists argue about realism in economics in terms of whether the unobservables exist or models should include the observables only, others insist that what really counts in terms of realism and economics is whether the essential causal mechanisms have or have not been included in the relevant theory (Hands 2001). However, causal mechanisms can be interpreted differently depending on whether the existence of a characteristic in discussion, such as some unobservable phenomenon, is recognised. In the case of the 2008 GFC, some consider bank run to be the causal factor for the crisis while others saw fear, distrust, non-transparency or ambiguity avoidance as the real and underlying true causes for the crisis given human survival mechanisms under radical uncertainty. In other words, while causal mechanisms are critical in determining realism in economics, recognition of the existence of the less observable, such as human psychological characteristics, is the fundamental stepping stone. In addition, the causal-effect relation is an evolving and dynamic process. The effect of a particular cause could subsequently become the cause of some other effects. For example, when a corporation had no capacity to borrow due to insufficient credit history at T_1, it subsequently depleted its reserves at T_2. The depletion of its reserves then became the cause for not being able to borrow again at T_3 even though the company had earned some good credits. Here, though the reasons for loan rejections were correlated, the causal factors varied at different time periods.

Perhaps the search for true causal factors leading to economic events, combined with the emotional, psychological and other less observable impacts on the market witnessed by the mind's eye of humans, led to the development of the field of behavioural economics for *Homo sapiens*. In many cases, these less observable but regular mechanisms given human characteristics in a particular environmental structure predict and provide explanations and understandings more profoundly than what posterior data can allude. The recognition of less observable realities as a result of human intentions and interactions in time, space and change is in line with Lawson's transcendental realism.

In behavioural economics, however, human behaviour relating to intentions, interactions or survival mechanisms is considered in the context of environmental structures beyond the assumptions of the existence of less observable phenomena. The closest methodological and philosophical guide and principles to the contextual behavioural approach in economics searching for causal factors and explanations of economic events in the real world is the theorem of causal holism initiated by Boylan and O'Gorman. Contrary to reductionism, causal holism assumes a complex system where parts are understood as part of an entire system in context and in relation. The theorem takes Lawson's scientific realism while giving epistemic weight to constructive empiricism yet transcends the conflict between them.

How does causal holism solve the conflict? While it recognises van Fraassen's pragmatic criteria, it also accepts that scientific explanation, such as explanations for economic outcomes, lies in the non-epistemic dimension of science, as in the aleatory or environmental uncertainty, depending on the context or due to complexity. What causal holism rejects are transcendental realists' theory on causality, which is neither deductive nor inductive but retroductive, and empiricists' theory which reduces causality to correlations (Boylan and

O'Gorman 1995). What causal holism emphasises, in constructing economic models, is accurate descriptions. So given the allowance of knowledge and time, effective economic models are not only about observable events but also about observable causes in an interactive and structural environment that can reveal hidden events and mechanisms. While the guiding principle of causal holism limits its commitment to what is observable and claims that no economic observation statement taken in isolation can mirror image any portion of the real world (Boylan and O'Gorman 1995), Boylan and O'Gorman acknowledge that our knowledge of causes is limited to what is in principle observable. However, they did not specify how, what and by what means we observe. This is where behavioural economics can fill the void and expand the knowledge of observable causes not only from scientific experiments but also through real-world events with the mind's eye. And to this end, human judgement cannot be avoided in a world of radical uncertainty (Kay and King 2020).

Given a non-centralised or non-coordinated, quasi-free and somewhat regulated capitalist market with ever more innovative products generating many grey areas, economic outcomes can be uncertain and the realities in terms of the final outcome are difficult if not impossible to project in advance without knowing all the steps and changes in the development in the process. Instead of looking into these steps and processes in finding possible and plausible causes, such as specific market mechanisms with human interactions, conflicts, incentive structures, limits of regulation and other bounded rationality, leading to a particular outcome, Friedman et al. had chosen a path of circular reasoning with some desired outcome as illustrated by the archer boy or a gambler who bet on a positive outcome of an expected reality given survival urges. The 'as if' or other super-simplified approaches in economic modelling prevented economists from understanding what is actually happening in an economy, which needs to be explored and understood to better anticipate the economic and market outcomes with explanations. This is especially the case when *Homo economicus* is in focus while *Homo sapiens* is ignored – it neglected what human fears or a survival mechanism from a counter-party could do in a complex, changing and interconnected environment for survival among multiple parties. To Friedman, 'the entirely valid use of "assumptions" in *specifying* the circumstances for which a theory holds is frequently, and erroneously, interpreted to mean that the assumptions can be used to *determine* the circumstances for which a theory holds' (Blaug 1992). From the behavioural perspective, however, assumptions made by behavioural actors can influence decisions and consequently circumstances!

This is where behavioural methods, as part of the meta-economics seeking holistic understandings of a complex and dynamic system, can make valuable contributions to the explanations of economic events turning unreal assumptions in modelling to higher levels of descriptive adequacy through knowledge in human attributes in a particular environment. They will not only look at the skills and capacities of the archer, the distance to the tree and the quality and features of his instrument, but also the speed and directions of the wind in the environment that may facilitate or prevent his arrow from travelling to the target as causes to the outcome. Subsequently, the inquiries into what is actually happening in economic events in the real world are not just about predictions; more importantly, they are about explanations and understandings of how various economic factors work together in generating economic events. The as-if method, however, not only refuses to offer any causal mechanisms linking business behaviour to the maximisation of returns as it presumes; it positively rules out the possibility of such an explanation (Boylan and O'Gorman 1995).

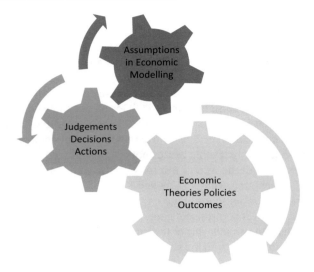

Figure 4.1   The impact of assumptions in economic modelling

BEHAVIOURAL APPLICATIONS AND ENLIGHTENMENT ON ASSUMPTIONS

Rationality Assumptions and Bounded Rationality

Perhaps the most salient assumption in conventional theory that is reflected in economic modelling, between the 'as if' and the rational expectation hypotheses (Ghisellini and Chang 2018), is the 'rational' and omniscient *Homo economicus*, who has a) unbounded knowledge along with b) unbounded computational skills to translate that knowledge into decisions and c) unbounded willpower to materialise those decisions into actions. In reality, these prescribed internal human capabilities and accessibility are bounded not only by the hard facts and limits of time, information and the make-up of our physiques but also are in relative and contextual terms to external conditions in dynamic, which are fundamentally uncertain and unobservable most of the time in an open market system. Ignoring these contemporaneous constraints at both internal and external levels, the positive economic outcome expected in normative terms in conventional theories also assumes that the knowledge and computational skill we acquired are always relevant to the decision under examination and that the desired opportunity is accessible for certain with the amount of willpower needed in execution. These assumptions laid foundations and conditions such as perfect knowledge and information in the development of conventional economic and financial theories and models about markets.

Nonetheless, the reality in market exchanges is depicted well by Herbert Simon in the theory of bounded rationality with the two blades of scissors – the two-way working mechanism of a successful economic event as a corollary of both the internal capacity and the external circumstance in the moving process. Nonetheless, conventional methods as well as the mainstream behavioural theorists continue to assume that only the internal blade exists with a unilateral cut in Simon's scissors, misinterpreting the essence of his theory, which weighs equally if not more on the external conditions that bound an individual or a firm's 'rationality' in knowledge and computational terms in decision-making. Here, external conditions in reality embrace behaviours of all market participants in changing forms, and bounded rationality virtually assumes and means ecological rationality, a term originated by Vernon Smith, the 2002 Nobel laureate.

In defining human rationality, Vernon Smith categorised the concept into two types: constructive rationality and ecological rationality. In the former, assumptions are made on behaviour on given

> social structures generated by emergent institutions that we observe in the world, and proceeds to model it formally. These assumptions might be correct, incorrect, or irrelevant, and the models may or may not lead to rational action in the sense of serving well the needs of those to whom the models apply.

For the latter, it

> uses reason or rational reconstruction to examine the behavior of individuals based on their experience . . . to understand the emergent order in human cultures; to discover the possible intelligence embodied in the rules, norms, and institutions of our cultural and biological heritage that are created from human interactions but not by deliberate human design.
>
> (Smith 2008)

For a smart decision-maker, the applications of ecological rationality not only represent the kind of rationality or skills one finds appropriate in the internal or personal toolbox in coping with the external challenges utilising both blades of the scissors but also makes the invisible hand, a remark by Adam Smith on the mechanisms of a decentralised economy, more visible or transparent and aware so any outsized shocks and damages in an economy may be prevented.

Since Smith, however, the narrow definition of rationality that follows strict mathematical logic and the assumption that this definition is the only one that is universally agreed upon in economics had caused serious divisions and disparate conclusions in the field of behavioural economics. In *Behavioral Economics: Moving Forward*, Ghisellini and Chang (2018) distinguish the German and the American Schools reflecting this divide in behavioural economics, where the former is represented by Gerd Gigerenzer trailing Herbert Simon and the latter by Amos Tversky and Daniel Kahneman as in the mainstream. While these brilliant psychologists from both schools recognise that humans do not behave strictly as what economic models predict or prescribe, the methodologies used in their respective research were vastly different. The German School builds its methods based on interdisciplinary and broader studies in fields such as biology, behavioural science and philosophy in addition to mathematics, statistics and economic concepts, while the American School draws its research findings from experimental psychology assuming constructive or axiomatic rationality as in the conventional and mainstream economics. The shortcomings of the latter school in methodology are that it assumes that fundamental uncertainty can always be reduced to a measurable risk and that heuristics are only the second-best. The division of the two schools led to disparate conclusions on how humans should behave along with policy ramifications.

Utility Maximisation and the Expected Utility Theory

The assumptions in the rational theory and hypothesis, such as the unbounded and all relevant computational skills with complete information gathered through unlimited time and effort, had paved the way for theories on utility since the old days. Utility in conventional terms assumes material wealth only and those who do not maximise the monetary wealth are irrational, irrespective of other personal and subjective values and criteria. But contrary to this belief, empirical study shows that one only lives one's life to the fullest if s/he lives in all five dimensions – career, social, financial, health and community. In addition, the assumption of maximising one's utility by choosing something rather than nothing has been proven otherwise in the ultimatum game tested across the globe in various cultures.

Another assumption on utility is about the value of goods: the value of a particular good is independent of the value of other goods to the same consumer. Would the total utility of two goods that are complimentary to each other equal the summation of the utilities measured independently? Suppose one has a Stradivarius as well as a Guarnerius violin along with an F.N. Voirin bow, which is a necessary and complimentary good for a stringed instrument like a violin. While the Stradivarius is generally higher in monetary value, the Guarnerius produces much better sound than that of the former with this Voirin bow (a bow contributes to about 20 per cent of the sound quality on a particular instrument). How do we measure the utility of this Voirin bow and the respective utilities of these two instruments with the same bow while there may be a less expensive bow that makes better sound on the Stradivarius than the Voirin? Is it irrational to claim that the Stradivarius has less utility than the Guarnerius to a particular player with the Voirin bow?

According to the expected utility theory (EUT, see Ghisellini and Chang 2018), choice in quantitative logic, e.g., 95 per cent chance of $30K > 100 per cent certainty of $25K, is assumed to be consistent and is independent of decision-making processes in qualitative measures. However, in reality, and as illustrated in the Allais paradox, the description of a choice with 100 per cent certainty of $25K is preferred, even though it has a lower value than 95 per cent chance of $30K. So people tend to give a higher value of utility when there is an absence of uncertainty. As Vernon Smith put it: 'Expected utility theory is for . . . the constructivist modeling of consistent choice. It seems inadequate for the prediction, or the ecological understanding, of behavior' (2008). This strict adherence to the EUT modelling of a 'rational' agent may have cost global finance dearly in determining the default probability of the subprime mortgage loans prior to 2008.

In the realm of gains or losses relating to utility, EUT assumes that the agent is only 'rational' if s/he responds to either of the prospects, gain or loss, equally and symmetrically. So you are indifferent to bets on the prospect of a 90 per cent chance of a $100 gain or the same probability of a $100 loss. In the conventional theory, where risk measures are assumed to be absolutely quantifiable with precision, utility or disutility is assumed to be similar when encountering monetary gains or losses. In reality, however, risk almost always involves some level of immeasurable uncertainty. It is the fundamental uncertainty that leads to the behaviour of loss aversion, which predicts that for the same amount of loss vs. gain, people suffer about twice as much from loss with disutility than they rejoice from a gain in utility. This also leads to the discovery that utility comes from relative wealth, unlike what is in the conventional theory, which assumes some absolute level of wealth, say one million, as the source of utility. So in reality and along with other environmental factors, utility comes from how one reaches some level of wealth from a particular reference point.

In the well-known concave line in gain and convex shape in loss of the 'value function' in the prospect theory, people have varied risk-taking attitudes in gains and losses, which defeats the assumption that risk is the same as uncertainty. People are risk-averse when a gain is less certain, e.g., a 100 per cent gain of $50 for certain is preferred to a 50 per cent chance of $120 (or there is in essence a loss aversion to a guaranteed gain of $50 vs. a possible less amount). On the contrary, people are risk-seeking or avoid sure loss when facing expected or probable loss, e.g., they prefer a 50 per cent chance of losing $100 to a sure loss of $50. The speculation here is that there may be a possibility of a lower than 50 per cent chance of losing $100. This is the rationale behind the risk-seeking tendency in a loss scenario, as in reality, there is always an element of uncertainty which cannot be exactly pinned down in measurement – it could be a downside risk or an upside opportunity. These findings point to a critical problem in economic projections that mainly fit parameters to data, rather than out-of-sample predictions and competitive testing of theories of profoundly different natures.

Social, Cultural and Emotive Dimensions that Influence Economic Outcomes

For a *Homo economicus* in utility terms, it is assumed that more is always preferred to less or it is better to have something than nothing. This monist approach in conventional economics, often in monetary and material terms, in determining the path to wealth and happiness excludes other drivers in humans in seeking life goals and purposes. The ultimatum game, which was experimented with worldwide with consistent results, proved that accepting a reward is not necessarily better than rejecting one in maximising one's utility in a particular social setup that affects the utility of a counter-party. While the second player has no control over how rewards are divided, s/he has the power of either accepting or rejecting the offer and in most cases, s/he would reject if the offer is less than 30 per cent, in which case both receive nothing. From this game, we could see clearly that there are utilities beyond monetary or material gains and these other types of utilitarian-induced acts are behavioural driven by social, moral, emotional or ideological factors.

According to neural scientists and findings in brain research, people who had the emotional part of the brain damaged have no decision-making capabilities. These brain-damaged patients share the same problem with people who have marginal emotional capacity albeit with computational skills but still have no sight for a decision. This endless pursuit in calculations is rather irrational than rational in decision-making as circumstances change with hidden conflicts, misunderstandings and surprises in varied timeframes in reality. Human emotion, which is a complex system by itself combining other valuable sources such as intuitions and short- and long-term memories from past experience, is the trigger and a critical component in making decisions. In the case of a policeman or a soldier, the demand for quick responses or decisions is part of human survival mechanisms in which actions and convictions are needed instantaneously. This indispensable mechanism with a huge emotional component in it, as in Damasio's somatic marker, also plays out vividly in financial markets from equity traders to regular investors. Without emotion, on a large or small scale, knowledge accumulated from one's past experience may have depressed value or cannot be expressed at its fullest potential in decision-making.

Nonetheless, conventional economics assumes that decision-making can only be based on meticulous calculations and that emotions are negative inputs or hindrances to good decisions as they lead to 'irrational' behaviour and subsequently bad choices. Careful calculations may be beneficial at some level when time is not a factor in a quasi-closed system. For behavioural economics, however, emotion is often necessary for making good decisions, especially in urgent and complex situations. It is a neutral mechanism from an aggregate perspective, the outcome of which depends on the specific individual with unique past experience in a particular situation. Emotions, along with intuitions and other less observable mechanisms that can be deliberate, often add value to decisions. As Nietzsche put it: why think there is no reason in emotions? He sees emotions as both a tool and effect of social forces and central to how individuals understand and situate themselves in the world (Kerruish 2009).

Aside from relative income or price as exhaustive in determining consumer choice behaviour, conventional economics also assumes that people's decisions are independent of their opinions of others. On the cultural front, this may be a special case for a specific sector in a particular social structure such as in a more individualistic society. While herd behaviour is more pronounced in the financial market, especially under situations of fear, than in other sectors in an individualistic world such as the US, following others' choices is common in a more collective culture such as in China. These differences also reflect differences in social structures, people relations and attitudes in terms of personal space or distance, tolerance for risk-taking, levels of trust and homogeneity. Cultural beliefs and traditions also determine behaviours in savings, investments and how and where people consume that reflect a particular spending pattern and a value system, all of which are silent in conventional economics.

At the organisational and institutional levels, conventional theories assume that employee effort is fixed and firms are x-efficient in production or firms are doing their best given factor inputs (Altman 2012). Differences in culture are reflected not only in hiring, whether it is political, social or merit-based, but also in relationships among workers, whether in a competitive or cooperative structure. Only in the latter case can x-inefficiency, where workers do not make their best effort in maximising firm output given resources, be eliminated (Altman 2012). From the behavioural perspective and given the cooperative nature of the institutional structure, perhaps with fewer 'animal spirits' or concerns of survival, mainstream behavioural focuses of 'biases' and 'irrationality' may not be applicable here as decisions are made in a coordinated fashion with more transparency through both vertical and lateral communications of all involved. Indeed, culture often plays a critical role in the success of an institution or an economy at large.

Institutional Implications

One of the most serious negligences made in the field of economics, aside from meta-economics, is that it had largely ignored the impact and the power of institutions in terms of rules of games and other structural mechanisms on individual behaviour to either promote or destroy an economy. Conventional theories assume that institutions are set up to be efficient or by default, they maximise profits and productivity. These assumptions were made without questioning how firms accomplish these objectives taking into account the human elements among various parties such as shareholders or owners, managers and workers; all have their respective interests and incentives to pursue, with explicit and implicit conflicts. Related, conventional theories assume that markets are efficient and inherently stable. Noises and conflicts, which are considered exogenous factors albeit drivers of market dynamics, are assumed to be temporary and the system adjusts by itself with invisible hands. Nonetheless, Douglas North found these assumptions to be flawed and that institutions do have independent roles in economic events and they are not necessarily designed to achieve efficient outcomes by default, and therefore cannot be ignored in economic analysis (Altman 2012). In the real world and as in the 2008 GFC and other economic crises, institutions were the sources of these mishaps, as they inherently involve incentive-related and risk-taking behaviour at both individual and firm levels, from financial over-leveraging to stock bubbles leading to crashes.

While conventional macroeconomic theories are based on micro-foundations, which concern incentives and risk-taking aspirations and assume 'rational' individuals in isolation with exogenous shocks only, they disregard any endogenous crisis. But are these shocks exogenous or endogenous?

The error made in assuming exogenous shock is in line with the error in assuming that institutions are set up to let people achieve their respective needs, wants and desires while maximising firm profits without any endogenous clashes among them due to conflicts of interest. The 2008 GFC was a case in point on how regulatory change at the institutional level led to more risk-taking with opacity and conflicts of interest among parties leading to a behaviour-related confidence crisis that caused the liquidity crisis, market fragility and eventually failure. In subprime mortgage lending, it assumed incentives for all where:

- Retail banks earn the origination fee while avoiding any losses from defaults as loans were taken off the books after extension
- Investment banks and real estate agents make commissions in the securitisation and home purchase transactions
- Homeowners achieved the 'American dream' of homeownership
- Investors expect to earn higher but 'safer' returns in mortgage-backed securities
- Rating agencies have shares of the fees in promoting the structured products
- Risks are 'diversified' or spread out and therefore 'reduced'

Subprime mortgage lending started with the intent to solve social and political problems for the lower income groups in homeownership. How did institutions contribute to the system's fragility and failure? It started from the repeal of the Glass Steagall Act that separated banking on the investment from retail, in which case money becomes more fungible and allows for more risk-taking such as using short-term deposits for long-term mortgage lending sliced and diced in securities offered to investors who were in fact the lenders. From the aforementioned list, all parties would promote subprime lending in pursuit of their respective incentives in an uncoordinated market structure. However, when there were first signs of loan defaults after interest rate increases, the 'rationality' assumption in the algorithms did not exactly apply due to the opaqueness of the product. Instead, sell-off was the mechanism of ambiguity aversion in a complex market with fundamental uncertainty, when the assumed incentives outlined earlier turned into conflicts of interest among market participants.

These issues and gaps that fall among institutions, market participants and economic events are exactly what behavioural economics and finance question: are institutions the rules of the game in the real world in managing uncertainty among human interactions and in determining efficiency and outcomes? What are the confluences of behaviour among economic actors at both intra- and inter-institutional levels in the structure? In other words, behavioural economics and finance ask how market participants would behave in a particular environment with varied economic incentives, where institutions are assumed to be important enforcers of the rules of these games, or lack thereof, as part of the environment. This is the other critical blade in Herbert Simon's scissors representing situations or environment that is often ignored in conventional economics.

In the subprime lending case, institutions as rules of games were apparently not set up properly. Deregulation and other shifts away from traditional lending practices had rendered power not only to the banks but also to various agents in over-extending financial capacities while

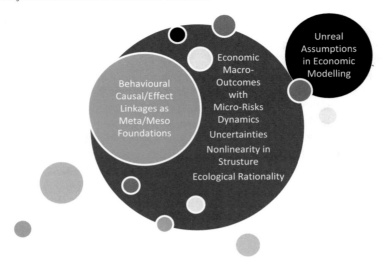

Figure 4.2   Behavioural economics as meta- and meso-economic foundations

maximising their respective incentives. These acts, however, victimised individual investors as there was no protective mechanism for the investment – the collateral did not exist – homes cannot be sliced and diced in pieces, let alone the fact that there was no designated home for a particular investment. These behavioural perspectives on institutions are in line with the claim that there should be three structural frameworks in the economy, macro, micro and meso (Chen 2010), where meso is the intermediate level represented by institutions, the design of which has a deterministic role in how market participants behave.

Risk versus Uncertainty and Financial Modelling with Time Factors

For many decades, if not for centuries, risk and uncertainty are assumed to be and regarded as the same in concept, in practice, and in experiments where both can be anticipated and tested utilising quantitative methods with precision ex-ante. Methodologies of probability and related, such as Bayesian or Bayesian updating, are taught and practised in higher education and the financial world as the only method for managing both risk and uncertainty. However, Camera and Loewenstein, among others, found that Bayes's rule has several features that are cognitively unrealistic and is unlikely to be correct descriptively (Camera and Loewenstein 2004).

How do we distinguish risk from uncertainty, or can they be clearly separated? Conceptually and for understanding from a cognitive perspective, while the outcome is unknown for both, the probability distribution governing that outcome is known for risk but not for uncertainty (Groot and Thurik 2018). There are other ways of categorising the two in various shades, from certainty or complete knowledge to total ignorance or complete uncertainty with risk next to the former and fundamental uncertainty next to the latter, and possibly other finer labellings in between. While risk may be considered as part of the uncertainty, it is at the lower end of the spectrum and therefore can largely be captured with quantitative methods. But how do we know whether we face a situation of risk or uncertainty in a particular instance?

In general, risk applies to matters in a rather closed environment while uncertainty is relevant to matters in an open system. In reality, however, we rarely encounter situations of either in absolute terms. For example, in a world of consumer credit in banking in the US, secured or unsecured, where there are ample data available on the historical nature of managing risk that allow for relatively rigorous analyses in both the selection (whom to extend credit to) and managing processes (whether borrowers are in good credit standing). So we could say that banking on consumer credit is a relatively closed system. It is relatively speaking, however, as it is not a completely closed system since variables such as interest rate and borrower employment status, among others, could change due to conditions of the overall economy and therefore impact the credit standing of the borrower and therefore the bank's risk profile. When secured lending in subprime mortgages is migrated to the investment world where investors, as lenders, could sell off if borrowers default, this relatively closed system is transformed into a more open one with a higher grade of uncertainty. While the 2008 GFC was certainly a liquidity crisis in technical terms, it was triggered by a crisis of investor confidence with sell-offs under uncertainty, a variable that is absent in the calculations of risk. Are these investors irrational? In Gigerenzer and Volz's words:

> Claims that the rational brain always works by Bayesian calculations are founded on the assumption that what is rational in a world of risk is also rational in an uncertain world . . . Bayesian inference works in small worlds where there are reliable data for probabilities and only a few alternatives and cues.
>
> (qtd. in Ghisellini and Chang 2018)

In Hertwig and Gigerenzer's research (Ghisellini and Chang 2018), they conclude that it is an error to impose the rules of probability as the norm for making rational inferences under uncertainty, and researchers have mistaken intelligent inferences, such as investor sell-offs in response to borrower default in the example earlier, as reasoning errors. This conclusion is generated from the belief and assumption that sound reasoning follows the rules in probability theory and that norms should be content-blind, which overlooks human intelligence in dealing with uncertainty in the real world. The benchmark using probability as the norm for all in projecting future events is a problem not only in determining 'rational' behaviour in risk vs. uncertainty, but also in ignorance of reality or the 'overfitting' problem in practice since unlike risk, fundamental uncertainty is unquantifiable in exact terms ex-ante; the latter is deceivingly reduced to the former for purposes of tractability, observability and convenience in executions.

In addition to problems such as zero-risk and turkey illusions found in economic and financial modelling that contributed to the 2008 GFC, content-blind norms are also issues for the validity and reliability of conclusions from scientific experiments in determining whether certain viewpoints or behaviours are biased or not, e.g., the deposition effect or loss aversion (see Ghisellini and Chang 2018). As we are semantically able to distinguish risk from fundamental uncertainty, the latter, which is classified to include both the aleatory or environmental as the source of uncertainty and epistemic or incomplete knowledge as the degree of uncertainty (Hertwig, Pleskac and Pachur 2019), cannot be fully captured in experiments which are mostly prescribed in settings. Under these environments, the possible outcome and probability distributions are mostly known or 'rehearsed'. Such choices are exceptions rather than the rule (Hertwig, Pleskac and Pachur 2019) as reality is experiential with both aleatory and epistemic uncertainties working in interactions. As in Daoist philosophy, a path in prescription is often not a path in experience.

Aside from the more explicit assumptions of a rational man who has all the unbounded capabilities in his computational skills, knowledge and willpower, the implicit assumption made here is that these capabilities would be sufficient in making optimal and rational decisions without error. However, as we have defined that fundamental uncertainty is comprised of both the aleatory and epistemic forms working in integration, the unbounded capabilities of the rational man, namely his computational skills, knowledge and willpower, belong only to the epistemic realm in determining the degree of uncertainty. Or the assumptions about the rational man have excluded the existence of the aleatory realm or the source of uncertainty that the rational man may not have access to, given constraints such as intentions, behaviours of counter-parties and the factor of time which embraces all unforeseen activities in development with irreversibility. Thus the very fundamental problem of the conventional theory is the assumption that the economic system operates largely in quantifiable risk instead of in fundamental uncertainty. It is this uncertain world that humans have to work with most of the time and this system has grown in more severe forms as markets develop in recent decades.

This mistreatment of fundamental uncertainty as a measurable risk in research and application may explain some of the profound issues contributing to non-realism in the conventional as well as mainstream behavioural theories and in turn economic modelling. In practice, risk management involves mostly epistemic acquisitions. The ignorance about the aleatory uncertainty and its contemporaneous interactive components of epistemic uncertainty on the part of the modeller, albeit assuming full knowledge with all possible measurement tools, blindfolds and detaches models from economic relevance hence reality with cumulative effects. Here, time is the pivotal element under fundamental uncertainty, which involves the velocity or speed of change of information demanded and supplied in the process of decision-making.

As the study of behavioural economics in the last decades primarily focused on the areas of consumer behaviour and the financial markets, assumptions and claims made on human biases and irrationality, however, may not be transferable between these two areas or applicable from one to the other given the nature of their distinctive market environment with the disparate speed of interactions on existing knowledge and of change along with the need for a judgment in a particular timeframe that drives behaviour. For instance, claims of biases, e.g., availability and representativeness, on consumer behaviour may be less applicable to behaviours in the financial market given differences in decision environment and market structures with the urge to act and to convict. Behaviour such as market sell-off in an extraordinary circumstance may not be considered 'irrational' because of fear of survival in fundamental uncertainty, as the claim is measured according to models utilising methods for a calculable risk. In this case, it mistook an immeasurable problem for a largely measurable one. This problem resonates in works by influential behavioural scholars who continue to adopt a conventional mean-variance method in finance, which is applicable under the assumption of risk aversion. In behavioural finance, however, investors are assumed to be loss averse (Ghisellini and Chang 2018), where the fear of loss in investment under fundamental uncertainty cannot be captured in the mean-variance framework.

CONCLUSION

Perhaps the fundamental setback in conventional methods in understanding economic outcomes lies in the adoption of classical mechanics from the field of physics with restrictive yet unrealistic assumptions in achieving mechanistic and deterministic measures. Closer to more realistic assumptions, however, are found in the field of quantum theories taking into account cognitive validities in behavioural economics. These assumptions include discrete values in movement, the uncertainty principle, the concept of duality and complementarity and the notion of entanglement given the effects of human interactions. While conventional economists call for 'anomalies' for justification of classical models, others foresee the same as normalcies in quantum models, which are expected to generate a less partial, more real-world-based and sustainable economy.

NOTES

1. In *Behavioral Economics: Moving Forward*, Ghisellini and Chang (2018) discuss how Brasser-Pereira (2009) distinguishes methodological sciences such as mathematics and statistics, which do not have an object but are instrumental to reasoning, and substantive sciences such as natural and social sciences (including economics), which have a clear object to analyse. The latter adopts the historical-deductive method from observations of realities and in contrast, methodological sciences are based on the hypothetic-deductive method such as a theory assessed not with reference to reality but to its mathematical validity. What new classical economists did was use the 'wrong' method (the hypothetical-deductive method) to build models that had no correspondence to reality, but were useful to claim that such models were scientific and could fully support hypotheses such as market efficiency. Unfortunately, science and mathematical formalisation are *not* the same thing (Ghisellini and Chang 2018).
2. Logical positivism's central tenets are: 1) scientific knowledge (math logic) is the only valid form of knowledge (knowledge: justifiable/verifiable belief of truth); 2) normative statements, value judgements and opinions are not valid knowledge; 3) empirical data is the only valid source of knowledge; 4) valid knowledge can only be obtained from natural sciences, particularly physics, using math and logic; 5) generalisation/principles/theories in science can only be derived from empirical data through induction expressed in math and logic; 6) item 2) should not be part of the empirical data collection theory formulation or verification; and 7) item 4) holds true for all fields of experience (unity of scientific methods; Boylan and O'Gorman 1995).

REFERENCES

Altman, Morris. 2008. "Behavioral economics, economic theory and public policy." *Australasian Journal of Economic Education* **5**: 1–55.
Kerruish, Erika. 2009. "Interpreting feeling: Nietzsche on the emotions and the self, Minerva - An Internet." *Journal of Philosophy* **13**(2009): 1–27.
Altman, Morris. 2012. *Behavioral Economics for Dummies* (pp. 23–25). Canada: John Wiley.
Blaug, Mark. 1992. *The Methodology of Economics or How Economists Explain* (pp. 42–104). Cambridge: Cambridge University Press.
Boylan, Thomas A. and Paschal F. O'Gorman. 1995. *Beyond Rhetoric and Realism in Economics: Towards a Reformulation of Economic Methodology* (pp. 13, 97–193). London: Routledge.
Bresser Pereira, L. (2009). *Globalization and Competition: Why Some Emergent Countries Succeed while Others Fall Behind*. Cambridge: Cambridge University Press.
Camera, Colin and George Loewenstein. 2004. *Behavioral Economics: Past, Present and Future in Advances in Behavioral Economics* (p. 9). New York: Russell Sage Foundation.
Chen, Ping. 2010. *Economic Complexity and Equilibrium Illusion: Essays on Market Instability and Macro Vitality*. London: Routledge.
Cohen, J. and Ian Stewart. 1995. *The Collapse of Chaos: Discovering Simplicity in a Complex World*. London: Penguin Books.
Ghisellini, Fabrizio and Beryl Y. Chang. 2018. *Behavioral Economics: Moving Forward* (pp. 15–176). London: Palgrave Macmillan.

Groot, K. D. and R. Thurik. 2018. "Disentangling Risk and Uncertainty: When Risk-Taking Measures are Not about Risk." *Frontiers in Psychology* https://www.ncbi.nlm.nih.gov/pmc/articles/PMC6249320/?report=classic

Hands, D. Wade. 2001. *Reflection without Rules: Economic Methodology and Contemporary Science Theory* (p. 331). Cambridge: Cambridge University Press.

Hausman, Daniel M. 1994. *The Philosophy of Economics: An Anthology* (p. 216). Cambridge: Cambridge University Press.

Hertwig, R., T. Pleskac and T. Pachur. 2019. *Taming Uncertainty* (p. 47, 349). Cambridge, MA: MIT Press.

Kay, J. and M. King. 2020. *Radical Uncertainty: Decision-Making beyond the Numbers*. New York: W. W. Norton & Company.

Kerruish, Erika. 2009. "Interpreting feeling: Nietzsche on the emotions and the self, Minerva - An Internet." *Journal of Philosophy* **13**(2009): 1–27.

Lawson, Tony. 1997. *Economics and Reality* (Ch. 3). London: Routledge.

Maki, Uskali. 2002. *Fact and Fiction in Economics: Models, Realism and Social Construction* (p. 95, 123). Cambridge: Cambridge University Press.

Smith, Vernon L. 2008. *Rationality in Economics: Constructivist and Ecological Forms* (pp. 32–36). Cambridge: Cambridge University Press.

Wilkinson, Nick. 2008. *An Introduction to Behavioral Economics* (p. 439). London: Palgrave Macmillan.

PART II

REAL-WORLD ECONOMICS

5. Realeconomik: Using the messy human experience to drive clean theoretical advance in economics

Gigi Foster and Paul Frijters

INTRODUCTION

One way to advance knowledge is to look for small improvements upon what one already holds to be true. The peer review system in modern economics rewards that practice, and we see it too in economic theories of altruism that start from the 'accepted' position that people have fixed 'selfish' preferences and hence cannot become altruistic towards something new but must already be so at birth. Outside of economics, this is viewed as absurd. Other social sciences view altruism and self-sacrificial behaviour as something that emerges, and hence is dynamic rather than fixed. Yet, within the valley of current economics, the incremental-change approach to advancing our understanding of altruism cannot escape the absurdity of fixed altruism. Retaining the minimum economic concept of the human as evolutionarily 'selfish', we describe how an economically tractable understanding of love can be built from a research methodology that includes introspection, participation, playfulness and ruthless musing, all necessary to escape from the pull of the valley in which we find ourselves.[1]

At the dawn of the discipline, philosophers like Jean-Jacques Rousseau, David Hume and Adam Smith laid the groundwork for modern economics by building overlapping storylines (theories) from a wide range of considerations and methods. They were willing to relate the building blocks of their theories to very wide and sometimes vague phenomena, such as when Adam Smith spoke of the importance of 'empathy' which he linked to 'something in [our] nature' (Smith 1759, p. 9). Rousseau similarly discussed reason in the context of the difficulty of thinking 'nobly' (Rousseau 1782/1998, p. 338). Hume talked of 'passions' as part of the 'primary constitution of the mind' (Hume 1739–40, p. 286). Their inquiries took them far from others' ideas, such as when Hume disagreed with other early philosophers when he said that reason was the slave of the 'passions', rather than being in the service of some fixed truth. The early economists engaged in inquiries that were wide and loose, allowing them to take large strides in their thinking.

These founding builders of economic thought were deeply involved in the concerns of their society, trying to see general patterns in whatever material they had. They spoke of social ills like inequality, abuse of power, envy, lack of liberty and inadequate education, using what their small-N observations of humans led their minds to suspect was true in general. Their wide inquiries were married with constant real engagement with the concerns of their societies, feeding the theories with what they learned from that engagement, and engaging on the basis of their theories. They aimed to take the measure of man and society not in formal mathematical models but in elegant verbal expression, which at the time was thought to be enough to guide generations of further thinkers ever closer to a truer representation of the tendencies of the species.

In their quest to understand and engage, they took no prisoners and saw that trait as helpful in the pursuit of their objective. For example, speaking of his contemporary Rousseau, David Hume remarked that he 'has not had the precaution to throw any veil over his sentiments' (Gay 1969, p. 72). Adam Smith was by character well known to be unconcerned with the opinions of others and devoted instead to a precise articulation of his thoughts on a wide range of social and political matters. Similarly, the institutional economist Thorstein Veblen was famously rude and cared little for his academic position, yet quite deeply for his ability to express his ideas. These proto-economists shared a commitment to their own personal truth, based on close observation of humans and their groups, and in spite of potential social disapproval for doing so. Rousseau even elevated his non-conformist nature into a philosophical doctrine: 'Why should we build our happiness on the opinions of others, when we can find it in our own hearts?' (Rousseau 1762/1913, p. 142). In today's academic environment, where to be taken seriously academics need to please peer reviewers, ethics boards and the image managers of their departments, this kind of thinking is not tolerated. Indeed, the modern academy might well deem the approach of these early thinkers insensitive, arrogant, elitist and out-of-touch. The accused might well have agreed with these characterisations, perhaps retorting that 'that stance is what you need to dare to think something interesting'.

The latter-day loss of the aristocrat mindset of these early economists carries implications for the breadth of modern thinking. Today's generation of economic thinkers has little incentive to present in published form a set of evidence-based thoughts galloping across individuals' nature and social patterns. Instead, they have strong incentives to follow in narrow lockstep with what beliefs, founded or not, have been pounded into stylised mathematical straitjackets by prior researchers. Those incentives are seen in the need to please peer reviewers: such reviewers demand that their thoughts are acknowledged and respected, and this enforces an incremental, 'stick to your patch' approach to discovery. True innovation, or even challenging mainstream untruths, is nearly impossible, with reward flowing not from speaking one's mind regardless of the social consequences but rather, in the extreme, from following, citing and fawning over the writings of others in the field. The 'room to manoeuvre' is evident more in accepted attempts to muscle out other disciplines, rather than slack granted within what is viewed as economists' common territory.

In the first section of this chapter, we review several examples of attempts to explore big ideas by modern economists who have been hampered in their intellectual travels by large bits of dysfunctional theoretical luggage. Examples of this luggage include the existence within human minds of fixed individual preferences; a representation of the future built on weighing up the 'utils' obtainable by some future self; and an absence of competing loyalties. These assumptions seem on the surface to allow a clean and tidy representation of decision-making and altruism, but in fact close down the path of deeper inquiry into decision-making and hamper any exploration of the dynamics of altruism. Yet, this luggage is compulsory for any economist wishing to have influence today, meaning that no real advance is possible. The same holds for many other areas of inquiry: the discipline is stuck with the same basic ideas it had in the 1950s, ideas shared across many sub-disciplines, taught in undergraduate texts that have not meaningfully changed since the 1950s. To get away from the stagnation inherent in hoisting useless luggage around, we advocate a new way of doing research, incorporating some of the classical methods that largely have been lost to modern academia.

In the second section of this chapter, we describe such a new way, illustrating it using the specific example of how to understand the human phenomenon of love. Love underpins many if not most of our resource allocation decisions and hence its nature is in the direct sight line of economic research. We illustrate the power of a grassroots-led, observational and experiential approach to gaining an understanding of how and why we love, starting with how life is lived rather than with whatever mathematical model of love someone else managed to publish.

Armed with a reminder of how research could be done and what it might yield, we then reassess the pathologies of modern economics and social science. We illustrate how our discipline has become stuck in performance rituals, exemplified by pre-registration plans that represent and enforce a sterile view of science in which everything important – including formulating theories and hypotheses that hold the key to knowledge advancement – supposedly happens before doing science, rather than during it.

FOOLS' ERRANDS

What follows is a critique of a selection of the dominant 'as-if' assumptions used in most conventional economic analysis today and how those assumptions have misdirected theoretical advances in understanding choice behaviour and altruism.

The Lack of Falsifiability of Fundamental Microeconomic Assumptions

The standard economic advice given today to governments worldwide, to the extent that it has microeconomic models of individual behaviour to back it up, is built on microeconomic models that assume a variety of unfalsifiable assumptions. In this subsection, we briefly review the most common of these, as a precursor to illustrating the incrementalist approach which takes such assumptions as given.

The first 'as-if' assumption is the notion of fixed preference maps. The fixation on fixity of preferences infected the discipline early in the 20th century, with axiomatic formalisations in the 1950s. Today we still teach students, even in graduate courses, that fixed preferences are a useful assumption in thinking about all choices (Mas-Colell, Whinston and Green 1995, p. 42; Jehle and Reny 2000, p. 70). Students are given no real counterargument and are told that these formulations have been a 'success', so students in the main do not question the notion of fixed preference maps as an 'explanation' of choice behaviour. Indeed, they go on to form the next generation of vocal proponents of this fiction. A survey of all pure theory papers published in the 'top five' journals in economics between November 2020 and October 2021 reveals that a large majority invokes fixed preferences (the fraction in each case is as follows: *American Economic Review*, 88 per cent; *Econometrica*, 78 per cent; *Journal of Political Economy*, 79 per cent; *Review of Economic Studies*, 79 per cent; *Quarterly Journal of Economics*, 60 per cent).

The problem is that fixed preference maps are nonsense from a neuroscientific point of view. No such maps have ever been found in human brains, and experiments on how the brain comes up with decisions show that all the main elements of the fixed preference story are untrue (see, e.g., Clark, Frijters and Shields 2008, p. 121; Bault et al. 2015). Humans do not 'look up in their brain' whether they prefer this car or that car when buying one, but construct a preference at the moment they are shopping for cars (for further discussion of the determinants of the choice process from a consumer psychology standpoint, see Simonson 2008). That 'just-in-time' preference construction involves the evolving personality of the person and all the environmental factors around car sales, meaning that people do not choose the same thing in situations that seem broadly the same, because they themselves change and wider circumstances also change in a myriad of unmeasured ways (see, e.g., Pugach, Leder and Graham 2017; Sharot et al. 2012). Axioms one proposes for preference maps (which themselves are fictional) are typically rejected by experimental evidence (see, e.g., Loomes, Starmer and Sugden 1991; Hoeffler and Ariely 1999; Jacobs 2016), which should come as no surprise. For example, people do not always choose the same bundle of goods if given the same choice, nor are their choices transitive or independent of the non-chosen options.

Not only do preference maps not exist, but the very idea that people have fixed desires removes from view the many areas of human behaviour in which desires are fluid. That includes most forms of social behaviour and motivators, such as mimicry, jealousy, empathy, hate, discovery, group formation and love. These all involve changes in how people see themselves and what they prefer, something that cannot be squared with the existence of fixed preferences over all goods. Hence, the assumption of fixed preferences is a hindrance in inquiries about these kinds of motivations and behaviours.

While the brain has no preference map but instead features many mechanisms to allow the human to change what she wants in reaction to social cues, the land of economic theory has not abandoned the idea of fixed preferences, but rather has moved the whole question of preference formation out of empirical sight completely (see Frijters and Foster 2013, chapter 1, for an extensive discussion). One way to insist that preferences are fixed, but not to allow any empirical check of that claim, is to suggest that an empirical researcher must discover the categories of things over which preferences might be fixed. Economic theorists might for example admit that people do not have fixed preferences over types of cars or types of breakfast, but then insist that they must have fixed preferences over, say, 'composite social goods' or 'self-affirming goods', leaving the empiricists to work out which goods fall into which of those baskets. One can move the goal posts endlessly in such a fashion, which is exactly what has happened. Since one can always claim that empirical researchers cannot measure the true objects over which fixed preferences exist, one thereby removes the possibility of being proven wrong. In this way, convenient redefinitions have made the idea of fixed preferences into an article of faith that cannot be disproven. This only makes the luggage heavier and more constraining.

A second example of a standard assumption that has become not falsifiable is the idea that people maximise a utility function to arrive at choices. Ever-present in the models economists build and the language economists use to speak about human motivation is the view that people walk around as so many incompletely filled vats of pleasing utils, making choices at every moment based only on what they expect will add the greatest additional utils from amongst some finite number of goods or activities. This is a useful depiction for many research purposes, but fanciful for many others and thus highly constraining when it becomes a compulsory piece of intellectual luggage.

The first problem with the notion of a utility function is that mistakes cannot be accommodated by the tautology implicit in the utility function: anything that people choose can be argued to be consistent with some utility function, of whatever convoluted form is required to fit their choices, unknown (though perhaps seductively estimable, given enough data!) to the observer but presumably known and used to drive choices by the individual. In this sense, mistakes are presumed not to exist and cannot be identified.

Second and more damningly, the types of utility functions taken seriously by policymakers normally include no more than a small handful of alternative options, meaning that the vast array of other things on which people could choose to spend time, money, or effort is simply swept under the carpet and assumed not to influence the choice under analysis by any given researcher or government analyst. In mainstream economic calculations of costs and benefits, for example, social externalities involving jealousy or joy are conspicuous in their absence.[2]

Third, and related to the earlier discussion of preference maps, a fixed utility function assumes a fixity of perception and preference unlike that seen amongst real humans, whose abilities and wishes change with the seasons, the menstrual cycle, the social environment and so on. The whole business of selective perception and observation is thereby swept away from view, in the style of marketing and politics rather than science.

Fourth, as with preference maps, the assumption that the utility function is fixed negates at the first post all inquiry into its sources or determinants, and hence all deeper inquiry regarding how people's motivations might be manipulated. The idea that a car might be made more desirable if its photo includes an attractive person is basically dismissed out of hand by the idea of a fixed utility function, despite being treated as an obvious truth by the car salesman. Unable to accommodate these and many other real features of human motivation, the utility function jolts like a marionette figurine through pages of academic work, dancing at the behest of his ever-changing masters, and perennially incapable of taking the lead and guiding the researcher towards true progress in understanding what makes people do things.

What is perhaps worst about the notion that people consciously maximise expected utility is that it makes no sense from an evolutionary point of view simply because it takes far too much effort for an individual to make choices in that fashion. No human really does all that conscious or subconscious maximising. An animal dumb enough to try to calculate the expected utility of all choices available at each moment would be outcompeted by another one that has lots of little mental short-cuts to support quick decision-making. Experimental work in zoonotic neurology has produced results in 'general agreement with an account of goal-directed behavior according to which the outcome should be represented already at the time at which the behavior toward the outcome is performed' (Hassani, Cromwell and Schultz 2001, abstract), or in other words, that animals appear to make choices in response to an imagined outcome, rather than in response to an imagined stream of future utilities dependent upon that outcome. Researchers in zoology have been unable to reconcile animals' choices on vital tasks like when to leave a hunting patch with the 'time preferences' derived from their responses to simple intertemporal choice problems (which by economic logic present animals with essentially an identical trade-off), also indicating that there is no 'expected utility' formula that animals are calculating and then maximising through their choices on survival-relevant tasks (see, e.g., Hayden 2016).

Similarly, the person following a routine in the morning (shower, breakfast, coffee) is not wasting time calculating the expected utilities of various alternative choices but is simply sticking to behaviours that worked out reasonably well most of the time in the past, thereby freeing his mind to be engaged with more rewarding tasks. Sticking to a routine is in this sense not a form of stupidity, but rather a superior form of behaviour, compared to maximising expected utility. The deep flaw is that on closer inspection, any science operating with the 'maximising expected utility' view of the world implicitly assumes that there is no cost to mental effort. As bizarre as it sounds, this centrepiece of modern economic theorising is a model in which a crucial good – mental effort – is presumed to have a price of zero. The early economists would probably have dismissed this presumption as inherently uneconomical.

The intellectual trap of the idea of zero costs to mental effort is nowhere clearer than in how behavioural economists in recent years have portrayed the now hundreds of behavioural phenomena that violate the implications of people maximising expected utility. Behavioural economists call these deviations 'anomalies', 'irrationalities', 'biases' and even 'fallacies'. In this class is the 'certainty illusion', referring to how people do not accommodate many sources of uncertainty in their mental models, but simply take lots of things as if they are certain. There is also the 'focusing illusion', whereby people involved in a specific task do not consider lots of things deemed irrelevant. Others include 'present bias' and 'framing bias'. The conceit inherent in these labels is that there is something inherently suboptimal about these behaviours, which is only true in the make-believe world of zero costs to calculating everything that could possibly matter in a choice setting.

Instead of talking about anomalies and biases that need 'correction' back towards some pre-fabricated, fictional baseline (i.e., utility maximisation), behavioural economists have the option to view behaviour from an evolutionary point of view. Economists studying humans' deviations from maximising utility behaviour could more profitably ask what deviations are good for, rather than trying to denounce them as a problem.

A final word is needed on two powerful meta-defences of such assumptions, often offered by their users, that there is no other game in town and/or that some tractability must be brought to the science of human behaviour in order to make any progress at all. This is both a conceit and an untrue sleight of hand. The conceit is that if something is the only game in town at the moment, it must be a good game. With that attitude, we would never have abandoned the religious certainties that preceded science. The sleight of hand of the many defenders of the utility-function-and-preference-map habit is the claim that it is tractable or that it explains choices. Quite the opposite is true: by their nature, preference maps and utility functions are not tractable at all but merely assume a reason for choices, without explaining or predicting anything. Preference maps are not observed and thus do not explain anything, but simply drag economic theory into the realm of undoubted religion. These assumptions endure in the place of useful explanations.

Realeconomik Incentives in Economic Research

Those who have tried in the past to question some of these assumptions have faced either the indifference of established mainstream scholars (e.g., virtually the entirety of the 'heterodox economics' community in Australia) or their disapprobation. Foss (2000) sums up the reality facing young scholars by saying 'Extreme specialization rules the roost among academic economists, and eclecticism and the broad view are shunned as the plague'. With extreme specialisation has come the demise of broad progress on the shared core, simply because broad thinking is not done, rewarded, or even recognised when someone does do it.

In a paper in the *American Economic Review*, Daniel Kahneman also noted how the 'church of economics' has a stable core that has not changed for decades despite huge changes in almost every subfield (Kahneman 2003): while every subfield has changed, the whole valley (or 'church' (p. 165)) has not. This is still true today, as reflected in the fact that the main textbooks in use in 2020 (e.g., Mankiw 2021; Acemoglu, Laibson and List 2018), are still in essence the Samuelson-derived textbooks of the 1950s (Samuelson 1948).

One deep reason for this conservatism is the classic argument by Hotelling (1929): a club becomes more conservative if its members divide into sub-specialisations because as the diversity increases, the middle ground (the median) moves less and less with any change in opinion by any person or sub-group. In every corner of the club, the specialists can then say something that is non-mainstream, while what is taught to the next generation does not change at all even though no individual sub-group any longer agrees with it. What then happens is that every generation of subfield specialists essentially starts from scratch and has little hope of ending up intellectually anywhere else, because by themselves they cannot move the whole discipline, tethered as they all are to the need to remain known as 'an economist', the brand from which they derive their attraction to students and politicians. The next generation also has every incentive to ignore the previous generation's work, and instead claim territory in their speciality afresh by starting from 'sound principles', by which is meant the shared (and stagnant) mainstream view.

We think modern economics is in this trap. Modern economics essentially consists of small sub-territories on which little sandcastles are built, while as a whole the grand sandbar on which all these territories stand remains exactly the same. Any sub-territory that tries to shift significant amounts of sand is purely seen as a threat. The only real sand-shifting encouraged is sand pinched from the sandbar of another discipline like psychology.

How is this orthodoxy kept intact? One leading visible way is via the inherently self-referential peer review system. Economic papers are not judged by society, government, business or other ultimate 'users' of economic insights, but by other academic economists. In their roles as editors and referees, these academics have no incentive to care about societal use, but they have strong incentives to force 'new contributions' to acknowledge their own prior work and not to destroy the value of the personal investments they themselves have made. This makes peer review into a kind of beauty pageant that rewards external appearances of innovation and technical prowess and punishes the actual destruction of current orthodoxy. The omission of external judges from the peer review process removes the incentive to innovate, while the fixed human capital possessed by all gatekeepers in the system leads to aversion to change, resulting in the reward of form over substance.

Another lock-in mechanism is that the media and students constantly look for signals of academic quality as part of their evaluative activities, since they cannot perfectly monitor quality. For reasons of efficiency and comparability, such outside actors typically use signals that emerge from within the peer review system rather than from any notion of usefulness to the outside world. This leads to the winners in the peer review beauty pageant being asked to talk about broad issues even though they have been trained and selected for the opposite. Paul Krugman is a perfect example: a hyper-specialist in fairly obscure and arguably policy-irrelevant trade models, who has morphed into an eagerly sought-after general commentator on society, complete with his own *New York Times* column.[3] That reality in turn takes away the incentive for ambitious young scholars to invest significant effort in developing broader views and pushes them instead to simply invest in the peer review game as a means of obtaining rewards in many arenas that seem to matter, both within and outside of academia.

An even more pernicious lock-in mechanism is embodied in the relatively recent development of empirical economics as a monoculture, wherein students and academics are told that science is about formulating hypotheses, gathering data and methods to test those hypotheses, and then accepting or rejecting those hypotheses based on formal tests. That view of science, which on the face of it sounds highly rational and sensible, is exemplified in 'pre-registration' plans for experiments and empirical inquiries. It is also the view mandated by many research funding agencies that simply demand, often in pre-set section headings, that an applicant list hypotheses, planned methods and intended tests, with consent plans and ethical 'approval' for each step in the process.

This view of science mandates that the scientist knows, before the journey begins, the nature of the thing that will be found. Is this how science truly proceeds or has proceeded in the past? Adam Smith, David Hume and even Paul Krugman did not in fact start out with precise hypotheses, but were instead on journeys of discovery that only far later led to insights and thoughts that one might be able to formulate as 'hypotheses'. Most of what historical economists are known and admired for would be rejected by the formal tests mandated by modern funding agencies. In light of that, even the notion of offering falsifiable hypotheses is not a reasonable description of the output of useful economic thinking. Rather, useful economic thinking provides maps that help describe a terrain in which difficult decisions have to be made, even though those maps are demonstrably inaccurate in every detailed section when one looks more closely. The hopeless quest for accurate maps within economics has in fact proven totally futile, with the old quip that 'economists have predicted nine out of the last five recessions' being just as true today as when it was first uttered (Samuelson 1966). If you doubt this, consider the unpredicted GFC, or the fruitless search for preference maps in neuroscience.

Having sketched the basic underpinnings of the essential deceit that mainstream empirical economics now entails, we proceed to offer two examples of the meagre fruits that have been produced in this environment in relation to our understanding of important, complex and unwieldy phenomena. This is followed by a fuller description of the contrastingly rich nature of real science.

Incrementalism on Groups and Power

One popular line of research in applied economics, spearheaded by Rachel Kranton and George Akerlof, has tackled the notion of group identity. Their basic framework was first published in a paper in the prestigious *Quarterly Journal of Economics* in 2000 (Akerlof and Kranton 2000) and has since been cited more than 6,500 times in the literature according to Google Scholar, making it Rachel Kranton's highest-cited work. This framework starts from the following simple mathematical assertion (p. 719):

$$U_j = U_j\left(a_j,\ a_{-j}, I_j\right)$$

where the 'a' terms denote the actions of self and others, and the I term captures 'identity'. The authors proceed to assert that identity can be to some extent chosen by individuals, who select membership in the social categories from which identity (and social status, the core good available from group membership in a social category) is then derived, based on the expected payoffs to the individual that flow from a high match between the social norms for a given category and the individual's own nature.

We do not wish to throw everything about Akerlof and Kranton's efforts under the bus. Many of the elements of their argument are promising – such as the implicit notion that social norms are kept alive via groups, and that people to some extent choose the groups they identify with based on what those groups offer. The problem is not with the ideas, but with the constricting mathematical form into which they need to be shoehorned in order for the valley of economics to take their work seriously. The paper's promising discussion about the ideas involved with groups, identity and power, and examples of human behaviours that are consistent with the importance of such phenomena in motivating people, are the highest-value parts of the paper

– but what got the paper published in an economics journal is its stroll through the various mathematical derivations of their changed utility function, matching preference model and comparative statics. In spite of the 6,500 citations it has received, Akerlof and Kranton's basic utility-based formulation has not enabled economists to learn more about groups, power and identity because rather than explaining anything, it represents things already known to non-economists, and does so in a straitjacketed way that clamps down on deeper investigation or innovation. Essentially their model removes from view the key questions, such as how groups arise and how group morality emerges.

Another offering in this line of work is Benabou and Tirole's *American Economic Review* paper of 2006 entitled 'Incentives and Pro-Social Behavior'. This work is again the top-cited work of Roland Benabou according to Google Scholar, with over 3,500 citations since it first appeared. As with Akerlof and Kranton's effort, this paper includes much interesting discussion about group-related phenomena including reputation, other-regarding behaviour, social norms and imperfect monitoring. In order to get published, the authors also had to include pages full of mathematical exposition into which some bits of these interesting ideas are shoved in ways that pleased the court. This begins with formulations for 'preferences and information' and 'intrinsic valuations' (p. 1656) and winds through expected rewards, equilibria (including for social norms) and social welfare functions. As with Akerlof and Kranton's work, the results of this exercise are difficult to truly build upon, as they offer no way to proceed to analyse the ideas in more depth. What is yielded instead by this performance is a mathematical formulation of some static echoes of important human processes, designed to seem as flexible and general as possible but in reality stifling further innovation because they essentially fit something fluid (group formation and identity) into a theoretical apparatus in which everything is fixed (preferences).

As a final example in the area of economists trying to stuff complex group dynamics into the requirements of utility functions and preference maps, consider Gary Becker's *Treatise on the Family*. Becker correctly identified that households are different from individuals and that this should be respected in the economic treatment of those two phenomena. Working almost entirely with the simple basic ingredients of utility functions and stable preferences, and their associated progeny such as market-level equilibria, Becker essentially shoehorned the complex phenomenon of local group influence into the 'household utility function'. Along the way he purported to 'explain' with his equations diverse real-world behaviour such as divorce, polygamy and child care choices, and his success is seen in his influence on later scholars, evidenced in the 22,000+ citations to this initial work. As with the earlier two examples, the stories told and the examples provided are appealing, but the line of true inquiry for future researchers is blocked by the narrow mathematical formulations that only by sleight of hand can be seen to capture the power of the ideas at play. One simply cannot explain the emergence of love for a child or a partner from a theory in which there are no emotional bonds but only the wish of individuals to keep a stream of goods and services towards themselves going.

Incrementalism on Love

Perhaps the most well-known modern economic researcher concerning himself with love is James Andreoni, with his most-cited work entitled 'Impure Altruism and Donations to Public Goods: A theory of warm-glow giving' (Andreoni 1990). The distinction he draws between unselfish behaviour resulting from a 'warm glow' motivation versus unselfish behaviour resulting from 'pure altruism' is shown via the usual suspects of utility functions and fixed preferences.

This paper begins with a lengthy quotation from David Hume in respect of the 'social virtues', followed by a short quip from the American Red Cross: 'Feel good about yourself – Give blood!' This clever artifice implies at the outset that the complex phenomena studied by long-ago thinkers can actually be reduced to pithy statements, thereby helping to prepare the reader's mind for the mathematical assault on the complex phenomenon of love that ensues. Not only the mathematics in this case, but Andreoni's distinction between 'warm glow' and 'pure' altruism too, is at the end of the day unhelpful: the reason for an individual to choose pure altruism as he defines it is omitted, with care for others just built into some people. His definition of pure love thus asks people to be saints in order to love, which any man on the street can say with confidence that they are not. Moreover, Andreoni's notion of pure altruism is totally undirected, and hence describes a person who makes no judgement at all about the world, 'giving' as much to the Nazi camp guard as to the Jew heading towards the gas chamber. He sets up a phenomenon that does not exist, thereby once again removing from view the question of how altruism develops. So Andreoni too tries to present water (fluid loyalty) as an unusual type of stone (pure altruism).

Even prior to Andreoni, of course, economists thought seriously about love. Fontaine (2000) reviews much of this work, recognising the often split-screen approach taken by economic historians compared to modern theorists, with the former recognising almost exclusively contributions made before 1970 and the latter almost exclusively contributions after that date. Fontaine opines that the modern convention of tethering long-ago thinkers' ideas about altruism to intertwined utility functions and proceeding forthwith is often self-serving and restrictive. We agree.

Many researchers in non-economics disciplines trying to come to terms with the nature of love are stuck in the early-stage 'aha!' moment of recognising that what seems to be self-sacrifice may in fact be a strategic investment in the hope of achieving socioemotional returns (e.g., Florczak 2004), without a discussion of when, how or why that expected bargaining takes place, nor how long or in what circumstances it endures. The analysis is descriptive rather than explanatory, and based on a model of the human not as cold himself – after all, he craves socioemotional rewards – but as a conscious, cold decision-maker. Others see love as an outgrowth of features of culture or politics and yet again fixate on description rather than explanation in general terms (Jankowiak and Fischer 1992; Schmitt 2019).

A common pitfall of researchers examining love is to ascribe a disproportionate amount of 'explanatory' power regarding love to factors difficult or impossible to manipulate in the short to medium term, like evolution or kinship ties (e.g., Alger and Weibull 2010). While the legitimacy of the influence of these factors on our capacity to love may be significant across whole human populations, recognising this 'additional variation explained' of love does not help us understand the everyday realities that we observe about love, and that are relevant to its influence on human choice: it varies in level across and within people, it is uncontrolled at a conscious level in the short to medium run (e.g., we do not choose to fall in love), and it lives across various windows, sometimes lasting a lifetime and sometimes only a week. Top theoretical research in our home discipline of economics has been virtually shut down on questions of love, with only two of the pure theory papers published in our 'top five' journals in the past year even mentioning the possibility of altruistic preferences (Newton 2021; Smith, Sørensen and Tian 2021).

REALECONOMIK

What alternative pathways towards theoretical advance in social science, other than incrementalism of the types sketched above, are consistent with the incentives facing researchers today?

What has been possible for a few lucky souls is to craft stories of depth rather than incrementalist mimicry while preserving some degree of reputation through engagement in other, parallel research agendas. The polymath Herb Simon was one such figure, illustrating the possibility of touching true advance (in Simon's case, regarding the nature, use and consequences of power within organisations (1947)) when one can convince the establishment through other, lesser works (e.g., in relation to the unavoidable reality of incomplete information (1982)) that one really is a genius.[4] This is a sort of 'through the back door' entrée into theoretical advance, available only to a select few people of truly exceptional intellect and energy. Nonetheless, it risks leaving the true innovation on the doorstep of history, never penetrating into the mainstream, left as something to be discovered and rediscovered again down the ages, in a merry-go-round of 'aha!' moments experienced by successive generations of scientists. Indeed, while Simon was very interested in power and was rewarded for his works on it, mainstream economics does not talk about the nature of power and how it is related to group processes anywhere in the conventional undergraduate program of study. So Simon's innovation was essentially left to starve on the doorstep, ignored because it does not fit in. The same fate has befallen many hundreds of other attempts to take power seriously within mainstream economics (see Frijters and Foster 2013). The essential reason for this is that discussing power automatically challenges power. Likely for an evolutionary reason, openly challenging power has slipped off the economic scientific radar, making something of a mockery of the names of many of the oldest economic journals containing the phrase 'political economy'.

Despite the present lack of welcome for truly challenging ideas, the barrenness of the incrementalist approach and the stagnancy of many of the dominant mainstream assumptions lead us to remain optimistic. Perhaps moments of crisis such as the recent COVID-19 mania, coupled with an explicit embrace of a viable alternative, may lead eventually to a shift in the priorities of the discipline such that real advance starts to become normalised.

The alternative we have in mind is not completely new. It harkens back directly to the modes of thought of early philosophers, who understood well that the subject matter of their observation was complex, emotive, difficult to pin down and susceptible to understanding only through directed, long-term observation and consideration. This approach respects the subject – the human and his society – rather than privileging technique, formalisation, extreme simplicity or tether to pre-fabrications or methodological fads.

Lost Research Methods: What We No Longer Do to Discover Things

Consider the actions of Charles Darwin, perhaps the most influential scientist in all of history. All he knew about what he was looking for when he set off around the world is that it had something to do with how species came about. His interest in this general topic drove him to want to see what could be found on exotic islands to help aid his understanding of the topic. On the Galapagos Islands and elsewhere, he prodded, examined, observed and experimented. He combined his observations on iguanas with observations he had made back home on pigeon breeding and the diversity of cows. Building up a story of how it might fit together, he combined close observations by his own eyes with stories of social evolution borrowed – believe it or not – from the early economists and their theories of how competitive forces lead to specialisation.[5] You can see an example of that borrowing in *On the Origin of Species by Means of Natural Selection* (1859), which used the idea of natural selection that Darwin found in Thomas Malthus' book from 1798, *An Essay on the Principle of Population*. On page 79 of the 1909 reprint of *Origin of Species,* Darwin writes that his own theory of the struggle for existence is 'the doctrine of Malthus applied with manifold force to the whole animal and vegetable kingdom'. Similarly, Darwin adopts the idea of the invisible hand of the market leading to optimal production methods when he claims that the particular wax hexagons found in beehives reflect an 'economy of wax' (p. 285), a technological discovery that he says came about via natural selection of bees and their beehives, not any conscious agency of bees. Darwin saw the same driving force of what made an optimal economy in many traits and behaviours of animals, from how canopies use all the available light to how particular snouts were useful in gathering nectar from particular flowers.

In the modern day, what Darwin did would be considered illegal, immoral and not science at all. He asked no permission to experiment on animals, did not articulate in a grant application exactly what he thought he was going to find, developed no testable hypotheses, used ad-hoc rather than pre-determined methods and then took 20 years to write up what he had discovered.

Consider three elements in Darwin's approach that were common at his time and are now almost as extinct as the dodo within mainstream social science, despite being extremely important in coming up with ideas and large-scale theories about how humans and societies function.

One lost element is playfulness with the methods and data one has. Playfulness is seen in an astronomer gazing through a telescope for years at random spots in the sky, looking to notice something of interest to then explain. Playfulness is seen in randomly trying stuff, like feeding one's dog something unusual and seeing how that works out. Playfulness is seen in combining data on stork nests with data on economic development, seeing whether the data line up and then reflecting on whether the accidental correlations are of any real use. These types of activities might be called 'random search', with entertainment as the immediate goal but with the longer-term scientific benefit that one is in fact sampling the entire space of possibilities. 'Looking for something interesting' and only then 'wondering what it might be' is a time-tested scientific activity. A famous example of its fruits is the discovery of bacteria when the early developers of the microscope simply looked through their instruments and noted what they saw (Bell 1966). Other famous examples include the discovery of cosmic background radiation, or of the fact that smoking kills, which was initially stated purely as a correlation found in mortality data, with no idea why it could be causal (US Public Health Service 1967).

Playfulness and the undirected search evidenced by it is also an obvious way to find out about love. One can read about the feelings of people who love, and one can choose to be around those falling in love. Observing young military recruits becoming loyal to their army, or new hires in a company becoming loyal to the company hierarchy, is similarly a form of 'just looking'. Crucially, these activities do not start from any prior theory or tether to a proper 'way of doing science', but simply consist of mainly random searching through the space containing the phenomenon in which one is somewhat interested.

A second lost element is what we might term 'ruthless musing', an armchair process wherein one builds an independent view in one's own mind – beholden to no particular prior thinker, framework or convention – of what might be going on, informed by lots of different influences. This too is a form of playfulness, akin to building sandcastles inside one's own head, but here the 'sand' can come from all kinds of places and one does not censor one's own thoughts no matter what others might think.

Darwin himself combined thoughts of friends, insights from different disciplines, personal observations, religious reading, random conversations and probably many other sources (Darwin 1876/1958, pp. 48–50), and combined them in an ongoing iterative process towards the building of a grand story of how species come about. As Jeff Wallace notes in his introduction to the 1998 reprint of *Origin of Species*, the whole book shifts perspectives and settings constantly, such as between the reality of pigeon breeding in England and the characteristics of beetles in the rainforest of Latin America, then to religious debates on a divine origin of diversity versus the implications of variation and family heredity, then to the theories of Darwin's early benefactors and mentors, like the evolutionist thinker Robert Grant. Darwin was apparently keenly aware of how ruthlessly far away from his contemporaries his thoughts were leading him. In his letters, Darwin worried whether he was devoting his life to 'phantasies' (Darwin 1859).

This internal musing and combining is a highly creative process but has many characteristics no longer explicitly taught to many students because it is inherently disrespectful. It inevitably contains a ruthless disregard of previous thought, exemplified by Darwin's realisation that his thinking was leading him to reject the religious doctrine he himself had believed in most of his life, something that made him extremely hesitant to publish his works (Darwin 1876/1958, p. 85). In his letters, he shows how he struggles immensely with how his thoughts are leading him away from religion, particularly as his father wanted him to be a priest and his initial benefactor was a reverend. He thus describes his own theories as if confessing 'a murder' (Darwin 1844).

To nevertheless arrive at his theories, Darwin allowed himself to think anything in his own mind, whether or not that meant the rejection of his whole culture. The equivalent today would be a type of thinking where flows of thought would not shy away from racism, sexism, deceit, murder, paedophilia, blasphemy or anything else about which our modern societies are sensitive. In the realm of the free-thinking mind, all thoughts are allowed and uncensored, with all judgements suspended until afterwards.

Fundamental scientific creation requires this sort of extreme freedom from accepted wisdom and accepted cultural norms. The reason it is not taught in mass education is that it is potentially destructive and would certainly never pass modern-day ethics procedures or requirements of grant-funding bodies. There is a grandiosity and aristocracy about this 'ruthless musing' activity, effusing almost an arrogance towards the elements being combined. Darwin not only failed to respect the values embedded in him since childhood, but also did not 'respect' in their full glory the economic theories he was playing with, as he distilled them into simpler patterns that he could apply in his own field.

For example, Darwin was interested in the implications of Malthus's argument on different sub-groups having differential rates of fertility, but wholly jettisoned the moralising of Malthus about whether there was anything noble about having more or fewer children (Malthus deplored the supposed slide towards 'vice' that he thought inevitable if the poor would have more children) (Darwin 1876/1958, p. 120; Malthus 1798, p. 170). That kind of brutal 'select, slice off, and ignore the rest' attitude towards accepted theories would be unacceptable nowadays and regarded as 'misinterpretation', 'over-simplification' or, worse, 'appropriation'. We venture that the peer review process would have seen Darwin's work sent to a disciple of Malthus who would have made mincemeat of Darwin's blasé treatment of prior 'wisdom'. Fortunately for the ensuing generations of scientists who benefitted from his pathbreaking work, Darwin's era had no peer review for books of the constricting modern form that rewards territorial games (Speir 2002): he just convinced a publisher (John Murray) to take his manuscript.

Thirdly, there is the lost habit of 'throwing myself personally into unfamiliar situations that feature the phenomenon in which I am interested, to see if I can figure out what is going on, partly by using myself as a source of information'. Darwin did this by physically travelling to islands and lying in the mud with the animals he was observing. Throwing themselves into the fray is also how whole generations of social scientists made discoveries on the nature of revolutions, dictatorships, markets, and so on.[6] Karl Marx famously railed against the Prussian government, engaged in multiple campaigns, and travelled to Paris to engage in revolutionary change, being at once scholar, journalist and radical. Henry George in America did not merely write on land rents but witnessed suffering in his own family due to the power dynamics he wrote about and actively campaigned about, even sacrificing his life for the cause when he died on the campaign trail. John Maynard Keynes did not merely theorise about economics: he participated in running Britain's economy during the Second World War and also helped in setting up new economic institutions after the war ended (Keynes 1940).

Like journalists, the social scientists of old travelled to places in the grip of revolutions, hyperinflation, and other social upheavals, to look around and notice what seemed to be of importance, checking candidate causal storylines on the spot, asking others what was going on and participating in the events of their time. Anthropologists still do this kind of personal immersion and participation today, though American anthropologists have to ask prior permission and keep to 'ethical professional relationships'.[7] Such rules implicitly prohibit sex, high risks or the use of information one accidentally comes across (Vivanco 2016). Such rules limit the extent to which true immersion and participation can occur.

Random playfulness, ruthless musing and immersion coupled with self-experimentation are but three of the many methods that scientists as a group used to value and teach. Nowadays, none of these three time-tested and effective means of doing science is taught to students, ostensibly because these methods are considered risky, immoral and inappropriate. Yet, we venture that it is nearly impossible to arrive at interesting theorising in the well-trodden land of social science today without the brutality inherent in these methods: one needs the big jumps that come from them in order to make more than incremental changes. One also needs them to bring back a bit of joy in social science, something essential to keep scientists motivated.

There are more methods to 'science as it was and can be' than just the three described here. Amongst others is the habit of making and then ex-post evaluating predictions about one's own preferences or behaviour, in order to curate the habit of honesty about oneself. There is the extraction of mental short-cuts from engagements with emotionally challenging experts or representative types. There is the use of 'to-and-fro sieving' of data through very different perspectives to gauge the reliability of different types of data. There is the running of prediction races between different viewpoints or formal models of real-world outcomes to gauge which theories work best and to encourage new methods to be developed and tested for usefulness. There is the application of emotional short-cutting leading to rules of thumb to lighten the cognitive load posed by applying and testing fleshed-out theories in complex environments. There is the ruthless requirement that the social scientist applies any theory to her own life, which unlocks the entirety of that person's life as a means of learning and sifting through theories. We leave fuller explanations of these methods and their importance to future papers.

An Alternative Story of Love (and Greed), and How It Came About

In 2013 after many years of work, the authors of this chapter published a living story of people and their societies, entitled *An Economic Theory of Greed, Love, Groups, and Networks* (Frijters with Foster 2013). In Chapter 2 of this book, in what we believe to be the only raw ingredient to our synthesis that is new to social science, we presented our theory of love without mathematics but in simple written form. Our 'love principle', as it was termed, was buttressed and explained using appeals to human love as it has emerged, grown and died across time and culture. The principle itself and the primary means of distinguishing between a greedy response and a loving response was explained via a graphical illustration, reproduced as Figure 5.1. We did not use a utility function or a preference map in presenting our theory, although in subsequent work we have shown how the implications of our theory could be demonstrated using conventional tools (e.g., Foster et al. 2019; Frijters and Foster 2017).

When theorising about love, we ourselves drew inspiration and analogies from far and wide. We considered the stories in the Bible of how Jesus and Moses found their gods while subjecting themselves to harsh circumstances, seeing such stories as mere stylised data points. The common experience of young men being trained for army service was taken as a universal data point. The stories in literature, such as Shakespeare's *Romeo and Juliet*, of how being in love is akin to an obsession were combined with the results in scientific papers measuring the obsessive features of people in love. Reams of data on who ends up with whom in romantic partnerships were used to weed out stories that were unlikely, such as that there are no patterns to love. Evolutionary stories on the possible role of 'bonding' were combined with stylised stories of how early humans actually lived. We brutally mused, and did so on a large canvas, with no regard to what evolutionary biologists themselves thought was most important. We deliberately simplified, for example by ignoring categorisations of different types of love such as the distinction between maternal love and romantic love, even though it was completely clear that the neuro-biological pathways underpinning those two types of love are not exactly the same. We also did not spend time doing full justice to everything that had been

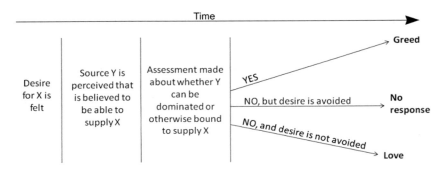

Figure 5.1   The stylised dichotomy between the strategies of dominance and submission

thought before on the subject of love, but instead sifted through the available evidence looking for patterns and testing candidate theories that at every point seemed partially to fit. Like Darwin, we were interested in a simple, general theory that would explain a lot while leaving room for expansion by later researchers.

So too did we throw ourselves wholeheartedly into the phenomenon of love using our personal experiences of various forms of love as additional data points. This did not merely mean reflecting on how it felt to be spouses, parents, citizens, economists and so forth. We consciously experimented with ourselves and others, seeing how loyalty could be created or lost if we changed this or that aspect of our own behaviour towards others. We even experimented with changing our own behaviour towards romantic partners, going so far as observing how we ourselves became more or less 'loving' in this or that circumstance. Such actions would never pass a modern ethics board, but they are indispensable for arriving at a deep understanding of the phenomenon. Our best sources of information are inside us, since we scientists are activated just as other humans are activated. Like medics injecting themselves with experimental vaccines, so too do we play with our own psychology and social position, observing our own emotional reactions much like a medic measures heart rates, in order to advance our knowledge.

Revisiting the Problems of Modern-day Research Culture

We now return to reflect in more detail upon the problems of modern economics, focusing on the problems in empirical economics which has become shackled to the notion that scientists follow divine inspiration. The quintessential implicit image underpinning the institutions and norms that now pervade empirical economics is of Archimedes sitting in his bathtub having a eureka moment of inspiration about water levels and things floating on the water, after which he 'tests' his 'new theory' with experiments, 'confirming' that his theory is 'correct'. Newton and the apple is another such example: science is implicitly seen to start with divine inspiration, preferably followed by a randomised controlled experiment.[8]

As should be clear from our discussions thus far, very little of historical science or actual empirical economics is like this, and yet students and academics are now almost universally forced to pretend otherwise. Research funding agencies nearly all want scientists to list their research questions or hypotheses, present the methods for checking those hypotheses, and outline their dissemination plans for telling the world whether they were right or wrong.

Think of how this view has come to dominate our teaching, our grant application activities and our research process.

Our teaching of the ways of science is a pale shadow of what it might be. Just ask yourself: which university will allow a lecturer to take students on a field trip to Syria in order to see how a civil war affects people? The answer is 'none'. It would run against an arm's-length worth of policies and norms to do so. The days of risky participatory field trips and immersion are over, replaced by the simpler view that science consists of the trifecta 'hypothesis, test and result'. Such a pat, dry method is easier to teach and easier to examine, but it neglects entirely the process via which an interesting hypothesis emerges, confining that process to divine inspiration in the bathroom.

Teaching also lacks the arrogance and ruthless playfulness of previous generations of economists. Nowadays, lecturers have to walk on eggshells lest they offend their snowflake students or 'trigger' them emotionally by presenting challenges to any preconceived idea, identity, belief system or desire that a student might possibly hold. Academics now move in intellectual minefields in which they fear for their jobs and sometimes even their freedom if they broach subjects that their students deem sensitive. This turns both the idea of social science and the search for truth on their heads: not merely is scientific discovery shackled to some notion of divine prior inspiration, but the very set of topics that is seen as acceptable to present and consider when exploring the world is shackled to the sensitivities of students when they are only starting out. That elevates those prior sensitivities to the 'real truth', and makes discovery an enemy of that real truth because discovery might lead to an emotionally uncomfortable recognition that those initial sensitivities were inappropriate, misguided, selfish or just blocking the path, rather than the 'real truth'.

The aristocratic mindset of the scientists of yesteryear took the emotional pain of being challenged as crucial for one's development as a thinker, and would even have used it as a data point, informative about the 'mental baggage' that one initially carried around and hence something to learn from. Nowadays that classical mindset and its implications for how to approach emotional challenges would be seen as insensitive, aggressive, hurtful and disrespectful. These are no longer traits to be admired and even demanded, but instead, grounds for dismissal.

Let us further consider the 'divine inspiration' view of research. The main problem with this view is that it requires a divinity to whisper something in our ears, while in reality, most new ideas do not come to us in a bathroom and then later get 'tested'. Rather, new ideas have typically occurred to scientists when looking at and experiencing lots of things they happen to be interested in, not fully knowing what they are looking at or experiencing or what they might find, using their wits and their knowledge of many other things, including their own nature. Even the notion of proving something later on rather than during discovery is odd when you reflect on it: for example, the proof that there are such things as tiny moving objects like bacteria happens before one's very eyes as one sees them crawling about under a microscope.

The notions of 'prior hypotheses', 'appropriate methods' and so on can then be seen largely as a form of ex-post explanation in many empirical sciences. They do not describe how you discover something, but how you pretend you discovered something – when in reality the discovery process itself was much messier, less controlled, less certain and much more personal.[9]

This pretence has further deepened in recent decades, particularly in social science and medicine. The rules of 'ethics' committees that now constrain the work of empirical scientists in many universities demand that one pretends that science is divine inspiration: the ethics committee only allows one to gather data or analyse existing data if one has 'prior hypotheses', 'consent plans' and a ream of other materials prepared in advance. They thus demand that you know beforehand what you are looking for. Only within the world of divine inspiration can one possibly know beforehand what data one wants to gather and thus what consent or other things one might need of 'participants'. This means that the implicit view underpinning the protocols of the modern university ethics committee is that true new knowledge can only come via divine inspiration, far before any interaction with the committee.

A major reason why this has developed is that it allows for what Nicholas Gruen (2019) and others have called 'accountability theatre': the divine inspiration model allows every aspect of research to be controlled, checked and mandated, which holds great appeal to university administrators while turning scientists into producers of a very particular form of scientific theatre.

It gets much, much worse. Not only do administrations and funding agencies now demand a kind of 'play science' from all actors involved, but scientists themselves have begun visiting these theatrical demands upon one another. The divine inspiration model is what many teach as the 'scientific method' to students, particularly in business and medicine. The latest invention in this self-immolating slide is the notion of 'pre-registration plans', not only to underpin laboratory experiments but as a requirement for all forms of 'approved' empirical discovery. In an increasing number of (top) journals, one is frowned upon if one has not pre-registered the planned analysis in a paper. The bizarre reasoning behind this is that if you didn't go looking for something in particular, then it's not science if you discover it.

Once again, this view implicitly leaves divine inspiration as the *only* valid form of science: divinity whispered ideas into one's head, after which one wrote down the tests and the data to go check on that idea, performed the appropriate tests and reported the answer. It makes any other approach, such as combining observations from different quasi-accidental empirical sources, unacceptable and even unethical because one did not ask permission for those sources to be probed for knowledge. The science of old was clearly not pre-registered, so by this new norm, it was not science. The chain of logic evidently need not go far to arrive at absurdity.

Pre-registration plans do not help science, but rather constrict scholars into play-acting science. The pantomime of pre-registration is just another form of accountability theatre, and one, tragically, not visited upon scientists by ethics committees or evil university managers but by the group of scientists themselves, telling each other and external parties that this is 'purer' and a way to 'prevent abuse'.

In economics, play science has now crystallised into what is known as the *randomista* culture:[10] if a piece of empirical research cannot be presented as a 'clean experiment', it has very little chance at top journals unless it is of innate concern to the country in which that journal is based. Unsurprisingly hence, young scientists have learned not even to look at important events or to think about the big picture, but rather to scan the world for what looks like an experiment. This trend has led to the production of huge numbers of papers showing estimated causal relations in highly specific contexts, often useless, but conforming to the image of science as running experiments based on divinely inspired ideas.

The reduction of science to a pantomime performance can also be seen in how scientists now communicate their results to others. In many disciplines, a very particular form of communication has arisen: the scientific article. Many journals and disciplines have developed quite fixed, narrow notions of what such an article should look like. In economics, for example, most journals expect a particular length, an abstract, an introduction, a methods section, a results section, conclusions and a reference list. Other disciplines and journals have other habits, but they are just as proscriptive. There are very particular rules on what to reference, how to reference, what to include in the methods, how to report results and many other small elements of the communication endeavour that scientists hoping to get published must obey.

Deviations from the norm are punished, even if the deviation is purely in style and in fact functional. For example, if a scientist would send an economics journal a video in which some market phenomenon is explained far better than could be done in words, she would have no chance of seeing it published as a stand-alone piece. Videos are not considered 'real science', at least not in economics, even if moving images can be a more powerful explanation than the non-moving images inherent in texts. Smells, artworks and other non-verbal communication forms are also deemed non-scientific. A collection of pictures with annotations and explanations is similarly not seen as a stand-alone piece of scientific communication, a reality to which we can firmly attest based on personal rejection experiences.

Still, scientific museums are full of artefacts used by scientists past and present to demonstrate scientific truths and explain things to the next generation and to their colleagues. Readers of sufficient age will remember the famous video of someone in a black gorilla suit going completely unnoticed by onlookers who were instructed to count the number of times the white-shirted people in the video passed a basketball around to each other.[11] This was a very powerful way of communicating to an audience the point that our visual perceptions are related to what we expect to see, rather than to what we actually see. Yet, stand-alone videos are not seen in today's economics because it is not 'how it is done' in our discipline.

Conforming in their communication efforts to the quasi-religious strictures associated with 'scientific articles' is the means by which individual scientists are rewarded for their research by the gatekeepers who, in the peer review system, are naturally their peers on editorial boards and in reviewer pools. This means that conformity and monoculturalism are not kept alive by outsiders, but by insiders, and not out of evil intent but out of the heart-felt notion, passed down from teacher to student, that this is 'how it should be'.

The perniciousness goes deeper still. Nearly every sentence of what scientists write in modern articles is a performance of sorts, with an element of deceit. A well-known example is the required acknowledgement of powerful figures in a discipline via prescribed forms of flattery, such as by writing words like, 'the seminal paper by X showed . . .,' where X is someone powerful in the discipline, and sometimes even the editor of the journal to which a paper is sent in hopes of publication. Writing instead something more honest, such as 'it was probably widely known for centuries, but X's name has recently become associated with the following piece of common sense knowledge', one might in a strict sense be more scientific, but it would never get past the refereeing process.[12] Dividing knowledge neatly into packages of 'truths' that were each 'discovered and then proven' by someone in particular is now a pretend view of the world that one cannot avoid playing into when writing an article, as just another part of the overall pantomime. It is a practice that is unscientific but completely fits the 'hypothesis, test, result' mantra.

The same goes for the issues of what counts as a contribution, what is deemed a 'significant result', how much evidence is required (which depends on what the audience already believes), and so on. Scientific papers, particularly in top journals, are now more like a leisurely walk through the subconscious prejudices of the editors and referees than a reflection of good science.

Junior scientists actively try to second-guess the subconscious of their judges, and this second-guessing is often encouraged by well-meaning supervisors who naturally want their students to succeed. Anything is potentially relevant, from the font type to the particular Latin phrase an intended referee would appreciate, based on analyses of which school she attended and what she wrote in her last five editorials. That is not even the worst we have seen. There is the 'seminar dance', the 'first draft slant', the 'after conference-dinner pitch' and of course the 'hiring of the student of the editor'. The scientifically bereft process of scientific publication has become essentially a beauty pageant now, complete with secret acts of sabotage and sex (Naezer, van der Brink and Benschop 2021).

Turning to what this means for individual scientists, they are nowadays nearly all degraded into performance monkeys. They no longer own science but instead have to continuously earn their place by appearing to be the right sort of monkey. They are forced into theatre and must become well practised in the art of deception towards colleagues, grant agencies, themselves and the general public. This theatre is not conducive to discoveries based on interest, let alone to major theoretical advances. These tragic realities have degraded many parts of economics, including the 'altruism industry'.

CONCLUSION

Economics is, if not uniquely amongst the sciences, then particularly burdened with complexity. Unlike the physical phenomena studied by physicists and chemists, economic phenomena are always entangled and interdependent, making an individual scientist's progress less promising than in other disciplines when he tries to discern and elucidate global truths. The seeming hopelessness at the enormity of this task produces pressure towards specialisation on the ambitious individual economist with limited time and energy. If not to seek a global truth, he may reason, then to seek a local one will have to suffice! Unfortunately, this dynamic produces at the macro level a discipline of thinkers who cannot progress together. Every small question worth asking in a corner of the economic world is inseparable from the wider picture of entanglements, which makes progress via specialisation impossible. In other sciences for which global truths are easier to discern, that is not true: the whole gets shifted by progress on the small. In economics, we need to rediscover our courage and patience to face and stomach – in our own individual research agendas – the enormity of the task of discovering what humans and their societies are really like.

The need for a realeconomik approach to investigation in our discipline was recognised almost 30 years ago by Herbert Simon (1993, p. 160):

> Instead of political science or history as derivative of economic analysis, there is a need for economics based upon the facts of history and political and social life. Such an economics will have little to say a priori but will reason from numerous painfully gathered facts. It will have the merit of describing the world in which we actually live. Altruism, especially altruism derived from group and organizational loyalties, will play a major role in it.

How can we push towards a world that allows 'economics based upon the facts of history and political and social life', in light of the massive social, cultural and institutional forces that have developed against this type of economics? One way is to model it ourselves, which it is possible to achieve through the construction of dual-pronged research agendas, in which one branch of one's research is seen to fit what the established norms call for and garners funding, published papers and other accolades, while the other and far more important branch is cross-subsidised by the first and takes place mainly behind closed doors and in one's own time. Both of us have pursued this strategy in our own work.

Yet in the longer run, it is the institutions and culture that must change in order to open the door to the vast quantity of untapped creative potential of scientists – including many of those who today would never dream of a career in science, and excluding many who today call themselves scientists – to explore and discover new deep truths about humans and our world. For this large-scale change, we suggest it is (as usual) the economics and politics of the situation that must be nudged. As a small step along that way, we advocate reducing the salaries of university management; the violent and unconditional defence of academic freedom by academics and their employers (Foster 2016; Frijters 2020); and the disbandment of potted-plant 'ethics committees' that serve little purpose other than to hamper true theoretical advance in economics and other social sciences (Foster 2015). Following that, the reintroduction of free speech and immersive field trips as regular parts of academic life would be a good second step, followed by many others. We await such changes with bated breath.

NOTES

1. We thank Thomas Houlden and Jason Baena-Tan for excellent research assistance. All errors remain ours.
2. See, e.g., https://austriaca.at/?arp=0x003c4646.
3. See www.nytimes.com/column/paul-krugman.
4. Simon (1993) also ventured into discussions of love but suffered in those discussions from many of the same ills as others (e.g., descriptivism and over-reliance on conjectural arguments about evolutionary fitness) but also a presumption of his own making and highly linked to his favoured idea of 'bounded rationality': that behaviour not in accord with the individual's best interests is a natural result of the inability of the human mind to think through everything for itself.
5. In addition to being directly influenced by the work of Thomas Malthus, Darwin was aware of the works of Adam Smith, David Hume and Dugald Stewart (Orr 2009).
6. Other examples include Karl Wittfogel (1957) in his travels to produce an analysis of despotic power in Asia, and Karl Marx and Friedrich Engels in their travels to revolutionary Germany (Riazanov 1974).
7. Since 2012, the American Anthropological Association's Principles of Professional Responsibility have stated:
   - Do no harm
   - Be open and honest regarding your own work
   - Obtain informed consent and necessary permissions
   - Weigh competing obligations due collaborators and affected parties
   - Make your results accessible
   - Protect and preserve your records
   - Maintain respectful and ethical professional relationships
8. Note, however, how each scientist in these stories was cognisant of being personally in amongst the phenomenon he was studying and relied on that personal immersion (with apologies to Archimedes) directly for his discovery, in a way that few modern social scientists can claim to.
9. As stated by Jacob Bronowski in *The Ascent of Man* (BBC documentary series, 1973): 'Every judgement in science stands on the edge of error and is *personal*'.
10. www.nature.com/articles/d41586-019-03125-y.
11. Now encased in a book, the message of the video and the video itself – dubbed 'the selective attention test' – were produced by Christopher Chabris and Daniel Simons (www.theinvisiblegorilla.com/videos.html).
12. Britain's Science Council defines science as 'the pursuit of knowledge and understanding of the natural and social world following a systematic methodology based on evidence' (https://sciencecouncil.org/about-science/our-definition-of-science/).

REFERENCES

Acemoglu, D., Liabson, D. I., & List, J. A. (2018). *Microeconomics*. New York: Pearson.
Akerlof, G. A., & Kranton, R. E. (2000). Economics and Identity. *Quarterly Journal of Economics*, 115(3), 715–753. Doi:10.1162/003355300554881
Alger, I., & Weibull, J. W. (2010). Kinship, Incentives, and Evolution. *American Economic Review*, 100(4), 1725–1758. Doi:10.1257/aer.100.4.1725
Allen, D., & Berg, C. (2014). *The Sharing Economy: How Over-Regulation Could Destroy an Economic Revolution*. Sydney: Institute for Public Affairs.
Andreoni, J. (1990). Impure Altruism and Donations to Public Goods: A Theory of Warm-Glow Giving. *The Economic Journal*, 100(401), 464–477. Doi:10.2307/2234133
Bault, N., Pelloux, B., Fahrenfort, J. K., Ridderinkhof, K. R., & van Winden, F. (2015). Neural Dynamics of Social Tie Formation in Economic Decision-Making. *Social Cognitive and Affective Neuroscience*, 10(6), 877–884, https://doi.org/10.1093/scan/nsu138
Becker, G. (1981). *A Treatise on the Family*. Cambridge, MA: Harvard University Press.
Bell, C. S. (1966). The Early History of the Compound Microscope. *Bios*, 37(2), 51–60.

Bénabou, R., & Tirole, J. (2006). Incentives and Prosocial Behaviour. *The American Economic Review*, 96(5), 1652–1678. Doi:10.1257/aer.96.5.1652

Benjamin, D. J., Kimball, M. S., Heffetz, O., & Szembrot, N. (2014). Beyond Happiness and Satisfaction: Toward Well-Being Indices Based on Stated Preference. *The American Economic Review*, 104(9), 2698–2735. Doi:10.1257/aer.104.9.2698

Bronowski, J. (1973). The Ascent of Man [BBC Documentary].

Clark, A. E., Frijters, P., & Shields, M. A. (2008). Relative Income, Happiness, and Utility: An Explanation for the Easterlin Paradox and Other Puzzles. *Journal of Economic Literature*, 46(1), 95–144.

Darwin, C. (1998). *On the Origin of Species by Mean of Natural Selection, or the Preservation of Favoured Races in the Struggle for Life*. (T. Griffith, Ed.) Ware: Wordsworth Editions. (Originally published in 1859).

Darwin, C. (1958). *The Autobiography of Charles Darwin*. (N. Barlow, Ed.) London: Collins. (Originally published 1876).

Darwin Correspondence Project. (2021, March 14). Letter no. 729. Retrieved from https://www.darwinproject.ac.uk/letter/DCP-LETT-729.xml

Darwin Correspondence Project. (2021, March 14). Letter no. 2543. Retrieved from https://www.darwinproject.ac.uk/letter/DCP-LETT-2543.xml

Florczak, K. L. (2004). An Exploration of the Concept of Sacrifice. *Nursing Science Quarterly*, 195–200. Doi:10.1177/0894318404266423

Fontaine, P. (2000). Making Use of the Past: Theorists and Historian on the Economics of Altruism. *The European Journal of the History of Economic Thought*, 407–422. Doi:10.1080/09672560050192125

Foss, N. J. (2000). The Dangers and Attractions of Theoretical Eclectisism. *Journal of Macromarketing*, 20(1), 65–67.

Foster, G. (2015, March 19). A New Model for Research Ethics Reviews. Retrieved from The Conversation: https://theconversation.com/a-new-model-for-research-ethics-reviews-38296

Foster, G. (2016, June 10). The Public Should be Concerned When Academics Must Battle Bureaucrats for Academic Freedom. Retrieved from The Conversation: https://theconversation.com/the-public-should-be-concerned-when-academics-must-battle-bureaucrats-for-academic-freedom-54039

Foster, G., Pingle, M., & Yang, J. (2017). Are We Addicted to Love? A Parsimonious Economic Model of Love. *Journal of Economic Behaviour and Organization*, 165(C), 70–81. Doi:10.1016/j.jebo.2019.07.009.

Frijters, P. (2020, May 20). How can the University of Queensland Recover from the Drew Pavlou affair? Retrieved from Club Troppo: https://clubtroppo.com.au/2020/05/30/how-can-the-university-of-queensland-recover-from-the-drew-pavlou-affair/

Frijters, P., & Foster, G. (2013). *An Economic Theory of Greed, Love, Groups, and Networks*. Cambridge: Cambridge University Press.

Frijters, P., & Foster, G. (2017). Is it Rational to Be in Love? In M. Altman (Ed.), *Handbook of Behavioural Economics and Smart Decision-Making: Rational Decision-Making within the Bounds of Reason* (pp. 205–232). Cheltenham: Edward Elgar Publishing.

Gay, P. (1969). *The Enlightenment: An Interpretation* (Vol.2). New York: Alfred A. Knopf.

Gruen, N. (2019, June 26). Accountability: From Above and Below. Retrieved from The Mandarin: https://www.themandarin.com.au/110549-the-accountability-trap-how-to-avoid-low-trust-and-low-performance-because-everyones-shifting-responsibility-and-protecting-themselves-not-collaborating/

Hassani, O. K, Cromwell, H. C., & Schultz, W. (2001). Influence of Expectation of Different Rewards on Behavior-Related Neuronal Activity in the Striatum. *Journal of Neurophysiology*, 85(6), 2477–2489. doi: 10.1152/jn.2001.85.6.2477. PMID: 11387394.

Hayden, B. Y. (2016). Time Discounting and Time Preference in Animals: A Critical Review. *Psychonomic Bulletin Review*, 23, 39–53. https://doi.org/10.3758/s13423-015-0879-3

Hoeffler, S., & Ariely, D. (1999). Constructing Stable Preferences: A Look into Dimensions of Experience and their Impact on Preference Stability. *Journal of Consumer Psychology*, 8(2), 113–139. https://doi.org/10.1207/s15327663jcp0802_01

Hotelling, H. (1929). Stability in Competition. *The Economic Journal*, 49(153), 41–57.

Hume, D. (1739–40). *A Treatise of Human Nature*. London: Published for John Noon.

Hunt, S. (1999). *A General Theory of Competition: Resources, Competences, Productivity, Economic Growth*. Thousand Oaks: Sage Publications, Inc.

Jacobs, M. (2016). Accounting for Changing Tastes: Approaches to Explaining Unstable Individual Preferences. *Review of Economics*, 67(2), 121–183. https://doi.org/10.1515/roe-2015-1007.

Jankowiak, W. R., & Fischer, E. F. (1992). A Cross-Cultural Perspective on Romantic Love. *Ethnology*, 31(2), 149–155. Doi:10.2307/3773618

Jehle, G. A., & Reny, P. J. (2000). *Advanced Microeconomic Theory* (3rd ed.). Boston: Addison-Wesley.

Kahneman, D. (2003). A Psychological Perspective on Economics. *American Economic Review, Papers and Proceedings* 2, 162–168.

Keynes, J. M., & Maynard, J. (1940*)*. *How to Pay for the War: A Radical Plan for the Chancellor of the Exchequer*. London: Macmillan.

Layard, R., Mayraz, G., & Nickell, S. (2008). The Marginal Utility of Income. *Journal of Public Economics*, 96(8–9), 1846–1857. doi:10.1016/j.jpubeco.2008.01.007

Loomes, G., Starmer, C., & Sugden, R. (1991). Observing Violations of Transitivity by Experimental Methods. *Econometrica* 59(2), 425–439. https://doi.org/10.2307/2938263

Malthus, T. (1798). *An Essay on the Principle of Population*. London: Printed for J. Johnson.

Mankiw, N. G. (2021). *Principles of Economics* (9th ed.). Boston: Cengage.

Mas-Colell, A., Whinston, M. D., & Green, J. R. (1995). *Microeconomic Theory*. New York: Oxford University Press.

Naezer, M., van der Brink, M., & Benschop, Y. (2021). Harassment in Dutch Academia. Commissioned by the Dutch Network of Women Professors.

Newton, J. (2021). Conventions under Heterogeneous Behavioural Rules. *The Review of Economic Studies*, 88(4), 2094–2118. https://doi.org/10.1093/restud/rdaa063

Orr, H. A. (2009). Darwin and Darwinism: The (Alleged) Social Implications of The Origin of Species. *Genetics*, 183(3), 767–772. doi:10.1534/genetics.109.110445

Oswald, A. J., & Powdthavee, N. (2008). Does Happiness Adapt? A Longitudinal Study of Disability with Implications for Economists and Judges. *Journal of Public Economics*, 92(5–6), 1061–1077. doi:10.1016/j.jpubeco.2008.01.002

Productivity Commission. (2017). *Rising Protectionism: Challenges, Threats and Opportunities for Australia*. Canberra: Commission Research Paper.

Pugach, C., Leder, H., & Graham, D. J. (2017). How Stable are Human Aesthetic Preferences Across the Lifespan? *Frontiers in Human Neuroscience*, 11, 1–11.

Riazanov, D. (1974). *Karl Marx and Friedrich Engels: An Introduction to Their Lives and Work*. (J. Kunitz, Trans.) New York: Monthly Review Press.

Rousseau, J. J. (1998*)*. *The Confessions and Correspondence, Including Letters to Malesherbes*. (C. Kelly, Trans.) Hanover: University of New England Press. (Original work published 1790).

Rousseau, J. J. (2002). *The Social Contract and Discourses*. (S. Dunn, Trans.) New Haven: Yale University Press. (Original work published 1762).

Samuelson, P. A. (1948). *Economics: An Introductory Analysis*. New York: McGraw-Hill.

Samuelson, P. A. (1966, September 9). *Science and Stocks*. Newsweek, p. 92.

Schmitt, D. P. (2019). Evolutionary and Cross-Cultural Perspectives on Love: The Influence of Gender, Personality, and Local Ecology on Emotional Investment in Romantic Relationships. In R. J. Sternberg & K. Sternberg, *The New Psychology of Love* (2nd ed., pp. 249–273). Cambridge: Cambridge University Press.

Science Council. (2015, May 10). Our Definition of Science. Retrieved from Science Council: https://sciencecouncil.org/about-science/our-definition-of-science/

Sharot, T., Fleming, S. M., Yu, X., Koster, R., & Dolan, R. J. (2012). Is Choice-Induced Preference Change Long Lasting? *Psychological Science*, 23(10), 1123–1129. Doi:10.1177/0956797612438733

Simon, H. A. (1947). *Administrative Behavior: A Study of Decision-Making Processes in Administrative Organization*. London: Macmillan.

Simon, H. A. (1982). *Models of Bounded Rationality*. Cambridge: MIT Press.

Simon, H. A. (1993). Altruism and Economics. *The American Economic Review*, 83(2), 156–161.

Simonson, I. (2008). Will I Like a "Medium" Pillow? Another Look at Constructed and Inherent Preferences. *Journal of Consumer Psychology*, 18, 155–169.

Smith, A. (1759). *The Theory of Moral Sentiments*. London: Printed for A. Millar, A. Kincaid and J. Bell.

Smith, L., Sørensen, P. N., & Tian, J. (2021). Informational Herding, Optimal Experimentation, and Contrarianism. *The Review of Economic Studies*, 88(5), 2527–2554, https://doi.org/10.1093/restud/rdab001

Speir, R. (2002). The History of the Peer-review Process. *Trends in Biotechnology*, 20(8), 357–358. doi:10.1016/S0167-7799(02)01985-6.

United States Public Health Service. (1967). *The Health Consequences of Smoking: A Public Health Service Review*. Washington: US Department of Health, Education, and Welfare, Public Health Service.

van der Deijl, W. (2018). Can Welfare be Measured with a Preference-Satisfaction Index? *Journal of Economic Methodology*, 25(2), 126–142. doi:10.1080/1350178X.2017.1413586

Vivanco, L. A. (2016). Fieldwork Ethics Forum. Retrieved from Companion Website for Field Notes: A Guided Journal for Doing Anthropology: https://global.oup.com/us/companion.websites/9780190642198/ethics/

Wittfogel, K. (1957). *Oriental Despotism: A Comparative Study of Total Power*. New Haven: Yale University Press.

6. The common-sense economy
Pascal Moliner and Patrick Rateau

INTRODUCTION

Almost every day we are exposed to information about the economy, whether of our country or of the world in general. The media regularly tells us about the state of stock markets, growth rates, long-term interest rates, the consequences of a particular crisis, the employment and unemployment situation, etc. The high media coverage of the economy and its omnipresence in our daily lives are probably due to the fact that many of us think it is important. Eurobarometer surveys[1] conducted by the European Commission confirm this intuition. In 2019, of the 13 issues that Europeans were most concerned about, six were directly related to economic issues (economic situation, public finances, unemployment, cost of living, pensions, and taxes). In the 2020 survey, 48 per cent of respondents thought that the priority for the European Parliament should be to reduce poverty and inequality. These figures show how important economic issues are to us collectively. But, as laypersons and despite the fact that we value the economy, are we able to understand it as experts do? Obviously not – not any more than a layperson is able to understand epidemiology like an epidemiologist or demography like a demographer. But since we have a vague feeling that these are important things, we must create an idea or, more precisely, a representation of them.

As *social psychologists*, we ask ourselves what the contents of this kind of representation are. What are their specificities? How are they developed and used by the 'general public'? With what effects? To answer these questions, the theory of social representations (Moscovici 1976, 2008) seems essential as it is a theory of lay knowledge. It describes how individuals develop systems of knowledge and beliefs about objects, events or situations in their environment. It also describes how these systems are used.

In this chapter, we will base ourselves on this theory and describe the main characteristics of social representations and the way they emerge in a society. We will then present some research that has explored the content of social representations of economic objects. Finally, we will show how, in some cases, behaviour or decisions normally subject to economic rationality can be significantly affected by social representations.

PHENOMENOLOGY AND THEORY OF SOCIAL REPRESENTATIONS

What Is a Social Representation?

Every day we use lay knowledge and attributions to explain and understand the world around us. In order to understand and control our environment, we need to make it predictable and find a certain coherence and stability. Otherwise, we would be constantly moving in a territory of emptiness, without any landmarks or cardinal points indicating the path to follow. This coherence and stability cannot be achieved without attributing meanings to the events, behaviours, ideas and exchanges that we have with others and with society as a whole. The environment we live in daily is extremely complex, at least in two ways: on the one hand, because it is made up of countless situations and multiple events, individuals and groups; on the other hand, because we are constantly called upon to make decisions, to give our opinion on any subject or to explain any event. In other words, we are constantly immersed in an environment that is saturated with information that we need to understand, deal with and communicate about.

Because of this complexity, we cannot see the environment as it is: we have to constantly simplify it, schematise it and make it more predictable and familiar. In short, we must reconstruct it in our own way (Abric 1987). However, this reconstruction is never done in isolation, and we always do it in the context of our interactions with others. From childhood, we are exposed to places, situations and information vectors such as school, family, institutions or the media. These encounters and exchanges give rise to a certain vision of the things that surround us, to what is considered good or bad, fair or unfair, acceptable or unacceptable, licit or illicit, to be confessed or kept quiet. In short, and to a very large extent, we are simply learning the already regulated construction of the world in which we evolve, the values that invest it, the categories that order it and the very principles of its understanding. This is our share of social heritage.

Subsequently, our membership in social groups, our status and our roles within the society we live in, in turn, shape our perception of the environment. It is therefore above all through our exchanges and communications with others that our reality of the surrounding world is constituted and becomes the 'truth' of it. It is through this communication that we acquire, transmit and perpetuate knowledge, beliefs and values that allow us to share a common conception of things and of others. In this sense, this reconstruction or representation of reality, which has a role of truth, is above all social, i.e., it is elaborated according to our characteristics and shared by a group of other individuals with the same characteristics.

This point is of the utmost importance. Although not all social groups share the same values, norms, ideologies or practical experiences, they all develop representations that are closely linked to them. This has two consequences: on the one hand, social representations bear the mark of the social belonging of the individuals who carry them and guarantee their identity; on the other hand, they play an important role in social differentiation in that they allow these same individuals to distinguish 'the others' – those who do not share the same representations and who appear to them at best as different, at worst as enemies (Deschamps & Moliner 2012).

Ultimately, social representations can be defined as systems of opinions, knowledge and beliefs that are specific to a culture, a category or a social group and relating to objects in the social environment (Moliner, Rateau & Cohen-Scali 2002). Let us look at this definition as it implies that the distinction between the notions of 'opinion', 'knowledge' and 'belief' are obsolete in relation to social representations. Indeed, if opinion rather belongs to the domain of position-taking, knowledge to the domain of skill and experience, and belief to that of conviction, everything in our daily experience shows us that confusions between these three notions are recurrent. Indeed, we regularly observe that beliefs become attested information or that opinions strangely resemble beliefs. In this way, the borderline between 'I think', 'I know' and 'I believe' is often blurred. Consequently, the contents of a representation can be indifferently qualified as opinions, information or beliefs and we can note that a social representation is concretely presented as an undifferentiated set of 'cognitive elements' relating to a social object.

How Is a Social Representation Constructed?

In his seminal work, Serge Moscovici (1976, 2008) proposed a description of the genesis and development of social representations. According to him, it is the appearance of a new, innovative situation, an unknown phenomenon or an unusual event that leads to the emergence of a social representation. Because of the novelty of the object or phenomenon, information about it is limited, incomplete and widely scattered among the different social groups involved in the emergence of this object. This is what Moscovici calls the *dispersion of information*. Moreover, this novelty disrupts the usual course of events and arouses concern and attention (an example is the introduction of the euro at the beginning of the 2000s). It therefore motivates intense cognitive activity aimed at understanding, mastering, explaining and even defending the object. In short, it constitutes a *pressure to inference* and, at the same time, gives rise to a multiplicity of debates and interpersonal and media communications. These debates take place through various communication channels and are accompanied by a pooling of information, beliefs, hypotheses or speculations leading to the emergence of majority positions in the different social groups. The appearance of these majority positions reflects the emergence of a consensus which is facilitated by the fact that individuals process information about the object or situation in a selective way, focusing on a particular aspect according to the expectations or orientations of their groups. This is what Moscovici calls the *focus phenomenon*.

The gradual emergence of a representation, which occurs spontaneously, is therefore based on three orders of phenomena constituting the conditions for its appearance: information dispersion, focus and pressure to inference. But these phenomena themselves develop against the backdrop of two major processes defined by Moscovici: *objectification* and *anchoring*.

Objectification refers to the way that the new object is rapidly simplified, imagined and schematised through communication related to it. Through a phenomenon of selective construction, the different facets of the object are first extracted from their context and sorted according to cultural criteria (not all groups have equal access to information about the object) and normative criteria (only those that are consistent with the group's value system are considered). The various aspects of the object are thus detached from the field that they belong to in order to be appropriated by the groups, which can better control them by projecting them into their own universe. Then, these selected elements form what Moscovici calls a figurative core, i.e., an imagined and coherent whole which reproduces the object in a concrete and selective way. Through this process, individuals transform a concept into a simplified image – a figurative core. Finally, by penetrating the social sphere through communications and by becoming generalised in a collective way, this schematisation of the object replaces the reality of the object itself and becomes 'naturalised'. We observe a 'commodification', a 'reification' or even an ontologisation of the concept which becomes an element, a being of reality. The representation is thus constituted and takes on the status of evidence. It constitutes an 'autonomous theory' of the object which serves as a basis for orienting judgements and behaviours relating to it.

The anchoring process complements the objectification process. It accounts for the way that the new object finds its place in the pre-existing thought system of individuals and groups. According to an elementary mode of knowledge production based on the principle of analogy, the new object is assimilated to already known forms, to familiar categories. At the same time, it becomes part of an already existing network of significations. The hierarchy of values specific to the different groups constitutes a network of significations which allows one to situate and evaluate the object. Thus, depending on the social group, the object gives rise to various interpretations, always in relation to an identity issue. Moreover, this interpretation extends to everything that is closely or remotely related to this object. Indeed, each social group links the object to its own networks of signification, which guarantee its identity. In this way, a very vast set of collective significations of the object is formed. In this way too, the object becomes a mediator and plays an important role in relations between groups. However, and this is an essential aspect of anchoring, this integration of the new into an already existing system of norms and values does not take place smoothly. The result of this contact between the old and the new is a mixture of innovation and persistence. The unknown object is indeed integrated and at the same time reactivates customary frames of thought in order to incorporate it. This shows that a social representation always appears to be both innovative and persistent, moving and rigid (Abric 1993).

Social representations are thus always indebted to a 'before' that they draw significations from and which is itself transformed in the light of the contemporary issues raised by the object. In fact, its fundamental property is that it is historical. On the one hand, it stems from history, and on the other hand, it itself has a history that articulates genesis, transformation and decay. Representation is thus both a product of becoming and a product in the process of becoming; change is not an accident; it belongs to its essence (Rouquette 1994). Consequently, to grasp a representation is above all to grasp its state at a given moment.

Phenomenology of Social Representation

As we have seen, once constituted, the contents of a representation can be qualified as opinions, information or beliefs. A social representation is therefore concretely presented as an undifferentiated set of 'cognitive elements' relating to a social object. This set has four main characteristics (cf. Rateau et al. 2011):

1. First of all, it is *organised*. It is not a succession of cognitive elements placed end to end, but a 'structure'. This means that these elements have relationships or links which make them interdependent. These relationships can be considered in many ways: in terms of equivalence or reciprocity, but also in terms of antagonism and contradiction. Opinions can be compatible with some beliefs and in opposition to others. The structural approach to representations, proposed by Abric (1993), also considers that this set of elements is hierarchical according to two complementary systems: a system designated as 'central' (or central core) and a system designated as 'peripheral'. Inherited from the figurative core, the central system is composed of a limited number of elements that play two essential roles: an organising role for all the links between the elements of the representation, and a role in managing the signification of the whole. Directly linked to the values, norms and history of the group, the central system appears to be rather abstract, stable, consensual and not very sensitive to variations in context. Conversely, the peripheral system, more directly linked to the concrete practices that the group maintains regarding the object, is presented as a set of concrete, flexible and heterogeneous elements that can be adapted to changes in the contexts in which the social representation is expressed.
2. Secondly, this set is *shared* within the same social group. However, it is important to specify that this consensus is always relative as it depends on both the homogeneity of the group and the position of individuals in relation to the object. Thus, the consensual character of a representation is generally partial and often reduced to a small number of elements of the representation which constitute the central core.

3. Thirdly, it is *collectively produced* in a global process of communication. The pooling of the elements at the origin of the formation of the social representation, and thus the sharing of these elements, depends closely on inter-individual exchanges and on exposure to communications internal and external to the group. Moreover, sharing allows for the possibility of discovering and bringing to the knowledge of others new information, but above all, it allows for realising the convergences that tend to create the conditions for the appearance of consensus and to confer social validity on the various opinions, information and beliefs that are shared.
4. Lastly, this set has a fourth characteristic, referring to its purpose, which is to be *socially useful*. As we have seen, this is firstly due to the fact that social representations constitute grids for reading, deciphering and therefore understanding the reality that we face. They are therefore socially useful as they give significations to our environment. But they also constitute guides during our social interactions and are massively involved in our exchanges and relations with other groups. In addition, social representations provide criteria for evaluating the social environment which make it possible to determine, justify or legitimise certain behaviours. In this perspective, they fulfil a function of orientation of social practices and constitute, as such, systems of expectations or anticipation which make it possible to influence and adjust behaviours. Conversely, they also intervene *a posteriori* and thus constitute systems for justifying our behaviour and that of others.

Finally, let us add that social representations generally unfold within a broader ideological system and around a certain number of epistemic schemes referred to as themata by Holton (1981) and then introduced by Moscovici and Vignaux (1994) in the field of social representations. A thema is defined as 'a pre-established epistemic formats, a preoccupation of immemorial origin which gives practical knowledge its framework of possibility and the framework of its organisation' (Flament & Rouquette 2003, p. 19). Transmitted from generation to generation, the themata are presented in the form of spontaneous oppositions with two poles (e.g., masculine/feminine, good/evil, right/wrong, fair/unfair, ideal/actual) which organise thought, predetermine it, extend it, feed it and argue it. They enable simple hierarchical classifications to be established based on a single criterion, from strong extreme positions (such as good versus evil). Stable over time and identifiable in all cultures, they appear as principles that generate social representations. They make it possible to organise and hold together a set of values, norms and beliefs (Rouquette 1996) and directly feed the content of social representations, which they determine, organise and justify.

SOCIAL REPRESENTATIONS OF OBJECTS OR ECONOMIC PHENOMENA

The theory of social representations has often been used to study how people think about economic objects or phenomena. Researchers have, for example, explored representations of work and unemployment (Milland 2002; Flament & Milland 2010), taxes (Kischler 1998, 2007), savings (Roland-Lévy, Boumelki & Guillet 2010), economic crises (Gangl et al. 2012) or globalisation (Viaud, Patiño & Ávila 2007). Unsurprisingly, this research has revealed significant differences between the way these objects are socially thought of by ordinary people and the descriptions or explanations given by economic experts. Overall, two types of results emerge from this work. The first type refers to the idea of a simplification of economic objects, while the second type suggests a simplification of the causalities that link these objects together.

Simplification of Objects

One of the reasons for the existence of the process of social representation is to enable a better understanding of the environment through familiarisation with the objects that are composing it. However, for many reasons (historical, social, technical) economic objects or phenomena are rarely simple objects. Therefore, in the social representations of these objects as they are thought of by ordinary people, we can expect to observe traces of a simplification work allowing their familiarisation. This simplification of objects is a phenomenon inherent to the process of social representation and several forms can be distinguished. We will discuss simplification by categorisation, anchoring and trivialisation.

Simplification by categorisation allows individuals to have classification systems that enable them to arrange the environment. For example, in a study on the representations of money (Vergès 1992), a representative sample of the French population was questioned using a verbal association method. The analysis of the associations collected clearly reveals a classification process operated by the social representation. Thus, money is considered in its different forms of appearance and use (e.g., money in the domestic budget, money as a means of exchange between economic actors, money as a symbol of power) or in its different concrete materialisations (e.g., banknotes, coins, credit cards). Apart from the fact that this type of classification is frequently encountered in studies of social representations, whatever the objects represented, it should be borne in mind that, on the cognitive level, the categorisation process that underlies it obviously corresponds to a desire to simplify the environment in order to control it (Rosch & Lloyd 1978).

Simplification by anchoring allows individuals to think about complex objects from a small amount of simple and general schemas. An example of this can be found in a study conducted on globalisation (Viaud, Patiño & Avila 2007), with participants from five countries (Brazil, France, Mexico, Portugal and Tunisia). The analysis revealed two opposing representations of the phenomenon. One is positive; recurring themes are technical progress, world unification and communication. The other is rather negative; recurring themes are opposition between rich and poor and the domination of North American capitalism. However, in these representations, the researchers note above all the absence of elements that constitute the history and dynamics of the phenomenon of economic globalisation. Thus, when talking about globalisation, the participants do not mention any symbolic locations[2] relating to it, even though these were mentioned in the news at a time (e.g., Porto-Alegre, Seattle), nor the movements that oppose the phenomenon (e.g., World Social Forum) or the institutions that support it (e.g., International Monetary Fund, World Trade Organization). These absences are in themselves a simplification of globalisation, but this simplification can also be achieved through an anchoring process, allowing one to reduce the object to a few easily mastered conceptual frameworks. Indeed, taking their analysis to a more qualitative level, the authors of this research finally suggest the presence of two encompassing and ambivalent themes about globalisation: 'progress' and 'exchange', both of which have positive and negative aspects.

Simplification by trivialisation consists in reducing an object of representation to everyday concerns. For example, in a study on representations of the 2008 economic crisis (Galli et al. 2010), the authors note that in the four countries where the study was carried out (France, Greece, Italy and Romania), unemployment appears to be a central element of the representation. On the other hand, the dysfunction of the real estate and credit markets in the United States and the contamination of the European financial markets are barely mentioned by the participants, despite being the main explanatory factors of this crisis. In other words, for the individuals interviewed, the 2008 crisis is primarily thought of in terms of the immediate consequences it may have on their daily lives. But this trivialisation process is probably not immediate when a social representation emerges, especially when the object of representation appears in the public sphere along with discourses (scientific, political, media) that are supposed to guide its perceptions. For example, regarding the euro, Meier-Pesti, Kirchler and El-Sehity (2003) interviewed Austrian individuals in 1997, 2001 and 2002. They noted that, between 1997 and 2001/2002, there has been a shift from a vision of the euro centred on the national consequences of the single currency to an individualised vision centred on the consequences of the euro in everyday life. It can therefore be assumed that in its initial form, the social representation is above all fed by the political and media discourse on the euro but that, as time goes by, individuals gradually base their common-sense knowledge on their daily practice of the single currency.

Causalities Simplification

Obviously, a naive understanding of economic objects requires an understanding of their reciprocal links. From this point of view, laypersons and experts do not differ from each other, even if their ways of considering economic causalities are obviously not the same. In this respect, the work of Leiser and Aroch (2009) is particularly illuminating. These researchers considered 19 economic variables (e.g., unemployment rate, growth rate, average wage, inflation rate, etc.) and asked their participants (first-year psychology students) to indicate a score reflecting their understanding of each of these 19 variables. They then presented the participants with all possible pairs of the 19 variables and asked them the following question: 'if the first variable in the pair increases, how does it affect the second variable in the pair?' (e.g., 'if the unemployment rate increases, how does it affect the inflation rate?').

To answer each question, participants were given four possible answers: 'the second variable increases', 'the second variable decreases', 'the second variable is not affected' and 'I don't know'. Finally, the researchers asked another group of participants to comment on whether an increase in each of the 19 variables would be positive or negative (e.g., 'for each of these variables, indicate whether an increase is a good thing or a bad thing'). Based on this protocol, the authors made several observations. First, they noted that participants organised the 19 variables into two subsets: those whose increase is a good thing (e.g., average wage, growth rate) and those whose increase is a bad thing (e.g., inflation rate, unemployment rate). The researchers then noted that when two variables belong to the same subset (e.g., average wage and growth rate), participants considered that an increase in the level of one leads to an increase in the level of the other. However, when two variables each belong to a different subset (e.g., average wage and inflation rate), participants consider that an increase in the level of one leads to a decrease in the level of the other.

Based on these findings, Leiser and Aroch suggest the existence of a heuristic used by participants to answer the questions they are asked, which they call 'good-begets-good'[3] (see also Leiser & Shemesh 2018). Clearly, this heuristic allows for a simplification of the understanding of economic causality. But it should be noted that this simplification is only possible if the different components of the economy are thought of through a simplified classification system. Finally, it should be added that these simplifications of economic causalities are not necessarily always inaccurate. They sometimes converge with certain laws identified by experts. For example, the opposition that laymen establish between growth rates and unemployment rates corresponds to an empirical reality that is well known to experts, namely Okun's law (see Lamla, Dräger & Damjan 2015).

Thema of Good and Evil

When we review the research carried out on the social representations of economic objects and phenomena, we are struck by the omnipresence of dichotomous social thinking that opposes good and evil (e.g., De Rosa, Bocci & Bulgarella 2010; Leiser & Aroch 2009; Poeschl, Campos & Ben Alaya 2007). One might fear that this observation is ultimately the result of the work of the researchers themselves. Researchers too often focus on exploring the evaluative aspects of the representations they study. However, we must consider that each study of representation is unique. It always highlights a system of knowledge and beliefs specific to a particular group and relating to a given object, as it appears at a given moment in the history of this group. To be convinced of this, it is sufficient to note that, contrary to what is done for other psychosocial phenomena (e.g., stereotypes or attitudes), there is no standardised scale for 'measuring' or 'evaluating' a social representation. Thus, in most cases, even if the researchers do not always specify it, a study of representation is generally preceded by an exploratory phase which makes it possible to identify, at least on a hypothetical basis, the paths that are about to be followed. It seems that with regard to the representations of economic objects or phenomena, these exploratory phases regularly reveal the presence of evaluative thinking. It is therefore appropriate to consider the possible reasons for this observation. For our part, we distinguish two complementary reasons.

The first is the very purpose of the process of social representation, which, it should be remembered, is to enable a practical understanding of objects in the social environment. From this perspective, it is understandable that the thema of good and evil is probably one of the most universal and one of the simplest to implement. That being said, not all social representations are organised according to this dichotomy. Then, what could be the specificity of representations of the economy?

The answer to this question leads us to the second reason which, in our opinion, explains the recurrent presence of the thema of good and evil in the representations of economic objects and phenomena. Basically, these objects and phenomena have always been thought of in terms of the consequences they could have on individuals. The very concept of *homo oeconomicus* (Smith 1776), which can be considered the foundation of expert economic thinking, describes a subject concerned with his pleasures and pains (Bentham 1789). In other words, for individuals and groups, understanding economics means being able to identify what is good and what is evil for each individual.

THE ROLE OF REPRESENTATIONS IN ECONOMIC BEHAVIOUR

Investing or saving, deciding to buy a particular product and speculating on the rise or fall of a share are all economic behaviours because they are all supposed to be the result of a cost/benefit calculation aimed at obtaining an advantage. According to the classical model of *homo oeconomicus* (Smith 1776), the individual would seek to obtain a maximum benefit for a minimum cost. However, numerous studies in psychology have shown that this rationality of economic behaviour is probably more complex (Dichter 1961; Kahneman & Tversky

1979, 1984; Katona 1974). More precisely, while engaging in an economic behaviour can be considered as the result of a cost/benefit calculation, it seems that this calculation is affected by numerous cognitive biases and modulated by contextual and psychological factors. From this perspective, we can ask ourselves what role social representations play here.

Field Approaches

In an attempt to answer the question of the role of social representations in economic behaviour, several studies have implemented investigative approaches aimed at identifying the content and/or structure of a particular representation and the behaviours that may be associated with this content.

An example is a study of 68 individual investors (Süer & Minibas-Poussard 2015). Participants were divided into two groups (risk-taker investors versus risk-averse investors) according to their investment practices (e.g., investment diversification, investment in shares or mutual funds). They were then asked about their representation of various economic objects including 'investment'. The results show that among risk-averse investors, the core of the investment representation is composed of the elements 'money', 'future', 'savings' and 'time deposit account'. For risk-taker investors, the core contains only the elements 'money' and 'future'. In other words, it seems that among risk-averse investors, investment is mainly thought of as a necessarily secure practice ('time deposit account', 'savings').

In another study, this time of inhabitants of the rural Las Vegas area, 301 participants were questioned about their representation of the impact of tourist activity (Suess & Mody 2016). It was found that those for whom tourism has mainly economic effects were in favour of the development of gaming tourism, but also the development of alternative forms of tourism (nature, culture, festivals). However, participants for whom tourism has more positive social or environmental effects are not in favour of developing gaming tourism. But whatever the type of tourism development desired, the participants who were in favour of this development declared themselves ready to pay more taxes to encourage it. This shows that depending on the way the inhabitants see the benefits of tourism activity, they are willing to pay more taxes to finance this or that type of development.

However, the links between social representations and behaviour are rarely simple. In the New York and Pennsylvania area, 590 residents were interviewed about the development of hydraulic fracturing for shale gas extraction (Bugden, Evensen & Stedman 2017). They were asked to write down any words or phrases that came to mind about this issue. Their answers were categorised according to whether they indicated an environmental view of the problem or an economic view. This technique therefore made it possible to identify the type of anchoring of the representation of hydraulic fracturing. The results of the study show a positive link between economic anchoring and declared support for the development of the shale gas industry, and a negative link between the environmental anchorage of the representation and the declared support for the industry. However, there is no significant link between the type of anchoring of the representation and the engagement in actual behaviour (participation in demonstrations, activism, petitioning, voting, etc.). This type of result illustrates quite well the limitations of the methodology of the survey when it comes to highlighting the links between social representations and behaviour (see also Roland-Lévy, Boumelki & Guillet 2010). In addition to the fact that this methodology often struggles to capture all the determinants of behaviour, when it succeeds in identifying some of them, it simply enables correlational links to be highlighted.

Experimental Approaches

Undoubtedly, one of the first researchers to undertake experimental exploration of the links between social representations and behaviour was Jean-Claude Abric. From the 1970s onwards, he developed a series of studies within the framework of the Prisoner's Dilemma paradigm (Abric & Kahan 1972; Abric 1976). According to Abric, this game situation places each player before a cooperative choice (choosing to deny a crime which one is accused of, in the hope that the other player, supposedly an accomplice, will make the same choice) or a competitive choice (choosing to confess to the crime which one is suspected of). For Abric, it is therefore a 'mixed-motivation' game (Abric 1987) where the combination of each player's choices determines the gains of each player. In many respects, the choice made by each player is similar to economic behaviour in that it is based on speculation aimed at maximising a gain. In one of his experiments, Abric manipulates the representation of the game partner. Some participants believe that they are playing against another player, while others believe they are playing against a computer programme.[4] In reality, all participants are confronted with the same succession of game phases determined by the experimenter themselves.[5] The results show that when participants believe that they are playing against another player, 54 per cent of their choices are cooperative, whereas when they believe that they are playing against a programme, the percentage drops to 35 per cent. Abric therefore concludes that the representation of the game partner guides the players' decisions. But we can wonder about the social nature of this representation. Is it not simply a cognitive (and therefore individual) representation?

To prevent this type of objection, Abric duplicated his original experiment. This time, it is the status of the partner that is manipulated. Thus, the high school students who participate in this second study believe, depending on the case, that they are playing against a peer (another high school student) or against a teacher. With this categorical assignment, the pitfall of the first experiment is avoided. Indeed, by indicating to the participants that they are playing against a peer or against a teacher, different 'intergroup representations' are induced in them (Deschamps 1973; Doise 1973). Intergroup representations are particular types of social representations concerning groups of individuals. Although their emergence is based more on a process of social categorisation (Tajfel 1972) than on the processes of anchoring and objectification, their functions and structuring are comparable to those of social representations. It is therefore difficult to speak of them only as cognitive representations. In this second version of the experiment, Abric also observes that when the participants believe that they are playing against a teacher, they make more cooperative choices than when they believe that they are playing against another student. These results therefore support the idea that, in an interaction involving the adoption of an economic behaviour, i.e., aiming at the maximisation of a gain, the representations relative to the protagonist of this interaction guide the decisions of individuals. But what exactly are the beliefs that could guide individuals' choices?

The work of Hidalgo (2012) provides some answers to this question. In one of her experiments, Hidalgo asks students to play Prisoner's Dilemma for research purposes. Depending on the case, the participants believe that they are playing against another student or against a partner from the Romani community. This choice is explained by the fact that some research studies conducted in France from the 2000s onwards have shown that for most people from outside the community, romanis are perceived as dishonest individuals

(Guimelli & Deschamps 2000). In the Prisoner's Dilemma, the adoption of a cooperative strategy is only possible if the players trust each other. But how can you trust someone that you think is dishonest? Hidalgo therefore expected to observe fewer cooperative choices among participants who believe that they are playing against a member of the Romani community than among those who believe that they are playing against another student. This is what the results indicated. It is therefore understandable that if a given representation is likely to guide a decision or an economic behaviour, it is because it induces a belief that allows this decision or behaviour to be justified or legitimised in those who are led to adopt it. From this perspective, the field studies mentioned above can be seen in a new light. What could be more legitimate than avoiding risky investment if one believes that investment must necessarily preserve savings? And what could be more legitimate than declaring oneself ready to pay more taxes to encourage the development of a form of tourism in one's region, the benefits of which one approves?

CONCLUSION

It would be an illusion to believe that we now have a perfect understanding of the social representations of economic objects and phenomena. Despite the research undertaken on this issue over the last 30 years, many questions remain unanswered. What exactly are the sociological or cultural determinants of these representations? What is the role of the media in their dissemination? What is the role of crises (political, economic, health, etc.) in their dynamics? These questions obviously await answers, but the growing amount of work on the subject can only convince us of the reality of a phenomenon: about the economy, as well as about many other subjects, individuals have knowledge that is based on common sense. Starting from this observation and going beyond a legitimate desire to better understand the world around us, we can ask ourselves what the usefulness could be of knowing more about the contents and processes of these social representations which form the basis of the common-sense economy. From our point of view, it is possible to distinguish at least four areas where this common-sense economy should be taken into consideration.

The Communication of Major Economic Actors

Here we refer to the thoughts of Darriet and Bourgeois-Gironde (2015), who explain that the major economic actors (e.g., central banks) should take greater account of the general public's perceptions in their strategic communication. Especially when this communication accompanies decisions aimed at impacting expectations, which play a primordial role in economic functioning. In this respect, Lamla, Dräger and Damjan (2015) show, for example, that the announcement of a target inflation rate by the Federal Reserve in the United States in 2012 had positive effects on the accuracy of the expectations that American consumers could make about their income.

The Teaching of Economics

As Legardez (2004) notes, many of the economic concepts and phenomena taught in the school context refer to issues of concern to society (e.g., unemployment, rising prices, globalisation, etc.). It is therefore not surprising that students who are taught economics are already imbued with the representations that circulate in society about these issues, even before the teaching begins. Thus, it can be expected that these representations will sometimes interfere with the learning of scientific concepts that contradict common sense. From this perspective, it could be useful to identify the dominant contents of these representations, especially their central elements, in order to define the pedagogical strategies best able to neutralise or bypass them.

Analysis of Interactions between Economic Actors

In a well-known study, Tajfel et al. (1971) set up two groups of schoolchildren according to their alleged aesthetic preferences. After this initial categorical assignment, each pupil was given a small amount of money and asked to divide it between two of their peers as a reward. But depending on the experimental conditions, 1. their two peers had the same aesthetic preferences as them; 2. Their two peers had different aesthetic preferences; or 3. one of their peers had the same preferences as them and the other had different preferences. The results show that 'the clearest effect on the distribution of rewards was due to the subjects' attempt to achieve a maximum difference between the ingroup and the outgroup even at the price of sacrificing other "objective" advantages' (Tajfel et al. 1971, p. 148). In this experiment, participants were placed in an interaction situation where they could expect a benefit for their group members (the peer having the same aesthetic preferences as the schoolchildren making the distribution). It is therefore a situation that induces economic behaviour in the sense already mentioned earlier. However, some participants behave in a way that is not at all consistent with the logic of *homo eoconomicus* – they go so far as to choose a loss for their own group in order to maximise the difference in gain between their group and the outgroup. The participants' representation of the situation that they are in (probably in terms of intergroup competition) is probably at the origin of this behaviour. The question then arises as to the extent to which this type of representation could explain the behaviour of real economic actors. An example is some of the economic decisions that have been taken by the US administration towards China in recent years. For some economists, these decisions, taken in the logic of trade war, have finally had rather negative consequences for the US economy (Fajgelbaum et al. 2020).

The Role of Social Classes

Classically, sociology conceptualises social class as determined by dimensions that are economic (the level of material resources of individuals), symbolic (the prestige associated with the status of the groups that they belong to) and cultural (the level of access to cultural objects and diplomas; cf. Bourdieu 1979). These dimensions determine membership in a particular social class, which in turn shapes the life experiences of individuals as it determines a coherent set of practices, values and tastes. For example, the probability of going to the opera, appreciating classical music or playing golf is not the same according to the economic capital, symbolic capital and cultural capital that individuals have in the social space. These contexts of existence closely influence the social representations and psychological functioning of individuals. Thus, the work of Mullainathan and Shafir (2013) shows that the scarcity of economic resources, relative to their abundance, influences the way individuals think and act from an economic point of view. For individuals confronted with financial difficulties, issues related to the management of resource scarcity (e.g., unpaid rent) appear to be central and highly salient. While these may have positive short-term consequences (e.g., increased efficiency in the immediate management of resources aimed at saving expenditure), they have negative long-term consequences, encouraging decisions that compromise the chances of escaping from poverty (e.g., taking out a high-interest loan). It is clear here that these effects are not a function of negligence or lack of capacity, but of a constraining life experience that determines specific ways of thinking.

As can be seen, the work is still in progress and leaves the way open to multiple and fertile research studies aiming at deepening the links that unite the thought of common sense and the issues linked to the economy.

NOTES

1. www.europarl.europa.eu/at-your-service/fr/be-heard/eurobarometer.
2. These places are symbolic because the meetings that took place there were marked by violent protests that many still remember. They were both a sign of the inexorable progress of the globalisation process and of the strong opposition that this process aroused in a part of the population.
3. In this study, Leiser and Aroch also interviewed third-year economics students. Their stated understanding of the 19 variables differs from that of the psychology students, although they also use the 'good-begets-good' heuristic. But the authors of the research point out that although both groups of participants give approximately the same answers, only the economics students are able to explain these answers correctly.
4. In experiments conducted in social psychology, it is common to deceive participants about the real nature of the situations in which they are placed. The important thing is to consider that the perception they have of a situation constitutes for them the reality of this situation.
5. In Abric's experiments, participants were confronted with a succession of 100 game phases.

REFERENCES

Abric, J.C. (1976), *Jeux, conflits et représentations sociales*, Thèse d'État, Aix-en-Provence, Université de Provence.
Abric, J.C. (1987), *Coopération, compétition et représentations sociales*, Cousset: Delval.
Abric, J.C. (1993), "Central system, peripheral system: Their functions and roles in the dynamic of social representations", *Papers on Social Representations*, **2**, 75–78.
Abric, J.C. and J. Kahan (1972), "The effects of representations and behavior in experimental games", *European Journal of Social Psychology*, **2(2)**, 129–144.
Bentham, J. (1789), "A utilitarian view", *Animal Rights and Human Obligations*, 25–26.
Bourdieu, P. (1979), *La distinction, critique sociale du jugement*, Paris: Éditions de minuit.
Bugden, D., D. Evensen and R. Stedman (2017), "A drill by any other name: Social representations, framing, and legacies of natural resource extraction in the fracking industry", *Energy Research and Social Science*, **29**, 62–71. https://doi.org/10.1016/j.erss.2017.05.011
De Rosa, A.S., E. Bocci and C. Bulgarella (2010), "Économie et Finance durant la crise financière mondiale: représentations sociales, métaphores et figures rhétoriques dans le discours des médias de l'automne 2008 au printemps 2010", *Les cahiers internationaux de psychologie sociale*, **3**, 543–584.
Deschamps, J.C. (1973), "L'attribution, la catégorisation sociale et les représentations intergroupes", *Bulletin de psychologie*, **13–14**, 710–721.
Deschamps, J.C. and P. Moliner (2012), *L'identité en psychologie sociale: des processus identitaires aux représentations sociales*, Paris: Armand Colin.
Doise, W. (1973), "Relations et représentations intergroupes", in S. Moscovici (Ed.). *Introduction à la psychologie sociale,* Paris: Larousse, pp. 195–214.
Fajgelbaum P.D., P.K. Goldberg, P.J. Kennedy and A.K. Khandelwal (2020), "The Return to protectionism", *The Quarterly Journal of Economics*, **135(1)**, 1–55. https://doi.org/10.1093/qje/qjz036
Flament, C. and M.L. Rouquette (2003), *Anatomie des idées ordinaires. Comment étudier les représentations sociales*, Paris: Armand Colin.

Galli I., B. Bouriche, R. Fasanelli, M. Geka, L. Iacob and G. Iacob (2010), "La représentation sociale de la crise économique dans quatre pays européens [The social representation of the economic crisis in four European countries]", *Les Cahiers Internationaux de Psychologie Sociale*, **3**, 585–620.

Gangl, K., B. Kastlunger, E. Kirchler and M. Voracek (2012), "Confidence in the economy in times of crisis: Social representations of experts and laypeople", *Journal of Socio-Economics*, **41(5)**, 603–614.

Guimelli, C. and J.C. Deschamps (2000), "Effets de contexte sur la production d'associations verbales: le cas des représentations sociales des Gitans", *Cahiers internationaux de psychologie sociale*, **47(48)**, 44–54.

Hidalgo, M. (2012), *Représentations sociales et contextes: études autour de l'expression et des comportements en lien avec les éléments masqués*. Thèse de doctorat, Aix-Marseille Université.

Holton, G. (1981). *L'imagination scientifique*, Paris: Gallimard.

Kahneman, D. and A. Tversky (1979), "Prospect theory: An analysis of decision under risk", *Econometrica*, **47**, 263–291.

Kahneman, D. and A. Tversky (1984), "Choices, values and frames", *American Psychologist*, **39**, 341–350.

Katona, G. (1974), "Psychology and consumer economics", *Journal of Consumer Research*, **1**, 1–8.

Kirchler, E. (1998), "Differential representations of taxes: Analysis of free associations and judgments of five employment groups", *Journal of Socio-Economics*, **27**, 117–131.

Kirchler, E. (2007). *The Economic Psychology of Tax Behaviour*, Cambridge, UK: Cambridge University Press.

Lamla, M., L. Dräger and P. Damjan (2015), "Are Consumer Expectations Theory-Consistent? The Role of Macroeconomic Determinants and Central Bank Communication", Annual conference of the Association for social politic. Leibniz.

Legardez, A. (2004), "L'utilisation de l'analyse des représentations sociales dans une perspective didactique: l'exemple de questions économiques", *Revue des sciences de l'éducation*, **30(3)**, 647–665.

Leiser, D. and R. Aroch (2009), "Lay understanding of macroeconomic causation: The good-begets-good heuristic", *Applied Psychology International Review*, **58**, 370–384.

Leiser, D. and Y. Shemesh (2018), *How We Misunderstand Economics and Why It Matters: The Psychology of Bias, Distortion and Conspiracy*, London and New York: Routledge.

Meier-Pesti, K., E. Kirchler and T. El-Sehity (2003), "The euro as a source of European identity Changes of social representations from 1997 to 2002", in *Vortrag gehalten beim IAREP (International Association for Research in Economic Psychology) Euro-Workshop*, Wien, 3rd – 5th of July 2003.

Milland, L. (2002), "Pour une approche de la dynamique du rapport entre représentations sociales du travail et du chômage", *Revue Internationale de Psychologie Sociale*, **15(2)**, 27–57.

Milland, L. and C. Flament (2010), "Les facettes d'une représentation sociale: nouvelle approche des effets de masquage", *Les Cahiers Internationaux de Psychologie Sociale*, **86(2)**, 213–240.

Moliner, P., P. Rateau and V. Cohen-Scali (2002), *Les représentations sociales. Pratique des études de terrain*, Rennes: Presses universitaires de Rennes.

Moscovici, S. (1961), *La psychanalyse, son image et son public*, Paris: Presses Universitaires de France.

Moscovici, S. (2008), *Psychoanalysis: Its Image and Its Public*, Cambridge: Polity Press.

Moscovici, S. and G. Vignaux (1994), "Le concept de thêmata", in C. Guimelli (Ed.), *Structures et transformations des représentations sociales*, Neuchâtel: Delachaux et Niestlé, pp. 25–72.

Mullainathan, S. and E. Shafir (2013), *Scarcity: Why Having Too Little Means so Much*, New York: Henry Holt.

Phillips, A. (1958), "The relation between unemployment and the rate of change of money wage rates in the United Kingdom, 1861–1857", *Economica*, **25(100)**, 283–299.

Poeschl, G., P.H.F. Campos and D. Ben Alaya (2007), "Appartenances nationales et prises de position sur la mondialisation", *Bulletin de psychologie*, **(1)**, 11–19.

Rateau, P., P. Moliner, C. Guimelli and J.C. Abric (2011), "Social representation theory", in P.A.M. Van Lange, A. Kruglanski and J. Higgins (Eds.), *Handbook of the Theories of Social Psychology*, Thousand Oaks: Sage, pp. 478–498.

Roland-Lévy, C., F.E.P. Boumelki and E. Guillet (2010), "Representation of the financial crisis: effect on social representations of savings and credit", *The Journal of Socio-Economics*, **39(2)**, 142–149.

Rosch, E. and B.B. Lloyd (Eds.) (1978), *Cognition and categorization*, Hillsdale: Lawrence Erlbaum.

Rouquette, M.-L. (1994). *Sur la connaissance des masses*, Grenoble: Presses Universitaires de Grenoble.

Rouquette, M.-L. (1996), "Représentations et idéologie", in J.C. Deschamps & J.L. Beauvois (Eds.), *Des attitudes aux attributions. Sur la construction de la réalité sociale,* Grenoble: Presses universitaires de Grenoble, pp. 163–173.

Süer, Ö. and J. Minibas-Poussard (2015), "Social representations of risk: A comparison between risk-taker and risk-averse investors", *Actual Problems of Economics,* **4(166)**, 314–324.

Suess, C. and M. Mody (2016), "Gaming can be sustainable too! Using Social Representation Theory to examine the moderating effects of tourism diversification on residents' tax paying behaviour", *Tourism Management,* **56**, 20–39.

Tajfel, H. (1972), "La catégorisation sociale", in S. Moscovici (Ed.), *Introduction à la psychologie sociale,* Paris: Larousse, vol. 1, pp. 272–302.

Tajfel, H., M.G. Billig, R.P. Bundy and C. Flament (1971), "Social categorization and intergroup behaviour", *European Journal of Social Psychology,* **1(2)**, 149–178.

Vergès, P. (1992), "L'evocation de l'argent: une méthode pour la définition du noyau central d'une représentation", *Bulletin de psychologie,* **XLV**, 203–209.

Viaud, J., F.J.U. Patiño and M.T.A. Ávila (2007), "Représentations et lieux communs de la mondialisation", *Bulletin de psychologie,* **(1)**, 21–33.

PART III

BEHAVIOURAL MACROECONOMICS

7. Behavioural methods for macroeconomics: Modelling investment
Michelle Baddeley

INTRODUCTION

Behavioural macroeconomics is growing as a sub-discipline of behavioural economics, yet its progress is slowed by the methodological limitations faced by macroeconomics generally. From an empirical perspective, these methodological limitations are not of direct interest to policy-makers and, thus, this chapter embeds a different behavioural approach to macroeconomics, as explicated in Tobias F. Rötheli's contribution to this edited volume – 'The business cycle and cycles of behavioural economics' – which builds on macroeconometric insights developed from Cowles Commission to develop an empirically informed, tractable and policy-oriented behavioural model of the macroeconomy.[1] In contrast, this chapter presents a theoretical analysis of fixed asset investment and its behavioural drivers in the context of macroeconomic trends. The different approaches presented in these two chapters are complementary to each other in representing different perspectives on aggregation and uncertainty.

To a limited extent, some insights from behavioural economics have been incorporated into macroeconomic models, for example via analyses of learning, limited attention and mimetic contagion (Gabaix 2020; Acemoglu 1993; Topol 1991). These models can be understood in terms of 'softer' forms of rationality than those associated with traditional macroeconomic models. Nonetheless, these embellishments to the mainstream models are still limited in their approach to modelling decision-making in the context of risk and uncertainty.

In terms of aggregation and uncertainty, behaviour at the level of an individual is relatively easy to model. But, at the aggregate macroeconomic level, risk and uncertainty limit the construction of plausible models – especially as one of the key insights from behavioural economics is that decision-makers will behave in different ways in different circumstances. Even the same decision-maker may make different choices depending on the context of their choices, how their choices are framed and the time horizon over which the consequences of their decisions will unfold. All these factors complicate the construction of intuitively plausible and analytically tractable models of macroeconomic outcomes, given that these outcomes are determined by large numbers of diverse and interacting individuals.

The solution adopted in the predominant macroeconomic paradigms, including rational expectations approaches as exemplified by dynamic stochastic general equilibrium (DSGE) models, is to design microeconomic foundations which are scaleable by embedding simplifying assumptions about all individuals being identical (at least on average) and operating rationally, independently and selfishly. Although DSGE models have been adapted to incorporate heterogeneous agents and the interdependencies between them, the basic idea is to take simple microeconomic relationships and describe the macroeconomy essentially as if it operates in the same way in which an individual agent would operate.

From a behavioural perspective, this approach is problematic. Shifting time and risk preferences; heuristics, bias and risk misperceptions; individual differences; learning; social influences, feedback effects and other interdependencies – all mean that coherent behavioural macroeconomic models cannot be captured just by aggregating individuals as if all individuals are the same. These problems are particularly profound for macroeconomic models of business investment and production because the behaviours driving investment and production for small and medium-sized enterprises (SMEs) are very different from those characterising large businesses. Also, whilst the simplified DSGE models have a neat logical structure, they do not rest easily with our intuitions about human behaviour, especially in the context of risk and uncertainty.

All these complexities mean that the macroeconomic whole cannot be described as the sum of its behavioural microeconomic parts. Therefore, in building strong foundations for a behavioural macroeconomic theory that overcomes some of the limitations associated with rational expectations models, an important set of insights revolve around how decision-makers adapt to risk and uncertainty, a key focus in behavioural economic analysis. In terms of broad macroeconomic implications, the behavioural anomalies which defy aggregation will be magnified in the macroeconomy, generating substantial deviations between *ex-ante* and *ex-post* consumption, investment and rates of profit – with significant implications for productivity growth and macroeconomic performance.

In addressing these gaps, this chapter explores some of the challenges in building behavioural macroeconomic models. Specifically, insights from behavioural economics can be embedded within macroeconomic analyses of investment – a key building block of macroeconomic theory because of its role in production, employment, expenditure generation and growth – founded on realistic behavioural assumptions about decision-making. Embedding strong and more realistic behavioural foundations will address some of the limitations of the rational expectations models associated with the mainstream micro-founded aggregative approach.

BEHAVIOURAL MACROECONOMICS AND THE AGGREGATION PROBLEM

In mainstream macroeconomic analysis, the aggregation problem pertains to the limitations associated with building large, multi-factor macroeconomic models using smaller, simpler models from microeconomic theory (Klein 1946; Peston 1959; Fisher 1987). Building macroeconomic models based on microfoundations requires a series of restrictive assumptions associated with microeconomic theories of optimising behaviour with respect to households' and businesses' decisions about consumption, labour–leisure trade-offs, investment and production. These assumptions are founded on very specific behavioural assumptions associated with rational choice and homogeneous, representative agents. There is no doubt that, whatever its flaws may be, this is a pragmatic approach because, if all decision-makers in an economy are assumed to be the same, then the macroeconomic model can be mapped directly onto simple microeconomic foundations and the task of building a macroeconomic model becomes much easier.

This micro-founded approach is associated most strongly with dynamic stochastic general equilibrium (DSGE) models. Variants of DSGE models do allow some relaxation of the restrictive assumptions but the key principles include the rational expectations hypothesis

(REH) – which simplifies the challenge of capturing complex behaviours by assuming that rational agents are fully informed, forward-looking, independent and self-interested maximisers (Muth 1961). According to the REH, rational agents learn instantaneously from any mistakes they make so that they do not repeat their mistakes. These restrictive behavioural assumptions about rationality work together with the representative agent hypothesis – that each group of economic agents (whether households/workers or firms/employers) can be represented by one highly stylised, homogeneous type – thus abstracting from individual differences. This enables all agents of each type to be captured within the model as if they are all the same. Thus, there is no fundamental difference between the macroeconomic aggregate of individuals' decisions and the microeconomic behaviours of strictly rational individuals. The difference between microeconomics and macroeconomics is reduced to a problem of scale, not substance.

Aggregation problems have been explored in the heterodox literature, specifically in the context of aggregate production functions (Felipe and Fisher 2008; Felipe and McCombie 2013) and there are additional problems for behavioural macroeconomic models given the complexities of economic behaviour which are the essential focus of behavioural economics. Rules which fit in a perfect world in which there is no uncertainty, in which expectations are fulfilled and in which the rate of profit is unambiguous do not fit so well in the real world in which distortions such as uncertainty, disappointed expectations and ambiguities in the rate of profit lead to significant differences between the *ex-post* and *ex-ante* rate of profit (Harcourt 1965). In these circumstances, there will be no simple rule of thumb to enable adjustment because rates of profit are greatly influenced by irrelevant factors, even under ideal conditions (Harcourt 1965, p. 80). Accounting rates of profits do not capture relative profitability and the relationships between investment and profits are too complicated to devise rough rules of thumb to enable approximations based on adjustments for the life of machines, patterns of rising and falling quasi-rents (temporary profits), rates of growth and depreciation methods used. Nor is it possible to generalise rates of profits in different countries and/or different industries. These microeconomic problems are magnified at an aggregate scale. Specifically, accountants' measures of profit at a microeconomic level will not accurately represent profits at a macroeconomic scale in four main cases: when distorted by quasi-rents from individual machines in the capital stock; when distorted by anomalies in the depreciation rate across businesses; when there is growth in the capital stock; and when the assets included in the capital stock are shifting (Harcourt 1965).

Similarly, constraints on expectations formation under conditions of fundamental uncertainty have also been explored in the heterodox post-Keynesian literature (for example see Crotty 1992; Fontana and Gerrard 2004; Gerrard 1994; Howitt 1979/1997; Meeks 1991, 2003; Baddeley 2014, 2017). Whilst some of these heterodox literatures have touched on behavioural factors, bringing these insights together into a coherent behavioural economic framework remains an overarching challenge for behavioural macroeconomic theory and analysis. An important starting point, connecting these heterodox literatures, is the behavioural analyses of decision-making under risk and uncertainty – as explored in the following.

BEHAVIOURAL APPROACHES TO RISK, UNCERTAINTY AND EXPECTATIONS

In spite of the aggregation problems outlined so far, behavioural economics has the potential to provide a stronger foundation for behavioural macroeconomics than traditional macroeconomics because it has developed out of a focus on choices and decisions when the future is uncertain and information is complex and unclear. Many of the fundamental insights from behavioural economics explore the constraints on decision-making under risk and uncertainty and the complexities generated by shifting risk and time preferences. These factors will dampen the key drivers of macroeconomic activity – including consumption and investment. Capturing the behavioural influences determining how households and businesses plan consumption and investment decisions, the consequences of which will unfold over long time horizons, is a key challenge for macroeconomic theory. Rational expectations models (for example as seen in the rational expectations models of consumption smoothing and investment decision-making) do not connect well with behavioural analyses and microeconomic experimental evidence about the limits on decision-makers' ability to plan for the future. Addressing these behavioural divergences from the assumptions embedded within rational expectations models is especially pressing in the context of macroeconomic theory. Whilst there is broad consensus from across the spectrum of macroeconomic theory that uncertainty impedes economic decision-making, debates have emerged around the relevance of different types of uncertainty, specifically Knightian risk versus Knightian uncertainty – a distinction contemporaneously identified by Knight and Keynes (Keynes 1921, 1937; Knight 1921). The differences in the theories emerge in the ways in which risk and uncertainty are defined and modelled. In mainstream models, uncertainty is conceptualised as a quantifiable risk, that is 'Knightian risk' – defined as a measurable, knowable form of uncertainty – for example, knowable from frequency distributions capturing the incidence of similar events in the past. Complex economic decisions are often associated with 'Knightian *uncertainty*' – more likely to be relevant to macroeconomic analysis given the complexity of real-world macroeconomic influences. For example, under Knightian uncertainty, future prospects and expected profits from capital investments will be unquantifiable and unknowable. In terms of macroeconomic consequences, the dampening impacts of risk misperceptions and uncertainty may reflect economic and/or information constraints – such as those preventing business managers from forming reliable expectations of future sales and other economic variables. In a macroeconomic context, this theme is a key feature of Keynes's analyses of the psychological foundations of decision-making and its implications for the macroeconomy (1930, 1936, 1937). Uncertainty triggers sluggishness in entrepreneurs' animal spirits, dampening their plans for the future – an insight originally explored by Keynes (1936) and also Katona (1946). These animal spirits, albeit in a re-imagined form distinct from Keynes's original conception, are now the centrepiece of many behavioural macroeconomic models (de Grauwe 2011, 2012; Farmer and Guo 1994; Gabaix 2020; Howitt and McAfee 1992; Baddeley 2014, 2016, 2019).

Departures from an analysis of rational choice in the context of Knightian risk do not, however, necessarily imply that decisions are formed irrationally. Departures from the assumptions of perfect rationality – in the sense of making complete use of available information and avoiding systematic mistakes – can more accurately be conceptualised in line with Herbert Simon's analysis of bounded rationality in the context of Knightian uncertainty, when optimising is not possible because of the bounds on optimising behaviour (Simon 1955). In other words, with Knightian uncertainty, decision-makers will be bounded by constraints on information and/or their cognitive processing capacity and so their decisions will diverge from what the far-sighted rational optimisers who inhabit rational expectations models would decide.

From the perspective of behavioural economics, the negative impacts of uncertainty will be magnified by behavioural constraints and biases – some of which have been brought into behavioural macroeconomic models. Keynes's analyses connect with Herbert Simon's distinction between different forms of rationality and their relevance depending on levels and types of uncertainty. Simon distinguishes substantive rationality, which can still operate well in a quantifiable world of Knightian risk, and procedural rationality, operating in a world of Knightian uncertainty (Simon 1979, p. 67). The substantively rational decision-maker will behave as described within standard economic theory, and they will focus on achieving objectively quantifiable goals of utility or profit maximisation in the face of fixed, knowable constraints. For example in a macroeconomic context, if business decision-makers are substantively rational, then they will form quantifiable expectations of the future and will make decisions using constrained optimisation techniques. In other words, they will utilise complex mathematical rules embedding forward-looking expectations to estimate the discounted flows of expected future utility or profit from their fixed asset investment decisions. But Simon (1979, p. 68) responds to the mathematical approaches subsumed within the substantively rational approaches associated with traditional economics by arguing that economic decisions are often the product of a 'procedurally rational' process – that is a process which operates from a basis of bounded rationality rather than the strict rationality associated with optimal decision-making. In much of economic decision-making, optimising behaviour is not achievable because of limits to information and/or cognitive processing ability. In this sort of world, decisions will be based on a broad reasoning process rather than the achievement of a given representative agent's goals (Simon 1979, p. 68).

HEURISTICS, ALGORITHMS AND BEHAVIOURAL BIAS

Developing insights about heuristics in a world of uncertainty, a key focus in behavioural economics is on the ways in which economic decision-makers use simple rules of thumb – i.e., heuristics – to navigate complex decision-making challenges, information overload and choice overload (for example, see the seminal paper by Tversky and Kahneman 1974). More precisely in economics, two distinct 'styles' of decision-making are highlighted (Baddeley 2006). First, heuristical approaches: these allow that decision-makers will use heuristics – simple rules of thumb – to guide them. For example, Gigerenzer and Brighton (2011) conceptualise heuristics as devices that save decision-makers time and energy in thinking through complex algorithmic calculations (Gigerenzer and Brighton 2011). Second, algorithmic approaches: these assume that any decision-maker, with access to the same information set, will form identical expectations centred around some objective probability distribution of outcomes. Decision-makers who are forward-looking and consistent in their discounting of future prospects – as seen in rational expectations versions of consumption and investment theory – are utilising algorithms.

Heuristics and algorithms can be distinguished in terms of their complexity: an algorithm is a complex analytical solution requiring a high degree of rationality. A heuristic is defined by Simon as a common-sense rule of thumb based on experience and intuition and is much more likely to be used by the majority of decision-makers because implementing heuristics in practice is much simpler and more feasible than implementing complex algorithms. Under conditions of fundamental uncertainty, heuristics will often be the best decision-making tool because so little is known about what is going on or what might happen in the future (Todd and Gigerenzer 2012). In other words, when uncertainty is profound and expectations cannot be quantified under any scenario, then it is much more reasonable to rely on heuristics than on spurious optimisation techniques.

In a macroeconomic context, heuristics will be especially useful in understanding SMEs' investment activity – and SMEs play an especially important macroeconomic role because they contribute significantly to macroeconomic performance in terms of production and employment. But whilst heuristics might be useful approximations on average at a microeconomic level, they are also associated with systematic biases (Tversky and Kahneman 1974; Kahneman and Tversky 1979) which, when magnified at an aggregate macroeconomic scale, can create significant problems for behavioural macroeconomic analysis. The presence of these biases implies that real-world macroeconomies are likely to diverge significantly from the stylised models of macroeconomies analysed via mainstream models grounded in principles of optimisation and rational expectations.

In capturing bias in behavioural macroeconomic models, there are a number of key questions to address. Assuming away unexpected events, why do businesses and households make mistakes in practice? What explains their behavioural biases? What are the macroeconomic implications of biases magnified on an aggregate macroeconomic scale? There may be mistakes or omissions at a number of stages of consumers' and businesses' decision-making processes: in gathering information about the various options available today; in forming expectations to predict future events and consequences. Households may make mistakes in balancing the future consequences of their decisions around balancing consumption versus savings today with implications for their income on retirement. Businesses planning to invest for the future may make mistakes in their expectations of future sales revenues, relative costs of labour versus capital in the future and/or the cost of borrowing, especially as information about these factors will be clouded by unpredictable macroeconomic events and shifting labour market conditions. Poor information about inherently uncertain future events will increase the reliance of businesses and households on heuristics and therefore increase their susceptibility to heuristical bias. If information is missing or misinterpreted, if there are asymmetric information and principal-agent problems associated with adverse selection and moral hazard, then there will be a widening divergence between the macroeconomic reality and the predictions from rational expectations macroeconomic models.

In terms of the key sources of bias that might lead to the widest divergences from the stylised rational expectations models, these include status quo bias, conventions and herding; shifting time and risk preferences; business heuristics; and optimism bias and animal spirits – as explored in the following.

Status Quo Bias, Conventions and Herding

The static expectations hypothesis is a macroeconomic corollary of status quo bias in behavioural microeconomics. A form of status quo bias, i.e., the bias which makes decision-makers slow to shift away from their reference points, is seen in mainstream models of business investment. For example, Jorgenson's early models of fixed asset investment assumed static expectations – businesses assume that the current state of affairs will continue into the future, and this decision inertia parallels status quo bias. Also, Keynes (1936) focused on the extent to which the current situation dominates decision-making: 'it is reasonable, therefore, to be guided to a considerable degree by the facts about which we feel somewhat confident, even though they may be less decisively relevant to the issue than other facts about which our knowledge is vague and scanty' (Keynes 1936, p. 148). Whilst static expectations are found in early versions of neoclassical theory (including Jorgenson's early versions of neoclassical investment theory) it is an assumption that is in essence more consistent with Keynesian principles. For example, it fits well with the Keynesian consumption function constructed via Keynes's (1936, 1937) 'fundamental psychological law': that the propensity to consume will be determined as a fixed proportion of current income (in contrast to monetarist and rational expectations models of consumption smoothing based on far-sighted expectations of future income). The principle of a static relationship between consumption and income also forms the foundation for multiplier-accelerator theories of output and investment.

In terms of social influences in mainstream macroeconomic models, behavioural macroeconomic analyses of these influences also build up from Keynes's macroeconomic analyses of herding and conventions in financial markets and their impact on real activity, especially fixed asset investment (Keynes 1930, 1936, 1937). The concept of a convention connects with behavioural economics' heuristics because following others is a quick decision-making shortcut which people use when information is complex and difficult to navigate and interpret (Baddeley 2018, 2019). The macroeconomic implications link with Keynes's insight that conventions in the macroeconomy are 'established as the outcome of the mass psychology of a large number of ignorant individuals [and are] liable to change violently' (Keynes 1936, p. 154). Psychological factors underlie the maintenance of conventions because people prefer stable routines; conventions lull anxiety created by uncertainty about the future (Earl 1983; Lawson 1995).

These conventions also connect with status quo bias because conventions are associated with the continuance of current conditions. Thus, conventions will become self-fulfilling prophecies and, once the convention is established, assuming that its continuance is not unreasonable and is consistent with Simon's procedural rationality.[2] Also, it is reasonable for an ignorant individual to rely on conventions because other economic actors may be acting on better information and, then, 'we endeavour to fall back on the judgement of the rest of the world which is perhaps better informed' (Keynes 1936, p. 217).

In the aggregate context of macroeconomics, conventions introduce complexities in terms of the overlap between the microeconomic decisions of households and businesses and the macroeconomic consequences: feedback effects ensure that individuals are affected by aggregate outcomes, and aggregate outcomes are affected by individuals' decisions. For example, social drivers of consumption on a macroeconomic scale include the interactions of Veblen effects and demonstration effects, triggering conspicuous consumption of luxury goods which spreads through the macroeconomy as consumers make their own decisions about luxury consumption on the basis of observing what others are doing – themes explored in macroeconomic models constructed on insights about consumer sentiment; for example, see Curtin (2019) and Wärneryd (1999).

Learning in the context of multiplier-accelerator models is analysed by Acemoglu (1993), who combines a rational expectations approach with a macroeconomic accelerator model in analysing the role played by output as a signal to businesses of what other businesses are planning. The positive externalities generated by technological innovations, learning by doing, innovation and growing aggregate demand will generate output growth. Businesses will use this output growth as a type of heuristic – as a signal that other businesses are investing. Thus, this herding heuristic will encourage businesses to follow the crowd, triggering copying behaviour as businesses follow each other with their investment plans.

Shifting Risk and Time Preferences

Macroeconomic drivers are also affected by biases associated with shifting time and risk preferences – for example, as identified by Strotz (1955), Ainslie (1991), Laibson (1997) and others in the context of time preference, and by Tversky and Kahneman (1974), Kahneman and Tversky (1979) and others in the context of risk preferences. These approaches contrast with rational expectations models of the macroeconomy which are founded on the idea that households smooth their consumption over their lifetimes. In rational expectations models, households' consumption smoothing is enabled by the presence of perfect financial markets via which households can borrow or save at a real interest rate that reflects their rate of time preference, i.e., the discount rate capturing the extent to which they value future consumption over present consumption. This discount rate is assumed to be a stable constant, unchanging over time.

But a key insight from behavioural economics is that the discount rate is not a stable constant. Microeconomic behavioural analyses of consumption include Thaler's mental accounting model, which focuses on the idea that money is not completely fungible (Thaler 1985, 1990). In contrast to a rational expectations world in which rational agents' decisions do not change unless information changes, decision-makers will treat the same amount of money in different ways depending on the context and framing. For example, Thaler's experimental evidence demonstrates that people will spend a windfall gain of $2,400 in different ways depending on how they receive the windfall. A windfall received as a series of monthly payments results in spending $1,200. A windfall received in a single lump sum results in spending £785. A windfall received as an inheritance will not be spent at all. Thaler interprets this experimental evidence as reflecting the fact that people's perceptions of the money they receive and their decisions to consume versus save are not treated as if they are a single optimisation problem. It is as if people have different mental accounts into which they allocate the money they receive in different ways. This explains why people build up credit card debt at very high interest rates whilst, at the same time, they put their savings away in accounts earning just very low interest rates.

Another anomaly from the behavioural literature which is inconsistent with rational expectations macroeconomic models is reflected in a large volume of experimental evidence from psychology as well as economics. This experimental evidence shows that people do not have stable discount rates. Instead, they tend to exhibit present bias – their discount rates are higher when making decisions over a short time horizon than when they are making decisions over a longer time horizon. In addition, there may be significant individual differences in people's planning for the future. This insight has external validity and has been seen also in natural experiments. For example, a study of the retirement decisions of US military personnel showed that military personnel had heterogeneous preferences when deciding between pensions received as a lump-sum payment versus pensions received as a regular stream of annuities over time; the choices between these two options were driven by individual differences in terms of military rank, education and age (Warren and Pleeter 2001).

Behavioural life-cycle models blend together elements of the rational expectations macroeconomic models, replacing standard exponential discount functions (which are consistent with stable discount rates) with quasi-hyperbolic discount functions (which allow discount rates to vary) with the aim of building a model which can capture the anomalous propensity of households to accumulate high-cost revolving debts, e.g., via credit cards, whilst simultaneously holding large stores of illiquid wealth or saving at low interest rates (Angeletos et al. 2001; Laibson, Repetto and Tobacman 2007). These models are then used to simulate macroeconomic outcomes in a methodology similar to the methods used in calibrating DSGE real business-cycle models. The empirical limitations include the absence of reliable and objective methods for quantifying the parameters embedded within the simulations.

Alternative behavioural approaches to consumption include macroeconomic behavioural analyses of consumer sentiment, as pioneered by George Katona, and these approaches are consistent with the idea that the psychology of consumers is also an important driver of consumption in the macroeconomy, with the psychology underlying the formation of expectations operating as an 'intervening variable' (Katona 1951; Wärneryd 1999; Curtin 2019).[3] In contrast to rational expectations models which focus on economic and financial drivers, behavioural economic analyses of consumer sentiment capture the impact of non-economic drivers – including emotions such as fear, nervousness, optimism and euphoria.

Emotional influences on the macroeconomy are likely to be stronger and more complex than when Keynes and Katona were writing and there is a burgeoning interest amongst macroeconomists in news-based measures of sentiment and uncertainty (for example, see Baker, Bloom and Davis 2016; Curtin 2019). The easy access to credit which is a feature of modern, financially deregulated economies means that the purchase of consumer durables and luxuries can pick up quickly when positive consumer sentiment is driven by buoyant macroeconomic conditions. In very recent times, news is having a much quicker and more destabilising impact on emotions because of online social media – with implications for consumption's impact on aggregate demand.

Business Investment Heuristics

In this section, in order to illustrate some key insights, the behavioural economic insights explored above are applied specifically to the role of business in the macroeconomy – in terms of employing workers and investing in capital and/or production. Business investment decisions can be understood in terms of the ways in which entrepreneurs and business managers use heuristics versus algorithms to guide their investment, employment and production decisions. As explored above, algorithms are more likely to be associated with a rational expectations model and heuristics are more likely to be associated with a behavioural approach – as explained in the following.[4]

The starting point for algorithmic, rational expectations approaches to business investment is Jorgenson's neoclassical model of fixed asset investment (Jorgenson 1963) and its variants. These models embed assumptions that firms are operating within a rational choice framework, using complex mathematical techniques of constrained optimisation to identify analytical solutions for maximising profits and minimising costs. In these mainstream investment models, built on assumptions of perfect information and rational choice, businesses invest in fixed assets to maximise their profits over an infinite time horizon by calculating the net present value (NPV) of a project using calculations of an investment project's expected discounted cash flow (DCF) relative to its capital cost. The starting point for these models is a production function via which firms' decisions are made within a 'black box'. Investors calculate the inputs going in and the outputs coming out but do not know, or care, what happens in between (Cobb and Douglas 1968).[5] In addition, Jorgenson's investment theory assumes constant returns to scale and homogeneity of capital, as captured in the Cobb-Douglas production function (CDPF). The overall result is that profit-maximising firms will invest up to the point where the user cost of capital and the marginal productivity of capital are equalised. Jorgenson uses a range of simplifying assumptions. Essentially, in Jorgenson's model behavioural/psychological factors are confined to the error term of the CDPF. There are limitations associated with the restrictive assumptions of Jorgenson's approach, but the specific and central limitation of Jorgenson's model is twofold: it does not consistently capture expectations and uncertainty, and it does not capture the ways in which real-world entrepreneurs and investors decide.

To capture expectations and uncertainty, rational expectations theory has evolved analytically rigorous models to capture the impacts of expectations and uncertainty on investment. These models are roughly consistent with neoclassical investment theory's rational optimiser framework because they are generally built on models of quantifiable uncertainty i.e., Knightian risk. Starting with expectations, Jorgenson's baseline neoclassical model is founded on the assumption of static expectations – businesses assume that the current state of affairs will continue into the future, and this decision inertia parallels status quo bias: businesses are slow to adjust their expectations. This first set of limitations associated with Jorgenson's model has been partly addressed via subsequent refinements from the rational optimiser perspective, for example, various versions of q theories, many of which focus on the existence of adjustment costs within a stock-flow consistent model (e.g., see Abel 1983). In q theories, marginal q pertains to the marginal benefits of an incremental investment in terms of discounted expected future profits from the investment relative to its marginal cost but the empirical problem is that marginal q is unobservable and therefore uncertain.

Transposing these insights into macroeconomic theory, assuming constant returns to scale and homogeneity of capital, the expectations of dividends and profits for marginal investments will proxy dividends and profits in aggregate and thus stock market capitalisations across an economy's stock markets will give an unbiased measure of rational investors' expectations of the discounted streams of future profits from current investment activity, at least for listed companies (Hayashi 1982). Average q is used as an empirical proxy for marginal q with immeasurable expectations proxied by stock market valuations. In practice, average q is equivalent to a valuation ratio, i.e., the ratio of stock market capitalisations to the current replacement cost of capital. This connection between stock markets and fixed asset investments is grounded on the assumption that stock markets reflect all relevant and currently available information about the value of a firm's capital stock. In this way, share prices and stock market valuations are used as proxies for expected future profits and dividends. A further limitation, however, is that this solution also depends on the empirically fallible efficient markets hypothesis assumption that financial markets are informationally efficient, i.e., adjust rapidly in response to news, enough to process all currently available information about future profits and dividends so that asset prices will reflect forward-looking rational expectations of profits and dividends from fixed asset investments (Brainard and Tobin 1977).

Another group of rational expectations models capture the impact of uncertainty on business decision-making, for example as outlined in Dixit and Pyndyck in the context of fixed asset investment models (Pindyck 1991; Dixit and Pindyck 1994). Uncertainty is embedded within a rational optimising framework by extending Jorgenson's model and the q models to capture the depressing impact of uncertainty on fixed asset investment in a world in which sunk costs are large and so problems of irreversibility in investment are substantial. Uncertainty is likely to affect large, capital-intensive projects more than smaller scale, less capital-intensive projects because the negative relationship between investment and uncertainty is driven by the interplay between uncertainty and irreversibility. When uncertainty and irreversibility coincide, businesses will be reluctant to commit to large-scale fixed asset investment projects because significant uncertainty means that they have limited reassurances that they will be able to recoup the sunk costs of their investments and the opportunity cost of exercising an option to invest rises accordingly. Larger investment projects involve larger sunk costs and irreversibility. The 'trigger rate of return' – that is, the rate of return needed to ensure that an investment project pays for itself in terms of discounted future cash flows – will be elevated and, with uncertainty having an aggregate impact across the macroeconomy via its inverse relationship with business confidence, investment activity will falter, with negative consequences for employment, production and growth in the macroeconomy. These real options theories reconcile limits on planning for the future by assuming that businesses will build buffers into their investment appraisal rules, raising the trigger/hurdle rates of return at which they are prepared to implement investment projects to take account of uncertainty – with the consequence that fewer investment projects will be implemented – thus leading to lower rates of investment both at the firm level and at an aggregate macroeconomic scale.

The Jorgenson, q and real options models outlined earlier are set in a world of quantifiable Knightian risk rather than fundamental, immeasurable Knightian uncertainty. In reality, uncertainty is not measurable and so it is not feasible for businesses to use complex rules/algorithms. In reality, Knightian uncertainty will transform the way in which businesses decide about their fixed asset investments.[6] Complexities are especially salient in the context of macroeconomic investment models. Risk and uncertainty are especially pertinent to the analysis of business fixed asset investment because investment is by its nature a forward-looking activity the success of which is determined by how accurately business decision-makers are able to forecast the future. In turn, investment is critical to macroeconomic growth and production. Understanding how business investors' expectations are formed in a world of risk and uncertainty is therefore a key challenge for macroeconomic theory.

Once a macroeconomist allows that uncertainty is immeasurable, the capacity for substantive rationality is removed. Thus, the distinction between heuristics and algorithms can be used to separate the different types of investment decision rules used by real-world businesses. In the context of fixed asset investment, procedurally rational investors will use common sense rather than complex mathematical techniques in assessing investment plans. A procedurally rational investor operating in a world of bounded rationality (in which the sensible application of mathematical constrained optimisation techniques will be impossible because nothing is precisely measurable) will not be able to quantify an NPV/DCF algorithm. Different investors, faced with the same information, may form different expectations reflecting arbitrarily assigned margins of error.

In the real world, many businesses, especially smaller businesses, will be unwilling and/or unable to implement complex optimising algorithms and will prefer techniques that require just simple assumptions based on current conditions. Consistent with this preference, businesses can do this by utilising simple business decision rules anchored around payback periods (PBP)[7] and accounting rates of return (ARR),[8] both of which fit within the behavioural economics conception of a heuristic (Baddeley 2006). These heuristics can help businesses in guiding their decisions about embarking on a new project, expanding or contracting their workforce, or investing to boost their capital stock. They are simple rules of thumb that are possible to implement without stringent requirements. They are relatively quick and easy to calculate and so will be a relatively simple way to navigate information problems and cognitive constraints.

In fact, PBP and ARR techniques approximate complex algorithms under certain conditions (Gordon 1955; Harcourt 1968; Sarnat and Levy 1969; Baddeley and Harcourt 2021) and so can be used to approximate NPV and DCF algorithms, sometimes without generating significant differences in investment decisions. Also, NPV and DCF algorithms are difficult to use properly and effectively. First, there is the problem of missing information. Questions around how to forecast future revenues and/or how to identify a 'correct' discount rate are far from settled questions, meaning that there are practical gaps in implementing these techniques in practice. There is no single robust method for forecasting future revenues or identifying an appropriate discount rate.

Moreover, and consistent with Todd and Gigerenzer's (2012) insight that heuristics will be better than complex decision rules in a fundamentally uncertain world, PBP and ARR heuristics may be more helpful than NPV and DCF algorithms because they do not require complex information about expected future cash flows, discount rates and forward-looking rational expectations. A fixed asset investor may not want to worry about identifying their discount rate either because they do not realise that the value of money changes over time and are ignorant about the trade-offs between present value and current value, or because they judge that current information is fallible and the future is too uncertain for calculations and predictions based around discounting procedures to be of much use. Either way, whether an inappropriate discount rate is used deliberately or by mistake, the consequent flows of fixed asset investment will not be consistent with the optimal decision-making highlighted in the Jorgenson, q and real options models. Overall, business decision-makers may make a procedurally rational judgement that the computational and cognitive costs of using sophisticated algorithms are too high relative to the likely benefits in terms of better investment decisions for the future.

In terms of the empirical evidence, interviews conducted in conjunction with the surveys of business leaders in Cambridgeshire (Baddeley 1996, 2006) indicated that some firms' managing directors just did not think that NPV and DCF were valid techniques to use when uncertainty was limiting the availability of clear, reliable information about the future. This survey evidence also showed that not only are DCF methods less commonly used in practice, but when they are used they are sometimes misused suggesting that decision-making biases are likely to distort the correct application of NPV/DCF techniques. For example, survey evidence from Baddeley (1996, 2006) shows that many businesses claimed to use discounted cash flow methods but had anomalously answered 'not applicable' when asked how they selected a discount rate. Those who did nominate a discount rate used the post-tax cost of capital or borrowing costs as a discount rate. They were not using higher discount rates to allow for impacts of uncertainty on sunk investments, as would be consistent with real options theories of investment. This suggests significant sources of bias are associated with the use of discounting techniques. If these types of bias and mistakes are widespread, then there will be negative implications not only for businesses and their employees but also for public sector infrastructure investment, and the macroeconomy as a whole.

Optimism Bias and Animal Spirits

Shifting risk and time preferences will affect consumption, inconsistent risk preferences may affect businesses in terms of cycles of optimism bias and pessimism bias, and both sets of impacts will have implications for macroeconomic confidence (Baddeley 2016, 2017). Entrepreneurs building their businesses via their fixed asset investments have a significant impact on the macroeconomy via aggregate demand, and behavioural influences drive entrepreneurial decision-making even when uncertainty limits entrepreneurs' ability to form accurate expectations of future prospects from investments. With uncertainty, the future is not easily quantifiable and so entrepreneurs cannot estimate with any accuracy their expectations of the future benefits from their entrepreneurial investments.

As noted earlier, Keynes's concept of animal spirits parallels insights from behavioural economics about optimism bias and pessimism bias. Animal spirits are psychological urges to act and intervene which are neither rational nor irrational. Keynes observes that decisions:

> to do something positive, the full consequences of which will be drawn out over many days to come, can only be taken as a result of animal spirits – of spontaneous urge to action rather than inaction, and not as the outcome of a weighted average of quantitative benefits multiplied by quantitative probabilities. Enterprise only pretends to itself to be mainly actuated by the statements in its own prospectus, however candid and sincere. Only a little more than an expedition to the South Pole, is it based on an exact calculation of benefits to come . . . [animal spirits drive entrepreneurs] so that the thought of ultimate loss which often overtakes pioneers . . . is put aside as a healthy man puts aside the expectations of death.
>
> (Keynes 1936, pp. 161–162)

In the context of business investment plans, Keynes (1936) observes that predicting long-term prospects of new investments is all but impossible and so entrepreneurs are unlikely to be driven by their quantified estimates of their best choices for maximising expected future profits. Instead, Keynes describes the entrepreneurial personality in terms of a 'sanguine temperament and constructive impulses' and people embarking on business ventures reflecting 'business as a way of life' not as a means to make a profit. Thus the entrepreneurial personality influences macroeconomic outcomes – and animal spirits play a central role in this (Keynes 1936).[9] In aggregate, animal spirits will drive the macroeconomy in periods of optimism and confidence; however, entrepreneurs are also easily discouraged psychologically by crises of confidence in times of economic adversity and social changes. So, during pessimistic, recessionary/deflationary periods, the reversion of entrepreneurs' animal spirits will slow entrepreneurial investment with magnified impacts on the macroeconomy via slumps in aggregate demand and employment:

> if the animal spirits are dimmed and the spontaneous optimism falters, leaving us to depend on nothing but a mathematical expectation, enterprise will fade and die; – though fears of loss may have a basis no more reasonable than hopes of profits had before.
>
> (Keynes 1936, p. 162)

So whilst animal spirits at first inspection seem like a force for good in the macroeconomy if, on balance, they do no more than amplify macroeconomic volatility, then the positive role of animal spirits is more ambiguous unless animal spirits' contribution to upswings in good times outweighs their depressing impacts during downswings.

CONCLUSIONS

To conclude, behavioural economic influences will have profound impacts on the macroeconomy. Biases associated with heuristics and inconsistencies in time and risk preferences will distort future planning by households and businesses. The macroeconomic implications will be substantial and complex because, when biases are aggregated, become systemic and/or are exhibited by a large proportion of businesses and consumers in the real world, they will combine in magnifying under-investment, unemployment and sluggish production during recessionary periods. Present bias will magnify current consumption to the detriment of future consumption, potentially triggering long-term shifts in inequality if poorer households are less able to accumulate wealth to pay for their retirement. Uncertainty will dampen businesses' investments, with knock-on effects on production, employment and growth. So, what are the behavioural macroeconomic policy solutions? As explored earlier, traditional macroeconomic models have not allowed for behavioural biases and psychological influences. The problem from a behavioural economics perspective is that biases are not just random noise. They are systematic biases which will not cancel out in aggregate and, in fact, are likely to be magnified when the herding and conventions outlined earlier are driving the decisions and choices of businesses and households.

This leads to the broader question of how behavioural macroeconomic policy should differ from conventional macroeconomic policies founded on assumptions of rational decision-making. Behavioural macroeconomic policies designed to take into account behavioural fallibilities (by policy-makers as well as households and businesses) could address issues of time inconsistency and present bias by embedding pre-commitments into decision-making, thus limiting the extent to which decision-makers shift decisions in response to short-term factors. Behavioural policies designed to boost animal spirits and optimism via improving business confidence and consumer sentiment could have a positive impact on macroeconomic activity, especially through downturns, recessions and depressions. In this, expansionary policies will have benefits beyond the standard multiplier effects if they boost confidence more generally via their impact on optimism and confidence. More generally, behavioural macroeconomic policy provides a potential route out of the political and ideological biases and rhetoric which have driven the pendulum-like oscillation of macroeconomic policy prescriptions in line with political trends – characterised by a series of contests between free-market 'hands-off' policy prescriptions and Keynesian interventionist policy prescriptions. In the first instance, more empirical evidence is needed to establish which behavioural influences are important, what sort of impacts they have and how beneficial impacts can be leveraged and negative impacts can be ameliorated. There is a growing range of promising data and techniques that could feed into this sort of research agenda. With more evidence about behavioural and psychological impacts on the macroeconomy, this might hopefully lead to a more scientific and less polemical approach to macroeconomic policy-making.

NOTES

1. With thanks to Tobias Rötheli for his comments and advice on an early draft.
2. See also Pesaran (1990) and Lawson (1995).
3. See also Earl (2005) on some of the connections and barriers between economics and psychology in the context of psychological economics more generally.
4. See also Baddeley (2003) for a survey of alternative approaches to modelling macroeconomic investment.
5. There is a separate and important literature on behavioural theories of the firm; for example, see Cyert and March (1992).
6. See Meeks (1991) on rationality and uncertainty in investors' decisions.
7. The length of time it takes to generate (undiscounted) cash flows from a project which are sufficient to cover the initial investment cost.
8. The ratio of (undiscounted) cash flows to the initial investment cost.
9. See also Katona (1946) and Akerlof and Shiller (2009) for a modern interpretation.

REFERENCES

Abel A.B. (1983), 'Optimal investment under uncertainty', *American Economic Review*, **73**(1), 228–233.
Acemoglu D. (1993), 'Learning about others' actions and the investment accelerator', *Economic Journal*, **103**(417), 318–328.

Ainslie G. (1991), 'Derivation of "rational" economic behavior from hyperbolic discount curves', *American Economic Review*, **92**(3), 411–433.

Akerlof G.A. and Shiller R. (2009), *Animal Spirits: How Human Psychology Drives the Economy, and Why It Matters for Global Capitalism*, Princeton: Princeton University Press.

Angeletos G.M., Laibson D., Repetto A. and Tobacman J. (2001), 'The hyperbolic consumption model: Calibration, simulation, and empirical evidence', *Journal of Economic Perspectives*, **15**(3), 47–68.

Baddeley, M.C. (1996), *Rationality, Expectations and Investment: The Theory of Keynes Vs. Neo-Classical Theory*, PhD thesis, supervised by G.C. Harcourt, Faculty of Economics and Politics, University of Cambridge.

Baddeley M.C. (2003), *Investment: Theories and Analysis*, London: Palgrave Macmillan.

Baddeley M.C. (2006), 'Behind the black box: A survey of real-world investment appraisal approaches', *Empirica*, **33**, 329–350.

Baddeley M.C. (2014), 'Rethinking microfoundations of macroeconomics: Insights from behavioural economics', *European Journal of Economics & Economic Policies*, **11**(1), 99–112.

Baddeley M.C. (2016), 'Behavioral macroeconomics: Time, optimism and animal spirits', in Frantz R., Chen S.-H., Dopfer K., et al. (eds), *The Routledge Handbook of Behavioral Economics*, Abingdon: Routledge, pp. 266–278.

Baddeley M.C. (2017), 'Keynes' psychology and behavioural macroeconomics: Theory and policy', *Economic and Labour Relations Review*, **28**(2), 177–196.

Baddeley M.C. (2018), *Copycats and Contrarians: Why We Follow Others and When We Don't*, London/New Haven: Yale University Press.

Baddeley M.C. (2019), *Behavioural Economics and Finance* (2nd ed.). Abingdon: Routledge, pp. 255–261.

Baddeley M.C., Curtis A. and Wood R.A. (2004), 'An introduction to prior information derived from probabilistic judgments', in Curtis A. and Wood R.A. (eds), *Geological Prior Information*, London: Geological Society, Special Publication, pp. 1–26.

Baddeley M.C. and Harcourt G.C. (2021), 'A behavioural model of investment appraisal and its implications for the macroeconomy', Economics Working Paper Series No. 2021/5, Economics Discipline Group, UTS Business School, University of Technology, Sydney.

Baker S.R., Bloom N. and Davis S.J. (2016), 'Measuring economic policy uncertainty', *Quarterly Journal of Economics*, **131**(4), 1593–1636.

Brainard W.C. and Tobin J. (1977), 'Asset markets and the cost of capital', in Nelson R. and Balassa B. (eds), *Economic Progress: Private Values and Public Policy (Essays in Honor of William Fellner)*, Amsterdam: North Holland, pp. 235–62.

Cobb C.W. and Douglas P.H. (1928), 'A theory of production', *American Economic Review*, **18**(1), 139–165.

Crotty J. (1992), 'Neoclassical and Keynesian approaches to the theory of investment', *Journal of Post Keynesian Economics*, **14**(4), 483–496.

Curtin R. (2019), *Consumer Expectations: Micro Foundations and Macro Impacts*, New York/Cambridge: Cambridge University Press.

Cyert R. and March J.G. (1992), *A Behavioral Theory of the Firm* (2nd ed.). Hoboken, NJ: Wiley-Blackwell.

Davidson P. (1991), 'Is probability theory relevant for uncertainty? A post Keynesian perspective', *Journal of Economic Perspectives*, **5**(1), 51–72.

de Grauwe P. (2011), 'Animal spirits and monetary policy', *Economic Theory*, **47**(2–3), 423–457.

de Grauwe P. (2012), 'Booms and busts in economic activity: A behavioural explanation', *Journal of Economic Behavior and Organization*, **83**(3), 484–501.

Dixit A.K. and Pindyck R.S. (1994), *Investment under Uncertainty*, Princeton: Princeton University Press.

Earl P. (1983), *The Economic Imagination: Towards a Behavioural Analysis of Choice*, New York: Sharpe.

Earl P. (2005), 'Economics and psychology in the twenty-first century', *Cambridge Journal of Economics*, **29**(6), 909–926.

Farmer R.E.A. and Guo J.-T. (1994), 'Real business cycles and the animal spirits hypothesis', *Journal of Economic Theory*, **63**, 42–73.

Felipe J. and Fisher F.M. (2008), 'Aggregation (production)', in Vernengo, M., Perez Caldentey, E. and Rosser Jr, B.J. (eds), *The New Palgrave Dictionary of Economics* (2nd ed.). London: Palgrave.

Felipe J. and McCombie J.S.L. (2013), *The Aggregate Production Function and the Measurement of Technical Change: 'Not Even Wrong'*, Cheltenham: Edward Elgar.

Fisher, F.M. (1987), 'Aggregation problem', *The New Palgrave: A Dictionary of Economics*, **1**, 53–55.

Fontana, G. and Gerrard B. (2004), 'A post Keynesian theory of decision-making under uncertainty', *Journal of Economic Psychology*, **25**(5), 619–637.

Gabaix X. (2020), 'A behavioral new Keynesian model', *American Economic Review*, **110**(8), 2271–2327.

Gerrard B. (1994), 'Beyond rational expectations: A constructive interpretation of Keynes's analysis of behaviour under uncertainty', *Economic Journal*, **104**(423), 327–337.

Gigerenzer G. and Brighton H. (2011), 'Homo heuristicus: Why biased minds make better inferences', in Gigerenzer G., Hertwig R. and Pachur T. (eds), *Heuristics: The Foundations of Adaptive Behavior*, Oxford/New York: Oxford University Press, pp. 107–143.

Gordon M.J. (1955), 'The payoff period and the rate of profit', *Journal of Business*, **28**(4), 253–260.

Harcourt G.C. (1965), 'The accountant in a golden age', *Oxford Economic Papers*, **17**(1), 66–80.

Harcourt G.C. (1968), 'Investment-decision criteria, investment incentives and the choice of technique', *Economic Journal*, **78**(309), 77–95.

Harcourt G.C. (1969), 'Some Cambridge controversies in the theory of capital', *Journal of Economic Literature*, **7**(2), 369–405.

Harcourt G.C. (1972), *Some Cambridge Controversies in the Theory of Capital*, Cambridge: Cambridge University Press.

Hayashi F. (1982), 'Tobin's marginal q and average q: A neoclassical interpretation', *Econometrica*, **50**(1), 213–224.

Heiner R.A. (1983), 'The origin of predictable behaviour', *American Economic Review*, **73**(4), 560–595.

Howitt P. (1997), 'Expectations and uncertainty in contemporary Keynesian models', in Harcourt G.C. and Riach P.A. (eds), *A 'Second Edition' of the General Theory*, London: Routledge, pp. 238–260.

Howitt P. and McAfee R.P. (1992), 'Animal spirits', *American Economic Review*, **82**(3), 493–507.

Jorgenson D.W. (1963), 'Capital theory and investment behaviour', *American Economic Review*, **53**(2), 247–259.

Kahneman D. and Tversky A. (1979), 'Prospect theory - an analysis of decision under risk', *Econometrica*, **47**(2), 263–292.

Kahneman D. and Tversky A. (1982), *Judgement under Uncertainty: Heuristics and Biases*, Cambridge: Cambridge University Press.

Katona G. (1946), 'Psychological analysis of business decisions and expectations', *American Economic Review*, **36**(1), 44–62.

Katona G. (1951), *Psychological Analysis of Economic Behavior*, New York: McGraw-Hill.

Keynes J.M. (1921), *A Treatise on Probability*, London: Macmillan/Royal Economic Society.

Keynes J.M. (1930), *A Treatise on Money*, London: Macmillan/Royal Economic Society.

Keynes J.M. (1936), *The General Theory of Employment, Interest and Money*, London: Macmillan/Royal Economic Society.

Keynes J.M. (1937), 'The general theory of employment', *Quarterly Journal of Economics*, **51**(2), 209–233.

Klein L.R. (1946), 'Macroeconomics and the theory of rational behaviour', *Econometrica*, **14**(2), 93–108.

Knight F.H. (1921), *Risk, Uncertainty and Profit*, Boston: Houghton Mifflin.

Laibson D. (1997), 'Golden eggs and hyperbolic discounting', *Quarterly Journal of Economics*, **112**, 443–478.

Laibson D., Repetto A. and Tobacman J. (2007), Estimating discount functions with consumption choices over the lifecycle, NBER Working Paper 13314, National Bureau of Economic Research.

Lawson T. (1995), 'Expectations and economics', in Dow S. and Hillard J. (eds), *Keynes, Uncertainty and Knowledge*, Cheltenham: Eldward Elgar, pp. 77–106.

Meeks J.G. (1991), 'Keynes on the rationality of decision procedures under uncertainty: The investment decision', in Meeks J.G. (ed), *Thoughtful Economic Man*, Cambridge: Cambridge University Press, pp. 126–144.

Muth J. (1961), 'Rational expectations and the theory of price movements', *Econometrica*, **29**(3), 315–335.

Pesaran M.H. (1990), 'Expectations in economics', Department of Applied Economics Working Paper No. 9016, Cambridge.
Peston M.H. (1959), 'A view of the aggregation problem', *Review of Economic Studies*, **27**(1), 58–64.
Pindyck R.S. (1991), 'Irreversibility, uncertainty and investment', *Journal of Economic Literature*, **29**(3), 1110–1148.
Sarnat M. and Levy H. (1969), 'The relationship of rules of thumb to the internal rate of return: A restatement and generalisation', *Journal of Finance*, **24**(3), 479–490.
Simon H.A. (1955), 'A behavioral model of rational choice', *Quarterly Journal of Economics* **69**(1), 99–118.
Simon H.A. (1979), 'From substantive to procedural rationality', in Hahn F. and Hollis M. (eds), *Philosophy and Economic Theory*, Oxford: Oxford University Press, pp. 65–86.
Strotz R.H. (1955), 'Myopia and inconsistency in dynamic utility maximisation', *Review of Economic Studies* **23**, 165–180.
Thaler R.H. (1985), 'Mental accounting and consumer choice', *Marketing Science*, **4**(3), 199–214.
Thaler R.H. (1990) 'Anomalies: Saving, fungibility, and mental accounts', *Journal of Economic Perspectives*, **4**(1), 193–205.
Todd P.M. and Gigerenzer G.E. (2012), *Ecological Rationality: Intelligence in the World*, New York/Oxford: Oxford University Press.
Topol R. (1991), 'Bubbles and volatility of stock prices: Effect of mimetic contagion', *Economic Journal*, **101**(407), 786–800.
Tversky A. and Kahneman D. (1974), 'Judgement under uncertainty: Heuristics & biases', *Science*, **185**, 1124–1131.
Tversky A. and Kahneman D. (1982), 'Judgements of and by representativeness', in Kahneman D. and Tversky A. (eds), *Judgement under Uncertainty: Heuristics and Biases*, Cambridge: Cambridge University Press, pp. 84–98.
Warner J.T. and Pleeter S. (2001), 'The personal discount rate: Evidence from military downsizing programs', *American Economic Review*, **91**(1), 33–53.
Wärneryd K.E. (1999), 'The role of macroeconomic psychology', *Applied Psychology*, **48**(3), 273–296.

8. The business cycle and the cycles of behavioural economics

Tobias F. Rötheli[1]

INTRODUCTION

This chapter offers insights into the economic fluctuations called the business cycle. In particular, I present an account of behavioural theorising of what underlies economic expansions and what causes them to end. Given the vast literature on business cycle theory and empirics, this chapter needs to be selective. Hence, the emphasis will be on the description of mechanisms and a comparison of theoretical explanations. By way of a historical point, it is important to note that business cycle analysis predates the field of macroeconomics. The 19th century, for example, was a period with regularly recurring booms followed by financial crises. These crises went together with insolvencies and high unemployment. The most pressing concern for the field of economics was to gain an understanding of the fluctuations in economic activity, particularly in view of the burdens of unemployment in the major industrialised economies of the time. Furthermore, industrial firms making major investments were eager to learn better ways to improve the timing of their decisions. Investing in a downturn could easily wipe out any enterprise.[2] Hence, both the social question and the profit motive fuelled the quest for insight into the drivers of economic boom and bust.

The present analysis follows a historical approach to develop an understanding of the issues. This method serves several purposes: first, we will encounter the emergence and re-emergence of concepts under new guises. This pertains in particular to the notion that an understanding of human behaviour – or psychology – should be helpful in explaining economic fluctuations. Second, it should become apparent that over time economic science has indeed progressed. Concepts have been refined, testing has become routine and new data have been gathered. The relevant new data typically come from surveys and from laboratory experiments. Third, a historical perspective shows that few if any views regarding behavioural factors affecting the cycle have been conclusively eliminated. But, arguably, this is a common feature in the history of economics: deficits and inconsistencies indeed weaken the validity of a theory. However, theoretical concepts have a way to come back as events, particularly economic crises, demand new answers.

Before getting started, it helps to have a rough idea of what the business cycle actually is. Samuelson gives a lower bound of a sensible understanding of the economic cycle (1988, p. 34): '[I]f you mean by a business cycle a periodic oscillation like the swing of a pendulum or the orbit of a planet, then in economics no business cycle ever did exist'. In line with much of the thinking of his time, Keynes suggested the following characterisation of the cycle which prepares us for the next section. He suggests that the essential characteristic of the (trade) cycle is (1936, p. 313) 'the regularity of time-sequence and of duration which justifies us in calling it a *cycle*'. Yet, today even the issues of time sequence and particularly duration are seen differently than in Keynes' time. In particular, the 20th century produced much less regular cycles than the 19th century. Just to fix ideas concerning the issue at hand, in the US since World War II the average (peak to peak) cycle is somewhat longer than six years.[3]

EARLY AND VERY EARLY CONTRIBUTIONS

A recurrence of financial crises and panics has generated a flow of analyses over the centuries. Clemens Juglar (1862), trained as a medical doctor, is often singled out as the first theorist of the financial or credit cycle. His was a clear conception of a sequence of events that led from a period with a (partially false) sense of prosperity to a period of overtrading with large increases in banks' credit supply, and finally to the inevitable crisis and a period of liquidation. In this process, human tendencies towards mania (in the upswing) and panic (as the crisis begins) played key roles. Yet, the disease metaphor was widely used before Juglar. The literature perceiving analogies between booms and crises with (mental) disease goes back at least as far as the 17th century. A very informative account of these early contributions is given by Besomi (2011). He details how 'diseases' of human excesses (the tendencies for mania and panic) were seen as amplified by contagion, multiplying individuals' failures of rational thinking. Further, the notion of the fever of speculation led some analysts to view the boom as the phase of disease while others saw the crisis as the diseased state.

EARLY 20TH-CENTURY CONTRIBUTIONS

Here, we start with the contribution of Arthur Cecil Pigou (1929). The key element of Pigou's and older approaches to studying economic tides is the desire to explain the course of an economy from the depth of the recession through the end of the boom as driven by a series of interlocking processes. This is not the same as the concept of an endogenous and perpetual business cycle that also has its supporters (Kalecki, 1933; Kaldor, 1940). The dynamics of interlocking processes instead need an initial impulse of one type or another to get started. Without the arrival of impulses (or shocks) coming from, e.g., technical inventions, monetary policy, natural resources or international trade or finance, the economic system would arguably follow a smooth growth path. Just a few years after Pigou's writing, Ragnar Frisch (1933) coined the term shock to capture this idea. In this perspective, shocks (impulses) working through the system by way of propagation mechanisms are seen to generate the cycle.

In Pigou's (1929) classic 'Industrial Fluctuations' published just before the onset of the great depression, he proposes an expectations-based account of the business cycle. An initial impulse (like an innovation) sparks expectations and leads to an expansion of production. As the expansion progresses, business people become over-optimistic, i.e., optimism is overdone. Importantly, undue optimism leads to over-investment (an over-accumulation of capital goods) and in time this process leads to frustrated profit expectations as expanded production capacity meets limited demand for final goods. Over-optimism is not corrected early on because it can take years for many investments to become profitable. Figure 8.1 illustrates the situation of a firm engaged in the production of a good with a lengthy production period. Here, the firm operates under the expectation of a high and rising return in the future. However, much time can pass before a discrepancy between expectations and facts arises. Eventually, though, a critical threshold of frustration regarding the return on investment is reached. Clearly, it does not much matter whether the long production type of good (typically a capital good) is produced for later sale on a spot market or whether it is ordered at a fixed price. In the latter case,

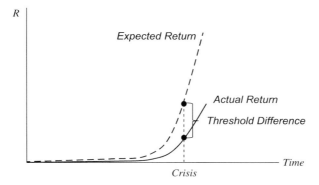

Figure 8.1   Error of optimism: long production lag

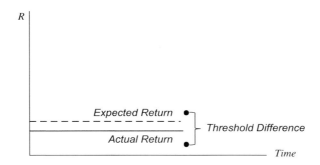

Figure 8.2   Error of optimism: short production lag

the firm ordering this type of good will eventually experience an error in its return expectations that surpasses its threshold. By contrast, Figure 8.2 shows the situation of an enterprise engaged in the production of a consumer good. This is a short production time type good. The producer holds a (per period) return expectation that systematically exceeds the expected return. However, period by period the error of optimism does not exceed a psychological threshold (return shortfall) that would trigger a crisis and a change in business planning and investments.[4]

The tech boom of the 1990s with its new ways of doing business and the related major investments offers an example. If financiers can be convinced to finance an entirely new way of doing business (e.g., the introduction of online sales of books by Amazon) they become willing to accept years with zero or even negative returns in the expectation of high rewards later. While some investments may merit this patience and optimism (as indeed Amazon's did), many projects started around the same time will experience the fate depicted in Figure 8.1.[5] Naturally, at a time when many long-term producers miss their expectations and curb their demand for goods, other types of producers (of the sort illustrated in Figure 8.2) will also be negatively affected and will curb production.

As the crisis occurs, presumably the process goes into reverse. In Pigou's words (1929, p. 85), 'the dying error of optimism gives birth to an error of pessimism'. Losses lead to liquidations and reductions of orders. Moreover, the thwarting of previously high expectations leads to a strong (indeed overly strong) recalibration of expectations. Production of goods, particularly of the long-lasting, long production time type, stalls. The stronger the drop in expectations, the sooner this error of pessimism is in turn detected and corrected. Some firms start to unexpectedly make money and thus expand operations again. It would appear that this mechanism has the potential to keep the cycle going on its own. However, as Pigou (1929) indicates (p. 42), 'with everything repeating itself regularly, rational beings would be bound to realise that this was happening, and so could not fall into error'. Keynes's (1936, chapter 22) perspective of the 'trade cycle' essentially follows Pigou's account with the addition of giving more detail to explaining variations in investment by fluctuations of the marginal efficiency of capital driven by sudden and violent changes in long-term expectations. However, Keynes's position as to what sparks a recession is tenuous (Rötheli, 2015). Even if long-term expectations are in fact precarious and unstable, and if expectations gyrations are behind stock prices movements (which affect the marginal efficiency of capital), we face the conundrum that, empirically, stock prices have little explanatory power for investment (Morck et al., 1990).[6]

Hence, there are several loose ends as to what, according to a behaviourally inspired theory, causes recessions. We will return to these issues when discussing more recent contributions about the financial cycle. As for the early phase of contributions, Haberler (1939) summarises the relevant views in economic science under the term 'inevitability of the cycle' (p. 83): 'The fact that oscillations are large is to be explained by the cumulative nature of the expansion and contraction process, which again is largely due to psychological reactions. Expansion creates optimism which stimulates investment and intensifies expansion. Contraction creates pessimism, which increases contraction'. Schumpeter (1939) puts the emphasis of his explanation of the business cycle on entrepreneurs who, with their visions for making money from technical innovations, ignite the cycle. Schumpeter's perspective which puts emphasis on single important actors may well be an underrated research topic with potential for behavioural economists (McCraw, 2007).

Before turning the page and describing the stage of mathematical modelling there is a point to be clarified. The phases of theorising described here cannot be neatly separated into historical epochs. Instead, the relevant developments overlap. A good example of this point is the business cycle analysis of Walter Jöhr. In a time already dominated by mathematical economics Jöhr (1952) proposed that social contagion among decision-makers (particularly entrepreneurs) make up the core process driving the business cycle. He based his notion mostly on intuition and his close acquaintance with business leaders.[7]

THE FIRST ROUND OF MATHEMATICAL EXPECTATIONS MODELLING

With respect to the mathematical and statistical analysis of business cycles, including the great depression, the contributions of Irving Fisher are central. In his debt-deflation theory of the depression (Fisher, 1933) he builds on his earlier work studying the link between inflation and interest rates, both nominal and real. He conceived of expectations as the weighted average of past observations. With respect to inflation expectations (his central concept), these past values were seen to reach as far back as two decades or more. With the obvious limitations of statistics of his time, Fisher was nevertheless able to contribute to the understanding of the determination of nominal and real interest rates in a number of countries. The contractionary force from deflation (in fact from declining inflation) stems partially from the slow adjustment of expectations and nominal interest rates. Accordingly, in such times real rates rise and debtors carry a higher burden paying interest.

The modelling of expectations continued with extrapolative views of expectations. Tinbergen (1940, p. 147) formulates it simply with 'the statement that expectations are, in my opinion, products of the human mind which are based on past experience, even though they relate to future moments'. Subsequent contributions that generalised modellers' notions of expectations came from Cagan (1956) and Nerlove (1958) on adaptive expectations. These models of expectations (heuristics because of their simplicity) would be the standard for modelling expectations in subsequent empirical work on macroeconomic relationships. An interesting feature of theory development in this early period of mathematical model building would later be repeated: models are first developed to explain cycles on agricultural markets before being generalised and applied to the question of economy-wide fluctuations. With these clarifications, the stage was set for the blossoming of macroeconometrics.

THE HEYDAY OF MACROECONOMETRICS

The project of macroeconometrics that built on Keynes's work has generated many important advances (Tinbergen, 1937; Koopmans, 1941; Klein, 1950). In particular, macroeconometric models clarify relationships of cause, effect and simultaneity and proceed to empirically estimate the relevant relationships. A parametrised model in this tradition typically has several dynamic relationships, e.g., the accelerator effect in the investment function. Further, and centrally important, effects from past variables on current outcomes are due to expectations or delayed responses.

To some observers, these models appear overly restrictive, e.g., in their typical linear structure. Yet, the discipline imposed by the need to make relationships explicit is a purifying exercise. It exposes some intuitively appealing behavioural ideas as circular. Also worth pointing out as a methodological advance is the approach of assessing the merits of so-called 'behavioural equations' in macroeconomic models. Behavioural equations are relationships between economic variables that are affected by human decisions and are not necessarily behavioural in the modern sense of the word.[8] These are relationships like the money demand function that go beyond mere accounting definitions. The test of the contribution of representing human decisions is to simulate the cyclical feature of the entire macroeconomic model by replacing the behavioural part with simple statistical projections of variables. Based on such an assessment it turns out that accounting identities alone can account for part of the cycle. However, the behavioural part of a (Keynesian) macroeconomic model adds significantly to track the business cycle (Adelman, 1960).

MEASURING EXPECTATIONS THROUGH SURVEYS

The macroeconometric movement sparked an important innovation in behavioural macroeconomics as regards expectations. This development is best introduced with the assessment of Katona and Klein (1952, p. 11):

> Two basic problems are involved in the theory of business cycles. (1) How do psychological variables influence economic decisions? (2) What is the process by which the psychological variables originate and are determined? Business cycle theory has certainly taken account of the first question

and has, in some measure, attempted to answer it. The second and more difficult question has largely been ignored.

It is this second question where surveys of expectations began to fill a gap. An early and very notable development here was initiated by George Katona (1946) who developed and organised the survey of consumers at the University of Michigan. Curtin (2019) gives a detailed account of the various economic variables surveyed over the years and the kind of studies that were made possible with these measures.[9]

A further important survey for studies related to business cycles is the survey of professional forecasters (Croushore and Stark, 2019). Surveys of expectations essentially serve two purposes. First, they measure up-to-date views of economic agents, particularly with a view to a real-time assessment of economic conditions. Second, the collected historical data can be used in econometric studies where expectations play a role. Part of this second point is the use of such data for testing models of expectations. A major drawback of survey data is their relatively short historical track record. Few surveys exist that go farther back than 40 or 50 years.[10] This severely limits the use of such measures in historical investigations.

THE SECOND ROUND OF EXPECTATIONS MODELLING: RATIONAL EXPECTATIONS

The 1960s saw one particularly important innovation in economic theory. John Muth (1961) introduced the concept of rational expectations. The rational expectations hypothesis proposes that people are able to use all relevant data in combination with economic theory and optimal statistical methods to form predictions. It took a decade for this revolutionary concept developed within the framework of a model of an agricultural market to influence macroeconomics and business cycle analysis (Lucas, 1972; Sargent, 1973). But when the change eventually came, it almost completely replaced earlier concepts of expectations. What could be held against the proposition that expectations should be guided by the same optimising principles that presumably guides all economic decisions? With respect to the explanations of the economic tides one thing is clear: if economic agents actually form rational expectations, then fluctuations cannot be the result of systematic expectations errors. According to a rational expectations view, people still make errors but not avoidable, i.e., systematic, errors. This tenet does not rule out that expectations errors can have effects that last for some time. However, it does rule out the sort of cycle that writers of earlier times saw at work.

Arguably, the implications on the nature of the cycle (or what appears to be a cycle) were not the key position of rational expectations business cycle theorists. Rather, the focus of attack pertained to the possibilities of economic policy (particular monetary policy) to smooth the economic cycle. Here, initial contributions held that monetary policy could be totally ineffective.[11] In contributions from the new Keynesian side (Akerlof and Yellen, 1985; Mankiw, 1985) these stark implications of rational expectations were corrected. These contributions in the Keynesian tradition, while strictly following rational expectations, made the point that actual prices might be sluggish because small and frequent adjustments do not pay off for producers. Furthermore, the tendency of labour to base wage demands on a comparison with wages of the cohort of workers that recently set their wages tends to generate sluggishness in wages (Taylor, 1979).

Challenges to rational expectations also came from the empirical front where studies rejected rational expectations again and again (for a survey see Rötheli, 2020). Besides empirical evidence, it was the fundamental critique from cognitive psychology that changed the tide against rational expectations. It was Herbert Simon (1978) who laid the groundwork pointing out that people have limited cognitive abilities and that decisions are guided by procedurally rational as opposed to substantively rational decisions. Furthermore, Daniel Kahneman (2003) identified the roles of System 1 (fast and automatic) and System 2 (analytic and slow) in information processing and decision-making. In everyday routine situations System 1 controls behaviour. Thus, in normal times, simple routines actually guide human anticipation.

For sure, the criticism aimed at rational expectations has not stopped the use of this concept. The idea is simply too appealing analytically and fits perfectly into the modern perspective of economic agents as sophisticated intertemporal optimisers. An additional toolbox for business cycle theory from the rational expectations side is the concept of 'sunspots'. A modern interpretation of the term sunspots describes a variable outside the economic system which helps people to coordinate their expectations.[12] Importantly, this variable has no effect on economic activity other than helping the public to choose expectations in a situation where there are many rational expectations equilibria. Hence, according to theory, changes in the sunspot variable induce people to adjust to a new equilibrium which implies a shift in economic activity. This is an extreme form of (self-fulfilling) expectations driving the business cycle. With this concept, the field cycles back to beliefs fashionable in the 1920s. Notably, the notion of animal spirits has not been supported by empirical evidence at the level of the individual. Hence, sunspots in the modern form are simply the deus ex machina of rational expectations theorists.

A more general argument about multiple macroeconomic equilibria related to expectations can be made in the framework of the Keynesian cross familiar from undergraduate textbooks. Figure 8.3 conveys the idea: investment demand as part of aggregate demand Z is a (possibly linear) rising function of expected income. Expected income, in turn, is a non-linear rising

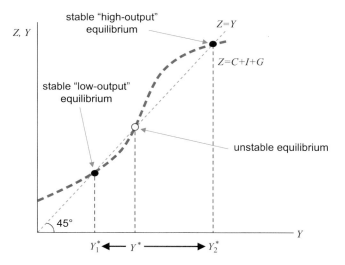

Figure 8.3   *Multiple expectations equilibria*

function of actual income.[13] Accordingly, aggregate demand can repeatedly intersect with aggregate supply (i.e., the 45-degree line). In the display, there are three such equilibria. As it turns out, two of these equilibria are stable and one (the middle one) is unstable. Hence, if income expectations are high (low), investment is elevated (depressed) and the economy operates at a high (low) output level. It is unlikely (but possible) that some of these equilibria are self-fulfilling in terms of expectations and thus rational expectation equilibria. The graphical analysis is also effective in clarifying a further interesting notion, i.e., the idea that good times (the high income equilibrium, Y_2^*) may be resilient to negative shocks as long as these shocks are not too large (i.e., do not temporarily reduce income below Y^*). Further along these lines, a relatively small positive shock may be sufficient to pull the economy out of a recession, i.e., upward from Y_1^*.

A very notable point about the period of theorising from the 1960s through the 1990s is the scant attention to the idea of a recurrent sequence of events that guides events from the upswing through to the downswing and crisis. In this sense the business cycle rested, if it was not altogether dead, as some claimed it to be in practical terms. This view was objected to by historically astute professional observers (Zarnowitz, 1998). In terms of theorising, it took the bursting of the tech bubble in 1999 and financial markets crashing in 2007 to turn the tide towards the notion of a cycle once again.

CREDIT BOOMS, BUBBLES AND THE RETURN OF THE CYCLE

As reported before, excesses of credit were an essential part of early accounts of economic cycles. With the program of macroeconometrics augmented by rational expectations in full bloom, this sort of analysis heeded little attention. By contrast, among financial historians, the idea of the credit cycle with its elements of mania, panic, and crash had never gone out of fashion (Kindleberger, 1978). Here, the stages of euphoria, lending excesses and eventually a financial crisis going together with large losses of banks on their credit portfolios were the elements of the financial cycle. In the field of economic theory, Hyman Minsky was a lonely voice who argued that times of prosperity lay the seeds for crises. Minsky (1964) described a tendency towards a growing instability of the financial system on the upswing. As household debts rise relative to income, as prices of stocks and real estate surge and liquidity declines, the system becomes increasingly susceptible to possible downturns in income. This analysis was mostly geared at explaining severe recessions. Yet, the tech boom of the 1990s, and even more so the financial crisis that broke out in 2007, led to a revival of Minsky's ideas.

The financial crisis also led to an updated account of Kindleberger's explanations of financial crises in the analysis of Reinhart and Rogoff (2009). Under the title 'This time is different', these authors propose that banks' and investors' mistaken beliefs cause excesses in return expectations and risk tolerance despite grim historical warnings. Likewise, Eichengreen and Mitchener (2004) and Rötheli (2013) are among the contributions that see the Great Depression as the result of credit expansion misguided by overconfidence in the 1920s. Empirical regularities concerning bank behaviour and credit cycle were already documented by Asea and Blomberg (1998). Nofsinger (2012) in turn showed how extrapolation bias, groupthink and changing social norms spur the boom in lending. The strong buildup of debt in turn magnifies the bust that typically follows the boom phase.

In terms of the psychological mechanism involved with the buildup of credit booms, several contributions revolve around the notion of forgetting previous losses. According to Berger and Udell (2004), the institutional memory of banks gradually diminishes recollections of credit defaults from earlier times of distress. In Rötheli (2012), this process of learning and unlearning is made explicit in a Markov switching model of the business cycle. Even if bank management responsible for credit decisions formed expectations about states of the economy (with high and low default probabilities) in a Bayesian manner, this probability updating would only be fully rational if decision-makers incorporated all of the historical data available. If bankers' assessments are instead based on a limited window of professional experience, views of default risk over the course of the expansion will by necessity turn over-optimistic as they turn over-pessimistic as the recession drags on. Strengthening the effect of banks' near-sightedness are tendencies of consumers to indulge in debt-driven consumption (Mian and Sufi, 2018). These behavioural elements are actually strong and systematic enough to make financial crises at least partially predictable (Greenwood et al., 2020).

Similarly to the excessive ups and downs in lending and debt, analysts have pointed to systematic movements in valuations of stocks and real estate that are not explainable by rational decision-making. The term 'bubble' came to be used to describe such developments.[14] With their accounts of historic housing bubbles, particularly the episode of the early 2000s (Case and Shiller, 2003; Mayer, 2011; Shiller, 2014; Lambertini et al., 2017) and stock price bubbles (Shiller, 2014), researchers once more concluded that human tendencies for exaggerations induce a dynamic path from optimism to crash. Here, the evidence against the efficiency of capital markets amassed by the field of behavioural finance (Thaler, 2016) is critical. In fact, these inefficiencies challenge the position that market economies move on efficient trajectories steered by rational investors who decide on the use of society's savings.

It is only logical that with the return of the notion of cycles, there were also other elements from earlier analyses that resurfaced. In this vein, the concept of 'animal spirits' saw a renewal. Introduced by Keynes (1936), animal spirits refer to motivational factors that spur activity. In a state where the future is very uncertain, a spontaneous urge for action might arise that is not based on rational thought. By contrast, with animal spirits dimmed, entrepreneurs fail to take action even if the objectively same conditions rule that otherwise would go with positive action. It is a short way from this idea to developing the notion that cognitive and emotional factors and forces unexplained by economic (or other measurable) variables drive the ups and downs of economic activity. Shortly after the financial crisis Akerlof and Shiller (2009) suggested this sort of perspective. While reviewing much experimental work the two authors failed to develop a coherent concept that could match the theoretical rigour established in the field of behavioural economics. Animal spirits became a catch-all for everything mainstream economics presumably had failed to incorporate – failures, too, that were understood to explain why economists had not been able to foresee the financial crisis.

Other writers took the concept of animal spirits in different directions to suit their inclinations. De Grauwe (2012) built on his earlier work and conceived of animal spirits as time-varying expectations where agents would switch between variants of forecast heuristics according to their relative forecast performance.[15] Simulated versions of such models succeed in generating cyclical characteristics that mimic actual economies. Yet, no computable model for historical expectations based on this approach was presented, and the conception of agents as simultaneously tracking the success and failure of various forecast models is not grounded in psychological research concerning how humans use their limited cognitive resources.

Notions inspired by the concept of animal spirits had their followers even before the financial crisis. These earlier efforts resulted in studies that are only loosely connected to formal economic theory. This work typically applies data from consumer surveys. The key concept here is 'confidence' constructed as an index of responses to several questions (like the prospect of employment). Empirical research has reported mixed evidence regarding the question of whether such an index can systematically explain variables like consumer spending (Ludvigson, 2004).[16] A further, and rather different, form of cyclical tendency comes from the side of policy. Monetary policy in particular shows a short-sighted tendency to engage in go-stop type dynamics. Frequently, central banks pursue low interest rate policies in order to pull their economy out of a recession but then continue to keep the interest low for too long. This causes inflation to rise and thus, eventually, policy has to break the inflationary cycle with contractionary measures. This once more leads the economy into recession. The generalised version of this sort of cycle is the subject of the "political business cycle" literature (Nordhaus et al., 1989).

THE THIRD ROUND OF EXPECTATIONS MODELLING: NEW IDEAS ON EXTRAPOLATION

Even among the adherents of optimisation as the overarching principle of economic behaviour, rational expectations of the Muthian type lost devotees in the aftermath of the tech boom of the 1990s. In response, several modified versions of rational expectations emerged. They all describe expectations formation as a routine behaviour without explicitly referring to Kahneman's concepts. In Sims' (2003) account, there is a notion of rational inattention, and in Carrol's (2003) version, people presumably follow a slow updating of their expectations to professional forecasters' views. So let us turn to entries in the competition of ideas concerning economic expectations that are more closely linked to psychological work.

In these new contributions the process of extrapolation – the basis of earlier mathematical expectations models – again became the focus of attention. Increasingly, researchers became convinced that the rational expectations revolution had thrown the baby out with the bath water. Yes, the early models of extrapolative or adaptive expectations have shortcomings. However, these problems can be fixed. A starting point for new models of extrapolative expectations is the accumulated experimental work on the subject.[17] Several key points stand out in these empirical findings. For one, it is the recent past of a time series that people rely on when forming expectations. Typically, decision-makers rely on just a few (three or four) past observations to assess the future of a series. Hence, Fisher's (1930) notion of experiences 20 years and older influencing extrapolation does not square with the data. Further, extrapolation is not well captured by a simple linear extension of recent experiences. Studies based on surveys of expectations suggest similar elements. Gennaioli et al. (2016) investigate the expectations of chief financial officers and find them based on past information. Such expectations concerning firms' profits then explain firms' investment decisions.

The new versions of extrapolative expectations come in several variants: there is the concept of naturalistic expectations suggested by Fuster et al. (2010), diagnostic expectations developed by Bordalo et al. (2018) and pattern-based expectations proposed by Rötheli (1998, 2020). All of them have the advantage, at least in principle, of being computable and thus useful in time series analyses. This is of key importance for much of the empirical work in macroeconomics. Importantly, with the improved understanding of the determinants of expectations, the notion that inexplicable variations in expectations (of the animal spirit type) are important drivers of economic activity is losing support.

CONCLUSIONS

As this survey documents, there is a long history of contributions of behavioural thoughts to the analysis of business cycles. Interestingly, concepts like human excesses tend to resurface in different forms. As an example consider the description of mental states in booms. This changes historically from 'mania' to 'over-optimism', and more recently, to 'cognitive heuristics'. Hence, the course of research shows more layers than just the cycle of scientific progress described by Thomas Kuhn (1962). According to Kuhn's perspective, a theory goes through a cycle that is somewhat similar to the cycle of a new consumer product: it arises as a challenge to something that already exists, may have a hard time overcoming rigidities, but will eventually become the ruling paradigm. By contrast, the history of business cycle research and the history of related behavioural ideas suggest an additional and longer cycle. Many of the relevant ideas have been around for a very long time. Some of these ideas are intuitively appealing but hard to put into a coherent theoretical framework. Others are still in a slow process of development. Collectively, they remain in the reservoir of potentially useful concepts.

The text of this chapter should have made clear that the just described cycle actually generates distinct insights and not merely old wine in new bottles. Admittedly, this process is sluggish and replete with confusion and sometimes even delusion. A critical bottleneck inhibiting or slowing progress, I would claim, is the interplay of economics and psychology. An example here is the use of cognitive psychology in the formulation of economic theories of expectations and risk. Too much work, even of the behaviourally oriented type, continues in the armchair approach described by Simon and Bartel (1986, p. 20):

> [I]n order to move from the economist's substantive rationality to the psychologist's procedural rationality requires a major extension in the empirical foundations of economics. Economists will have to observe decision-makers in the actual process of making decisions in the real world or in laboratory experiments, or study the actors' beliefs, their expectations and their methods of calculation and reasoning.[18]

It is also apparent that psychology does not produce concepts that are tailor-made for use by economists. Rather it is a difficult and time-consuming process to shape psychological insights for the modelling requirements of macroeconomists.

So, where are the cycles of economic activity and economic theorising going? The safest bet is, they will both continue. Still, I would be willing to take the riskier bet that the amplitude at least of the scientific cycle will decline. Science, after all, does show progress and what we call mainstream theory over time incorporates ideas that initially seem hard to formalise and test. Nevertheless, over time, clarifying elements regarding human decision-making have enriched analysis. Hence, business cycle theory always was and will continue to be behavioural economics.

NOTES

1. I would like to thank Michelle Baddeley, Jannick Plaasch and Matthias Priester for helpful comments.
2. Rötheli (2007) gives a historical account of the interplay of analysis and practice in the development of business cycle theories.

3. Zarnowitz (1985) and Claessens et al. (2009) give a more detailed empirical description of the business cycle drawing on US and international data, and Shapiro and Watson (1988) provide an eclectic account of sources of the business cycle. Longer cycles of around 50 years of length have been discussed in the literature (see Kondratieff and Stolper, 1935). Sterman (1985) has proposed a behavioural explanation of this Kondratieff cycle.
4. 'Thresholds' and 'triggers' were not explicit elements in the analysis of the time.
5. McCarthy (2004) documents the excesses of investment in the tech boom of the 1990s.
6. In fact, a more plausible explanation of revisions of expectations in line with the thinking of Keynes's times would draw on ideas as exposed in Figures 8.1 and 8.2 of this chapter.
7. At a later stage of theorising agent-based modellers found new ways of making use of this sort of concept (Lux, 2008). Yet, the evidence for this approach is tentative. While parameters of a contagion process can be estimated from aggregated data, the evidence on the level of decision-makers is lacking. Clearly, the notion of a contagion of views (as opposed to the more familiar interdependencies among businesses) could be tested with survey data. Yet, to my knowledge, no evidence has been presented that firms that are close together (geographically or product-wise) tend to affect their neighbours' expectations more strongly than does other information.
8. 'Behavioural' in the modern sense of the word typically refers to the modelling of deviations from substantive rationality in the sense of Simon (1976).
9. Manski (2004) describes the range of theoretical questions that can be addressed with expectations survey data and possible extensions of the survey method.
10. One survey that goes back somewhat farther was initiated in 1946 by Joseph Livingston, who was a columnist at the *Philadelphia Inquirer*. His survey is continued by the Federal Reserve Bank of Philadelphia under www.philadelphiafed.org/surveys-and-data/real-time-data-research/livingston-historical-data.
11. The so-called policy ineffectiveness proposition has been made in various forms. One important contribution is from Sargent and Wallace (1975). It is worth mentioning here that the first generation of rational expectations models tended to emphasise a different point. Many of them were in a classical tradition and critical of the Keynesian approach particularly as regards the notion of sticky prices and wages.
12. In an older perspective sun spot activity was claimed to drive the business cycles based on the possibly relevant notion that sun activity affects earth's temperature and thus harvests (Jevons, 1878; Gallegati and Mignacca, 1994).
13. The depicted demand function in Figure 8.3, in particular, can be derived from an S-shaped function for expected income depending on actual income. Hence, at a low income level, an increase in income raises expected income less than proportionally. This is followed by a middle range of income where expectations rise over-proportionally. At a high level of income, once again, expected income increases less than one-to-one with an increase in income.
14. Hence, the present use of the term bubble does not include the sort of rational expectations bubble solution described, e.g., by Blanchard (1979).
15. A related analysis is presented in Jaimovich and Rebelo (2007) where a combination of rational and optimistic agents gives rise to cycles.
16. Ilut and Schneider (2014) show how this can be brought into a model frame building on Knightian uncertainty.
17. The relevant experimental work comes from psychology and economics (Tversky and Kahneman, 1973; Wagenaar and Timmers, 1979; Harvey et al., 1994; Oskarsson and Hastie, 2009; Rötheli, 1998, 2011; Roos and Schmidt, 2011).
18. This attitude is also responsible for the systematic neglect of economic theorists to take notice of the growing field of business forecasting when formulating theories of the cycle in the early decades of the 20th century (Rötheli, 2007).

REFERENCES

Adelman, I. (1960), 'Business Cycles-Endogenous or Stochastic?', *Economic Journal*, **70** (280), 783–796.
Akerlof, G. A. and J. L. Yellen (1985), 'A Near-Rational Model of the Business Cycle, With Wage and Price Inertia', *Quarterly Journal of Economics*, **100** (Supplement), 823–838.

Akerlof, George A. and R. Shiller (2009), *Animal Spirits: How Human Psychology Drives the Economy, and Why It Matters for Global Capitalism*, Princeton, Princeton University Press.
Asea, P. K. and B. S. Blomberg (1998), 'Lending Cycles', *Journal of Econometrics*, **83** (1–2), 89–128.
Berger, A. N. and G. F. Udell (2004), 'The Institutional Memory Hypothesis and the Procyclicality of Bank Lending Behavior', *Journal of Financial Intermediation*, **13** (4), 458–495.
Besomi, D. (2011), 'Disease of the Body Politick. A Metaphor for Crises in the History of Nineteenth Century Economics', *Journal of the History of Economic Thought*, **33** (1), 67–118.
Blanchard, O. (1979), 'Speculative Bubbles, Crashes, and Rational Expectations', *Economic Letters*, **3** (4), 387–389.
Bordalo, P., Gennaioli, N., and A. Shleifer (2018), 'Diagnostic Expectations and Credit Cycles', *Journal of Finance*, **73** (1), 199–227.
Cagan, P. (1956), 'The Monetary Dynamics of Hyper-Inflation', in M. Friedman (ed.), *Studies in the Quantity Theory of Money*, Chicago, University of Chicago Press, pp. 25–117.
Carroll, C. D. (2003), 'Macroeconomic Expectations of Households and Professional Forecasters', *Quarterly Journal of Economics*, **118** (1), 269–298.
Case, K. E. and R. J. Shiller (2003), 'Is There a Bubble in the Housing Market?', *Brookings Papers on Economic Activity*, **2**, 299–342.
Claessens, S., Kose, M. A., and M. E. Terrones (2009), 'What Happens during Recessions, Crunches and Busts?', *Economic Policy*, **24** (60), 653–700.
Croushore, D. and T. Stark (2019), 'Fifty Years of the Survey of Professional Forecasters', *Economic Insights*, **4** (4), 1–11.
Curtin, Richard T. (2019), *Consumer Expectations: Micro Foundations and Macro Impact*, Cambridge, Cambridge University Press.
De Grauwe, P. (2012), *Lectures on Behavioral Macroeconomics*, Princeton, Princeton University Press.
Eichengreen, B. and K. Mitchener (2004), 'The Great Depression as a Credit Boom Gone Wrong', *Research in Economic History*, **22**, 183–237.
Fisher, I. (1930), *The Theory of Interest*, New York, Macmillan.
Fisher, I. (1933), 'The Debt-Deflation Theory of Great Depressions', *Econometrica*, **1** (4), 337–357.
Frisch, R. (1933), 'Propagation Problems and Impulse Problems in Dynamic Economics', in K. Koch (ed.), *Economic Essays in Honour of Gustav Cassel*, London, Allen & Unwin, pp. 171–205.
Fuster, A., Laibson, D., and B. Mendel (2010), 'Natural Expectations and Macroeconomic Fluctuations', *Journal of Economic Perspectives*, **24** (4), 67–84.
Gallegati, M. and D. Mignacca (1994), 'Jevons, Sunspot Theory and Economic Fluctuations', *History of Economic Ideas*, **2** (2), 23–40.
Gennaioli, N., Ma, Y., and A. Shleifer (2016), 'Expectations and Investment', *NBER Macroeconomics Annual*, **30**, 379–442.
Greenwood, Robin M., Hanson, Samuel G., Shleifer, A., and J. Sørensen (2020), Predictable Financial Crises, NBER Working Paper No. w27396.
Haberler, G. (1939), *Prosperity and Depression: A Theoretical Analysis of Cyclical Movements*, Lake Success, League of Nations.
Harvey, N., Fergus, B., and A. McClelland (1994), 'On the Nature of Expectations', *British Journal of Psychology*, **85** (2), 203–229.
Ilut, C. L. and M. Schneider (2014), 'Ambiguous Business Cycles', *American Economic Review*, **104** (8), 2368–2399.
Jaimovich, N. and S. Rebelo (2007), 'Behavioral Theories of the Business Cycle', *Journal of the European Economic Association*, **5** (2–3), 361–368.
Jevons, William S. (1878), 'Commercial Crises and Sunspots', in Jevons, William S. (ed.) (1884), *Investigations in Currency and Finance*, ed. By H. S. Foxwell, London, Macmillan.
Jöhr, Walter A. (1952), *Die Konjunkturschwankungen: Theoretische Gundlagen der Wirtschaftspolitik*, Bd. II, Tübingen, J. C. B. Mohr.
Juglar, C. (1862), *Des Crises Commerciales et de Leur Retour Périodique*, Paris, Guillaume et Cie.
Kaldor, N. (1940), 'A Model of the Trade Cycle', *Economic Journal*, 78–92. Reprinted in Kaldor, N. (ed.) (1960), *Essays on Economic Stability and Growth*, New York, Holmes and Meier Publishers, Inc., pp. 177–192.
Kahneman, D. (2003), 'Maps of Bounded Rationality: Psychology for Behavioral Economics', *American Economic Review*, **93** (5), 1449–1475.

Kalecki, M. (1933), 'Próba Teorii Koniunktury', ISBCP, Warsaw, translated as 'Essay on the Business Cycle Theory', in Osiatyński, Jerzy (ed.) (1990), *Collected Works of Michał Kalecki*, Volume I, Capitalism: Business Cycles and Full Employment, Oxford, Clarendon Press.

Katona, G. (1946), 'Psychological Analysis of Business Decisions and Expectations', *American Economic Review*, **36** (1), 44–62.

Katona, G. and L. R. Klein (1952), 'Psychological Data in Business Cycle Research', *American Journal of Economics and Sociology*, **12** (1), 11–22.

Keynes, John M. (1936), *The General Theory of Employment, Interest and Money*, Cambridge, Macmillan.

Kindleberger, C. (1978), *Manias, Panics, and Crashes: A History of Financial Crises*, New York, Basis Books.

Klein, Lawrence R. (1950), *Economic Fluctuations in the United States 1921-1941*, New York, John Wiley & Sons.

Kondratieff, N. D. and W. F. Stolper (1935), 'The Long Waves in Economic Life', *Review of Economics and Statistics*, **17** (6), 105–115.

Koopmans, T. (1941), 'The Logic of Econometric Business-Cycle Research', *Journal of Political Economy*, **49** (2), 157–181.

Kuhn, Thomas S. (1962), *The Structure of Scientific Revolutions*, Chicago, University of Chicago Press.

Lambertini, L., Mendicino, C., and M. T. Punzi (2017), 'Expectations-Driven Cycles in the Housing Market', *Economic Modelling*, **60** (C), 297–312.

Lucas, R. E., Jr. (1972), 'Expectations and the Neutrality of Money', *Journal of Economic Theory*, **4** (2), 103–124.

Ludvigson, S. C. (2004), 'Consumer Confidence and Consumer Spending', *Journal of Economic Perspectives*, **18** (2), 29–50.

Lux, T. (2008), 'Rational Forecasts or Social Opinion Dynamics? Identification of Interaction Effects in a Business Climate Survey', *Journal of Economic Behavior and Organization*, **72** (2), 638–655.

Mankiw, G. N. (1985), 'Small Menu Costs and Large Business Cycles: A Macroeconomic Model of Monopoly', *Quarterly Journal of Economics*, **100** (2), 529–538.

Manski, C. F. (2004), 'Measuring Expectations', *Econometrica*, **72** (5), 1329–1376.

Mayer, C. (2011), 'Housing Bubbles: A Survey', *Annual Review of Economics*, **3**, 559–568.

McCarthy, J. (2004), 'What Investment Patterns across Equipment and Industries Tell Us about the Recent Investment Boom and Bust', Current Issues in *Economics and Finance, Federal Reserve Bank of New York*, **10** (6), 1–7.

McCraw, Thomas K. (2007), 'Business Cycles, Business History', in *Prophet of Innovation*, Cambridge, Harvard University Press, pp. 251–278.

Mian, A. and A. Sufi (2018), 'Finance and Business Cycles: The Credit-Driven Household Demand Channel', *Journal of Economic Perspectives*, **32** (3), 31–58.

Minsky, H. P. (1964), 'Longer Waves in Financial Relations: Financial Factors in the More Severe Depressions', *American Economic Review*, **54** (3), 324–335.

Morck, R., Shleifer, A., and R. W. Vishny (1990), 'The Stock Market and Investment: Is the Market a Sideshow?', *Brookings Papers on Economic Activity*, 2, 157–202.

Muth, J. F. (1961), 'Rational Expectations and the Theory of Price Movements', *Econometrica*, **29** (3), 315–335.

Nerlove, M. (1958), 'Adaptive Expectations and Cobweb Phenomena', *Quarterly Journal of Economics*, **72** (2), 227–240.

Nofsinger, J. R. (2012), 'Household Behavior and Boom/Bust Cycles', *Journal of Financial Stability*, **8** (3), 161–173.

Nordhaus, W. D., Alesina, A., and C. L. Schultze (1989), 'Alternative Approaches to the Political Business Cycle', *Brookings Papers on Economic Activity*, **2**, 1–68.

Oskarsson, Van B. and R. Hastie (2009), 'What's Next? Judging Sequences of Binary Events', *Psychological Bulletin*, **135** (2), 262–285.

Pigou, Arthur C. (1929), *Industrial Fluctuations*, London, Macmillan.

Reinhart, Carmen M. and K. Rogoff (2009), *This Time Is Different: Eight Centuries of Financial Folly*, Princeton, Princeton University Press.

Roos, M. W. and U. Schmidt (2011), 'The Importance of Time-Series Extrapolation for Macroeconomic Expectation', *German Economic Review*, **13** (2), 196–210.

Rötheli, T. F. (1998), 'Pattern Recognition and Procedurally Rational Expectations', *Journal of Economic Behavior and Organization*, **37** (1), 71–90.
Rötheli, T. F. (2007), 'Business Forecasting and the Development of Business Cycle Theory', *History of Political Economy*, **39** (3), 481–510.
Rötheli, T. F. (2011), 'Pattern-Based Expectations: International Experimental Evidence and Applications in Financial Economics', *Review of Economics and Statistics*, **93** (4), 1319–1330.
Rötheli, T. F. (2012), 'Boundedly Rational Banks' Contribution to the Credit Cycle', *Journal of Socio-Economics*, **41** (5), 730–737.
Rötheli, T. F. (2013), 'Innovations in Banking Practices and the Credit Boom of the 1920s', *Business History Review*, **87** (2), 309–327.
Rötheli, T. F. (2015), 'Sudden and Violent Changes in Long-Term Expectations: Keynes and Reality', in H. Peukert (ed.), *Taking up the Challenge*, Festschrift for Jürgen Backhaus, Marburg, Metropolis-Verlag, pp. 141–156.
Rötheli, T. F. (2020), *The Behavioral Economics of Inflation Expectations: Macroeconomics Meets Psychology*. Cambridge, Cambridge University Press.
Samuelson, P. (1998), 'Summing Up on Business Cycles: Opening Address', in J. C. Fuhrer and S. Schuh (eds), *Beyond Shocks: What Causes Business Cycles?*, Federal Reserve Bank of Boston Conference Series, no. 42. Boston, Federal Reserve Bank of Boston, pp. 33–36.
Sargent, T. J. (1973), 'Interest Rates and Prices in the Long Run: A Study of the Gibson Paradox', *Journal of Money, Credit and Banking*, **5** (1), 385–449.
Sargent, T. J. and N. Wallace (1975), '"Rational" Expectations, the Optimal Monetary Instrument, and the Optimal Money Supply Rule', *Journal of Political Economy*, **83** (2), 241–254.
Schumpeter, Joseph A. (1939), *Business Cycles: A Theoretical, Historical, and Statistical Analysis of the Capitalist Process*, New York, McGraw-Hill.
Shapiro, M. D. and M. W. Watson (1988), 'Sources of Business Cycle Fluctuations', *NBER Macroeconomics Annual*, **3**, 1–148.
Shiller, R. J. (2014), 'Speculative Asset Prices', *American Economic Review*, **104** (6), 1486–1517.
Simon, H. A. (1976), 'From Substantive to Procedural Rationality', in S. Latsis (ed.), *Method and Appraisal in Economics*, Cambridge, Cambridge University Press, pp. 129–148.
Simon, H. A. (1978), 'Rationality as Process and as Product of Thought', *American Economic Review*, **68** (2), 1–16.
Simon, H. A. and R. D. Bartel (1986), 'The Failure of Armchair Economics', *Challenge*, **29** (5), 18–25.
Sims, C. A. (2003), 'Implications of Rational Inattention', *Journal of Monetary Economics*, **50** (3), 665–690.
Sterman, John D. (1985), 'A Behavioral Model of The Economic Long Wave', *Journal of Economic Behavior and Organization*, **6** (1), 17–53.
Taylor, J. B. (1979), 'Staggered Wage Setting in a Marco Model', *American Economic Review*, **69** (2), 108–113.
Thaler, R. H. (2016), 'Behavioral Economics: Past, Present, and Future', *American Economic Review*, **106** (7), 1577–1600.
Tinbergen, J. (1937), *An Econometric Approach to Business Cycle Problems*, Paris, Hermann et Company.
Tinbergen, J. (1940), 'On a Method of Statistical Business-Cycle Research. A Reply', *Economic Journal*, **50** (197), 141–154.
Tversky, A. and D. Kahneman (1983), 'Extensional versus Intuitive Reasoning: The Conjunction Fallacy in Probability Judgment', *Psychological Review*, **90**, 293–315.
Tversky, A. and D. Kahneman (1973), 'Availability: A Heuristic for Judging Frequency and Probability', *Cognitive Psychology*, **5** (2), 207–232.
Wagenaar, W. A. and H. Timmers (1979), 'The Pond-and-Duckweed Problem: Three Experiments on the Misperception of Exponential Growth', *Acta Psychologica*, **43** (3), 239–251.
Zarnowitz, V. (1985), 'Recent Work on Business Cycles in Historical Perspective: A Review of Theories and Evidence', *Journal of Economic Literature*, **23** (2), 523–580.
Zarnowitz, V. (1998), 'Has the Business Cycle Been Abolished?', *Business Economics*, **33** (4), 39–45.

PART IV

BEHAVIOURAL LABOUR ECONOMICS AND THE THEORY OF THE FIRM

9. Behavioural labour economics
Morris Altman[1]

INTRODUCTION

In this chapter, I elaborate on the contributions of behavioural economics to better understand how labour markets function, to the improved modelling of labour markets and, relatedly, to public policy. I pay special attention to alternatives to the standard model, where labour supply is a function of the wage rate and income, to a focus on labour supply determination as a function of an individual's target income.[2]

I also discuss the theoretical and policy implications of modelling the reality of boundedly rational individuals who have limited information processing capabilities and make decisions in a world of complex, costly and asymmetric information. Decisions are also affected by institutional parameters, norms, social context and past behaviour (path dependency). This can result in errors in labour market decisions, generating outcomes that are inefficient from both the individual's and society's perspective.[3]

From a nuanced behavioural economics perspective, the labour market is a social institution, a view promoted by Solow (1990). Behavioural economics enriches the standard demand and supply analysis of the labour market. From this perspective, the slopes and positions of the demand and supply curves are impacted by psychological, sociological and institutional variables, as they are in real-world labour markets, as well as by prices and income.

BEHAVIOURAL LABOUR ECONOMICS

Following in the tradition of Hebert Simon, behavioural labour economics builds models based upon more realistic simplifying behavioural assumptions by integrating insights from psychology, sociology and institutional analyses. These can be expected to generate more robust descriptions of labour market behaviour and more accurate analytical predictions and credible cause-and-effect analyses.

These assumptions are based on the reality of the brain as a scarce resource, with limited processing capabilities (bounded rationality), imperfect and asymmetric information, heterogeneous decision-makers, transaction costs, the importance of social norms for decision-making, effort variability and the significance of institutional parameters affecting the decision-making process, inclusive of bargaining power. This enriches the price and income focus of traditional economics (Akerlof 1982, 1984, 2002; Altman 2005, 2006, 2008a; Berg 2006; Gigerenzer 2007; on complex information, see Hayak 1945; Kahneman 2011; March 1978; Simon 1955, 1978, 1979, 1987; Smith 2003; Todd and Gigerenzer 2003).

Behavioural labour economics is influenced by two different but overlapping approaches to behavioural economics. One approach, pioneered by Daniel Kahneman and Amos Tversky (Kahneman and Tversky 1979; Kahneman 2003, 2011; and Tversky and Kahneman 1981, 1986), assumes that individuals tend to be error-prone and biased in decision-making because of how the brain is hardwired. This generates persistent sub-optimal outcomes from the individual's and society's welfare-maximising perspective. Such sub-optimal decisions need to be corrected by the intervention of experts, often through the auspices of government. This perspective forms the basis of the nudging literature (Thaler and Sustein 2008; Babcock et al. 2010).

In the alternative, bounded rationality approach pioneered by Simon (1955, 1978, 1979, 1987), individuals are not assumed to be hardwired to behave in a sub-optimal error-prone and biased manner. Hence errors can often be corrected by improvements in the decision-making environment and through education. Moreover, individuals can deviate from standard economic decision-making norms, but this often results in superior economic outcomes (Altman 2005; Gigerenzer 2007; Smith 2003).

MODELLING LABOUR SUPPLY: THE NEOCLASSICAL APPROACH

The standard model of labour supply is predicated upon a model of labour-leisure choice. It is based on the behavioural assumptions that: (1) leisure (nonmarket activities) is preferred to work and is modelled as a normal good whereby increases in real income increase the demand for leisure, thereby reducing market labour supply; (2) holding real income constant, making leisure more expensive by increasing the real wage, increases market labour supply, and lowering the real wage reduces it (Becker 1965). It is implicitly assumed that individuals gain no positive utility from labour market activities. However, in reality, this is not the case (Frey and Stutzer 2002; Helliwell and Huang 2011; Jahoda 1981; Sherman and Shavit 2009). It is also assumed that individuals can afford *not* to work in the market. So, they can and will withdraw from the labour market if the wage rate is too low.

Given these standard assumptions, the substitution effect predicts that as the price (wage rate) of leisure increases, market labour supply increases and therefore less leisure is consumed. But as the wage increases, income goes up, resulting in increasing the demand for leisure (income effect). The supply of labour is a product of the interaction of the substitution and income effects as the wage rate changes. Labour supply increases as wages increase – the labour supply curve is upward sloping – as long as the substitution effect dominates the income effect. But when the income effect dominates, this yields the 'classic' backwards-bending labour supply curve. This is illustrated in Figure 9.1, where the relationship between the real wage rate and the supply of market labour is illustrated. All along the labour supply curve, the individual is assumed to be maximising his or her utility, even if the individual is unemployed or is working seven days a week, 12 hours per day.

What underlies (the micro-foundations) this type of labour supply curve is the assumption that income and non-labour time ('leisure') are substitutes. The individual increases labour supply as the wage rate increases, which is the price of nonmarket time. Labour supply keeps on increasing as wages rise as long as the substitution effect outweighs the income effect. But when the wage rate diminishes, individuals substitute out-of-the-market labour into nonmarket time, thereby reducing market labour supply as long as this substitution effect outweighs the income effect of falling real income.

It is also assumed that individuals will accept a wage offer only if their reservation wage – the minimal acceptable wage – is high enough. This assumes that individuals can afford not to work and that individuals experience no positive utility from working in the labour market. Policy, such as improvements to minimum wages, unemployment insurance and social welfare, that increases the reservation wage will reduce the percentage of wage offers accepted,

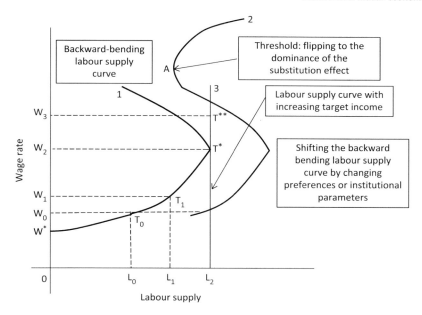

Figure 9.1 The backwards-bending labour supply curve

increasing unemployment, whereas policy that reduces that reservation wage has the opposite effect. Changes in the reservation wage can also affect the supply of labour, by affecting the expected cost of leisure time. Increases to the reservation wage will reduce the supply of labour to the extent that individuals expect a higher wage rate to compensate them for sacrificing a unit of leisure (shifting the labour supply curve to the left). Moreover, increases in the reservation wage are predicted to increase the overall wage rates paid by all firms irrespective of current wage levels, increasing average production costs and, thereby, increasing unemployment.[4]

A critical problem with the neoclassical model is that it fails to provide any reasonable predictions on the timing and direction of changes in labour supply. Rather, once one knows the shape of the labour supply curve, it is argued that a particular change in the relationship between the substitution and income effect 'caused' a change in labour supply. By assumption, other possible causal variables, even those that are more plausible from a reality-based perspective are not ever brought into consideration (this is a serious omitted variable problem).

There is no empirical or theoretical basis to predict when or the extent to which there should be a change in the relationship between income and substitution effects such that labour supply increases and then diminishes, yielding a backwards-bending labour supply curve, for example. The changing historical relationship between the substitution and income effect can also yield an s-shaped labour supply curve which requires explaining (see Figure 9.1). (For problems and issues with contemporary labour supply theory, see Altman 2001; Pencavel 1986; Prasch 2000; Dessing 2002; Sharif 2000.)

In the real world, we have witnessed such s-shaped labour curves, wherein hours worked per week initially fell in currently developed economies, in the late nineteenth century, when workers often worked six to seven days a week, often for more than ten hours a day, with little or no vacation time. More recently, in many of these economies, hours worked per week increased somewhat from lows of less than 40 hours per week (Messenger, Lee and McCann 2007). What is required is a model that ex-ante predicts labour market behaviour, generating analytical predictions using credible behavioural and institutional assumptions.

A BEHAVIOURAL MODEL OF LABOUR SUPPLY: A TARGET APPROACH

In the target approach, real target income and target nonmarket activities are introduced into the modelling of market labour supply (see Altman 2001; Camerer et al. 1997; Baxter 1993; Kaufman 1989, 1999, for more details).[5] Labour supply decisions can be more robustly modelled here by making the simplifying assumption that individuals are most concerned with their target income and their target nonmarket activities. This is opposed to the standard focus on the relative price of leisure and the capacity of individuals to purchase more leisure time. The notion that target income can be important is not new but has not had much impact on the standard labour supply literature. But the target income approach generates different and more robust analytical predictions that the income-leisure model.

One can write the target theory as market labour supply being a function of target market income, target nonmarket activities, nonmarket income and the real wage rate (Altman 2001). This argument can take the form of:

$$L^{SM} = F(TY, TNML, NMY, w)$$

TY is real target income, $TNML$ is target nonmarket time, NMY is real nonmarket income and w is the real wage rate. Market labour supply can be measured by hours supplied to the labour market. Given real target income, labour supply is given by the real wage rate, *conditional* upon target nonmarket time and real nonmarket income, or:

$$L^{SM} = \frac{TY - NMY}{W}, \text{ conditional upon } TNML$$

Given TY, NMY and W, market labour supply is determined. It is important to note the importance of $TNML$, such as childcare and care of disabled loved ones, for example, in determining TY. The higher the $TNML$, the lower the market labour supply. Such would be the case with single-parent female-led households with no affordable childcare. On the other hand, artists or musicians who are happy (maximising utility) at a low target income so that more time is devoted off-market to painting and music, will supply minimal labour to the labour market. Overall, ceteris paribus, one can model increasing target minimum nonmarket time as shifting the market labour supply curve to the left whilst reducing this target shifts the market labour supply curve to the right.

Real target income is defined as inclusive of expenses required to earn a particular level of target real income, such as taxes, daycare, appropriate clothing and transportation costs. Once target income is known, one can more accurately predict the price effect (the slope of the labour supply curve) of a change in wages. Moreover, ceteris paribus, changes in target income affect the extent to which changes in wages affect labour supply, since the ability to realise a given level of real target income is a product of real wages and hours worked.

For example, if real target income is met at a given real wage rate and number of hours worked, increasing real wages will reduce the supply of labour.[6] If real target income increases, on the other hand, the supply of labour would increase at any given real wage rate to meet the increased target income. Moreover, if real target income exceeds what can be realised at the current real wage and a given (maximum) labour supply, increasing real wage can be expected to have no effect on labour supply. If real target income increases, labour supply would not fall in the face of increasing real wages if these higher wages, in combination with the existing level of market labour supply, are required to either approach or realise the higher level of target income.

There is evidence supportive of the hypothesis that target income increases over time resulting in a persistent and sometimes growing gap between the actual real income of the individual or household and their real target income (Altman 2001; Berry 1994; Lebergott 1993, p. 65). This could be a function of sellers promoting new products by creating new wants (Frank 1985, 1999, 2005; Galbraith 1965; George 2001), the desire of individuals to maintain their income position in relation to their peers (Duesenberry 1949; Easterlin 2001; Leibenstein 1950) and the increasing material aspiration levels of individuals (Easterlin 2001; Lebergott 1993; Mack 1956; March and Simon 1968; Sanders 2008; Shane and Loewenstein 1999; Stutzer 2004). If real target income did not increase over time in developed economies, most people there would not have to work very much at all. No more than 10–15 hours of work per week would be required to achieve the average income of early twentieth-century Americans and no more than 10–15 minutes per week to reach the income levels of the Kapauku Papuans of the Pacific Islands (Altman 2001; Lebergott 1993, p. 65).

Hours worked have declined over the past 100-odd years in economies that are currently developed but not nearly as much as they should have if target real income had not increased. Moreover, hours of work tend to decline quite dramatically amongst developing low-income economies but only in a fashion consistent with increasing real income. And, amongst the developed wealthy economies there is little relationship between hours worked per week and increases in real wages (Messenger, Lee and McCann 2007). The evidence tends to support the hypothesis that real target income increases over time.

The fact that real target income keeps increasing is critically important to understand the evolution of market labour supply and to predict future movements in market labour supply. Here we have an evidenced-based variable (unlike the substitution and income effects) that drives market labour supply. And, evidence-based variables are critical components of behavioural economics analyses. This allows for more substantive economic predictions and causal analyses.

A key point of the target approach is that the market supply of labour is driven by the wants and desires of individuals.[7] Here, substitution effects are often of little analytical consequence. Indeed, when market labour supply is fixed for target income reasons the individual's indifference curve for income and nonmarket time is L-shaped as opposed to being convex to the origin as in the conventional approach. Here one has lexicographic indifference curves.[8] Illustrated in Figure 9.2, along indifference curve U_0, as the wage rate changes from 2 to 3 or from 3 to 2, there is no change in the preferred amount of nonmarket activities and, therefore, in market labour supply. Individuals are not willing to sacrifice real income to obtain more nonmarket activities when the wage rate falls. There are no 'income-leisure' trade-offs as there would be through the substitution effect in the conventional model. Price lines 1 and 3 represent the same wage (they are the same slope). In the conventional narrative, reducing

158 *Handbook of research methods in behavioural economics*

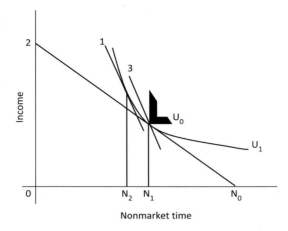

Figure 9.2 *Labour market indifference curves*

the price of labour from 1 to 2 (where 1 = 3) increases the demand for nonmarket time by N_1N_2, along convex indifference curve U_1. In the target income approach, labour supply changes, not as a consequence of changes in the price of nonmarket or 'leisure' time (substitution effect), but as a function of changes in target income and whether an increase in the wage rate yields a real income that exceeds the current target income. If the latter occurs, there is a decrease in labour supply as a result of target income being surpassed at the higher real wage and the given amount of hours worked. Once one knows an individual's target income, one can predict market labour supply as the real wage rate changes.

The trade-off between market income and nonmarket activities is illustrated in Figure 9.3. In the target income model, since the indifference curves are assumed to be L-shaped, the individual's market labour supply decision is based on target income, not income-'leisure' trade-offs in terms of substitution effects. As the wage rate increases, from 1 to 2, the individual can choose to maintain his or her prior supply of market labour (N_0N_1) and maximise income, at 0C. On the other hand, the individual can reduce market labour supply to N_0N_2, and increase income to 0B. In this case, BC of income is sacrificed in order to increase nonmarket activities from $0N_1$ to $0N_3$. These choices, based on an individual's target income, can all be utility maximising and are given by the tangency of indifference curves U_1, U_2, and U_0, to their respective price lines.

In one plausible scenario, one begins a market labour supply narrative at very low real wages and a very high level of market labour supply, such as 60 hours (a ten-hour workday of six days) per week, not uncommon in the nineteenth-century industrial world and prevalent in many developing economies today. Increasing nonmarket time as real wages increase *eventually* proves to be a higher-order need than a further increase in real income (Cross 1988). In Figure 9.3, utility is maximised at a low level of nonmarket activities, such as $0N_1$, in an attempt to meet target income. Initial increases in real wages can be expected to have no effect on target nonmarket activities if target income has yet to be met. But as real wages increase further, the next step in the hierarchy of needs and wants would be to increase nonmarket time from its very low levels, maximising utility at $0N_3$ of nonmarket time. In this case, both

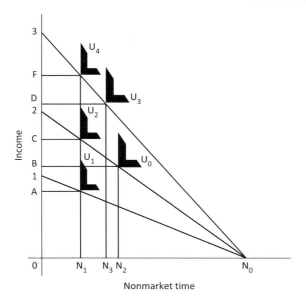

Figure 9.3   Income–nonmarket time trade-off

nonmarket time and real income increase (to 0D from 0C). Once the need for more nonmarket time is met, it becomes possible to meet higher-order needs as real wages increase, which can be either more nonmarket time or more market goods. If target real income increases whilst target nonmarket time is being met, further increases in real wages can be expected to have no effect on labour supply. In this scenario, utility can only be increased by increasing real income as wages rise. In this case, as the wage rate increase from 1 to 2 to 3, the labour supply remains at N_0N_1, whilst income increases from OA to OF. Increasing nonmarket time cannot compensate an individual for any reduction in income – the indifference curve is L-shaped. In this case, the substitution effect is zero while the income effect depends on the time-specific ranking of market income and nonmarket time.

The resulting labour supply curve, FGHJ, mapped out from this indifference curve analysis, is illustrated in Figure 9.4. This is a long-run market labour supply curve, where two independent variables are changing, both the wage rate and preferences for goods and services. At low levels of real income, the labour supply curve is perfectly inelastic, at $0L_1$, to changes in the real wage rate. There is a backward bend to the labour supply curve at point G, at wage rate W_2. Thereafter, as the wage rate increases from W_3, the labour supply curve is once again inelastic to increases in the real wage rate. This type of labour supply curve is consistent with the evidence across time and place (Messenger, Lee and McCann 2007, p. 33). Based on the target income theory, one would predict a drop in market labour supply only if target income no longer increases in pace with real wage growth.

This modelling of labour supply has not taken into consideration the utility that individuals obtain from market work (Frey and Stutzer 2002; Helliwell and Huang 2011; Jahoda 1981; Sherman and Shavit 2009). Quite rationally, the act of working and working with others, being part of a group, can make people feel better. This psychological variable, itself, can

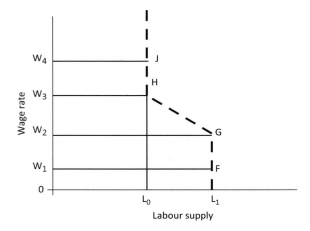

Figure 9.4   Labour supply curve and target income

set a floor to market labour supply. Even if real target income is met, labour supply may not diminish if the given level of labour supply is utility maximising in terms of the psychological kick the individual obtains from working. Any increase in the utility an individual obtains from market work can be modelled as an outward shift in the labour supply curve, such as from labour supply curve 1 to 2 in Figure 9.1. However, if the work environment is nasty, this does not imply that an individual will reduce her or his supply of labour. This is especially the case when a given amount of market labour is required to meet the real target income of the individual. Still, one could predict that a poor work environment can, on the margin, in higher-income societies, have the effect of shifting the labour supply curve inward to the left.

Another important psychological labour supply shift factor is the discouraged worker effect. An individual becomes discouraged if she loses confidence in her ability to find work and stops actively searching for work. This person drops out of the labour market even while still desiring market employment. This shifts the market labour supply curve to the left. On the other hand, increasing aggregate demand, invigorated animal spirits, and improved job search mechanisms reduce the discouraged workers' effect which shifts the economy-wide market labour supply curve outward to the right (on animal spirits, see Akerlof and Shiller 2009).

An important footnote to this target theory of labour supply is that individuals' ability to choose their preferred amount of labour supply, given the wage rate and their target income, is affected by the political-legal environment in which labour market decisions are made. Standard labour market theory assumes an institutional environment wherein individuals choose how much to work. But at one extreme, where free labour markets do not exist, such as with slavery or serfdom, individuals are not free to choose. Where free labour markets predominate, individuals legally own their labour power. Their market labour supply decisions are affected by institutional parameters such as labour unions and nonmarket income such as unemployment insurance and social security (social welfare payments). The target labour supply theory can incorporate various types of institutional parameters. For example, where labour has limited legal rights, labour supply can be constrained to the physiological maximum and the labour supply curve would be perfectly inelastic at this maximum supply, such as labour supply curve 3 in Figure 9.1. Where more labour rights obtain, workers can choose to supply less labour as real wages increase, if this choice set maximises their utility. Here, the slope of the market labour supply curve changes from being completely inelastic to somewhat elastic.

Labour market discrimination can also affect labour supply, shifting the economy-wide market labour supply curve to the left. If particular groups in society are precluded from labour market participation, members of these groups can't participate even if they are willing to work at prevailing wage rates. Their revealed preference for market work is stymied by institutional variables. Their absence from the labour market is not related to the substitution and income effects. Reducing labour market discrimination should shift the market labour supply curve to the right, as more individuals, women, for example, choose to seek employment to meet their target income and to meet their psychological need to participate in the world of work. The extent of this shift can be in part determined by estimating the shortfall between actual real income and target income.

NON-LABOUR MARKET INCOME AND LABOUR SUPPLY

Increasing nonmarket sources of income would not reduce labour force participation unless target income is met with the assistance of the nonmarket sources of income and market work has no positive effect on utility. This speaks to the potential impact of the introduction or increases in 'social welfare' payments or unemployment insurance on labour supply. The standard model predicts that such nonmarket increases in income (demogrants) will reduce labour supply whereas a decrease in such income will increase labour supply through the income effect, shifting the labour supply curve (Friedman 1968; Mulligan 2013). Such predictions pay no attention to individuals' target income, their target level of nonmarket time, their physical capacity to work, their hierarchy of wants and the rules and regulations that dictate the terms under which individuals are entitled to demogrants (Altman 2004a, 2004b). Also, no attention is paid to the utility gained from the act of engaging in market work (Sherman and Shavit 2009). Such utility diminishes the impact that demogrants might otherwise have on labour supply. The traditional model's predictions need to be modified to incorporate these non-economic variables.

The target approach predicts that as long as target income is *not* met, ceteris paribus, labour supply should not be reduced with the introduction or increases in the level of social welfare. This is especially true if the individual gains utility from working on the labour market (Sherman and Shavit 2009). In this case, social welfare would form a basis of economic support for individuals who prefer to work but are unable to obtain employment. The predicted impact of increases in social welfare on labour supply is much more complex than in the standard model, requiring information on target income and the utility of market work.

For work-capable individuals, the target approach suggests that they might be on social welfare because they have a low target income (covered by social welfare), do not gain utility from working, have a higher-order preference for nonmarket activities, or cannot find work. Behavioural economics would be open to the hypothesis that the lack of job opportunities can result in individuals being on social welfare even though they prefer to work. Also, market work might also be discouraged when jobs are available if the tax rate on market work results in net income being greater if one does not accept available and otherwise acceptable job offers. This is an important institutional parameter requiring consideration. Increasing labour supply here requires a change and/or restructuring of the tax rate and creating more job opportunities, not the elimination of social welfare (Organisation for Economic Co-operation and Development 2003; Starky 2006).

Individuals who are not in the labour market for psychological reasons might not increase their labour force participation even if, as a consequence, they must suffer economic losses (their target income drops). The psychological cost of entering the labour market might outweigh the possible benefits, especially if they have very negative views of labour market conditions. Reducing social welfare would, in this case, simply increase the level of economic deprivation among these individuals. Other means would be required to increase labour supply inclusive of overcoming individuals' biases and misinformation on the state of the labour market.

Overall, eliminating or reducing social welfare might increase labour supply, but realistically, not by much, given the small percentage of the population in most countries on social welfare. This increase in labour supply would have little to do with the income or substitution effects as specified in the standard model. What is critical to understanding labour market dynamics with regards to social welfare, from a behavioural perspective, is to better incorporate non-economic factors that underlie why individuals are outside of the labour market.

For example, the disabled who are not work-capable can't work, so reducing social welfare simply increases these individuals' level of economic deprivation. Stay-at-home moms might be on welfare (low target income) so as to take care of their children, absent childcare facilities, for example. Reducing social welfare might force some of these individuals onto the labour market, shifting the labour supply curve outward and reducing the wage rate, thereby reducing the level of economic sustenance provided by the market (Solow 2003). But this has nothing to do with traditional income effects. Rather, mothers are forced into the labour market to meet minimal target incomes at the opportunity cost of taking care of their children. This can also have the long-term effect of reducing the supply of labour, controlling for quality, by reducing the labour market capabilities of children. However, single mothers can reduce target income as social welfare is cut to take care of their children, increasing the economic deprivation within their household. In this case, any increase in labour supply predicted by the standard model would not take place or would be mitigated. Unless a vibrant labour market accompanies cuts to social welfare, the increased labour supply generated by such cuts, simply increases the number of unemployed and reduces the equilibrium wage. A key determinant of poverty and social welfare dependency is the absence or lack of work, hence the significance of vibrant labour markets (International Labour Organization 2010; Rice et al. 2013; Solow 2003).

UNEMPLOYMENT INSURANCE AND LABOUR SUPPLY

The preceding discussion is also pertinent to an understanding of unemployment insurance, which the standard model predicts should result in increasing unemployment. This increase is caused by attracting individuals into the labour market who intend to quit their new jobs to collect this benefit, by increasing the voluntary job search time of the unemployed workers already in the labour force, by inducing increasing quit rates of the currently employed so that they can search for better jobs, and by increasing the market wage thereby increasing the price of labour and reducing the competitiveness of the economy. Moreover, following upon the efficiency wage literature, unemployment insurance is expected to reduce the effort incentive effect of a given rate of unemployment (unemployment is viewed as a disciplinary device to keep effort levels at higher levels) (see the following on efficiency wages) (Altman 2004a; Holmlund 1998; Shapiro and Stiglitz 1984).

The standard approach also assumes that the increased duration of short-term job searches induced by unemployment insurance can have no positive effect on long-term employment rates. It is further assumed that higher real wages necessarily or typically generate higher production costs and thereby higher rates of unemployment. Neither of these assumptions needs to hold. It is further assumed that the marginal worker maximises utility or economic well-being at low levels of real income thus allowing unemployment insurance to serve as a utility-maximising 'wage of being unemployed'. Thus, some workers maximise their utility by getting themselves laid off so as to take advantage of this 'wage of being unemployed'.

The available empirical evidence provides no unambiguous support for the conventional proposition that unemployment insurance damages the economy (Altman 2004a; Holmlund 1998; Atkinson and Micklewright 1991; Howell and Azizoglu 2011; Howell and Rehm 2009). For example, to the extent that unemployment increases search time and this produces a better match between job searcher and job, this can reduce job turnover and thereby reduce the long-term unemployment rate (Altman 2004a). Also, since unemployment insurance is typically much less than market income, individuals won't quit their jobs to earn unemployment insurance unless their target income is relatively quite low and they attach little or no utility to market work. Moreover, most workers are not eligible for unemployment insurance if they simply quit their jobs. This institutional reality, critical to a behaviouralist analysis, often precludes unemployment insurance from actually directly causing an increase in the unemployment rate (Holmlund 1998; Atkinson and Micklewright 1991). Finally, one can't easily predict the extent to which unemployment insurance increases the market wage and the extent to which this increases costs and thereby unemployment. Efficiency wage theory and especially x-efficiency theory predicts different plausible outcomes wherein increasing wages has a positive effect on productivity that can offset any wage increases. This follows from the more realistic behavioural assumption that effort inputs per unit of labour are positively impacted the real wage rate and overall working conditions.

It is critically important from both an analytical and public policy perspective to develop a theoretical framework that incorporates the empirics suggesting that unemployment insurance generates no long-run negative economic effects. Introducing more realistic behavioural and institutional assumptions into one's modelling of unemployment insurance contributes to this task of developing and testing a variety of hypotheses relating unemployment insurance to labour supply and employment.

NON-ECONOMIC VARIABLES AND ERRORS OR BIASES IN LABOUR MARKET DECISION-MAKING

Labour supply can be affected by psychological variables such as inaccurate perceptions about labour market opportunities. Some behavioural economists define and interpret these as cognitive illusions (Babcock et al. 2010). This overlaps with the severely critiqued 'culture of poverty' literature wherein it is maintained that poverty persists because of the cultural (and related innate biases) of the poor (Gorski 2008; Wilson 1997). But these misperceptions can also be viewed as a product of poor or incorrect information sets, cognitive costs, loss or risk-averse behaviour in a world of uncertainty, peer effects, social capital or psychological depression, all consistent with Herbert Simon's perspective on behavioural economics (see also March 1978). In this case, one has rational individuals whose choices might be improved (even from their own perspective or objective function) with improvements in their decision-making environment. Either way, introducing non-economic variables into the analytical mix allows one to better explain certain aspects of behaviour and to suggest policy to improve labour market outcomes.

Of critical importance is the now-established fact that persistent involuntary unemployment causes depression and other mental health issues, including loss of self-esteem and loss of a sense of control among the unemployed. This also has negative, possibly long-term repercussions on the family of the unemployed. Moreover, long-term unemployment results in the depreciation of the human capital stock of the unemployed. This is one reason why the long-term unemployed tend to end up with jobs paying less than their former jobs. Long-term unemployment also reduces, on average, the long-run capital stock of family members. Moreover, such unemployment sends negative signals to prospective employers resulting in the long-term unemployed being less likely to secure future employment than individuals who are short-term unemployed. It appears that in a world of asymmetric information, employers use long-term unemployment as a signal for relatively poorer future performance and employability – a form of statistical discrimination. These variables cause a downward shift in the demand curve for labour.

Long-term unemployment also increases the probability of morbidity, reduces life expectancy and increases the probability of family violence. The mental health effects of unemployment feed into the human capital side of the story, contributing to reducing human capital stock, which reduces the probability of getting a job, which increases mental health problems, which reduces human capital stock. In addition, because of depression (related to this, loss of self-confidence), due to unemployment, there is a lower probability of job search amongst the long-term unemployed – this relates to the discouraged worker effect. Overall, long-term unemployment by reducing human capital stock per prospective employee reduces the employability of such individuals at any given real wage rate. For this reason, persistent long-term unemployment can have the effect of reducing the equilibrium rate of employment. This need not increase the official rate of unemployment if one is also increasing the number of discouraged workers sufficiently (Adams 2012; Babcock et al. 2010; Darity and Goldsmith 1996; Heikki and Venetoklis 2010; Jahoda 1981; Linn, Sandifer and Stein 1985; Paul and Moser 2009; Stuckler and Basu 2013; Zukin 2009).

Applied economics is increasingly integrating these findings into its corpus. And many economists recommend that it is critically important to reduce long-term unemployment, not only for the mental anguish it causes the unemployed and their families, but also because of the serious deleterious effects it has on productivity. So, a big public policy question relates to how can one most effectively and efficiently reduce the long-run unemployment rate by increasing employment, given the importance of these particular non-economic variables.

With regards to macroeconomic policy, behavioural economics places close attention on the importance of psychological variables, such as confidence and animal spirits, in moving the economy forward. It's not only about monetary and fiscal policy (Akerlof and Shiller 2009). Rather it is about such policy recognising the importance of psychological variables in determining the extent and timing of spending (see Chapters 4 and 9 of this book for a search and matching and post-Keynesian perspectives on macroeconomics, respectively).

Behavioural economics also pays close attention to informational concerns, capital market imperfections and uncertainty affecting labour market behaviour. Unemployed workers can and do underestimate the probability of securing employment at preferred real wage rates and annual income. This can be a product of individuals suffering from a loss of confidence who then might become discouraged workers. This market failure, related to errors in decision-making, can be corrected by more direct intervention by job search agencies and client-specific advisors who can provide individuals with more direct information on job prospects and facilitate the interview process. In this instance, the default is that the job search agency leads the job search process as opposed to the traditional default where the unemployed are left to take the initiative. The traditional default does not work effectively when workers are literally psyched out of the job search process and subject to imperfect and even misleading information. Workers may also not have the financial means to engage in an effective job search – inadequate funds for transportation, presentable clothing and childcare. This can be addressed by more direct intervention in the job search process, facilitating such individuals moving into the job market, to correct for market failure. In this case, the intervention increases the job search capabilities of the unemployed as opposed to building policy based on the conventional assumption that adequate capabilities are in place and the unemployed would rather engage in 'leisure' activities than find a job.

This approach does not assume that individuals are engaged in biased decision-making – an assumption made by many behavioural economists. Rather, 'real' variables generate correctable decision-making errors. Given these 'real' variables, changing the defaults affect decision-making in terms of how the new defaults provide better information, reduce uncertainty and transaction costs, and help compensate for underconfidence amongst the unemployed.

Moreover, behavioural economics, in the tradition of institutional economics pays close attention to components of long-run unemployment that are structural. Many unemployed will not find employment in jobs that require their former skill set because of the changing nature of the economy. To move forward in the job market, adequate job retraining is required as is accurate information on job opportunities and the necessary skill sets required for available jobs. In a world of asymmetric information and imperfect capital markets, individuals may not have the capacity to invest in skill upgrading. In this case, either subsidised or public job retraining programmes would be required to fix such a market failure.

But there is another approach to the causes of long-run unemployment embedded in the Kahneman-Tversky errors and biases approach to behavioural economics (for a survey of this see, Babcock et al. 2010). In this approach, individuals are assumed to suffer from a range of biases, such as present or status quo bias, loss aversion (losses weighted more heavily than gains) and hyperbolic discounting (procrastination). This results in such individuals not knowing what's in their own best interest. As a result, the unemployed engage in inadequate job searches and reject job offers that should be accepted given the objective labour market conditions. In this case, workers actually suffer from errors in decision-making based on an overconfidence bias. The unemployed set their reservation wage too high, based on the wages in their former jobs, which no longer reflects the objective reality of the labour market. The difference between their former wage and current and lower wage offers (the former wage is regarded as an anchor) is also treated as a loss of income by the unemployed. Given loss aversion, this type of framing of job offers incentivises the unemployed to reject what are objectively optimal job offers. In summary, these various biases result in too many of the unemployed procrastinating in their job search, not spending enough time searching for a job and rejecting what are the best possible jobs offers. All this causes the rate of unemployment to be greater than it should otherwise be – what it would be in a de-biased world.

One solution to this type of biased decision-making is providing wage-loss insurance to the unemployed that would temporarily subsidise a worker's income when he or she accepts a relatively low-paying job. This reduces perceived income loss (as well as loss aversion) and therefore incentivises individuals to increase their job search and increase the acceptance rate of relatively low-paying job offers. It is also argued that framing wage-loss insurance explicitly in the pay statement will help push wage expectations downwards towards an objectively given lower level. All of this would serve to reduce the long-run rate of unemployment by proactively dealing with the biased decision-making of the unemployed.

This errors and biases approach to long-run unemployment does not deny the importance of inaccurate information and information processing costs as possible causes of errors in decision-making. But the focus is on cognitive biases. The biased decisions of the unemployed are an important cause of persistent unemployment. A key prior assumption here is that there exists a supply of jobs available to meet the demand for jobs given that the price of labour is right – the real wage rate must be low enough. The demand side is not a problem, it is assumed. It is also assumed that there is no negative efficiency wage effect of dropping the wage rate, therefore a lower wage rate won't cause such a drop in productivity that employing the lower wage, less efficient worker becomes unprofitable.

In the bounded rationality approach to behavioural economics, where individuals are largely rational and smart, correcting information errors, more accurately framing information, providing less costly access to information, reducing job search costs, improving individual capabilities to engage in job search, job re-training and addressing depression-induced lack of confidence, is of greater importance to reducing long-run unemployment. From this perspective, correctable errors in decision-making and inadequate capabilities amongst the unemployed are thought to be the larger problem. This does not deny, however, the possibility of biases in decision-making. And, of course, given optimal conditions on the supply side, job offers must be available to the job searchers. Otherwise, these individuals will remain unemployed irrespective of ideal supply-side conditions that explicitly deal with decision-making problems related to cognitive, informational and transaction cost issues.

CONCLUSION

Behavioural models of labour markets are informed by how decision-making is affected by psychological, sociological and institutional variables. A common concern of behavioural economists is that there are all too many empirical occurrences that are inconsistent with key elements of standard labour economics theory. As well, standard labour economics can't explain all too many labour market phenomena. To better explain labour market behaviour and outcomes requires revisiting and revising some key simplifying modelling assumptions that are the mainstay of standard labour market theory.

In this chapter, I focus on two key areas where behavioural economics provides considerable theoretical insight. One area is the determinants of labour supply. This brings us to a discussion of a target theory of labour supply in contrast to the standard theory's focus on the income and substitution effects. Modelling target income and also and, relatedly, target nonmarket activities, allows for more robust predictions of the determinants and timing of labour supply. This also brings to the fore the determinants of individuals' targets, which are important economic and non-economic dimensions.

Secondly, I discuss the analytical and public policy insights that behavioural economics provide into what many behavioural economists refer to as errors and biases in decision-making that are said to produce inefficient labour market outcomes. In the standard modelling, individuals are assumed to be calculating and omniscient, not subject to errors or biases in decision-making. Decisions are assumed to be optimal and not subject to regret.

Each school of behavioural economics, based on different methodological approaches to decision-making, proffers different solutions to correct inefficient decision-making outcomes. If one assumes that individuals are fundamentally error-prone and biased then it becomes critical to de-bias decision-making. The alternative is to induce or force individuals to behave in a manner that's inconsistent with their preferences, but which is consistent with optimality and efficiency from the perspective of the expert (referred to as choice architects).

If one assumes that individuals are largely rational and unbiased but sometimes do make error-prone decisions or decisions that are not optimal socially or even from the perspective of the decision-maker, the public policy focus is on changing the incentive and information environment and the capabilities of the decision-makers. This stands a good chance of inducing and facilitating choices that are more in line with individuals' own self-interest and that of society at large.

Both approaches to behavioural economics recognise and identify the gaps in the standard approaches to labour market modelling. Both approaches also have implications for understanding both the supply and demand sides of the labour market. Behavioural dimensions to decision-making, rational or not, affect our understanding of how much labour is supplied on the market. Behavioural economics thereby enriches the price and income-focused standard economic toolbox, generating alternative hypotheses to be tested and public policy designs to be evaluated. What is not discussed in this chapter, in any detail, are the determinants of human capital formation. This relates to the quality of labour supply which has important non-market determinants. Also, not discussed in much detail, is how effort variability, important to behavioural economics, affects labour market outcomes and policy (see my chapter on the theory of the firm in this book (Chapter 11)).

NOTES

1. The author thanks Bruce Kaufman, Morris Kleiner and Louise Lamontagne for their many helpful comments and suggestions.
2. For broader surveys and ones with a different orientation from what's presented here, see, for example, Berg (2006), Charness and Kuhn (2011) and Dohmen (2014). See also, Pencavel (1986), Killingsworth and Heckman (1987) and Rogerson, Shimer and Wright (2005).
3. Errors in decision-making are inconsistent with the leading proponents of traditional economics, following upon the arguments of Alchian (1950) and Friedman (1953), that competitive markets will force efficiency. However, possible errors in decision-making are a focal point of contemporary behavioural economics and behavioural finance (Altman 2005; Akerlof and Shiller 2009; Thaler and Sustein 2008), especially given the pervasiveness of imperfect product markets. Behavioural economics attempts to explain such errors as well as resulting economic inefficiencies (Simon 1987).
4. Friedman (1968) and Mulligan (2013), respectively, provide the old and new versions of this perspective.
5. There are some points of intersection between the target theory and the arguments presented in Prasch (2000).
6. Camerer, Babcock, Lowenstein and Thaler's (1997) target model of labour supply focuses on taxi drivers where target income appears to be fixed, thus increasing wages reduces the labour supply.

This model builds on very short run objective functions. See Farber (2005) for a critique of the Camerer et al. (1997).
7. This target income modelling of labour supply is based on Altman (2001).
8. Kaufman (1989), building upon Maslow (1954), argues that labour market choices are largely determined by the hierarchy of needs of the individual, which typically overwhelms any predicted substitution and income effects, often generating lexicographical or L-shaped indifference curves.

REFERENCES

Adams, S. (2012). 'New study: Long-term unemployment viewed by hiring companies as worse than a criminal record', *Forbes Magazine*. Available at: http://www.forbes.com/sites/susanadams/2012/09/18/new-study-long-term-unemployment-viewed-by-hiring-companies-as-worse-than-a-criminal-record/.

Akerlof, G.A. (1982). 'Labor contracts as partial gift exchange', *Quarterly Journal of Economics*, 97: 543–569.

Akerlof, G.A. (1984). 'Gift exchange and efficiency-wage theory: Four views', *American Economic Review, Papers and Proceedings*, 74: 79–83.

Akerlof, G.A. (2002). 'Behavioral macroeconomics and macroeconomic behavior', *American Economic Review*, 92: 411–433.

Akerlof, G.A. and R.J. Shiller (2009). *Animal Spirits: How Human Psychology Drives the Economy, and Why It Matters for Global Capitalism*. Princeton: Princeton University Press.

Alchian, A.A. (1950). 'Uncertainty, evolution and economic theory', *Journal of Political Economy*, 58: 211–221.

Altman, M. (2001). 'Preferences and labor supply: Casting some light into the black box of income – leisure choice', *Journal of Socio-Economics*, 31: 199–219.

Altman, M. (2004a). 'Why unemployment insurance might not only be good for the soul, it might also be good for the economy', *Review for Social Economy*, 62: 517–541.

Altman, M. (2004b). 'The efficiency and employment enhancing effects of social welfare', in M. Oppenheimer and N. Mercuro (eds.), *Law and Economics: Alternative Economic Approaches to Legal and Regulatory Issues*. Armong, New York: M.E. Sharpe Publishers, pp. 257–285.

Altman, M. (2005). 'Reconciling altruistic, moralistic, and ethical behavior with the rational economic agent and competitive markets', *Journal of Economic Psychology*, 26: 732–757.

Altman, M. (2006). 'Involuntary unemployment, macroeconomic policy, and a behavioral model of the firm: Why high real wages need not cause high unemployment', *Research in Economics*, 60: 97–111.

Altman, M. (2012). *Behavioral Economics for Dummies*. Mississauga, Canada: Wiley.

Atkinson, A.B. and J. Micklewright (1991). 'Unemployment compensation and labor market transitions', *Journal of Economic Literature*, 29: 1679–727.

Babcock, L., W.J. Congdon, L.F. Katz, and S. Mullainathan (2010). 'Notes on behavioral economics and labor market policy', *Brookings Institute*. http://www.brookings.edu/research/papers/2010/12/29-behavioral-econ-labor-market-policy. Accessed May 10, 2012.

Baxter, J.L. (1993). *Behavioural Foundations of Economics*. New York: St. Martin's Press.

Becker, G.S. (1965). 'A theory of the allocation of time', *Economic Journal*, 75: 493–517.

Berg, N. (2006). 'Behavioral labor economics', in M. Altman (ed.), *Handbook of Contemporary Behavioral Economics*. New York: M.E. Sharpe, pp. 457–478.

Camerer, C., C. Babcock, G. Lowenstein, and R. Thaler (1997). 'Labor supply of New York cabdrivers: One day at a time', *Quarterly Journal of Economics*, 112: 407–441.

Charness, G. and P. Kuhn (2011). 'Lab labor: What can labor economists learn from the lab?', in *Handbook of Labor Economics*, Elsevier, vol. 4, Part A. San Diego: Elsevier Science, pp. 229–330.

Darity, W., Jr. and A.H. Goldsmith (1996). 'Unemployment, social psychology, and macroeconomics', *Journal of Economic Perspectives*, 10: 121–140.

Dessing, M. (2002). 'Labor supply, the family and poverty: The S-Shaped labor supply curve', *Journal of Economic Behavior and Organization*, 49: 443–458.

Dohmen, T. (2014). 'Behavioural labour economics: Advances and future directions', IZA Discussion Paper No. 8263. Available at: http://d.repec.org/n?u=RePEc:iza:izadps:dp8263&r=lab.

Duesenberry, J.S. (1949). *Income, Saving and the Theory of Consumer Behavior.* Cambridge, MA: Harvard University Press.
Easterlin, R.A. (2001). 'Income and happiness: Towards a unified theory', *Economic Journal*, 111: 465–484.
Farber, H.S. (2005). 'Is tomorrow another day? The labor supply of New York City cabdrivers', *Journal of Political Economy*, 113: 46–82.
Frank, R. (1985). *Choosing the Right Pond: Human Behavior and the Quest for Status.* New York: Oxford University Press.
Frank, R. (1999). *Luxury Fever Why Money Fails to Satisfy in an Era of Excess.* Princeton: Princeton University Press.
Frank, R. (2005). 'The mysterious disappearance of James Duesenberry', *New York Times.* Available at: http://www.nytimes.com/2005/06/09/business/09scene.html?_r=0.
Frey, B.S. and A. Stutzer (2002). *Happiness and Economics: How the Economy and Institutions Affect Human Well-Being.* Princeton: Princeton University Press.
Friedman, M. (1953). 'The methodology of positive economics', in M. Friedman, *Essays in Positive Economics.* Chicago: University of Chicago Press, pp. 3–43.
Galbraith, J.K. (1958). *The Affluent Society.* New York: New American Library.
George, D. (2001). *Preference Pollution: How Markets Create the Desires We Dislike.* Ann Arbor: University of Michigan Press.
Gigerenzer, G. (2007). *Gut Feelings: The Intelligence of the Unconscious.* New York: Viking.
Gorski, P. (2008). 'Myth of the culture of poverty', *Poverty and Learning*, 65: 32–36.
Hayek, F.A. (1945). 'The use of knowledge in society', *American Economic Review*, 35, 519–530.
Heikki, E. and T. Venetoklis (2010). 'Unemployment and subjective well-being: An empirical test of deprivation theory, incentive paradigm and financial strain approach', *Acta Sociologica*, 53: 119–139.
Helliwell, J.F. and H. Huang (2011). 'Well-being and trust in the workplace', *Journal of Happiness Studies*, 12: 747–767.
Holmlund, B. (1998). 'Unemployment insurance in theory and practice', *Scandinavian Journal of Economics,* 100, 113–141.
Howell, D. and B. Azizoglu (2011). 'Unemployment benefits and work incentives: The US labor market in the great recession'. Political Economy Research Institute, Working Paper No.257.
Howell, D. and M. Rehm (2009). 'Unemployment compensation and high European unemployment: A reassessment with new benefit indicators', *Oxford Review of Economic Policy*, 25: 60–93.
International Labour Organization (2010). *World Social Security Report 2010/11: Providing Coverage in Times of Crisis and Beyond.* Geneva: International Labour Organization.
Jahoda, M. (1981). 'Work, employment and unemployment: Values, theories and approaches in social research', *American Psychologist*, 36: 184–191.
Kahneman, D. (2003). 'Maps of bounded rationality: Psychology for behavioral economics', *American Economic Review*, 93, 1449–1475.
Kahneman, D. (2011). *Thinking Fast and Slow.* New York: Farrar, Strauss, Giroux.
Kahneman, D. and A. Tversky (1979). 'Prospect theory: An analysis of decisions under risk', *Econometrica*, 47, 313–327.
Kaufman, B.E. (1989). 'Models of man in industrial relations research', *Industrial and Labor Relations Review*, 43, 72–88.
Kaufman, B.E. (1999). 'Expanding the behavioral foundations of labor economics', *Industrial and Labor Relations Review*, 52, 361–392.
Killingsworth, M.R. and J.J. Heckman (1987). 'Female labor supply: A survey', in O. Ashenfelter and R. Layard (eds.), *Handbook of Labor Economics*, ed. 1, vol. 1. Amsterdam: Elsevier, pp. 103–204.
Lebergott, S. (1993). *Pursuing Happiness: American Consumers in the Twentieth Century.* Princeton: Princeton University Press.
Leibenstein, H. (1950). 'Bandwagon, Snob, and Veblen effects in the theory of consumers' demand', *Quarterly Journal of Economics*, 64: 183–207.
Linn, M.W., R. Sandifer, and S. Stein (1985). 'Effects of unemployment on mental and physical health American', *Journal of Public Health*, 75: 502–506.
Mack, R.P. (1956). 'Trends in American consumption and the aspiration to consume', *American Economic Review*, 46: 55–68.

March, J.G. (1978). 'Bounded rationality, ambiguity, and the engineering of choice', *Bell Journal of Economics*, 9: 587–608.
March, J.G. and H.A. Simon (1968). *Organizations*. New York: John Wiley.
Maslow, A.H. (1954). *Motivation and Personality*. New York: Harper and Row.
Messenger, J.C., S. Lee, and D. McCann (2007). *Working Time around the World: Trends in Working Hours, Laws, and Policies in a Global Comparative Perspective*. New York: Routledge.
Mulligan, C.B. (2013). *The Redistribution Recession: How Labor Market Distortions Contracted the Economy*. New York: Oxford University Press.
Organisation for Economic Co-operation and Development (2003). 'Making work pay, making work possible', Chapter 3 in *OECD Employment Outlook 2003: Towards More and Better Jobs*, pp. 113–170. Available at: http://www.oecd.org/dataoecd/62/59/31775213.pdf.
Paul, K.I. and K. Moser (2009). 'Unemployment impairs mental health: A meta analyses', *Journal of Vocational Behavior*, 74, 264–282.
Pencavel, J.H. (1986). 'Labor supply of men: A survey', in O. Ashenfelter and R. Layard (eds.), *Handbook of Labor Economics*, vol. 1. Amsterdam: North Holland, pp. 3–102.
Prasch, R.E. (2000). 'Reassessing the labor supply curve', *Journal of Economic Issues*, 34, 679–692.
Rice, J.K., K.F. Wyche, D. Bowker-Turner, H. Bullock, K. Gamble, B. Lott, D.L. McDonald, S. Riger, J.H. Rollins, L. Rubin, J. Sanchez-Hucles, and H. Spears (2013). 'Making "Welfare to Work" really work: Improving welfare reform for poor women, families and children', *American Psychological Association*. Available at: http://www.apa.org/pi/women/programs/poverty/welfare-to-work.aspx.
Rogerson, R., R. Shimer, and R. Wright (2005). 'Search-theoretic models of the labor market: A survey', *Journal of Economic Literature*, 43, 959–988.
Sanders, S. (2008). 'A pedagogical model of the relative income hypothesis'. Available at: SSRN: http://ssrn.com/abstract=1262991 or http://dx.doi.org/10.2139/ssrn.1262991.
Shane, F. and G. Loewenstein (1999). 'Hedonic adaptation', in D. Kahneman, E. Diener and N. Schwarz (eds.), *Well Being: The Foundations of Hedonic Psychology*. New York: Russell Sage Foundation, pp. 302–329.
Sharif, M. (2000). 'Inverted 'S' – The complete neoclassical labour-supply function', *International Labour Review*, 139, 409–435.
Sherman, A. and T. Shavit (2009). 'Welfare to work and work to welfare: The effect of the reference point: A theoretical and experimental study', *Economics Letters*, 105, 290–292.
Simon, H.A. (1955). 'A behavioral model of rational choice', *Quarterly Journal of Economics*, 69, 99–188.
Simon, H.A. (1978). 'Rationality as a process and as a product of thought', *American Economic Review*, 70, 1–16.
Simon, H.A. (1979). 'Rational decision making in business organizations', *American Economic Review*, 69, 493–513.
Simon, H.A. (1987). 'Behavioral economics', in J. Eatwell, M. Millgate and P. Newman (eds.), *The New Palgrave: A Dictionary of Economics*. London: Macmillan, pp. 266–267.
Smith, V.L. (2003). 'Constructivist and ecological rationality in economics', *American Economic Review*, 93, 465–508.
Solow, R.M. (1990). *The Labor Market As a Social Institution*. New York: Blackwell.
Solow, R.M. (2003). 'Lessons Learned from U.S. Welfare Reform', *Prisme,* Cournot Centre for Economic Studies. Available at: http://www.centre-cournot.org/index.php/2003/11/26/lessons-learned-from-u-s-welfare-reform/#more-276/.
Starky, S. (2006). 'Scaling the welfare wall: Earned income tax credits', *In Brief*, PRB 05-98E. Ottawa: Parliamentary Information and Research Service Library of Parliament.
Stuckler, D. and S. Basu (2013). *The Body Economic: Why Austerity Kills*. London: Allen Lane.
Stutzer, A. (2004). 'The role of income aspirations in individual happiness', *Journal of Economic Behavior & Organization*, 54, 89–109.
Thaler, R.H. and C. Sustein (2008). *Nudge: Improving Decisions about Health, Wealth, and Happiness*. New Haven and London: Yale University Press.
Todd, P.M. and G. Gigerenzer (2003). 'Bounding rationality to the world', *Journal of Economic Psychology*, 24, 143–165.

Tversky, A. and D. Kahneman (1981). 'The framing of decisions and the psychology of choice', *Science*, 211, 453–458.
Tversky, A. and D. Kahneman (1986). 'Rational choice and the framing of decisions', *Journal of Business*, 59, 251–278.
Wilson, W.J. (1997). *When Work Disappears*. New York: Random House.
Zukin, C. (2009). 'The anguish of the unemployed', Report, John J. Heldrich Center for Workforce Development, Rutgers, The State University of New Jersey. Available at: http://www.heldrich.rutgers.edu/sites/default/files/content/Heldrich_Work_Trends_.

10. Some implications of x-efficiency theory for the role of managerial quality as a key determinant of firm performance and productivity

Sodany Tong[1,2]

INTRODUCTION

The behavioural economics literature has grown in recent decades and its findings appear to be consistently incompatible with the neoclassical axioms of optimisation and profit maximisation. Studies examining the effect of firm ownership on firm performance, technical efficiency and productivity have frequently found a deficiency in management quality (Altman 2007; Frantz 1988; Leibenstein 1968). Rather than being fixed at an optimal level, as assumed by neoclassical firm theory, managerial quality varies and tends to be suboptimal, arising in part from market imperfections (Bloom et al. 2012; Bloom and Van Reenen 2010) and the lack of managerial entrepreneurship (Leibenstein 1968) or rational choice utility models (Lynne 2015). There is some degree of freedom in managerial choice and effort exertion (Argote and Greve 2007; Cyert and March 1963). Human behaviours and real-world decision-making do not typically fit into the optimal rational choice mould (Schwartz 2008). Managers are driven by goals other than the pursuit of profit, and they tend to operate less efficiently due to 'laziness' and the desire for cognitive ease. This mental folly causes managers to make irrational and non-optimal decisions, resulting in what Leibenstein (1966) terms 'managerial x-inefficiency' (see Frantz 2020; Schwartz 2008; Webber et al. 2018).

In Leibenstein's theory, a lack of effort and competitive ability lead to lower productivity and higher costs (also see Frantz 1980). Cost inefficiency leads to a waste of resources, lowering firm performance and productivity and negatively affecting firm value (Greene and Segal 2004). In an imperfect market, higher production costs may be protected from competitive market forces because inefficient firms typically remain unchallenged by relatively efficient firms and can survive, even in a competitive market economy (Altman 1999, 2007, 2013; Simon 1956). From the x-efficiency theoretical perspective, this means that persistent differences in managerial quality are possible and can be a potential source of performance variations and persistent productivity growth gaps across firms and countries over time (Cyert and March 1963; Leibenstein 1968).

A review of current long-term productivity growth trends reveals significant differences in productivity growth across Organisation for Economic Co-operation and Development (OECD) countries (Frantz 2020; Manyika et al. 2017). In a related study, Bloom and Van Reenen (2010) found significant differences in the quality of managerial practices across firms in the OECD and that these practices were strongly related to firm-level performance and productivity (see also Bloom et al. 2012, 2016). The development of organisational human capital (such as managerial quality) may improve employee effort levels, efficiency, performance and productivity (Frantz 1988; Tomer 2016).

This chapter proceeds as follows. The second section reviews the literature on managerial quality in the firm ownership–performance/productivity nexus and discusses the implications of x-efficiency theory for managerial quality as a determinant of firm performance and productivity from the behavioural versus neoclassical perspective. The third section presents the empirical models used to analyse the effect of managerial quality on x-efficiency as a potential source of firm performance and productivity variations for given ownership and country contexts. Applying Leibenstein's x-efficiency theory, the fourth section reports the empirical results for management x-efficiency as a source of performance variations and persistent productivity growth gaps of firms in OECD countries, including New Zealand (NZ). The use of OECD countries is appropriate for studying the role of managerial quality and x-efficiency in firm performance and productivity because they are characterised by high-quality institutions and unanticipated low performance and productivity growth. NZ is an extreme case of such a performance and productivity problem (see Tong 2019, pp. 38–55). The fifth section provides some conclusions and policy implications.

Managers' abilities and efforts are used as proxies to measure managerial quality in the analysis. Ability relates to managers' competency to manage the assets and resources under their stewardship to create value for shareholders. In addition to managerial ability, a firm's ownership structure has also been found to affect its performance by affecting managers' incentives and efforts (Hu and Izumida 2008; Jiang et al. 2009). Managers' efforts associated with particular ownership structures are related to their incentives and preferences to efficiently manage a firm's assets and resources to maximise or add value (Altman 2013; Frantz 2007; Leibenstein 1966).

For the country-level analysis, in which ability cannot be measured across firms, managerial quality is approximated by the association between ownership and performance, which is used as a proxy for managerial effectiveness in the ownership–performance literature (Hu and Izumida 2008). In the firm-level analysis of specific countries, where data on abilities (e.g., education, training and skills associated with labour market experience) are available, ability and effort can be used as proxies for managerial quality associated with a particular ownership structure.

Studies on the ownership–performance nexus have used a range of indicators to measure firm performance, with the two most common being accounting-based and market-based indicators. Given that accounting-based and market-based measurements of firm performance differ (Al-Matari et al. 2014), the model accounts for these differences when estimating the effect of managerial quality on x-efficiency as a source of between-study variations in the ownership–performance nexus. Given that firm performance and productivity may be interrelated through the concept of efficiency (Fiordelisi et al. 2010; Janssen and McLoughlin 2008), a measure of firm performance and productivity that incorporates efficiency parameters is ideal—that measure is total factor productivity (TFP) (see Tong 2019, pp. 30–33).

This chapter's findings contribute to the x-efficiency literature and emphasise the need to modify neoclassical models to incorporate managerial quality and efficiency in firm performance and productivity research. The outcome provides a cornerstone for behavioural economics, showing that the realism of assumptions is fundamental in model building and the empirical testing of management matters in the determination of firm performance and productivity.

LITERATURE REVIEW

Neoclassical Perspectives

The key focus of the neoclassical firm theory is cost minimisation, thus increasing the gap between revenue and costs to maximise profits. Firms are modelled as 'black boxes', with firm efficiency assumed to be fixed at an optimal level (Friedman 1984). Employees are assumed to work as hard and as effectively as possible. Suppose the neoclassical view, with its underlying economic assumption of optimal input decisions, is accepted. In this case, it should be possible to fix managerial quality at an optimum level so that x-inefficiency (managerial slack and technical inefficiency) may be disregarded as a possible cause of (i) performance variations and (ii) productivity growth gaps between firms in different ownership structure and country contexts. In this case, the null hypotheses are:

H_0^i : *Managerial quality does not affect the relationship between ownership structure (managerial and ownership concentration) and firm performance.*
H_0^{ii} : *Managerial quality is not a determinant of firm productivity growth.*

However, in practice, individuals may choose not to behave in a neoclassical cost-minimising/profit-maximising manner. Thus, alternative theories have been developed to embrace and make sense of the economics of firm behaviour and inefficiency.

Behavioural Perspectives

Among the behavioural perspectives of firm theory, Leibenstein's (1966) x-efficiency theory offers an alternative to the neoclassical theory by recognising that, in reality, management may be less efficient and productive because individual effort and efficiency are variable. Leibenstein maintained that the one-to-one relationships between inputs and outputs assumed by neoclassical models do not exist because, in practice, the market is less than perfect, 'contracts for labor are incomplete, the production function is not completely specified or known, and not all factors of production are marketed' (Leibenstein 1968, p. 72). This means that firm performance and productivity may be lower than that assumed by the optimal profit-maximising position because managerial quality may be x-inefficient (XI). Indeed, there is frequently a shortfall in the quality of management (Bloom et al. 2012; Bloom and Van Reenen 2010), a lack of managerial entrepreneurship and inefficiency (Leibenstein 1968).

Unlike transaction cost economics and agency theory, Leibenstein's (1966, 1973) x-efficiency theory recognises that, in practice, inertia, slothfulness, satisficing behaviour and poor competitive ability are a normal part of human functioning. X-efficiency theory also allows for the quality of managerial decisions and entrepreneurship to enhance firm performance and productivity by compensating for market deficiencies (Leibenstein 1968). The x-inefficiency dimension of this theory also offers flexibility in modelling and understanding the dynamics of managerial quality. In this case, managerial quality, efficiency, performance and productivity are interrelated through the concept of x-efficiency because XI managers and firms are relatively less productive by performing below those operating at the x-efficient (XE) production frontier.

Such flexibilities of the x-efficiency theoretical framework make it appropriate for analysing the effect of managerial quality on x-efficiency as a potential source of performance variations and persistent productivity growth gaps across firms and countries. Using x-efficiency in the measurement of firm performance and decomposition of TFP means that improvements in managerial quality may reduce management x-inefficiency, thus improving firm performance and TFP growth. These factors are not accounted for in neoclassical modelling, which assumes that there can be no variation in effort or technical efficiency (Altman 2007; Frantz 1988; Leibenstein 1968). Thus, the alternative behavioural x-efficiency hypotheses are:

H_1^i : *Managerial quality affects the relationship between ownership structure (managerial and ownership concentration) and firm performance.*
H_1^{ii} : *Managerial quality is a determinant of firm productivity growth.*

The literature on firm ownership and performance indicates that information asymmetries arising from the separation of ownership and control can lead to managers exploiting shareholders, resulting in suboptimal firm outcomes. This is known as managerial inefficiency in the existing literature (Berle and Means 1991; Jensen and Meckling 1976; White 2015). Among market and corporate governance mechanisms, ownership structure is a key determinant of firm performance and for understanding the dynamics of managerial effort and quality (Boyd and Solarino 2016). Variations in managerial quality may explain why some studies have found that increased managerial ownership and large shareholder ownership concentration enhance firm performance because of the convergence of interests and improved monitoring efficiency (Berle and Means 1991; Jensen and Meckling 1976), while others have found that they can impede firm performance because of entrenchment and expropriation (Jiang et al. 2009; Yunos 2011). If the effectiveness of ownership structure as a corporate governance mechanism depends on its influence on managerial quality, which in turn affects firm performance, acknowledging the existence of managerial quality as a variable may help to reconcile the mixed empirical results regarding the ownership–performance nexus. Applying this framework to sampled OECD countries may provide meaningful insights into the importance of managerial quality under different ownership structures as a factor influencing firm performance.

The empirical productivity literature has also long recognised the importance of managerial input and that failing to consider this biases the parameter estimates for production functions (Hoch 1962; Mundlak 1961). Recent studies by Bloom and colleagues (Bloom et al. 2012; Bloom et al. 2016; Bloom and Van Reenen 2010) show that persistent productivity differences at firm and national levels primarily result from variations in managerial practices. A study by Manevska-Tasevska et al. (2017) found that the quality of managerial practices shapes long-term productivity. Baumol (1996) also found that upward and downward swings in management may account for unprecedented expansions and declines in productivity growth. He argued that because managerial roles can vary, they may be reallocated to influence firm performance and productivity. This function means that managers can obtain and use factors of production and compensate for deficiencies in the market economy, the outcomes of which are influenced by the quality of management. Consequently, there is room for managerial and firm technical inefficiencies, which can vary over time (Kumbhakar et al. 2015). Given that managerial quality is a significant human capital variable that can compensate for market and firm inefficiencies, improvements in managerial quality should enhance the growth of TFP and its components when applied to firms in NZ.

EMPIRICAL MODEL

Managerial Quality, Ownership Structure and Firm Performance

The empirical model used to measure the effect of managerial quality on the ownership structure–firm performance nexus is based on meta-regression analysis, controlling for differences in estimation techniques and measurements between studies:

$$Zr_{js} = \beta_o + \Sigma a_o O_o + \Sigma a_c C_c + \Sigma a_p P_p \\ + \Sigma a_m M_m + \Sigma a_f F + a_d D_d + \xi_{js} \quad (10.1)$$

where $j = 1, 2, \ldots, s$, and $Zr = 1/2 \log_e [1 + r/1 - r]$ is the dependent variable, representing the Fisher z-transformation of the effect size partial coefficient ($r = [e^{2Zr} - 1/e^{2Zr} + 1] = \sqrt{t^2/[t^2 + df]}$) calculated from statistics in primary studies.[3] A rule of thumb for interpreting effect size (r) is that 0.1, 0.3 and 0.5 represent small, medium and large effect sizes, respectively (Walker 2008). The two types of ownership structures examined are managerial ownership (Zr_inown) and ownership concentration (Zr_owncon). O and C are the indicator variables representing ownership characteristics (i.e., directors, board members, managers/insiders, top one, top five and top ten shareholders, outside large shareholders, Herfindahl index and others) and country (i.e., Canada, Australia, NZ and others), respectively, as reported in the studies. M is the indicator variable for the choice of estimation method (e.g., ordinary least squares, two-stage least squares, three-stage least squares, generalised least squares, generalised method of moments, fixed effects, random effects and others). F is the indicator variable reflecting the model used in the study (linear, nonlinear, polynomial, piecewise or spline). P is the indicator variable for the definition of firm performance (e.g., Tobin's Q, profitability, efficiency and others). D is the indicator variable representing multiple firm-specific control variables.

Equation 10.1 tests for heterogeneity between studies in terms of the size of the effect of ownership structure on firm performance, as detected by the I^2 index (Higgins et al. 2003), arising from differences in ownership and country characteristics. This model explores the level of variation in managerial quality in different ownership and country contexts, with weighted least squares contributing to the heterogeneity in the ownership–performance effect sizes across studies (R^2), controlling for various methodological and measurement differences between studies.

If firms are fully XE as neoclassical models assume, there should be no variations in the ownership–performance nexus associated with different ownership and country characteristics. The presence of heterogeneity, in which effects are either positive or negative but never zero, suggests the existence of variations in effort and efficiency associated with particular ownership and country characteristics.

Managerial Quality, Technical Efficiency and Firm Productivity

The production function must be modified to incorporate managerial quality and measure firm productivity by TFP – which incorporates efficiency parameters – to directly estimate the effect of managerial quality on efficiency and productivity.[4] It then follows that by decomposing TFP growth, it is possible to clarify the component of TFP growth that was attributable to managerial quality and related x-efficiency.

The production function model (denoted by XIE) for the XI frontier–counterfactual growth with external factors and management technical inefficiencies is:

$$y_{it}^B = f(d_{it}^B, t) \exp(-u_{it})$$

In logarithm:

$$
\begin{aligned}
&= \hat{\beta}_0 + \hat{\beta}_k k_i + \hat{\beta}_l l_i + \hat{\beta}_m m_i + \frac{1}{2}\left(\hat{\beta}_{ll} l_i^2\right) + \frac{1}{2}\left(\hat{\beta}_{kk} k_i^2\right) \\
&+ \frac{1}{2}\left(\hat{\beta}_{mm} m_i^2\right) + \hat{\beta}_{lk} l_i k_i + \hat{\beta}_{lm} l_i m_i + \hat{\beta}_{km} k_i m_i + \hat{\beta}_t t_i \\
&+ \frac{1}{2}\hat{\beta}_{tt} t_i^2 + \hat{\beta}_{tk} t_i k_i + \hat{\beta}_{tl} t_i l_i + \hat{\beta}_{tm} t_i m_i + g(q_{it}') \\
&+ a_i + h_i + \varepsilon_{it}
\end{aligned}
\quad (10.2)
$$

Where d_{it}^B is a vector of standard factor (S) inputs (k_{it}, l_{it}, m_{it}), accounting for managerial quality (q_{it}') and firm-specific and external factors of firm i in period t (i = 1, ..., N; t = 1, ..., T); and $f(.)$ is the production technology, allowing for technical inefficiency and a time trend (t). The q_{it}' managerial quality covariates are treated like the standard inputs k_{it}, l_{it} and m_{it} and measured in standardised z-scores. The output (y_{it}^B) is in logarithm, β is the output elasticity of the S inputs specified (parametric) and $g(q_{it}')$ is unspecified (nonparametric) – a semi-parametric estimation approach in which managerial quality acts as a proxy for firm productivity. The production function in Equation 10.2 assumes that (i) the inclusion of q_{it}' changes the productivity of available technology, (ii) management shifts technology neutrally (Griffith et al. 2004; Mundlak 1961) and (iii) growth is time-varying (Kumbhakar et al. 2015). This accounts for the potential importance of management to productivity, management input and quality in the estimation of the production function (Triebs and Kumbhakar 2012). The variables a and h denote firm-specific and external factors beyond the manager and firm's control, respectively, while ε is the error term. The firm-specific control variables are leverage, firm age, firm size and industry, all of which may affect firm productivity (see Tong 2019, pp. 123–124). Apart from internal managerial quality factors directly affecting TFP, external factors affecting a firm's business environment may affect the management–TFP relationship because of their influence on managerial incentives (Frantz 2007; Leibenstein 1966, 1976). Recent empirical evidence on the external factors affecting the firm management–productivity relationship has found that competition, internationalisation and trade liberalisation have implications for managerial quality and firm productivity (see Tong 2019, pp. 157–160). These external factors are employed in this analysis.

The process to separate TFP growth into its components is as follows. Under the TFP change approach, TFP growth with multiple inputs is defined as output growth minus the growth of a combination of the measured factor inputs (i.e., $T\dot{F}P = \dot{y} - \sum_s P^a \dot{d}_s$, where $P_s^a = w_s d_s / \sum_s w_s d_s$, with w_s being the price of input, and d_{it} being a vector of S inputs, denoted d_s for simplicity). In a single-output production function with panel data, output is defined as a function of the measured factor inputs multiplied by the expected efficiency over time (i.e., $y_{it} = f[d_{it}, t] \exp[-u_{it}]$, where d_{it} is a vector of S inputs). The component $u_{it} > 0$ is output-oriented technical inefficiency, which is used as a measure of x-inefficiency. In the neoclassical production model, which assumes no x-inefficiency ($u_{it} = 0$) (thus, $\exp[-u_{it}] = 1$), a firm is viewed as being fully XE. Subsequently, $\dot{TFP}$ can be expanded and separated into technological change (TC) and efficiency change (EC) components using:

$$\dot{TFP} = \partial \ln f(.)/\partial t + \left(-\partial u/\partial t + \sum_s [f_s d_s / f - P_s^a] \dot{d}_s\right) = TC + EC$$

Which is derived by substituting a total differentiation of the output equation (i.e., $\dot{y} = f(d_{it}, t) \exp(-u_{it})$) into the definition of TFP growth ($\dot{TFP}$). The EC component can be decomposed further into technical efficiency change (TEC), scale and allocative efficiency as:

$$EC = -\partial u/\partial t + \sum_s [f_s d_s / f - P_s^a] \dot{d}_s$$

$$= -\partial u/\partial t + (RTS - 1) \sum_s \lambda_s \dot{d}_s + \sum_s (\lambda_s - P_s^a) \dot{d}_s$$

$$= TEC + Scale + Allocative$$

where:

$$RTS = \sum_s [\partial \ln y / \partial \ln d_s] = \sum_s [\partial \ln f(.)/\partial \ln d_s]$$

$$= \sum_s [f_s(.) d_s / f(.)] \equiv \sum_s b_s$$

RTS is a return to scale measure, and b_s is the input elasticity defined by the production frontier $f(d,t)$, with d being the factor of production accounting for managerial quality and firm-specific and external factors. $\lambda_s = f_s d_s / \sum_k f_k d_k = b_s / RTS$ when f_s is the marginal product of input d_s (for details see Kumbhakar et al. 2015).

Thus, as proposed by Leibenstein's x-efficiency theory, this framework allows for the separation of TFP growth into four components and the possibility of TEC affecting TFP over time because of the time-varying effects of technical inefficiency (a measure of x-inefficiency), expressed as $\exp(-u_{it})$. This model provides a measure of x-inefficiency or relative x-efficiency as a determinant of measured TFP growth:

$$\dot{TFP} = \partial \ln f(.)/\partial t + (-\partial u/\partial t) + (RTS - 1) \sum_s \lambda_s \dot{d}_s$$

$$+ \sum_s (\lambda_s - P_s^a) \dot{d}_s \quad (10.3)$$

$$= TC + TEC + Scale + Allocative$$

where TFP = total factor productivity, TC = technological change, TEC = technical efficiency change, $Scale$ = scale and $Allocative$ = improvements in allocative efficiency.

In the neoclassical approach to TFP growth decomposition, the traditional null hypothesis assumes that all technologies should be adopted because all firms and managers are fully XE (Friedman 1984). The neoclassical model assumes no managerial slack or technical inefficiency, thus $TEC = 0$. In the neoclassical view, there can be no TEC because technical inefficiency is assumed to be time-invariant with management changes.

In contrast, the behavioural x-inefficiency approach to TFP growth decomposition allows for managerial slack and technical inefficiency and recognises that firms and managers can be XI (Leibenstein 1966, 1978). In this case, $TEC \neq 0$ and can change over time with managerial quality (i.e., $TEC = -\partial u / \partial t \neq 0$). That is, improvements in management quality that compensate for market and firm inefficiencies can affect the estimated rate of TEC in the determination of TFP growth.

Consequently, TFP growth decomposition incorporating TEC in the measurement framework, as specified in Equation 10.3, and bias in TFP growth estimation from the missing managerial quality–TEC effect is estimated as:

$$\kappa_{\dot{C}}^* = \frac{\dot{C}_{\dot{u} \geq 0}^{XIE \text{ no TEC}} - \dot{C}_{\dot{u} \geq 0}^{XIE \text{ with TEC}}}{\left| \dot{C}_{\dot{u} \geq 0}^{XIE \text{ with TEC}} \right|} \quad (10.4)$$

where $\dot{C}$ denotes the components of TFP growth, and XIE denotes XI frontier–counterfactual growth with external factors and management technical inefficiencies.

If deficiencies in management technical efficiency make no difference to TC and TFP growth with changes in the external business environment, as assumed by the traditional model with no TEC, then $\kappa_{\dot{C}=\dot{T}C}^*$ and $\kappa_{\dot{C}=\dot{T}\dot{F}P}^*$ computed using Equation 10.4 will both be 0. However, if $\kappa_{\dot{C}=\dot{T}C}^*$ and $\kappa_{\dot{C}=\dot{T}\dot{F}P}^*$ are not 0, then there is evidence for the alternative model, which assumes that managerial quality and TEC affect TC and TFP growth in productivity determination.

RESULTS AND DISCUSSION

Managerial Quality, Ownership and Performance in some OECD Countries

A meta-regression analysis of data from 46 studies on OECD countries was conducted (for details of primary studies and data sources, see Tong 2019, pp. 84–86). Table 10.1 summarises the variations in the size of the effect of managerial ownership and ownership concentration on firm performance by country after controlling for various methodological differences (see Equation 10.1). In Table 10.1, *MRA1* shows the meta-regression results of the estimated effect size (Zr) of the ownership structure–firm performance relationship based on different ownership and country characteristics. *MRA1* shows the dependent variable (Zr) meta-regression results based on ownership and country characteristics and controlling for differences in estimation methods between studies. The results reported for *MRA1* and *MRA1* reveal that 91 per cent of the 99 per cent between-study variation (heterogeneity) in the effect of ownership structure on firm performance nexus, as detected by Higgins et al.'s (2003) I^2 index, may be attributable to differences in managerial quality. Only 1.29 per cent is explained by methodological heterogeneity (related to differences in estimation techniques and measurements), with the remaining 6.8 per cent attributable to residual heterogeneity and no more than 0.8 per cent of this attributable to sampling error. Analysis of the relationship between managerial and

Table 10.1 Meta-regression analysis of ownership–performance relationship

Variable	MRA1 Zr	MRA1 Zr	MRA2 Zr_inown	MRA3 Zr_owncon
N	525	525	372	153
τ^2	0.089	0.068	0.005	0.172
I^2	99.30%	99.20%	78.10%	99.70%
$Adj.R^2$	91.10%	93.20%	90.80%	94.10%
Prob>F	0	0	0	0
Sampling error		0.80%	8.70%	11.29%
_cons	0.424**	0.281	0.036	0.662
Country (C)				
Australia	0.138	−0.054	0.03	−0.119
Canada	−0.012	−0.181	0.195***	−0.396
France	5.480***	4.818***		5.635***
Germany	−0.03	−0.212		−0.409
Japan	0.103	−0.051	0.03	0.211
South Korea	0.398**	0.083		0.655
Mexico	0.054	−0.056		
Netherlands	1.903***	1.597***		1.770**
New Zealand	0.384***	−0.028	−0.026	−0.216
Spain	0.17	−0.108	−0.091	−0.11
Sweden	0.12	−0.076	−0.096	
Switzerland	0.065	−0.096	0.145	−0.4
Turkey	0.153	−0.081	−0.041	
United Kingdom	0.153	−0.089	−0.066	−0.258
United States	0.019	−0.064	−0.054	0.125
Ownership characteristic (O)	Yes	Yes	Yes	Yes
Performance specification (P)	No	Yes	Yes	Yes
Estimation method (M)	No	Yes	Yes	Yes
Functional form (F)	No	Yes	Yes	Yes
The control indicator (D)	No	Yes	Yes	Yes

Note: Zr = dependent variable in the full meta-regression; Zr_inown = dependent variable in the managerial ownership subsample; Zr_owncon = the dependent variable in the ownership concentration subsample. The meta-regression analysis was carried out in Stata. τ^2 = restricted maximum likelihood estimates of between-study variance. I^2 = residual variation due to heterogeneity. Adjusted R2 = proportion of between-study variance explained by the covariates. ***, ** and * denote p < 1 per cent, p < 5 per cent and p < 10 per cent, respectively. All firms included in this study meta-analysis were publicly listed; hence, data reported are annual. The Fisher z-transformation effect size was calculated as $Zr = 1/2 \log_e\left[1+r/1-r\right]$, and $r = \left[e^{2Zr}-1\right]/\left[e^{2Zr}+1\right]$. Data source: Tong (2019, pp. 84–86).

ownership concentration and firm performance (in $\overline{MRA2}$ and $\overline{MRA3}$, respectively) revealed similar patterns.

The existence of substantial effect size variations (heterogeneity beyond that arising from methodological differences) between different countries and ownership structures suggests that the effect of ownership on performance may be primarily influenced by management variables. Managers have some degree of freedom in making decisions, which may enhance or impede efficiency; thus, firm performance depends on the ownership structure as a corporate governance mechanism.

Using the ownership structure information available in the *OECD Corporate Governance Factbook 2015* (OECD 2015), the countries shown in Table 10.1 can be characterised into three types of firm ownership based on their systems of corporate governance: diffused ownership (i.e., Australia, Canada, Japan, United States [US], United Kingdom [UK] and the Netherlands), concentrated ownership (i.e., France, South Korea, Mexico, New Zealand [NZ], Spain, Sweden, Switzerland and Turkey) and duopolistic ownership (a mix of concentrated and diffused ownership structures) (i.e., Germany).

The rest of this section discusses how managerial quality as a variable helps to reconcile the mixed empirical results regarding the ownership–performance nexus in sampled OECD countries. This application provides meaningful insights into the importance of managerial quality under different ownership structures as a factor influencing firm performance.

Entrenchment and expropriation effects

The financial needs of firms in countries with relatively diffused firm ownership are typically fulfilled through capital markets with strong external governance mechanisms, such as corporate control and management discipline. Thus, increasing managerial ownership in countries characterised by diffused ownership does not provide managers with incentives to work harder and improve firm performance if a firm is owned by a significant core of insiders, meaning that the entrenchment effect is more likely to emerge, and the incentive effect is likely to be ineffective when fewer directors are involved (Cosh et al. 2008). The entrenchment effect was evident in the US and the UK, but its magnitude was small, with $Zr^{inown}_{United\ States} = -0.054$ and $Zr^{inown}_{United\ Kingdom} = -0.066$. This result is consistent with findings on the large shareholder expropriation effect on the ownership concentration–performance nexus in the UK, with $Zr^{owncon}_{United\ Kingdom}$ being negative at −0.258. There is a less active corrective market for corporate control mechanisms against management entrenchment; thus, large shareholder monitoring of management was also relatively inefficient in Australia at $Zr^{owncon}_{Australia} = -0.119$ and Canada at $Zr^{owncon}_{Canada} = -0.396$.

For countries in which there is relatively concentrated ownership, thus less rigorous regulatory systems, firms' financial needs are frequently fulfilled through bank finance, resulting in a weaker management discipline via the securities market. Thus, to control suboptimal managerial quality, much emphasis is placed on internal control mechanisms (e.g., the monitoring and discipline of management by boards) (Coffee 2012; Koen and Mason 2005). In this case, increasing managerial ownership also fails to incentivise managers to work harder and improve firm performance if the problem relates to large shareholders creating challenges in monitoring and controlling for suboptimal managerial quality. Such a result was evident in the case of NZ, Spain, Sweden and Turkey.

In NZ, the effects of both managerial ownership and ownership concentration on firm performance were negative at $Zr^{inown}_{New\ Zealand} = -0.026$ and $Zr^{owncon}_{New\ Zealand} = -0.216$, respectively. Jiang et al. (2009) identified a potential threat to management practices in that the largest institutional investors in NZ were more tolerant and accommodating of suboptimal top management compensation packages. This outcome indicates the preference for a close large shareholder–management relationship arising from the advantage of individual control in the absence of stringent regulatory disclosure and transparency, irrespective of costs to firm performance. Another possible reason for large institutional investors' passivity in monitoring management in NZ may be the geographical separation of these shareholders from the firms in which they own stocks. On 31 March 2001, foreign institutions and corporations collectively held 54 per cent of NZ equities, while local institutions only held a meagre 15 per cent (Healy 2001). A study by Rad et al. (2013) found that NZ's managerial (insider) ownership was 12 per cent, while outsider block ownership was approximately 49 per cent. Although NZ's publicly listed firms had begun to revert to the mid-range of outside block ownership, the issue of ineffective monitoring remained (Jiang et al. 2009).

In Spain, monitoring is ineffective because of the likelihood of rent expropriation at high ownership concentration levels (de Miguel et al. 2004). The high level of ownership concentration and the lack of independent boards and management teams in Spanish firms, resulting in a lack of competent control mechanisms, make it easier for large shareholders to expropriate rent. Boards of directors in Spain are also one-tiered, meaning that board members both manage and supervise the firm. Such board members usually lack the information and freedom to make decisions (Ricart et al. 1999). Ineffective internal control mechanisms can result in poor monitoring and control of managers and the increased risk of expropriation activities by large shareholders. Hence, the effect of managerial ownership on firm performance was negative at $Zr^{inown}_{Spain} = -0.091$ and that of ownership concentration was negative at $Zr^{owncon}_{Spain} = -0.110$.

In Turkey, increased managerial ownership decreased firm performance ($Zr^{inown}_{Turkey} = -0.041$). This entrenchment effect may be related to Turkey's high level of state ownership concentration. The lack of competition and high level of industry protection and administrative management provide more scope for suboptimal activities and less pressure for improved managerial quality when protected from competitive market forces. A similar argument is evident in the case of Sweden, where $Zr^{inown}_{Sweden} = -0.096$ (OECD 2015; Önder 2003).

In Switzerland, increased ownership concentration had a reasonable expropriation effect on firm performance ($Zr^{owncon}_{Switzerland} = -0.400$). This result may be related to the fact that a significant number of shares in publicly listed firms are concentrated in the hands of controlling shareholder groups (Barroso Casado et al. 2016), thus making it difficult to rely on Swiss boards to monitor large shareholders' expropriation activities.

In Germany, the moderate negative association between ownership concentration and firm performance ($Zr^{owncon}_{Germany} = -0.409$) may be attributable to the inefficient German system of mandatory parity or quasi-parity codetermination. In this system, significant control rights are ceded to employees without them having to make any coalition-specific investments. The worker-directors supervising and influencing managerial decisions in this duopolistic management system do not bear the total costs of their decisions because they have no direct income rights, cannot transfer property rights to others and do not share directly in residual claims of the firm's output. These conditions explain why the incentive structure to motivate the supervisory board's efficiency-enhancing monitoring may be relatively ineffective in Germany (Addison and Schnabel 2009).

Incentive and monitoring effects
In countries characterised by diffused ownership, increased managerial ownership may incentivise managers to work harder if relatively dispersed shareholders hold the share of ownership. Small incentive effects were evident in the managerial ownership–firm performance relationships in Canada, Australia and Japan (Zr^{inown}_{Canada}, $Zr^{inown}_{Australia}$ and Zr^{inown}_{Japan} were 0.195, 0.03 and 0.03, respectively).

Studies show that increasing the number of active external large shareholders may induce better monitoring of management and improve firm performance, but this effect may be lower than expected because of weak internal control mechanisms (Edmans and Holderness 2017). This result is consistent with the small but positive monitoring efficiency of large external shareholders in the US ($Zr^{owncon}_{United States} = 0.125$).

In the Netherlands, the suboptimal activities of managers may be limited by increasing shareholder ownership concentration if the shareholders are active external large shareholders with significant business shareholdings. This outcome suggests a large positive significant association between large shareholder ownership and improved managerial quality and firm performance. The estimated effect size of ownership concentration on firm performance in the Netherlands was $Zr^{owncon}_{Netherlands} = 1.770$. A relatively more concentrated control structure in the Netherlands (38 per cent) with significant trust office ownership corresponds to its relatively high and considerable monitoring efficiency effect of ownership concentration on firm performance. The disproportionately large institutional holding in a small country with large financial centres, brought about by the nation's ultra-flexible tax policies, management-friendly governance laws and home court advantages suffusing the legal system, is key to such a large and significant positive effect size. The existence of two distinct corporate governance systems in Japan – one among independent firms and the other among firms with a *keiretsu* structure of corporate ownership – may explain why the aggregate effect size of ownership concentration on firm performance was relatively small and less significant in Japan ($Zr^{owncon}_{Japan} = 0.211$) than that observed in the Netherlands ($Zr^{owncon}_{Netherlands} = 1.770$).

Among countries characterised by concentrated ownership, the case of France reveals that concentrated ownership in the hands of a single large shareholder (or group) could limit managers' suboptimal activities by inducing monitoring efficiency with effective corporate governance regulations and rules (Lakhal 2005). The effect of ownership concentration on firm performance was positive and relatively high in France ($Zr^{owncon}_{France} = 5.635$). This result means that a standard deviation increase in concentrated ownership shareholding z-score above the mean is associated with a greater than a one-to-one increase in firm performance. The positive large shareholder monitoring effect was smaller in the case of South Korea ($Zr^{owncon}_{Korea} = 0.655$), which could be related to the existence of multi-firm conglomerates, which have significant government influence and substantial family involvement in management (Choi et al. 2018; Lim and Kim 2005).

These findings suggest that the relationship between ownership and performance varies from firm to firm depending on management quality. Thus, empirical models and methods used in the analysis of firms should include managerial quality when measuring firm performance in given ownership and country contexts.

MANAGERIAL QUALITY, TECHNICAL EFFICIENCY AND FIRM PRODUCTIVITY IN NZ

Using stochastic frontier modelling and a longitudinal microdata set (2001–2012) from NZ, the effect of managerial technical efficiency on firm productivity in NZ from the perspective of x-efficiency theory was investigated (for details on data sources, see Tong 2019, pp. 160–165). The results presented in Table 10.2 highlight that managerial quality in NZ is not fully XE, implying the existence of technical inefficiency; thus, the use of a neoclassical model that ignores improvements in TEC with better management will underestimate TC and TFP growth.

Table 10.2 shows that at a 1.03 per cent rate of TEC, based on XIE frontier growth and ignoring TEC, the average TC rate was underestimated by a factor of 2.1 ($\kappa^*_{\dot{C}=\dot{T}C} > 0$), thus TFP growth by a factor of 2.4 ($\kappa^*_{\dot{C}=T\dot{F}P} > 0$). These findings highlight the potential effects of managerial quality in determining efficiency and productivity gaps, and that failing to consider such a link biases the parameter estimates of the production function and consequently the estimated rate of change of TFP and its components. Thus, a behavioural x-efficiency model based on a more realistic assumption about the link between managerial quality and technical efficiency will yield better estimates of TEC rates and efficiency-enhancing technological progress and correct for biases in the estimation of the scale and allocative components of TFP. Thus, TFP growth decomposition shows that managerial quality is a determinant of firm TFP by affecting the rates of TEC and TC.

The existence of a TEC–TC–TFP link is consistent with the notion that new or existing technologies may not be adopted in a given external business environment because firms and countries are not operating at an optimal level of efficiency (Altman 2009; Rosenberg 1982). Inefficiencies in XIE sub-frontier firms will impede the growth of TEC, TC and TFP if management was otherwise more XE. This outcome aligns with x-efficiency theory (Leibenstein

Table 10.2 *Estimating the effect of managerial quality on firm productivity and its components: behavioural technical x-efficiency model (with TEC) v. neoclassical model (without TEC)*

Model		Variables (C)				
		Scale	TC	TEC	Allocative	$T\dot{F}P^{NZ}_{\dot{q} \leq 0}$
Behavioural technical x-efficiency model	$\left(TEC = -\dfrac{\partial u}{\partial t} \neq 0\right)$	−2.00%	0.66%	1.03%	1.66%	1.35%
Neoclassical ordinary least squares production model	$(TEC = 0)$	−1.63%	−0.59%	–	1.28%	−0.94%
Modelling biases (in factor): $\kappa^*_{\dot{C}}$		0.2	2.1	1.0	0.3	2.4

Note: The models control for firm-specific effects and external influences. External influences = industry competition (Herfindahl–Hirschman Index), internationalisation (export intensity and scope) and the distortionary trade effect of the tariffs (ad valorem equivalent). TFP = total factor productivity; TEC = technical efficiency change; TC = technological change; NZ = New Zealand. Data source: Statistics New Zealand's longitudinal microdata for the period 2001–2012 (see Tong 2019, pp. 160–165).

1966, 1968) and helps us to better understand the uneven technological diffusion and persistent productivity gaps across firms and countries, which cannot be explained by the neoclassical theory of the firm (Baumol 1986; DeLong 1988; Leibenstein 1969).

The analyses presented in this chapter could be applied to other jurisdictions grappling with the productivity problem. There is room to suggest that better managerial quality may improve the TFP of firms in other countries by accounting for the negative relationship between underskilling and lower within-firm productivity (McGowan and Andrews 2015). The increasing availability of firm-level microdata and ongoing efforts to connect databases and information systems in OECD and European Union countries should facilitate the exchange of microdata for statistical purposes in future international research projects (Eurostat 2019).

CONCLUSIONS

The findings of this chapter highlight that by affecting x-efficiency, managerial quality is a crucial determinant of firm performance variations, TFP gaps and TEC and TC rates. Such a critical linkage reinforces the behavioural economic approach to firm theory that firms and managers are not fully XE. Managerial decisions and quality differ significantly between organisational contexts, as suggested by the substantial variations (beyond methodological differences) between countries and types of organisational ownership. Such variations mean that the assumptions underlying managerial quality and efficiency are important for the validity of x-efficiency theory and modelling firm-level data in testing the effect of management technical efficiency on firm performance variations and TFP gaps. The empirical results emphasise the importance of improving the quality of management to enhance the performance and TFP of firms in NZ and elsewhere.

The findings have critical implications for public policies and managerial practices in laggard firms aiming to close their performance and productivity gaps with frontier firms.

To discourage suboptimal management behaviours, the government should develop policies for greater accountability and transparency of management decisions. Policies should promote systems to measure and manage managerial quality, firm performance and productivity. Central and regional government systems for monitoring firms' activities and performance will increase top management accountability and facilitate large shareholders' monitoring efforts by providing a transparent information platform. Suboptimal management behaviours could further be limited if there is no close relationship between large shareholders and managers.[5]

Managerial efficiency could also increase with high-yield work cultures and practices associated with more active employee participation,[6] greater cooperation between employees and management,[7] employee compensation related to productivity and long-term job security.[8] The development of policies to promote an outward-facing and engaged tertiary education system with strong links to industry, the community and the international economy is also critical to the development of the managerial human capital resources of firms. Better management education, training (both formal and informal) and job matching should improve managerial quality, providing managers with skills to drive new work practices that effectively integrate new technologies and reallocate resources to more productive uses, enabling firms to successfully operate in the international marketplace.

NOTES

1. The author would like to thank Professor Morris Altman and Professor Roger Frantz for providing comments on the first draft of this chapter. This research was supported by an Australian Government Research Training Program (RTP) Scholarship.
2. The results are not official statistics. They have been created for research purposes from the Integrated Data Infrastructure (IDI) and Longitudinal Business Database (LBD) which are carefully managed by Statistics New Zealand (Stats NZ). For more information about the IDI and LBD please visit www.stats.govt.nz/integrated-data/. The results are based in part on tax data supplied by Inland Revenue to Stats NZ under the Tax Administration Act 1994 for statistical purposes. Any discussion of data limitations or weaknesses is in the context of using the IDI for statistical purposes, and is not related to the data's ability to support Inland Revenue's core operational requirements.
3. The variables t and df denote t-statistics and residual degrees of freedom, respectively. In studies that did not report t-statistics, t was computed using the reported standard error, p-value or z-statistics ($r = z/\sqrt{n}$, where n = sample size) (Rosenthal 1991). Using the Fisher z-transformation, r was transformed to make it independent from the unknown population of partial correlation coefficients (ρ) because large ρ values can skew the distribution of r (Wang and Shailer 2015).
4. That is, x-efficient firms may be more productive by performing better than the 'ideal' performance of firms operating at the production frontier, and vice versa.
5. If a close relationship between large shareholders and managers exists, management policies should aim at more decentralised organisational structures to improve monitoring among management (North 1990).
6. Giving employees more voice could increase efficiency (Altman 2005; Gordon 1996).
7. A less hierarchical management system could increase efficiency (Lee and Edmondson 2017; Pfeffer 1995).
8. Efficiency wages and long-term employment relationship are associated with higher efficiency and productivity (Altman 2002; Fehr et al. 2009)

REFERENCES

Addison, John T. and Claus Schnabel (2009), 'Worker directors: A German product that didn't export?', http://ftp.iza.org/dp3918.pdf.

Al-Matari, Ebrahim M., Abdullah K. Al-Swidi and Faudziah H. B. Fadzil (2014), 'The measurements of firm performance's dimensions', *Asian Journal of Finance & Accounting*, **6** (1), 24–49.

Altman, Morris (1999), 'The methodology of economics and the survival principle revisited and revised: Some welfare and public policy implications of modeling the economic agent', *Review of Social Economy*, **57** (4), 427–449.

Altman, Morris (2002), 'Economic theory and the challenge of innovative work practices', *Economic and Industrial Democracy*, **23** (2), 271–290.

Altman, Morris (2005), 'Behavioral economics, power, rational inefficiencies, fuzzy sets, and public policy', *Journal of Economic Issues*, **39** (3), 683–706.

Altman, Morris (2007), 'Effort discretion and economic agency and behavioral economics: Transforming economic theory and public policy', in Roger Frantz (ed.), *Renaissance in behavioral economics: Essays in honor of Harvey Leibenstein,* New York, US: Routledge, pp. 105–145.

Altman, Morris (2009), 'A behavioral–institutional model of endogenous growth and induced technical change', *Journal of Economic Issues*, **43** (3), 685–714.

Altman, Morris (ed.) (2013), *Economic growth and the high wage economy: Choices, constraints and opportunities in the market economy,* London, UK and New York, US: Routledge.

Argote, Linda and Henrich R. Greve (2007), 'A behavioral theory of the firm—40 years and counting: Introduction and impact', *Organization Science*, **18** (3), 337–349.

Barroso Casado, Raúl, Michael Burkert, Antonio Dávila and Daniel Oyon (2016), 'Shareholder protection: The role of multiple large shareholders', *Corporate Governance: An International Review*, **24** (2), 105–129.

Baumol, William J. (1986), 'Productivity growth, convergence, and welfare: What the long-run data show', *The American Economic Review,* **76** (5), 1072–1085.

Baumol, William J. (1996), 'Entrepreneurship: Productive, unproductive, and destructive', *Journal of Business Venturing,* **11** (1), 3–22.

Berle, Adolf A. and Gardiner C. Means (eds) (1991), *The modern corporation and private property,* New York, US: Transaction Publishers.

Bloom, Nicholas, Christos Genakos, Raffaella Sadun and John Van Reenen (2012), 'Management practices across firms and countries', *Academy of Management Perspectives,* **26** (1), 12–33.

Bloom, Nicholas and John Van Reenen (2010), 'Why do management practices differ across firms and countries?', *Journal of Economic Perspectives,* **24** (1), 203–224.

Bloom, Nicholas, Raffaella Sadun and John Van Reenen (2016), 'Management as a technology?', https://www.nber.org/system/files/working_papers/w22327/w22327.pdf.

Boyd, Brian K. and Angelo M. Solarino (2016), 'Ownership of corporations: A review, synthesis, and research agenda', *Journal of Management,* **42** (5), 1282–1314.

Choi, Daeheon, Chune Y. Chung, Kyung S. Kim and Jason Young (2018), 'The impact of institutional investor trading on income smoothing: Evidence from the Korean stock market', *Transylvanian Review,* **1** (1), 1221–1249.

Coffee, John C., Jr. (2012), 'Dispersed ownership: The theories, the evidence, and the enduring tension between "lumpers" and "splitters"', in Dennis C. Mueller (ed.), *The Oxford handbook of capitalism,* New York, US: Oxford University Press, pp. 463–507.

Cosh, Andy, Paul Guest and Alan Hughes (2008), 'UK corporate governance and takeover performance', in Klaus Gugler and Burcin B. Yurtoglu (eds.), *The economics of corporate governance and mergers,* Cheltenham, UK and Northampton, US: Edward Elgar, pp. 226–261.

Cyert, Richard M. and James G. March (1963), *A behavioral theory of the firm.* Engelwood Cliffs, US: Prentice Hall.

DeLong, Bradford J. (1988), 'Productivity growth, convergence, and welfare: Comment', *The American Economic Review,* **78** (5), 1138–1154.

de Miguel, Alberto, Julio Pindado and Chabela de la Torre (2004), 'Ownership structure and firm value: New evidence from Spain', *Strategic Management Journal,* **25** (12), 1199–1207.

Edmans, Alex and Clifford G. Holderness (2017), 'Blockholders: A survey of theory and evidence', in Benjamin E. Hermalin and Michael S. Weisbach (eds.), *The handbook of the economics of corporate governance,* Oxford, UK: North Holland, pp. 541–636.

Eurostat. (2019), 'Micro data linking: 2019 edition', https://ec.europa.eu/eurostat/documents/3859598/10295208/KS-GQ-19-013-EN-N.pdf/5e2fdf0a-2bf9-7430-309a-3565fc1d329f?t=1575968597000.

Fehr, Ernst, Lorenz F. Goette and Christian Zehnder (2009), 'A behavioral account of the labour market: The role of fairness concerns', *Annual Review of Economics,* **1** (1), 355–384.

Fiordelisi, Franco, Philip Molyneux and Daniele Previati (2010), 'Introduction', in Franco Fiordelisi, Philip Molyneux and Daniele Previati (eds), *New issues in financial institutions management,* Hampshire, UK and New York, US: Palgrave Macmillan, pp. 1–10.

Frantz, Roger (1980), 'On the existence of x-efficiency', *Journal of Post Keynesian Economics,* **2** (4), 509–527.

Frantz, Roger (ed.) (1988), *X-efficiency: Theory, evidence and applications,* Boston, US: Kluwer Academic.

Frantz, Roger (2007), 'Introduction: Leibenstein as a behavioral pioneer', in Roger Frantz (ed.), *Renaissance in behavioral economics: Essays in honor of Harvey Leibenstein,* New York, US: Routledge, pp. 1–16.

Frantz, Roger (2020), 'The beginnings of behavioral economics: Katona, Simon, and Leibenstein's x-efficiency theory', in Morris Altman (ed.), *Perspectives in behavioral economics and the economics of behavior,* Oxford, UK: Elsevier.

Friedman, Milton (1984), 'The methodology of positive economics', in Daniel M. Hausman (ed.), *The philosophy of economics: An anthology,* New York, US: Cambridge University Press, pp. 145–178.

Gordon, David M. (ed.) (1996), *Fat and mean: The corporate squeeze of working Americans and the myth of managerial 'downsizing',* New York, US: Simon and Schuster.

Greene, William H. and Dan Segal (2004), 'Profitability and efficiency in the US life insurance industry', *Journal of Productivity Analysis,* **21** (3), 229–247.

Griffith, Rachel, Stephen Redding and John Van Reenen (2004), 'Mapping the two faces of R&D: Productivity growth in a panel of OECD industries', *The Review of Economics and Statistics*, **86** (4), 883–895.

Healy, J. (2001), 'New Zealand capital markets', paper presented at Ministry of Economic Development, Wellington, New Zealand.

Higgins, Julian P., Simon G. Thompson, Jonathan J. Deeks and Douglas G. Altman (2003), 'Measuring inconsistency in meta-analyses', *British Medical Journal*, **327** (7414), 557–560.

Hoch, Irving (1962), 'Estimation of production function parameters combining time-series and cross-section data', *Econometrica*, **30** (1), 34–53.

Hu, Yabei and Shigemi Izumida (2008), 'Ownership concentration and corporate performance: A causal analysis with Japanese panel data', *Corporate Governance: An International Review*, **16** (4), 342–358.

Janssen, John and Simon McLoughlin (2008), 'New Zealand's productivity performance', https://www.treasury.govt.nz/sites/default/files/2008-04/tprp08-02.pdf.

Jensen, Michael C. and William H. Meckling (1976), 'Theory of the firm: Managerial behaviour, agency costs and ownership structure', *Journal of Financial Economics*, **3** (4), 305–360.

Jiang, Haiyan, Ahsan Habib and Clive Smallman (2009), 'The effect of ownership concentration on CEO compensation-firm performance relationship in New Zealand', *Pacific Accounting Review*, **21** (2), 104–131.

Koen, Carla I. and Kate Mason (eds) (2005), *Comparative international management*, London, UK: McGraw-Hill Education.

Kumbhakar, Subal C., Hung-Jen Wang and Alan P. Horncastle (2015), *A practitioner's guide to stochastic frontier analysis using Stata*, New York, US: Cambridge University Press.

Lakhal, Faten (2005), 'Voluntary earnings disclosures and corporate governance: Evidence from France', *Review of Accounting and Finance*, **4** (3), 64–85.

Lee, Michael Y. and Amy C. Edmondson (2017), 'Self-managing organizations: Exploring the limits of less-hierarchical organizing', *Research in Organizational Behavior*, **37**, 35–58.

Leibenstein, Harvey (1966), 'Allocative efficiency vs. "x-efficiency"', *The American Economic Review*, **56** (3), 392–415.

Leibenstein, Harvey (1968), 'Entrepreneurship and development', *The American Economic Review*, **58** (2), 72–83.

Leibenstein, Harvey (1969), 'Organizational or frictional equilibria, x-efficiency, and the rate of innovation', *The Quarterly Journal of Economics*, **83** (4), 600–623.

Leibenstein, Harvey (1973), 'Note on x-efficiency and technical change', in Eliezer B. Ayal (ed.), *Micro aspects of development*, New York, US: Praeger, pp. 18–38.

Leibenstein, Harvey (ed.) (1976), *Beyond the economic man: A new foundation for microeconomics*, Rhode Island, US: Harvard University Press.

Leibenstein, Harvey (ed.) (1978), *General x-efficiency theory and economic development*, New York, US: Harvard University Press.

Lim, Ungki and Chang-Soo Kim (2005), 'Determinants of ownership structure: An empirical study of the Korean conglomerates', *Pacific-Basin Finance Journal*, **13** (1), 1–28.

Lynne, Gary D. (2015), 'On the economics of subselves: Toward a metaeconomics', in Morris Altman (ed.), *Handbook of contemporary behavioral economics*, London, UK and New York, US: Routledge, pp. 121–144.

Manevska-Tasevska, Gordana, Helena Hansson and Katarina Labajova (2017), 'Impact of management practices on persistent and residual technical efficiency–a study of Swedish pig farming', *Managerial and Decision Economics*, **38** (6), 890–905.

Manyika, James, Jaana Remes, Jan Mischke and Mekala Krishnan (2017), 'The productivity puzzle: A closer look at the United States', https://www.mckinsey.com/~/media/mckinsey/featured%20insights/employment%20and%20growth/new%20insights%20into%20the%20slowdown%20in%20us%20productivity%20growth/mgi-the-productivity-puzzle-discussion-paper.ashx.

McGowan, Müge A. and Dan Andrews (2015), 'Labour market mismatch and labour productivity: Evidence from PIAAC data', https://www.oecd.org/eco/growth/Labour-Market-Mismatch-and-Labour-Productivity-Evidence-from-PIAAC-Data.pdf.

Mundlak, Yair (1961), 'Empirical production function free of management bias', *Journal of Farm Economics,* **43** (1), 44–56.
North, Douglas C. (ed.) (1990), *Institutions, institutional change, and economic performance,* Cambridge, UK and New York, US: Cambridge University Press.
Önder, Zeynep (2003), 'Ownership concentration and firm performance: Evidence from Turkish firms', *METU Studies in Development,* **30** (2), 181–203.
Organisation for Economic Co-operation and Development (2015), 'OECD corporate governance factbook 2015', http://www.tkyd.org/files/downloads/PageFiles/%7Bf80611a8-5832-4cb0-9348-742a9eb32dea%7D/Files/Corporate_Governance_Factbook.pdf.
Pfeffer, Jeffrey (1995), 'Producing sustainable competitive advantage through the effective management of people', *Academy of Management Perspectives,* **9** (1), 55–69.
Rad, Salman A., Stuart Locke and Krishna Reddy (2013), 'Global financial crisis and role of ownership structure on cost of capital', *Asian Journal of Finance & Accounting,* **5** (1), 396–418.
Ricart, Joan, Jose Álvarez and Miguel Gallo (1999), 'Governance mechanisms for effective leadership: The case of Spain', *Corporate Governance: An International Review,* **7** (3), 266–287.
Rosenberg, Nathan (ed.) (1982), *Inside the black box: Technology and economics.* Cambridge, UK and New York, US: Cambridge University Press.
Rosenthal, Robert (Revised ed.) (1991), *Meta-analytic procedures for social research,* Newbury Park, US: Sage.
Schwartz, Hugh H. (ed.) (2008), *A guide to behavioral economics,* Reston, US: Higher Education.
Simon, Herbert A. (1956), 'Rational choice and the structure of the environment', *Psychological Review,* **63** (2): 129–138.
Tomer, John F. (2016), *Integrating human capital with human development: The path to a more productive and humane economy,* New York, US: Palgrave Macmillan.
Tong, Sodany (2019), 'Managerial quality, firm performance, technical efficiency and productivity in New Zealand', http://hdl.handle.net/1959.13/1408624.
Triebs, Thomas P. and Subal C. Kumbhakar (2012), 'Management practice in production', https://www.ifo.de/DocDL/IfoWorkingPaper-129.pdf.
Walker, Ian (2008), 'Null hypothesis testing and effect sizes', http://staff.bath.ac.uk/pssiw/stats2/page2/page14/page14.html.
Wang, Kun and Greg Shailer (2015), 'Ownership concentration and firm performance in emerging markets: A meta-analysis', *Journal of Economic Surveys,* **29** (2), 199–229.
Webber, Don J., Gail A. Webber, Sebastian Berger and Peter Bradley (2018), 'Explaining productivity in a poor productivity region', *Environment and Planning A: Economy and Space,* **50** (1), 157–174.
White, McCall M. (2015), 'Corporate governance', in Michael A. Hitt, R. Duane Ireland and Robert E. Hoskisson (eds), *Strategic management: Competitiveness and globalization: Concepts and cases,* ed. 11, Stamford, US: Cengage Learning, pp. 294–327.
Yunos, Rahimah M. (2011), 'The effect of ownership concentration, board of directors, audit committee and ethnicity on conservative accounting: Malaysian evidence', https://ro.ecu.edu.au/theses/155.

11. Behavioural theories of the firm with a focus on x-efficiency and effort discretion: Implications for analysis
Morris Altman

INTRODUCTION

Behavioural economics offers up theories of the firm which can be counterposed to those provided by conventional neoclassical economics. At least according to Simon, who pioneered contemporary behavioural economics, the starting point of any behavioural theory must be rooted in the realism of one's behavioural assumptions and the context within which decisions are made and firms operate. This includes institutional variables. Therefore, core to a behavioural theory of the firm requires modelling what happens inside the infamous black box of the firm (Simon 1955, 1978, 1979, 1987; Altman 2006a). One such approach is exemplified in Cyert and March's (1963) classic, *Behavioral Theory of the Firm*. Here the authors (close associates of Simon) ask the question of how firms, more specifically firm members, actually behave, and what motivates their behaviour. This question was also addressed earlier by Penrose (1959; on Penrose, see also Almeida and Pessali 2017; Pitelis 2004). Shefrin (1999, 2001) discusses and models financial decision-making in real-world firms. Leibenstein (1966, 1979) models firm performance by informing his model by expected behaviours of real-world decision-makers. Smith (2003) argues, along similar lines, for reality-informed modelling, from his experimental economics methodological approach, wherein he finds that rational and successful agents do not behave as predicted by conventional or neoclassical economics. Cyert, March, Leibenstein, Penrose, Shefrin and Smith, for example, all argue that economic theory needs to build on the empirical reality of the firm given the decision-making capabilities and environment of decision-makers within which decisions are being made.[1]

Firm members actually don't try to maximise profits by matching marginal costs to marginal benefits as standard (neoclassical) theory maintains or implies. Moreover, there is no evidence that such behaviour is key to building a successful firm. Actually, Smith (2003) argues that neoclassical-type behaviour will result in a failed or sub-optimally performing firm. And, behavioural models and narratives of the firm tend to assume that decision-makers don't behave in this fashion (neoclassically) and try to explain why this is the case. This assumption is empirically derived. Moreover, behavioural theories of the firm, at least in the Simon tradition, do not adopt the default assumption that firms, that is, firm decision-makers, should behave in a 'neoclassical' manner for their firm to meet with success. From a methodological perspective, behavioural economics' starting point is to better understand how 'firms' behave in the real world and model this behaviour – there is both an inductive and deductive side to the behavioural economics approach to the firm. This should allow one to better model and understand how and why particular decisions are made under particular circumstances, where economic and non-economic variables all matter in the decision-making process.

The focus of this chapter is to examine and draw out the implications of one important strand of a behavioural theory of the firm, embodied in x-efficiency theory and efficiency wage theory. The original versions of these theories were formulated by Harvey Leibenstein (1957, 1966) as a reality-based alternative to formulistic deductive neoclassical approaches to the firm. Leibenstein's method probes what motivates firm decision-makers and how this affects choices that ultimately impact the extent of firm efficiency. This particular methodological approach to the firm has been extended and enriched over the decades since first formulated many decades ago. What's significant methodologically about efficiency wage and x-efficiency theory is that it provides important building blocks of a theory that affords causal analyses of firm performance based on relatively realistic behavioural assumptions about human behaviour and the institutions that parameterise decisions made inside of the firm. Also, of analytical significance is that x-efficiency theory, in particular, makes no prior assumptions that firms must be economically efficient or that 'neoclassical' behaviour is the most rational and effective means by which economic efficiency can be achieved. This opens the analytical door to what determines efficiency and what choices result in a firm's relative inefficiency and how and why inefficient firms survive over time.

EFFICIENCY WAGE AND X-EFFICIENCY THEORY

Efficiency wage theory was originally formulated by Leibenstein (1957) to explain persistent unemployment in less developed economies. It specifies that there is a unique profit-maximising wage (the efficiency wage), yielding a unique profit-maximising level of effort input per unit of labour input. This was partially based on the argument that if wages were cut at low levels of nutrition, workers' effort input would collapse, cutting into firm profits. Thus, rational decision-makers maintain wages above their market-clearing rate, yielding persistent involuntary unemployment. In this narrative, Leibenstein assumes that firm decision-makers, in the farm or factory, are concerned about making as much profit as possible, and to achieve this end they will not attempt to cut real wages even if labour market conditions allow them to do so. Here, Leibenstein breaks with the conventional economic wisdom by assuming that effort inputs into the production process are not fixed. Rather they are variable, where this variability is a function of the nutritional level of workers which, in turn, is given by the real wage earned by workers. In this model, firm owners/managers will pay a relatively high wage, which is the efficiency wage, to 'maximise' their profits. The result is a higher rate of unemployment than would occur had effort been fixed, insensitive levels of nutrition. In this type of model, paying a wage that is not the efficiency wage would be inconsistent with profit maximisation. In this sense, rational employers, are forced to pay this unique and relatively high wage rate if they want to maximise profits.

Akerlof's contemporary rendering of efficiency wage theory makes the case for an above labour-market-clearing unique efficiency wage, constructed by rational decision-makers, for social and psychological as opposed to nutrition-related reasons. These include social norms or fairness, reciprocity, moral sentiment, insider power, asymmetric information and employers' fear of retaliation by employees for perceived unfair treatment (Akerlof 2002; Akerlof, Dickens and Perry 1996, 2000; Akerlof and Shiller 2009; Bewley 1999). This is the same type of narrative as Leibenstein's: where effort is variable, one has an efficiency wage. But here it is not determined by nutritional levels. Firms are expected to pay workers an efficiency wage, which is above what they would pay workers if fairness did not matter to the determination of effort levels. This would be the case if effort inputs were fixed irrespective of levels of fairness. Akerlof's (2002) project was to explain relatively high levels of involuntary unemployment for rational reasons, which he believed he did through efficiency wage theory. There's no theory of the firm here; however, Akerlof's methodology proffers predictions on how one should expect rational employers to behave with regards to the level of wage rates when effort is variable and fairness is important.

X-EFFICIENCY THEORIES OF THE FIRM

Pioneered by Leibenstein (1966, 1979, 1987; Frantz 1997), x-efficiency theory puts in place the basics of a behavioural theory of the firm that builds on the assumption of effort variability. There are other factors that are of importance to the determination of firm efficiency and productivity, but effort inputs were, for Leibenstein, a long-neglected variable. Simply put, x-inefficiency exists when productivity (labour productivity or total factor productivity) is less than it would be if effort inputs (quality and quantity) are fixed at some maximum, controlling for traditional factor inputs, such as hours worked, capital, land and technology. This sub-optimal level of output is a function of the quantity and quality of effort being inputted into the production process than would be the case under best practice industrial relations and a competitive (product market) environment.[2] For conventional theory, efficiency is typically relegated to the realm of allocative efficiency. In Leibenstein's model, a firm can be both allocatively efficient (in reality allocative inefficiency tends to be quite small) and x-inefficient if effort levels are below what they can be ideally.

Leibenstein's original rendition of x-efficiency theory offers a richer, more nuanced modelling of effort variability than what is modelled through efficiency wage theory and is situated directly on how a firm is organised and managed. It also directly links to the level of product market competitiveness and government subsidies as key determinants of effort input. Finally, Leibenstein links the preferences of firm decision-makers in traditional investor-owned firms as being of fundamental importance in determining the extent of firm efficiency. Unlike efficiency wage theory, there is no attention paid to wage rates as a determinant of economic efficiency. His theory of the firm relates to the preferences of owners and managers in relation to efficiency in production and the extent to which markets and institutional parameters facilitate persistent inefficiency. Leibenstein presents a theory of the firm that's specifically oriented towards explaining how firm inefficiency can persist over time by dropping the conventional assumption that effort inputs are fixed. This assumption of effort variability is a key methodological difference from conventional economics where a potential cause of economic inefficiency (related to effort variability) is assumed away through the assumption of fixed effort inputs.

In this chapter, Leibenstein's (1966) original x-inefficiency theory is briefly elaborated upon, and then key methodological revisions are discussed wherein wages and working conditions, power relations between firm members, mental models and technological change are linked to effort variability. Moreover, x-inefficiency is modelled such that different levels of x-inefficiency are possible for any given market structure even when product markets are heavily competitive. Therefore, one can have multi-equilibrium with regard to different sustainable levels of x-inefficiency. For example, both low- and high-wage firms can be sustainable at different levels of x-inefficiency, even with perfect product market competition. In contrast, for Leibenstein, 'perfect' product market competition would and should eliminate x-inefficiency. One can refer to this revision as representing an x-inefficiency plus theory or a holistic x-inefficiency theory of the firm. This holistic theory facilitates identifying and interrogating different variables that affect the level of effort inputs and, therefore, the extent of x-inefficiency. On the other side of the analytical coin, this theory facilitates identifying and examining variables that serve to make firms more x-efficient and, therefore, more productive even in the context of highly competitive product markets (Altman 1998, 2002, 2005, 2006a, 2009).

A MANAGERIAL X-EFFICIENCY THEORY OF THE FIRM

In the original specification of x-efficiency theory, Leibenstein (1966) focuses on the effort variability of management and owners. Ceteris paribus, reducing the quality and quantity of managerial effort increases unit production costs, by reducing firm productivity, making the firm less competitive, unless protected from competitive pressures. Managers' and owners' decisions on their own effort input drive firm productivity. In this modelling scenario, firm decision-makers, members of the firm hierarchy, might very well be maximising their utility by reducing their effort levels below some reasonable potential high. Leibenstein assumes that members of the firm hierarchy have, on average, a strong preference for leisure. This is because, in Leibenstein's narrative, their utility is not related to the firm achieving x-efficiency. It is also not necessarily related to their firm somehow maximising profits. Even if they know how to maximise efficiency, they will choose not to do so. But such x-inefficient preferences must be consistent with their firm being competitive and their achieving some high level of target income. But realising this target need not require their firm to achieve x-efficiency. To sustain x-inefficiency in production, the firm must be operating in an imperfect product market environment or obtain protection or support from the government to survive as a high-cost firm. Or, such firms can survive if their competitor firms are no more x-efficient than they are. That is to say, their competitors are not characterised by lower average costs.[3] In Leibenstein's model, being x-inefficient results in higher average or unit costs.

One way of illustrating this particular approach to x-efficiency theory is in terms of a very simple economy where labour is the only costed input (Altman 2005).

$$AC = \frac{w}{\left(\frac{Q}{L}\right)} \tag{11.1}$$

where AC is the average cost, w is the wage rate, (Q/L) is the average product of labour, Q is total output and L is labour input measured in terms of hours worked. If managerial effort input is reduced, firm productivity falls (Q/L) and this yields, ceteris paribus, higher average costs. Of course, increasing effort levels increase firm productivity, thereby reducing average costs. The average cost is lowest for the most x-efficient firms. In a more complex model where labour is not the only input in the production function, the implications of varying effort inputs remain the same (see, for example, Altman 2006a). In this model, the competitively sustainable minimum effort levels are given by the extent to which x-inefficient firms are protected from competitive pressures. Therefore, I would argue, based on the assumptions of this model, one can predict that there is an array of levels of x-inefficiency consistent with an array of product market competitiveness wherein managers and owners are the causal intermediaries. The level of competitiveness and the level of x-inefficiency are negatively related.

One of the key predictions from this model is that more competitive markets yield, ceteris paribus, higher levels of x-efficiency. This is achieved through the intermediary of firm managers and owners. Competitive pressures force firm decision-makers into increasing their effort levels, even if this higher level is not preferred. This, however, I would argue, might end up being an unstable equilibrium with regards to the higher effort levels forthcoming from firm decision-makers if their preferences for lower effort levels remain stable. Therefore, if environmental constraints change and are relaxed, one would predict a reversion to lower levels of effort and higher levels of x-inefficiency. Another prediction flowing from this model is that firms (members of the firm hierarchy) with preferences for x-inefficient levels of effort input invest in sheltering activity (a point made by Leibenstein) to preserve an institutional environment where they can choose lower levels of effort input thereby increasing their level of utility. But this would be at the cost to the firm and to society wherein there would be higher average costs and lower levels of x-efficiency, and a smaller economic pie.

Some of these arguments are illustrated in Figure 11.1. Average cost curve 1 is given by managers maximising their level of effort input which maximises the level of x-efficiency (minimising x-inefficiency). This is given, in Leibenstein's narrative, by the extent of product market competition. At average cost curve 1, competition is being maximised. As the extent of competition is reduced, the extent of managerial effort input is reduced, thereby increasing the extent of x-inefficiency. This is given by outward shift in the average cost curve from average cost curve 1 to 2 to 3 to 4. At 4, managerial effort input is being minimised, resulting in minimising the level of x-efficiency, thereby increasing average cost.

Leibenstein extended his model beyond the determinants of managerial and owners' effort supply. Leibenstein (1982) introduces the multi-agent firm, where conflict and conflict resolution in the context of cultural and institutional variables (inclusive of power relationships across

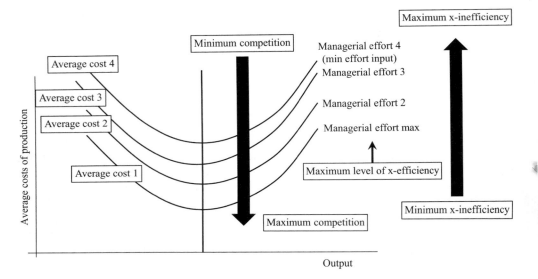

Figure 11.1   Managerial output and average cost

agents) play a key role in determining the levels of effort levels supplied across agents to the firm (Commons 1934, 1950; North 1991; Rothschild 2002; Veblen 1894, 1904). Leibenstein regards the determinants of principle-agent related x-inefficiency as analogous to a potential Prisoner's Dilemma-type problem that can only be resolved by changing the industrial relations system – injecting trust, honesty, fairness, transparency, legal recourse to conflict resolution and conventions into the system – so that agents make choices consistent with Golden Rule or maximum x-efficiency outcomes. Co-operation and trust across agents are the penultimate solutions to maximising the effort dimension of labour supply whilst minimising various transaction costs related to effort monitoring (Leibenstein 1978, 1982, 1983). The alternative, adversarial method of managing the firm incentivises agents to veer towards the low productivity solution (Nash equilibrium) to the firm-based Prisoner's Dilemma problem.[4] But a methodological gap in this model relates to how and why managers and owners should prefer the Golden Rule outcome if this requires more effort input on their part and if their firm's survival and their target income can be achieved without constructing a more cooperative work environment. However, an important point here is that x-efficiency is obtained only in a Golden Rule work environment. And this raises the question of under what conditions such an environment can be obtained. Is the Golder Rule solution realised only through particular preferences of managers and owners? Or, would this require highly competitive product markets either as a necessary or sufficient condition? Moreover, can the Golden Rule solution be obtained under a particular firm ownership structure, such as an employee ownership/cooperative organisational form, or under a particular industrial relations system within the parameters of the traditional investor-owned firm?

AN X-EFFICIENCY PLUS THEORY OF THE FIRM: INTEGRATING MANAGERS, OWNERS AND EMPLOYEES IN THE DETERMINATION OF FIRM X-EFFICIENCY

In a more generalised x-efficiency theory (Altman 1992, 1996, 1998, 1999, 2001b, 2002), unlike in the efficiency wage literature, the wage rate is only one determinant of effort as part of the overall system of industrial relations. In Leibenstein's x-efficiency theory, wage rates are not modelled as a determinant of the level of x-efficiency. Moreover, in the more generalised x-efficiency theory, management and owner preferences for effort are not the primary drivers of the level of x-efficiency, nor is the extent of product market competition. X-efficiency is maximised given the appropriate mix and level of material and nonmaterial incentives, although material incentives are typically quite important. In this x-inefficiency plus model, x-efficiency can be achieved even if product markets are not extremely competitive. Increasing x-efficiency can be a product of voluntary cooperation across agents to maximise output and economic payoffs to workers and members of the firm hierarchy. Or it can be a product of shocks to the system such as increasing wages and improved working conditions, which can occur even if product markets are not highly competitive. Increasing x-efficiency can also be a product of increased competitive pressures that force firm decision-makers as well as agents (workers) to resolve Prisoner's Dilemma-type problems to remain competitive given the new binding constraints facing the firm.

In the x-inefficiency plus model, wages and overall labour compensation play a critical role in determining the level of x-inefficiency. This is part and parcel of the industrial relations system within the firm. There is much evidence that a more cooperative work environment is critical to realise the achievement of the Golden Rule solution to the productivity problem (Altman 1998, 2002, 2005, 2006a; Buchele and Christainsen 1999; Falk and Fehr 2003; Gordon 1998; Helliwell and Huang 2011; Kaufman 2008; Levine and Tyson 1990; Logue and Yates 1999; McKersie and Klein 1983; Organisation for Economic Co-operation and Development 2003; Pfeffer 1995; Solow 1990; Tomer 1987; and Winther and Marens 1997).

This revises the original Leibenstein formulation that focuses on managerial preferences with regard to own-effort provision. There is no consideration given, in Leibenstein's original model, for how employees are incentivised to work harder or smarter to increase the level of x-efficiency. Leibenstein assumes that managerial preferences for more own-efforts yield more x-efficiency. However, any increase in the quality and/or quantity of managerial effort would have to be accompanied by the same on the part of employees. Managerial and employee effort provisions are joint inputs into the production process. Simply increasing managerial effort inputs unaccompanied by increases in employee effort is unlikely to yield increases in the extent of x-efficiency in both the quality and quantity dimensions. However, increasing employee effort typically comes at a cost (wages, benefits, for example). Increasing effort input is not a free-ride. The relationship between managerial/owner and employee effort and the cost of changing effort levels, which is critical to understanding the determination of the level of x-efficiency, is not modelled in the Leibenstein narrative.

It is important to recall that in Leibenstein's model the level of x-efficiency is determined by the extent to which product markets are competitive. One has a simplified model where cost considerations are, in a sense, held constant, and what varies is the level of product market competitiveness. The latter determines the extent of discretion managers and owners have to reduce their effort levels, as this affects the average cost (Figure 11.1). Although Leibenstein does not speak to this point, there is implicit in his narrative that there is a unique equilibrium level of x-efficiency and, therefore, of x-inefficiency, given by manager/owner preferences and the extent of product market competitiveness. But this predicted equilibrium is contingent on the impact that changing effort levels have on average cost. This original x-efficiency model's predictions are significantly affected by enriching this model by introducing employees, their preferences and their bargaining power into the modelling discourse.

Given the introduction of labour and related costs into the effort-contextualised modelling of the firm, the x-inefficiency plus behavioural model presented in this chapter allows for multiple equilibria with regards to the wage and the overall compensation package and work environment and minimum average cost. This is unlike with efficiency wage theory, with its unique equilibrium wage. Efficiency wage theory assumes a traditional convex u-shaped production function with its unique maximum. In the behavioural plus model, there is a wide array of levels of labour compensation consistent with some unique unit cost of production. Average unit cost is inelastic with respect to changes in the level of x-efficiency if productivity increases are just offset by changes in the level of labour compensation, inclusive of the costs related to changes in the work environment. Increasing wages, for example, need not increase unit cost, while cutting wages need not reduce unit cost (see equation 11.1). For this reason, changes in the rate of labour compensation need not affect the competitive position of the firm. More specifically, increasing the level of x-inefficiency need not make a firm less competitive, whilst reducing the level of x-inefficiency need not make a firm more competitive, where labour and related costs are brought into the modelling of the firm and the methodological design of x-efficiency theory. This is in contrast with the analytical predictions that follow Leibenstein's modelling narrative.

In this revised modelling scenario, more or less competition need not affect the level of x-inefficiency, since changes in the level of x-inefficiency need not affect average cost. Cost-minimising firms can choose from a relatively large set of wage rates (or more comprehensively, compensation packages and work environments), contingent on the preferences of firm decision-makers and the power relationships across agents, for example. Therefore, in this model, there is no unique efficiency wage that must be chosen by rational cost-minimising, profit-maximising decision-makers. This behavioural model provides an analytical framework that allows for the persistence of x-efficiency under different competitive environments as well for multiple equilibria in terms of levels of x-efficiency and in-firm work conventions and norms. In this model, product markets can even be perfectly competitive or at least contestable. Moreover, wages can vary across firms without there being any difference in average costs. But if wages and compensation packages do vary, then there must be a compensating variation in effort inputs related to such variations in systems of industrial relations.

This type of effort-related modelling of the firm can help explain how and why firms and economies with different wage rates and working conditions can persist over time and, related to this point, how x-inefficient firms can persist over time. The survival of the fittest (or the most x-efficient) does not hold when changes in effort inputs compensate for changes in labour costs. Decision-makers can choose a utility-maximising combination of x-inefficiency and wages and working conditions that maximise their utility. An x-inefficient utility-maximising choice for firm managers and owners can be consistent with competitive average costs and profits, but could be well below the x-efficient level of production and could yield relatively low levels of utility or well-being to the firms' workers. On the other hand, the most x-efficient firm need not be more competitive than firms that are characterised by lower levels of x-efficiency when the costs associated with higher and lower levels of x-efficiency are brought into the modelling narrative.

In this modelling narrative, as in Leibenstein's, the preferences of managers and owners play an important role in determining the level of x-efficiency. But in the revised model, in the x-efficiency plus model, these preferences are not simply related to the desire to work less hard, where Leibenstein assumes a very strong preference for 'leisure' amongst firm managers (and even owners), which results in x-inefficiency. Here, members of the firm hierarchy can maximise own-benefits whilst the benefits to employees are much lower than they would be in a more x-efficient firm, more oriented towards a Golden Rule, cooperative solution to the productivity challenge. Preferences can also be oriented towards improving the well-being of all firm members (Golden Rule solution) if such preferences are consistent with the firm achieving target or competitive average cost and target rates of return. Both x-efficiency and x-inefficient preferences are consistent with members of the firm hierarchy being rational and 'utility maximising' in their orientation.

It is important to note this model is not only pertinent to traditional investor-owned firms. One can also have member-owned/employee-owned firms (that is, cooperative organisations) where the preferences of employees dominate the decision-making process. Employees would tend to have preferences oriented towards maximising benefits to all firm members. For this to occur productivity must increase to cover the cost of such benefits. In other words, the firm must be more x-efficient. In this case, employee ownership and the objective function embodying the preferences of employee-owners incentivise firms to become more x-efficient thereby realising the Golden Rule solution to the productivity problem. Therefore, who owns the firm and the preferences of these owners (the firm's organisational form) play a critical role in determining the firm's level of x-efficiency.

Some of the points are illustrated in Figure 11.2. In the conventional neoclassical approach, given the assumptions being made about effort variability, any increase in wages or improvements to working conditions generates an increase in average cost. Any decrease in the value of these variables results in a drop in average cost. This is given by ACW. The slope of this curve is determined by production function parameters. The efficiency wage story is illustrated by curve EW. There exists some unique wage, W_1, that yields a unique minimum average cost at A, given by e_1. Any wage that differs from the efficiency wage generates a higher average cost. No neoclassically rational cost-minimising firm would choose a wage that differs from the efficiency wage, in this case, W_1.

The more general behavioural (x-efficiency plus) narrative is illustrated by curve BM. As wages increase or fall from a to e_5, there are no changes to the average cost. There exists some horizontal constant cost linearity to this particular average cost function. This is based on the assumptions being made with regard to the causal relationship between wages, overall working conditions, industrial relations, effort inputs and productivity. After a certain point, effort increases as a function of increases in costs and hits a wall of seriously diminishing returns, and the behavioural narrative and cost curve reverts to the standard one wherein increases in wages and related costs generate increasing average costs.

Output consistent with wage W_3 would be consistent with the Golden Rule outcome or solution to the productivity problem. In this case, the pie size is maximised. On the other hand, at wage W_0, for example, the pie size is much smaller, and one is veering towards a Prisoner's Dilemma solution to the productivity problem. Firm decision-makers have a choice in determining how x-efficient their firm happens to be, even when product markets are highly competitive or contestable, given that average costs are constant over a certain domain. Much depends on the preferences of decision-makers. However, the investor-owned firms, preferences for 'low wage' firm configuration can be overwritten when employees have greater bargaining paper, forcing labour costs up which, in turn, incentivise firms into becoming more x-efficient, ceteris paribus.

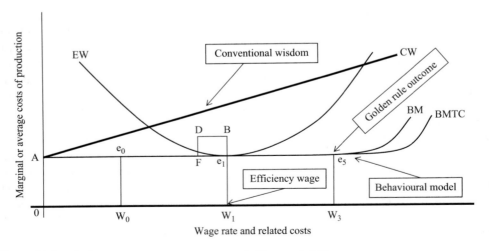

Figure 11.2   Labour costs, average costs and effort variability

X-EFFICIENT AND TECHNICAL CHANGE

In the x-efficiency plus model, the constraint of higher wages can also be predicted to incentivise technological change shifting the cost curve from BM to BMTC, allowing for wages higher than W_3 to be consistent with the competitive and prior average cost of 0A (Altman 2009). In this sense, the rate of technical change can be x-inefficient – below what it can be given the appropriate incentive environment. 'Low wages' facilitate firm decision-makers in investor-owned firms to avoid engaging in technical change since they meet their targets, inclusive of remaining competitive, without adopting or developing higher productivity-related technology. Technically speaking, it is important to note that I'm not referring to a movement along the production isoquant to reflect changing relative prices of factor inputs. Rather, I'm referring to inward shifts of the production isoquant.

Technical change need not generate improvements in average costs or profits in 'low wage' firms and technical change might initially only keep the higher wage firms competitive, although this serves to increase the size of the economic pie within the firm and society at large. Moreover, technical change might initially be viable only for firms that are sufficiently x-efficient. There is an important assumed positive causal linkage between increasing costs, the extent of x-efficiency and the rate of technical change (Altman 2009). The rate of technical change can also be affected by the organisational form of the firm. For example, if a firm is member-owned or a cooperative, the preferences of members for a high level of material well-being for all could require not only increasing the extent of x-efficiency but also technical change. Here the preferences of the firm hierarchy are derived from member preferences which are most conducive to increasing rates of technical change. Moreover, in investor-owned firms where owners have a preference for improving the well-being of their employees are incentivised to engage in more technical change to cover the costs of being more ethically inclined.

In much of the conventional treatment of technical change, technical change is exogenous. However, it can be argued that *one driver* (which does not rule out other drivers) of technical change can be increasing labour costs, the same variable that incentivises firms to increase their level of x-efficiency. This latter variable is not part of the methodological mapping of conventional wisdom. Once again, here I am referring to inward shifts in the production isoquant, not simply movements along the production isoquant. In the x-inefficiency plus model, endogenising technical change and linking its determinants with those of the extent of x-efficiency helps to enrich explanations of differences in growth rates across firms and countries by better identifying causal variables assumed away in the conventional economics narrative. It also underlies the importance of better and more accurately modelling how firm members behave under different incentives, preferences and institutional environments.

RATIONAL X-INEFFICIENCY

Further to the x-efficiency plus model, there are short-term costs involved in either increasing or decreasing the wage rate. This is given by FD or e_1B. This is one reason that efficiency wage scholars find the nominal wage rate is sticky downward over the business cycle (Bewley1999). Also, improving efficiency as wages increase involves short-term costs, which can deter firms from engaging in higher wage-x-efficient strategies on their own (utility maximising) volition, given trust levels and the uncertainty of future outcomes. These 'transaction' costs and uncertainty of outcomes can be predicted to impede improvements in x-efficiency and in the rate of induced technical change. One ends up with a form of rational x-inefficiency. In this narrative, decision-makers would prefer a more x-efficient firm, but the costs of making this transition are deemed to be too high. This being said, reducing transaction costs and uncertainty of outcomes can be expected to have the opposite effect. Also, of consequence would be improved bargaining power of labour which incentivises firm decision-makers to absorb short-term costs and take more calculated risks to become more x-efficient as a means to remain competitive and profitable.

One obstacle to working towards reducing the level of x-inefficiency by rational decision-makers would be changing their mental model about the impact of higher wages, for example, on average costs and the rate of return. If one subscribes to the view that higher wages and a more environmentally friendly firm, for example, require higher costs and lower profits in both the short and long run then even individuals supportive of a higher wage and more environmentally friendly firm would resist such a transformation if she or he is rational. This mental model still dominates in much of university teachings and corporate culture and is derived from conventional economic theory. A change in the mental model would, therefore, contribute to incentivising firm decision-makers with preferences sympathetic and supportive of higher wages and more environmentally friendly firms to transform their firm in the preferred and utility-maximising direction (Altman 2014).

Another important obstacle to moving towards greater firm x-efficiency would be the resistance from members of the firm hierarchy to a higher wage firm. This would be the case even if this is known to be completely consistent with the firm remaining competitive. This resistance could be embedded in decision-makers' preferences where the firm hierarchy members' utility is related to maximising their relative power with respect to employees and even the broader society (could also be related here to resistance to environmental regulation).[5] This is another example of rational x-inefficiency. In this case, changes in how competitive firm is organised and whether it becomes more or less x-efficient depends on the constraints faced by firm decision-makers. For example, when employees become more empowered, this can incentivise these types of decision-makers to organise their firms to become more x-efficient economic organisations to remain competitive if faced with higher labour costs.

As discussed earlier, one would expect member-owned firms or cooperatives to be relatively x-efficient if the preferences of members relate to improving their level of material well-being. In a cooperative, a fundamentally important means of achieving this end is to improve firm productivity by increasing the level of the firm's x-efficiency and engaging in more technical change. Only in this manner can the cost of improving members' level of material well-being be covered, allowing the firm to remain competitive. In the investor-owned firm, members of the firm hierarchy are afforded alternatives to improve their well-being and utility by, for example, reducing wages and benefits to employees.

QUALITY OF MANAGEMENT AND X-EFFICIENCY

The x-efficiency model, in its original formulation, pays special attention to management/owners' preferences for the determination of the extent of x-efficiency. But this approach also pays some attention to the quality of management as a determinant of the extent of x-efficiency. However, Leibenstein's focus is on preferences for different levels of effort which, in turn, affect the level of x-inefficiency. But Leibenstein (1968) also makes the point that the quality of management can be affected by educational and training parameters. Entrepreneurs and management tend to refer to individuals who manage a business as opposed to those who spearhead start-ups.

Leibenstein effectively makes the case that the quality of management is an independent variable in the production function, albeit he does not use these specific terms. Moreover, the quantity of management, controlled for quality, is an independent variable, in so far that there can be a shortage of quality management, and this affects the efficiency of the firm (its level of x-efficiency) through the production function. In this modelling scenario, given that effort discretion exists and that x-inefficiency is a possibility, x-efficiency can't be achieved, even if owners prefer this outcome, unless the management of an appropriate quality can be secured. In this modelling narrative, differences in levels of x-efficiency can be explained by differences in the quality of management and affected by the number of quality managers at the macro level. In terms of this methodological approach, the managerial variable and how it (the quality of management) can be enhanced is of critical importance. How the firm is managed affects the quantity and quality of effort input and the extent and quality of induced technical change are discussed earlier.

IMPLICATIONS OF THE X-INEFFICIENCY PLUS THEORY FOR EMPLOYMENT

In the x-inefficiency plus model, it is possible to have a multiple equilibrium in terms of a unique average cost across an array of wage rates. In this narrative, increasing wage rates need not increase average costs and lowering the real wage need not have the opposite effect. This modelling prediction has important implications for analyses of employment, firm-specific wage-employee benefit analyses and policy, and policy with regard to income support as well as with regard to unions and other aspects of worker rights. The notion that increasing real wages and labour benefits, more generally, need not have negative consequences on the firm's competitiveness and profits contravenes conventional predictions because they assume fixed effort inputs and no labour-cost-related induced technical change. But this modelling narrative also has consequences for the conventional predictions of the implications of increasing wages and labour benefits on employment.

The core conventional critique of minimum wages, labour unions, and tight labour markets is that they will result in long-term decreases to equilibrium employment, causing the most harm to the least skilled (more poorly endowed with human capital) and least productive members of the economy. The argument is very simple, increasing the real wage rate, ceteris paribus, increases the wage above the worker's marginal contribution (marginal product), which forces the profit-maximising firm (firm managers/owners) to fire these now relatively unproductive employees. However, this argument assumes away the possibility that firms facing the challenge of increasing labour costs will respond by organising and managing increases to the firm's level of x-efficiency and adopting and developing technologies that further compensate for such increasing labour costs. The rigid conventional behavioural assumption of fixed effort inputs and exogenous technical change, however, which is taken as common knowledge, does not have a strong reality-based foundation.

This conventional economic proposition is illustrated in Figure 11.3. One begins with the conventional marginal product of labour curve MP_2 at wage rate W_2 and equilibrium employment of L_2. Equilibrium is given by e_2. We're assuming, for simplicity, a perfectly inelastic

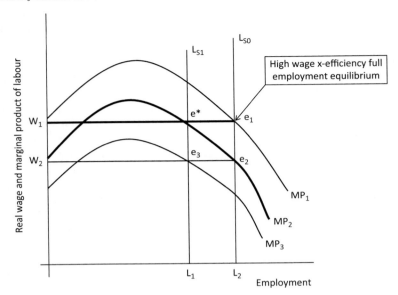

Figure 11.3 Labour demand, effort variability and x-efficiency

labour supply curve of L_{S0}, L_{S1}. Let's assume that this wage rate is below that which is consistent with achieving x-efficiency in the firm. Assume that one introduces a minimum wage above the current equilibrium wage, W_2, or that employees increase their bargaining power, increasing the wage above this equilibrium wage. In the conventional model, this will result in less employment (L_1) when the wage rate increases to W_1. But if there is an x-efficiency effect caused by the increase in the wage rate, resulting in an increase in the level of x-efficiency and induced technical change, this will cause the marginal product curve to shift outward, possibly to MP_2. In this case, the new equilibrium is at e_2, with employment remaining at L_2.

In this scenario, increasing the wage rate would not have a negative impact on the level of employment and, therefore, on the unemployment rate. On the other hand, efforts to reduce wage rates, which is often an acceptable strategy based on conventional economics to improve firm performance, need not have the predicted effect of increasing employment when effort is a variable in the production function. If employees react to wage cuts by reducing effort inputs this would shift the marginal product of the labour curve inward, such as to MP_3. In this case, there would none of the employment growth predicted by conventional economic theory. Indeed, if the marginal product curve shifted even further to the left, there would be a fall in employment.

When effort is variable and technical change is induced by labour cost pressures, higher wages and institutions that improve the bargaining power of workers should not be viewed as detrimental to employment. This simple black-and-white prediction is based on a very narrow and unrealistic assumption about effort discretion and technical change and what motivates or incentivises changes in effort levels and technical change. In the x-efficiency plus theory, the realistic assumption of effort discretion and induced technical change allows for the possibility that increasing labour costs will be compensated by reductions in the level of x-inefficiency and induced technical change. On average, this appears to be the case. What's important from a methodological perspective is that this behavioural economics model does not exclude, *by definition*, the possibility that improving the well-being of workers *does not* cause harm to employment and the firm. Indeed, it can have the opposite effect. What then also becomes important is to determine the conditions under which firms can increase their productivity to sustain higher levels of well-being of their workforce whilst remaining sustainable.

CONCLUSION

In this chapter, I focus on the role that effort variability has in modelling firm behaviour and performance, thereby providing a basis for a behavioural theory of the firm that relates to the assumption of effort variability and its determinants. This builds upon the early contributions of Leibenstein (x-efficiency theory and efficiency wages) and Akerlof (fairness and efficiency wages). This contrasts with the standard view that effort inputs are fixed. Introducing effort variability impacts one's understanding of how and why firms can be more or less economically efficient or more or less x-inefficient, even with the same set of traditional factor inputs. A critical methodological contribution of this approach to the theory of the firm is that it recognises and tries to explain how firms need not be economically efficient and still survive and even prosper in the marketplace. The market can't guarantee economic or x-efficiency in production.

This speaks to the importance of what actually transpires in the traditional black box of the firm. The x-efficiency-related theory discussed in this chapter, what I refer to as an x-efficiency plus theory, which extends the original contributions to this theoretical and methodological narrative, allows for precise analytical predictions as to why firms can be persistently x-inefficiency, how x-inefficient firms can compete with x-efficient firms, how changes in managerial and owner preferences can change the extent of x-inefficiency and how technical change can be endogenised and better explained through an effort variability–related theory of the firm. One can also address why rational decision-makers would and could prefer to have their firms remain x-inefficient even if an x-efficient alternative is achievable, cost competitive and profitable. One can have a form of rational x-inefficiency as an equilibrium solution to the productivity problem. On the other hand, the x-efficiency plus approach provides us with the tools to better understand how to achieve x-efficiency in production. This requires a detailed and nuanced understanding of how the firm functions in the real world and the institutional and social context that parameterise decision-making.

Amongst the highlights of the effort discretion–related behavioural theory of the firm are:

1. Effort variability comprises of both quality and quantity dimensions.
2. Technical change is induced by changing costs facing the firm.
3. Economically inefficient firms can survive and be profitable in long-term equilibrium.
4. Economically efficient firms need not be more competitive than x-inefficient firms.
5. Preferences of management and owners play a key role in determining how x-efficient a firm is. These agents' rational preferences need not be consistent with conventional notions of profit maximisation.
6. X-efficiency can be induced by empowering employees and incentivising cooperation between management, owners and employees.
7. Supply of quality management/entrepreneurs is a necessary but not sufficient condition to achieve x-efficiency.

8. X-efficiency requires a relatively cooperative and 'fair' work environment.
9. Golden Rule solutions to the productivity problem are not related to neoclassical behavioural norms but are rather derived from the social, institutional and human context within which the firm operates.
10. When x-inefficiency and induced technical change exist, improved worker benefits need not threaten the competitiveness of firms or employment.

NOTES

1. Coase (1937) introduced transaction costs to explain why firms exist and aspects of firm behaviour. Williamson (1975), influenced by Simon, used transaction costs to further explain aspects of firm behaviour and firm size that neoclassical theory could not explain, when assuming zero transaction costs.
2. Leibenstein (1982) makes this argument in passing in his elaboration of x-efficiency theory. But the notion that ideal systems of industrial relations are core to the realisation of x-efficiency is a critical methodological point of this chapter, wherein labour management co-operation in a win-win scenario (game theory modelling) is the key to the achievement of x-efficiency in production.
3. Simon (1987, p. 223) makes the point: 'In the biological world at least, many organisms survive that are not maximizers but that operate at far less than the highest achievable efficiency. Their survival is not threatened as long as no other organisms have evolved that can challenge the possession of their specific niches. Analogously, since there is no reason to suppose that every business firm is challenged by an optimally efficient competitor, survival only requires meeting the competition. In a system in which there are innumerable rents, of long-term and short-term duration, even egregious sub-optimality may permit survival'.
4. Leibenstein (1982) argues: 'The main general point is that merely obtaining an acquiescent nonshirking effort is of limited value. Freely offered effort, inclusive of attentiveness and caring about the quality of effort, in return for what is viewed as a good deal (in the long run) is likely to result in higher productivity'.
5. On the importance of relative positioning, see Duesenberry (1949) and Frank (1985, 2005).

REFERENCES

Akerlof, G.A. (1982), 'Labor contracts as partial gift exchange', *Quarterly Journal of Economics*, 97: 543–569.
Akerlof, G.A. (1984), 'Gift exchange and efficiency-wage theory: Four views', *American Economic Review, Papers and Proceedings*, 74: 79–83.
Akerlof, G.A. (2002), 'Behavioral macroeconomics and macroeconomic behavior', *American Economic Review*, 92: 411–433.
Akerlof, G.A. and J.L. Yellen (1990), 'The fair wage hypothesis and unemployment', *Quarterly Journal of Economics*, 105: 255–283.
Akerlof, G.A. and J.L. Yellen (1988), 'Fairness and unemployment', *American Economic Review, Papers and Proceedings*, 78: 44–49.
Altman, M. (1998), 'A high wage path to economic growth and development', *Challenge: The Magazine of Economic Affairs*, 41: 91–104.
Altman, M. (1999), 'The methodology of economics and the survivor principle revisited and revised: Some welfare and public policy implications of modeling the economic agent', *Review of Social Economics*, 57: 427–449.
Altman, M. (2002), 'Economic theory, public policy and the challenge of innovative work practices', *Economic and Industrial Democracy: An International Journal*, 23: 271–290.
Altman, M. (2005), 'Behavioral economics, rational inefficiencies, fuzzy sets, and public policy', *Journal of Economic Issues*, 34: 683–706.
Altman, M. (2006a), 'What a difference an assumption makes: Effort discretion, economic theory, and public policy', in M. Altman (ed.), *Handbook of Contemporary Behavioral Economics: Foundations and Developments*. Armonk, NY: M.E. Sharpe, pp. 125–164.

Altman, M. (2006b), 'Involuntary unemployment, macroeconomic policy, and a behavioral model of the firm: Why high real wages need not cause high unemployment', *Research in Economics*, 60: 97–111.

Altman, M. (2009), 'A behavioral-institutional model of endogenous growth and induced technical change', *Journal of Economic Issues*, 63: 685–713.

Altman, M. (2014), 'Mental models, Bargaining power, and institutional change'. World Interdisciplinary Network for Institutional Research, Old Royal Naval College, Greenwich University. London, UK, September 11–14.

Almeida, F. and H. Pessali (2017), 'Revisiting the evolutionism of Edith Penrose's The theory of the growth of the firm: Penrose's entrepreneur meets Veblenian institutions', *EconomiA*, 18: 298–309.

Baumol, W.J. (1990), 'Entrepreneurship: Productive, unproductive, and destructive', *Journal of Political Economy*, 98: 893–921.

Bewley, T. (1999), *Why Wages Don't Fall During a Recession*. Cambridge, MA: Harvard University Press.

Buchele, R. and J. Christainsen (1999), 'Labor relations and productivity growth in advanced capitalist economies', *Review of Radical Political Economics*, 31: 87–110.

Card, D. and A.B. Krueger (1995), *Myth and Measurement: The New Economics of the Wage*. Princeton, NJ: Princeton University Press.

Coase, R.H. (1937), 'The nature of the firm', *Economica*, 4: 386–405.

Commons, J.R. (1934), *Institutional Economics: Its Place in Political Economy*. New York: Macmillan.

Commons, J.R. (1950), *The Economics of Collective Action*. Madison, WI: University of Wisconsin Press.

Cyert, R.M. and J.C. March (1963), *A Behavioral Theory of the Firm*. Englewood Cliffs, NJ: Prentice Hall.

Duesenberry, J.S. (1949), *Income, Saving and the Theory of Consumer Behavior*. Cambridge, MA: Harvard University Press.

Falk, A. and E. Fehr (2003), 'Why labour market experiments?' *Labor Economics*, 10: 399–406.

Fehr, E. and S. Gachter (2000), 'Fairness and retaliation: The economics of reciprocity', *Journal of Economic Perspectives*, 14: 159–181.

Frank, R. (1985), *Choosing the Right Pond: Human Behavior and the Quest for Status*. New York: Oxford University Press.

Frank, R. (2005), 'The mysterious disappearance of James Duesenberry', *New York Times*. Available at: http://www.nytimes.com/2005/06/09/business/09scene.html?_r=0.

Frantz, R. (1997), *X-Efficiency Theory: Evidence and Applications*, 2nd ed. Boston/Dordrecht/London: Kluwer Academic Publishers.

Freeman, R.B. and J.L. Medoff (1984), *What Do Unions Do?* New York: Basic Books.

Friedman, M. (1953), 'The methodology of positive economics', in M. Friedman, *Essays in Positive Economics*. Chicago: University of Chicago Press, pp. 3–43.

Friedman, M. (1968), 'The role of monetary policy', *American Economic Review*, 58: 1–17.

Galbraith, J.K. (1958), *The Affluent Society*. New York: New American Library.

Gigerenzer, G. (2007), *Gut Feelings: The Intelligence of the Unconscious*. New York: Viking.

Gordon, D.M. (1998), 'Conflict and cooperation: An empirical glimpse of the imperatives of efficiency and redistribution', in S. Bowles and H. Gintis (eds.), *Recasting Egalitarianism: New Rules for Communities, States and Markets*. London: Verso, pp. 181–207.

Güth, W., R. Schmittberger and B. Schwarze (1982), 'An experimental analysis of ultimatum bargaining', *Journal of Economic Behavior and Organization*, 3: 367–388.

Hayek, F.A. (1945), 'The use of knowledge in society', *American Economic Review*, 35: 519–530.

Helliwell, J.F. and H. Huang (2011), 'Well-being and trust in the workplace', *Journal of Happiness Studies*, 12: 747–767.

Henrich, J., R. Boyd, S. Bowles, C. Camerer, E. Fehr, H. Gintis and R. McElreath (2001), 'In search of Homo Economicus: Behavioral experiments in 15 small-scale societies', *American Economic Review, Papers and Proceedings*, 91: 73–78.

Kahneman, D. (2003), 'Maps of bounded rationality: Psychology for behavioral economics', *American Economic Review*, 93: 1449–1475.

Kahneman, D. (2011), *Thinking Fast and Slow*. New York: Farrar, Strauss, Giroux.

Kaufman, B.E. (2008), *Managing the Human Factor: The Early Years of Human Resource Management in American Industry*. Ithaca, NY: Cornell University Press.

Leibenstein, H. (1957), 'The theory of underemployment in densely populated backward areas', in H. Leibenstein, *Economic Backwardness and Economic Growth: Studies in the Theory of Economic Development*. New York: John Wiley and Sons, pp. 58–76.

Leibenstein, H. (1966), 'Allocative efficiency vs. "X-efficiency"', *American Economic Review*, 56: 392–415.

Leibenstein, H. (1968), 'Entrepreneurship and development', *American Economic Review*, 58: 72–83.

Leibenstein, H. (1979), 'A branch of economics is missing: Micro-micro theory', *Journal of Economic Literature*, 17: 477–502.

Leibenstein, H. (1982), 'The Prisoner's Dilemma in the invisible hand: An analysis of intrafirm productivity', *American Economic Review*, 72: 92–97.

Leibenstein, H. (1987), *Inside the Firm: the Inefficiencies of Hierarchy*. Cambridge, MA and London: Harvard University Press.

Levine, D.I. and L. D'Andrea Tyson (1990), 'Participation, productivity, and the firm's environment', in Alan S. Blinder (ed.), *Paying for Productivity: A Look at the Evidence*. Washington, D.C.: Brookings Institute, pp. 183–237.

Logue, J. and J.S. Yates (1999), 'Worker ownership American style: Pluralism, participation and performance', *Economic and Industrial Democracy*, 20 (2): 225–252.

March, J.G. (1978), 'Bounded rationality, ambiguity, and the engineering of choice', *Bell Journal of Economics*, 9: 587–608.

March, J.G. and H.A. Simon (1968), *Organizations*. New York: John Wiley.

McKersie, Robert B. and Janice A. Klein (1983), 'Productivity: The industrial relations connection', *National Productivity Review*, 3: 26–35.

North, D.C. (1991), 'Institutions', *Journal of Economic Perspectives*, 5: 97–112.

Organisation for Economic Co-operation and Development (2003), 'Making work pay, making work possible', Chapter 3 in *OECD Employment Outlook 2003: Towards More and Better Jobs*, pp. 113–170. Available at: http://www.oecd.org/dataoecd/62/59/31775213.pdf.

Penrose, E.T. (1959/1995), *The Theory of the Growth of the Firm*, 3rd ed. Oxford: Oxford University Press.

Pfeffer, J. (1995), 'Producing sustainable competitive advantage through the effective management of people', *Academy of Management Executive*, 9: 55–69.

Pitelis, C. (2004), 'Edith Penrose's organizational theory of the firm: Contract, conflict, knowledge and management', in H. Tsoukas and N. Mylonopoulos (eds.), *Organizations as Knowledge Systems*. London: Palgrave Macmillan, pp. 238–251.

Rothschild, K.W. (2002), 'The absence of power in contemporary economic theory', *Journal of Socio-Economics*, 31: 433–442.

Shapiro, C. and J.E. Stiglitz (1984), 'Equilibrium unemployment as a worker discipline device', *American Economic Review*, 74: 433–44.

Shefrin, H. (1999), *Beyond Greed and Fear: Understanding Behavioral Finance and the Psychology of Investing*. Boston, MA: Harvard Business School Press.

Shefrin, H. (2001), 'Behavioral corporate finance', *Journal of Applied Corporate Finance*, 14: 113–126.

Simon, H.A. (1955), 'A behavioral model of rational choice', *Quarterly Journal of Economics*, 69: 99–188.

Simon, H.A. (1978), 'Rationality as a process and as a product of thought', *American Economic Review*, 70: 1–16.

Simon, H.A. (1979), 'Rational decision making in business organizations', *American Economic Review*, 69: 493–513.

Simon, H.A. (1987), 'Behavioral economics', in J. Eatwell, M. Millgate and P. Newman (eds.), *The New Palgrave: A Dictionary of Economics*. London: Macmillan, pp. 266–267.

Slichter, S.H. (1920), 'Industrial morale', *Quarterly Journal of Economics*, 35: 36–60.

Smith, V.L. (2003), 'Constructivist and ecological rationality in economics', *American Economic Review*, 93: 465–508.

Solow, R.M. (1979), 'Another possible source of wage stickiness', *Journal of Macroeconomics*, 1: 79–82.

Solow, R.M. (1990), *The Labor Market As a Social Institution*. New York: Blackwell.

Solow, R.M. (2003), 'Lessons learned from U.S. welfare reform', *Prisme,* Cournot Centre for Economic Studies. Available at: http://www.centre-cournot.org/index.php/2003/11/26/lessons-learned-from-u-s-welfare-reform/#more-276/.
Thaler, R.H. and C. Sustein (2008), *Nudge: Improving Decisions about Health, Wealth, and Happiness.* New Haven and London: Yale University Press.
Todd, P.M. and G. Gigerenzer (2003), 'Bounding rationality to the world', *Journal of Economic Psychology,* 24: 143–165.
Tomer, J. (1987), *Organizational Capital—The Path to Higher Productivity and Well-Being.* New York: Praeger Publishers.
Tversky, A. and D. Kahneman (1981), 'The framing of decisions and the psychology of choice', *Science,* 211: 453–458.
Tversky, A. and D. Kahneman (1986), 'Rational choice and the framing of decisions', *Journal of Business,* 59: 251–278.
Veblen, T.B. (1899), *The Theory of the Leisure Class: An Economic Study in the Evolution of Institutions.* New York: Macmillan.
Veblen, T.B. (1904), *The Theory of Business Enterprise.* New York: Charles Scribners.
Williamson, O.E. (1975), *Markets and Hierarchies: Analysis and Antitrust Implications.* New York: Free Press.
Winther, G. and R. Marens (1997), 'Participatory democracy may go a long way: Comparative growth performance of employee ownership firms in New York and Washington States', *Economic and Industrial Democracy,* 18: 393–422.

PART V

MONEY AND BEHAVIOURAL ECONOMICS

12. The psychology of money
Agata Gasiorowska and Tomasz Zaleskiewicz

INTRODUCTION

Although money is a relatively recent phenomenon (from the perspective of the evolution of humankind) – not older than a few thousand years – it has become an integral part of everyday modern life and contemporary market societies (Burgoyne & Lea, 2006; Sandel, 2012). Without exaggeration, barely a day passes without an economic transaction. Money is exchangeable for virtually all other goods in the marketplace and takes on significant importance in people's behaviour. This significance obviously results from the fact that money is a functional medium of exchange, as defined in economics. However, the importance of money comes also from its subjective value and its meaning, which go far beyond its economic functions (Kirchler & Hoelzl, 2017).

From an economic point of view, money is a universal, anonymous, fungible and market-driven force defined by the function it provides: a medium of exchange, a way to store value and wealth and a means of assessing the value of goods and services (Mishkin, 2019; Reddy, 1987). In this sense, the main economic functions of money are purely instrumental. Money is used to express the magnitude of the value of goods and services, and attach a precise number to represent such value. Hence, it is a common denominator making alternatives comparable in a simple, numerical dimension. Finally, money facilitates economic exchange, floating from one hand to another, connecting separate transactions in a long market chain. Therefore, from this point of view, money is desired because of its inherent involvement in trade, and not because it is an end in itself (Carruthers & Espeland, 1998; Lea & Webley, 2006).

Studies in psychology, anthropology and sociology suggest that a purely instrumental approach to money is not sufficient for explaining the role it plays in people's lives, as human attitudes and behaviour deviate from the rational assumptions underlying economic models (Belk & Wallendorf, 1990; Lea & Webley, 2006; Zelizer, 1994). From this point of view, money is not universal because, for example, some of its forms are strictly reserved for special occasions (Belk & Wallendorf, 1990; Zelizer, 1994), and it is not fungible because people treat it differently depending on its form, use and context (Thaler, 1990, 1999). However, the psychological research of money is not limited to the deviations from rationality observed in the process of economic exchange. Over 45 years ago, Becker (1975, p. 81) proposed that humans perceive money as a symbol of power – the power 'to increase oneself, to change one's natural situation from one of smallness, helplessness, finitude, to one of bigness, control, durability, importance'. In line with this view, researchers started looking into money as a symbol imbued with social and psychological meanings, and not as a direct instrument of consumption. The view that money does far more for people than just facilitating exchange is corroborated by a growing body of recent research showing that it serves important symbolic – emotional, psychological and social – functions, and it acts as a psychological resource for interpersonal and intrapersonal regulation in both adults and children (see Furnham, 2014;

Lea & Webley, 2006; Zaleskiewicz & Gasiorowska, 2017; Zaleskiewicz et al., 2018; Wang et al., 2020 for reviews).

The dichotomy between the instrumental and symbolic meanings or functions of money forms a basis for theories developed by psychologists and anthropologists, such as the theory of sacrum and profanum (Belk & Wallendorf, 1990) or the tool/drug theory of money (Lea & Webley, 2006). These theories suggest that in some situations people act in accordance with the instrumental nature of money (i.e., simply exchange money for other desirable goods), while in others they appear to pay more attention to its symbolic nature (Belk & Wallendorf, 1990; Lea & Webley, 2006). Moreover, the dual nature of money is also reflected in attitudes towards money – in relatively stable individual differences reflecting how people perceive the role of money in life and how they behave with respect to money across different situations (Furnham, 1984; Gasiorowska, 2015; Tang, 1992; Yamauchi & Templer, 1982).

This chapter summarises the current state of psychological literature on money, investigating both its instrumental and symbolic meanings and functions. In its first part, we describe how people assign value to money used in transactions, how they use money in transactions and manage their finances and, finally, how these processes differ from the assumptions underlying normative models of money. In the second part, we review studies on the symbolic, non-economic functions of money and provide insights into a range of research methods, including priming techniques and individual differences tests.

THE SUBJECTIVE VALUATION OF MONEY

The Objective vs Subjective Value of Money

One of the basic functions of money is that it serves as a means of evaluation – it is used for measuring and assessing the value of things and ideas. Hence, the value of money usually represents the quantity and quality of products or services that can be bought with a unit amount of money. Therefore, the real or objective value of money refers to its purchasing power, that is, the amount paid in exchange for a good or service. In other words, the consumer considers the purchase of a certain item as a trade-off between the worth of the money at hand and the worth of the item to be bought. The purchase would be made when the item is deemed more valuable than the money, while it would not occur if the money is considered to be worth more than the item. However, the perceived worth of items is not constant – for example, most goods and services have a so-called decreasing marginal utility, meaning that the marginal utility derived from each additional unit consumed declines (Mishkin, 2019). The same rule governs the subjective utility or value of money: although utility is supposed to be a growing function of the objective value, this growth is not linear, and the marginal utility of each additional unit of money also decreases (Mishkin, 2019; Von Neumann & Morgenstern, 1953). In other words, the difference between $50 and $100 appears larger than the difference between $1,000 and $1,050, even though it is literally the same.

The objective value of money is somewhat artificial in the sense that money usually does not have its own value (or its value is relatively small) but only substitutes for it as a symbol or sign. For example, the cost of producing a $100 note is around 10 cents, and the cost of storing $100 in an online bank account is even less than that, but in terms of the goods it can buy its value is much higher. Coins, banknotes and electronic accounts do not have any real (intrinsic) value, but are valuable only because people trust that they will be accepted by others in the market – so, they are valuable because people believe and agree that they are valuable. The objective, economic value of a unit of money might change over time depending on various situational factors, such as inflation, money redenomination or a switch from one currency system to another (as in the case of the introduction of the euro). Additionally, the way people subjectively value money depends on several individual factors, such as income, money attitudes or social comparisons (Buechel & Morewedge, 2014), but also on various features of money, such as its denomination, form, origin, state or whether the money is gained or lost. Even if the purchasing power of money does not change with these factors, people behave as if it does. This variability in money valuation in fact violates the fundamental economic assumption of the fungibility and universality of money (Von Neumann & Morgenstern, 1953, p. 8).

Difficulties in money valuations that people experience may originate from the fact that money serves as a unit of measure for comparing the value of other things, but in most cases cannot be a measure of value for itself. Hence, when measuring the subjective value of money in research, researchers cannot just ask participants what is the worth of half of $100, because they would get the obvious answer 'fifty dollars', and participants may possibly consider such a question extremely trivial. The problem is, therefore, to get people to scale not amounts of money, but rather the valuational effect that it produces – that is, the subjective value of money. That is why some studies measure this subjective value by asking people how happy they would be after receiving a specific amount of money, how much money they needed to feel twice as happy or upset as the specific amount (or loss of it) would make them feel (Brandstätter & Brandstätter, 1996; Galanter, 1962), how much they would like to own specific money (Tasimi & Gelman, 2020) or how valuable or important they consider this money to be (Devoe et al., 2013; Peetz & Soliman, 2016). The lower subjective value of money should also manifest itself in a higher propensity to part with money, for example in reckless spending, donating to charity or gambling (Arkes et al., 1994; Dolansky, 2014; Gourville & Soman, 1998; Henderson & Peterson, 1992; Liu et al., 2018; Soman, 2001; Tykocinski & Pittman, 2013; Vandoros, 2013), but also in putting less effort into earning or not wasting money (Devoe et al., 2013; Duclos & Khamitov, 2019; Gourville & Soman, 1998; Hur & Nordgren, 2016; Jonas et al., 2002). Finally, some researchers employ the willingness-to-pay technique, in which participants are instructed to provide a maximum buying price for the good(s) under consideration (Frederick, 2012; Li, 2002; Matthews et al., 2016; Mishra et al., 2006; Prelec & Simester, 2001; Raghubir & Srivastava, 2002, 2008, 2009; Tessari et al., 2011). The rationale behind this approach is that an individual will set a higher maximum buying price if the value of money seems to be lower than the value of the goods, and a lower maximum price when the value of cash seems higher. Hence, in such evaluations, a higher willingness to pay implies a lower value of money. In the simplified version of this technique, participants are asked whether the specific item is worth the price (Gourville & Soman, 1998), how many specific items people believe they could buy with a certain sum of money (Alter & Oppenheimer, 2008; Dolansky, 2014; Polman et al., 2018; Stellar & Willer, 2014), or how expensive a specific price or price increase is (Gamble, 2006; Gamble et al., 2002).

Irrespective of how it is measured, the subjective value of money assigned by a specific individual in a specific context might differ from its actual economic value or purchasing power. The same amounts of money can seem like subjectively higher or lower amounts, as though more or less valuable, depending on the situation. Thus, in the following part of this chapter, we focus on various factors that might affect people's valuation of money.

Factors Affecting the Subjective Value of Money

Money illusion

When evaluating the value of money, or the value of things expressed in monetary units, people are susceptible to various biases. One example is 'money illusion' – a bias in how people assess economic transactions because they overweight nominal values relative to real (purchasing) values (Shafir et al., 1997). Although individuals presumably know the usual price for a cup of regular coffee in their country, they probably do not know whether 70 bahts for a coffee in Bangkok is a rip-off or a bargain, since they might not know the scale or range of prices in Thailand. However, one might assume that paying 70 currency units for a coffee is quite a lot, since in their country it costs only slightly more than 2 units (dollars or euros, for example). In a similar vein, using a variety of scenarios, Shafir et al. (1997) showed that people making choices between monetary outcomes do not always choose the option with the highest objective value. Instead, they tend to choose the one with the greatest absolute (nominal) value, disregarding the influence of inflation on the real value of money, without accurately correcting for the appreciation or depreciation in objective value and purchasing power. In other words, people's judgements of the value of money often represent some combination of nominal and real values with a bias towards nominal representations, because they are relatively easier and more salient – even if the information necessary to make corrections for real values, such as inflation rates, is available (Shafir et al., 1997). Raghubir and Srivastava (2002) demonstrated a parallel effect using foreign currencies, calling it 'the face value effect'. They showed that even if people know the exchange rate and attempt to account for it in their spending decision, there is a systematic difference in their spending behaviour in the foreign currency, depending on whether this foreign currency is a fraction or a multiple of a unit of their home currency. More specifically, people tend to underspend when the face value of the foreign currency was a multiple of a unit of their home currency (such as 1 US dollar being equal to 30 Thai bahts), and to overspend when this face value is a fraction of their home currency (such as 1 US dollar being equal to 0.3 Kuwait dollars). Therefore, although 70 bahts, 2.35 US dollars and 0.7 Kuwait dollars have an equivalent objective value when their exchange rates are taken into account, coffee in Thailand would seem the most expensive (and probably not worth this money), while in Kuwait it would appear the cheapest.

A specific case of money illusion is called the 'euro illusion' and has been observed after the transition to the euro in many European countries (Del Missier et al., 2007; Desmet, 2002; Gamble, 2007; Gamble et al., 2002, 2005; Jonas et al., 2002). Research has documented that prices in euros were perceived to be cheaper and wages in euros were perceived to be lower than those expressed in the former, familiar currency when the nominal value of the euro was smaller than that of the former currency – which in fact was the case for most of the countries that introduced the euro currency.

The money illusion, the euro illusion and the face value effect are basically the same phenomenon in that the nominal representation influences the subjective value of money to a greater extent than it should. In the case of the money illusion, the subjective value of money does not change with real value changes because the nominal representation stays the same. In the case of the euro illusion or face value illusion, the nominal representation changes, even though the real value remains the same (Gamble et al., 2002; Raghubir & Srivastava, 2002; Shafir et al., 1997). These effects obviously mean it is not only the subjective value of money that is biased towards its nominal value, but everything that is related to this value: the perception of prices and salaries, donation behaviour, choice of consumer goods or behaviour on a stock market (Cannon & Cipriani, 2006; Gamble et al., 2002, 2005; Jonas et al., 2002; Raghubir & Srivastava, 2002; Soman et al., 2002; Svedsäter et al., 2007). However, one additional reason for the presence of the euro illusion effect might be the fact that the subjective value of money can be influenced by the expectation of the prices of consumer products rising in euros. For example, imagine that something cost 20 German marks before the transition to euros, and now you are asked to evaluate how much you would have to pay for the same item after the transition, assuming that the exchange rate was 1 euro = 2 German marks. Most German participants who were asked similar questions believed they would have to pay more than 10 euros – partially because of anchoring at nominal value before transition, but partially because they expected prices to rise after the introduction of the euro (Antonides, 2008; Greitemeyer et al., 2005; Traut-Mattausch et al., 2007). Even when prices remained stable, participants still evaluated them as significantly higher when they were expressed in euros than in German marks, and when they had actually fallen, they judged them to be stable (Greitemeyer et al., 2005). In other words, the lowered subjective value of money in this case was a result of both a lower nominal value of prices expressed in euros and people's expectations that the real value of money was diminished after the new currency was introduced.

Mental accounting

As we pointed out before, normative economic theories assume that money is indispensably fungible: it remains the same (this is, it has the same value) regardless of any contextual factors, including its form, denomination, source, purpose, particular social setting or the participants in the monetary exchange. That is, a dollar always has the same value regardless of whether it is in the form of a note or coin, was earned, found, received or stolen, or is new and crisp or old and dirty, and is always interchangeable with another single dollar – its physical form and history are insignificant (Thaler, 1990). However, almost 30 years ago, social scientists already noticed that people's judgements and behaviour strongly deviate from the notion of the fungibility of money. In fact, the principle of an abstract, substitutable currency is not fully compatible with human intuition, and a particular token of physical currency is in some cases unlike any other. One phenomenon that describes how people actually make decisions with respect to their nonfungible money is 'mental accounting'. Thaler (1999, p. 183) defines mental accounting as 'a set of cognitive operations used by individuals and households to organize, evaluate, and keep track of financial activities'. These operations sometimes lead to nonoptimal financial decisions on the one hand, but on the other, they are efficient in a sense of the economisation of time and effort and allow for dealing with self-control problems. Broadly speaking, people set up mental accounts of budgets for different expenses and they separately trace different sources of money (Thaler, 1985, 1990, 1999). Shefrin and Thaler (1988) indicated that individuals distinguish between wealth in categories such as 'current spendable income', 'current assets' and 'long-term savings' and are more likely to consume an increase in current income (e.g., a pay rise or a lottery reward) when compared to an increase in current assets (e.g., home equity) or in long-term savings (e.g., interest from one's child education account). People also label money as relevant for certain categories of goods and label goods as relevant for certain pools of money (Heath & Soll, 1996; Thaler, 1985). When they think that they have overspent in one mental account (for example, by eating out), they would possibly eschew further purchases in this specific category even while freely spending on items in other categories (for example, buying clothes). Moreover, people are less likely to purchase another $10 theatre ticket to see a play if they have just lost a $10 ticket than if they had just lost a $10 note that had not yet been allocated to any mental account – even though both situations involve the same objective monetary loss (Kahneman & Tversky, 1984). This is caused by the assignment of expenditures to different mental accounts, and is one of many instances of violating the economic assumption that money is fungible. Finally, when facing a dilemma between borrowing money at a high interest rate to pay for a home renovation and using the money that has been already saved in one's child's education account, or between maintaining an outstanding balance on a credit card that charges high interest and repaying it from a savings account earning virtually no interest, most people would rather decide not to pay off the loans or finance home improvements from savings, even if it seems an obvious financial opportunity. Thaler (2015, p. 77) even calls long-term saving accounts 'sacred', meaning that the money accumulated in such an account seems extremely nonfungible via a cognitive process that sets it apart from unrestricted funds like cash that, according to Thaler (2015, p. 76), 'seems to exist only to be spent'.

The mental accounting theory also posits that money that comes from different sources is treated in different ways as if it was valued differently. Generally speaking, windfall money – that is, money received unexpectedly – is spent more lavishly and freely than money earned through hard work (Arkes et al., 1994; Epley & Gneezy, 2007; O'Curry & Strahilevitz, 2001). Indeed, in a study by Arkes et al. (1994), a group of students was told in advance that they would receive a payment for participation, while another group was told about the money only after they arrived at the experimental laboratory. Those who were given no forewarning of the payoff bet significantly more money in the subsequent gambling game and spent more at a basketball game compared to those who anticipated the money. In another study, participants were more prone to spend on themselves money from a gift, lottery or found on the street than money than came from debt repayment or from selling their own stereo (Henderson & Peterson, 1992).

However, not all windfalls are the same. They may be consumed, valued and spent differently, depending on how they are framed. Income described as an upward departure from the status quo (such as a bonus) is more readily spent than objectively identical income that is described as a return to the status quo (e.g., a rebate), even if the two windfalls would be equally unexpected (Epley & Gneezy, 2007). Additionally, people distinguish between windfalls that are tagged with different emotions experienced in response to the receipt of money (Levav & McGraw, 2009). Windfall typically evokes positive feelings which might mitigate guilt arising from frivolous spending. For example, money received as a graduation gift could be tagged as 'happy money', since it was obtained in recognition of one's achievement and to celebrate a precious moment (Liu et al., 2018). Furthermore, when cash is given as a gift, in most cases it is given with the specific instruction to get something hedonic, 'special' or decadent, that the recipients would not normally allow themselves (O'Curry & Strahilevitz, 2001). Additionally, positive windfalls might have divergent effects on money valuations and one's propensity to spend them, depending on whether they are tagged with either 'pride' or 'surprise' (Liu et al., 2018). 'Pride-tagged money' is the money received as a reward for one's efforts, such as a bonus at work or a scholarship. In most cases, although it might be objectively unexpected, it is felt more 'earned' than other windfalls, especially those tagged as 'surprise money'. In this latter case, one's attention is directed to more situational than internal factors that caused the money reception. In experiments conducted by Liu et al. (2018), participants seemed to value 'pride-tagged money' more than 'surprised-tagged money', as they were more prone to spend it on themselves rather than on others, and preferred to abstain from donating it to a charity organisation.

Conversely, money obtained in a contentious life insurance settlement could be tagged as 'unhappy money' because of its associations with someone's death and the struggle of battling with an insurance company. Levav and McGraw (2009) showed that people tend to avoid buying hedonic products using money that came from a 'negative windfall' (for example, because they received it from a terminally ill uncle). In such a situation, people either avoid spending it at all or try to 'purify' it by using it to finance virtuous or utilitarian spending, such as paying for educational expenses instead of paying for a spring break beach trip, in order to reduce the negative affective component of the windfall (Levav & McGraw, 2009).

Another interesting example of a windfall is inheritance. Although inheritance is often indicated as an example of a windfall gain, the abovementioned results of the 'emotional accounting' studies suggest that the 'unhappy' origins of such a resource may set it apart from other kinds of windfalls. Tykocinski and Pittman (2013) propose that in the case of a legacy, the personality of the departed 'stamps' the money, and this association – together with the quality of the relationship one had with the departed – affects the way an inheritance is used. These authors use the terms 'money imbued with essence' and 'money with personality' to emphasise that inherited funds are not only tagged with a negative emotional valence by their connection to sad events, but also that they carry the 'essence' of the departed person's qualities, worldview or lifestyle, and bear the social relationships that existed between the parties. Tykocinski and Pittman (2013) demonstrated that, generally, people are more prone to spend inherited money in utilitarian and less risky ways and that this effect is more profound in the case of an endowment from a deceased beloved grandmother than from an unknown distant relative. However, such 'appropriate spending' might not always mean spending money in a nonfrivolous way – it would rather mean spending it in a way that would presumably be approved by the deceased. Indeed, participants were more willing to buy a ticket for a rock concert using money inherited from a vivacious grandmother who just two years before her death won the first prize in a golden age dance competition than when their deceased grandmother was described as an educated woman who worked as a senior high school teacher. Tykocinski and Pittman (2013) conclude that inherited money will receive special treatment as long as it maintains a strong association with the benefactor and the circumstances of the endowment – probably as long as people remember its history and expend the attention and energy to preserve its special character, but there is the possibility of 'an expiry date' when such money would become just an ordinary means of exchange.

The reasoning presented so far leads to the conclusion that when people think about money and its value, they think about it in terms of its source and its emotional, social and moral connotations. This view has been widely supported by sociologists. For example, Carruthers and Espeland (1998) suggested that money flows from one place to another as people use it in successive exchanges and different contexts, hence it can be contaminated – both in a positive and negative manner – by the social meaning of the places through which it moves. Bandelj et al. (2017) describe this process as relational earmarking and distinguish it from mental accounting by focusing on the social ties and dynamic interactions that shape how people make sense of money and perceive its value. In other words, money is attached to social relationships in the sense that people regularly differentiate (earmark) their money in correspondence with their definition of the sort of relationship that exists between the parties engaged in monetary transfers. In the example we used earlier – the dilemma on how to finance home renovation – people's reluctance to use the money from their child's education account is probably something more than just an example of mental accounting. Using this money would probably be not only a breach of mental account assignments, but also a relationally damaging violation, potentially affecting not only the relationship between a parent and a child but also between a parent and other family members (Zelizer, 2012, p. 162).

Moral history of money
Evidence from psychological research also endorses the proposition that people do not perceive money coming from different sources as fungible, but rather as carrying traces of its moral history, and as potentially morally contaminating. For example, in a series of experiments conducted by Tasimi and Gelman (2017), participants showed aversion to money that had been stolen, regardless of whether the sum was small ($1) or large ($100), whether it was traceable (notes with serial numbers) or not (unrecognisable coins of the same value), even when they were told that no one saw it being stolen, the owner was not aware of the theft or there was no way of getting into trouble for taking it. When asked about their real-life experiences, participants indicated that they would be more likely to accept money that was physically dirty than money that was metaphorically dirty: obtained by selling drugs or other illegal activities, offered as an emotional bribe, offered as payment for voluntary work, etc. It seems that negative moral associations can reduce the desirability and perceived value of money, mainly because of the threat of contaminating individuals' perceptions of their morality (Stellar & Willer, 2014). Moreover, people were less likely to spend morally tainted money on themselves, preferring to 'purify' such money by donating it to charity (Tasimi & Gelman, 2017).

The question one might ask is whether the belief that money carries traces of its moral history represents a foundational way of thinking. To explore this topic, Tasimi and Gelman (2020) conducted another series of experiments, this time with children aged five to nine. Children were more likely to prefer a non-stolen dollar offered by a bad character than a stolen dollar offered by a morally neutral character. Whereas older children were less eager to generally accept the bill than younger children, they consistently preferred the non-stolen over the stolen dollar, regardless of who was offering it. Younger children, in turn, wanted money more, and they only preferred non-stolen over stolen money when it was offered by a morally neutral individual. In sum, children treated monetary tokens as carrying traces of their moral history, and this pattern of thinking was largely consistent among older participants but weaker among preschoolers, suggesting a developmental process (Tasimi & Gelman, 2020). It seems that thinking about money in terms of its moral history and devaluing money from morally tainted sources does not even require experience with concepts such as dirty money or bloody money that only adults likely encounter (Tasimi & Gross, 2020).

Physical features of money
Other factors that impact the subjective valuation of money include its form, denomination and physical attributes. Concerning form, people are prone to spend more when paying with dematerialised money such as credit or debit cards than when using cash. This is obviously not surprising for payments with credit cards, since by using them people spend money that they do not actually own and behave like others' money is less valuable than their own (Frederick,

2012; Matthews et al., 2016; Polman et al., 2018). Indeed, Soman (2001) noted that payments by credit cards result in the disassociation of the payment from the purchase (due to a month-long payment cycle), so at the moment of purchase consumers myopically concentrate on the product-related benefit rather than on the unpleasantness of the following costs. Furthermore, dematerialised payments are relatively less memorable than cash payments: while consumers are able to recall *what* they purchased, many of them are unable to recall *how much* they paid (Soman, 2001, 2003). Hence, because of the resulting underestimation of past expenses at the time of making another purchase, consumers using cards or other electronic payments might feel like they still have resources available and show a greater likelihood of spending. Indeed, money, when in a cash form, feels more real, proximal, tangible, visceral and more valuable, which in turn makes it more psychologically painful to part with when compared to cashless forms (Prelec & Simester, 2001; Raghubir & Srivastava, 2008; Soman, 2001, 2003).

Does this mean that in the 'digitised' economy people are somehow doomed to overspend their undervalued money? Indeed, contemporary consumers make electronic transactions more often than ever before, but the use of cash in daily life still remains more common than people usually think. Despite the strong growth in the adoption of electronic payments since the 1990s, cash usage in most OECD counties remains substantial (Amromin & Chakravorti, 2009). Therefore, it is still important to understand how cash denominations and their physical attributes affect subjective valuations of money.

People seem to undervalue smaller denominations when compared to larger denominations of an equivalent amount of money: for example, they tend to value one $100 note more than ten $10 notes, and for that reason are more reluctant to part with the former than with the latter. Mishra et al. (2006) call it 'a bias for the whole' and argue that individuals perceive a higher value when money is in form of a large single denomination because of the heightened experience of processing fluency associated with higher denominations. This greater processing fluency translates into positive affect towards the money, which leads people to overvalue the whole, thereby making them less likely to spend it when compared to the parts (Mishra et al., 2006).

The fluency effect on subjective valuations of different denominations of money has also been found in experiments conducted by Alter and Oppenheimer (2008). Participants in their study were asked to estimate the purchasing power of a certain sum of money, while it was presented as either one $2 bill or two $1 bills. However, the effect found in this study was actually the opposite of the one predicted by 'a bias for the whole' – participants believed that two $1 bills would buy more items than one $2 bill. Alter and Oppenheimer (2008) explain that the subjective valuation in this case was affected by the familiarity of the bills rather than by 'the whole': what is familiar is more fluent because it is more easily mentally processed than the unfamiliar. Indeed, $2 bills are quite rare, as there are around ten $1 bills for every $2 in circulation. Raghubir and Srivastava (2009) provide an alternative explanation for 'a bias for the whole', proposing that it occurs because individuals perceive relatively large denominations as less fungible. Leveraging their lower perceived fungibility, people strategically choose larger denominations over smaller ones as a way to exert self-control and curb spending. Another explanation is that large denominations of money may be placed into a mental account of 'real money', while an equivalent amount in smaller denominations may be placed into a 'petty cash' or 'loose change' account (Raghubir & Srivastava, 2009).

Additionally, what seems to be of importance here is whether smaller denominations are expressed in banknotes or in coins. In addition to comparing one $2 note to two $1 notes,

Alter and Oppenheimer (2008) demonstrated that people believed that the $1 bill has a greater purchasing power than a $1 Susan B. Anthony coin. Again, although they may still be used as legal tender, $1 coins in the US are produced as collectibles and people are much less familiar with them than with the extremely common $1 bills. The difference between the subjective value of a coin and a bill of the same denomination might also stem not only from its prevalence. The term 'bills' might trigger associations with larger values than the term 'coins', just because of people's experiences with instances for each category. Therefore, due to the representativeness heuristics, just because people know that bills have higher values than coins, money expressed in bills might be believed to have even greater purchasing power than money expressed in coins (Dolansky, 2014). While asking participants to estimate the purchasing power of one unit of unfamiliar currency presented in either coins or banknotes, Dolansky (2014) found that the difference between the subjective value of a coin and a note was much larger for Americans than for Canadians. Relative to Canada, the US uses coins of smaller value; coin values in the US (in common circulation and use) only go as high as 25 cents, while coin values in Canada go up to two dollars, with the exchange rate between Canadian and US dollars being roughly 1:1 during the time of the experiment (Dolansky, 2014).

Another explanation for the fact that coins are given a lower subjective value is that people simply do not like carrying them around. Coins are heavier than banknotes, they jingle, require more space, are less organisable and more likely to drop out of the wallet when compared to banknotes or alternative forms of payment. It is not uncommon that people empty their pockets from coins when arriving home, keeping them in a box or jar – a sign that they are perceived as kind of useless. Interestingly, as a result, more coins need to be minted by the government to account for money 'lying around' (Dolansky, 2014). When Great Britain introduced the one-pound coin in April 1983, it was initially rejected by the citizens, and even called 'the pound Britain doesn't want' (Burgoyne et al., 1999, p. 97). The speculated reason behind this boycott was that exchanging the one-pound note with a coin represented a devaluation of sterling and had implications for the British sense of national identity. Moreover, according to the Royal Mint, the coins were being collected in jars and piggy banks rather than carried in wallets and pockets, as they were regarded as heavy, bulky and easy to lose (Burgoyne et al., 1999).

This relative disutility of coins caused by their physical features may then hamper their subjective value when compared to bills. Vandoros (2013) demonstrated in a field experiment that consumers were likely to forgo a small monetary value in order to avoid coins. He surveyed random people in a park in London and offered either a five-pound note or GBP 5.10 in 12 coins as compensation for their effort in filling out some questionnaires. Almost half of the participants chose to receive the lower payment in order to receive a more convenient banknote instead of a handful of coins. Interestingly, this preference for a banknote over coins was somehow smaller among respondents who carried a bag than for those who did not have one, speaking in favour of the inconvenience of carrying coins explanation (Vandoros, 2013).

To sum up, for many different reasons people perceive smaller denominations of money, especially coins, as less valuable than they actually are. This effect is so strong that a shift from bills to coins for a particular denomination could possibly have an impact on the overall perception of money, as individuals ascribe less purchasing power to a coin than to a bill even if both are of the same objective value. This is probably why the $1 coins in the US never succeeded: the US has committed to minting hundreds of millions of one-dollar coins every year, at a great cost of about 30 cents per coin, for citizens who do not value them (Benincasa & Kestenbaum, 2011).

Summary

As we demonstrated in this chapter, even if people do not think that others can tell the difference between one piece of money and another of the same form and denomination, and deem distinguishing them from each other illogical (Uhlman & Zhu, 2013), they actually behave as if it were possible and logical. From a psychological perspective, unlike classical economic models assume, money is neither fungible nor universal, and its value depends on factors such as comparison standards, the source it originates from, its physical form and state, etc. Money bears traces of its history and becomes contaminated by its previous uses and owners, both in positive and negative ways. That is why the subjective value of money is in the eye of beholder and it might seriously differ from its actual, objective purchasing power.

Although an analysis of the subjective value of money reveals discrepancies between what economic theory assumes and how people actually behave, it is still focused on investigating the functions or properties of money postulated by economists, like its purchasing power in transactions or its fungibility. However, as we mentioned at the beginning of this chapter, money might convey a subjective meaning that goes far beyond economic theories. In the following part of this chapter, we review both theories and evidence regarding the symbolic meaning of money that is present in people's minds.

THE SYMBOLIC MEANING OF MONEY

Although the primary theoretical explanation for the fact that money is an effective and desired reward is that the value of money rests on its exchange function or economic value, studies in both psychology and sociology demonstrate that the desire for money exceeds its economic meaning. The money people receive as a payoff for their work not only becomes a medium of exchange, but also might be seen as an indicator of their achievement, status, respect, power and competencies. Monetary rewards received at a workplace might achieve varied symbolic meanings depending on who distributes the reward, why it is given, how it is awarded and who receives it (Mickel & Barron, 2008). For example, when monetary bonuses are distributed to the highest performers in recognition of their achievements and handed out by an individual in a high position in the organisational hierarchy in a ceremony, they are salient and prized. The money in such a situation becomes associated with the achievement and may even increase intrinsic motivation. However, rewards given for years of practice that are just added to the person's regular paycheck are less likely to signal anything special about the recipient and their accomplishment, and hence such money is just a mundane means of exchange (Mickel & Barron, 2008).

Would that imply that the symbolic meaning of money is only the question of how money is transferred to a person? As we demonstrated in the previous part of this chapter, the social history of money does matter, but it does not seem to be an exclusive explanation. Money has different meanings for different people, and usually, these differences are operationalised as attitudes towards money. As such, the symbolic meaning of money might also be considered as an individual difference variable.

Money Attitudes

The most widely used scales for measuring money attitudes include the Money Attitude Scale (MAS) by Yamauchi and Templer (1982), the Money Beliefs and Behaviour Scale (MBBS) by Furnham (1984), the Money Ethics Scale (MES) by Tang (1995), later converted into the Love of Money Scale (Tang, 2007), and the Money Attitudes Questionnaire (MAQ; Gasiorowska, 2014, 2015). Despite the fact that these scales vary in their details, the elements common to all of them are that they measure two relatively independent aspects representing either the symbolic meaning assigned to money (money as an indicator of achievement, respect, freedom, power or prestige; as a basis for social evaluation; assessment of money as good or evil or a source of distrust and anxiety or obsession) or the way individuals manage their money (control over finances, saving, debt aversion, practical budgeting, or retention from spending). These two high-level aspects of money attitudes are orthogonal and have different psychological and behavioural correlates (Gasiorowska & Zaleskiewicz, in preparation; Tatzel, 2002). For example, frugal money management is associated with having more savings and insurance, financial literacy, conscientiousness and a higher sense of control. In turn, the symbolic meaning of money is related to materialism, financial contingency of self-worth, higher neuroticism and anxiety, lower self-esteem and lower sense of control (Gasiorowska & Zaleskiewicz, 2021). In one of our studies, we found that participants who highly valued money for its symbolic meaning showed an increased desire for money after being exposed to the salience of their mortality, while these existential anxiety-quelling properties of money were not present for participants who did not assign such denotations to money. This means that for people holding symbolic attitudes towards money, it has the potential to provide psychological resources such as meaning, security and self-esteem in the face of death (Zaleskiewicz et al., 2013).

Money Priming

The symbolic meaning of money has been investigated in experiments using money priming procedures (e.g., Vohs et al., 2006). In these experiments, participants are randomly assigned either to a money condition (e.g., handling banknotes or being exposed to pictures with money) or a control condition (e.g., handling pieces of paper with numbers on them or being exposed to pictures with non-monetary objects), and then the effects of these primes on variables of interest are tested. Recent reviews of money priming consequences reveal that money triggers a focus on the self, one's own goals and agency, and makes people more individualistically oriented. In parallel with this, money downplays empathetic relations with others and impairs communal relationships, because when they have money people do not need to cooperate with others to fulfil their needs to the same extent as when they do not (for recent reviews, see Wang et al., 2020; Zaleskiewicz et al., 2018; Zaleskiewicz & Gasiorowska, 2017). Money also affects social norms and values. As a result, it might produce tension between taking more than is fair and upholding codes of fairness, honesty and trust that are needed for the effective functioning of the market (Zaleskiewicz et al., 2018; Zaleskiewicz & Gasiorowska, 2017).

Although the effects of money priming have been demonstrated by independent researchers from different cultures, there are some controversies due to inconsistent findings and failures in replicating the results that caused substantial criticism towards their reliability (see Caruso et al., 2017; Crawford et al., 2019; Rohrer et al., 2015, 2019). However, a recent meta-analysis conducted on both published and unpublished money priming studies revealed that some methods of money priming work better than others: more explicit manipulations, such as counting or sorting money, tended to produce larger effects than more subtle manipulations, such as exposure to images of money or word-descrambling tasks (Lodder et al., 2019). Additionally, it seems that people's susceptibility to the effects of money priming depends on their attitudes to money, with those who assign symbolic meaning to money reacting more strongly to these manipulations, in contrast to those who perceive money in strictly economic, instrumental terms (Gasiorowska & Helka, 2012; Zaleskiewicz et al., 2013). This leads to the conclusion that the symbolic meaning of money we investigate by employing subtle primes and by measuring individual differences taps the same psychological construct.

CONCLUSION

The aim of this chapter was to provide insights into the psychology of money, an area that has witnessed a substantial increase in research attention over the last 30 years. Economic models typically define money in terms of a universal and fungible market force that is valued because it allows for buying goods and services. Psychological science, however, posits that people construe both the value and meaning of money in a variety of ways, not only via its purchasing power, and provides an empirical test that validates this claim. In this chapter, we discussed the issue of the subjective value of money and presented factors that might affect this valuation. Notably, the fact that people perceive money as non-fungible might have important practical implications, such as suboptimal decisions when borrowing and saving, or social resistance to the replacement of old notes with newer coins. We presented main ideas from recent research based on the technique of money priming, allowing for the examination of non-conscious associations with money. Finally, we pointed to research on money attitudes as another way of investigating the divergent meanings of money.

Although the area of the psychology of money is not new, some issues still remain unexplored. For example, one question that definitely requires further research is how people come to possess symbolic associations with money, and how early in life they develop biases in the subjective valuation of money and their symbolic attitudes towards money. Although some studies suggest that young children react to money priming in a similar way as adults do (see a recent review in Gasiorowska, 2019), there are still more questions than answers concerning the process of the development of these associations. However, a deeper understanding of how laypeople's theories of money develop, and especially at how early a stage of their development children acquire the symbolic meaning of money, could have practical implications for designing better programs for education about money and for helping people to develop more sustainable approaches to this desirable resource.

ACKNOWLEDGEMENT

This work was supported by Polish National Science Centre (Grant DEC-2016/21/B/HS6/01188).

REFERENCES

Alter, A. L., & Oppenheimer, D. M. (2008). Easy on the mind, easy on the wallet: The roles of familiarity and processing fluency in valuation judgments. *Psychonomic Bulletin & Review*, *15*(5), 985–990.

Amromin, G., & Chakravorti, S. (2009). Whither loose change? The diminishing demand for small-denomination currency. *Journal of Money, Credit and Banking*, *41*(2–3), 315–335.

Antonides, G. (2008). How is perceived inflation related to actual price changes in the European Union? *Journal of Economic Psychology*, *29*(4), 417–432.

Arkes, H. R., Joyner, C. A., Pezzo, M. V., Nash, J. G., Siegel-Jacobs, K., & Stone, E. (1994). The psychology of windfall gains. *Organizational Behavior and Human Decision Processes*, *59*(3), 331–347.

Bandelj, N., Wherry, F. F., & Zelizer, V. A. (Eds.). (2017). *Money talks: Explaining how money really works*. Princeton University Press.

Becker, E. (1975). *Escape from evil*. Free Press.

Belk, R. W., & Wallendorf, M. (1990). The sacred meanings of money. *Journal of Economic Psychology*, *11*(1), 35–67.

Benincasa, R., & Kestenbaum, D. (2011). *$1 billion in coins that nobody wants*. NPR.org. https://www.npr.org/2011/06/28/137394348/-1-billion-that-nobody-wants

Brandstätter, E., & Brandstätter, H. (1996). What's money worth? Determinants of the subjective value of money. *Journal of Economic Psychology*, *17*(4), 443–464.

Buechel, E. C., & Morewedge, C. K. (2014). The (relative and absolute) subjective value of money. In E. Bijleveld & H. Aarts (Eds.), *The psychological science of money* (pp. 93–120). Springer Science + Business Media.

Burgoyne, C. B., & Lea, S. E. G. (2006). Money is material. *Science*, *314*(5802), 1091–1092.

Burgoyne, C. B., Routh, D. A., & Ellis, A.-M. (1999). The transition to the euro: Some perspectives from economic psychology. *Journal of Consumer Policy*, *22*(1), 91–116.

Cannon, E. S., & Cipriani, G. P. (2006). Euro-illusion: A natural experiment. *Journal of Money, Credit, and Banking*, *38*(5), 1391–1403.

Carruthers, B. G., & Espeland, W. N. (1998). Money, meaning, and morality. *American Behavioral Scientist*, *41*(10), 1384–1408.

Caruso, E. M., Shapira, O., & Landy, J. F. (2017). Show me the money: A systematic exploration of manipulations, moderators, and mechanisms of priming effects. *Psychological Science*, *28*(8), 1148–1159.

Crawford, J. T., Fournier, A., & Ruscio, J. (2019). Does subjective SES moderate the effect of money priming on socioeconomic system support? A replication of Schuler and Wänke (2016). *Social Psychological and Personality Science*, *10*(1), 103–109.

Del Missier, F., Bonini, N., & Ranyard, R. (2007). The euro illusion in consumers' price estimation: An Italian–Irish comparison in the third year of the euro. *Journal of Consumer Policy*, *30*(4), 337–354.

Desmet, P. (2002). A study of the potential effects of the conversion to euro. *Journal of Product & Brand Management*, *11*(3), 134–146.

DeVoe, S. E., Pfeffer, J., & Lee, B. Y. (2013). When does money make money more important? Survey and experimental evidence. *ILR Review*, *66*(5), 1078–1096.

Dolansky, E. (2014). The subjective valuation of coins and bills. *Canadian Journal of Administrative Sciences*, *31*(2), 78–89.

Duclos, R., & Khamitov, M. (2019). Compared to dematerialized money, cash increases impatience in intertemporal choice. *Journal of Consumer Psychology*, *29*(3), 445–454.

Epley, N., & Gneezy, A. (2007). The framing of financial windfalls and implications for public policy. *The Journal of Socio-Economics*, *36*(1), 36–47.

Frederick, S. (2012). Overestimating others' willingness to pay. *Journal of Consumer Research*, *39*(1), 1–21.

Furnham, A. (1984). Many sides of the coin: The psychology of money usage. *Personality and Individual Differences*, *5*(5), 501–509.

Furnham, A. (2014). *The new psychology of money*. Routledge.

Galanter, E. (1962). The direct measurement of utility and subjective probability. *The American Journal of Psychology*, *75*(2), 208–220.

Gamble, A. (2006). Euro illusion or the reverse? Effects of currency and income on evaluations of prices of consumer products. *Journal of Economic Psychology*, *27*(4), 531–542.

Gamble, A. (2007). The "euro illusion": Illusion or fact? *Journal of Consumer Policy*, *30*(4), 323–336.

Gamble, A., Gärling, T., Charlton, J., & Ranyard, R. (2002). Euro illusion: Psychological insights into price evaluations with a unitary currency. *European Psychologist*, *7*(4), 302–311.

Gamble, A., Gärling, T., Västfjäll, D., & Marell, A. (2005). Interaction effects of mood induction and nominal representation of price on consumer choice. *Journal of Retailing and Consumer Services*, *12*(6), 397–406.

Gasiorowska, A. (2014). The relationship between objective and subjective wealth is moderated by financial control and mediated by money anxiety. *Journal of Economic Psychology*, *43*, 64–74.

Gasiorowska, A. (2015). The impact of money attitudes on the relationship between income and financial satisfaction. *Polish Psychological Bulletin*, *46*(2), 197–208.

Gasiorowska, A. (2019). Lay people's and children's theories of money. In K. Gangl & E. Kirchler (Eds.), *A research agenda for economic psychology* (pp. 11–25). Edward Elgar Publishing.

Gasiorowska, A., & Helka, A. M. (2012). Psychological consequences of money and money attitudes in dictator game. *Polish Psychological Bulletin*, *43*(1), 20–26.

Gasiorowska, A., & Zaleskiewicz, T. (2021). *Two-dimensional model of money attitudes*. Manuscript in preparation.

Gourville, J. T., & Soman, D. (1998). Payment depreciation: The behavioral effects of temporally separating payments from consumption. *Journal of Consumer Research*, *25*(2), 160–174.

Greitemeyer, T., Schulz-Hardt, S., Traut-Mattausch, E., & Frey, D. (2005). The influence of price trend expectations on price trend perceptions: Why the Euro seems to make life more expensive? *Journal of Economic Psychology*, *26*(4), 541–548.

Heath, C., & Soll, J. B. (1996). Mental budgeting and consumer decisions. *Journal of Consumer Research*, *23*(1), 40–52.

Henderson, P. W., & Peterson, R. A. (1992). Mental accounting and categorization. *Organizational Behavior and Human Decision Processes*, *51*(1), 92–117.

Hur, J. D., & Nordgren, L. F. (2016). Paying for performance: Performance incentives increase desire for the reward object. *Journal of Personality and Social Psychology*, *111*(3), 301–316.

Jonas, E., Greitemeyer, T., Frey, D., & Schulz-Hardt, S. (2002). Psychological effects of the Euro – Experimental research on the perception of salaries and price estimations. *European Journal of Social Psychology*, *32*(2), 147–169.

Kahneman, D., & Tversky, A. (1984). Choices, values, and frames. *American Psychologist*, *39*(4), 341–350.

Kirchler, E., & Hoelzl, E. (2017, November 23). *Economic psychology: An introduction*. Cambridge University Press. https://doi.org/10.1017/9781139629065

Lea, S., & Webley, P. (2006). Money as tool, money as drug: The biological psychology of a strong incentive. *Behavioral and Brain Sciences*, *29*(2), 161–209.

Levav, J., & McGraw, A. P. (2009). Emotional accounting: How feelings about money influence consumer choice. *Journal of Marketing Research*, *46*(1), 66–80. https://doi.org/10.1509/jmkr.46.1.66

Li, S. (2002). Do money-earning time and money-exchanging route matter? *Psychology and Marketing*, *19*(9), 777–782.

Liu, C., Choi, N. H., & Li, B. (2018). To buy for whom? The effects of money's pride and surprise tag on spending behaviors. *European Journal of Marketing*, *52*(5/6), 910–924.

Lodder, P., Ong, H. H., Grasman, R. P. P. P., & Wicherts, J. M. (2019). A comprehensive meta-analysis of money priming. *Journal of Experimental Psychology: General*, *148*(4), 688–712.

Matthews, W. J., Gheorghiu, A. I., & Callan, M. J. (2016). Why do we overestimate others' willingness to pay? *Judgment and Decision Making*, *11*(1), 21–39.

Mickel, A. E., & Barron, L. A. (2008). Getting "more bang for the buck": Symbolic value of monetary rewards in organizations. *Journal of Management Inquiry*, *17*(4), 329–338.

Mishkin, F. S. (2019). *The economics of money, banking, and financial markets*. Pearson Education.

Mishra, H., Mishra, A., & Nayakankuppam, D. (2006). Money: A bias for the whole. *Journal of Consumer Research*, *32*(4), 541–549.

O'Curry, S., & Strahilevitz, M. (2001). Probability and mode of acquisition effects on choices between hedonic and utilitarian options. *Marketing Letters*, *12*(1), 37–49.

Peetz, J., & Soliman, M. (2016). Big money: The effect of money size on value perceptions and saving motivation. *Perception*, *45*(6), 631–641.

Polman, E., Effron, D. A., & Thomas, M. R. (2018). Other people's money: Money's perceived purchasing power is smaller for others than for the self. *Journal of Consumer Research*, *45*(1), 109–125.

Prelec, D., & Simester, D. (2001). Always leave home without it: A further investigation of the credit-card effect on willingness to pay. *Marketing Letters*, *12*(1), 5–12.

Raghubir, P., & Srivastava, J. (2002). Effect of face value on product valuation in foreign currencies. *Journal of Consumer Research*, *29*(3), 335–347.

Raghubir, P., & Srivastava, J. (2008). Monopoly money: The effect of payment coupling and form on spending behavior. *Journal of Experimental Psychology: Applied*, *14*(3), 213–225.

Raghubir, P., & Srivastava, J. (2009). The denomination effect. *Journal of Consumer Research*, *36*(4), 701–713.

Reddy, W. M. (1987). *Money and liberty in modern Europe: A critique of historical understanding*. Cambridge University Press.

Rohrer, D., Pashler, H., & Harris, C. R. (2015). Do subtle reminders of money change people's political views? *Journal of Experimental Psychology: General*, *144*(4), e73–e85.

Rohrer, D., Pashler, H., & Harris, C. R. (2019). Discrepant data and improbable results: An examination of Vohs, Mead, and Goode (2006). *Basic and Applied Social Psychology*, *41*(4), 263–271. https://doi.org/10.1080/01973533.2019.1624965

Sandel, M. J. (2012). *What money can't buy: The moral limits of markets*. Farrar, Straus and Giroux.

Shafir, E., Diamond, P., & Tversky, A. (1997). Money illusion. *The Quarterly Journal of Economics*, *112*(2), 341–374.

Shefrin, H. M., & Thaler, R. H. (1988). The behavioral life-cycle hypothesis. *Economic Inquiry*, *26*(4), 609–643.

Soman, D. (2001). Effects of payment mechanism on spending behavior: The role of rehearsal and immediacy of payments. *Journal of Consumer Research*, *27*(4), 460–474.

Soman, D. (2003). The effect of payment transparency on consumption: Quasi-experiments from the field. *Marketing Letters*, *14*(3), 173–183.

Soman, D., Wertenbroch, K., & Chattopadhyay, A. (2002). *Currency numerosity effects on the perceived value of transactions*. Unpublished working paper. Hong Kong University of Science and Technology. http://www.ssrn.com/abstract=336206

Stellar, J. E., & Willer, R. (2014). The corruption of value: Negative moral associations diminish the value of money. *Social Psychological and Personality Science*, *5*(1), 60–66.

Svedsäter, H., Gamble, A., & Gärling, T. (2007). Money illusion in intuitive financial judgments: Influences of nominal representation of share prices. *The Journal of Socio-Economics*, *36*(5), 698–712.

Tang, T. L. P. (1992). The meaning of money revisited. *Journal of Organizational Behavior*, *13*(2), 197–202.

Tang, T. L. P. (1995). The development of a short Money Ethic Scale: Attitudes toward money and pay satisfaction revisited. *Personality and Individual Differences*, *19*(6), 809–816.

Tang, T. L. P. (2007). Income and quality of life: Does the love of money make a difference? *Journal of Business Ethics*, *72*(4), 375–393.

Tasimi, A., & Gelman, S. A. (2017). Dirty money: The role of moral history in economic judgments. *Cognitive Science*, *41*, 523–544.

Tasimi, A., & Gelman, S. A. (2020). A dollar is a dollar is a dollar, or is it? Insights from children's reasoning about "dirty money". *Cognitive Science*, forthcoming.

Tasimi, A., & Gross, J. J. (2020). The dilemma of dirty money. *Current Directions in Psychological Science*, *29*(1), 41–46.

Tatzel, M. (2002). "Money worlds" and well-being: An integration of money dispositions, materialism and price-related behavior. *Journal of Economic Psychology*, *23*(1), 103–126.

Tessari, T., Rubaltelli, E., Tomelleri, S., Zorzi, C., Pietroni, D., Levorato, C., & Rumiati, R. (2011). €1 ≠ €1: Coins versus banknotes and people's spending behavior. *European Psychologist*, *16*(3), 238–246.

Thaler, R. H. (1985). Mental accounting and consumer choice. *Marketing Science*, *4*, 199–214.

Thaler, R. H. (1990). Anomalies: Saving, fungibility, and mental accounts. *Journal of Economic Perspectives*, *4*(1), 193–205.

Thaler, R. H. (1999). Mental accounting matters. *Journal of Behavioral Decision Making*, *12*(3), 183–206.

Thaler, R. H. (2015). *Misbehaving: The making of behavioral economics*. WW Norton New York.

Traut-Mattausch, E., Greitemeyer, T., Frey, D., & Schulz-Hardt, S. (2007). Illusory price increases after the euro changeover in Germany: An expectancy-consistent bias. *Journal of Consumer Policy*, *30*(4), 421–434.

Tykocinski, O. E., & Pittman, T. S. (2013). Money imbued with essence: How we preserve, invest, and spend inherited money. *Basic and Applied Social Psychology*, *35*(6), 506–514.

Uhlmann, E. L., & Zhu, L. (2013). Money is essential: Ownership intuitions are linked to physical currency. *Cognition*, *127*(2), 220–229. https://doi.org/10.1016/j.cognition.2013.01.001

Vandoros, S. (2013). My five pounds are not as good as yours, so I will spend them. *Experimental Economics*, *16*(4), 546–559.

Vohs, K. D., Mead, N. L., & Goode, M. R. (2006). The psychological consequences of money. *Science*, *314*(5802), 1154–1156.

Von Neumann, J., & Morgenstern, O. (1953). *Theory of games and economic behavior.* Princeton University Press.

Wang, X., Chen, Z., & Krumhuber, E. G. (2020). Money: An integrated review and synthesis from a psychological perspective. *Review of General Psychology*, *24*(2), 172–190.

Yamauchi, K. T., & Templer, D. J. (1982). The development of a money attitude scale. *Journal of Personality Assessment*, *46*(5), 522–528.

Zaleskiewicz, T., & Gasiorowska, A. (2017). The psychological consequences of money for economic and social relationships. In C. Jansson-Boyd and M. Zawisza (Eds.), *The Routledge international handbook of consumer psychology* (pp. 312–326). Routledge.

Zaleskiewicz, T., Gasiorowska, A., Kesebir, P., Luszczynska, A., & Pyszczynski, T. (2013). Money and the fear of death: The symbolic power of money as an existential anxiety buffer. *Journal of Economic Psychology*, *36*, 55–67.

Zaleskiewicz, T., Gasiorowska, A., & Vohs, K. D. (2018). The psychological meaning of money. In R. Ranyard (Ed.), *Economic psychology: The science of economic mental life and behaviour* (pp. 107–122). John Wiley & Sons Ltd.

Zelizer, V. A. (1994). *The social meaning of money.* Basic Books.

Zelizer, V. A. (2012). How I became a relational economic sociologist and what does that mean? *Politics & Society*, *40*(2), 145–174.

13. Taking financial advice: Going beyond making good decisions

Tomasz Zaleskiewicz and Agata Gasiorowska

INTRODUCTION

One of the most important mental activities people engage in when making decisions – including decisions in the domain of finance – is the search for information.[1] For example, if consumers intend to make a choice that concerns investing money, they should first recognise what investing possibilities are available, how they differ from each other, what their expected returns and risks are and so on (Schiffman et al., 2010). Choices based on improper information are likely to turn out to be inaccurate. Decision makers can refer to a variety of information sources; some of them are internal and others external. The 'internal' category is related to decision makers' experience and knowledge (both general and that which is specific to the decision problem). Klein's (1998) recognition-primed decision model may be given here as an example of a theoretical approach that interprets decision making – mainly in experienced decision makers such as stock market traders, nurses or fire ground commanders – in terms of behaviour which is grounded in one's prior experience and the skill to recognise the extent to which the situation is prototypical. The 'external' category seems to be much broader than the 'internal' one because the range of external sources of information a decision maker can have access to is quite extensive. It includes other people (e.g., experts, coworkers, colleagues and family members); the Internet (e.g., social media, professional websites and comparison websites); published reports (e.g., professional magazines and scientific papers); statistics (e.g., results of market or social research) and so on.

The apparent explanation of why people turn to experts – one specific external source of information – is that experts know better and that relying on their knowledge, skills or competence increases the probability of achieving efficient decision outcomes (Bonaccio & Dalal, 2006; Harvey & Fischer, 1997; Inderst & Ottaviani, 2012; Yaniv, 2004a, 2004b). For example, when suffering different health problems, patients who do not have medical education take advice from a physician to learn which course of action offers the highest chance for recovery. Taking advice from experts is also very popular in financial markets. Statistical data indicate that more than 70 per cent of retail investors in the United States consult with an advisor before they buy shares (Hung et al., 2008). Similarly, Chater et al. (2010) have documented that almost 80 per cent of Europeans interested in financial products talk to an expert when making their decisions.

People especially tend to appreciate advice from those with greater age, education, experience and wisdom than themselves (Feng & MacGeorge, 2006) because all these characteristics are likely to positively correlate with advice quality. The assumption that relying on expert knowledge is useful is not unfounded. Evidence suggests that collecting advice from multiple sources of expertise which are independent of each other may indeed have a favourable impact on the accuracy of decision making (Budescu & Rantilla, 2000; Johnson et al., 2001;

Soll, 1999). Bonaccio and Dalal (2006), who presented an extensive review of research on advice giving and taking in their paper, concluded that 'In general, using advice has been found to increase decision accuracy' (p. 133). However, under certain conditions, basing a decision on expert advice may be unbeneficial. For example, as suggested by Inderst and Ottaviani (2012), 'Consumers seem to misunderstand, ignore, or overlook the potential conflicts of interest created when product providers either pay commissions or inducements to advisers or employ advisers directly' (p. 510). According to these authors, in such cases, a recommendation from an advisor may be more of a curse than a blessing for naïve decision makers. In the present chapter, we propose yet another source of potential bias in advice taking, and suggest that both searching for professional recommendations and evaluating the quality of the source of expertise may sometimes go beyond the need to only make optimal decisions and can be driven by motivations independent of accuracy. In particular, we argue that when people are confronted with the necessity to evaluate the quality of a certain expert and their advice, they use their own beliefs as a reference point and tend to depreciate such recommendations that are at odds with those beliefs. In other words, our idea, supported by the results of a series of studies, points to the psychological role of the confirmation effect in advice taking.

In the following sections of the chapter, first, we explain in more detail what we generally mean by saying that taking financial advice may serve different psychological needs, and also provide some specific examples related to the avoidance of regret and cognitive dissonance. Next, we introduce the idea that when lay decision makers face a range of experts whose recommendations can be used – as typically happens in the financial advice market – they strongly focus on how much these recommendations are consistent with their own beliefs, even if they are unqualified in the field. Finally, we review evidence not only showing that the need to confirm one's opinions is associated with evaluating the quality of expertise, but also suggesting that specific psychological mechanisms fixed to protect one's self-worth may be responsible for the entanglement of motivated reasoning in using financial advice.

Unlike a standard economic view on using expert recommendations (e.g., Inderst & Ottaviani, 2012), we represent a purely descriptive approach to the study of financial advice taking. Instead of offering any formal model, we review evidence collected mainly in cognitive and social psychology to propose a potential explanation behind advisees' engagement in motivations that deviate from a search for accuracy.

PSYCHOLOGICAL MOTIVATIONS IN FINANCIAL ADVICE TAKING

As we have already suggested in the introduction, turning to experts in financial decision making may be motivated by something more than only the need to ensure good decision making. Prior research suggests that relying on advice may be useful in regulating the emotion of regret or protecting oneself against the experience of cognitive dissonance.

Regret can be defined as the emotion that is 'experienced when looking back at decisions that went awry' and as being 'typically associated with feeling responsible for the bad outcome and kicking oneself over the mistake made' (Zeelenberg, 2018, p. 276). Regret undoubtedly has a negative valence (Saffrey et al., 2008), and its painful essence most likely arises from the fact that people experience it when they are aware that they made a wrong decision – the decision that produced harmful consequences (e.g., financial losses). However, regret can also be considered as an anticipated emotion, which means that people try to forecast how they will feel after making a certain decision (Baumeister et al., 2007; Lerner et al., 2015;

Zaleskiewicz & Traczyk, 2020). Therefore, they may feel strongly motivated to take actions which would defend them in advance against experiencing this unpleasant emotion, and turning to experts may be one such action. Kahneman and Tversky (1982, p. 173) analysed the following case of two investors who may have experienced regret:

> Paul owns shares in Company A. During the past year he considered switching to stock in Company B, but he decided against it. He now finds that he would have been better off by $1,200 if he had switched to the stock of Company B. George owned shares in Company B. During the last year he switched to stock in Company A. He now finds that he would have been better off by $1,200 if he had kept his stock in Company B.

As Kahneman and Tversky (1982) argued, both Paul and George are likely to experience regret because they are aware that they would be better off financially had they chosen differently. Even if they differ in whether they took action (George) or refrained from acting (Paul), they are similar in two ways: both of them suffer negative financial outcomes, and both are responsible for the decisions they made. What, however, would happen if both investors, instead of deciding individually, consulted with an independent advisor about their choices? Would they still experience regret after learning that their decisions turned out to be unbeneficial and 'kick' themselves over the mistake they made? Our suggestion is that in such a case they might have felt justified that the decision followed the expert's recommendation and experienced anger (i.e., the emotion directed towards an expert) instead of regret (i.e., the emotion oriented towards the decision maker themselves). This means that people sometimes may consult with experts to take responsibility away from themselves for the expected bad outcomes of the decisions they face and to protect themselves against feelings which could be harmful to their sense of self-worth.

Another example that illustrates how needs which are not directly associated with making good decisions may cause people to take advice from experts refers to protecting against cognitive dissonance. This psychological effect occurs when an individual holds at least two contradictory ideas simultaneously, thus producing the feeling of distress, and, therefore, the individual feels strongly motivated to take action in order to reduce the discomfort (Festinger, 1957). For example, individuals might perceive themselves as effective investors, but at the same time might be losing money. Such inconsistency generates the unpleasant feeling of cognitive dissonance that should be somehow diminished. The theory of cognitive dissonance suggests that in cases similar to the one we describe here, people are unwilling to change positive opinions about themselves ('I am a knowledgeable investor, so it is unlikely that I made a mistake') but rather they try to change their perception of the environment (e.g., 'Someone else gave me wrong advice and, therefore, is responsible for why I lost my money'). In a similar way to taking protective actions oriented to reduce future regret, people may want to decrease the probability of dissonance occurring after the decision is made. They may, for example, base their decision on an expert's recommendation in order to make the expert responsible for potential losses. In the case of financial decision making, one possibility is to invest in mutual funds in which managers are in the position of experts who make decisions on behalf of their clients. Empirical evidence seems to support the reasoning we propose here. Chang et al. (2016) reported that investing in delegated assets, such as mutual funds, reverses the disposition effect. The disposition effect is a robust behavioural phenomenon present in financial markets that manifests itself as selling winners too fast and keeping losers too long (Odean, 1998; Shefrin & Statman, 1985). As Chang et al. (2016) showed, investing in mutual funds significantly increases the readiness to sell losers quickly because responsibility can be moved to an expert who, in the view of the decision maker, ineffectively managed the portfolio. In an experiment, these authors additionally found that the effect they observed was amplified when the salience of delegation was increased (Chang et al., 2016).

In the opening paragraph of this chapter, we suggested that when people recognise their competence as not sufficiently adequate to make informed decisions individually, they may show the demand for support from advisors. Prior research has consistently indicated that people's financial literacy is inappropriate, and its low level might be a sufficient reason behind their interest in consulting with experts (Lusardi & Mitchell, 2011; van Rooij et al., 2011). However, the two examples presented here related to protecting against regret and cognitive dissonance seem to indicate that when decision makers turn to experts for advice, they must not necessarily be driven by the need to increase the chances for beneficial choices. Of course, we do not argue that when people take professional advice they are not interested in broadening their knowledge. Rather, we suggest that this obvious motivation is accompanied by other, less obvious motivations resulting from different psychological needs.

So far, we have discussed the issue of motivational and emotional effects associated with the decision to rely on financial experts. However, motivations that go beyond making good decisions may also regulate one's behaviour when needing to evaluate the quality of advisors to make sure that they can be considered a trustful source of information. We propose that in such cases people's behaviour may be determined by the need to confirm their own beliefs. We begin the next part of this chapter by developing the issue of laypeople's evaluations of expert authority, and then investigate the psychological functions of the confirmation effect in financial advice taking.

LAYPEOPLE'S EVALUATIONS OF EXPERT AUTHORITY

Before people start collecting information from experts, they have to decide which source of knowledge is trustworthy and reliable. This is not an easy task. For example, in the United States, the size of the financial advice industry has been consistently increasing in recent years, and currently, there are a few thousand firms that offer consumers the chance to consult about their financial decisions.[2] This implies that clients need to discover which cues indicate high-quality expertise in order to find a way of differentiating between better and inferior experts. Only those experts whose advice is perceived as valid and trustworthy are considered by people to be authorities in a particular field and can exert a determinative influence on their decisions (Kruglanski, 1989). However, the issue that remains problematic in this context refers to the question of how laypeople – not possessing professional knowledge and often being financially illiterate – get to know who a better and more competent expert is, and whom they should trust more. If uninformed people are not able to use analytical thinking, they must rely on intuitive processing and gut feelings, rendering their evaluations more susceptible to errors and bias (Bazerman & Moore, 2012; Kahneman, 2003). One such bias may result from people's desire to use motivated reasoning in general and confirmatory thinking in particular (Kunda, 1999; Nickerson, 1998).

Researchers in cognitive psychology have studied how people subjectively assimilate qualitative knowledge provided by different authorities (e.g., experts) and in which conditions they tend to rely on it (Kruglanski, 1989; Kruglanski et al., 2005). Lay epistemic theory (Kruglanski, 1989, 2012) introduced the concept of *epistemic authority* (EA) which 'denotes a source on whom an individual may rely in her or his attempts to acquire knowledge on various topics' (Kruglanski et al., 2005, p. 351). Experts or advisors can acquire EA to the extent that an individual believes they possess characteristics that give them such authority (Raviv et al., 1993). Once people recognise a certain source as an EA, they tend to accept the knowledge it provides as true and factual, assimilate it and then rely on it. People process the information from a source with greater EA more extensively, are more certain of it and tend to act in accordance with its implications. They are also more confident about decisions based on recommendations given by experts with high EA (Kruglansky et al., 2010). For example, if decision makers ascribe high EA to a particular financial consultant, they will make choices based on this consultant's advice (e.g., concerning investments, insurance or loans) without searching for other sources of knowledge.

As suggested by Kruglanski et al. (2005), the influence of EA may be so powerful that it overrides all other sources of information in decision making. This claim seems to be supported by the results of prior research by Engelmann et al., (2009) who investigated the neural mechanisms involved in taking advice in decision making under risk. In their study, participants made a series of financial choices between lotteries and were assigned to one of the two experimental conditions which differed as to whether the advice from a financial expert was present or not. For example, people made a choice between a smaller gain received with certainty and a larger but uncertain gain, and in the advice-present group, they were informed that the expert suggested choosing the former option. On the behavioural level, the authors showed that the expert's advice significantly influenced behaviour – participants were highly willing to follow the recommendations they received. On the neural level, they found that brain activations showing significant correlations with valuation were obtained only in the absence of the expert's advice. Interestingly, no such correlations with value were observed in the presence of advice. In the authors' interpretation, these results suggest not only that people may be prone to follow advisors' recommendations when making financially risky decisions, but also that the presence of advice has the capacity to 'offload' the calculation of the value of alternative decision options from the individual's brain. Later research indicated that this effect is especially pronounced among inexperienced decision makers (Engelmann et al., 2012). To summarise, people tend to use advice when they get it, therefore it is important to know that people recognise the authority of experts and the extent to which this process may be biased.

The importance of EA in knowledge formation and decision making has spurred researchers to try to find out what factors lend a source to EA. The characteristics that are used to identify a source as an EA can be general – a professional or social role (e.g., a leader or physician); level of education (e.g., the holder of a doctorate); an appearance in print (e.g., in a book or a newspaper) – or specific, as when EA is assigned to a particular person (Kruglanski et al., 2005). In the context of financial decision making, someone can ascribe greater EA to an advisor who holds a PhD in economics, has longer experience in the market or can document good prior results in giving recommendations to clients. Evidence indeed suggests that people tend to trust more experienced financial advisors to a larger extent than less experienced ones (Zaleskiewicz et al., 2016). However, when evaluating the authority of advisors, people use not only objective (truly informative), but also subjective (potentially uninformative) cues. Using the terminology proposed by the elaboration likelihood model (Petty & Cacioppo, 1986), we might say that decision makers process information about the value of an authority using either the central route (careful and thoughtful consideration of those aspects of the advice which are truly related to its quality), or the peripheral route (consideration of aspects which are generally unrelated to the true quality of the advice, but which may seem credible).

Probably one of the most extreme examples of how an uninformative cue may influence the perception of advice quality is the so-called white-coat effect in the domain of medical decision making. It has been found that patients react differently to doctors depending on the latter's attire. More precisely, people exhibit greater confidence in the competence of those doctors who are dressed formally and in a way that is typical for the medical profession (e.g., wearing a white coat) compared to those who are dressed casually (e.g., wearing jeans and a T-shirt) (Gledhill et al., 1997; Hennessy et al., 1993). In one of the studies (Brase & Richmond, 2004), participants were presented with photographs of three models dressed more or less formally, depending on the condition (e.g., a white coat with a plain white shirt and black dress trousers vs. blue jeans, a plain white T-shirt and trainers). In all conditions, the model held a clipboard, wore a stethoscope around their neck, and wore a name badge to avoid misunderstandings concerning participants' beliefs of whether the model was indeed a doctor or not. The authors found the highest authority ratings when the model was shown in a white coat and the lowest ratings when the model's attire was casual. Such outcomes clearly suggest that the way experts look has an impact on the manner they are perceived and evaluated.

The perception of experts' authority can be affected not only by physical aspects (how they are dressed, how their office looks, etc.) but also by factors that are related to experts' behaviour and how they express their opinions. One of these non-physical factors, which determines the credibility of experts' messages, is their self-confidence (Bonaccio & Dalal, 2006). Price and Stone (2004) even suggested that advisees use a 'confidence heuristic' to infer advisors' knowledge, ability and level of expertise. Evidence indicates that when advisors provide their recommendations with greater confidence, they have a better chance of their recommendations being followed (e.g., Sniezek & Van Swol, 2001; Van Swol & Sniezek, 2005). The heuristic does not have to produce an incorrect decision based on expert advice because high confidence can result from deep knowledge. However, prior research comparing financial forecasts given by professionals (e.g., financial analysts) and by novices (e.g., psychology students) has shown that even if the former express very high confidence, they are not necessarily more accurate in their predictions, revealing the overconfidence effect (Törngren & Montgomery, 2004; Zaleskiewicz, 2011). In other words, confidence does not always positively correlate with the level of expertise, suggesting that subjective cues that laypeople use when assessing the quality of expert advice may be uninformative and misleading.

In the following part of the chapter, we will elaborate on one more source of potential distortion in evaluating advisors' authority – the extent to which the recommendation provided by an expert overlaps with advisees' own opinions. First, we review results related to different forms of 'my-side' thinking and egocentric discounting of expert advice. Second, we summarise our original research showing how either consistency or inconsistency between people's opinions and recommendations they receive from experts can affect the perception of experts' authority. Finally, we provide evidence suggesting that the evaluation of the quality of financial advice may serve motivations that go beyond making good decisions.

EGOCENTRIC DISCOUNTING OF EXPERT ADVICE

When we use the term 'egocentric discounting of expert advice', we mean that people perceive advice based on their thoughts about the topic. More technically, those decision makers who reveal egocentric discounting and various forms of 'my-side' thinking in their evaluations of advice, place a higher weight on their own opinion than on the advisor's suggestion (Yaniv, 2004a; Yaniv et al., 2009; Yaniv & Kleinberger, 2000; Yaniv & Milyavsky, 2007). This means that such decision makers are vulnerable to the confirmation effect (Nickerson, 1998) in processing professional recommendations.

'My-side Thinking' in Social Cognition

Research in both social and cognitive psychology has shown for a long time that people are strongly determined to defend their beliefs and are reluctant to change them in the face of opposite opinions received from other sources. In a broader sense, the persistent adherence to one's system of beliefs and convictions reflects such psychological phenomena as motivated thinking and motivated reasoning (Haidt, 2012; Kunda, 1987, 1990; Lundgren & Prislin, 1998; Mercier & Sperber, 2011; Molden & Higgins, 2005). For example, the work on attitude polarisation revealed that people holding strong opinions on different issues process empirical evidence in a biased manner, revealing the *prior belief effect* (Edwards & Smith, 1996). Individuals tend to accept information supporting their initial beliefs and critically evaluate disconfirming evidence (Lord et al., 1979; Lundgren & Prislin, 1998). Edwards and Smith (1996) proposed the disconfirmation model. They provided empirical evidence showing that arguments inconsistent with prior beliefs related to such issues as the death penalty or abortion are scrutinised longer, subjected to more extensive refutational analysis, and perceived to be weaker than arguments congruent with prior beliefs. Similarly, Ditto and Lopez (1992) showed that people are motivated sceptics; specifically, they process and examine information inconsistent with their beliefs more critically and more carefully than beliefs-consistent information (see also Ditto et al., 1998). In other words, people experience greater uncertainty regarding the validity of preference-inconsistent information. Research in group behaviour also suggests that interpersonal cognitive consistency plays an important role in how people perceive and evaluate one another. Mojzich et al. (2014) studied collective decision processes and found that participants evaluated their partners in dyads as more competent when these partners communicated information that was consistent with participants' preferences. Preference-consistent information itself was also perceived as more important and accurate than preference-inconsistent information. In the same vein, Minson et al. (2011) and Liberman et al. (2011) have reported that people engaged in a dyadic collaboration failed to give due weight to their partner's estimates when these diverged from their own beliefs.

Egocentric Discounting of Advice

Research in social psychology described above has consistently documented that people are strongly motivated to defend their attitudes and beliefs, even at the price of the lower accuracy of judgements or evaluations they produce (Minson et al., 2011). Yaniv (2004a) proposed an analogy between attitude change and advice use and argued that similar psychological factors might be responsible for these two processes. Knowing that people are strongly determined to defend their opinions by ignoring disconfirming evidence, one might assume that a similar tendency would have an effect on an information search in the advice-taking context. Indeed, when participants provided their judgements on the basis of their own opinions and advice presented to them, they revealed egocentric discounting of another's opinion (Yaniv, 2004a; Yaniv & Kleinberger, 2000; Yaniv & Milyavsky, 2007). In one study (Yaniv & Kleinberger,

2000), participants' task was to answer a set of general knowledge questions related to a range of historic events (e.g., 'In what year were the Dead Sea scrolls first discovered?'). First, they provided their answers to the questions. In the next step, they responded again to the same questions, but this time they also received responses from an advisor, and thus they had a chance to revise their initial estimates. The results showed that the vast majority of participants did not revise their initial responses, revealing a strong 'my-side' thinking effect. Furthermore, the authors reported that the mean absolute error was lower for the combined estimate than for the initial estimate, which suggests that the egocentric discounting of advice led to more errors when answering the questions.

Yaniv et al. (2009) argue that advisees tend to overweight advice that is consistent with their preferences because congruence with advisors is rewarding and reduces cognitive effort. These authors also reported that when participants received advice close to their opinions, they were less willing to change their initial estimates and indicated greater confidence in their final estimates. Schultze et al. (2015) confirmed the aforementioned effects in their research and showed that decision makers weighted advice to a lesser degree when it deviated from their own initial opinions. Moreover, Ecken and Pibernik (2015) have shown that people's tendency to ignore advice due to their reluctance to update prior beliefs might be observed not only in lay evaluations but also in long-term professional judgements.

THE CONFIRMATION EFFECT IN EVALUATING ADVISORS' AUTHORITY

Decision makers who use advice may be vulnerable to the confirmation effect and 'my-side' thinking not only when they provide specific judgements but also when they have to recognise the quality of an advisor. As we have already suggested earlier in this chapter, such situations typically happen when decision makers can consult with several experts who differ in a range of characteristics that may be viewed as either objective (i.e., length of experience or prior results in advising), or subjective (i.e., self-confidence or appearance) cues in evaluating the authority of those experts. In this section, we briefly discuss the results of our experimental project that was intended to test the general hypothesis that people tend to favourably evaluate the quality of an advisor when they provide recommendations consistent with a decision maker's own opinions about the topic.[3]

In the first part of the project, we conducted experiments in which we manipulated both participants' opinions about the profitability of some financial products and experts' advice concerning these products (the expert presented in a scenario provided arguments in favour or against the profitability of a financial product). For example, in the investment scenario, participants were asked to imagine that they went to the bank just to change their telephone contact number, and while the advisor was changing the information in the bank system, the talk turned to a discussion of investing. In the 'advice against' condition, the advisor recommended against opening an investment account, as it was quite expensive and not profitable. In the 'advice for' condition, the advisor recommended opening the account, as it was inexpensive and very profitable. The recommendation provided by the advisor was again followed by a brief description of the client's opinion. In the 'positive opinion' condition, participants were asked to imagine that they were interested in individual investing in the stock market because they believed it was very profitable. In the 'negative opinion' condition participants realised that they were not convinced about the idea of individual investing because they believed that it was prone to making losses. After reading each scenario, participants answered six questions that together assessed the EA attributed to the advisor presented in the scenario, adjusted for the content of the scenario (e.g., 'To what extent do you think the financial advisor is an expert in investing?'). Higher EA ratings indicated participants' more favourable evaluations of advisors' authority in the field of finance.

The results were consistent with our predictions and showed that participants indeed attributed greater authority to financial consultants whose advice was congruent with their opinions. When advisors recommended action (vs. inaction), they were perceived as better experts by those participants who were induced to hold positive (vs. negative) opinions regarding purchasing two different financial products (i.e., an investment account or insurance). Because it may seem problematic that participants' opinions were manipulated, we also replicated our effects using a different approach. Instead of manipulating participants' financial beliefs, we simply measured them by asking a set of questions at the very beginning of the study before the scenarios were introduced (e.g., 'What is your opinion of investing in the stock market by someone with an average income?'). Irrespective of whether we manipulated participants' opinions or measured them, the results we found supported our hypothesis concerning the existence of the confirmation effect in evaluating financial experts' authority. Interestingly, the confirmation effect we observed was not moderated by the participants' subjective knowledge of finance. This might suggest that the impact of the 'my-side thinking' on experts' authority evaluations is universal and does not depend on how competent an individual feels in the financial domain (Zaleskiewicz & Gasiorowska, 2016).

The prediction that people tend to adjust their evaluations of experts in accordance with their opinions assumes that people do have opinions. What, however, happens when decision makers are highly uncertain about their beliefs or preferences? We proposed that in such cases decision makers might be motivated to confirm more general social norms related to a particular behaviour. If people did not have access to their own opinions in a particular domain but were aware of what behaviour is most valued by other people from their social group, they would form their preferences in line with the salient norms because they were trying to conform to the common rules (Aarts & Dijksterhuis, 2003; Cialdini et al., 1990; Nolan et al., 2008; Schultz et al., 2007). One of our experiments provided results confirming such reasoning. Again, we measured participants' opinions related to individual investing on the stock market and manipulated: (a) expert advice (in favour or against the profitability of investing), (b) the valence of a social norm (positive or negative) and (c) content of the social norm (related to finances or not related to finances). The reason for manipulating the norm content was based on the assumption that the norm must be related to a particular domain (the financial domain in our case) to evoke the confirmation effect. The most important result of this experiment was that while making their evaluations of the financial advisors' EA, laypeople expressed the confirmation effect even if their own opinions had not been made salient. We observed that greater authority was attributed to those financial consultants whose recommendations were consistent with the behaviour that is common and valued by people who are part of the same society as our participants. More precisely, when financial consultants' advice was congruent with the salient social norm, they were perceived as better experts than when their recommendation was inconsistent with this norm. This effect was exclusive to the norm related to investing and did not occur when the norm regarded non-financial behaviours. Once more, we showed the existence of the confirmation effect in lay evaluations of the authority of financial consultants and indicated another source of this effect in the perception of the experts' advice quality. Again, no moderation effect of the perceived self-knowledge in finance was found (Zaleskiewicz & Gasiorowska, 2016).

In the second phase of our project, we intended to not only replicate people revealing 'my-side thinking' in their evaluations of the quality of financial expert advice but also to show that such a psychological effect holds for different financial products and cultures (Zaleskiewicz & Gasiorowska, 2020). First, we found that the confirmation effect could be observed with respect to decisions concerning such products as insurance, investment accounts or health savings accounts. Second, we showed that the confirmation effect similarly influences evaluations of the authority of experts in personal finance in three different countries: the United States, the United Kingdom and Poland. This is notable in that these countries all differ from each other – not only in terms of their culture but also concerning the history and the size of their economic systems. Third, as already discussed earlier, we demonstrated that such a confirmation effect was present not only for those with no experience in finances but also for those whose education or profession was related to personal finance. These findings support the possibility that the confirmation effect – at least as it applies to financial advising – may be replicated in a cross-national sense and, further, cannot be approached as a bias present only in laypeople. In other words, our results seem to reveal basic psychological effects, as opposed to economic and/or political trends reflective of, and specific to, a certain country (or, alternatively, knowledge/experience possessed by a certain group of people).

Our reasoning proposes that people are vulnerable to the confirmation effect in evaluating experts. Still, it also suggests that this effect is determined by people's needs that are not directly associated with making good decisions. In the final part of this chapter, we summarise the results of our project which provide support for such an argument.

Psychological Motivations behind the Confirmation Effect in Evaluating Financial Advisors' Authority

One of our main theoretical arguments is that the susceptibility to 'my-side thinking' in the perception of financial advisors' authority can be considered as more than a cognitive bias interpreted in terms of an insufficient adjustment of one's beliefs to suggestions from external sources. Earlier in this chapter, we referred to Yaniv et al. (2009), who proposed that overweighting advice that is consistent with the decision maker's own preferences may occur because congruence with advisors is rewarding. Following this idea, we suggested that processing advice from experts can be associated with the regulation of advisees' self-esteem.

People are strongly motivated to maintain high self-esteem which is expressed by the overall subjective evaluation of one's own worth (Hewitt, 2009), showing 'a desperate and pervasive need to view oneself as valuable' (Greenberg et al., 1986, p. 197). One of the means of supporting high self-esteem is to find confirmation for one's knowledge and competencies (Pyszczynski & Greenberg, 1987). An interaction with an advisor, in which two parties exchange their opinions and predictions, may end in either consensus or disagreement. If individuals receive advice that is consistent with their a priori opinions, they can affirm their belief in being competent and intelligent – as competent as somebody who is recognised as an expert. On the contrary, receiving advice that is inconsistent with prior opinions might lead to activating psychological defence mechanisms to eliminate, or at least diminish, a threat to self-esteem. One such mechanism is to depreciate the source of advice and to convince oneself that such a source is a poor authority.

The outlined process of motivated advice taking seems to resemble two well-documented psychological effects: *self-serving attributional bias* (Mezulis et al., 2004) and *bias blind spot* (Pronin et al., 2002). In line with the former effect, people tend to see themselves in a favourable manner, which might lead to ascribing successes to one's abilities and efforts, on the one hand, and to ascribing failures to different external factors, on the other (Campbell & Sedikides, 1999). The latter effect is related to the more basic *naïve realism* phenomenon, which reflects people's claiming they perceive the world objectively and, at the same time, believe that others share their perceptions (Pronin, 2007, 2008; Ross & Ward, 1996). From this standpoint, if people realise that others disagree with those perceptions, they might come to believe these others are either uninformed or biased (Pronin et al., 2004; Scopelliti et al., 2015). Pronin et al. (2002) proposed that people exhibit a bias blind spot – they see others as more susceptible to biases and errors than they themselves are. In this vein, when recommendations given by experts deviate from a person's opinions, people may attribute the source of that disagreement to experts' inclination to biased reasoning, as opposed to their own lack of knowledge. For example, people might think that advisors do not have access to all the relevant information or that their recommendations are skewed by self-interest.

To investigate the previously discussed theoretical predictions, we conducted a series of experiments (see Zaleskiewicz & Gasiorowska, 2020) aimed at testing whether such psychological phenomena as self-esteem or bias blind spot are involved in the evaluation of expert authority and whether they may be indeed responsible for the 'my-side thinking' distortion in advice taking. Our main hypothesis was that people who evaluate the authority of financial experts favour advice confirming their beliefs because they are motivated to sustain self-integrity and maintain their positive view of themselves. In other words, we predicted that bolstering confirmatory advice and depreciating disconfirmatory advice might be interpreted as a psychological strategy initiated to defend one's feelings of self-worth and to attribute biased reasoning to those experts who provide recommendations incongruent with the decision maker's opinions.

In all studies, participants were asked about their beliefs concerning the profitability of some financial products and then received advice that was either consistent or inconsistent with their opinions. Their final task was to evaluate the authority of the expert from whom they received recommendations. In addition, we also measured participants' state self-esteem and their willingness to attribute biased thinking to the advisor. The latter measure asked participants how much they thought that the advisor was focused more on their own interest than on the client's profit, had omitted important information, and so on. Our findings indicated that both factors (i.e., self-esteem and attributing bias to advisors) mediated the relationship between (in)consistency between one's opinion and expert advice, on the one hand, and the evaluation of expert authority, on the other. Receiving financial advice that confirmed people's beliefs was related to higher self-esteem and less of a tendency to attribute biases to experts' judgements – both of which, in turn, led to ascribing greater authority to advisors. That is to say, we showed that an individual might form their evaluations of an expert's competence not based on objective facts but rather based on various psychological needs they wish to fulfil.

CONCLUSION

When making real-life decisions, people often must deal with complex – and, in most cases, frustrating – issues such as uncertainty, ambiguity, information overload, data scarcity, or, to put it more generally, lack of knowledge. Even professional decision makers, including managers or experienced entrepreneurs, may face problems with understanding, processing and applying available knowledge, as well as dealing with the challenges of predicting the consequences of their actions. In such cases, decision makers may want to turn for advice to experts whose proficiency can serve as a source of information essential to make reasonable and deliberate choices. It means that the main motivation behind turning to experts should be to acquire, extend, or verify knowledge to arrive at beneficial decision consequences. In the present chapter, we proposed, however, that both asking for and using financial advice, as well as evaluating advisors' authority, may be associated with satisfying needs that go beyond making accurate decisions. First, our review suggested that cooperating with advisors also serves such psychological needs as protection against expected regret and cognitive dissonance. If the outcomes of decisions people made individually turn out to be unsatisfactory, it is likely that they experience regret and engage in counterfactual thinking. In contrast, when a particular choice was suggested by an advisor, its negative consequences would rather evoke anger because the advisor was seen by a decision maker as being responsible for the action that was taken. Second, we provided evidence indicating that when people evaluate experts' authority, they become vulnerable to the confirmation effect. This vulnerability arises from people's need to maintain high self-worth and to protect against anything that might be threatening to it. Receiving advice that is inconsistent with the decision maker's opinions can be considered such a threat.

The fact that taking financial advice engages motivations going beyond making good decisions seems to generate consequences for both sides of the advising process – advisors and advisees. Advisors should be aware that receiving positive feedback from a client does not have to be informative of the quality of the advice they gave. It can only result from a high congruence between the advice and the client's opinion. Advisees should carefully consider reasons as to why they turn to an expert. For example, when information that will be useful for making a good decision can be found without taking costly advice, and one decides to pay for it anyway, this might signal that the behaviour is driven by a need, such as regret avoidance, that is independent of the objective decision quality. When negatively assessing the credibility of an expert, they should recognise if such unfavourable evaluation indeed results from the poor quality of the advice and not from the incongruence between their opinions and what they find out from that expert.

NOTES

1. The authors would like to thank Gerrit Antonides for comments on the first draft of this chapter. The preparation of this chapter was supported by the National Science Centre in Poland (grant UMO-2012/05/B/HS6/00268).
2. www.ibisworld.com/united-states/market-research-reports/financial-planning-advice-industry/ (retrieved on February 25, 2021).
3. The detailed results and their thorough interpretation can be found in: Zaleskiewicz et al. (2016), Zaleskiewicz and Gasiorowska (2018, 2020).

REFERENCES

Aarts, H., & Dijksterhuis, A. (2003). The silence of the library: Environment, situational norm, and social behavior. *Journal of Personality and Social Psychology*, *84*, 18–28.

Baumeister, R. F., Vohs, K. D., Nathan DeWall, C., & Liqing Zhang (2007). How emotion shapes behavior: Feedback, anticipation, and reflection, rather than direct causation. *Personality and Social Psychology Review, 11*, 167–203.

Bazerman, M. H., & Moore, D. A. (2012). *Judgment in Managerial Decision Making, 8th Edition*. Wiley.

Bonaccio, S., & Dalal, R. S. (2006). Advice taking and decision-making: An integrative literature review, and implications for the organizational sciences. *Organizational Behavior and Human Decision Processes, 101*, 127–151.

Brase, G. L., & Richmond, J. (2004). The White–Coat effect: Physician attire and perceived authority, friendliness, and attractiveness. *Journal of Applied Social Psychology, 34*, 2469–2481.

Budescu, D. V., & Rantilla, A. K. (2000). Confidence in aggregation of expert opinions. *Acta Psychologica, 104*, 371–398.

Campbell, W. K., & Sedikides, C. (1999). Self-threat magnifies the self-serving bias: A meta-analytic integration. *Review of General Psychology, 3*, 23–43.

Chang, T. Y., Solomon, D. H., & Westerfield, M. (2016). Looking for someone to blame: Delegation, cognitive dissonance, and the disposition effect. *Journal of Finance, 71*, 267–302.

Chater, N., Huck, S., & Inderst, R. (2010). *Consumer decision-making in retail investment services: A behavioural economics perspective*. Report to the European Commission/SANCO.

Cialdini, R. B., Reno, R. R., & Kallgren, C. A. (1990). A focus theory of normative conduct: Recycling the concept of norms to reduce littering in public places. *Journal of Personality and Social Psychology, 58*, 1015–1026.

Ditto, P. H., & Lopez, D. L. (1992). Motivated skepticism: Use of differential decision criteria for preferred and nonpreferred conclusions. *Journal of Personality and Social Psychology, 63*, 568–584.

Ditto, P. H., Scepansky, J. A., Munro, G. D., Apanovitch, A. M., & Lockhart, L. K. (1998). Motivated sensitivity to preference-inconsistent information. *Journal of Personality and Social Psychology, 75*, 53–69.

Ecken, P., & Pibernik, R. (2015). Hit or miss: What leads experts to take advice for long-term judgments? *Management Science, 62*, 2002–2021.

Edwards, K., & Smith, E. E. (1996). A disconfirmation bias in the evaluation of arguments. *Journal of Personality and Social Psychology, 71*, 5–24.

Engelmann, J. B., Capra, C. M., Noussair, C., & Berns, G. S. (2009). Expert financial advice neurobiologically "offloads" financial decision-making under risk. *PLoS ONE, 4*, e4957.

Engelmann, J. B., Moore, S., Capra, C. M., & Berns, G. S. (2012). Differential neurobiological effects of expert advice on risky choice in adolescents and adults. *Social Cognitive and Affective Neuroscience, 7*, 557–567.

Feng, B., & MacGeorge, E. L. (2006). Predicting receptiveness to advice: Characteristics of the problem, the advice-giver, and the recipient. *Southern Communication Journal, 71*, 67–85.

Festinger, L. (1957). *A theory of cognitive dissonance*. Stanford University Press.

Gledhill, J. A., Warner, J. P., & King, M. (1997). Psychiatrists and their patients: Views on forms of dress and address. *The British Journal of Psychiatry, 171*, 228–232.

Greenberg, J., Pyszczynski, T., & Solomon, S. (1986). The causes and consequences of the need for self-esteem: A terror management theory. In R. Baumeister (Ed.), *Public self and private self* (pp. 189–212). Springer.

Haidt, J. (2012). *The righteous mind: Why good people are divided by politics and religion*. Pantheon/Random House.

Harvey, N., & Fischer, I. (1997). Taking advice: Accepting help, improving judgment, and sharing responsibility. *Organizational Behavior and Human Decision Processes, 70*(2), 117–133.

Hennessy, N., Harrison, D. A., & Aitkenhead, A. R. (1993). The effect of the anaesthetist's attire on patient attitudes. The influence of dress on patient perception of the anaesthetist's prestige. *Anaesthesia, 48*, 219–222.

Hewitt, J. P. (2009). The social construction of self-esteem. In C. R. Snyder, & S. Lopez (Eds.), *Oxford handbook of positive psychology* (pp. 217–224). Oxford University Press.

Hung, A. A., Clancy, N., Dominitz, J., Talley, E., Berrebi, C., & Suvankulov, F. (2008). *Investor and industry perspectives on investment advisers and broker-dealers*. RAND Institute for Civil Justice Technical Report.

Inderst, R., & Ottaviani, M. (2012). Financial advice. *Journal of Economic Literature, 50*, 494–512.
Johnson, T. R., Budescu, D. V., & Wallsten, T. S. (2001). Averaging probability judgments: Monte Carlo analyses of diagnostic value. *Journal of Behavioral Decision Making, 14*, 123–140.
Kahneman, D. (2003). A perspective on judgment and choice: Mapping bounded rationality. *American Psychologist, 58*, 697–720.
Kahneman, D., & Tversky, A. (1982). The psychology of preferences. *Scientific American, 246*, 160–173. Retrieved from http://www.jstor.org/stable/24966506
Klein, G. A. (1998). *Sources of power. How people make decisions.* MIT Press.
Kruglanski, A. W. (1989). *Lay epistemics and human knowledge: Cognitive and motivational bases.* Springer Science+Business Media.
Kruglanski, A. W. (2012). Lay epistemic theory. In P. A. M. Van Lange, A. W. Kruglanski, & E. T. Higgins (Eds.), *Handbook of theories of social psychology* (Vol. 1) (pp. 460–482). SAGE.
Kruglanski, A. W., Orehek, E., Dechesne, M., & Pierro, A. (2010). Lay epistemic theory: The motivational, cognitive, and social aspects of knowledge formation. *Social and Personality Psychology Compass, 4*, 939–950.
Kruglanski, A. W., Raviv, A., Bar-Tal, D., Raviv, A., Sharvit, K., Ellis, S., Bar, R., Pierro, A., & Mannetti, L. (2005). Says who? Epistemic authority effects in social judgment. In M. P. Zanna (Ed.), *Advances in experimental social psychology* (pp. 345–392). Academic Press.
Kunda, Z. (1987). Motivated inference: Self-serving generation and evaluation of causal theories. *Journal of Personality and Social Psychology, 53*, 636–647.
Kunda, Z. (1990). The case for motivated reasoning. *Psychological Bulletin, 108*, 480–498.
Kunda, Z. (1999). *Social cognition: Making sense of people.* The MIT Press.
Lerner, J. S., Li, Y., Valdesolo, P., & Kassam, K. S. (2015). Emotion and decision making. *Annual Review of Psychology, 66*, 799–823.
Liberman, V., Minson, J. A., Bryan, C. J., & Ross, L. (2011). Naive realism and capturing the "wisdom of dyads". *Journal of Experimental Social Psychology, 48*, 507–512.
Lord, C. S., Ross, L., & Lepper, M. (1979). Biased assimilation and attitude polarization: The effects of prior theories on subsequently considered evidence. *Journal of Personality and Social Psychology, 37*, 2098–2109.
Lundgren, S. R., & Prislin, R. (1998). Motivated cognitive processing and attitude change. *Personality and Social Psychology Bulletin, 24*, 715–726.
Lusardi, A., & Mitchell, O. (2011). Financial literacy around the world: An overview. *Journal of Pension Economics and Finance, 10*, 497–508.
Mercier, H., & Sperber, D. (2011). Why do humans reason? Arguments for an argumentative theory. *Behavioral and Brain Sciences, 34*, 57–111.
Mezulis, A. H., Abramson, L. Y., Hyde, J. S., & Hankin, B. L. (2004). Is there a universal positivity bias in attributions? A meta-analytic review of individual, developmental, and cultural differences in the self-serving attributional bias. *Psychological Bulletin, 130*, 711–747.
Minson, J. A., Liberman, V., & Ross, L. (2011). Two to tango: Effects of collaboration and disagreement on dyadic judgment. *Personality and Social Psychology Bulletin, 37*, 1325–1338.
Mojzisch, A., Kerschreiter, R., Faulmüller, N., Vogelgesang, F., & Schulz-Hardt, S. (2014). The consistency principle in interpersonal communication: Consequences of preference confirmation and disconfirmation in collective decision making. *Journal of Personality and Social Psychology, 106*, 961–977.
Molden, D. C., & Higgins, E. T. (2005). Motivated thinking. In K. Holyoak, & B. Morrison (Eds.), *Handbook of thinking and reasoning* (pp. 295–320). Cambridge University Press.
Nickerson, R. S. (1998). Confirmation bias: A ubiquitous phenomenon in many guises. *Review of General Psychology, 2*, 175–220.
Nolan, J. M., Schultz, P. W., Cialdini, R. B., Goldstein, N. J., & Griskevicius, V. (2008). Normative social influence is underdetected. *Personality and Social Psychology Bulletin, 34*, 913–923.
Odean, T. (1998). Are investors reluctant to realize their losses? *Journal of Finance, 53*, 1775–1798.
Petty, R. E., & Cacioppo, J. T. (1986). *Communication and persuasion: Central and peripheral routes to attitude change.* Springer.
Price, P. C., & Stone, E. R. (2004). Intuitive evaluation of likelihood judgment producers: Evidence for a confidence heuristic. *Journal of Behavioral Decision Making, 17*, 39–57.

Pronin, E. (2007). Perception and misperception of bias in human judgment. *Trends in Cognitive Science, 11*, 37–43.
Pronin, E. (2008). How we see ourselves and how we see others. *Science, 320*, 1177–1180.
Pronin, E., Gilovich, T., & Ross, L. (2004). Objectivity in the eye of the beholder: Divergent perceptions of bias in self versus others. *Psychological Review, 111*, 781–799.
Pronin, E., Lin, D. Y., & Ross, L. (2002). The bias blind spot: Perceptions of bias in self versus others. *Personality and Social Psychology Bulletin, 28*, 369–381.
Pyszczynski, T., & Greenberg, J. (1987). Toward an integration of cognitive and motivational perspectives on social inference: A biased hypothesis-testing model. In L. Berkowitz (Ed.), *Advances in experimental social psychology* (Vol. 20) (pp. 297–340). Academic Press.
Raviv, A., Bar-Tal, D., Raviv, A., & Abin, R. (1993). Measuring epistemic authority: Studies of politicians and professors. *European Journal of Personality, 7*, 119–138.
Ross, L., & Ward, A. (1996). Naive realism in everyday life: Implications for social conflict and misunderstanding. In T. Brown, E. S. Reed, & E. Turiel (Eds.), *Values and knowledge* (pp. 103–135). Erlbaum.
Saffrey, C., Summerville, A., & Roese, N. J. (2008). Praise for regret: People value regret above other negative emotions. *Motivation and Emotion, 32*, 46–54.
Schiffman, L. G., Kanuk, L. L., Ramesh Kumar, S., & Wisenblit, J. (2010). *Consumer behavior* (10th ed.). Prentice Hall.
Schultz, P. W., Nolan, J. M., Cialdini, R. B., Goldstein, N. J., & Griskevicius, V. (2007). The constructive, destructive, and reconstructive power of social norms. *Psychological Science, 18*, 429–434.
Schultze, T., Rakotoarisoa, A., & Schulz-Hardt, S. (2015). Effects of distance between initial estimates and advice on advice Utilization. *Judgment and Decision Making, 10*, 144–171.
Scopelliti, I., Morewedge, C. K., McCormick, E., Min, H. L., Lebrecht, S., & Kassam, K. S. (2015). Bias blind spot: Structure, measurement, and consequences. *Management Science, 61*, 2468–2486.
Shefrin, H., & Statman, M. (1985). The disposition to sell winners too early and ride losers too long: Theory and evidence. *The Journal of Finance, 40*, 777–790.
Sniezek, J. A., & Van Swol, L. M. (2001). Trust, confidence, and expertise in a judge–advisor system. *Organizational Behavior and Human Decision Processes, 84*, 288–307.
Soll, J. B. (1999). Intuitive theories of information: Beliefs about the value of redundancy. *Cognitive Psychology, 38*, 317–346.
Törngren, G., & Montgomery, H. (2004). Worse than chance? Performance and confidence among professionals and laypeople in the stock market. *Journal of Behavioral Finance, 5*, 148–153.
van Rooij, M., Lusardi, A., & Alessie, R. (2011). Financial literacy and stock market participation. *Journal of Financial Economics, 101*, 449–472.
Van Swol, L. M., & Sniezek, J. A. (2005). Factors affecting the acceptance of expert advice. *British Journal of Social Psychology, 44*, 443–461.
Yaniv, I. (2004a). Receiving other people's advice: Influence and benefit. *Organizational Behavior and Human Decision Processes, 93*, 1–13.
Yaniv, I. (2004b). The benefit of additional opinions. *Current Directions in Psychological Science, 13*, 75–78.
Yaniv, I., Choshen-Hillel, S., & Milyavsky, M. (2009). Spurious consensus and opinion revision: Why might people be more confident in their less accurate judgments? *Journal of Experimental Psychology: Learning, Memory, and Cognition, 35*, 558–563.
Yaniv, I., & Kleinberger, E. (2000). Advice taking in decision making: Egocentric discounting and reputation formation. *Organizational Behavior and Human Decision Processes, 83*, 260–281.
Yaniv, I., & Milyavsky, M. (2007). Using advice from multiple sources to revise and improve judgment. *Organizational Behavior and Human Decision Processes, 103*, 104–120.
Zaleskiewicz, T. (2011). Financial forecasts during the crisis. Were experts more accurate than laypeople? *Journal of Economic Psychology, 32*, 384–390.
Zaleskiewicz, T., & Gasiorowska, A. (2018). Tell me what I wanted to hear: Confirmation effect in lay evaluations of expert authority. *Applied Psychology: An International Review, 67*, 686–722.
Zaleskiewicz, T., & Gasiorowska, A. (2020). Evaluating experts serves psychological needs: Self-esteem, bias blind spot, and processing fluency explain confirmation effect in assessing financial advisors' authority. *Journal of Experimental Psychology: Applied, 27*, 27–45.

Zaleskiewicz, T., Gasiorowska, A., Stasiuk, K., Maksymiuk, R., & Bar-Tal, Y. (2016). Lay evaluation of financial experts: The action advice effect and confirmation bias. *Frontiers in Psychology, 7,* 1476.

Zaleskiewicz, T., & Traczyk, J. (2020). Emotions and financial decision making. In T. Zaleskiewicz, & J. Traczyk (Eds.), *Psychological perspectives on financial decision making* (pp. 109–136). Springer.

Zeelenberg, M. (2018). Anticipated regret: A prospective emotion about the future past. In G. Oettingen, A. T. Sevincer, & P. M. Gollwitzer (Eds.), *The psychology of thinking about the future* (pp. 276–295). The Guilford Press.

PART VI

BEHAVIOURAL APPROACHES TO HEALTH ECONOMICS

14. Bounded rationality, imperfect and costly information and sub-optimal outcomes in the sports and health and fitness industries

Hannah Rachel Josepha Altman and Morris Altman

INTRODUCTION

A key insight of behavioural economics, as articulated, by Herbert Simon, is that humans make decisions in a world of incomplete or imperfect and costly information with limited information processing capabilities. For Simon, any modelling of decision-making must take this reality of human decision-making into consideration. Moreover, Simon points out the importance of different institutional environments (which includes power relationships across individuals), which contextualises the decision-making process and choices made by individuals. More realistic simplifying assumptions are required to build more robust models of decision-making which, in turn, facilitates the construction of more robust econometric models (Simon 1959, 1986, 1987; see also Altman 2006).

This chapter builds upon this insight of Simon to critically examine behavioural economics alternatives to conventional neoclassical economics methodological approaches to decision-making, with specific application to and implications for the health and fitness and sports industries and their clients. These interrelated industries are of increasing importance economically, and they hold considerable importance to the health and wellbeing of the population at large. Having an analytical frame that serves to better understand this industry, especially the decisions made within it (on both the demand and supply side) can, therefore, have important welfare implications.

The specific methodological focus of this chapter is on two fundamental streams in behavioural economics. One relates to the bounded rationality approach, pioneered by Simon, which speaks to the brain as a scarce resource (computational and information acquisition capabilities) and the decision-making environment and the other relates to the heuristics and biases approach which focuses on humans being hardwired towards making systemic errors in decision-making. The latter approach was pioneered by Kahneman and Tversky (Kahneman and Tversky 1979, 2000; Kahneman 2003, 2011). Its assumptions stem from the belief that human decision-makers are characterised by innate biases, which are often a by-product of using heuristics or decision-making shortcuts and relying on 'emotions' to drive decision-making. Both approaches suggest that one should not expect humans to make optimal decisions from either a private (the decision-maker) or social perspective. But both approaches suggest different policies to correct for sub-optimal decisions. The bounded rationality approach suggests policy which is more oriented towards improving the individual's decision-making capabilities and decision-making environment, whereas the heuristics and biases approach is more vested in nudging the individual, at different levels (soft versus hard), to behave in a manner consistent with expert advice on what optimal behaviour should be. However, there is some important overlap between the two approaches. But both of these methodological perspectives on decision-making differ substantively from the conventional economics perspective on decision-making which strongly infers that decisions should be optimal at least from the individual's perspective, if not from the group or team perspective as well.

We exemplify the behavioural economics methodological approaches to decision-making and policy using the example of the health and fitness industry, choices made that affect the level of obesity and the extent to which obesity can be eliminated, and athletes and trainers' and coaches' choices with regards to realising targeted levels of performance. Our narrative on the health and fitness industry directly feeds into our narrative about obesity and sports performance. We argue that it is important to go beyond a discourse on price and income (an important component of the conventional economics narrative) and also go beyond a focus on systemic cognitive-based errors in decision-making, which is very much the purview of the heuristics and biases approach to behavioural economics. It is critically important to take into consideration individuals' decision-making capabilities, which are very often socially affected if not determined, and the decision-making environment which has critical social and institutional determinants. Here, choices are not simply a function of relative price and real income, but also of non-economic determinants, which incorporate social and institutional variables, and even cognitive biases of decision-makers. This broader, more realistic, modelling methodology, makes for a more robust understanding of how decision-making takes place in the health and fitness and sports industries. This more holistic behavioural economics methodological perspective is rooted in the bounded rationality narrative.

We argue that significant problems related to health and wellbeing and which also relate to sub-optimal decisions and performance in the health and fitness and sports industries are most closely related to asymmetric and costly information as well as to institutional failures that make it difficult for optimal choices to be made (Altman and Altman 2022a, 2022b). We further argue that many of the problems in these sectors can be explained whilst retaining the assumption of rational or smart decision-makers, which is not the same as neoclassical rationality (Altman 2017; March 1978). One does not have to revert to the assumption of systemically biased behaviour by decision-makers to explain sub-optimal outcomes once one takes into consideration individuals' decision-making capabilities and their decision-making environment.

SOME BASIC METHODOLOGICAL UNDERPINNINGS OF BEHAVIOURAL ECONOMICS

For the purposes of this chapter, what is of fundamental importance is the emphasis by Simon on the importance of the realism of one's modelling assumptions. This is not an argument for the absolute realism of these assumptions, but rather for the realism of the simplifying assumptions. For example, related to this chapter, one should not assume perfect information, a correct understanding of what's best practice for coaching and player selection, the ability to know, automatically, if coaches and trainers are adequately or properly qualified, how best to lose weight, and the optimal (or close to optimal) environment to make optimal decisions in the health and fitness and sports industries.

This contrasts with the focus of much of contemporary economics on the importance of a model's predictive capabilities, irrespective of the realism of its assumptions. And this follows from Friedman's (1953) classic paper on the methodology of economics. But unrealistic assumptions can generate a poor causal analysis even if one's analytical prediction is strong

(Altman 1999). One might simply have a spurious correlation or prediction. Robust causal analysis, which also yields strong analytical predictions, also allows us to better understand which independent variables truly affect the dependent variable, such as the choice of trainers or coaches, how or even if one tries to lose weight, and how one goes about training and selecting one's athletes, for example. Related to this, focusing on prediction, with little or no attention to the realism of one's simplifying assumptions risks fundamental omitted variable problems wherein one inadvertently omits true causal variables because your model already does a good-enough job predicting or because your current independent variables best fit with one's prior theory or model of the determinants of, say, the choice of trainers, how best to lose weight or the causes of obesity.

The approach that we take in this chapter is to pay heed to the realism of one's behavioural assumptions as being core to a behavioural approach to key questions in health, fitness and sports. However, it should be noted, that there are economists who identify behavioural economics with adding non-economic variables into one's modelling narrative irrespective of whether or not these variables are realistic. They can be added simply to improve the predictive capacity of one's model or to provide an alternative behavioural analysis to a particular question (Berg and Gigerenzer 2010). What's critical to our approach and underlined by Simon is building models with an eye to improved causal and predictive analysis. The inclusion of psychological variables, in and of itself, does not make for a robust economic analysis. Our focus also goes beyond introducing psychological variables. Of critical importance are any pertinent non-economic variables, inclusive of institutional variables that make for a more robust model and analytical narrative.

Another important point of methodological focus in this chapter, because it has implications for policy, is one's prior assumptions about the rationality of decision-makers: whether decision-makers are in some broad sense smart or prone to systemic biases in their preferences and choices. The bounded rationality approach pioneered by Simon focuses on the decision-making capabilities of individuals and their decision-making environment. Decision-making capabilities relate to individuals' ability to rapidly process all information pertinent to making particular choices, quickly acquire all such pertinent information and be able to accurately predict the consequences of making such choices in the near and more distant future. The decision-making environment relates to external factors that either promote or impede optimal decisions. For Simon, optimal decision-making capabilities and environment should not be assumed a priori. For this reason, Simon rejects neoclassical rationality which tends to presume optimality of the decision-making capabilities and environment. Rather, Simon assumes that individuals make decisions in an imperfect world (which can be improved) – decisions are boundedly rational – and that individuals do the best that they can. They satisfice, as opposed to optimising, as they do and should in the conventional economics understanding of rationality. Policy embedded in the bounded rationality approach would be focused on improving individuals' ability to make better decisions.

The heuristics and biases approach pioneered by Kahneman and Tversky, also rejects the conventional assumption of rational decision-makers, that is that the typical individual behaves in accordance with conventional economics norms of rationality. However, this approach to behavioural economics assumes that individuals should be able to behave in accordance with the conventional norms of rationality. Individuals deviate from these norms because of ingrained systemic cognitive biases, to a certain extent because they adopt heuristics (decision-making shortcuts) to arrive at their decisions. This has given rise to the nudging approach to policy, pioneered by Thaler and Sunstein (2008), wherein experts or choice architects nudge individuals to make decisions that they deem to be in the individuals' best interest (optimal, or welfare maximising). Systemic biases dominate learnt decision-making capabilities and alterable decision-making environments as the key determinants of sub-optimal decisions. We argue that the boundedly rational approach is better grounded in reality, which is not to say individual biases can't negatively affect the choices made by individuals – overconfidence, confirmation and status quo biases, for example. But a larger question is whether these so-called cognitive biases can be affected by individuals' decision-making environment and even if one assumes biased behaviour it is actually sub-optimal capabilities and sub-optimal decision-making environments that yield errors in decision-making.

OBESITY AND BEING OVERWEIGHT: SOME FACTS[1]

Being overweight and especially being obese have been of increasing concern to many economists and policy leaders. To address these concerns from the perspective of behavioural economics it is important to first define what is the common understanding of these two concepts and how important being overweight and obese is from a health perspective.

Obesity is a medical condition where an individual has an extremely unhealthy amount of body fat for her or his height. This is usually determined by a person's body mass index or BMI. The BMI is calculated as BMI = kg/h^2 or, a person's weight in kilograms divided by the person's height squared (h^2). A BMI over 25 is defined as overweight, while a BMI over 30 is obese. A 50-year old male who is six feet tall or 182 centimetres and 100 kilograms or 220 pounds is just crossing the benchmark dividing the medically overweight from the medically obese. But it is important to recognise that these common BMI cut-offs may and should vary slightly for different racial/ethnic groups (Weir and Jan 2021). This being said, it is clear from the evidence that on average obesity reduces life expectancy by from one to two years for the American and European populations (University of Oxford 2009; Vidra, Trias-Llimós and Janssen 2009).

Whilst life expectancy is being reduced because of obesity and a larger percentage of the world's population is becoming obese, it is important to note that life expectancy at birth has increased quite dramatically throughout the world, even in those countries, such as the United States, where obesity rates have increased most dramatically. From 1975, life expectancy has increased by about ten years amongst the wealthier economies; in the United States by eight years. But in South Korea life expectancy has increased by 17 years, in China by 12 and in India by over 18 years. Therefore, obesity results in an obese individual's life expectancy increasing not as much as it would have increased if that individual was not obese. So, in the United States, the life expectancy of an obese person would have increased not by eight years, but by six to seven years and in China the increase would not be 12 years, rather it would be between ten and 11 years. This point becomes important when we ask the question of why might rational or smart individuals choose to overeat in a world where net life expectancy has been increasing. We address this choice question in the following. Smart people might be aware (without any detailed analysis) that people are living much longer, even if they are seriously overweight. This awareness and perception can effect their eating decisions.

However, it is clear that obesity is a problem. It accounts for around 15 per cent of deaths amongst wealthier countries, but much less amongst poorer countries and the more rapidly developing countries. In China and India, this percentage is around 7 per cent and rising.

The United States stands out as a wealthy country where obesity-related death rates are increasing, which is not the case in most wealthy countries. So, it is important to note that deaths attributable to obesity have fallen amongst the relatively wealthy countries in the world, with the exception of the United States.

Another bit of information that is pertinent to our theoretical discussion is that obesity rates are highly correlated to calorie consumption. This is, in turn, related to per capita GDP. Related to this, there is a positive relationship between food expenditure and per capita GDP and between calorie consumption and obesity rates. This type of relationship also holds true for overweight rates. Overall, this relationship between calorie consumption and obesity and overweight rates is most pronounced in the United States. These relationships are all averages. And there are very large variations in overweight rates, for example, for every given level of calorie intake. Therefore, consuming a large number of calories or more calories does not necessarily mean that one becomes overweight or obese. Other factors, not simply the consumption of more calories, are required to explain the growth and variation in overweight and obesity rates. Of course, consuming more calories can be more than neutralised by sufficient physical activity. An important question to be addressed is why more calorie consumption is not countered by more physical activity if individuals do *not* want to be overweight or obese (Altman and Altman 2022a).

Price Theory and Obesity

Price theory is the main tool that conventional economics employs to explain weight gain or losses and levels and to inform policy that encourages weight loss if being overweight or obese was deemed to be of social concern. Relative prices and real income and changes therein are what should determine choice behaviour with regard to the determinants of weight gain or loss (Grossman and Mocan 2011; Philipson and Posner 1999). If the price of foods which contribute most to weight gain per calorie consumed falls, then it is argued that this would be a key contributor to weight gain through the substitution effect – individuals tend to substitute into relatively less expensive foodstuffs. This further assumes that the income effect reinforces the substitution effect – that the more income one has the more 'unhealthy' foodstuffs one purchases. Also presumed is that even holding relative prices constant, increasing real income, will typically increase one's consumption of 'unhealthy' foodstuffs. This approach assumes that the preferences of consumers do not change over time and that one individual's preference does not influence the preferences of other individuals. Preference formation is assumed not to be interdependent. Therefore, even if preferences don't shift in favour of 'unhealthy' foods, one can explain a larger percentage of the population becoming overweight through relative changes in prices and increasing real income, especially if there is a prior preference for relatively 'unhealthy' foods. Moreover, an additional contributing variable to increasing obesity rates would be increasing the price of physical activity, where the price would include the price of time required to engage in sufficient physical activity to prevent individuals from being overweight or obese. Another, critical assumption in the conventional economics approach is that consumers have available to them all the relevant information to make an optimal decision and that they understand this information. And it assumed that the information available is truthful and accurate. It is also assumed that consumers can realise their true preferences and that their revealed preferences (what they purchase and the activities that they do or do not engage in) reflect their true preferences.

But this need not be the case. Consumers need not have the capabilities to realise their true preferences in terms of what they consume and the extent to which they engage in adequate and appropriate physical activity. For example, this would be the case if individuals do not have accurate information on healthy foods, food preparation or weight-reducing physical activity. Individuals might not have access to healthy foods or to safe facilities or safe outdoor locations to engage in physical activities, and individuals might not have the time or the income that allows for the realisation of preferences that would favour not being overweight or obese. Therefore, price theory, not adjusted for non-economic considerations and *differences* in income and time constraints, is incomplete with respect to its ability to explain the rise and persistence of being overweight or obese. It is quite possible for individuals to be maximising their utility or satisficing (either way doing the best they can, given the resources in hand), without these individuals realising their true preferences. So, for example, improving the information set available to individuals will facilitate individuals' satisficing 'equilibrium' being closer to their preferred preference, which could be being at a lower weight.

BEHAVIOURAL ECONOMICS AND OBESITY[2]

There are different behavioural economics perspectives on the causes of changes in the extent of obesity and more generally the extent of overweight. One approach which is more consistent with the heuristics and biases and nudging narrative maintains that individuals make decisions that are systemically biased against what experts (referred to as choice architects in the nudging literature) would regard as utility- or welfare-maximising choices. Individuals would make decisions that generate overweight or obesity. Individuals, in this scenario, have a preference for unhealthy foods. Realising this preference is utility maximising, given income and prices. Individuals, therefore, must be nudged towards behaviour that the experts deem to be in the best interest of these individuals. Public policy is related to changing individuals' tastes and preferences for unhealthy foods and/or constraining what individuals can consume (which is referred to as hard nudging). The nudging policy basket could also include changing relative prices and making unhealthy foods relatively more expensive (increasing the price of sugary drinks and processed foods) (see, for example, Tomer 2001, 2011, 2013). More often than not the income distribution effects of such policy are not taken into consideration. Lower income cohorts can be squeezed out of some markets (obviating their preferences), whilst the higher-income cohort's behaviour might be little affected.

Fundamentally important to this approach is the assumption that individuals are fairly easily manipulated by the unhealthy food industry (comprised of large and powerful profit-maximising corporations) towards the consumption of relatively unhealthy foods that are highly profitable to produce. In addition, individuals are prone to adapt their behaviour to their group and community which might have a preference for unhealthy foods (such as fast foods). Your sports team goes for a Big Mac. You tag along to be part of your group. You're contributing towards building a team spirit. In the process, more unhealthy food is being consumed. An underlying assumption is also that individuals have a 'natural' preference for unhealthy foods – for many these are sweet and tasty. So, even if individuals know that certain foods are unhealthy, they can't resist the temptation to consume more unhealthy foods. This reinforces any impact that taste manipulation might have on consumption patterns. This sub-optimal consumption behaviour is reinforced by the *assumed* relative fall in the price of unhealthy foods. This assumption is not correct. Rather, what we've seen is a trend decrease in the relative price of food and beverages. Reference is also made to food-related education. In other words, consumption patterns can be changed with improved education. Also, information on food content might be false or misleading, generating a greater consumption of unhealthy foods than might otherwise occur. These variables, combined (which include a set of behavioural variables), yield an increase in overweight and obesity rates. Relatively little attention is directed to the role that physical activity can play in controlling or reducing overweight and obesity rates.

An alternative behaviour approach to overweight and obesity stems from what we refer to as the bounded rationality approach. This complements important aspects of price theory. In other words, prices and income matter to behaviour but so do non-economic variables. In this approach, one recognises that increasing overweight and obesity rates have been consistent with increasing real income some of which is a product of the relative fall in the price of foodstuffs. This approach also recognises that increasing income is not always and everywhere consistent and correlated with increasing overweight and obesity rates. Finally, this approach recognises that overweight and obesity rates tend to increase amongst the wealthier segments of society as their income grows and then these rates typically decrease as individuals appear to adjust to their higher levels of income. Then this pattern tends to be repeated amongst the relatively lower income cohorts. However, there also tends to be a trend increase, *on average*, in overweight and obesity rates as real per capita income increases over time across countries and income cohorts. Amongst the important outliers to this trend, with persistent and significant increases in overweight and obesity rates, is the United States (Altman and Altman 2022a). We argue that one important non-economic variable that helps explain both high and low overweight and obesity rate outliers, a variable most pertinent to this chapter, is the level of extent of physical activity, a subset of which is engagement in sports activities at different levels.

One important point of differentiation between this bounded rationality approach and the heuristics and biases approach (upon which the nudging approach is constructed), is in the bounded rationality approach the prior initial assumption is that decision-makers deciding on their calorie consumption and physical activity are rational, more specifically, smart decision-makers. Being overweight or obese should not, in the first instance, be attributable to systemic errors in decision-making. If decision-makers are smart then the reason for being or becoming overweight or obese should be located in the socio-institutional constraints over which they have limited control. This bounded rationality approach yields a different set of policy recommendations than the heuristics and biases approach, although there is some overlap between the two.

Critical to the bounded rationality approach is that one recognises that smart people can make decisions that are error-prone given imperfect and costly information. Based on this type of information environment, if misleading or conflicting information is available to decision-makers, individuals will make food and physical activity choices that they would not otherwise make in a more perfect information environment. And these error-prone choices contribute towards increasing overweight and obesity rates.

Related to this, individuals might adopt 'bad' heuristics (decision-making shortcuts) in this sub-optimal decision-making environment. Individuals might make food choices based on what certain thought leaders profess, even if these leaders are incorrect from a scientific point of view. Here one has a form of herding-based decision-making, where what one decides is based on what one *believes* to be true given that other people appear to believe this information to be credible, and so on (Baddeley 2018). Keynes (1936) identified this type of behaviour, based on ideas, as opposed to objective facts, to have been a critical determinant of financial booms and busts. These types of error-prone decisions would still be rational in this sub-optimal decision-making environment. Policies emanating from this understanding of particular causes of errors in decision-making would suggest improving the information environment, which could involve regulating the quality of information and making the information available to decision-making more understandable (points made by Akerlof and Shiller, 2015).

One variable that contributes to lowering obesity is accurate and easily understood food and beverage product labels that include information on calories. For example, Zagorsky and Smith (2017a; see also, McCarthy 2004) find that checking nutrition food and beverage labels frequently tends to reduce fast-food consumption. But this requires easily located, easy-to-read, easy-to-understand and accurate labels and literacy amongst consumers. Moreover, more specifically, better information yields food consumption that is less calorically intensive. One should note that there is no evidence that eating fast foods per se is the leading cause of increasing overweight and obesity rates, exemplified in the United States, which remains well above the average of relatively wealthy economies. Consuming too many calories in fast-food outlets and or in fancy and expensive restaurants contribute to gaining weight. Indeed, consuming too many healthy foods, if one can afford these, can also contribute towards weight gain. In this sense, being food-healthy does not solve the overweight-obesity problem. And information that suggests that eating healthy food is the solution can result in the unintended consequence of weight gain.

In this bounded rationality methodological approach, where policy is oriented towards improving the information environment, individuals retain the freedom of choice in decision-making, but this free choice would be expected to yield outcomes consistent with lower overweight and obesity rates. Improved information would shift individuals' present or revealed preferences (or choices) which would better reflect their true preferences (being healthier in terms of weight), without the necessity of nudging individuals towards the preferences of choice architects.

Another institutional variable important to determining what foodstuffs individuals choose to purchase is a person's location and access to low-cost transportation. Amongst lower income cohorts there is very limited access to healthy foods, or such foodstuffs are highly expensive in their neighbourhoods (denoted as food deserts). In this case, even if individuals preferred healthy foods, and information issues are not a problem, such foods are not readily available. Therefore, these individuals can't realise their true preferences for consuming healthier foods. One reason for rising obesity amongst the lower income cohorts is related to the constraints they face in terms of healthy food availability and price (being priced out of the market). These represent clear institutional constraints on healthy eating. In addition to this, the poor tend to be cash poor and will purchase high-energy unhealthy food when cash is available. This can contribute to obesity but is sensible or rational for individuals who are poor, residing in food deserts, and facing high prices for healthy foods. In this case, what is required are changes in the incentive environment to attract food stores that supply healthier foods at lower price points into low-income cohort areas.

More to the point of this chapter, critical to reducing overweight and obesity rates is the extent of physical activity given the extent of an individual's calorie consumption. This is consistent with the fact that there is very large variability in overweight and obesity rates for given levels of calorie consumption as real per capita income increases. Sufficient and appropriate physical activity should burn off sufficient calories to neutralise the impact of calorie intake on weight and even reverse the process of being overweight. Sufficient and appropriate physical activity can flip an individual from being overweight into being in the relatively healthy range of weight measured by BMI, for example. Appropriate refers to the fact that not all physical activity has the same effect on a person's health and weight. And, some forms of physical activity can be dangerous for one's wellbeing.

There is considerable evidence to support the argument that physical activity can play an important role in weight control and loss. For adolescents, across income cohorts, overweight and obesity rates would fall by 11 and 26 per cent respectively if they played on at least two sports teams per year. Obesity rates would drop by over 20 per cent if adolescents walked or biked to school four to five times per week (Drake, Beach and Longacre 2012). But this requires sports facilities in school and outside of school, qualified instructors and safe spaces to walk, jog or run (Levine 2011; Noonan 2018; O'Mara 2019). It might also require the ability to purchase sports equipment, or this must be supplied by schools or local authorities. In some cases, for walking or jogging, no expensive equipment is required. For wealthier individuals with time-intensive jobs, being time-poor is a constraint on engaging in adequate and sufficient physical activities. Another study (Levine 2011), based on American data, found that sedentary individuals move two hours less per day than more active individuals (broadly defined), therefore expending less energy and burning fewer calories. According to this study, more than 50 per cent of the variance in obesity rates across counties (in the USA) is accounted for by the variance in the extent to which individuals are relatively sedentary. This point relates to the more specific evidence on the relationship between particular physical activities and overweight and obesity rates.

Overall, there are environmental constraints on individuals' ability to engage in physical activity to burn off the necessary calories to either lose weight or prevent weight gain. One does not need to refer to irrationality or systemic biases of decision-makers to explain overweight and obesity rates. Environmental factors play an important role in determining overweight and obesity rates. And, from an individual's perspective, they help explain the extent to which a particular individual is at a healthy weight or not. What we've discussed here supplements objective constraints related to imperfect and costly information.

However, these types of environmental constraints are not usually faced by individuals in higher income cohorts and are often not faced by individuals above the lower income cohorts. These individuals have the opportunity to take out a gym membership and seek the advice of health and fitness professionals, which include exercise scientists, trainers and dieticians. But this typically comes at an income and time cost. This raises the question of whether these higher-income individuals choose not to be more physically active even when the opportunities to do so are more readily available.

However, the evidence suggests that there was a growing demand for gym memberships in the United States from 2010 to 2019, for example, at a time when obesity rates were increasing in the United States (Altman and Altman 2021a). From 2010 to 2016 the American obesity rate increased by about 6 per cent and gym activity increased by over 20 per cent. By 2019, 25 per cent of Americans were gym members. Over 40 per cent of these members earned over $100,000 USD per year. These individuals were also the most active gym members. These estimates suggest that individuals who could afford to were attempting to engage in physical activity (through gym memberships) that could at least partially counteract weight gain. The important point here is that individuals are making an effort to become healthier but, these efforts, in the aggregate, do not appear to have borne fruit.

This evidence insinuates that individuals have increasingly made efforts to become physically active, which could be attributed to the significant rise in the overweight and obesity rates in a large number of countries, especially in the United States. Being more physically active would be a rational response of individuals to the unwanted prospect of becoming obese or overweight. But the obesity and overweight rates keep rising, or at least not diminishing, especially in the United States. It is important to recognise that with some exceptions overweight and obesity rise and then adjust to relatively lower levels as per capita income increases. But even these rates, some would argue, are problematic and should be lowered if possible, as this lowering would have positive health consequences (Templin et al. 2019). It is apparent from the evidence that individuals adjust their behaviour to their higher income circumstances. This takes time. This adjustment is what one would expect from rational individuals if they have the capacity and capability to engage in this adjustment process.

In the United States, however, there is no trend of decline in obesity. This can, in part, be related to the lack of quality assurance in the health and fitness industry. Given imperfect and costly information, the lack of quality assurance can mean that attempts at becoming more physically fit, inclusive of weight loss, will not generate the expected results. Individuals end up choosing fitness facilities and health and fitness professionals that they believe will help them lose weight based on credentials and other signals that can be false or misleading given the lack of appropriate quality assurance. With sub-optimal health and fitness industry professional support, one ends up with sub-optimal outcomes for clients (H. Altman 2020). Moreover, *accurate knowledge* as to how sports and physical activity in general can contribute to weight loss may not be available. This relates to the health and fitness advice industry. In this environment, anticipated weight loss will not be achieved by rational or smart decision-makers even if they have the means to do so because of the sub-optimal decision-making environment.

The bounded rationality approach suggests that it is important to recognise the importance of institutional failures that preclude optimal weight loss from being achieved, given the preferences of individuals seeking to lose weight. Biased decision-making need not be the dominant cause of overweight and obesity rates not declining or not declining by as much as they can, given the preferences of individuals and the resources available to them, such as membership in gyms and access to health and fitness professionals.

This is not to say that psychological and other non-economic variables are not important and should not be considered: variables such as self-control and commitment, peer pressure and, relatedly, identity. But from the bounded rationality methodological perspective, the decision-making environment must be considered even prior to other considerations. Ceteris paribus, repairing the decision-making environment to optimise physical activity would represent an important step forward in facilitating reducing overweight and obesity rates. Without an appropriate decision-making environment, individuals simply can't realise their true preferences to lose weight, even given relative prices and their real income or purchasing power. And, the latter two variables, important to the conventional economic narrative, can further explain overweight and obesity rates given psychological variables.

Aspects of this argument are illustrated in Figure 14.1. The Body Mass Index (BMI) is measured along the horizontal axis. Calorie consumption is measured along the vertical axis where we use the origin to proxy maximum calorie intake. Increasing calorie intake

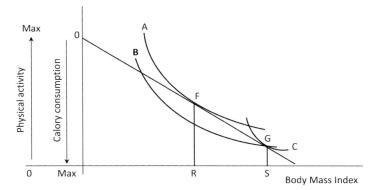

Figure 14.1   Determinants of overweight and obesity rates

translates into a higher BMI. The sub-optimal equilibrium is given by indifference curve B and C at point G, with a high BMI of S, which we assume represents an obese person. The individual is maximising her utility at point G given her environmental constraints. But this is an *unstable* equilibrium that the individual is stuck at (in conventional economic terms the indifference curve is not tangent to the price line). But this constrained equilibrium is a form of satisficing – the individual is doing the best that she can, given the constraints that she faces. This satisficing equilibrium is given by indifference curve C. This individual would prefer to be at point F at a BMI of R with indifference curve A. A yields a higher level of utility than B. Change the decision-making environment, and the BMI would be lower, which is what our rational individual would prefer under a different set of decision-making circumstances. With regards to physical activity, this is measured along the vertical axis where the origin designates 0 physical activity. The more physical activity, the lower the BMI. We have a sub-optimal equilibrium at G, yielding obesity at point S. The individual prefers point R given by indifferent curve A. But the individual is locked out of this preferred equilibrium because of a lack of the facilities and capabilities to engage in sufficient physical activity.

SUB-OPTIMAL CHOICES IN THE HEALTH AND FITNESS INDUSTRY

The preceding discussion highlights the importance of the health and fitness industry to weight loss. But it is also important to improvements to health as well as to improvements to individuals' sports performance at any level. If this industry is sub-optimal, as is suggested here, then this specific sub-optimality can help contribute to explaining sub-optimal behaviours or choices in health and fitness and sports outcomes, and in variations of outcomes across jurisdictions and even individuals. This approach to understanding sub-optimal or poor outcomes is rooted in the bounded rationality methodological narrative in behavioural economics. An alternative explanation for sub-optimal outcomes is that individuals engage in systemic errors in decision-making, largely based on inherent biases, which are more aligned with the heuristics and biases methodological narrative. But the bounded rationality methodological approach presented in this chapter first addresses the question of the decision-making environment since with serious shortfalls in this environment rational decision-makers will make error-prone decisions with regard to the selection of health and fitness professionals and training protocols.

This section also pays attention to the fast and frugal heuristics approach to decision-making, pioneered by Gigerenzer (2007; see also Todd and Gigerenzer 2003) which, he argues is closely aligned with the bounded rationality approach to decision-making. In this case, heuristics (decision-making shortcuts) tend to generate superior outcomes as opposed to errors in decision-making (the argument put forth in the heuristics and biases methodological narrative) given that individuals make choices given their decision-making capabilities and their decision-making environment. Indeed, from the perspective of the fast and frugal methodological approach, using heuristics is the optimal approach to decision-making and neo-classical behavioural norms should not be the benchmark for optimal choice behaviour. Heuristics are an evolutionary by-product of the reality of real-world human decision-making capabilities and the decision-making environment. Therefore, individuals will invariably use heuristics to decide on which gyms to go to, which trainer or exercise scientist service to engage and which health and fitness literature to trust. We argue, however, that there are good and bad heuristics and the latter can be a product of rational choices given imperfect, asymmetric and costly information (see also Kahneman 2011). And these bad heuristics can generate sub-optimal outcomes with regard to health and also sports performance as they are affected by and mediated through the health and fitness industry, for example.

The health and fitness industry is one of the fastest growing amongst the relatively economically advanced countries in the world. This can be taken to represent a revealed preference on the part of consumers, given their income or purchasing power, for services that help them achieve improvements to their health. It can also present a preference to look 'beautiful' or 'sexy' through engaging in physical activity mediated through health and fitness professionals. A side effect of more and higher quality physical activity should be better health outcomes. In sports, amongst athletes, health and fitness professionals should contribute to improved performance outcomes. But, as we've seen earlier, this rapid growth in the demand for health and fitness industry services does not appear to have the expected positive effect on health and wellbeing, exemplified by its lack of impact on overweight and obesity rates. The counterfactual here would be that given the increase in these services one would have expected better outcomes than actually transpired. It should also be the case for individuals who have access to free outdoor facilities where they can engage in physical activities by applying the knowledge from health and fitness professionals.

Conventional economics would assume that there is no reason for the services of the health and fitness sector to be sub-optimal or for decision-makers or prospective clients to choose health and fitness facilities and professionals who will generate sub-optimal outcomes. It is assumed that these prospective clients would be purchasing services with full information and a full understanding of this information. Hence, one would assume that the revealed preferences of consumers should be consistent with their true preferences – what they really want with regard to the type and quality of services provided. Consumers get what they truly want according to this worldview.

However, behavioural economics recognises that information is far from perfect and quality information is difficult to identify and obtain. Moreover, individuals often do not have the capability to understand or interpret the information at hand. The health and fitness industry is situated in this real world of imperfect, asymmetric and costly information. The implications of this type of decision-making environment are discussed and modelled from different methodological perspectives by Stigler (1961; see also Spence 1973, 2002, who pioneered signalling theory) and then by Akerlof (1970). In his market of lemons narrative, he modelled the implications for decision-making based on false and misleading signals, which are hard or costly to detect (see also Akerlof and Shiller 2015). Gigerenzer (2007) pioneered the evolutionary development of optimal heuristics in a world of bounded rationality as opposed to heuristics as a decision-making error-generating machine, as it is in conventional economics and in the heuristics and biases approach to behavioural economics. Of particular interest to us is that Akerlof's modelling narrative explores how, in a world of costly and asymmetric information, one can end up with sub-optimal outcomes (such as in the used car market) without credible government or industry self-regulation.

The reality of the health and fitness industry is that it has been characterised by unacceptable levels of injury to clients and, on average, sub-optimal outcomes for clients (H. Altman 2020; Bowen 2018; Caldwell 2017; Cleaver 2016; Clent 2019; Marshall and Guskiewicz 2003; Shephard 2003). This is exemplified by our discussion of the challenge of high overweight and obesity rates internationally, which this sector does not appear to have successfully addressed given the client uptake of the services provided by this sector. Moreover, evidence suggests that there is a problem of underqualified health and fitness professionals being employed in this sector and their ability to successfully market their service to prospective clients. And, these prospective clients appear to believe that these professionals are duly qualified. Hence any failure to achieve goals, such as weight loss or improved sports performance, could be attributable to the client's choices as opposed to the vendor of health and fitness services. In a world of complete information, this might very well be the case. And sub-optimal outcomes could then also be a function of behavioural considerations (or behavioural independent variables as would be the case in the heuristics and biases narrative) (H. Altman 2020).

From the heuristics and biases methodological perspective, consideration would be given to prospective clients or decision-makers making systematically biased decisions and this could be attributed to using fast heuristics to make decisions as opposed to taking a more careful, calculating and considered approach (Kahneman 2011). It could be attributed to both wanting to be in better health and choosing beauty as the dominant signal in one's heuristic for choosing a health and fitness professional. Beauty is a 'natural' draw to decision-makers (Hamermesh 2013), but *not* one that objectively indicates the qualifications and capabilities of a health and fitness professional (Altman et al. 2022c). Therefore, such non-economic considerations can help explain why the health and fitness sectors do not appear to have provided services that have generated optimal outcomes in terms of health and performance.

But, as with our discourse on obesity rates, some mindful focus on decision-making capabilities and environmental factors might shed a brighter light on why the health and fitness sector does not provide optimal outcomes for clients. Consistent with the bounded rationality methodological perspective and following from Akerlof's 'market for lemons' narrative, it is important to think through the implications of the health and fitness sector not issuing reasonably accurate signals on the quality of services provided and the overall qualifications of the providers of these services.[3] Sellers know the true quality of services provided and the qualifications and quality of the health professionals. And, these sellers can very well be health and fitness professionals who are independent contractors. In this asymmetric information decision-making environment, sellers have better information than buyers. And, sellers can exploit this information advantage to market sub-optimal services (a form of adverse selection). These sellers can be modelled as 'profit maximisers' or profit satisficers (borrowing from Simon's bounded rationality narrative). This supply-side condition must then be twinned with the demand side, in terms of how poor or misleading signals affect the demand for particular health and fitness professionals and the services provided.[4] Here too one can assume that prospective clients are rational or smart and are trying to do their best with the resources at hand and their preferences: they are attempting to satisfice.

We start with the working assumption that the typical individual (client) wants to be in good health or, as an athlete, wants to optimise performance outcomes. Given the information at hand, the clients choose health and fitness professionals who they *believe* will help them achieve their objectives. In sports teams, team leaders will often do the selection, but with the same assumed objective of optimising performance outcomes. The demand for quality services is, in part, predicated on the signals issued on the supply side of the market. This can be certificates of qualification, for example. This would be a rational heuristic given the asymmetric decision-making environment that clients are facing. But if there is no quality control over the quality of these certificates then clients might very well engage the services of individuals who they *believe* will facilitate the meeting of their objectives. In a world of asymmetric information and adverse selection, clients stand a high chance of purchasing lemons in the market for health professionals. And, in this decision-making environment, it can be difficult to distinguish lemons from high-quality health and fitness professionals. This can take time and can be a costly process. The absence of clear and unambiguous signals can result in market failure and a market for lemons in the health and fitness sector (H. Altman 2020). Indeed, there is significant evidence that this is the case (H. Altman 2020).

From this methodological perspective, failures in the health and fitness sector resulting in sub-optimal health and sports performance outcomes can be located in the sub-optimal decision-making environment, related to asymmetric information and adverse selection. Biased behaviour need not play a determining role in sub-optimal outcomes emanating from the health and fitness sector. In this context, the absence of quality and trustworthy regulation to correct market failures is a primary cause of this type of market failure. On the supply side, rewarding sub-optimal health and fitness professionals, who have invested less in their human capital formation, can be expected to reduce the pool or reduce the growth rate of the pool of the most qualified health and fitness professionals. One has a race to the bottom (see Akerlof and Shiller (2015) for a more generalised argument).

This sub-optimal information environment can also result in psychological and sociological variables worsening health and performance outcomes, given a sub-optimal decision-making environment and sub-optimal decision-making capabilities. One example of this would be choosing health and fitness professionals based on their 'looks', whether one regards them as more or less beautiful or sexy (Altman et al. 2022c). Beauty as a heuristic might be consistent with a client's preferences and sellers of health and fitness services might then pay undue attention to beauty to sell their services. This is in spite of the fact that beauty, per se, is not an indicator of quality service. In this case, beauty is an often-used bad heuristic, wherein this heuristic does not generate desired health and performance outcomes. However, it can be consistent with rational behaviour on the part of the decision-maker. This would be especially true when prospective clients believe that the health and fitness professionals they are considering are equally qualified and 'beauty' is the wrapping of a high-quality health and fitness professional service package.[5] In other words, in this scenario, clients don't believe that there is a trade-off between beauty and the quality of health and fitness-related services. To address this problem, the information decision-making environment must be improved. Otherwise, rational choice yields lemon outcomes.

Also, accentuating these sub-optimal outcomes would be status quo bias, regret aversion and herding. The former two 'biases' relate to individuals not being willing to reverse bad decisions for psychological reasons. The psychological costs are considered too great relative to the health performance benefits. Here, individuals are willing to sacrifice health and performance benefits so as not to suffer the embarrassment ensuing from reversing past bad decisions. From the heuristic and biases-nudging methodological perspectives, one would need to locate means to nudge individuals towards moving to choose better health and fitness professionals. In this case, individuals actually do want to improve their health or performance outcomes, but they are stuck in a sub-optimal health and performance disequilibrium for psychological reasons. But from our bounded rationality modelling perspective, these individuals ended up in this disequilibrium in the first place, because of a sub-optimal decision-making environment.

Herding is a heuristic that can yields either positive or negative outcomes, depending on the direction in which the herd and herd leaders are heading. Herds are influenced by the behaviour of herd leaders, and these can be exemplified by what celebrities (including Instagram and Twitter leaders or influencers) choose in the health and fitness industry. Given imperfect and asymmetric information it is possible for clients to rationally adopt herding heuristics to make their choices in the hope or belief that the herd or herd leaders know best. Keynes (1936) developed the herding methodological framework to help explain movements in financial asset prices which have no substantive roots in reality (see also Shiller (2019) on narrative economics). Beliefs and believing in particular individuals can have a significant impact on demand. In the case of the health and fitness industry, what information or advice individuals use to improve their health and performance, is also heavily influenced by the herd. This can result in poor decisions and sub-optimal outcomes for clients. Herding can also result in significant benefits to the sellers of health and fitness-related services. Lemons can be sold on the market, whilst clients believe that these lemons are top-of-the-line products. The herding heuristics yield such sub-optimal outcomes when clients can be easily deceived because of imperfect and asymmetric information and adverse selection. There is no biased behaviour here; no irrationality. As with Akerlof's market for lemons, this market failure can be corrected by quality assuring the information provided to clients in the health and fitness industry.

X-EFFICIENCY THEORY AND SUB-OPTIMAL SPORTS PERFORMANCE[6]

One important cause of sub-optimal sports performance by teams and by individual athletes competing in individualised sports such as powerlifting, golf, tennis and K1 sprint kayaking and rowing, is related to our above discussion of imperfect and asymmetric information and adverse selection. Here one selects sub-optimal health and fitness professionals and consults advisory handbooks, for example, that provide incorrect and misleading information for rational reasons. Psychological and sociological factors then lock the athlete into an overall support network that yields sub-optimal outcomes that can persist over time. Lemons for input yield lemons for output. One has a production function for sports performance outcomes wherein inputs can range in quality from lemons to the highest quality of inputs (for example, in terms of the quality of the services provided by health and fitness professionals). Inputs which are lemons at one level or another yield performance outcomes which are below what they would be if one used the highest quality health and fitness providers and advice.

In this sense, one has x-inefficiency in performance outcomes (Altman and Altman 2015a). Leibenstein (1966; see also Altman 1990, 1992) first developed this concept to explain variations in the quantity and quality of output given traditional inputs. Such variations are assumed away in the conventional theory of the firm. Rather, effort is assumed to be maximised or fixed at some optimal level. Leibenstein focuses on variation in the level and quality of effort inputs by firm members as the key determinant of variations in output levels and in the quality of output. Firms are x-efficient when they are producing less than they can (sub-optimally), controlling for quality. We are referring to sub-optimal outcomes as a function of sub-optimal inputs related to the health and fitness industry as a function of imperfect and asymmetric information. In this case, outcomes are sub-optimal, holding effort inputs constant. One can also have sub-optimal inputs yielding sub-optimal effort inputs as well.

The bounded rationality methodological perspective suggests improvements to the decision-making environment to minimise the probability of choosing lemons as inputs into the sports performance production function in the first place. Improvements in the decision-making capabilities of clients can also serve to drive decision-makers out of a sub-optimal performance equilibrium. However, psychological and sociological obstacles to breaking out of this sub-optimal performance equilibrium trap might have to be overcome as well (as discussed above). This brings to the fore the potential importance of nudging techniques to shift behaviour away from what becomes a preference for lemon inputs. This is given the sunk costs involved in choosing lemons for rational reasons and the psychological costs of changing one's preferences and choices (see Becker 1996).

In the conventional model, inefficiencies of the sort discussed earlier should be eliminated by market forces. X-inefficiency, by lowering productivity, increases the average cost of production, making x-inefficient firms uncompetitive.[7]

To remain competitive, firms must revert to x-efficiency in production. Market forces serve to discipline the firm. But Leibenstein argues that in the real-world product markets aren't sufficiently competitive to maintain market discipline, hence the persistence of x-inefficiency. Imperfect product markets serve to protect x-inefficient firms as would tariffs and government subsidies. Other factors, such as low wages can also serve to protect inefficient firms and contribute to the inefficiency of the firm as well (Altman 1990, 1992). A key point made by Leibenstein, which also serves as a basis for Simon's bounded rationality methodological approach, is that one should not make the prior assumption that firms or organisations are efficient or performing optimally. Much depends on what transpires inside the firm and the preferences of firm 'members' (Cyert and March 1963). With regards to the realm of sports, when it comes to athletes and sports teams, market forces can't drive performance efficiency.

We address two basic questions here:

- If you wish to be a successful athlete at any level why would you persist with sub-optimal inputs or determinants of your performance outcomes?
- If you manage and/or own a sports team, why would you persist with sub-optimal inputs or determinants of your team's performance outcomes?

To address these questions, we link our narrative related to the health and fitness industry to the choices that decision-makers make with regards to health and fitness professionals and advice sought and obtained to improve performance outcomes. We make the initial prior assumption that decision-makers are rational or smart and have a preference for being x-efficient in performance outcomes. We briefly model individual athletes in individualised sports and then sports organisations (see also Altman and Altman 2015a, 2022b).

Performance outcomes can be measured by the ranking of players and teams, percentage wins, major tournament wins, the number of championships within a specified time frame and awards, for example. Given imperfect and asymmetric information it is costly and difficult to identify best practice providers of health and fitness services and advice, especially in unregulated markets where it is relatively easy to provide prospective clients with misleading information on quality. We have a type of market for lemons. As discussed earlier, one can explain levels of performance and differences in the extent of performance x-inefficiency through an understanding of such sub-optimal decision-making environments and decision-making capabilities. Changing other independent variables are also of importance and this brings to the fore the importance of psychological and sociological variables. Once one is in a sub-optimal performance position, athletes under different sets of pressures and imbued with different work ethics, for example, might be prone to search for higher quality health and fitness professionals and sets of advice, if it is understood that their sub-optimal performance is a product of sub-optimal health and fitness service inputs. This requires that decision-makers have the capabilities to identify lemons and also to identify higher quality services and information in a world of imperfect and asymmetric information, adverse selection, and possible deceit. But it is clear from this bounded rationality methodological narrative there is no reason to expect optimality in performance, but there is a way forward here in terms of policy as to how to improve performance, largely with respect to the decision-making environment and the decision-makers' (clients') decision-making capabilities.

Aspects of this argument are illustrated in Figure 14.2. Here we examine the demand and supply of quality health and fitness professionals. This can also be used as a proxy for the supply of higher quality athletes. This is measured along the horizontal axis. Also, along this axis, we measure the level of performance (performance index). Along the vertical axis, we have price. The supply of quality health and fitness professionals is assumed price sensitive

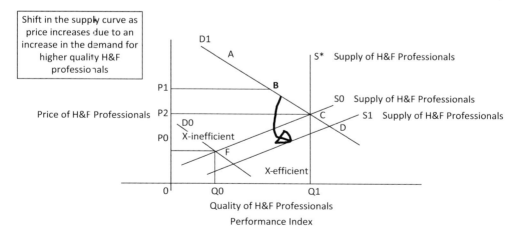

Figure 14.2 The demand and supply for quality health and fitness professionals

as is the demand. Given asymmetric and costly information and the sub-optimal decision-making capabilities of individuals and in the absence of an appropriate regulatory framework, clients are at a sub-optimal equilibrium at F, with an equilibrium quality at Q0. Therefore, on the market, other clients are demanding relatively poorly qualified health and fitness professionals who are being incorrectly assumed to be of a much higher level of quality, yielding a lower level of performance outcomes than should be the case. Significant improvements to the decision-making environment and capabilities result in a shift outward in the demand for quality to D1, yielding a new quality equilibrium at Q1. If this was the current market, in equilibrium, for qualified health and fitness professionals, there would be an x-efficient outcome – the highest possible performance rating given inputs. Once health and fitness professionals realise that clients can identify quality from lemons, one would expect more individuals of quality to enter the market and more investment in human capital in this domain shifting the supply curve to S1, yielding a new equilibrium at D in the longer run.

With regards to sports teams, especially those that must be financially sustainable, it is clear that there can be errors in decision-making in the first instance resulting in sub-optimal or x-inefficient performance outcomes. Sports teams can remain economically viable even if their performance is sub-optimal. Your team does not have to be the best to be profitable. It can even be a relatively poor-performing team and be profitable. And a successful team can be unprofitable if its success relies on expensive talent where the marginal costs outweigh the marginal benefits. Moreover, sports teams can be owned by larger economic organisations, where the sports team is a vanity or positional good, where the value of the teams is in owning a sports team. The larger corporation's profit is generated elsewhere, and the ownership of the sports team can also serve to market the corporation's many other outputs. From the x-inefficiency modelling perspective, sports teams are 'protected' from market forces and can survive even if they are performance inefficient (see also Scully 1994). In addition to the aforementioned, the fan base of the team, and the extent of fans' loyalty, provide an additional layer of protection to the sports team, to the extent that loyalty remains intact even in the face of their team remaining performance-x-inefficient. Fans purchase the tickets and add-ons (like team clothing and other paraphernalia) and provide the basis (market) for TV rights, for example.

This type of modelling allows for a wide variation in performance x-inefficiency (from highly x-inefficient to x-efficient). And this ties into a wide variation in the choice of health and fitness professionals and sought-after performance-related information. This relates to imperfect and asymmetric information and adverse selection and the market for lemons in this domain given insufficiently regulated markets and inadequate decision-making capabilities amongst decision-makers. There is a direct and positive causal relationship between the health and fitness industry and the multifaceted services that they provide and the extent to which sports teams are performance x-efficient. And this relationship is mediated by the seller and client through the decision-making environment and the decision-making capabilities of the clients. Sub-optimality as a quasi-equilibrium is arrived at for rational reasons given a bounded rationality universe. As in the earlier discussion, psychological and sociological variables can keep the sports organisation in this sub-optimal, x-inefficient equilibrium unless the extent of protection diminishes. An example of this would be a sufficient diminution of the fan base as fans become frustrated with their team doing poorly year in and year out.

The level of performance x-efficiency is determined by a variety of important variables apart from inputs from the health and fitness industry, which has been our point of focus.

How the sports team is organised and managed is also critical. For example, is it more or less hierarchical in organisational structure? An organisational structure that allows for the dominance of a strong-willed leader with no or little voice from other members of the team can result in the choice of sub-optimal inputs (such as players and health and fitness services) and a sub-optimal combination of inputs (Sheffrin 2008). Such lack of voice (Hirschman 1970) also facilitates remaining in a sub-optimal equilibrium once it is chosen. This is a form of hysteresis, where the current and future state of affairs depends on past decisions, even when history yields sub-optimal outcomes. Also of importance would be whether or not the sports team is community-owned (a type of cooperative organisational form) as compared to the traditional investor-owned organisational form. They yield different types of incentives. Also, of consequence is the balance, or lack thereof, between using metrics (in the form of statistical analysis) for decision-making and experience-based decision-making (which has typically made use of data, albeit not in terms of applying strict statistical analysis) (Altman and Altman 2022c).

All of this takes into consideration the too often neglected black box of the firm, which is critical to the bounded rationality methodological approach (Cyert and March 1963). Overall, how a firm is managed and, relatedly, the quality of management, affects the extent to which the highest quality health and fitness services are engaged in sports teams. This relates to their decision-making capabilities. As discussed earlier, this has a significant effect on the teams' level of performance x-efficiency. The significance of the bounded rationality approach to an understanding of sports team performance is underscored by the recognition that sports organisations can survive without being x-efficient and team decisions can result, even if unintentionally, in performance x-inefficiencies which can persist over time. And, this persistence can be explained by psychological and sociological factors with respect to firm decision-makers. One important psychological variable that needs to be taken into consideration is that key decision-makers of sports organisations need not be interested in maximising performance outcomes. One can then have organisational slack in a protected environment. This is an important point emphasised by Simon and by Leibenstein (1996).

CONCLUSION

This chapter casts its eye on how behavioural economics can explain some key issues related to health and wellbeing and sports. We focus on the bounded rationality methodological approach, but also pay critical attention to the heuristics and biases approach which currently holds a more dominant position in the literature and is often identified with the nudging methodological narrative. Both are differentiated from the conventional wisdom which focuses on relative prices and real income as the key independent variables and makes extreme assumptions about information perfections, the decision-making capabilities of individuals and the foresight of individuals. The bounded rationality approach pioneered by Simon assumes that individuals are smart, but their decisions are bounded by their decision-making environment and their decision-making capabilities. It also pays attention to the reality that sub-optimal decisions and outcomes can be pervasive and persist for institutional, sociological and psychological reasons. The heuristics and biases approach focuses on errors in decisions which are assumed to be systemic and very much part of the human condition. It also pays little heed to economic variables being possibly an important determinant of decision-making.

We argue that the causes of overweight and obesity and differences in overweight and obesity rates across individuals, regions and nations are most effectively located in differences in the decision-making environment and decision-making capabilities of individuals. This is as opposed to the strict focus on relative prices and real income in the conventional economics methodological narrative and on biased behaviour in the heuristics and biases narrative. This being said, an important barrier to overcoming overweight and obesity can be related to the inability of decision-makers (those who are overweight or obese) to choose appropriate health and fitness services and advice given an imperfect and asymmetric information and decision-making environment, giving rise to adverse selection issues and, relatedly, to a market for lemons. Even when individuals want to improve their health it is difficult to do so given a sub-optimal decision-making environment and capabilities. Price and income are also important independent variables. And psychological and sociological variables intervene to lock individuals into a sub-optimal equilibrium.

Methodologically, we argue, it's important to pay careful attention to the overall decision-making environment and capabilities as this approach allows for smart individuals not being able to realise their preferences due to exogenously determined circumstances, where the latter can be affected by policy. A focus on systemic biases makes the prior assumption that non-psychological variables are not of first-order importance and that what needs to be changed are the biased preferences of individuals. Although 'biases' might be of some analytical importance, if exogenously determined factors remain sub-optimal, health outcomes will remain sub-optimal irrespective of whether or not decision-makers are biased.

It is important to pay attention to the well-established determinants of sub-optimal outcomes emanating from the health and fitness industry given its importance to improving the health and welfare of the population, where overweight and obesity is one such important area requiring significant improvement. We argue that of critical importance to the sub-optimal outcomes in this sector is imperfect and asymmetric information with adverse section, yielding a type of market for lemons, especially given sub-optimal decision-making capabilities amongst clients and prospective clients. This negatively impacts the supply and demand side of the market for health and fitness professionals and services. Fundamentally important here is that *even if clients want* to improve their health outcomes, if quality signals from the industry are fuzzy, incorrect or misleading, clients end up choosing sub-optimal service provision yielding sub-optimal (inclusive of damaging) health outcomes. This bounded rationality methodological approach suggests regulatory intervention in this sector by governments and/or industry to improve health outcomes (Lloyd 2005; Lloyd and Payne 2018; see also Altman 2020). But one should note that sub-optimal outcomes for clients are consistent with the profitability of the providers of sub-optimal services in the health and fitness industry. Hence, the sustainability of sub-optimality from the supply side of the market.

Finally, we link sub-optimality in the health and fitness sector with sub-optimality amongst athletes and sports teams. We apply the bounded rationality methodological narrative here as well. But this is contextualised by the reality modelled by Leibenstein, following upon Simon's insights, that inefficient organisations (which include sports teams) can survive and persist over time in the market. One can end up with sub-optimal or x-inefficient performance outcomes amongst sports teams. The same is the case for individual athletes competing in individualised sports. This can be related to the choice of sub-optimal inputs from the health and fitness industry which, in turn, is related to a sub-optimal decision-making environment and decision-making capabilities. Other factors are also important here as determinants of sub-optimality in performance. But critical to the bounded rationality approach is to address the issue of the exogenously determined constraints on decision-making. Analyses of psychological and sociological determinants of sub-optimal performance should not be addressed independently of these exogenously determined constraints on decision-making. Moreover, it is important to appreciate the significance of relative prices and real income to the decision-making toolbox. In the realm of the health and fitness industry and sports, behavioural economics should complement and enrich the conventional economics toolbox.

Table 14.1 summarises some of the main points of this chapter. Once again, a key distinguishing feature of the two behavioural economics methodological approaches relates to whether bred-in-the-bone behavioural biases are the main cause of sub-optimal and x-inefficient decisions and outcomes as opposed to a sub-optimal decision-making environment and decision-making capabilities. This relates to exogenous variables that yield sub-optimal outcomes. The heuristics and biases approach focuses on biased decision-making, which is internal to the individual and part of the human condition, which yields sub-optimal outcomes. We argue that important to achieving improved health and fitness and sports outcomes is a concerted focus on the health and fitness industry and those critical variables, which relate mainly to the decision-making environment and decision-making capabilities, that

Table 14.1 Behavioural economics and the health and fitness and sports industries

Bounded rationality approach		Heuristics and biases approach	
Decision-making environment		Use of heuristics	Biased decisions
Decision-making capabilities	Inadequate education	Individual biased choices	Sub-optimal outcomes
Imperfect and asymmetric information	Market for lemons	Choice architects	
Misleading signals			
Adverse selection	Inadequate regulation		
Bad heuristics (rational)	Sub-optimal choices	Bad heuristics (biased)	Sub-optimal choices
X-inefficiency	Sub-optimal sports outcomes	X-inefficiency	Sub-optimal sports outcomes
	Sub-optimal rational choices made by sports team leaders		Biased choices
	Significance of how the team is managed		Choice architects and improving decisions
Rationality	Reform of decision-making environments and capabilities	Systemic biases	Nudging
Importance of prices and incomes		Focus on non-economic variables	

affect health and fitness and sports outcomes. Ultimately, the quality and quantity of physical activity and related choices and their management are critically important to improving these outcomes as well as the wellbeing of society.

NOTES

1. This section is drawn from Altman and Altman (2022a). The estimates related to obesity and life expectancy are derived from www.ourworldindata.org and discussed in Altman and Altman (2022a). For the data, see Ritchie (2017), Roser and Ritchie (2013) and Roser, Ospina and Ritchie (2013).
2. The obesity section of this chapter draws heavily from Altman and Altman (2022a).
3. Aspects of this argument is based on H. Altman (2020). See also, Boulding and Kirmani (1993), Chan (2013) and Jordon et al. (2017).
4. In Akerlof's (1970) original lemons paper, in a world of asymmetric information consumers can't easily distinguish lemons in the used car market from higher quality cars. Lemon dealers pretend (signal) that their vehicles are high quality. Then consumers, in this world of confusing signals with no quality control, assume the worst, that the cars on the market are all lemons, and they are only willing to pay a lemon price for all cars. This drives out of the market the sellers of higher quality cars. One has a race to the bottom in terms of quality of cars and price. All choices in this market are rational or smart given the sub-optimal decision-making environment.
5. Becker and Murphy (1993) make the important point that rational or smart individuals will purchase based on the packaging of the product, but they are assuming that the product purchased of high quality. Quality packaging add utility to the decision-maker or customer.
6. See Altman and Altman (2015a and 2015b), for more details.
7. $Average\ cost = \dfrac{wage\ rate}{\dfrac{Output}{Labour\ Input}}$, in a simple model of the firm, with one factor input. Labour productivity $\left(\dfrac{Output}{Labour\ input}\right)$, ceteris paribus, is determined by the extent of x-inefficiency.

REFERENCES

Akerlof, G. (1970). "The Market for Lemons: Quality Uncertainty and the Market Mechanism," *Quarterly Journal of Economics,* 84(3), 488–500.
Akerlof, G.E. and R.J. Shiller (2015). *Phishing for Phools: The Economics of Manipulation and Deception.* Princeton, NJ: Princeton University Press.
Altman, H. (2020). *The Behavioural Economics of Organisational Inefficiency: The Example of the New Zealand Fitness Industry.* Master of Philosophy Thesis, Queensland University of Technology. Brisbane: Australia. https://eprints.qut.edu.au/198038/1/Hannah_Altman_Thesis.pdf.
Altman, H. and M. Altman (2015a). "Sport Economics and Performance Inefficiencies," in M. Altman, ed., *Real World Decision Making: An Encyclopedia of Behavioral Economics.* New York: Praeger, ABC-CLIO: 410–412.
Altman, H. and M. Altman (2015b). "Sports Economics and Economic Psychology," in M. Altman, ed., *Real World Decision Making: An Encyclopedia of Behavioral Economics.* New York: Praeger, ABC-CLIO: 412–415.
Altman, H. and M. Altman (2022a). "Obesity, Wellbeing, Freedom of Choice, and Institutional Change," in M. Altman, ed., *Constructing a More Scientific Economics: John Tomer's Pluralistic and Humanistic.* New York: Palgrave Macmillan: 197–234.
Altman, H. and M. Altman (2022b). "Sports Performance, Procedural Rationality and Organizational Inefficiency," in H. Altman, M. Altman and B. Togler, eds., *Behavioural Sport Economics.* New York: Routledge: 52–77.

Altman, H., M. Altman, B. Torgler and S. Whyte (2022c). "Beauty and Preferences and Choice Exemplified in the Sports Market," in H. Altman, M. Altman and B. Togler, eds., *Behavioural Sport Economics*. New York: Routledge: 201–221.

Altman, H. and M. Altman (2022d). "Moneyball and Decision-Making Heuristics: An Intersection of Statistics and Practical Expertise," in H. Altman, M. Altman and B. Togler, eds., *Behavioural Sport Economics*. New York: Routledge: 222–240.

Altman, M. (1990). 'Interfirm, Interregional, and International Differences in Labor Productivity: Variations in the Levels of 'X-Inefficiency' as a Function of Differential Labor Costs," in M. Perlman and K. Weiermair, eds., *Studies in Economic Rationality: X- Efficiency Examined and Extolled*. Ann Arbor: University of Michigan Press: 323–350.

Altman, M. (1992). "The Economics of Exogenous Increases in Wage Rates in a Behavioral/X-Efficiency Model of the Firm," *Review of Social Economy*, 50, 163–192.

Altman, M. (1999). "The Methodology of Economics and the Survivor Principle Revisited and Revised: Some Welfare and Public Policy Implications of Modeling the Economic Agent," *Review of Social Economics*, 57, 427–449.

Altman, M. (2006). "What a Difference an Assumption Makes: Effort Discretion, Economic Theory, and Public Policy," in M. Altman, ed., *Handbook of Contemporary Behavioral Economics: Foundations and Developments*. London: Routledge: 125–164.

Altman, M. (2017) "A Bounded Rationality Assessment of the New Behavioral Economics," in R. Frantz, S.H. Chen, K. Dopfer, F. Heukelom and S. Mousavi, eds., *Routledge Handbook of Behavioral Economics*. Routledge: London and New York: 179–193.

Arrow, K.J. (1973). "Higher Education as a Filter," *Journal of Public Economics*, 2, 193–216.

Baddeley, M. (2018). *Copycats and Contrarians - Why We Follow Others, and When We Don't*. London/New Haven: Yale University Press.

Becker, G.S. and Kevin M. Murphy (1993). "A Simple Theory of Advertising as a Good or Bad," *Quarterly Journal of Economics*, 108, 941–964.

Becker, G.S. (1996). *Accounting for Tastes*. Cambridge and London: Harvard University Press.

Berg, N. and G. Gigerenzer (2010). "As-If Behavioral Economics: Neoclassical Economics in Disguise?" *History of Economic Ideas*, 18, 133–166.

Boulding, W. and A. Kirmani (1993). "A Consumer-Side Experimental Examination of Signaling Theory: Do Consumers Perceive Warranties as Signals of Quality?" *Journal of Consumer Research*, 20(1), 111–123

Bowen, J. (2018, February 12). "Gym Injuries not a Fit Use for Public Money. Dominion Post." Retrieved from https://www.stuff.co.nz/national/101832723/gym-injuries-cost-taxpayers- 33m-in-2017-including-brain-injuries-hernias-and-burns?rm=a.

Caldwell, O. (2017, July20). "Sport Injury Costs Soar to $542m-that's More to ACC than Road Crashes." Retrieved from https://www.stuff.co.nz/sport/94891232/sports-injuries-cost-nz- 500m--more-than-road-carnage.

Chan, A.L. (2013). "Signal Jamming in the Translation Market and the Complementary Roles of Certification and Diplomas in Developing Multilateral Signaling Mechanism," *Translation and Interpreting*, 5(1), 211–221.

Cleaver, J. (2016, March 23). "Unqualified Trainers Giving us All a Bad Name." Retrieved from https://tewahanui.nz/health/unqualified-trainers-giving-us-all-a-bad-name.

Clent, D. (2016, May12). "Fitness Injuries on the Rise, Misinformation Online Could be Partly to Blame." Retrieved from https://www.stuff.co.nz/life-style/112534010/fitness-injuries-on- the-rise-misinformation-online-could-be-partly-to-blame.

Cyert, R.M. and J.C. March (1963). *A Behavioral Theory of the Firm*. Englewood Cliffs, NJ: Prentice Hall.

Drewes, M. (2003). "Competition and Efficiency in Professional Sports Leagues," *European Sport Management Quarterly*, 3(4), 240–252.

Friedman, M. (1953). "The Methodology of Positive Economics," in M. Friedman, *Essays in Positive Economics*. Chicago, IL: University of Chicago Press: 3–43.

Gigerenzer, G. (2007). *Gut Feelings: The Intelligence of the Unconscious*. New York: Viking.

Grossman, M. and N.H. Mocan, eds. (2011). "Introduction to 'Economic Aspects of Obesity'," in Michael Grossman and Naci H. Mocan, eds., *Economic Aspects of Obesity*. Chicago: University

of Chicago Press: 1–16. Accessed December 12, 2020, Available at: http://www.nber.org/chapters/c11814.
Hamermesh, D. (2013). *Beauty Pays: Why Attractive People Are More Successful*. Princeton, NJ: Princeton University Press.
Hirschman, Albert O. (1970). *Exit, Voice, and Loyalty: Responses to Decline in Firms, Organizations, and States*. Cambridge, MA: Harvard University Press.
Jordon, J.J., R. Sommers, P. Bloom and P.G. Rand (2017). "Why do We Hate Hypocrites? Evidence for a Theory of False Signaling," *Psychological Science*. Doi:101177/0956797616685771.
Kahneman, D. and A. Tversky (1979). "Prospect Theory: An Analysis of Decisions Under Risk," *Econometrica*, 47, 313–327.
Kahneman, D. and A. Tversky, eds. (2000). *Choices, Values and Frames*. New York: Cambridge University Press & Russell Sage Foundation.
Kahneman, D. (2003). "Maps of Bounded Rationality: Psychology for Behavioral Economics," *American Economic Review*, 93: 1449–1475.
Kahneman, D. (2011). *Thinking, Fast and Slow*. New York: Farrar, Straus and Giroux.
Keynes, J.M. (1936) [2007]. *The General Theory of Employment, Interest and Money*. London: Macmillan.
Leibenstein, H. (1966). "Allocative Efficiency vs. X-efficiency," *American Economic Review*, 56, 392–415.
Lloyd, C. (2005). "Training Standards as a Policy Option? The Regulation of the Fitness Industry," *Industrial Relations Journal*, 36(5), 367–385.
Lloyd, C. and J. Payne (2018). "Licensed to Skill? The Impact of Occupational Regulation on Fitness Instructors," *European Journal of Industrial Relations*, 24(1), 91–108.
March, J.G. (1978). "Bounded Rationality, Ambiguity, and the Engineering of Choice," *Bell Journal of Economics*, 9, 587–608.
Marshall, S.W. and K.M. Guskiewicz (2003). "Sports and Recreational Injury: The Hidden Cost of a Healthy Lifestyle," *Injury Prevention*, 9: 100–102.
North, D.C. (1990). *Institutions, Institutional Change and Economic Performance*. Cambridge: Cambridge University Press.
North, D.C. (2016). "Institutions and Economic Theory," *American Economist*, 61, 72–76.
Ritchie, H. (2017). "Obesity," *Published online at OurWorldInData.org*. Accessed December 19, 2020, Available at: https://ourworldindata.org/obesity.
Roser, M., E. Ortiz-Ospina and H. Ritchie (2013). "Life Expectancy," *OurWorldInData.org*. Accessed January 3, 2021, Available at: https://ourworldindata.org/life-expectancy.
Roser, M. and H. Ritchie (2013). "Food Prices," *OurWorldInData.org*. Accessed January 3, 2021, Available at: https://ourworldindata.org/food-prices.
Scully, G.W. (1994). "Managerial Efficiency and Survivability in Professional Team Sports," *Managerial and Decision Economics*, 15, 403–411.
Sheffrin, H. (2008). *Ending the Management Illusion: How to Drive Business Results Using the Principles of Behavioral Finance*. New York: McGraw-Hill.
Shephard R.J. (2003). "Can We Afford to Exercise, Given Current Injury Rates?" *Injury Prevention: Journal of the International Society for Child and Adolescent Injury Prevention*, 9, 99–100.
Shiller, R. and G. Akerlof (2015). *Phishing for Phools: The Economics of Manipulation and Deception*. Princeton, NJ: Princeton University Press.
Shiller, R. (2019). *Narrative Economics: How Stories Go Viral and Drive Major Economic Events*. Princeton, NJ: Princeton University Press.
Simon, H.A. (1959). "Theories of Decision Making in Economics and Behavioral Science," *American Economic Review*, 49, 252–283.
Simon, H.A. (1986). "Rationality in Psychology and Economics," *Journal of Business*, 59, S209–224.
Simon, H.A. (1987). "Behavioral Economics," in John Eatwell, Murray Millgate, & Peter Newman, eds., *The New Palgrave: A Dictionary of Economics*. London: Macmillan: 221–225.
Spence, M.A. (1973). "Job Market Signalling," *Quarterly Journal of Economics*, 87, 355–374.
Spence, M.A. (2002). "Signalling in Retrospect and the Informational Structure of Markets," *American Economic Review*, 92, 434–459.
Stigler, G.J. (1961). "The Economics of Information," *Journal of Political Economy*, 69, 213–225.

Thaler, R.H. and C.R. Sunstein (2008). *Nudge: Improving Decisions about Health, Wealth, and Happiness*. New York: Penguin Books.
The Press (2018, February 8). "Editorial: Unregulated Fitness Industry's Cost to Taxpayers Jump as Injury Numbers Rise." Retrieved from https://www.stuff.co.nz/the-press/opinion/101232614/editorial-unregulated-fitness-industrys-cost-to-taxpayers-jumps-as-injury-numbers-rise.
Todd, P.M. and G. Gigerenzer (2003). "Bounding Rationality to the World," *Journal of Economic Psychology*, 24, 143–165.
Tomer, J.F. (2001). "Addictions are Not Rational: A Socio-Economic Model of Addictive Behavior," *Journal of Socio-Economics*, 33, 243–261.
Tomer, J.F. (2011). "What Causes Obesity? And Why Has It Grown So Much?," *Challenge*, 54, 22–49.
Tomer, J.F. (2013). "Stemming the Tide of Obesity: What Needs to Happen," *Journal of Behavioral and Experimental Economics* (formerly The Journal of Socio-Economics), 42, 88–98.

15. Empirical methods and methodological developments in economics of health and health behaviour: A discussion of theory and applications

Nazmi Sari

INTRODUCTION

Policymakers have widely implemented new policies or revised the existing ones to influence the behaviour of individuals. In recent decades, there have been substantial changes in public health policies and regulations promoting healthy lifestyles (Chaloupka & Warner 2000; Humphreys & Ruseski 2007; Miller et al. 2016). Indoor smoking bans in public places became one of the common regulations in most countries around the globe (see Chaloupka & Warner 2000; Sari 2013). Other policies to increase access to parks and green spaces or to design and implement more active modes of transportation (i.e. bike lanes and walkable cities) are also routinely implemented in several countries (see Saelens et al. 2003; Sallis et al. 1992). Additional forms of policies using financial incentives (i.e. providing tax credits for participation in sports and physical activities) are also used in selected countries including Canada (Spence et al. 2010).

While we have seen changes in policies taking place during recent decades, there has been also a growing interest among social scientists to examine the effect of these changes in policies and regulations on the intended outcomes. Given the nature of the research questions, and the fact that there are limited controlled research environments in social sciences, estimating the causal effect of these policies on intended outcomes has been an ongoing challenge. To overcome these challenges in social science research, various methods based on observational data have been developed in the economics field and applied in economics as well as in other social science research. In this chapter, we will provide a review of selected methodological developments that are most relevant to health economics and the economics of health behaviour.

Our objective is to review the relevant methodological developments with specific examples derived from the related literature on health economics and economics of health behaviour. As widely documented in the literature, healthy lifestyles (i.e. obesity, physical activity and smoking) not only influence health outcomes (Lechner 2009; Humphreys et al. 2014; Raglin 1990; Ruseski et al. 2014; Sari & Lechner 2015) but also affect individuals' labour market outcomes through productivity gain (Cawley 2000; Lechner 2009; Lechner & Sari 2015; Morris 2006, 2007; Norton & Han 2008; Sari & Osman 2018). Therefore, we present findings on how policies potentially influence individuals' health behaviour that impacts their health and labour market outcomes.

In the next section of the chapter, we start with the theory and applications of randomised controlled trials (RCTs). Applications of RCTs and their limitations are also discussed in this section. Due to its experimental nature, implementations of RCTs in health economics and economics of health behaviour are limited to a few well-known examples. The RAND Health Insurance Experiment (HIE) is one of the first well-known examples of an RCT designed and implemented in the field of health economics (Manning et al. 1987; Newhouse 1993). The HIE project is the most important experiment conducted in the 1970s to investigate the impact of health insurance on the use of healthcare services. Following this example, there have been other small-scale experiments implemented in health economics research. We will provide a few of these examples in the second section.

As a research method, RCTs are considered the gold standard in estimating the causal effect of an intervention or a change in policy. While it is relatively easier and feasible to design and implement in biological sciences, as discussed in the second section, there are methodological challenges that become harder to overcome in social science research. As an alternative to RCTs, regression-based methods based on observational data have been developed and applied in the economics literature. These alternative methods and their applications in the economics of health and health behaviour are presented in the third and fourth sections. The final section of the chapter provides a summary and conclusion.

RANDOMISED CONTROLLED TRIALS AND SELECTED APPLICATIONS

This section provides a brief overview of the methodological issues of RCTs and their applications. We provide a discussion of limitations that are most relevant in social science research and highlight these issues using a few examples of RCTs implemented in this literature. We limit our discussion to a brief overview and provide further references for interested readers for more detailed discussions on this issue.

A Methodological Overview of Randomised Controlled Trials

RCT is an experimental research method implemented in various fields. It was developed as a research method to examine the (causal) effect of an intervention, policy or programme on the corresponding outcome of interest. While it is widely used in medicine and biological sciences (i.e. drug development, effectiveness of new technology or treatment for diseases), it has been also implemented in social sciences including in economics (for a list of studies in economics literature, see Burtless 1995). In RCT applications, each discipline, however, has been using its own discipline-specific jargon. These terms (i.e. impact, effectiveness, effect, treatment effect, intervention effect) in various disciplines are used for the same meaning (i.e. causal effect of an intervention or programme or policy on the corresponding outcome of interest). For the remainder of this chapter, I use *effect* (or intervention effect) interchangeably for impact, effectiveness, effect or treatment effect, and *intervention* for intervention, experiment, treatment or change in policy or programme.

In the most general setup, researchers design the RCT so that participants are randomly allocated or assigned to one of the two groups in order to estimate the causal effect of the corresponding intervention. The first group is the intervention (experimental or treatment) group while the second one is the control group. In an application of RCTs, randomisation of participants is the key aspect in obtaining reliable estimated causal effects of the intervention (Burtless 1995; Stolberg et al. 2004). Given that all consented participants of an RCT are randomly assigned to one of the two groups, each group would be similar (or statistically identical) in terms of the characteristics that may be relevant to the outcome of interest intended by the intervention. As a result, any observed differences in outcome variable(s) after the intervention between the two groups would be solely attributable to the intervention. While randomisation is the most important strength of an RCT, it could also create a detrimental failure in estimating the effect of an intervention if one would fail to strictly follow the research protocols expected in an RCT design. We will discuss these issues in the following section.

To illustrate an empirical model and discuss the estimation issues for an RCT, we start with the assumption that there are two periods in the implementation of the intervention. In the first period (also known as baseline, t = 0), RCT participants are invited to participate in the intervention. Given that each participant will be in one of the two states (i.e. exposed to the intervention or not), but not in both, we will not be observing the outcome variable(s) in the absence of the intervention for a participant assigned to the intervention group. This issue, known as the missing data problem in evaluation research, is discussed in the following.

D stands for the states associated with receiving the intervention and Y denotes the outcome variable as follows:

$$\text{Intervention, } D = \begin{cases} 1 & \text{if particiant received the intervention} \\ 0 & \text{if participant did not receive the intervention} \end{cases}$$

$$\text{Outcome variable, } Y = \begin{cases} Y_1 & \text{if } D = 1 \\ Y_0 & \text{if } D = 0 \end{cases}$$

The observed outcome for participant i can be defined as $Y_i = DY_1 + (1-D)Y_0$. The gain from participating in the intervention for participant i would be $(Y_1 - Y_0)$. In an ideal research setting, we need to observe both states for participant i (with and without the intervention, Y_{1i} and Y_{0i}) to estimate the intervention effect. However, in reality, we can only observe one of the two potential outcomes (either the intervention or the control outcome, Y_{1i} or Y_{0i}) for each participant in the RCT. As suggested in the programme evaluation literature, the estimation of an intervention effect for causal inference requires researchers to deal with this missing data problem (Imbens & Rubin 2015; Rosenbaum & Rubin 1983; Ding & Li 2018).

In order to deal with the missing data problem, each participant, after providing a signed consent to be part of the intervention, is randomly assigned to one of the two groups (intervention and control). The purpose of the randomisation is to assign the same chance to each participant to be in either of the states. Therefore, the average differences in outcome variable(s) after the intervention between both groups would reflect the impact of the intervention. After data on outcome variable (Y) is collected from each participant, one could easily estimate the intervention effect using the following regression model:

$$Y_i = \alpha + \beta D_i + \varepsilon_i \qquad (15.1)$$

where each participant is randomly assigned to the intervention or the control group. This randomisation implies that participants in each group do not systematically differ from each other (i.e. $E(D_i, \varepsilon_i) = 0$). Given the randomisation, the intervention effect can be determined with the estimated coefficient (β) associated with D_i in equation (15.1). While the randomisation would make both groups similar at baseline ($t = 0$) in terms of their characteristics and the outcome variable, one could compare the baseline characteristics, and include a baseline outcome variable as an additional variable in the right-hand side of equation (15.1) (Twisk & De Vente 2008). While an RCT is the best research design to estimate the causal association of an intervention on an outcome variable, it is prone to potential biases. These issues will be discussed in the next subsection.

Applications and Limitations of Randomised Control Trials

There are several studies in health economics applying RCT design in order to assess the impact of an intervention (i.e. Manning et al. 1987; Miller et al. 2016; Newhouse 1993). For interventions with a focus on physical activity, diet and nutrition, RCTs are used to estimate the effect of the corresponding health behaviour on participation in healthy lifestyles or health and labour market outcomes. In these studies, either the participants or learning centres (i.e. school, daycare centres) are randomly assigned to control or intervention arms of the study, and the participants are followed up for a period of time to observe the differences in outcome variables.

One of the setups used for RCTs is preschool children attending early childcare centres (Binkley & Specker 2004; for a review see Hesketh & Campbel 2010; Trost et al. 2008). For instance, in a study examining the impact of physical activity and diet programmes implemented in childcare settings in the province of Saskatchewan, Canada, the centres were stratified by their location (rural and urban), and then were invited to participate in the study (Belanger et al. 2016). With the invitation, the centres were provided with details about the intervention. After receiving consent from the centres, the parents in these selected centres were also required to provide consent for their children to take part in the study. Once consent was obtained from the centres and parents, the centres were randomly assigned to both arms of the study (Belanger et al. 2016; Sari et al. 2016; Sari et al. 2019). The intervention included education and information for families and educators to actively incorporate physical activity as well as a healthy diet in the daily lives of the children, parents and educators themselves. The training sessions regarding nutrition and physical activity for educators, and daycare staff including directors and cooks were an essential component of the intervention. For centres assigned to the control arm of the study, no training sessions, support or monitoring was provided. The implementation period was between six and eight months for the corresponding year with the first phase of implementation taking place during the 2013–2014 academic year and the second over the 2015–2016 academic year. The data were collected before and after each of these time periods. Each centre in the intervention arm received the intervention only once even though the centres were constantly motivated to put into practice what they had learned during the implementation and evaluation stages. The results from this intervention show about 17 minutes/day increase in moderate-to-vigorous physical activity and 15.3 on the gross motor quotient scale for locomotor skills among children in centres located in small communities. In other centres located in cities and larger communities, there was no significant difference in outcome variables between intervention and control centres (Sari et al. 2019). These relatively weak and mixed results are somewhat similar to other studies examining the impact of physical activity and nutrition-based interventions in childcare centres (i.e. Reilly et al. 2006; Ward et al. 2008).

There are other studies assessing the impact of interventions with a specific focus on nutrition and healthy eating. These interventions were applied through the school-based lunch programmes to influence the food selection of the students. In these studies examining the impact of school-based lunch programmes, students in the same school were randomly assigned to the intervention or control arm of the study, and their food choices have been observed (i.e. Miller et al. 2016; Smith & Cunningham-Sabo 2014). In the study examining the effects of pre-ordering on fruits, vegetables and low-fat milk selections by participants of the National School Lunch Program in a Florida school, Miller et al. (2016) find that the students in the intervention group ordered significantly more fruits, vegetables and low-fat milk compared to the students in the control group.

Given the social context and potential interactions among study participants in both arms of the study, there are significant limitations of RCTs in these settings where participants in the control and intervention arms of the RCTs may have close communications (i.e. when participants in both arms are in the same school). Through communications, participants in the control group may learn from the intervention participants, and they may change their behaviour accordingly. As a result, this leads to underestimation of the intervention effect. As also indicated by Ward et al. (2008), there are factors affecting the intervention design (i.e. participants can observe their assignment status) and potential issues in the implementation of the intervention, selection and measurement of outcome variables, and timeline for the follow-up period that contribute to the shortcomings in the application of RCTs in these settings.

As widely indicated in earlier literature, most of the advantages of RCTs may not be maintained in social science experiments (Burtless 1995). While random assignment removes any systematic correlation between the intervention status and participants' observed or unobserved characteristics (also known as selection bias), it becomes difficult to maintain it following the randomisation in real-life applications. The participants, after being randomly assigned to either arm of the study, will be observing their intervention status, and therefore they may adjust their behaviour accordingly (for further discussion on blinding in RCTs and its impact on research findings, see Burtless 1995; Stolberg et al. 2004). If the participants' response differs from each other based on assignments to intervention or control arms of the study, these differences would affect the outcome variable in a way that it may not be possible to make any correction or even prediction for the direction of the bias generated from this response. Especially for the case of experiments implemented in school settings, it is likely that the students in each arm of the study will learn from each other and may adjust their health behaviour. As it is consistently shown in peer effect literature (i.e. Falk & Ichino 2006; Hoxby 2000; Sacerdote 2011), it is plausible to expect that there will be strong learning effects in these settings. As a result, observed differences in outcome variables after the intervention could capture the learning effects as well as the intervention effects. To decrease the learning effects among students within the same schools, one of the common approaches is to assign each school or daycare centre as an intervention or control group. For instance, in the study assessing the impact of physical activity and nutrition-based intervention in daycare settings in Saskatchewan, each centre was assigned to either arm of the study (Belanger et al. 2016; Sari et al. 2019). While this approach potentially eliminates the peer effects among the students, there is still anecdotal evidence suggesting that the staff and administrators in centres assigned to control groups were learning from intervention centres and potentially implementing their version of the intervention in the control centres.

RCTs are the gold standard when the design of research and implementation of the interventions are not prone to any aforementioned issues. While this is relatively straightforward and somewhat easy in biological sciences, dealing with learning effects among control and intervention group participants is very hard to achieve in social experiments including the

RCTs implemented to influence the health behaviours of the individuals. As an alternative to RCTs, there are regression-based methods developed and applied in the field of economics. They are non-experimental options and therefore provide less costly and more feasible alternatives. Given that these methods are based on observational data that are available through large-scale household surveys, they have been routinely applied in the economics of health and health behaviour. We will present these alternative methods with selected examples of applications in the following sections.

INSTRUMENTAL VARIABLE METHODS AND SELECTED APPLICATIONS

The instrumental variable (IV) approach is an empirical technique developed to estimate the causal effect of an intervention. It is one of the regression-based alternatives to overcome some of the problems of RCTs (Angrist & Pischke 2014; Angrist et al. 1996; Imbens & Rubin 2015). Given its applications using readily available observational data sets, the IV method is relatively easier to apply in examining issues in social sciences. This section presents an overview of the method and its empirical applications in the economics of health and health behaviour.

An Overview of the Instrumental Variable Methods

As explained in the previous section, the random assignment of participants to different arms of an RCT is an effective method to make sure that measured or unmeasured confounders are no different in both groups. While this is an easy target to achieve in experimental studies, confounders are not easy to control in observational studies, potentially leading to biased estimates of the intervention effect. One common source of bias is known as selection bias, which occurs when individuals with certain characteristics select themselves for a specific exposure (Heckman 1990; Lousdal 2018; Vella 1998). In the economics of health and health behaviour, there are various examples of selection bias. For instance, individuals who expect to use more healthcare services in the future are more likely to buy health insurance compared to relatively healthy people (Cutler & Zeckhauser 1998; Waters 1999). Observed differences in the use of healthcare services could be because of differences in having insurance as well as differences in unobserved healthcare needs (Manning et al. 1987; Newhouse 1993). The same kind of selection may also occur among individuals with differences in health behaviour. It is likely that participants in healthy lifestyle activities are relatively healthier than non-participants. While some of their characteristics could be observed differences, there could be unobserved differences as well. It is plausible that the participants such as those who are physically active could be disproportionally more health-conscious, motivated and following other preventive health measures. In the absence of reliable RCTs, these unobserved confounders create methodological challenges in estimating the causal effect of health behaviours. To deal with these methodological issues, the IV method has been developed in economics (Angrist & Pischke 2014; Angrist & Krueger 2001; Stock & Trebbi 2003) and employed in the context of the economics of health and health behaviour.

To illustrate an IV analysis, let us use the following regression model. This model is used in the context of observational data collected from individuals for their outcome variable (Y_i), and the exposure (treatment) variable (X_i).

$$Y_i = \alpha + \beta X_i + W_i \delta + \varepsilon_i \tag{15.2}$$

where W_i stands for all other observed characteristics, and ε_i shows the error terms for individual i. The object of interest is to estimate the causal effect of exposure (i.e. participation and/or intensity of participation in healthy behaviour) on outcome variables (health and/or labour market outcomes). As long as there is no correlation between error terms and exposure variable (i.e. $E(X_i, \varepsilon_i) = 0$), the estimated coefficient of X_i from an ordinary least square (OLS) regression analysis provides the causal effect of the exposure on outcome variables. While this assumption of independence between X_i and ε_i is maintained with the random assignment in RCTs, it is very difficult to achieve in observational studies.

There are at least three common sources in observational studies where the assumption of no correlation between error terms and the exposure variable mentioned above is violated. The first one is due to omitted variables. To deal with this issue, one could include a rich set of observable confounders (i.e. W_i in equation (15.2)) in the regression. While this approach decreases the size of bias, it is likely that there are still unobserved factors not captured with the included observable confounders. In the case of health behaviours, it is plausible to expect that the individuals participating in healthy behaviour would have differences in their observed and unobserved characteristics. As a result, these differences in unobserved characteristics (i.e. motivation and unobserved efforts to stay healthy) create a bias in the estimation of the causal effect of the exposure variable. The second source would be measurement error for the exposure variable. If the measurement error for the exposure variable and ε_i are correlated, then the independence assumption of X_i and ε_i will be violated. The third source, simultaneity bias (or reverse causality), is relatively more common in observational studies. As the exposure variable would affect the outcome variable, it is likely that the outcome variable may also impact the exposure variable, therefore leading to a simultaneity bias or reverse causality. This is a potential bias often indicated in health economics literature (Cawley 2000; Morris 2006, 2007; Norton & Han 2008; Sari & Osman 2018). While health behaviour would affect health outcomes, being healthy could also directly influences individuals' health behaviour. Therefore, the causality runs in both directions leading to a bias for the estimated coefficient from an OLS analysis.

In the field of economics, the IV approach has been used for decades to deal with the three sources of bias mentioned earlier (Angrist & Pischke 2014). To employ this method, researchers need to identify an IV (variable Z_i) that satisfies the following three conditions (Greene 2000; Rassen et al. 2009; Wooldridge 2002): the IV (i) needs to predict exposure variable, X_i (relevance assumption), (ii) only affects the outcome variable through X_i (exclusion restriction), and (iii) has no relationship with the outcome variable through a measured or unmeasured path (independence assumption). It is usually not easy to find a valid IV that satisfies these conditions. While assumption (i) is a testable hypothesis, other assumptions are not testable, therefore they need to be assumed and justified using relevant economic and social theory.

To show that the variable Z_i predicts X_i (condition i), and therefore it is valid as an IV, one can estimate equation (15.3) by regressing X_i on the IV and all other control variables. From this regression, an estimated non-zero coefficient of Z_i shows that this condition is satisfied. This needs to be tested with a t-test (or F-test if there is more than one IV) that rejects the null hypothesis of $\theta = 0$.

$$X_i = \gamma + \theta Z_i + W_i \varphi + u_i \tag{15.3}$$

This IV estimation described is commonly known as the two-stage least squares (2SLS) method. In the first stage, equation (15.3) is estimated to show that the IV is valid. After estimating equation (15.3), predicted values of X_i are computed to be used in the second stage. In the second stage, equation (15.2) will be estimated using predicted values of X_i rather than observed values of X_i. As long as assumptions (ii) and (iii) hold, the estimated coefficient $(\widehat{\beta})$ from the second stage shows the causal effect of X_i on the outcome variable.

When the exposure and outcome variables are continuous variables, 2SLS is the standard application of the IV method. However, in applications of health behaviour literature, both outcome and exposure variables could be binary variables rather than continuous variables (i.e. participation in labour market and physical activity). In these cases, researchers use IVs in the context of a bivariate regression model. In the next section, we present a few applications of both 2SLS and IV methods in the bivariate context. Detailed discussions on methodological issues on bivariate regression models and the use of IVs in bivariate context are discussed extensively in a large body of literature (see Greene 2000; Sari & Osman 2018; Wooldridge 2002), therefore these methodological discussions will not be presented in this chapter.

Applications of Instrumental Variable Methods

IV techniques have been widely used in studies that examine the impact of a healthy/unhealthy lifestyle (i.e. obesity, physical activity and smoking) on labour market outcomes (i.e. wages and/or participation in the labour market) (i.e. Cawley 2000; Morris 2006, 2007; Norton & Han 2008; Sari & Osman 2018). Various types of IVs are used in this literature ranging from genetic and biological information of the individuals to location choices and prevalence of corresponding health behaviour in the neighbourhood or regions individuals live (i.e. Morris 2006, 2007; Norton & Han 2008).

The first group of IVs explores genetic information (Burgess et al. 2013; Norton & Han 2008; Shelton Brown et al. 2005). One example is the use of these IVs in estimating the impact of obesity on labour market outcomes. Using the evidence from studies in behavioural genetics that suggest a strong genetic effect on variation in body mass index (BMI), several studies employ these variables as IVs (i.e. Norton and Han 2008; Shelton Brown et al. 2005). For instance, Norton and Han (2008) use six genes identified from the DNA samples submitted by a subset of participants in the National Longitudinal Study of Adolescent Health. Their 2SLS estimations indicate no effect of obesity on employment probability or wages.

As much as genetic information may seem to be a plausible IV, it is harder to obtain in observational data sets. Alternatively, other studies explored related concepts using relatively easy-to-find biological information about family members. Given that the family members share common genes, these studies argue that the BMI of family members (i.e. biological mother, father or siblings) is a strong predictor for individual BMI within the family. For instance, Brunello and d'Hombres (2007) use the BMI of a biological family member as an instrument for individual BMI and show that body weight has negative effects on earnings in Europe that become even stronger in Southern Europe when the authors employ subsample analysis.

In exploring the gender-based obesity effect on labour market outcomes, Cawley (2000) uses the weight of a child as an IV for the BMI of the child's mother. As also argued in other papers (i.e. Norton & Han 2008; Shelton Brown et al. 2005), these genetic variants among family members are not correlated with the labour market outcomes of the individuals. This study shows a differential effect of body weight on wages by race among women. While the study shows that weight lowers wages for white women, this negative effect is weak for Hispanic women, and there is no impact of weight on wages for black women. Similar to Norton and Han (2008), Cawley (2000) also concludes that there is no effect of weight on employment probability.

The second group of IVs explore the individuals' neighbourhood choices to live in based on their expectations of healthcare utilisation or health behaviour (Brock & Durlauf 2001, 2002; Ioannides & Zabel 2008; Manski 2000). As indicated in earlier literature, individuals may choose their place of residence based on the distance to physical fitness and activity centres and access to green spaces, parks and other recreational centres. A number of studies examining the impact of the built environment on the level of physical activity show a positive association between the availability of parks, sports facilities, playgrounds and recreational centres and the physical activity level of the individuals (Babey et al. 2008; Brownson et al. 2001; Saelens & Handy 2008; Sallis et al. 1992; Cerin & Leslie 2008; Cohen et al. 2007). There are other studies providing additional evidence to show a strong correlation between physical activity and transportation infrastructure, well-maintained sidewalks (see Limstrand 2008; Kaczynski & Henderson 2008; Kaczynski et al. 2008; Owen et al. 2004) and other factors, such as traffic noise, green space quality, land use mix and government spending on parks and recreational centres (Brownson et al. 2001; Rodriguez et al. 2006; Craig et al. 2002; Huston et al. 2003; Humphreys & Ruseski 2007; Sallis et al. 2016; Saelens et al. 2003). The overall conclusion from this body of literature indicates a positive association between a favourable built environment for physical activity and healthy lifestyles including participation in leisure time physical activity.

There are two plausible channels by which a favourable built environment (i.e. density of exercise facilities, parks and green space) encourages physical activity and healthy lifestyles (i.e. lower body weight). The first channel is that easy access to the facilities and availability of a favourable built environment creates a direct effect by reducing physical barriers associated with exercise. This is seen, for example, as a reduction in travel time cost and traffic-related stress. Consistently, some studies in economics of health behaviour use the distance to the closest sports and fitness facilities (Ruseski et al. 2014; Sari & Osman 2018) or the density of sports and physical fitness facilities within a fixed radius from an individual's residence (Brechot et al. 2017) as an IV for participation in physical activities and individual weight. For example, Brechot et al. (2017) and Ruseski et al. (2014) estimate the effect of participation in physical activity and sports on health and subjective well-being using a 2SLS regression method with a data set from Switzerland and Germany. Both studies showed that participation in sports activities increases health, well-being and happiness. In a study examining the impact of obesity on labour market participation, Sari and Osman (2018) use an IV approach in the bivariate probit regression context using various Canadian population health surveys. Their results showed that the probability of employment has a negative association with the body weight of women. Obesity decreases employment probability by about 25 percentage points for women in Canada.

There is another plausible channel for the built environment to influence healthy lifestyles. It is likely that individuals living close to the environment promoting or influencing healthy lifestyles will be more frequently observing other people with healthy lifestyles. As a result, this may strengthen the perception of healthy lifestyles being the norm (Sallis et al. 1990). If complementarities exist between the individual choice and average choices by others (i.e. increase in the marginal utility of physical activity due to an increase in other individuals' physical activity level), living close to a favourable built environment creates a boost in exercise levels and healthy lifestyles for individuals through this channel. As suggested in Bernheim (1994), these types of complementarities among individuals may lead to a convergence in homogeneous behaviour even if they have heterogeneous preferences. As expected, there could be stronger consumption complementarities among family members, therefore this effect could be even stronger among them (Sari 2021). A number of studies have been using the evidence from this line of research to determine a potential IV for individuals' health behaviour (i.e. Morris 2006, 2007; Sari & Osman 2018). For instance, prevalence of obesity and average BMI in the area where the individuals live are IVs used in studies examining the impact of obesity on labour market outcomes. The results from these studies show that obesity reduces the employment probability of women by about 21–25 percentage points (Morris 2006, 2007; Sari & Osman 2018).

As indicated in the previous section, a valid IV needs to have a strong correlation with the exposure variable (i.e. obesity) and not to have any other correlation with the outcome variable (i.e. labour market outcomes). If the IVs have a weak correlation with the exposure variable, then even a weak correlation between the IVs and the error terms leads to a large inconsistency in IV estimations (Bound et al. 1995). While the correlation between the IVs and exposure variable can be verified with a Wald test, the second and third assumptions mentioned earlier cannot be tested but need to be assumed. Due to this potential bias with the IV approach, and difficulties in finding valid IVs satisfying the assumptions mentioned earlier, an alternative approach would be to use data from natural experiments in order to estimate the causal effects of an intervention or policy change (Angrist & Pischke 2014; Card & Krueger 2015; Imbens & Rubin 2015; Rosenzweig & Wolpin 2000). This method is presented in the next section.

DIFFERENCE-IN-DIFFERENCES REGRESSION APPROACH

The difference-in-differences (DID) regression approach has been developed as an alternative to RCTs or IV methods (Angrist & Pischke 2014; Ashenfelter & Card 1985; Card 1992; Card & Krueger 1994; Card & Krueger 2015). In this section, we provide an overview of the DID method in the context of natural experiments, followed by the application of DID derived from the literature on the economics of health and health behaviour.

An Overview of the Difference-in-Differences Method

Designing an RCT or finding a valid IV is a challenge for researchers in social sciences including the economics of health and health behaviour. As an alternative, researchers commonly explore quasi-experimental settings to examine the effect of an intervention or policy change. To conduct research designed to be executed using a DID method, researchers need to identify a change in policy, practice or an intervention implemented in some jurisdictions (municipal, regional, state or provincial level) but not in other jurisdictions with similar characteristics relevant for the outcome of interest (i.e. Nuti et al. 2016). In countries with Federal systems such as in the United States or Canada, provincial or state governments may differ from each other in terms of the types and timing of policies implemented. It is likely that a policy change may take place in one province (or state) but not in another comparable province. As long as these provinces are similar in their other characteristics potentially relevant for outcome variables, one could explore the differences in outcome variables between these provinces to estimate the causal impact of a policy change on outcome variables. It is also likely that within the same province, a change in policy may be relevant for a subgroup of people but not for others (i.e. Li et al. 2014; Sari & Osman 2015). These variations in policies also provide an opportunity for researchers to estimate the effect of the policy change.

Similar to RCTs, the underlying assumption for the identification of the policy (intervention) effect is that these two groups are similar other than the fact that only one group was exposed to the policy. Random assignment of individuals to intervention and control groups in RCTs guarantees this assumption to hold, but in DID design, individuals are not assigned to either group. Instead, they just happen, for example, to be living in the corresponding province with or without the policy change. Therefore, the assumption that the outcome variable for both groups over time would be the same if there was no change in policy needs to hold. This assumption, known as a common trend assumption in the DID approach, cannot be easily testable. In some cases, if the researchers have multiple-year data prior to the policy change, then a comparison of outcome variables over time between the groups can be used to test if the common trend assumption is plausible. But otherwise, it is an assumption that needs to hold to obtain an unbiased estimated impact of the policy change (Wooldridge 2002).

To illustrate a DID model within a simple linear regression approach, assume that we have a cross-sectional individual-level data set available for two periods ($t = 0$ or 1) with a set of variables measuring outcome variable (Y) and a set of control variables (W). Suppose that a policy change (or an intervention) is implemented at the end of the first period in one of the two provinces. To indicate the timing of the policy implementation, we will use T as a binary indicator for time indicating the period prior to the policy change ($T = 0$) or the period after the policy change ($T = 1$). D_i, a binary variable, takes a value of 1 for individuals living in the province with the policy change, and it is zero for individuals who live in the other province. Using similar terms used in RCTs, $D_i = 1$ for individuals in the intervention group (for example, where the policy or law change takes place) and $D_i = 0$ for individuals in the control group (no change). We can use the following regression model to estimate the impact of the policy change:

$$Y_{it} = \alpha + \gamma D_i + \delta T + \beta D_i * T + \delta W_{it} + \varepsilon_{it} \qquad (15.4)$$

where Y_{it} indicates the outcome variable for individual i at time t. The coefficient of the interaction term between D_i and T will show the impact of the policy change on the corresponding outcome variable. To increase the precision of the estimated effect and control for any observable differences between groups, we include W_{it}, a vector of control variables, in the regression model above (for discussion on further details on methodological issues see Angrist & Pischke 2014; Bertrand et al. 2004; Conley & Taber 2011; Lechner 2010). The last term on the right-hand side of the model (ε_{it}) is the error term. As long as both groups have similar characteristics (i.e. socio-economic, demographic factors) at the baseline (prior to the policy change, t = 0), and the trends in outcome variables for both intervention and control groups would be the same in the absence of the intervention (both groups would be affected by time-varying confounding variables in a similar way), estimated coefficient $\left(\widehat{\beta}\right)$ will show the effect of the intervention.

Selected Applications of Difference-in-Differences Methods

Following earlier papers using DID methods in labour economics (i.e. Ashenfelter 1978; Ashenfelter & Card 1985; Card & Krueger 1994), similar methods have been applied in other subfields in economics including health economics and economics of health behaviour (i.e. Carpenter & Dobkin 2011; Del Bono & Vuri 2018; Li et al. 2014; Nelson 2015; Page et al. 2012). In health economics applications of DID methods, various policy changes affecting the reimbursement of the physicians, the impact of specific education campaigns for patients, policy changes in relation to indoor smoking regulations or tax incentives for certain kinds of health behaviour have been studied.

In a recent study examining the impact of the pay for performance (P4P) programme on primary care services provided by physicians, Li et al. (2014) explore a policy change in P4P in Ontario, Canada. This policy change did not affect all physicians in the province since participation in the programme was voluntary. While some physicians were not eligible (control physicians) to participate (i.e. physicians in traditional fee-for-service practices), all other physicians in primary care reform practices were eligible (intervention physicians). Therefore, the study explores variations in primary care services provided by each physician group (with and without the policy change) to estimate the impact of P4P. The authors concluded that physicians' response to the policy is modest and their response changes based on the types of services provided (a modest improvement in Pap smears, mammograms, senior flu shots and colorectal cancer screenings, but no impact on toddler immunisations).

Other studies used DID approach to estimate the impact of smoking ban policies on foetal outcomes and maternal smoking (i.e. Page et al. 2012) and smoking prevalence (i.e. Del Bono & Vuri 2018). As discussed in the earlier section, these studies explore natural experiments in order to identify intervention and control subjects based on their locations, or period of data collection. In Page et al. 2012, two sites are used to identify intervention (Pueblo, Colorado) and control (El Paso County) groups. This study showed that the odds of maternal smoking and preterm births were significantly lower among the intervention group compared to the control group. Del Bono and Vuri (2018), however, use a combination of the period before and after the bar policies implemented in Italy, and the interview months. By teasing out the seasonal variation in smoking rates, they showed that the smoking ban in Italy had no impact on smoking behaviour for the overall population but only had an impact on some subgroups.

There are other studies using a DID approach but with a somewhat different approach. For instance, instead of natural experiments, these studies exploit interventions specifically designed for and implemented for a group of individuals (i.e. Diamond & Chapman 2001; Sari & Osman 2015). During the design and implementation of the intervention, it is likely that a control group may not be identified. In these cases, researchers could use alternative techniques to generate a control group, and then employ a DID approach to estimate the intervention effect. For instance, in a recent study, Sari and Osman (2015) examine the impact of an intervention (effective and high-quality asthma and COPD education for both patients and healthcare professionals and spirometry use) implemented by the Lung Association of Saskatchewan on medication use among asthma and COPD patients. When this intervention was implemented, the Lung Association followed up and collected data from intervention patients but there was no control group identified. To deal with this issue Sari and Osman (2015) applied a propensity score (PS) matching strategy to identify a control group (see also Lechner & Sari 2015). The purpose of PS matching was to identify similar groups of participants (i.e. control and intervention) in terms of their characteristics that would be relevant to the outcome variables (see Imbens & Rubin 2015; Rosenbaum & Rubin 1983 for details on PS matching). After creating the control group, and using existing administrative databases Sari and Osman (2015) employed a DID approach to estimate the impact of this intervention. While this study uses PS matching to generate a control group, there are other studies using matching to estimate the impact of a policy or an exposure variable. The details of this alternative approach are beyond the scope of this chapter and can be found in other studies (i.e. Imbens & Rubin 2015; Rosenbaum & Rubin 1983; Dehejia & Wahba 2002; Caliendo & Kopeinig 2008).

CONCLUSION

In an effort to estimate the causal effect of an intervention or policy change, there has been a growing interest in developing and applying various empirical methods in social sciences including in economics of health and health behaviour. This chapter presented a review of the three main methodological developments relevant to the field of economics of health and health behaviour. After providing an overview of the corresponding empirical techniques, the challenges and applications of each method and examples from the literature were discussed for each of the methods.

As discussed in the second section, RCTs are commonly applied in biological sciences but their applications in social sciences are relatively rare due to difficulties in applying large-scale social experiments, ethical issues or the financial burden of these experiments. While conducting social experiments and collecting experimental data are not always feasible for issues relevant to social sciences, observational data sets are routinely collected through large-scale household surveys covering various topics relevant to the economics of health and health behaviour. As a result, regression-based techniques utilising secondary data sets have been standard alternatives to RCTs. During the last few decades, IV and DID regression analyses have been developed and applied in economics to estimate the causal effect of an intervention or a change in policy.

As discussed in this chapter, these methods offer easier alternatives to RCTs, but each method depends on a set of restricting assumptions. The IV and DID methods are easier to apply as they generally use readily available secondary data sets. However, their reliability in estimating the intervention effects depends on the validity of the corresponding assumptions imposed in each method. Some of these assumptions are not easily testable; therefore, any violations of these restricting assumptions could lead to even greater bias in the estimated intervention effects. Researchers applying these alternatives need to evaluate the specific circumstances and conduct sensitivity analysis to minimise the bias or to identify the direction of the bias, if there is any, in estimated coefficients. The readers of this literature should consider these potential empirical limitations when making inferences based on estimated intervention effects provided in studies examining intervention effects relevant to the economics of health and health behaviour.

REFERENCES

Abadie, A. (2005). Semiparametric difference-in-differences estimators. *The Review of Economic Studies*, 72(1), 1–19.
Angrist, J. D., Pischke, J. S. (2014). *Mastering Metrics: The Path from Cause to Effect*. Princeton University Press.
Angrist, J. D., Krueger, A. B. (2001). Instrumental variables and the search for identification: From supply and demand to natural experiments. *Journal of Economic Perspectives*, 15(4), 69–85.
Angrist, J. D., Imbens, G. W., Rubin, D. B. (1996). Identification of causal effects using instrumental variables. *Journal of the American Statistical Association*, 91(434), 444–455.

Ashenfelter, O. (1978). Estimating the effect of training programs on earnings. *The Review of Economics and Statistics, 60*(1), 47–57.

Ashenfelter, O., Card, D. (1985). Using the longitudinal structure of earnings to estimate the effect of training programs. *The Review of Economics and Statistics, 67,* 648–660.

Babey, S. H., Hastert, T. A., Yu, H., Brown, E. R. (2008). Physical activity among adolescents: When do parks matter? *American Journal of Preventive Medicine, 34*(4), 345–348.

Bélanger, M., Humbert, L., Vatanparast, H., Ward, S., Muhajarine, N., Chow, A. F., Leis, A. (2016). A multilevel intervention to increase physical activity and improve healthy eating and physical literacy among young children (ages 3-5) attending early childcare centres: The Healthy Start-Départ Santé cluster randomised controlled trial study protocol. *BMC Public Health, 16*(313), 1–10.

Bernheim, B. D. (1994). A theory of conformity. *Journal of Political Economy, 102*(5), 841–877.

Bertrand, M., Duflo, E., Mullainathan, S. (2004). How much should we trust differences-in-differences estimates? *The Quarterly Journal of Economics, 119*(1), 249–275.

Binkley, T., Specker, B. (2004). Increased periosteal circumference remains present 12 months after an exercise intervention in preschool children. *Bone, 35*(6), 1383–1388.

Bound, J., Jaeger, A. D., Baker, M. R. (1995). Problems with instrumental variables estimation when the correlation between the instruments and the endogenous explanatory variables is weak. *American Statistical Association, 90*(450), 443–450.

Brechot, M., Nüesch, S., Franck, E. (2017). Does sports activity improve health? Representative evidence using local density of sports facilities as an instrument. *Applied Economics, 49*(48), 4871–4884.

Brock, W. A., Durlauf, S. N. (2001). Discrete choice with social interactions. *The Review of Economic Studies, 68*(2), 235–260.

Brock, W. A., Durlauf, S. N. (2002). A multinomial-choice model of neighborhood effects. *American Economic Review, 92*(2), 298–303.

Brownson, R. C., Baker, E. A., Housemann, R. A., Brennan, L. K., Bacak, S. J. (2001). Environmental and policy determinants of physical activity in the United States. *American Journal of Public Health, 91*(12), 1995–2003.

Brunello, G., d'Hombres, B. (2007). Does body weight affect wages?: Evidence from Europe. *Economics & Human Biology, 5*(1), 1–19.

Burgess, S., Butterworth, A., Thompson, S. G. (2013). Mendelian randomization analysis with multiple genetic variants using summarized data. *Genetic Epidemiology, 37*(7), 658–665.

Burtless, G. (1995). The case for randomized field trials in economic and policy research. *Journal of Economic Perspectives, 9*(2), 63–84.

Caliendo, M., Kopeinig, S. (2008). Some practical guidance for the implementation of propensity score matching. *Journal of Economic Surveys, 22*(1), 31–72.

Card, D. (1992). Using regional variation in wages to measure the effects of the federal minimum wage. *Ilr Review, 46*(1), 22–37.

Card, D., Krueger, A. B. (1994), Minimum wages and employment: A case study of the fast-food industry in New Jersey and Pennsylvania. *American Economic Review, 84,* 772–793.

Card, D., Krueger, A. B. (2015). *Myth and Measurement: The New Economics of the Minimum Wage-Twentieth-Anniversary Edition.* Princeton: Princeton University Press.

Carpenter, C., Dobkin, C. (2011). The minimum legal drinking age and public health. *Journal of Economic Perspectives, 25*(2), 133–156.

Cawley, J. (2000). Body weight and women's labor market outcomes. *National Bureau of Economic Research. Working paper # 7841.*

Chaloupka, F. J., Warner, K. E. (2000). The economics of smoking. In A. Culyer, J. Newhouse (Eds.), *The Handbook of Health Economics.* Amsterdam: Elsevier, pp. 1541–1612.

Cohen, D. A., McKenzie, T. L., Sehgal, A., Williamson, S., Golinelli, D., Lurie, N. (2007). Contribution of public parks to physical activity. *American Journal of Public Health, 97*(3), 509–514.

Conley, T. G., Taber, C. R. (2011). Inference with "difference in differences" with a small number of policy changes. *The Review of Economics and Statistics, 93*(1), 113–125.

Craig, C. L., Brownson, R. C., Cragg, S. E., Dunn, A. L. (2002). Exploring the effect of the environment on physical activity: A study examining walking to work. *American Journal of Preventive Medicine, 23*(2), 36–43.

Cutler, D. M., Zeckhauser, R. J. (1998). Adverse selection in health insurance. *Forum for Health Economics & Policy,* 1(1): doi.org/10.2202/1558-9544.1056

Dehejia, R. H., Wahba, S. (2002). Propensity score-matching methods for nonexperimental causal studies. *The Review of Economics and Statistics*, *84*(1), 151–161.

Del Bono, E., Vuri, D. (2018). Smoking behaviour and individual well-being: A fresh look at the effects of the 2005 public smoking ban in Italy. *Oxford Economic Papers*, *70*(3), 741–762.

Diamond, S. A., Chapman, K. R. (2001). The impact of nationally coordinated pharmacy-based asthma education intervention. *Canadian Respiratory Journal*, *8*(4), 261–265.

Ding, P., Li, F. (2018). Causal inference: A missing data perspective. *Statistical Science*, *33*(2), 214–237.

Falk, A., Ichino, A. (2006). Clean evidence on peer effects. *Journal of Labor Economics*, *24*(1), 39–57.

Greene, W. H. (2000). *Econometric Analysis*. Upper Saddle River: Prentice Hall Inc.

Heckman, J. (1990). Varieties of selection bias. *American Economic Review*, *80*(2), 313–318.

Hesketh, K. D., Campbell, K. J. (2010). Interventions to prevent obesity in 0–5 year olds: An updated systematic review of the literature. *Obesity*, *18*(S1), S27–S35.

Hoxby, C. M. (2000). Peer effects in the classroom: Learning from gender and race variation. *NBER Working Papers, No: 7867*.

Humphreys, B. R., Ruseski, J. E. (2007). Participation in physical activity and government spending on parks and recreation. *Contemporary Economic Policy*, 25, 538–552.

Humphreys, B. R., McLeod, L., Ruseski, J. E. (2014). Physical activity and health outcomes: Evidence from Canada. *Health Economics*, *23*(1), 33–54.

Huston, S. L., Evenson, K. R., Bors, P., Gizlice, Z. (2003). Neighborhood environment, access to places for activity, and leisure-time physical activity in a diverse North Carolina population. *American Journal of Health Promotion*, *18*(1), 58–69.

Imbens, G. W., Rubin, D. B. (2015). *Causal Inference in Statistics, Social, and Biomedical Sciences*. Cambridge: Cambridge University Press.

Ioannides, Y. M., Zabel, J. E. (2008). Interactions, neighborhood selection and housing demand. *Journal of Urban Economics*, *63*(1), 229–252.

Kaczynski, A. T., Henderson, K. A. (2008). Parks and recreation settings and active living: A review of associations with physical activity function and intensity. *Journal of Physical Activity & Health*, *5*(4), 619–632.

Kaczynski, A. T., Potwarka, L. R., Saelens, B. E. (2008). Association of park size, distance, and features with physical activity in neighborhood parks. *American Journal of Public Health*, *98*(8), 1451–1456.

Li, J., Hurley, J., DeCicca, P., Buckley, G. (2014). Physician response to pay-for-performance: Evidence from a natural experiment. *Health Economics*, *23*(8), 962–978.

Lechner, M. (2010). The estimation of causal effects by difference-in-difference methods. *Foundations and Trends in Econometrics*, *4*(3), 165–224.

Lechner, M. (2009). Long-run labour market and health effects of individual sports activities. *Journal of Health Economics*, 28, 839–854.

Lechner, M., Sari, N. (2015). Labor market effects of sports and exercise: Evidence from Canadian panel data. *Labour Economics*, 35, 1–15.

Limstrand T. (2008). Environmental characteristics relevant to young people's use of sports facilities: A review. *Scandinavian Journal of Medicine & Science in Sports*, *18*(3): 275–287.

Lousdal, M. L. (2018). An introduction to instrumental variable assumptions, validation and estimation. *Emerging Themes in Epidemiology*, *15*(1), 1–7.

Manning, W. G., Newhouse, J. P., Duan, N., Keeler, E. B., Leibowitz, A. (1987). Health insurance and the demand for medical care: Evidence from a randomized experiment. *American Economic Review*, *77*(3), 251–277.

Manski, C. F. (2000). Economic analysis of social interactions. *Journal of Economic Perspectives*, *14*(3), 115–136.

Miller, G. F., Gupta, S., Kropp, J. D., Grogan, K. A., Mathews, A. (2016). The effects of pre-ordering and behavioral nudges on National School Lunch Program participants' food item selection. *Journal of Economic Psychology*, 55, 4–16.

Morris, S. (2006). Body mass index and occupational attainment. *Journal of Health Economics*, *25*(2), 347–364.

Morris, S. (2007). The impact of obesity on employment. *Labour Economics*, 14, 413–433.

Nelson, J. P. (2015). Binge drinking and alcohol prices: A systematic review of age-related results from econometric studies, natural experiments and field studies. *Health Economics Review*, *5*(1), 1–13.

Newhouse, J. P. (1993). *Free for All?: Lessons from the RAND Health Insurance Experiment* (Vol. 172). Cambridge, MA: Harvard University Press.

Norton, E. C., Han, E. (2008). Genetic information, obesity, and labor market outcomes. *Health Economics, 17*(9), 1089–1104.

Nuti, S., Vola, F., Bonini, A., Vainieri, M. (2016). Making governance work in the health care sector: Evidence from a natural experiment in Italy. *Health Economics, Policy and Law, 11*(1), 17–38.

Owen, N., Humpel, E., Leslie, A., Bauman, J. F., Sallis, J. F. (2004). Understanding environmental influences on walking: Review and research agenda. *American Journal of Preventive Medicine, 27*(1), 67–76.

Page, R. L., Slejko, J. F., Libby, A. M. (2012). A citywide smoking ban reduced maternal smoking and risk for preterm births: A Colorado natural experiment. *Journal of Women's Health, 21*(6), 621–627.

Raglin, J. S. (1990). Exercise and mental health. *Sports Medicine, 9*(6), 323–329.

Rassen, J. A., Brookhart, M. A., Glynn, R. J., Mittleman, M. A., Schneeweiss, S. (2009). Instrumental variables I: Instrumental variables exploit natural variation in nonexperimental data to estimate causal relationships. *Journal of Clinical Epidemiology, 62*(12), 1226–1232.

Reilly, J. J., Kelly, L., Montgomery, C., Williamson, A., Fisher, A., McColl, J. H., Conte, R. L., Paton, J. Y., Grant, S. (2006). Physical activity to prevent obesity in young children: Cluster randomised controlled trial. *BMJ, 333*(7577), 1041.

Rodriguez, D. A., Khattak, A. J., Evenson, K. R. (2006). Can new urbanism encourage physical activity?: Comparing a new Urbanist neighborhood with conventional suburbs. *Journal of the American Planning Association, 72*(1): 43–54.

Rosenbaum, P. R., Rubin, D. B. (1983). The central role of the propensity score in observational studies for causal effects. *Biometrika, 70*(1), 41–55.

Rosenzweig, M. R., Wolpin, K. I. (2000). Natural "natural experiments" in economics. *Journal of Economic Literature, 38*(4), 827–874.

Ruseski, J. E., Humphreys, B. R., Hallman, K., Wicker, P., Breuer, C. (2014). Sport participation and subjective well-being: Instrumental variable results from German survey data. *Journal of Physical Activity and Health, 11*(2), 396–403.

Sacerdote, B. (2011). Peer effects in education: How might they work, how big are they and how much do we know thus far?. In E. A. Hanushek, S. Machin, L. Woessmann (Eds), *Handbook of the Economics of Education* (Vol. 3, pp. 249–277). Amsterdam: Elsevier.

Saelens, B. E., Sallis, J. F., Frank, L. D. (2003). Environmental correlates of walking and cycling: Findings from the transportation, urban design, and planning literatures. *Annals of Behavioral Medicine, 25*(2): 80–91.

Saelens, B. E., Handy, S. L. (2008). Built environment correlates of walking: A review. *Medicine and Science in Sports and Exercise, 40*(7 Suppl): S550–S566.

Sallis, J. F., Hovell, M. F., Hofstetter, C. R., Elder, J. P., Hackley, M., Caspersen, C. J., Powell, K. E. (1990). Distance between homes and exercise facilities related to frequency of exercise among San Diego residents. *Public Health Reports, 105*(2), 179–185.

Sallis, J. F., Hovell, M. F., Hofstetter, C. R. (1992). Predictors of adoption and maintenance of vigorous physical activity in men and women. *Preventive Medicine, 21*(2), 237–251.

Sari, N. (2013). On anti-smoking regulations and tobacco consumption. *Journal of Socio-Economics, 43*, 60–67.

Sari, N. (2021). Socio-economic and demographic correlates of sports participation in Canada. In H. Altman, M. Altman, B. Torgler (Eds), *Behavioural Sports Economics: A Research Companion*. Abingdon, UK: Routledge (Taylor & Francis Group), Chapter 17 (in press).

Sari, N., Muhajarine, N., Froehlich Chow, A. (2016). The SK/NB Healthy Start-Départ Santé intervention: Implementation cost estimates of a physical activity and healthy eating intervention in early learning centers. *BMC Health Services Research, 17*(57) 1–14.

Sari N., Sakyi, G., Frimpong, F. (2019). A social return on investment analysis for the Saskatchewan/New Brunswick Healthy Start/Départ Santé intervention. Final report to the Public Health Agency of Canada.

Sari, N., Osmar, B. A. (2018). The effect of body weight on employment among Canadian women: Evidence from Canadian data. *Canadian Journal of Public Health, 109*(5), 873–881.

Sari, N., Osman, M. (2015). The effects of patient education programs on medication use among asthma and COPD patients: A propensity score matching with a difference-in-difference regression approach. *BMC Health Services Research*, *15*(1), 1–9.

Sari, N., Lechner, M. (2015). Long-run health effects of sports and exercise in Canada. *CCHE/ CCES Working Paper* No. 150018. Toronto, ON: Canadian Centre for Health Economics.

Shelton Brown III, H., Pagán, J. A., Bastida, E. (2005). The impact of diabetes on employment: Genetic IVs in a bivariate probit. *Health Economics*, *14*(5), 537–544.

Smith, S. L., Cunningham-Sabo, L. (2014). Food choice, plate waste and nutrient intake of elementary- and middle-school students participating in the US National School Lunch Program. *Public Health Nutrition*, *17*(6), 1255–1263.

Spence, J. C., Holt, N. L., Dutove, J. K., Carson, V. (2010). Uptake and effectiveness of the children's fitness tax credit in Canada: The rich get richer. *BMC Public Health*, *10*(1), 1–6.

Stock, J. H., Trebbi, F. (2003). Retrospectives: Who invented instrumental variable regression? *Journal of Economic Perspectives*, *17*(3), 177–194.

Stolberg, H. O., Norman, G., Trop, I. (2004). Fundamentals of clinical research for radiologists. *AJR*, *183*, 1539–1544.

Trost, S. G., Fees, B., Dzewaltowski, D. (2008). Feasibility and efficacy of a "move and learn" physical activity curriculum in preschool children. *Journal of Physical Activity and Health*, *5*(1), 88–103.

Twisk, J. W., De Vente, W. (2008). The analysis of randomised controlled trial data with more than one follow-up measurement. A comparison between different approaches. *European Journal of Epidemiology*, *23*(10), 655–660.

Vella, F. (1998). Estimating models with sample selection bias: A survey. *Journal of Human Resources*, *33*(1), 127–169.

Ward, D. S., Benjamin, S. E., Ammerman, A. S., Ball, S. C., Neelon, B. H., Bangdiwala, S. I. (2008). Nutrition and physical activity in child care: Results from an environmental intervention. *American Journal of Preventive Medicine*, *35*(4), 352–356.

Waters, H. R. (1999). Measuring the impact of health insurance with a correction for selection bias – a case study of Ecuador. *Health Economics*, *8*(5), 473–483.

Wooldridge, J. M. (2002). *Econometric Analysis of Cross-Section and Panel Data*. Cambridge, MA: MIT Press.

16. The behavioural impact of pandemics: Incomplete markets and the supply chain
David A. Savage and Derek Friday

Disaster planning is only as good as the assumptions it is based upon.

(Auf der Heide 2004, p. 340)

INTRODUCTION

Most natural disasters are calamitous because of their unexpected occurrence or rapid onset, but COVID-19 was more akin to an invisible slow-speed tsunami where the only real evidence of its passing was the wave of casualties after it had hit. And like most modern events, this was live-streamed around the world, across news and social media platforms, to the point that most people knew exactly where the virus was, including a live infection and fatality counter. However, this also meant that individuals could see the impact of the disaster elsewhere and gain a sense of what might be coming; it was not if COVID would arrive, but when, and with it issues such as lockdowns, potential shortages and travel restrictions. And unlike a 'normal' disaster, the foreshadowing of the COVID-19 pandemic enabled many people to prepare for the eventuality rather than react to it afterwards. While this may seem like a fairly unimportant difference, what it did do was trigger consumer behaviour labelled as 'panic buying' and the eventual stockouts[1] of a limited number of product lines in supermarkets.

One of the most unusual things about the COVID-19 pandemic (2020) was that even with widespread media coverage and early foreshadowing of what was likely to come, it somehow still managed to catch the world completely unprepared for its impacts on markets. It highlighted that in our very interconnected world this pandemic exposed a much more complex relationship between supply and demand than what is traditionally included in our thinking. The pandemic exposed two fundamental flaws: in the way economists think about markets and in the way that international supply chains operate. Firstly, the economic problem came about due to the assumptions economists make when we abstract and simplify our models; generally speaking, we assumed an automated (instantaneous) transfer from manufacturer or producer to market. This is not to imply that we were unaware of its existence, as there is a whole stream of economic and supply chain literature dedicated to that exact phenomenon. However, behavioural economists have focused their attention on the demand side, i.e., the choices and behaviour of the consumers, but have mostly left alone the behavioural aspects of the manufacturer and their suppliers/contractors. More importantly, economists have not explored the way in which behavioural biases impact the supply side or examined the modelling from a behavioural viewpoint.

Secondly, the supply chain problem was known to economists as they had made this one before: the lack of humans in a system attempting to predict human needs! Supply chain systems had become so good at understanding exactly how to move, stock and monitor goods that we forgot that the ultimate end goal was a human, a consumer, an individual whose choices and preferences make up the demand function. This should of course sound very familiar to economists and those who work in finance. For decades, macroeconomic theory omitted humans and relied on just so (or as-if) models (Friedman 1953)[2] that assumed completely rational human behaviour – which included stable preferences, transitivity and of course total self-interest (in short, the *Homo economicus*). The Global Financial Crisis (GFC) is a good example of what happens to long-running 'stable' markets when they are hit with a shock event and humans are not included in the modelling.[3] The 2019–2020 COVID-19 pandemic made it painfully clear that these shortcomings could not continue and that as a discipline behavioural economics needed to rethink our role in understanding areas not traditionally thought of as economics – this includes disasters and supply chains.

While there are usually copious amounts of analyses regarding *what* happened during any particular disaster event (i.e., outcomes of actions), what is often lacking is a detailed discussion regarding *why* those outcomes or actions occurred. This is where behavioural economics has been able to make major contributions to the disaster literature in recent years (Frey, Savage and Torgler 2010a; Chan et al. 2020b; Savage 2019). Rather than the simplistic abstract models we are used to running, we need to adopt more complexity in order to understand the behavioural factors behind the unanticipated demand shocks resulting in stockouts. In line with this, we explore the conceptual relationship between human behaviour and the market/supply chain problems exposed by the COVID-19 pandemic which were driven by so-called 'panic buying' and resulted in stockouts in numerous countries around the world. This is done using the same approach outlined in Savage (2019) and viewed through a lens of complex systems to link individuals and group behaviours to demand, supply and the supply chain side problems caused by the pandemic. In order to accomplish this, the chapter is divided into five main sections, as follows: i) an overview of complex systems and how they could be used to map the pandemic behaviour; ii) a discussion of the factors impacting individual decision-makers; iii) a discussion of the feedback and factors that impact groups and other decision-makers; iv) a discussion of the supply chain factors that impacted supply; and v) an economic view of the market failures and stockouts. The chapter concludes with a discussion of potential solutions and ways in which insights from behavioural economics could assist supply chain modelling in the future.

COMPLEX SYSTEMS AND PANDEMIC BEHAVIOUR

In recent years a broad range of disaster-related disciplines (from social sciences to health) have begun to realise that simple models and the one-size-fits-all solutions are no longer sufficient to deal with the complexities that exist within the context of disasters (O'Sullivan et al. 2013; Bergström, Uhr, and Frykmer 2016). Meanwhile, a more than substantial amount of evidence has been generated that suggests motives other than self-interest, such as altruism, fairness and morality, have a profound effect on the behaviour of individuals.[4] Experiments have shown that strategic incentives may be critical to understanding whether self-regarding or other-regarding preferences dominate (Camerer and Fehr 2006). When it comes to disaster (or pandemic) behaviour, individuals are capable of both *other-regarding unselfish-type behaviours* as well as the *more self-interested type of actions*. One of these strategic incentives that could cause a switch in individual behaviour from other- to self-regarding is likely to include access to or the lack of resources, which could include food and medical supplies, among other goods. Research has shown how actual behaviour and outcomes regularly deviate from our simplified models that have long been the workhorses of economics (e.g., *Homo economicus*). However, the strength of these models is also their major weakness (simplicity). While the models have been easy to apply and thus easy to gain insights and predictions, deviations and flaws in everyday situations can become major problems in extreme or unusual ones (e.g., Black Swan events, disasters and pandemics). Savage (2019, p. 773) highlighted the need for more complexity in our models in order to understand behaviour in disasters (pandemics) as the 'explanatory power limit of simple models has been reached, as they are no longer sufficient in explaining behaviour and often lead to erroneous or invalid predictions'. Our models would be more aligned with what we observe in the real world if we included interactions between multiple entities and then provided them with the ability to deliver feedback, engage in learning and adapt to changes (just as most humans do when presented with new information). In line with this, it would be important to begin exploring the links between individual characteristics of the changes in environments and the impact on consumer behaviours, resulting in how they would impact markets through the supply chain. However, it is possible to overcome many limitations by building behavioural models based on complex adaptive systems (CAS) that could include the interaction between distinct elements such as individuals, groups, consumer behaviour and the supply chain systems.

One of the earliest economic proponents of CAS was Hayek (1967) who described the four major attributes 1) it consists of a set of elements which are related to each other in a specific way; 2) the whole has properties which are different than those found in its individual parts (i.e., when viewed in isolation); 3) these properties are difficult to predict from knowledge of the elements; 4) it is an evolutionarily adaptive process which is able to adjust to its own environment. In line with this, individual and group behaviours are linked to consumption choices and ultimately to *demand*, while on the other end of the system we can link the producers and the supply chain system to the market and *supply*. Unlike the assumptions of simpler models, elements in a CAS model are structured such that the properties of the whole and the elements can be different, i.e., the total does not need to be the sum of the parts. Specifically, the properties of an individual are not the same as those of the whole system, and the overall properties are different from the elements.[5] Additionally, such a system is adaptive so it can adjust to environmental changes such that individuals and groups can change their behaviour in response to changes in the system around them. There is already a strong theoretical foundation supporting the separate parts of CAS such as agent-based modelling (Bonabeau 2002; Miller and Page 2007), feedback loops (Sterman 1994) and network theory (Newman 2010; Newman, Barabási, and Watts 2006) with extended concepts from economics and game theory. Additionally, CAS can achieve something that has been virtually impossible in traditional economic models – it can include micro-specification to explore the evolution of individual behavioural characteristics based on predefined (local) channels or rules (bottom-up approach) while still observing the macro-structure and the supply and demand system implications (Railsback and Grimm 2012).

What's more, it includes a temporal aspect which gives the system the time required to attain equilibrium or observe out-of-equilibrium dynamics (e.g., the long-lived transient behaviours suggested by Epstein (2006, p. 23)).[6] Figure 16.1 presents a stylised overview of a CAS model that links together the various aspects which will be discussed in more detail in the following sections.

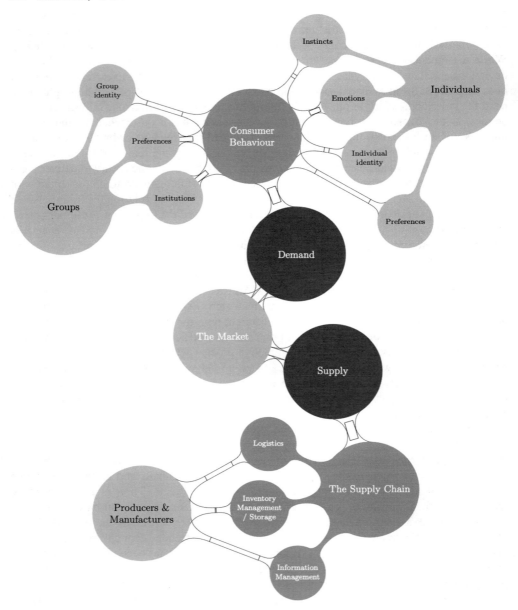

Figure 16.1   Conceptual model – a stylised overview of how a complex adaptive systems model links together the various aspects

BEHAVIOUR AND DECISION-MAKING

Until recently a disproportionate amount of research concentrated on what decisions individuals make but not on why they do so, which can be the difference between life and death in environments (Savage 2016a: 2016b) characterised by high risk, conflict or disasters (pandemics). Understanding why allows researchers to decouple the behaviour being observed from the context, enabling the decision-making to be separated from the environment making results more generalisable. The decision-making of individuals can be influenced by a range of factors – either separately or interactively – which can include (but are not limited to) emotions, instincts, identity, preferences and knowledge (see Figure 16.2). Many of these individual-level factors form the basis of group behaviour and decision-making and have a symbiotic feedback system between them. While obvious and tautological, a group is made up of a number of individuals, and a number of individuals make up a group. This is represented in Figure 16.1 in an abstract way via consumer behaviour, such that identity and preferences are in a constant feedback loop between the individual and the group. The stylised depiction

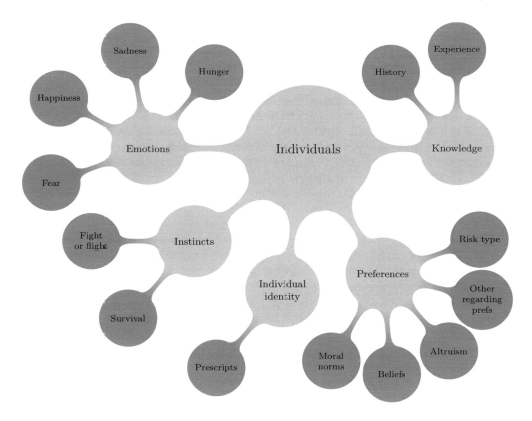

Source: Savage 2019, p. 5.

Figure 16.2   Factors influencing the decision-making of individuals – either separately or interactively

in Figure 16.2 is only supplied to demonstrate how complex relationships exist and is not a conclusive all-inclusive model, as there exists a range of other factors that influence individual behaviour and are not included. The following section explores some of these aspects in more detail and discusses how they are relevant to human (consumer) behaviour.

There is a plethora of behavioural economics research identifying that emotions, experience, identity and preferences[7] impact decision-making and behaviour and that they are neither isolated nor independent of each other as single- or bi-directional linkages and feedback loops are present. This is in line with Kahneman (2011) who believed that the decision-maker has knowledge about their world but is constrained (by intuition, emotion and physiological factors) when acting on this knowledge. If we extend this to include Bayesian updating then decision-makers are acting much more realistically as they actively update their knowledge of the world, along with their preferences and decision-making processes in context to the changes (e.g., a looming disaster).

Humans (even economists) are social animals, capable of handling a lot of different stresses, but we do not like being isolated and alone whilst doing so – there are a few true hermits in society but are considered to be very much a minority. Being forced into social isolation (even in small family groups) goes against our nature and being isolated during these types of events only increases our stress (Mawson 2005). Long periods of high stress have a detrimental impact on our mental and physical health (Cannon 1929a, 1929b, 1935; Seyle 1936), which is an accurate description of social isolation and lockdown policies[8] widely implemented in 2020. The complex interaction of our biological, psychological, social, emotional and (boundedly) rational selves has adapted over millennia to increase survival fitness and guided human reasoning and decision-making (Lawrence and Nohria 2002). However, along with the adaptions that increased our survival fitness, we have also inherited a few other instinctual behaviours and biases that do not often serve us that well in the modern era. Unfortunately, this includes a strong preference for leaving things as they currently are or a status quo bias, i.e., we don't like change even if what we are currently doing is not the best choice (Thaler and Sunstein 2008). Our modern lives have included very public habitual activities, whether it be going to work, shopping, the weekend markets, clubbing or gym attendance, and like all habits, they can be very difficult to break or deviate from.[9]

Unlike most other natural disasters (e.g., fires or floods), a pandemic does not have clear lines of infection or impact; this fundamental difference has a direct impact on uncertainty, as the more random that transmission appears to be, the greater the levels of uncertainty it generates. Risk, perception and uncertainty are key factors driving our decision-making and risk is little more than the probability of something occurring – or to be more precise, it entails complete probabilistic knowledge, knowing the probability of something occurring and then choosing what action to take. Furthermore, humans are boundedly rational, as we have serious limits on our ability to make complex decisions and limits on the amount of information we are able to access and process. We have a poor innate grasp of statistics and probabilities, especially if they do not follow linear patterns or well-known functional forms. Our risk attitudes play an important role in decision-making as research has shown that risk aversion can result in the overweighting of risk factors and risk seeking can result in the underweighting of risk (Charness, Gneezy and Imas 2013; Kahneman and Tversky 1992; Pratt 1964; Rabin 2000; Wakker 2010). Additionally, the pandemic was something outside the experience of nearly all individuals,[10] such that it created an ambiguity problem, as people couldn't infer any subjective probability of risk – that is, they do not have sufficient information about the problem to even guess as to the range or probabilistic nature of the risk being faced.[11] However, our risk preferences and attitudes are not static but can be impacted by other factors such as our identity, social norms, perceptions and our experience generating second- or third-order feedback loops inside individual decision-making.

We have a societal problem where most public policy related to disasters or pandemics remains based on the belief that the public is prone to panic or mass panic (Mawson 2005). Individual panic is actually rare as four conditions must be present for it to occur: 1) victims perceive an immediate threat of entrapment; 2) the escape routes appear to be rapidly closing; 3) flight seems the only way to survive; and 4) no one is available to help/no help is coming (Auf der Heide 2004). Additionally, in order for group panic to occur, access to escape routes needs to be either closing or very limited and major physical danger needs to be present (imminent) as well as the previous conditions (Mawson 2005). As such, the probability of all four conditions being present for panic to occur in individuals and/or the six for groups is highly unlikely (not impossible, just very rare). Even though the long-held misconception of panic has been empirically refuted (e.g., Frey, Savage and Torgler 2010), it is still commonly believed that hysteria or uncontrolled emotion, such as fear,[12] results in uncontrollable behaviour or random actions.

The fear of contracting the virus during a pandemic and the risk of it occurring should not be conflated, especially as the invisible nature of the COVID-19 pandemic was such that individuals would have been unable to use local transmission (infection) rates as a proximity guide or to the level of threat it posed. Calculating the probability of risk is not the same as how we perceive it, and humans use less accurate heuristics to make judgements which also include the perception[13] of risk. Our biases often disrupt our risk assessments in both positive and negative directions through limiting access to information (searches), limited cognitive understanding (noise) and through our own personal experiences. While it is relatively simple to estimate the a priori risks for certain events (such as flooding, earthquakes or pandemic spreads) so long as they fit within certain 'normal' parameters, rare events like estimating the likelihood of an individual being in the right location to be impacted by a one-in-a-hundred-year flood or other extreme outlier (or 'black swan') events are all but impossible (Taleb 2007). As a result, we would expect that over time individuals would not continuously monitor risks (Rosenboim et al. 2012) and slowly increase their likelihood of risky behaviours.

This becomes more complicated if we consider how events are framed (Kahneman and Tversky 1979) or if we have just experienced gains or losses such as prospect theory (Page, Savage and Torgler 2014; Thaler and Johnson 1990). Individuals are more likely to adopt risk-averse behaviour when faced with choices involving gains but become more risk-seeking when faced with choices involving losses. This fits in relatively well with choices to remain in isolation; many people are feeling the loss of freedom and mobility in reference to their 'normal' activities. Those with high levels of mobility prior to a lockdown would have the largest relative losses and we should observe this group being the most risk-seeking and breaking the lockdown rules. Alternatively, those who had the least amount of social mobility have in relative terms only suffered a small loss – and should be much less likely to break the lockdown rules.[14] Sitting just below this are other factors with significant impacts on decision-making: socio-demographic factors (e.g., education, religiosity, income, health); well-being; individual personality types (Digman 1990; McCrae 1992); and an individual's belief about the level of control they can exert over their future via their perceived 'locus of control' (Rotter 1966). Additionally, research has demonstrated that on average women are less risk-taking (seeking) than men (Charness and Gneezy 2012) and that risk preferences can change over time as older individuals are more risk-averse than their younger counterparts (Moore and Viscusi 1988).

INDIVIDUAL AND GROUPS IMPACT ON CONSUMER BEHAVIOUR

We do not make decisions or operate inside a vacuum, as a significant amount of behavioural information and prompts come from the world around us – for example, the behaviour of other individuals, our institutions and the information presented to us. As such it is important to include not only the individual in the decision-making process but also the groups or institutions around them. As pointed out in the previous section there is an obvious tautology that exists between individuals and groups, but it needs to be elucidated that while the beliefs and preferences of an individual are part of that of a group, they may not actually be the norm of that group; i.e., society may believe that certain behaviour is acceptable but you as an individual may not. In a similar vein to the first section, this section explores how aspects of group behaviour can influence individual decision-making and consumer behaviour (see Figure 16.3).

While not explicitly shown here, Figures 16.2–16.3 are linked via feedback loops between a number of nodes, e.g., individual and group *preferences* are linked between social and moral

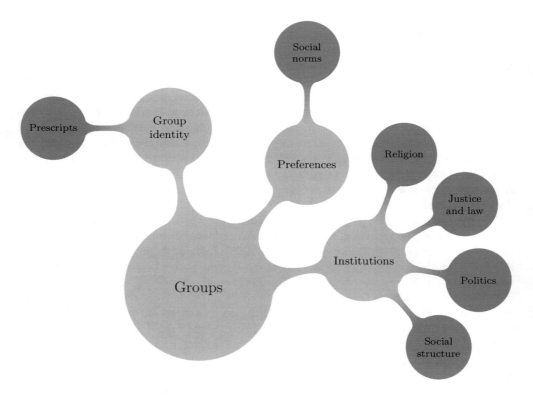

Source: Savage 2019, p. 11.

Figure 16.3 *Aspects of group behaviour that influence decision-making and consumer behaviour*

norms; this is also present for *identity* which is linked through their prescripts (and many others not listed in either figure) – which sit behind consumer behaviour in Figure 16.1. Akerlof and Kranton (2000) demonstrated that there are strong links between/from other individuals, our social norms and how they interact with our identities. Social norms are the foundations of our societies and form the rules by which all individuals in a society are expected to behave and interact with each other (Elster 2007). Furthermore, it is the interaction between who we are (our identity) and how we are supposed to behave (social norms) that influences our choices (Elster 1985). As the name implies, social norms are conditional and are influenced by the presence and behaviour of others around us, and conformity to these norms is influenced by observation (Banerjee 1992). However, moral norms are internalised social norms that have become unconditional and no longer require the presence of others to be enacted upon (Elster 2007, p. 104), such that if we observe individuals ignoring social distancing and isolation protocol, or not wearing protective equipment such as facemasks, then they are likely to be copied by others. Unlike other signals, mask-wearing is very visible, and as such, the absence of people wearing them in public places is very likely to trigger herd-type behaviours (Banerjee 1992) or social norms (Elster 1985). The more individuals that follow or break a particular norm will escalate the likelihood that others will also do so, i.e., if 1 per cent of the population are not wearing masks then the social norm would likely be for all to wear them, but if more than 50 per cent are not wearing masks then more and more would also stop.

Formal and informal institutions have a significant impact on how humans behave; this includes everything from informal social groups and organisations right up to the institutions of government, religion and the legal fraternity. It is important to recognise that the way we fit into our societies is a very complex set of interconnections and rather than just being some abstract concept, it consists of complex amorphous economic and social structures that can grow or die depending on the conditions facing it. However, this can create unforeseen externalities when events like disasters or pandemics occur as the institutions to which we belong frame how we act or perceive events around us. For example, the spread of COVID-19 was not just a physical disease, as it corresponded with a metaphysical contagion of the mind (Eichenberger et al. 2020). The spread of the pandemic coincided with two forms of virus fixation which become a behavioural contagion, infecting the collective consciousness and transferring from person to person.

Government institutions and health (medical) bodies became obsessed with stopping the virus at all costs, advocating for curfews, widespread lockdowns, social isolation and travel bans all in the name of saving the lives of approximately 1.5 per cent[15] of the infected populations from death. The at-all-costs approach has likely resulted in large losses in life years[16] in the number of non-COVID-related deaths stemming from elective surgery cancellations and delays or the negative impacts of isolation on mental health and its related outcomes. Alternatively, in recent years there has been a growing movement of anti-intellectualism and anti-science, which became very visible during 2020, i.e., these fundamentalists actively supported 'alternative fact' views on the pandemic, mostly with an anti-vaccination stance. Many took the position that the virus was no worse than the common cold and fought against any suggestion of social isolation, face masks and travel bans. These views became most noticeable in the USA and fractured mostly along the left vs. right political ideology where mask-wearing was associated with left-wing pro-science Democrats, while those refusing to do so were associated with right-wing anti-science Republicans.

DEMAND-DRIVEN SUPPLY PROBLEMS AND STOCKOUTS

We tend to fear what we don't understand and in many cases, we look to those around us for cues and insights on how we should react. But in disasters and pandemics, there is a large amount of uncertainty and a lack of information which are reinforced by lockdowns and social isolations as we are no longer able to obtain cues from others. The knock-on impact of this is that the general public reactions will be more volatile (i.e., have a greater spread) than what we would usually observe and that can create behavioural biases and changes in decision-making. This manifests itself in disruptions to everyday activities – reaction to the pandemic became quickly visible as many people began to avoid public places like shopping centres and community events, even before lockdown or social isolation rules were put in place (Chan et al. 2020). Even though the risk was unknown (or low) many people changed their normal behaviours as a way for individuals to minimise their perceived exposure to danger and reduce the likelihood of them becoming a victim themselves.

As these individuals became less engaged in public activities and spent more time isolated at home in an attempt to gain control of their situation, they changed their normal consumption patterns. While these small changes in consumption patterns may not appear to be important, when aggregated across a nation or across the world they quickly escalate in size and value. A perfect example of this was seen after the 9/11 attacks on the World Trade Center. While the overall damage amounted to little more than 0.2 per cent of the physical US assets (Becker and Murphy 2001), the behavioural reaction of the general public led to significant economic damage and many more lives lost (Becker and Murphy 2001; Mehmood 2014; Rose et al. 2017). For example, many people avoided flying following 9/11, resulting in plummeting airline share prices (Kaplanski and Levy 2010). And as more people chose to drive rather than fly, there was a resulting spike in road fatalities as driving is inherently more dangerous than flying (Blalock, Kadiyali and Simon 2009). One could argue that fear[17] and risk aversion was the significant factor behind both the economic consequences and the additional fatalities (Cevik and Ricco 2018; Herzenstein, Horsky and Posavac 2015; Rose et al. 2017).

One of the most commonly seen impacts of consumer behaviours was observed on markets shelves, specifically the number of products missing off them or stockouts, in what was incorrectly labelled as 'panic buying'. Consider that many people were uncertain if or when the virus will spread to their region; they did not know the risk (probability) of themselves becoming infected, which also means they did not know if or when they might need to go into isolation and if they would need several weeks' worth of supplies. The compounding of risk and uncertainty with some advance warning that the virus was becoming a worldwide pandemic prompted many people to take some precautionary action.[18] Panic buying is very similar to what happens during a run on a bank, when some individuals believe that the institution may be in financial trouble and seek to withdraw all their holdings from the institution – starting a downward spiral or a self-fulfilling prophecy. Others observe this behaviour, and they speculate that the bank may be in financial trouble, for why else would people be trying to withdraw all their money? So they also withdraw all their holdings. As the number of people trying to withdraw grows, the bank eventually reaches the cash holding limits (i.e., banks only hold a small percentage of total holding in cash) and puts limits on withdrawals. This is seen as verification that the bank is in financial trouble, hence creating a widespread rush on the bank to withdraw money that is no longer available and that now places the bank in financial jeopardy. The observed behaviour that seemed to trigger other individuals to take the same actions is known as herd behaviour; when we see others acting in a certain way, we want to conform with the group or at the very least we stop and think about the behaviour and consider if we should be doing the same. The reason people start to flock to withdraw their holding is caused by loss aversion, i.e., people overweight the probability that something negative will occur and act to avoid it (even if it causes a worse outcome for themselves).

We can apply the same insights for a 'run' on supermarket shelves; when we hear that another lockdown has been called we consider what it is that we need to stock up on and recollect that shelves cleared out in previous lockdowns. At this point, some people will begin to worry (anxiety) that they may miss out on 'essentials' so they race to supermarkets, but rather than only buying enough to cover a potential lockdown period, anxiety and/or fear kicks in and they overbuy (or hoard). And just like the bank example, this is observed by still more people, who then worry that if they do not act now, they may now miss out. The situation snowballs until supply chains and distribution stores cannot keep shelves stocked fast enough or run out of in-store stock. However, now the really ugly problem rears its head – when the shelves are empty, even if only for a few hours, the shortage problem appears to have become a reality and vindicates those that started the problem with overbuying and hoarding. The first media reports of a shelf being empty or a product being in short supply further fuel the downward spiral of pandemic buying – essentially another pandemic of the mind spreads among humans by preying on emotions which are ill-equipped to deal with the problem.

Consider an insight from game theory called backward induction, that is, you start at the result and work backwards to figure out what you should do. Now if we think that the shelves will be empty a few hours after a lockdown is called, and we don't want to miss out, then we want to get in a little earlier than everyone else – say two hours. But what if everyone else is smart like us and wants to get in a little earlier as well? So we decide to get in even earlier (say three hours earlier). And again, so does everyone else; if you play this scenario over and over, eventually people would act immediately rather than risk others getting in before them. The problem is not necessarily that people wish to overstock in preparation for the likely arrival of the lockdown, but rather, natural instincts of anxiety and fear so well-honed for survival kick in and drive some people to 'panic-buy' or what could be more accurately described as 'anxiety'-driven supermarket runs. Unfortunately for us modern humans, the evolutionary gift of fear and anxiety cannot be returned and will occasionally drive us into behaviour that would be deemed irrational to those sitting outside the event from the comfort of history or distance.

ECONOMICS AND THE SUPPLY CHAIN

The supply chain has been an underexplored topic by economists who have mostly assumed the supply side of the market, i.e., goods just materialise in time to interact with consumers to form markets. However, the pandemic exposed a weakness in the supply chain and its ability to adapt to sudden demand side shocks resulting in an incomplete market. In general, economists would describe supply chain models as inward-looking (seeking to maximise efficiency within the supply system), and that it is because of these inward-looking models that changes in the market (consumers, groups or changes in the environment) have been missing. Additionally, much like supply chain systems, economics became obsessed with constrained optimisation problems (Foster 2004, p. 4). And while simpler models are more mathematically tractable, we know that these interactions are neither fixed nor static and are dependent on how individuals view the world, which is itself changed by learning and knowledge generation (Boulding 1961). Unfortunately, these models failed to place the work inside the broader context of the society(s) in which they operated but focused on the internal working of the supply system.

Unlike other recent localised disease epidemics (such as SARS, Ebola and swine flu), COVID-19 become a truly global pandemic event which we have not seen in over 100 years – since the last comparable pandemic was the Spanish Flu (H1N1) pandemic of 1918 with approximately 500 million infected and 50 million deaths (Snowden 2016). The long duration between events exposed a major problem with a generational loss of knowledge and understanding of what occurred and how it affected the market space. Even before the pandemic had been declared, the local 'epidemics' brought to light some relatively unexplored problems within local supply chains. However, when it became a pandemic, it exposed a number of weaknesses within the global supply chain – the most prominent being identification of choke points or single points of failure in a globalised chain. For the most part, global and local chains are affected differently given that manufacturing (including components) tends to be via global chains, while production of foodstuffs tends towards more localised (national) supply chains. This also demonstrated that single points of failure can occur when global manufacturing and supply funnel through a single point (e.g., China) or if a part of the up or downstream manufacturing process funnels through a single point and that point is unable to function.

Nearly all supply chains from grocery retail all the way up to global commodities work on forecasts, which are generally based on extrapolations of past trends with a margin of safety stock if the firms think it appropriate or necessary. Built into these forecasts are allowances for seasonal spikes caused by busy periods (Easter, Christmas, Thanksgiving, etc.) where retailers know from historical experience that they will need to carry extra stock and/or increase delivery frequency or quantities. Large organisations like Walmart have learned that a great deal of the cost of managing a large-scale supply chain can be tied up in safety stock (or warehoused inventory). In an attempt to maximise profits and limit money tied up in warehouses, these large organisations have attempted to squeeze their supply chains through better information and better coordination (e.g., CPFR), and some rely on just-in-time shipments to eliminate most if not all safety stock. This concept works well with stable systems and no shocks, other than the predicted seasonal ones or minor events that fall within the margin of error or limits of safety stock. However, these models have ignored the possibility of 'black swan' (random events or unknown unknowns) events and had no mechanism built into the model to allow feedback for shocks that occur outside the system. In line with macroeconomics having to rethink models, this also requires a general reconsideration of what risks are and how they should be incorporated with respect to supply chains.

While the pandemic created the shock, it did not directly cause a problem for the supply side or for the supply chain (other than chains locked up in China); rather it was the unanticipated consumer behaviour that created the problem. From an economic perspective, we see that a shock event has occurred outside the supply chain system but has created a problem within it, and it is a problem that requires a system solution that extends beyond the current supply chain management thinking. This unique event has demonstrated that supply chain management systems and models assume a simplistic form of rationality and do not inherently include the behaviour of the customer. Specifically, the rate of consumer-driven change was faster than the supply chain could handle, and the rate of consumption was greater than the supply chain could deliver. It is important to note that we use the term handle rather than react to, as the current models do not include complex feedback mechanisms – so they do not react to change. Furthermore, it takes time to add capacity, assuming that we can access adequate stocks of raw materials among other factors of production (e.g., labour). Economics theory shows that in the short run, the only thing that can be done is to facilitate increased output, and only in the longer run can manufacturing production increase capacity (increased machinery or processes). Even if the shock was small enough to be within the scope of a short-run increase in labour, the pandemic revealed an additional problem which was the increase in production required a proportional increase in logistics, i.e., delivering such a large increase in output would require an equally large increase in logistics. In short, the current systems would be virtually incapable of responding to the sudden upsurge in demand and even less likely to predict if or when one would occur.

INCOMPLETE AND STOCKOUT MARKETS

One of the market failures economists rarely cover is that of incomplete markets, where the market has a clear supply (or demand) but due to some impediment the two sides of the market don't meet. As a result, the market is not operating as it should or at times not at all. A good example of this was the insurance industry after the events of 9/11, where the claim for losses became virtually insurmountable and was driving many firms into bankruptcy. Even though there was a definite need and demand for the product, insurance companies were not willing to supply the market, resulting in an incomplete market (supply and demand were unable to intersect to create a market). Governments ended up underwriting insurance companies for a while as it was the only solution to getting that market out of failure. Basic economic theory suggests that markets respond to changes in demand by regulating the price mechanism via the law of demand (see Figure 16.4).

We would generally state that an increase in demand (a move of the demand function) from D_1 to D_4 would be accompanied by an increase in price, but in most normal markets it is illegal to increase the price of goods in response to a disaster. This is generally considered to be price gouging and is considered an unfair practice by the public (Kahneman, Knetsch and Thaler 1986) and illegal in most western governments. Alternatively, we consider that the market is more in line with a perfect competition model – such that the price is fixed regardless of changes in demand but that the supply of the good is actually fixed and finite. In this stockout model, it would be possible for demand to increase beyond the limit of the short-run supply curve – creating the classical incomplete market failure scenario. We observe this in Figure 16.5 where the demand exceeds its ability to resupply – the market becomes incomplete at point (C) and the quantity available falls to zero (a stockout). However, like all Marshallian markets, this does not capture any sense of the temporal aspects, so in order to capture this, we provide a stylised supply timeline (see Figure 16.6), with an upper level of stock (safety stock) and a minimum level of stock wanted to be held. What we observe over time is the actual level of stock bouncing between the ceiling and floor levels as stock is consumed and resupply increases inventory levels. However, when a demand shock occurs it quickly overcomes the resupply ability and drives the quantity to zero (creating a stockout).

Figure 16.6 also highlights that the first attempts at a regular restock are quickly wiped out (returning to zero) and even the second much larger attempt quickly does the same. These stockouts don't necessarily occur only at the market shelves and can occur at a number of different points in the supply chain and could include local and/or global logistic problems,

298 *Handbook of research methods in behavioural economics*

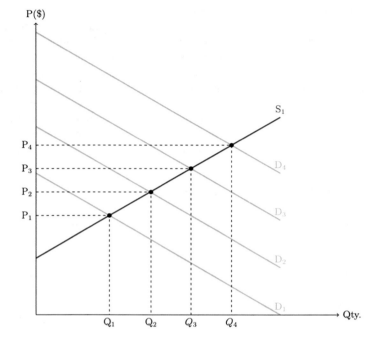

Figure 16.4 Illustration of how markets respond to changes in demand by regulating prices

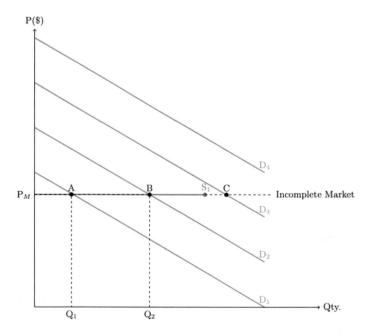

Figure 16.5 Illustration of how demand exceeds its ability to resupply the market

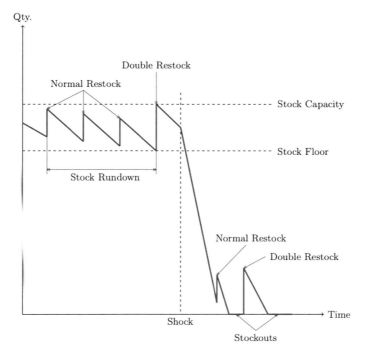

Figure 16.6   Illustration of how demand shock quickly overcomes resupply ability

supply failure points (e.g., no trade with a single country in lockdown) or local problems associated with manufacture/harvesting of goods.

CONCLUSION

The aim of this chapter was to explore the conceptual relationship between human behaviour and the market/supply chain problems exposed by the COVID-19 pandemic (driven by the so-called 'panic buying') and the resulting incomplete market failures in numerous countries around the world. We started by building a discussion around the need to adopt complexity into the economic modelling of behaviour and demonstrated the links between individual and group behaviours that led to unpredictable demand spikes and incomplete markets (e.g., Savage 2019). We also highlighted that economic models and assumptions on the mechanics of markets have been very useful to create abstractions from which we can model the interactions of supply and demand and that they may not be overly helpful when extrapolating to the real world. Additionally, while there is a broad comprehensive microeconomic literature exploring a range of consumer decision-making processes and behaviours, there appears to be a shortfall when it comes to decision-making and behaviours on the supply side. This becomes particularly important in relation to disasters if they result in extreme shifts in individual preferences or consumer behaviour and incomplete markets. We assume that most disasters are black swans or events derived from the unknown unknowns, i.e., unpredictable, and as a consequence, they are reacted to, not prepared for. However, this does not need to be the case as it may be possible to incorporate widely used tracking and sensing systems that already exist in much of the world's supply chain with external data to help address this problem.

One possible solution to this intractable problem is to turn to technologies such as big data, machine learning (ML), artificial intelligence (AI) and next-generation quantum computing capabilities that are already proving it possible to solve problems previously thought to be beyond the scope of current technology. The reason this may ultimately be more useful is that 'machine learning isn't about looking backwards at scientific data and trying to decide what conclusions are viable. It's about looking forward and asking what we can predict about the future and what will happen in various scenarios'.[19] This closely describes the problem at hand, current supply chain systems are using historical data and backwards-looking algorithms to predict future requirements, but what is needed is a way to incorporate live big data from numerous sources to sense what is occurring outside the current system to predict what is happening now and may be coming. Companies like Target are already using big data and ML to predict their customer current and future circumstances, e.g., while possibly apocryphal, Target was able to predict a teenage girl was pregnant and send her marketing material before she had even told her parents (Forbes 2012).[20] Regardless of the veracity of this story, the sophistication and advancements of both AI and ML have surged forward in leaps and bounds, e.g., Google's AI system Alpha Go has been able to learn one of the world's most complex games and beat human masters in a game that requires an understanding of intuition and the human decision-making process. If an AI can learn to understand human behaviour in one context, it would be possible to redirect the focus onto other areas – this should include looking for and identifying data sources that could be used as markers for potential upheavals.

Historical vision is almost always perfect (20/20) such that when we examine disasters after the fact, we can nearly always find a turning point or a marker that probably should have been identified as being a significant indicator of what followed. In line with this, we suggest that supply chain systems adopt the concept that there are markers we are currently missing in our day-to-day analysis of data, and through the use of AI and ML, we should be able to identify them either at the time (or close to) or before the event itself. While this may not be able to predict the exact nature of the event that is about to occur, it may be enough to provide stakeholders with an incentive to pay more attention to and more closely monitor their systems for anomalies to see if it is their systems being impacted. While many running under the current supply chain paradigm may be happy to maintain the status quo, the plethora of events and disasters in recent decades should be a wake-up call to look outside the limitations of the current supply chain systems and start thinking outside the box. We hope that supply chain systems can learn from the mistakes of economics by not only including consumer behaviour but also to stop using as-if models for optimising efficiency and predicting future market needs. If the pandemic has taught us nothing else, failing to understand human behaviours is the surest way to ensure more incomplete market failures and stockout problems.

NOTES

1. Stockouts is a general term to describe the unavailability of a good on shelves, which could be the result of any number of supply side or demand issues.
2. These models were very good at status quo markets predictions, e.g., GDP forecasts where there were no unforeseen shocks or changes to the system.

3. Macroeconomic finance has also been guilty of forgetting that all the 'data points' in their work are actually human beings that are at times not predictable nor perfectly rational; even predictable irrationality would have been better.
4. See for example Andreoni and Miller (2002); Becker (1974); Bolton and Ockenfels (2000); Dufwenberg and Kirchsteiger (2004); Fehr and Schmidt (1999); Frey (1997); Rabin (1993); Sobel (2005); Kahneman, Knetsch and Thaler (1986).
5. Such that it may be possible to predict consumer choices from individuals as they are directly related, but very difficult to predict overall demand changes from a single individual.
6. Theoretically such a system should be able to use historical supply chain data to see if the model would have successfully predicted similar supply chain shocks over the last 20 years, such as pandemics (SARS and Ebola), financial disasters (GFC) or terrorist attacks (9/11).
7. These broad categories can be broken down further such that 'preferences' includes beliefs (faith), moral norms or risk attitudes, and 'experience' can differentiate between what one learns and what one has experienced.
8. Social isolation and lockdowns are a tried and proven method of limiting the spread of any pandemic, as analysis of the 1919 Spanish Flu pandemic demonstrate (Snowden 2016).
9. Ask any ex-smoker or one who has tried to quit several times how hard it is to break the habit formation; for several years after I quit smoking I would find myself patting down my pockets looking for my cigarettes and lighter. This was not about a nicotine fix, but simply an automated habitual response learned over many years when leaving the house.
10. While Cameron and Shah (2015) showed that repeated experience with a specific type of disaster event can create risk aversion, we believe that the lack of prior experience with pandemic type events (e.g., Ebola or SARS) would not have been enough to create a heightened level of background risk aversion.
11. The classic Ellsberg paradox is a perfect example of ambiguity, as participants not only have no idea how many red or black balls may be in the urn, but they do not know the composition (ratio) of red to black
12. An analysis of both soldiers and students in Gaza (Israel) demonstrated that fear of attack impacted how the groups perceived the threat enabling them to willingly stay in areas of heightened risk (Lerner and Keltner 2000; Shahrabani et al. 2012)
13. An individual's risk type and their perception of risk are likely to be highly correlated and interact to exacerbate the underlying risk type. That is, risk seekers are likely to have a worse perception of risk such that not only are they willing to accept more gambles, but their estimations of the gambles are also underweighted, leading to a greater adoption of risk than the individual intended (Slovic 1993).
14. However, this should adjust over time as individuals habituate the changes and reset their reference points. This fits nicely into the suggestion that 'a person who has not made peace with his losses is likely to accept gambles that would be unacceptable to him otherwise' (Kahneman and Tversky 1979, p. 287).
15. Ioannidis (2021) included 61 studies (74 estimates) and eight preliminary national estimates. He reported that the infection fatality rates ranged from 0.00 per cent to 1.63 per cent and that the median rate was 0.27 per cent.
16. This is likely not going to be truly known until long after the pandemic as passed and we are able to estimate not only the total number of lives lost, but also the losses in Quality Adjusted Life Years (QALY) or Welfare Adjusted Life Years (WALY).
17. Fear can cause behaviour that can lead to individuals disregarding the probability of harm occurring following 'vivid' or 'visceral' factors (Sunstein and Zeckhauser 2011) or it can the opposite effect where individuals overweight the probability of harm and completely shut down.
18. It is rational to prepare for something bad if it looks likely to occur, but it may not be seen as rational to buy 500 cans of baked beans for what would likely be a two-week isolation period.
19. Ted Dunning cited in Marvin, R. (2018). 'The Business Guide to Machine Learning', *PC Magazine* (Australia), available from: https://au.pcmag.com/enterprise/47684/the-business-guide-to-machine-learning.
20. Sourced from www.forbes.com/sites/kashmirhill/2012/02/16/how-target-figured-out-a-teen-girl-was-pregnant-before-her-father-did/?sh=413b33046668.

REFERENCES

Aarle, B. van and Kappler, M. (2012). Economic sentiment shocks and fluctuations in economic activity in the Euro Area and the USA. *Intereconomics/Review of European Economic Policy*, 47(1), 44–51.

Akerlof, G. A. and Kranton, R. E. (2000). Economics and identity. *The Quarterly Journal of Economics*, 115(3), 715–753.

Akerlof, G. A. and Yellen, J. L. (1990). The fair wage-effort hypothesis and unemployment. *Quarterly Journal of Economics*, 105(2), 255–284.

Aspinwall, L. G. (1998). Rethinking the role of positive affect in self-regulation. *Motivation and Emotion*, 22(1), 1–32.

Aspinwall, L. G. (2004). Dealing with adversity: Self-regulation, coping, adaptation, and health. *Applied Social Psychology*, 1, 3–27.

Axelrod, R. and Cohen, M. D. (2000). *Harnessing complexity: Organizational implications of a scientific frontier.* New York: Basic Books.

Banerjee, A. V. (1992). A simple model of herd behavior. *The Quarterly Journal of Economics*, 107(3), 797–817.

Becker, G. S. and Murphy, K. M. (2001). Prosperity will rise out of the ashes. *Wall Street Journal* (Eastern edition), October 29, 2001.

Becker, G. S. and Rubinstein, Y. (2004). Fear and the response to terrorism: An economic analysis. *University of Chicago*, 93(1).https://EconPapers.repec.org/RePEc:cep:cepdps:dp1079

Bergström, J., Uhr, C. and Frykmer, T. (2016). A complexity framework for studying disaster response management. *Journal of Contingencies and Crisis Management*, 24(3), 124–135.

Blalock, G., Kadiyali, V. and Simon, D. H. (2009). Driving fatalities after 9/11: A hidden cost of terrorism. *Applied Economics*, 41(14), 1717–1729.

Bonabeau, E. (2002). Agent-based modeling: Methods and techniques for simulating human systems. *Proceedings of the National Academy of Sciences*, 99(3), 7280.

Bondt, G. J. and Schiaff, S. (2015). Confidence matters for current economic growth: Empirical evidence for the Euro Area and the United States. *Social Science Quarterly*, 96(4), 1027–1040.

Botzen, C., Wouter, W. J., Kunreuther, H. and Michel-Kerjan, E. (2015). Divergence between individual perceptions and objective indicators of tail risks: Evidence from floodplain residents in New York City. *Judgment and Decision Making,* 10(4), 365–385.

Brodeur, A. (2018). The effect of terrorism on employment and consumer sentiment: Evidence from successful and failed terror attacks. *Applied Economics*, 10(4), 246–282.

Cameron, L. and Shah, M. (2015). Risk-taking behavior in the wake of natural disasters. *Journal of Human Resources*, 50(2), 484–515.

Campbell, J. and Cochrane, J. (1999). By force of habit: A consumption-based explanation of aggregate stock market behavior. *Journal of Political Economy*, 107(2), 205–251.

Cannon, W. B. (1929a). *Bodily changes in pain, hunger, fear and rage.* New York: D. Appleton & Co.

Cannon, W. B. (1929b). Organization for physiological homeostasis. *Physiological Reviews*, 9(3), 399–431.

Cannon, W. B. (1935). Stresses and strains of homoeostasis. *American Journal of Medical Science*, 189(1), 13–14.

Cevik, S. and Ricco, J. (2018). Shock and awe? Fiscal consequences of terrorism. *Empirical Economics*, 58, 723–748. https://link.springer.com/article/10.1007/s00181-018-1543-3

Chan, H. F., Brumpton, M., Macintyre, A., Arapoc, J., Savage, D. A., Skali, A., Stadelmann, D. and Torgler, B. (2020a). How confidence in health care systems affects mobility and compliance during the COVID-19 pandemic. *PloS one*, 15(10), e0240644.

Chan, H. F., Moon, J. W., Savage, D. A., Skali, A., Torgler, B. and Whyte, S. (2020b). Can psychological traits explain mobility behaviour during the COVID-19 pandemic? *Social Psychological and Personality Science.* 12(6), 1018–1029. https://doi.org/10.1177/1948550620952572

Chan, H. F., Skali, A., Savage, D. A., Stadelmann, D. and Torgler, B. (2020c). Risk attitudes and human mobility during the COVID-19 pandemic. *Scientific Reports*, 10(1), 1–13.

Charness, G., Gneezy, U. and Imas, A. (2013). Experimental methods: Eliciting risk preferences. *Journal of Economic Behavior & Organization*, 87, 43–51.

Cheng, Z., Mencolia, S., Paloyo, A. R., Savage, D. A. and Tani, M. (2021). Working parents, financial insecurity, and childcare: Mental health in the time of COVID-19 in the UK. Forthcoming in *Review of the Economic Household*. 19, 123–144.

Drakos, K. (2010). Terrorism activity, investor sentiment, and stock returns. *Review of Financial Economics*, 19, 128–135.

Drakos, K. and Kallandranis, C. (2015). A note on the effect of terrorism on economic sentiment. *Defence and Peace Economics*, 26(6), 600–608.

Eckel, C., El-Gamal, M. and Wilson, R. (2009). Risk loving after the storm: A bayesian-network study of Hurricane Katrina evacuees. *Journal of Economic Behavior & Organization*, 69(2), 110–124.

Eichenberger, R., Hegselmann, R., Savage, D. A., Stadelmann, D. and Torgler, B. (2020). Certified coronavirus immunity as a resource and strategy to cope with pandemic costs. *Kyklos*, 73(3), 464–474.

Elster, J. (1989). Social norms and economic theory. *The Journal of Economic Perspectives*, 3(4), 99–117.

Elster, J. (1998). Emotions and economic theory. *Journal of Economic Literature*, 36(1), 47–74.

Elster, J. (2007). *Explaining social behavior. More nuts and bolts for the social sciences*. Cambridge: Cambridge University Press.

Epstein, J. M. (2006). *Generative social science: Studies in agent-based computational models*. Princeton: Princeton University Press.

Epstein, J. M. and Axtell, R. (1996). *Growing artificial societies: Social science from the bottom up*. Washington, DC: Brookings Institution Press.

Fauci, A. S., Lane, H. C. and Redfield, R. R. (2020). COVID-19 — Navigating the Uncharted. *New England Journal of Medicine*, 382(13), 1268–1269.

Foster, J. (2004). Why is economics not a complex systems science? School of economics, The University of Queensland Discussion Paper # 336.

Frey, B. S., Savage, D. A. and Torgler, B. (2010a). Interaction of natural survival instincts and internalized social norms exploring the Titanic and Lusitania disasters. *Proceedings of the National Academy of Sciences*, 107(11), 4862–4865.

Frey, B. S., Savage, D. A. and Torgler, B. (2010b). Noblesse oblige? Determinants of survival in a life and death situation. *Journal of Economic Behavior and Organization*, 74(1), 1–11.

Frey, B. S., Savage D. A. and Torgler, B. (2011). Behavior under extreme conditions: The Titanic disaster. *Journal of Economic Perspectives*, 25(1), 209–222.

Friday, D., Savage, D. A., Melnyk, S. A., Harrison, N., Ryan, S. and Wechtler, H. (2021). A collaborative approach to maintaining optimal inventory and mitigating stockout risks during a pandemic: Capabilities for enabling health-care supply chain resilience. *Journal of Humanitarian Logistics and Supply Chain Management*, 11(2), 248–271.

Friedman, M. (1953) *Essays in positive economic*. Chicago: University of Chicago Press.

Greenland, A., Proux, D. and Savage, D. A. (2020). Dying for the cause: The rationality of martyrs, suicide bombers and self-immolators. *Rationality and Society*, 32(1), 93–115.

Hayek, F. (1967). Notes on the evolution of systems of rules of conduct. In F. Hayek (ed.), *Studies in philosophy, politics and economics*. London: Routledge & Kegan Paul, pp. 66–81.

Hennet, J.-C. and Arda, Y. (2008). Supply chain coordination: A game-theory approach. *Engineering Applications of Artificial Intelligence*, 21(3), 399–405.

Herzenstein, M., Horsky, S. and Posavac, S. S. (2015). Living with terrorism or withdrawing in terror: Perceived control and consumer avoidance. *Journal of Consumer Behavior*, 14(4), 228–236.

Ioannidis, J. (2021). Infection fatality rate of COVID-19 inferred from seroprevalence data. *Bulletin World Health Organization* 99(1), 19.

Kahneman, D. (2011). *Thinking, fast and slow*. New York: Farrar, Straus and Giroux.

Kahneman, D., Knetsch, J. L. and Thaler, R. (1986). Fairness as a constraint on profit seeking: Entitlements in the market. *The American Economic Review*, 76(4), 728–741.

Kahneman, D., Slovic, P. and Tversky, A. (1982). *Judgment under uncertainty: Heuristics and biases*. Cambridge: Cambridge University Press.

Kahneman, D. and Tversky, A. (1979). Prospect theory: An analysis of decision under risk. *Econometrica*, 47(2), 263–291.

Kahneman, D. and Tversky, A. (1992). Advances in prospect theory: Cumulative representation of uncertainty. *Journal of Risk and Uncertainty*, 5(4), 297–323.

Kaplanski, G. and Levy, H. (2010). Sentiment and stock prices: The case of aviation disasters. *Journal of Financial Economics*, 95, 174–201.

Klein, L. R. and Ozmucur, S. (2002). Consumer behavior under the influence of terrorism within the United States. *Journal of Entrepreneurial Finance and Business Ventures*, 7(3), 1–15.

Kolaric, S. and Schiereck, D. (2016). Are stock markets efficient in the face of fear? Evidence from the terrorist attacks in Paris and Brussels. *Finance Research Letters,* 18, 306–310.

Lawrence, P. R. and Nohria, N. (2002). *Driven: How human nature shapes our choices*. San Francisco: Jossey-Bass.

Lerner, J. S. and Keltner, D. (2000). Beyond valence: Toward a model of emotion-specific influences on judgment and choice. *Cognition and Emotion*, 14, 473–493.

Ludvigson, S. C. (2004). Consumer confidence and consumer spending. *Journal of Economic Perspectives*, 18(2), 29–50.

Mawson, A. R. (2005). Understanding mass panic and other collective responses to threat and disaster. *Psychiatry*, 68(2), 95–113.

Mehmood, S. (2014). Terrorism and the macroeconomy: Evidence from Pakistan. *Defence and Peace Economics*, 25(5), 509–534.

Miller, J. H. and Page, S. E. (2007). *Complex adaptive systems: An introduction to computational models of social life*. Princeton: Princeton University Press.

Mitchell, M. (2009). *Complexity: A guided tour*. Oxford: Oxford University Press.

Nagarajan, M. and Sošić, G. (2008). Game-theoretic analysis of cooperation among supply chain agents: Review and extensions. *European Journal of Operational Research*, 187(3), 719–745.

Newman, M. E. J. (2010). *Networks: An introduction*. Oxford: Oxford University Press.

Newman, M. E. J., Barabási, A.-L. and Watts, D. J. (2006). *The structure and dynamics of networks*. Princeton: Princeton University Press.

O'Sullivan, T. L., Kuziemsky, C. E., Toal-Sullivan, D. and Corneil, W. (2013). Unraveling the complexities of disaster management: A framework for critical social infrastructure to promote population health and resilience. *Social Science & Medicine*, 93, 238–246.

Page, L., Savage, D. A. and Torgler, B. (2014). Variation in risk seeking behaviour following large losses: A natural experiment. *European Economic Review*, 71, 121–131.

Pratt, J. W. (1964). Risk aversion in the small and in the large. *Econometrica*, 32(1–2), 122–136.

Proulx, D. and Savage, D. A. (2020). What determines end-of-life attitudes? revisiting the Dutch experience. *Social Indicators Research*, 152(3), 1085–1125.

Rabin, M. (2000). Risk aversion and expected-utility theory: A calibration theorem. *Econometrica*, 68(5), 1281–1292.

Reilsback, S. F. and Grimm, V. (2012). *Agent-based and individual-based modeling*. Princeton: Princeton University Press.

Rose, A., Avetisyan, M., Rosoff, H., Burns, W. J., Slovic, P. and Chan, O. (2017). The role of behavioral responses in the total economic consequences of terrorist attacks on U.S. air travel targets. *Risk Analysis: An International Journal,* 37(7), 1403–1418.

Rosenboim, M., Ben-Zion, U., Shahrabani, S. and Shavit, T. (2012). Emotions, risk perceptions and precautionary behavior under the threat of terror attacks: A field study among Israeli college students. *Journal of Behavioral Decision Making*, 25, 248–256.

Savage, D. A. (2016a). Surviving the storm: Behavioural economics in the conflict environment. *Peace Economics, Peace Science and Public Policy*, 22(2), 105–129.

Savage, D. A. (2016b). Those left behind: Euthanasia, suicide and other regarding preferences. *Rationality and Society*, 28(4), 439–452.

Savage, D. A. (2019). Towards a complex model of disaster behaviour. *Disasters*, 43(4), 771–798.

Savage, D. A., Chan, H. F., Moy, N., Schaffner, M. and Torgler, B. (2020). Personality and individual characteristics as indicators of lifetime climbing success among Everest mountaineers. *Personality and Individual Differences*, 162, 110044.

Savage, D. A. and Torgler, B. (2013). The emergence of emotions and religious sentiments during the September 11 disaster. *Motivation and Emotion*, 37(3), 586–599.

Savage, D. A. and Torgler, B. (2021). Methods and insights on how to explore human behaviour in the disaster environment. In *Economic effects of natural disasters*, 191–209. Elsevier. https://www.sciencedirect.com/science/article/pii/B9780128174654000133

Schelling, T. C. (1978). *Micromotives and macrobehavior.* New York: W. W. Norton.
Selye, H. (1936). A syndrome produced by diverse noxious agents. *Nature*, 138(3479), 32.
Simon, H. (1991). Bounded rationality and organizational learning. *Organization Science*, 2(1), 125–134.
Slovic, P. (1993). Perceived risk, trust, and democracy. *Risk analysis*, 13(6), 675–682.
Smith, A. D. (1991). *National identity.* Reno: University of Nevada Press.
Snowden, F. M. (2019). *Epidemics and society: From the black death to the present.* New Haven: Yale University Press.
Sterman, J. D. (1994). Learning in and about complex systems. *System Dynamics Review*, 10, 291–330.
Sunstein, C. and Zeckhauser, R. (2011). Overreaction to fearsome risks. *Environmental & Resource Economics,* 48(3), 435–449.
Taleb, N. N. (2007). *The black swan: The impact of the highly improbable.* New York: Random.
Verdelhan, A. (2010). A habit-based explanation of the exchange rate risk premium. *Journal of Finance*, 65(1), 123–146.
Wakker, P. (2010). Prospect theory: For risk and ambiguity. Cambridge: Cambridge University Press.
Whyte, S., Savage, D. A. and Torgler, B. (2017). Online sperm donors: The impact of family, friends, personality and risk perception on behaviour. *Reproductive Biomedicine Online*, 35, 723–732.
Wilson, E. O. (1975). *Sociobiology: The new synthesis.* Cambridge: The Belknap Press of Harvard University Press.
Yao, J. M. (2013) Scheduling optimisation of co-operator selection and task allocation in mass customisation supply chain based on collaborative benefits and risks. *International Journal of Production Research*, 51(8), 2219–2239.

PART VII

'EMOTIONS', MORALS AND BEHAVIOURAL ECONOMICS

17. Economics of trust: Its nature, measures, determinants and application

Jefferson Arapoc

INTRODUCTION

In today's intricate worldwide economy, trust is an important aspect of the conduct of any human affairs. The presence of trust ensures social interactions run smoothly, even without formal contracts (Sutter & Kocher, 2007). Without trust, dealings of varying natures would be problematic as doubt would surface among the participants. Therefore, trust is essential for any economic transaction to work efficiently. While its importance has already been established by existing literature, the definition of trust remains a source of debate across many disciplines. The significant attention it received in recent years has resulted in an assortment of definitions.

Grasping the concept of trust is more complex than we think. In fact, the pursuit to further understand trust has produced an extensive body of literature, but there are inconsistencies in their empirical findings and conclusions. The long history of debate among social scientists regarding its definition, categorisation and key determinants has inspired this research to unify the concept of trust by revisiting previous assertions of past empirical workings and exploring some of its unchartered domains. This chapter aims to present a concise literature review on what trust is and its importance from a societal perspective and discuss the formal definition of trust, its categorisation and how it is being measured. It will be followed by reconciling its different types with existing measurement methodologies. This chapter will also discuss trust as social capital, its determinants and its relevance in the real world.

DEFINITION OF TRUST ACROSS DISCIPLINES

In the second half of the twentieth century, the concept of trust grew as a topic of inquiry in various social sciences. While each discipline offers a distinctive perspective that enriches the concept of trust, it also creates perplexity in the conceptualisation of its definition (Colquitt et al., 2007). Trust has always been associated with many familiar words that are used in day-to-day conversation, such as reliance, confidence and dependence (Shapiro, 1987). Most studies frame the concept of trust around the cognitive, emotional and behavioural dimensions of human psychology vital to various social interactions (Lewis & Weigert, 1985). For example, trust is often regarded as a personal or interpersonal aspect of human interactions reinforced by personal bonds, social norms, community rules and formal and informal institutions, among many others (Granovetter, 1985; Geertz, 1978).

Disparities in the idea of trust across disciplines can be traced to their respective inherent assumptions (Rousseau et al., 1998). In psychology, trust can either be classified as an intrapersonal or an interpersonal phenomenon (Blomqvist, 1997). The former considers trust as a personal trait affected by internal cognition processes (Deutsch, 1958; Rotter, 1967). On the other hand, the latter viewed trust as the ability to expose oneself in a potentially vulnerable situation to another person (Blomqvist, 1997; Luhmann, 1979). In philosophy, the concept of trust can be traced back to ancient moral philosophers' workings (Blomqvist, 1997). Plato indirectly introduced trust through his seminal book *The Republic*. The book suggests that for a republic to thrive, the majority of its citizens must be able to trust a group of wise people – known as philosopher-kings – to rule them wisely (Baier, 1986). Philosophers formally defined trust as an individual's capacity to place confidence in other people to act reliably even if potential personal gains are possible at his expense (Pettit, 1995).

In economics, the assumption of perfect information caused traditional economists to turn a blind eye to the role of trust in market transactions (Platteau, 1994). This assumption makes it impossible for economic agents to engage in any form of fraud which makes the concept of trust irrelevant (Blomqvist, 1997). However, a paradigm shift in economic analysis uncovered the unrealistic assumptions of classical models, exposing that real-world markets are plagued with market imperfections (Stiglitz, 2002). The growing interest in market imperfections led subsequent studies to focus on the concept of trust (Gambetta, 1988). In modern economic literature, trust is defined as a voluntary reallocation of a good or favour from one person to another, with an expectation of reciprocation but without guarantee (Gunnthorsdottir et al., 2002).

The concept of trust in economics is relatively straightforward in comparison with that in psychology and philosophy. Economics' perspective on trust only focuses on the actual action of trusting and reciprocation, unlike the aforementioned fields that also consider its forms and incitements (Blomqvist, 1997; Rousseau et al., 1998). Nevertheless, the concept of trust in economics and philosophy is congruent with the interpersonal viewpoint of trust in psychology. Trust in an interpersonal perspective is regarded as an expectation in a situation where an individual decides to transact in an imperfect environment characterised by risk and uncertainty or asymmetric information (Blomqvist, 1997; James, 2002).

CONCEPT OF TRUST IN ECONOMICS

The definition of trust varies not only across disciplines but also within them. Trust can be defined as either a process or a condition. In economic literature, the concept of trust is dependent on the subfield in which it is being used. In game theory, trust is commonly viewed as a calculative process of action associated with risk. The act of trusting presumes a situation of risk which entails a person exposing himself to possible opportunistic action by another individual (Coleman, 1990; Luhmann, 2000). Thus, game-theoretic models evaluate trusting behaviour by looking at the possible payoff. Coleman (1990) formalised the condition that fosters an individual's trusting behaviour using equation 17.1.

$$G*p > (1-p)L \qquad (17.1)$$

Where:

G is the potential gain if the other agent acts honestly.
p is the probability that the other agent acts honestly.
L is the potential loss if the other agent acts dishonestly.

An agent enters the transaction if the potential gain, when the other agent acts honestly, is greater than the potential losses when the other agent acts dishonestly. It suggests that trust is an ex-ante condition based on subjective probabilities of how the other agent will behave. In the game Prisoner's Dilemma, two players are interviewed separately about their involvement in a crime and each must decide whether (or not) to confess. In this context, trust can be viewed as the degree of confidence by one player in the other player's propensity to cooperate even without the possibility of collusion (Dasgupta, 1988; Platteau, 1994). Game theory reveals how trust can be conceptualised as a calculative process; however, game theory as an analytical framework assumes that rules are exogenous to each player's decision-making process. The assumption that players have an existing disposition towards certain behaviours (e.g., trusting behaviour) undermines the existing body of literature that supports the idea that social and cultural factors shape people's attitudes and value systems – which in turn influence their behaviour.

It is important to look at trust in a social context in which people's interpersonal endeavours are taking place. Economic transactions are considered a particular case of interpersonal endeavour, where an agent and a principal enter a contract or an agreement (Hosmer, 1995). The transaction between a principal and an agent is formalised by agency theory, which states when a principal employs an agent, where some decision-making permission is established, a possible agency problem exists (Alston & Higgs, 1982). If both the principal and the agent desire to maximise their utility, it is assumed that the agent will act independently and not always in the principal's best interests (Jensen & Meckling, 1976). For economic transactions to occur, the principal must be able to find ways to safeguard and motivate the agent to behave favourably to the former's interests. Providing proper incentives and behaviour monitoring are just some of the long-standing approaches to solving the agency problem. However, these strategies are often difficult and costly to implement. One natural way to solve the agency problem is to ensure that a certain level of trust must transpire between a principal and an agent. Trust occurs when a principal is willing to become vulnerable to an agent's action, even if the former cannot control the behaviour of the latter (Zand, 1972). Therefore, trust is classified as a desirable condition for the economic transaction to run smoothly.

Economic transactions can occur among individuals, groups, firms, or based on any combination of these economic players (Freeman, 2010). The level of mutual trust among these players determines the success of these transactions that drive the productive capacity of a society. In 2006 estimates of the United States, trust was worth $12.4 trillion USD a year, approximately 9.5 per cent of the country's income (Harford & Knack, 2006). Economic transactions that require interpersonal trust include trading of goods and services, employment, investments and savings decisions (Knack & Keefer, 1997). Societies with higher degrees of trust among economic agents incur fewer transaction costs (Knack & Zak, 2003), suggesting that they are less dependent on formal institutions to enforce contracts and agreements.

CATEGORISATION OF TRUST

Aside from its definition, there is also a rudimentary categorisation in the existing literature on trust. Psychology has classified trust into intrapersonal and interpersonal trust (Blomqvist, 1997). The former views trust as a personal trait affected by internal cognition processes (Deutsch, 1958; Rotter, 1967), while the latter views it as the ability to expose oneself in a potentially vulnerable situation to another person (Blomqvist, 1997; Luhmann, 1979).

Economic literature often refers to interpersonal trust since trusting behaviour is often viewed in the context of economic transaction. However, it is important to disaggregate trust into different categories (Uslaner, 2002). Within the interpersonal trust domain, the literature identifies two distinct types of trust based on their social scope: localised trust and generalised trust (Stolle, 2002; Uslaner, 2003).

Localised trust, also known as particularised trust, functions in small and intimate communities with healthy social controls and where people can interact closely with one another (Gambetta, 1988; Portes & Landolt, 1996). It is found in close social proximity or the same neighbourhood – such as family members, friends and neighbours. Generalised trust, on the other hand, is a somewhat more abstract view towards people in general. It is a type of trust that functions in complex societies that involve numerous daily interactions among unfamiliar people (Nannestad, 2008; Zmerli et al., 2007). It covers people's perception of others beyond immediate familiarity, including strangers – such as fellow citizens and foreigners. To put it simply, the clear distinction between localised and generalised trust is that the former refers to a trust 'in closely related people' while the latter is trust in people in a more general sense (Yamagishi & Yamagishi, 1994). Several empirical studies support the idea that localised and generalised trust are different from one another. For example, by employing a factor analysis on trust survey data, it was revealed that there are distinct factors for localised and generalised trust. Out of the 32 factors identified to be related to trust in different groups of people, it was found that trusting people in a more general sense versus trusting those closely related were not associated with the same factor (Uslaner, 2002; Yamagishi & Yamagishi, 1994).

To further distinguish the difference between these two types of trust, it is vital to recognise the difference in their radius and level. Localised trust resonates from cooperative norms in close social circles, while generalised trust resonates from more distant social circles where cooperative norms are operating (Fukuyama, 1995). The radius of trust is a significant aspect of civic cooperation. A wider trust radius ensures a society's cooperation circle is more inclusive (Delhey et al., 2011). Moreover, the level of trust is as important as its radius since a greater intensity of trust produces more cooperation. The radius of trust defines the range of the cooperation circle, while the level of trust defines the intensity of civic cooperation within a social circle.

MEASURING TRUST

Measuring trust is a focal point of empirical work in social sciences, particularly in Economics (Holm & Nystedt, 2008). There are two main approaches in measuring trust: through surveys and experiments, each approach has its own merits and drawbacks. The first approach measures trust through a survey instrument (Jøsang et al., 2007), of which the general social survey (GSS) and the WVS are examples. The implementation of this method uses Likert scales or attitudinal survey questions to elicit the respondents' trust (Glaeser et al., 2000). In the United States, trust in their government is measured through attitudinal surveys (Doherty et al., 2017).

While this approach might be relatively easier to implement, the reliability of subjects' responses depends on the survey instrument's design and how the survey proper is conducted. For example, GSS and WVS questions are framed to measure people's expectations of others' trustworthiness rather than trust per se. While expectations regarding trustworthiness matter in deciding whether to trust or distrust people, the question seems to measure cautiousness rather than the ability to trust. Yamagishi et al. (1999) argued that the survey questions seem to offer respondents a choice between trust and caution – not a choice between trust and distrust nor between cautious and incautious behaviour. Even if trust and caution are difficult to disentangle, it is important to treat them as two different concepts since they are not necessarily mutually exclusive.

The interpretation of the survey question may differ across different countries. A study revealed that Japanese students are more likely to be more trusting than their American counterparts when trust is measured using the questions from the GSS (Miller & Mitamura, 2003). However, when trust and caution are measured separately, the study found that American students are more trusting and cautious than Japanese students. These inconsistent results from the separate surveys validate the interpretation problems related to survey questions as a measure of trust. Moreover, answers to survey questions are merely stated preferences prone to different biases – a hypothetical bias that could lead to measurement overestimation or underestimation (Ben-Ner & Halldorsson, 2010).

Contrastly, the second known approach to measure trust is through experiments and games to elicit actual trusting behaviour (Berg et al., 1995). The trust game is a good example of an investigational approach extensively used in experimental economics. In this game, a transaction will occur between two players. The first mover is the trustor, while the second mover is the trustee. The trustor is given an initial monetary endowment equivalent to X and decides how much of this endowment to transfer to the trustee. The trustor send rate could range from sending zero amount to sending all X. Once the transfer is completed, the trustor can no longer withdraw any amount given to the trustee. The trustee, on the other hand, is receiving the transferred amount by a factor of $K > 1$ (e.g., doubled or tripled). For example, if the trustor sends $10AUD, the trustee is receiving $20AUD if doubling or $30AUD if tripling, depending on the factor K setting. Upon receiving the factored amount sent by the trustor, the trustee has the option to return any amount to the trustor, ranging from zero to the full amount. In a laboratory setting, the roles of the trustor and trustee are randomly assigned, and the same is true in matching the players. Also, all trustor–trustee interactions are typically done virtually through a programmed computer application. While this game is now universally known as the trust game, it was originally called the investment game by Berg et al. (1995), where they used $10USD as their initial endowment ($X = 10$) with a transfer factor of 3 ($K = 3$).

Experiments are said to be less exposed to self-serving biases compared to the previous approach. This procedure measures trust based on the actual actions of players in a specific game. Since players face real monetary incentives; it discourages them from deviating from their real perceptions and preferences (Johansson-Stenman et al., 2005). However, there is still an ongoing debate among researchers on the validity of trust measured using games. The risk attitudes of players also influence their respective strategies in a game which may lead to questionable inferences about trust (Houser et al., 2010). Moreover, many studies suggest that experimental games do not measure trust, but rather the concept of reciprocity (Falk & Fischbacher, 2006; Glaeser et al., 2000; Holm & Nystedt, 2008).

Both experiments and survey-based measures are widely used in economic literature to measure trust. Some economists have devoted time to scrutinising how these two approaches correlate with one another and whether they are measuring the same type of trusting behaviour. Some studies suggest a significant correlation between the survey and the experimental approach as a measure of trust (Bellemare & Kröger, 2003; Sapienza et al., 2013; Vyrastekova & Garikipati, 2005). On the other hand, some studies provided empirical evidence that the questions used in GSS and WVS do not correlate with trusting behaviour in a trust game (Ashraf et al., 2006; Glaeser et al., 2000; Holm & Nystedt, 2008). Evidence suggests that the response to the WVS trust question correlated with the trustor's trust behaviour in laboratory experiments but not with the trustee's trustworthiness (Bellemare & Kröger, 2003; Fehr, 2002).

Other studies suggest that the WVS question about trust is not correlated with trust in laboratory experiments but with trustworthiness (Glaeser et al., 2000; Lazzarini et al., 2005). These assertions were challenged by another study suggesting that the WVS survey question on trust does not measure the trust or trustworthiness of the survey participants, but their belief about the trustworthiness of other people (Sapienza et al., 2013). Meanwhile, another study argued that the WVS question about trust is more of a proxy measure of cooperative preferences than trust (Thöni et al., 2012).

This conflicting evidence in the literature poses a crucial question on the validity and reliability of both experimental and survey approaches in measuring trust. Several studies have questioned the reliability of the GSS survey as a measure of trust. They found that the question that aims to elicit trust is somehow imprecise because of the numerous possible answers that are not necessarily mutually exclusive from one another (Glaeser et al., 2000; Miller & Mitamura, 2003; Yamagishi et al., 1999). For the experimental approach, little is still known about the sensitivity and validity of trust games when performed in large and heterogeneous populations. However, since the conduct of a large-scale incentivised trust game with full representation of different nationalities is expensive and logistically impossible to implement, most studies relied on the use of the WVS trust question to measure trust (Naef & Schupp, 2009).

TRUST AND ECONOMIC DEVELOPMENT

Empirical studies have supported the idea that trust is one of the primary drivers of economic growth and development (Algan & Cahuc, 2010, 2013; Fukuyama, 1995; Holm & Nystedt, 2008; Knack, 2001; Zak & Knack, 2001). Trust is believed to oversee the distinction between the wealthiest and the poorest nations, presuming that trust is the logic behind the disparity between the per capita income of the United States and Somalia (Harford & Knack, 2006). The link between trust and a country's economic performance can be explained by looking at trust's micro and macro channels (Knack, 2001). On a micro level, trust reduces transaction costs, reinforces contracts and facilitates exchanges between buyers and sellers across different market types. Market players in higher trust societies are expected to use fewer resources to guard themselves against possible exploitation during economic transactions. It only means that these societies have less tendency to enter formal contracts, engage in bribe, or invest in private security services and equipment (Fukuyama, 2001).

Most developing countries are unable to develop effective, low-cost measures to enforce contracts, which causes both historical stagnation and underdevelopment of these countries (North, 1990). The absence of trust-dependent trades discourages players to engage in transactions that rely on future payments, which causes several market problems. For example, the notion of the unreliability of future payment mechanisms – due to the lack of trust – can delay the provision of goods and services. It can also lead to limited creditors willing to provide loans on the promise of future repayment. Moreover, the lack of trust is also a deterrent to innovation. Imagine entrepreneurs devoting more resources – such as money, time, and effort – to monitoring the actions of other market players (e.g., suppliers and employees), rather than using it for innovation of new products and process improvement (Zak & Knack, 2001). Thus, the economic backwardness in some economies can be ascribed to the lack of trust and mutual confidence among market players (Arrow, 1972).

Meanwhile, on a macro level, trust as a social capital is believed to foster democratic and good governance, boost economic efficiency and improve economic policies (Easterly & Levine, 1997; Putnam et al., 1994; Verba & Almond, 1963). The macro-level effects of trust are more speculative, where it indirectly improves economic efficiency through political channels. Societies with higher trust and social cohesion have a better political climate which leads to improved governance and better economic policies. For example, regional governments in more trusting parts of Italy, mostly in northern and central parts, were found to deliver more effective public services than those in the less trusting southern regions (Helliwell & Putnam, 1995; Putnam et al., 1994). Moreover, trust also promotes a healthy relationship between the government and its opposition. Granato et al. (1996) found empirical evidence of a strong positive correlation between trust and the stability of democratic institutions through cross-country data. In essence, it can be deduced that trust fosters economic development by improving efficiency at both micro and macro levels.

DETERMINANTS OF TRUST

Although trust is a determinant of economic growth, it is partially an endogenous variable (Fehr, 2009). Factors such as religion, tradition, and national history play an important role in forming social capital and trust (Fukuyama, 2001). Socio-demographic characteristics like gender and age are also linked with individual trusting behaviour. Several studies have investigated the difference in trusting behaviour between males and females. Evidence suggests that men are more trusting than women because men tend to perform strategic behaviour. Such behaviour is driven by their motivation to increase the payoff by the potential gains in the game (Buchan et al., 2008). However, women were found to be more trustworthy than men, due to a higher tendency to honour the trust displayed by their counterparts.

A cross-country analysis among the United States, China, Japan and Korea found no significant difference in trusting behaviour between men and women (Croson & Buchan, 1999). Experimental trust games were used to investigate the relationship between trust and age. A study assessed the level of trust and trustworthiness across different age groups – ranging from eight-year-old primary school students to retired persons in their late sixties (Sutter & Kocher, 2007). Key findings of the study suggest that trustworthiness exists in all age groups, but its level seems to increase along with age. Trust, on the other hand, was observed to be considerably higher in adult age groups compared to the groups of children and adolescents. On the contrary, a study in Sweden using a mail-based trust game found that people in their twenties are more trusting than people in their seventies (Holm & Nystedt, 2008). Also, the participants notably favoured placing trust when their counterparts belonged to the same age group.

Aside from socio-demographic characteristics, several bodies of literature also examined the link between trust and wealth and individuals' cognitive ability. A study devised a game where eliciting trust and trustworthiness is dependent on one's wealth and the average wealth of the population (Bac, 2009). Evidence suggests that in equilibrium, wealthy individuals exhibit higher trusting behaviour but lower trustworthiness, while relatively poor individuals display higher trustworthiness but lower trusting behaviour. For the case of an individual's cognitive ability, a study devised a trust game that incorporates the participants' intellectual ability through the cognitive reflection test (Corgnet et al., 2016). Results suggest there is a positive relationship between cognitive ability and trust. It implies a higher probability for players with more advanced cognitive ability to employ dominant strategies in the presence of social preferences. It must also be noted that risk preferences do not seem to explain the presented findings.

While studies on its socio-demographic determinants are interesting, studies on how social systems and institutions shape people's behaviour offer a more novel contribution to the growing literature on trust. For example, the rule of law and an independent judiciary system are found to influence trust in government (Johnston et al., 2006; Knack & Zak, 2003). Trust in government is important in situations, such as economic crises, political unrest or adverse natural phenomenon. During a major crisis, a lack of trust may impede the government's implementation of emergency and recovery plans because people might choose to act independently, causing greater harm to society (Lee, 2009). Meanwhile, external factors, such as uncertainty and ambiguity, are seen to dampen an individual's trusting behaviour (Clots-Figueras et al., 2016). Smaller stake size and group identity are observed to increase an individual's propensity to trust (Becchetti et al., 2013; Johansson-Stenman et al., 2005).

TRUST AND INEQUALITY

Literature also identifies social distance and inequality as a key determinant of trust. Evidence suggests that income inequality tends to diminish trust at the individual level, where countries with lower levels of income inequality have relatively higher trust ratings than countries with severe inequality problems (Korpi & Palme, 1998). Nations with a relatively high-income dispersion show considerably lower values for a trust measure derived from surveys conducted within the country (Knack & Keefer, 1997). The negative link between higher income disparity and trust was further supported by a study in Sweden. It was found that high income inequality between people in the lower half of the income distribution hampers trust (Gustavsson & Jordahl, 2008). Furthermore, empirical evidence also suggests that the negative link between social distance and trust thrives in heterogeneous communities (Alesina & La Ferrara, 2002).

Inequality, be it in wealth or education, affects the interaction of people across different social classes. An experimental study found that inequality affects people's perceptions of the broader climate in society, making them more individualistic than cooperative (Sánchez-Rodríguez et al., 2019). Another experimental study showed that visible inequality decreases wealthy people's propensity to cooperate with others (Nishi et al., 2015). Differences in wealth as a barometer of success may lead to social comparisons and competitiveness that diminishes cooperation. From a macroeconomic perspective, a study found that polarised countries due to income inequality are more likely to default on sovereign debt (Berg & Sachs, 1988). However, there is literature that contradicts the aforementioned findings of inequality and trust. A cross-country study of western developed economies revealed that inequality has no significant effect on trust when considering each nation's national wealth (Steijn & Lancee, 2011). In addition, an experimental study conducted in the United States where show-up fees given to the participants were randomly varied, also found no strong evidence for the hypothesis that inequality dampens trusting behaviour.

It must be noted that inequality may not necessarily have a direct impact on trust, but rather, it influences several channels that eventually shape an individual's ability to trust. According to social psychology, inequality is a welfare state that shapes a person's value judgment (Dutta, 2002), and since value judgments are susceptible to the 'reference effect', people tend to evaluate their current wealth levels in relative terms rather than in absolute terms (Frank, 1989). This evaluation process may lead to subjective value judgements that shape an individual's idea or perception of what is 'fair'. Even though the perception of fairness is based on evaluating a neutral reference outcome, individuals have different prosocial preferences that dictate their subjective idea of fairness (Fehr & Schmidt, 1999). Thus, low fairness perception may directly incentivise people to gain wealth by taking it from others rather than producing it. According to Kamas and Preston (2012), fairness perception can be categorised into two: distributive and reciprocal fairness. Distributive fairness aims to achieve equality in the final distribution of wealth – regardless of people's productivity level. Reciprocal fairness, on the other hand, aims to achieve equitable wealth distribution by basing incentives on people's contributions and productivity. Thus, the concept of 'fair' lies in the individual's preference for the wealth distribution system.

In behavioural economics, there is a notion that people, in general, are 'inequity averse'. Studies on equity theory suggest that the desire to uphold perceived equity motivates people to either reward or punish others for behaviour that they perceive to be just or unjust, respectively (Konow, 2003). People tend to do deplorable actions during 'unfair' situations as a way of achieving justice (Baumol & Fischer, 1986). These kinds of behaviour have been observed in various laboratory games, particularly in trust games (Fehr & Schmidt, 1999; Savage & Torgler, 2010). Therefore, the perception of fairness fosters social cohesion and trust among people.

TRUST IN THE CONTEXT OF SOCIETIES

The lives of people in organised societies are affected by the actions and choices of different political actors and institutions (Hakhverdian & Mayne, 2012). Institutional trust, most commonly known as political trust, is defined as the ability of citizens to place their faith in different political players and institutions. These include the government, the judiciary system, the police, politicians and many others – to act in ways that will not place them in danger or jeopardy (Levi & Stoker, 2000; Newton, 2001). Theoretically, citizens' ability to trust other people is informed by the rules and regulations that govern a society. However, their effectiveness relies on the credibility of state institutions (e.g., the police, judiciary and government) that are perceived to be fair and efficient, breeding a culture of trust among people by signalling those untrustworthy behaviours – such as dishonesty and corruption – are rare and unusual. It also assures the public that violators of the existing rules and regulations will be punished (Rothstein & Stolle, 2003).

Past literature on institutional trust has tried to uncover its economic significance in society. Several empirical studies pointed out that institutional trust is regarded as an important measure of a nation's democratic and political health (Dalton, 2004; Pharr & Putnam, 2000). Findings show that individual trust in the political actors and institutions generates a society that is leaning more towards democratic principles (Seligson & Carrión, 2002). People tend to judge an institution's performance based on its ability to deliver its promises by promoting political fairness and equality through an effective set of rules and regulations. Political institutions are also expected to pursue policies and social services that reflect the public's preferences and priorities. When political actors and institutions are able to keep up with their promises, citizens reward these positive performances with trust. In contrast, the underperformance of political actors and institutions induces low levels of institutional trust. (Hakhverdian & Mayne, 2012). Lack of institutional trust affects people's involvement in political and civic activities – such as participation in mass demonstrations, protests and political consumerism (Micheletti & Stolle, 2004; Mishler & Rose, 2005). It also affects people's public policy preferences (Chanley et al., 2000; Hetherington, 2005) and dampens generalised trust (Zmerli & Newton, 2008).

CONCLUSION

This chapter encapsulates the idea of trust by evaluating its nature, measurement, determinants and application. It presented how the conceptualisation of trust in economics leads to its different categorisations (e.g., interpersonal vs. intrapersonal and generalised vs. localised trust) and its measurement methodologies (i.e., surveys vs. games and experiments). It also surveyed its existing determinants ranging from socio-demographics (e.g., age and sex) to endogenous and exogenous factors (e.g., income class and institutions). Most importantly, it also bared the real-world economic implications of trust as a desirable condition for any kind of social interaction. It dictates our day-to-day decisions, from deciding what goods to buy to choosing who to vote for in an election. Trust ensures social interactions run smoothly even without the existence of formal contracts. Without trust, all kinds of dealings are problematic since everyone eyes each other with doubt. Future researchers on the topic of trust could build on the studies presented in this chapter. One good example would be addressing its methodological issues, particularly searching for better proxy measures of trust that could help improve future empirical workings in this research area. This could range from devising more detailed survey trust questions to improve the standard trust game procedure to reconciling the difference between stated and revealed trusting behaviour. Another interesting angle would be deconstructing the concept of interpersonal trust in the context of social relations. It would be thought-provoking to understand how people trust others in and outside their social circles and how people trust existing institutions.

REFERENCES

Alesina, A., & La Ferrara, E. (2002). Who trusts others? *Journal of Public Economics*, 85(2), 207–234.
Algan, Y., & Cahuc, P. (2010). Inherited trust and growth. *The American Economic Review*, 100(5), 2060–2092.
Alston, L. J., & Higgs, R. (1982). Contractual mix in southern agriculture since the Civil War: Facts, hypotheses, and tests. *The Journal of Economic History*, 42(2), 327–353.
Arrow, K. J. (1972). Gifts and exchanges. *Philosophy & Public Affairs*, 1(4), 343–362.
Ashraf, N., Bohnet, I., & Piankov, N. (2006). Decomposing trust and trustworthiness. *Experimental Economics*, 9(3), 193–208.
Baier, A. (1986). Trust and antitrust. *Ethics*, 96(2), 231–260.
Baumol, W. J., & Fischer, D. (1986). *Superfairness: Applications and theory*. MIT Press.
Becchetti, L., Castriota, S., & Conzo, P. (2013). Cooperative membership as a trust and trustworthiness reinforcing device: Results from a field experiment in the Philippines. *Journal of Development Studies*, 49(3), 412–425.
Bellemare, C., & Kröger, S. (2003). *On representative trust*. CentER Discussion Paper Series No. 2003-47, Tilburg University. https://pure.uvt.nl/ws/portalfiles/portal/545418/47.pdf
Ben-Ner, A., & Halldorsson, F. (2010). Trusting and trustworthiness: What are they, how to measure them, and what affects them. *Journal of Economic Psychology*, 31(1), 64–79.

Berg, A., & Sachs, J. (1988). The debt crisis structural explanations of country performance. *Journal of Development Economics*, 29(3), 271–306.

Berg, J., Dickhaut, J., & McCabe, K. (1995). Trust, reciprocity, and social history. *Games and Economic Behavior*, 10(1), 122–142.

Blomqvist, K. (1997). The many faces of trust. *Scandinavian Journal of Management*, 13(3), 271–286.

Buchan, N. R., Croson, R. T., & Solnick, S. (2008). Trust and gender: An examination of behavior and beliefs in the Investment Game. *Journal of Economic Behavior & Organization*, 68(3), 466–476.

Chanley, V. A. Rudolph, T. J., & Rahn, W. M. (2000). The origins and consequences of public trust in government. A time series analysis. *Public Opinion Quarterly*, 64(3), 239–256.

Clots-Figueras. I., Hernan Gonzalez, R., & Kujal, P. (2016). Trust and trustworthiness under information asymmetry and ambiguity. *Economics Letters*, 147(1), 168–170.

Coleman, J. (1990). *Foundations of social theory*. Belknap Press.

Colquitt, J., Scott, B., & LePine, J. (2007). Trust, trustworthiness, and trust propensity: A meta-analytic test of their unique relationships with risk taking and job performance. *Journal of Applied Psychology*, 92(4), 909–927.

Corgnet, B., Espín, A. M., Hernán-González, R., Kujal, P., & Rassenti, S. (2016). To trust, or not to trust: Cognitive reflection in trust games. *Journal of Behavioral and Experimental Economics*, 64, 20–27.

Croson, R., & Buchan, N. (1999). Gender and culture: International experimental evidence from trust games. *American Economic Review*, 89(2), 386–391.

Dalton, R. J. (2004). *Democratic challenges, democratic choices* (Vol. 10). Oxford University Press.

Dasgupta, P. (1988). Trust as a commodity. In D. Gambetta (Ed.) *Trust: Making and breaking cooperative relations*. Basil Blackwell Publishing.

Delhey, J., Newton, K., & Welzel, C. (2011). How general is trust in "most people"? Solving the radius of trust problem. *American Sociological Review*, 76(5), 786–807.

Deutsch, M. (1958). Trust and suspicion. *Journal of Conflict Resolution*, 2(4), 265–279.

Doherty, C., Kiley, J., & Johnson, B. (2017). *Public trust in government remains near historic lows as partisan attitudes shift,* Discussion Paper 2017-05-03, Pew Research Center. https://www.pewresearch.org/politics/2017/05/03/public-trust-in-government-remains-near-historic-lows-as-partisan-attitudes-shift/

Dutta, B. (2002). Chapter 12 Inequality, poverty and welfare. In *Handbook of social choice and welfare* (pp. 597–633). Elsevier.

Easterly, W., & Levine, R. (1997). Africa's growth tragedy: Policies and ethnic divisions. *The Quarterly Journal of Economics*, 112(4), 1203–1250.

Falk, A., & Fischbacher, U. (2006). A theory of reciprocity. *Games and Economic Behavior*, 54(2), 293–315.

Fehr, E. (2002). A nation-wide laboratory: Examining trust and trustworthiness by integrating behavioral experiment into representative surveys. *Journal of Applied Social Science Studies*, 122(4), 519–542.

Fehr, E. (2009). On the economics and biology of trust. *Journal of the European Economic Association*, 7(2–3), 235–266.

Fehr, E., & Schmidt, K. M. (1999). A theory of fairness, competition, and cooperation. *The Quarterly Journal of Economics*, 114(3), 817–868.

Frank, R. H. (1989). Frames of reference and the quality of life. *The American Economic Review*, 79(2), 80–85.

Freeman, R. E. (2010). *Strategic management: A stakeholder approach*. Cambridge University Press.

Fukuyama, F. (1995). *Trust: The social virtues and the creation of prosperity* (Vol. 99). Free Press.

Fukuyama, F. (2001). Social capital, civil society and development. *Third World Quarterly*, 22(1), 7–20.

Gambetta, D. (1988). *Trust: Making and breaking cooperative relations* (Vol. 52). Basil Blackwell Publishing.

Geertz, C. (1978). The bazaar economy: Information and search in peasant marketing. *The American Economic Review*, 68(2), 28–32.

Glaeser, E. L., Laibson, D. I., Scheinkman, J. A., & Soutter, C. L. (2000). Measuring trust. *The Quarterly Journal of Economics*, 115(3), 811–846.

Granato, J., Inglehart, R., & Leblang, D. (1996). Cultural values, stable democracy, and economic development: A reply. *American Journal of Political Science*, 40(3), 680–696.

Granovetter, M. (1985). Economic action and social structure: The problem of embeddedness. *American Journal of Sociology*, 91(3), 481–510.

Gunnthorsdottir, A., McCabe, K., & Smith, V. (2002). Using the Machiavellianism instrument to predict trustworthiness in a bargaining game. *Journal of Economic Psychology*, 23(1), 49–66.

Gustavsson, M., & Jordahl, H. (2008). Inequality and trust in Sweden: Some inequalities are more harmful than others. *Journal of Public Economics*, 92(1–2), 348–365.

Hakhverdian, A., & Mayne, Q. (2012). Institutional trust, education, and corruption: A micro-macro interactive approach. *The Journal of Politics*, 74(3), 739–750.

Harford, T., & Knack, S. (2006, 7/21/2010). *The economics of trust*. Forbes Magazine – Online, https://www.forbes.com/2006/09/22/trust-economy-markets-tech_cx_th_06trust_0925harford.html

Helliwell, J. F., & Putnam, R. D. (1995). Economic growth and social capital in Italy. *Eastern Economic Journal*, 21(3), 295–307.

Hetherington, M. J. (2005). *Why trust matters: Declining political trust and the demise of American liberalism*. Princeton University Press.

Holm, H., & Nystedt, P. (2008). Trust in surveys and games - A methodological contribution on the influence of money and location. *Journal of Economic Psychology*, 29(4), 522–542.

Hosmer, L. T. (1995). Trust: The connecting link between organizational theory and philosophical ethics. *The Academy of Management Review*, 20(2), 379–403.

Houser, D., Schunk, D., & Winter, J. (2010). Distinguishing trust from risk: An anatomy of the investment game. *Journal of Economic Behavior & Organization*, 74(1–2), 72–81.

James, H. S., Jr. (2002). The trust paradox: A survey of economic inquiries into the nature of trust and trustworthiness. *Journal of Economic Behavior & Organization*, 47(3), 291–307.

Jensen, M. C., & Meckling, W. H. (1976). Theory of the firm: Managerial behavior, agency costs and ownership structure. *Journal of Financial Economics*, 3(4), 305–360.

Johansson-Stenman, O., Mahmud, M., & Martinsson, P. (2005). Does stake size matter in trust games? *Economics Letters*, 88(3), 365–369.

Johnston, W., Krahn, H., & Harrison, T. (2006). Democracy, political institutions, and trust: The limits of current electoral reform proposals. *Canadian Journal of Sociology/Cahiers canadiens de sociologie*, 31(2), 165–182.

Jøsang, A., Ismail, R., & Boyd, C. (2007). A survey of trust and reputation systems for online service provision. *Decision Support Systems*, 43(2), 618–644.

Kamas, L., & Preston, A. (2012). Distributive and reciprocal fairness: What can we learn from the heterogeneity of social preferences? *Journal of Economic Psychology*, 33(3), 538–553.

Knack, S. (2001). *Trust, associational life, and economic performance*, MPRA Paper No. 27247. Munich Personal RePEc Archive. https://mpra.ub.uni-muenchen.de/27247/1/MPRA_paper_27247.pdf

Knack, S., & Keefer, P. (1997). Does social capital have an economic payoff? A cross-country investigation. *The Quarterly Journal of Economics*, 112(4), 1251–1288.

Knack, S., & Zak, P. J. (2003). Building trust: Public policy, interpersonal trust, and economic development. *Supreme Court Economic Review*, 10, 91–107.

Konow, J. (2003). Which is the fairest one of all? A positive analysis of justice theories. *Journal of Economic Literature*, 41(4), 1188–1239.

Korpi, W., & Palme, J. (1998). The paradox of redistribution and strategies of equality: Welfare state institutions, inequality, and poverty in the Western countries. *American Sociological Review*, 63(5), 661–687.

Lazzarini, S. G., Madalozzo, R., Artes, R., & Siqueira, J. d. O. (2005). Measuring trust: An experiment in Brazil. *Brazilian Journal of Applied Economics*, 9(2), 153–169.

Lee, K. (2009). How the Hong Kong government lost the public trust in SARS: Insights for government communication in a health crisis. *Public Relations Review*, 35(1), 74–76.

Levi, M., & Stoker, L. (2000). Political trust and trustworthiness. *Annual Review of Political Science*, 3(1), 475–507.

Lewis, J. D., & Weigert, A. (1985). Trust as a social reality. *Social Forces*, 63(4), 967–985.

Luhmann, N. (1979). *Trust and power: Two works*. Wiley.

Luhmann, N. (2000). Familiarity, confidence, trust: Problems and alternatives. *Trust: Making and breaking cooperative relations*, 6(1), 94–107.

Micheletti, M., & Stolle, D. (2004). Politics, products, and markets: Exploring political consumerism past and present. *Transaction Publishers*, 84 (1), 123–125.

Miller, A. S., & Mitamura, T. (2003). Are surveys on trust trustworthy? *Social Psychology Quarterly*, 66(1), 62–70.
Mishler, W., & Rose, R. (2005). What are the political consequences of trust? A test of cultural and institutional theories in Russia. *Comparative Political Studies*, 38(9), 1050–1078.
Naef, M., & Schupp, J. (2009). Measuring trust: *Experiments and surveys in contrast and combination*, SOEPaper No. 167, Deutsches Institut für Wirtschaftsforschung. http://dx.doi.org/10.2139/ssrn.1367375
Nannestad, P. (2008). What have we learned about generalized trust, if anything? *Annu. Review of Political Science*, 11, 413–436.
Newton, K. (2001). Trust, social capital, civil society, and democracy. *International Political Science Review*, 22(2), 201–214.
Nishi, A., Shirado, H., Rand, D. G., & Christakis, N. A. (2015). Inequality and visibility of wealth in experimental social networks. *Nature*, 526(7573), 426–429.
Pettit, P. (1995). The cunning of trust. *Philosophy & Public Affairs*, 24(3), 202–225.
Pharr, S. J., & Putnam, R. D. (2000). *Officials' misconduct and public distrust: Japan and the liberal democracies*. Princeton University Press.
Platteau, J. P. (1994). Behind the market stage where real societies exist (Part I): The role of public and private order institutions. *The Journal of Development Studies*, 30(3), 533–577.
Portes, A., & Landolt, P. (1996). Unsolved mysteries: The Tocqueville files II. The downside of social capital. *The American Prospect*, 7(26), 18–21.
Putnam, R. D., Leonardi, R., & Nanetti, R. Y. (1994). *Making democracy work: Civic traditions in modern Italy*. Princeton University Press.
Rothstein, B., & Stolle, D. (2003). Social capital, impartiality and the welfare state: An institutional approach. In M. Hooghe & D. Stolle (Eds.) *Generating social capital: Civil society and institutions in comparative perspective* (pp. 191–210). Palgrave.
Rotter, J. B. (1967). A new scale for the measurement of interpersonal trust. *Journal of Personality*, 35(4), 651–665.
Rousseau, D. M., Sitkin, S. B., Burt, R. S., & Camerer, C. (1998). Not so different after all: A cross-discipline view of trust. *Academy of Management Review*, 23(3), 393–404.
Sánchez-Rodríguez, Á., Willis, G. B., & Rodríguez-Bailón, R. (2019). Economic and social distance: Perceived income inequality negatively predicts an interdependent self-construal. *International Journal of Psychology*, 54(1), 117–125.
Sapienza, P., Toldra-Simats, A., & Zingales, L. (2013). Understanding trust. *Economic Journal*, 123(573), 1313–1332.
Savage, D. A., & Torgler, B. (2010). Perceptions of fairness and allocation systems. *Economic Analysis and Policy*, 40(2), 229–248.
Seligson, M. A., & Carrión, J. F. (2002). Political support, political skepticism, and political stability in new democracies: An empirical examination of mass support for coups d'etat in Peru. *Comparative Political Studies*, 35(1), 58–82.
Shapiro, S. P. (1987). The social control of impersonal trust. *American Journal of Sociology*, 93(3), 623–658.
Steijn, S., & Larcee, B. (2011). *Does income inequality negatively affect general trust. Examining three potential problems with the inequality trust hypothesis*, Discussion Paper Number 20, GINI Growing Inequalities Impact. https://core.ac.uk/reader/6273040
Stiglitz, J. E. (2002). Information and the change in the paradigm in economics. *The American Economic Review*, 92(3), 460–501.
Sutter, M., & Kocher, M. G. (2007). Trust and trustworthiness across different age groups. *Games and Economic Behavior*, 59(2), 364–382.
Thöni, C., Tyran, J.-R., & Wengström, E. (2012). Microfoundations of social capital. *Journal of Public Economics*, 96(7–8), 635–643.
Uslaner, E. M. (2002). *The moral foundations of trust*. Cambridge University Press.
Uslaner, E. M. (2003). Trust, democracy and governance: Can government policies influence generalized trust? In M. Hooghe & D. Stolle (Eds.) *Generating social capital: Civil society and institutions in comparative perspective* (pp. 171–190). Springer.
Verba, S., & Almond, G. (1963). *The civic culture: Political attitudes and democracy in five nations*. Princeton University Press.

Vyrastekova, J., & Garikipati, S. (2005). *Beliefs and trust: An experiment,* CentER Discussion Paper No. 2005-88, Tilburg University. https://pure.uvt.nl/ws/portalfiles/portal/775010/88.pdf

Yamagishi, T., Kikuchi, M., & Kosugi, M. (1999). Trust, gullibility, and social intelligence. *Asian Journal of Social Psychology,* 2(1), 145–161.

Yamagishi, T., & Yamagishi, M. (1994). Trust and commitment in the United States and Japan. *Motivation and Emotion,* 18(2), 129–166.

Zak, P., & Knack, S. (2001). Trust and growth. *Economic Journal,* 111(470), 295–321.

Zand, D. E. (1972). Trust and managerial problem solving. *Administrative Science Quarterly,* 17(2), 229–239.

Zmerli, S., & Newton, K. (2008). Social trust and attitudes toward democracy. *Public Opinion Quarterly,* 72(4), 706–724.

Zmerli, S., Newton, K., & Montero, J. R. (2007). Trust in people, confidence in political institutions, and satisfaction with democracy. In J. Van Deth, J. Montero & A. Westholm (Eds.) *Citizenship and involvement. European democracies: A comparative analysis* (pp. 35–65). Routledge.

18. Intuition and behavioural economics: A very brief history
Roger Frantz

INTRODUCTION

Kahneman and Tversky revolutionised economics in part by recognising our cognitive limits and by their ability to write about it in a way which attracted the attention of economists as a group. Our cognitive limits lead us to use heuristics, or shortcuts, and intuition was used as a synonym for heuristics. Kahneman and Tversky commented that intuition can be very useful, but it also leads to errors in decision-making. Economics thus began travelling down a 'road' in which economic man, the errorless, bias-less 'unicorn', to use the term for economic man brilliantly uttered by Richard Thaler, was replaced by error-and-biased man, in which seemingly everything we do from morning to night involves errors and biases. Let's accept the fact that intuition involves errors in decision-making. As Kahneman and Tversky have shown, humans make mistake after mistake when it comes to analytical/logical thinking. So, everything we do, our System 1 and our System 2 thinking, creates errors.

Not all economists in the history of economic thought, for example, Adam Smith, John Maynard Keynes, Herbert Simon and Frank Knight, among many others, saw intuition as being synonymous with errors or irrationality. This chapter will discuss what these four economists in the history of economic thought have said about intuition and behavioural economics.

ADAM SMITH: OUR FATHER WHO ART IN SCOTLAND

Smith believed that much of our mental life is unconscious processes. As such, the mind generates intuitions about many things including the way we should act. Smith thus drew the distinction between intuition and reflective processes. He also found that the two processes (intuitive and reflective) may lead to different behaviours in the same circumstances and that our intuitions are clearly non-utilitarian. There is a distinction between reason and passion, or reason and imagination. This implies a distinction between unconscious, implicit and effortless mechanisms on one hand and conscious, explicit and effortful mechanisms on the other – or, what Kahneman referred to as System 1 and System 2.

Smith lived during a time when the community of the Middle Ages was giving way to a commercial 'society of strangers' (Frantz, 2005)). How can social bonds be maintained in this new social form? Smith's answer was through sympathy and the impartial spectator, both of which have characteristics of intuition. Sympathy is imagining what it is like to be in another's 'shoes'. You can never know what it is like to be your brother 'on the rack'. However, you can imagine what it would be like to be your brother on the rack. This allows the 'sympathiser' to understand what others consider to be right and wrong. Sympathy with another allows us to imagine what their life is like. Smith says that people who sympathised with the wealthy imagined their lives to be wonderful. The result is that people would strive to be wealthy in order to have the life of a wealthy person, at which time others would sympathise with them. Smith adds that this is an illusion about the wealthy, but it is a 'trick' which God plays on us in order to increase the wealth of nations from which everyone can have a decent standard of living. The impartial spectator is the objective part of ourselves; it is our conscience, the inhabitant in the breast, the great judge and arbiter of our conduct, a moral sense. It is experienced, not logically, but intuitively. It plays a positive role in society; more about this in the following.

Dual Processing: Intuition and Analysis

The use of the impartial spectator (IS) is done intuitively because when you use the IS you 'divide yourself' into two persons, the examiner and the examined, the judge and the one being judged. Dividing yourself into two is not the result of an analytical and logical process. It is an intuitive process, the work of the imagination. Without the IS we are left to 'the selfish and original passions of human nature' (Smith, 1969, p. 233). The impartial spectator and sympathy are designed so that we will consider the welfare of others as well as our own welfare. To ignore others is an act of impropriety: it is rude, indecent, unseemly, in bad taste and is bad behaviour. We process selfish desires and benevolent affections. We process pleasure and pain. We process life from our point of view and that of another. Without the impartial spectator, we will over-exaggerate our pain and rejoice excessively about our joy. Doing so is the 'fatal weakness of mankind, is the source of half the disorders of human life' (p. 263).

On the first page of the text of *The Theory of Moral Sentiments*, Smith says that we are self-interested and altruistic:

> How selfish so ever a man may be supposed, there are evidently some principles in his nature, which interest him in the fortune of others, and render their happiness necessary to him, though he derives nothing from it, except the pleasure of seeing it. Of this kind is pity or compassion, the emotion we feel for the misery of others, when we either see it, or are made to conceive it in a very lively manner. That we often derive sorrow from the sorrows of others, is a matter of fact too obvious to require any instances to prove it; for this sentiment, like all the other original passions of human nature, is by no means confined to the virtuous or the humane, though they perhaps may feel it with the most exquisite sensibility. The greatest ruffian, the most hardened violator of the laws of society, is not altogether without it.
>
> (Smith, 1969, p. 45)

He continues, 'to feel much for others, and little for ourselves, that to restrain our selfish, and to indulge our benevolent, affections, constitutes the perfection of human nature; and can alone produce among mankind that harmony of sentiments and passions in which consists their whole grace and propriety' (Smith, 1969, pp. 71–72). We are self-interested and altruistic. We are moved by passion and logic. We are analytical and intuitive. We do *not* have a moral sense, a sixth sense or a seventh sense. We have moral feelings from sympathy and the impartial spectator.

Cognitive (Optical) Illusions

Kahneman and Tversky developed their ideas about cognitive illusions or errors from reading the literature about optical illusions. Smith discussed these in *The Theory of Moral*

Sentiments. He says that only by using the impartial spectator 'can we ever see what relates to ourselves in its proper shape and dimensions' (Smith, 1969, p. 232). For example, 'to the eye of the body, objects appear great or small, not so much according to their real dimensions as according to the nearness or distance of their situation' (p. 232). So the body's eye makes it 'appear that large mountains in the distance can fit inside a small glass window that is one foot away' (p. 232). You can fix this by 'transporting' yourself via your imagination, halfway between the window and the mountains. This is currently referred to as 'spatial intelligence' (Gardner, 1982) – an intelligence controlled by the right hemisphere of the neocortex – intuition.

There is a rough similarity between this and studies done in behavioural economics which try to get people to appreciate the future more so that they save more. Hal E. Hershfield et al. (2011) used samples of students who were shown visual representations of their future selves at retirement age. The result was that all the students, upon seeing their future selves, reduced the discounting of their future selves and began saving more money. And this result was not due to thinking about ageing per se, but from simply seeing a representative of their future self (Hershfield et al., 2011).

Loss Aversion

How do we process pleasure and pain? Smith implies what we now refer to as loss aversion.

> Pain . . . is, in almost all cases, a more pungent sensation than the opposite and correspondent pleasure. The one almost always depresses us much more below the ordinary, or what may be called the natural state of our happiness, than the other ever raises us above it. A man of sensibility is apt to be more humiliated by just censure than he is ever elevated by just applause.
> (Smith, 1769, p. 218)

The natural state of our happiness is our reference point. Smith says that we dislike losing more than we like winning, even when the amount gained and lost are the same amount.

> To be deprived of that which we are possessed of, is a greater evil than to be disappointed of what we have only an expectation. Breach of property, therefore, theft and robbery, which take from us what we are possessed of, are greater crimes than breach of contract, which only disappoints us of what we expected.
> (Smith, 1959, p. 163)

Modern behavioural economics refers to this as valuing out-of-pocket costs more than opportunity costs. It also leads to a gap between willingness to pay and willingness to receive.

Optimism Bias and the Overconfidence Effect

Smith uses the term 'overweening conceit' to describe people's beliefs about their own abilities. We are overconfident. In addition, we have an 'absurd presumption in their own good fortune'. We believe that good things are more likely to happen to us, and that bad things are less likely to happen. Behavioural economists refer to this as the optimism bias. Smith says that

> There is no man living who, when in tolerable health and spirits, has not some share of it. The chance of gain is by every man more or less over-valued, and the chance of loss is by most men under-valued, and by scarce any man, who is in tolerable health and spirits, valued more than it is worth.
> (Smith, 1776/1976, p. 120)

The fact that men are overconfident about winning at risky ventures is obvious from the success of lotteries. Smith says confidently, that there never has been a 'perfectly fair' lottery. That people undervalue the chance of losing is obvious from the moderate profit rates of insurers.

Fairness

Not using the impartial spectator is the cause of much illness in the world. In a related statement, Smith says that the IS will also not abide by unfairness or excessively unequal distribution of income, especially when the moral conduct of both rich and poor is considered the cause of wealth and poverty. He says that the

> disposition to admire, and almost to worship, the rich and the powerful, and to despise, or, at least, to neglect, persons of poor and mean condition, though necessary both to establish and to maintain the distinction of ranks and the order of society, is, at the same time, the great and most universal cause of the corruption of our moral sentiments. That wealth and greatness are often regarded with the respect and admiration which are due only to wisdom and virtue; and that the contempt, of which vice and folly are the only proper objects, is often most unjustly bestowed upon poverty and weakness, has been the complaint of moralists in all ages.
> (Smith, 1776/1976, p. 126)

Sympathy and the impartial spectator are *not* experienced via a conscious logical process. They are experienced intuitively, via a subconscious and non-logical process. However, intuition is not, per se, rational or irrational. Smith emphasised the positive role of both sympathy and the impartial spectator.

JOHN MAYNARD KEYNES

> Keynes' General Theory was the greatest contribution to behavioural economics before the present era. Almost everywhere Keynes blamed market failures on psychological propensities (as in consumption) and irrationalities (as in stock market speculation).
> (Akerlof, 2002, p. 428)

John Maynard Keynes's (1883–1946) publications include *The Economic Consequences of the Peace* (1919), *A Treatise on Probability* (1921), *A Tract on Monetary Reform* (1923), *The End of Laissez-Faire* (1926), *A Treatise on Money* (1930), *Economic Possibilities for Our Grandchildren* (1930), *Essays in Persuasion* (1931), *Essays in Biography* (1933) and *The General Theory* (1936). He was one of the chief negotiators for England after World War I. He was Chair of the World Bank and a central figure in the creation of the Bretton Woods system of international finance after World War II. He served as the editor of the *Economic Journal* from 1912 to 1944. Keynes had an intellect par excellence, but he also had a strong intuition. George Akerlof says that Keynes's achievements were due to Keynes's 'intuitive understanding of psychology' (Akerlof, 2002, p. 420).

Keynes's synonyms for intuition included self-evident or a priori knowledge, vision, mind's eye, eye of common sense, the peering eye of philosophy and direct judgement (Frantz, 2005). One of the things intuition does, according to Keynes, is to see the destination of your thoughts even before you see the path. It also shows how things are related to each other. It provides a vision which is a basis for analysis, and developing expectations about the future. How do scientists make discoveries? Keynes says that it is a three-step process. First, perceive the details. Second, hold the details together in your mind for a long time. And, third, 'with a kind of sudden insight', all the details fall into place so the connections among them become clear. Keynes considered Newton to be an expert in this three-step process, which is one reason he referred to Newton as the 'last of the magicians' (Frantz, 2005, p. 83). In another place, Keynes says that creativity begins as a 'grey, fuzzy, woolly monster' (p. 83) inside your head leading to the use of language to make your thoughts more useful. Because economics is not an exact science it must consider more vague forms of reasoning such as intuition. It must appeal to the readers' intuition. Without intuition, 'one is helpless'.

Why do we need intuition? First, because our knowledge and experience are related. Second, and related, our knowledge of the future is limited. Because of this Keynes did not want to forego current benefits for future ones. In other words, Keynes was subject to the status quo bias. Third, logical analysis has its limits. As it turns out, not only do heuristics – intuitions – have their limits, as Kahneman and Tversky said repeatedly, but so does logical analysis, as Keynes said repeatedly.

Keynes's Early Beliefs

In 1938, Keynes (2010) wrote an essay, 'My Early Beliefs'. It reveals some of Keynes's explicit and implicit beliefs about psychology (and economics). Speaking of his years at Cambridge, Keynes (2010) says that it was the 'habits of feeling' which set Keynes and his colleagues in the Bloomsbury group apart from the other people at Cambridge. Keynes and his friends were disciples of Cambridge philosopher G.E. Moore, a philosopher who placed a lot of attention on intuition. All that mattered was states of mind, not associated with achievement or consequences, but with 'timeless, passionate states of contemplation and communion' (ibid., p. 436). After reading Moore for the first time, Keynes said that he 'saw everything quite clearly in a flash' (ibid., p. 79). In other words, Keynes had an 'ah-ha' experience, aka an intuition.

Which states of mind were good? In 'My Early Beliefs', Keynes (2010) says that goodness is known only by direct inspection, of direct unanalysable intuition. Keynes referred to intuition as a 'unique non-sensory, cognitive faculty' (ibid., p. 437). Synonyms for Smith's term sympathy are all of the following: feeling sorry for another person, imagining being in another's shoes and using the impartial spectator. For Keynes, economics was a moral science, not a mechanical science. Newton was associated with mechanical science. However, for Keynes, Newton was a 'magician', an alchemist, who made intuitive leaps to prove what he already knew. He used mathematics to communicate. For Keynes, intuitive leaps could form the basis of rational beliefs.

Keynes on Long-Term Expectations and Investment

Our knowledge of the world is very limited, says Keynes. But, at the same time, we have to rely on uncertain events when we formulate our expectations. We face a tradeoff: rely on facts we feel confident in even though they are relatively less relevant to what we are trying to attain or rely on facts which are more relevant but our knowledge of which is vague. What do we do? We project the current situation into the future unless we have very good reasons for expecting a change requiring a different approach. And our long-term expectations depend on the 'most probable forecast we can make' and on our confidence in the forecast. 'Practical men' put the utmost importance on confidence. Economists, however, have not analysed the topic of confidence with any specificity. Their conversations are more general. Similar to Pigou, Keynes talks about the time gap in making forecasts. Keynes (1936/1965) insists on the limits of our knowledge and the illusion that we know more than we do. The knowledge which we use in our forecasts is its overall extreme precariousness. For forecasts of several years in the future, it is 'very slight and often negligible', 'little and sometimes nothing'.

On what basis do we make forecasts? '[W]e have tacitly agreed , as a rule, to fall back on what is, in truth, a conventions . . . assuming that the existing state of affairs will continue indefinitely, except in so far as we have specific reasons to expect a change' (Keynes (1936/1965, p. 152). Such conventions are arbitrary and precarious and this is one reason why investment falls short of sufficiency. Behavioural economists refer to this as the status quo bias.

What heightens the precariousness of our knowledge? First, owners of capital are different from managers, and the owners have no special knowledge of capital investment. Second, day-to-day changes in profits are not significant but have an 'altogether excessive, and even absurd, influence on the market' (Keynes (1936/1965, p. 154). Third, the mass psychology of 'ignorant individuals' creates a convention based on irrelevant information. This convention changes suddenly as irrelevant information changes. What we have here is a combination of bounded rationality, irrationality and errors and biases: a combo of Simon, Leibenstein and Kahneman and Tversky.

Fourth, and perhaps most important is that investors and speculators are concerned not with making above-average forecasts as they are with predicting changes in the prevailing convention before others predict these changes. Why try to beat others than make better forecasts?

'Investment based on genuine long-term expectation is so difficult to-day as to be scarcely practicable. He who attempts it must surely . . . run greater risks than he who tries to guess better than the crowd how the crowd will behave' (Keynes (1936/1965, p. 157).

Animal Spirits

Adam Smith asked why the (market) economy is essentially stable. His answer is that rational people pursuing their own interests will take advantage of all mutually beneficial opportunities in production and consumption. And this results in full employment. So long as Smith restricts himself to rational behaviour then his analysis is rational. However, at least in *The Wealth of Nations*, Smith minimised or neglected non-rational behaviour and non-economic motives. In short, Smith ignored animal spirits. Keynes did not ignore animal spirits. Why is investment spending unstable? Besides speculation, instability in investment is due to animal spirits. Keynes (1936/1965, p. 161) explains it this way:

> the instability due to the characteristic of human nature that a large proportion of our positive activities depend on spontaneous optimism rather than on a mathematical expectation . . . Most . . . of our decisions to do something positive . . . can only be taken as a result of animal spirits.

The alternative to animal spirits is the method of orthodox economics: a weighted average of quantitative benefits multiplied by quantitative probabilities. Keynes says that organisations 'fade and die' if they depend on mathematical expectations in the wake of the 'death' of animal spirits. Keynes is clear that long-term expectations are not prisoners to 'irrational psychology'. But, at the same time, decisions about the future 'cannot depend on strict mathematical expectation, since the basis for making such calculations does not exist' (Keynes 1936/1965, p. 163). But we have an 'innate urge to activity', and when we can calculate we do. But, for the most part, we fall back upon 'whim, or sentiment, or chance' (Keynes 1936/1965, p. 163). Why do economic crises occur? What about changing thought patterns? Orthodox economic theory says what? But changes in confidence, and other changing thought patterns, are, according to Akerlof and Shiller (2009), a good reason for the 2008–2009 crises.

FRANK KNIGHT: RISK, UNCERTAINTY AND CONSCIOUSNESS

> Eighty years before there was such a thing called behavioral economics, Frank Knight pondered the limitations of the scientific treatment of human data . . . As a social philosopher – as well as an economic theorist, Knight was skeptical of the trend in social scientific thinking.
> (Smith and Wilson, 2019, p. 49)

Frederich Kershner, President of Milligan College and professor of Frank Knight, said of Knight, 'From the standpoint of quickness of perception, or of that rare capacity, which enables a person to see through things almost at a glance, he is the best student I have had' (Howey, 1983, p. 165). Knight had a well-developed intuition.

Knowledge

In 'The Truth About Economics' (1940), Knight says that our knowledge is limited and can be categorised into here are three types of knowledge: knowledge of the external world, knowledge of the truths of logic and mathematics and the knowledge of human conduct. The last one-third is about economics, the knowledge of human conduct, motives and interests – the knowledge of maximisation, which is the 'fundamental proposition' of economics. Economic behaviour, maximisation, is the result of an intention or an intended result, which is not amenable to observation in any admissible use of that term. Satisfaction, psychic income or utility, the stuff of economics, is a 'mental fact', an intuition, and is not measurable, at least the same way that physical magnitudes are measured. More than that, no one achieves the maximum. The gap between the maximum and actual behaviour is due to ignorance, error and prejudice, all of which affect real, human choices. This knowledge of maximisation or economic behaviour can neither be observed nor inferred from observations.

Knowledge of Self and Others

Economic knowledge is a social activity and a social phenomenon. This means that economic knowledge depends on self-knowledge and the knowledge of others, specifically, others' minds. Hence economic knowledge requires intercommunications between and among minds. This is Hayek's (Hayek 1952) view that some human knowledge requires what might be referred to as mind reading. At the end of 'Facts and Metaphysics in Economic Psychology', Knight says that

> we can learn about human phenomena . . . chiefly by studying, und practicing, communication with other minds, the process of which activity is art in its various forms, in contrast with science . . . we do know other minds, and in them know our own, and vice versa. In this knowledge vastly more than observation is involved; we know from the inside as well as the outside, by identifying ourselves in a real sense with the object of knowledge. The understanding, prediction and control of human 'behavior' is an art.
> (Knight, 1925, p. 266)

In 'What Is Truth in Economics', Knight says that

> intercommunication between our own minds and other minds, which is the fundamental basis of all knowledge, whether of the world or of mind (meaning human minds, primarily normal), and the basis of intelligence itself.
>
> (Knight, 1940, pp. 21–22)

Mind reading is an intuitive process but not a logical and analytical process.

Rationality

Scientific economics requires an answer to the question of how far life is rational, meaning that life is governed by the means–end relationship. Knight says that life is not very rational. People don't have tastes and preferences or values which are given and stable. However, economics is forward-looking and organisations must anticipate what people will want. To anticipate correctly, tastes must be, according to Knight, stable. But, they are not, again, according to Knight, stable. Our tastes are discovered through activity. Knight says that We strive to 'know ourselves', to find out our real wants, more than to get what we want. We want interesting experiences which often come from the unanticipated, from novelty and surprise. This fact sets what may be the first and most sweeping limitation to the conception of economics as a science (McKenzie, 1983, p. 99).

ECONOMIC THEORY

Economic theory must, but doesn't, examine the assumptions about human behaviour. Until it does, it cannot bridge the gap between the ideal and the actual conditions of society. Knight viewed neoclassical theory as studying the abstract ideal world of perfect competition which included a rational economic man with perfect knowledge efficiently satisfying his preferences through the market.

Economic Man

What is economic man? He acts with 'complete rationality'. To say that someone is perfectly rational 'would be equivalent to saying that they are accurate mechanisms of desire satisfaction. In fact, human activity is largely impulsive, a relatively unthinking and undetermined response to stimulus and suggestion' (Knight, 1923, p. 590). In another place, he says that 'The economic man neither competes nor higgles – nor does he co-operate, psychologically speaking; he treats other human beings as if they were slot machine' (Knight, 1939, p. 18).

The assumption of economic man reduces the market process and human behaviour to a mechanical process. In 'Economic Theory and Nationalism', Knight says that 'The view of human behavior as a mechanical process . . . is impossible to human beings . . . This is one of the main differences between the economic man and the real human being' (Emmett, 2009, p. 93).

As Knight (1921/1965, pp. 76–77) argues: "By this we do not mean that they are to be 'as angels, knowing good from evil'; we assume ordinary human motives (with the reservations noted in the following paragraphs), but they are supposed to 'know what they want' and to seek it 'intelligently'. Their behaviour, that is, is all 'conduct', as we have previously defined the term; all their acts take place in response to real, conscious, stable and consistent motives, dispositions or desires; nothing is capricious or experimental, everything deliberate. They are supposed to know absolutely the consequences of their acts when they are performed, and to perform them in the light of the consequences."

RISK, UNCERTAINTY AND PROFIT

> A scientific world view has no possible place for the intuitive, or any other foresight of new truth, in advance of perception.
> (Knight, 1924, p. 103)

In *Risk, Uncertainty, and Profit*, Knight lists the conditions necessary for perfect competition. The reason? To understand the theoretical tendencies of a free enterprise society. Among them are that human beings are completely rational. People know what they want and they seek it intelligently. They know the consequences of their behaviour and act accordingly. Second, every member of a competitive society or system possesses 'practical omniscience' (Knight, 1921, p. 197). Third, 'Productive operations must not form habits, preferences, or aversions, or develop or reduce the capacity to perform them' (Knight, 1921, pp. 77–78). In other words, x-efficiency is 100 per cent (Leibenstein, 1966).

Errors in Judgement

We are not *Homo economicus* and hence we are subject to making errors in judgement. Knight goes further. We don't want to live in a world inhabited by only ECONS—by humans devoid of emotion and imperfections. In that world everything is mechanistic, humans are reduced to automatons, which means they cease to be human. Life, says Knight, is more interesting in the face of uncertainty. There are two types of errors. The first is errors in reaching a goal, and the second is errors in the conception of the goal. Everyone makes errors. For example,

> As Knight (1921, p. xxxii) argues: "We 'intellectuals' may condemn the crowd-mind for unintelligent conceptions of economy, but we should recognise that the more vital problems are not problems of economy, but of maintaining social unity in the face of economic interests. And the foundations of unity lie not in intelligence, but in habit, emotion, and ideals of value."

The Limitations of Theoretical Economics

Economics is a human science about human behaviour. As such it 'must begin with some observations on the psychology of human conduct which controls economic life' (Knight 1921, p. 52). An important limitation is that it assumes that human behaviour is based on conscious motives. Hence, 'The conclusions of economic theory must in general be admitted subject to the qualification, in so far as men's economic activities are rational or planned' (Knight 1921, p. 52). But this is correct about human behaviour only to a 'limited extent' (Knight 1921, p. 52). Hence, Knight refers to himself as an 'irrationalist' when it comes to studying human behaviour scientifically. He says that 'In this view the whole interpretation of life as activity directed toward securing anything considered as really wanted, is highly artificial and unreal' (Knight, 1921, p. 53). Thus, the second limitation of economic theory is that almost all activities of human beings towards gratifying needs or desires are based on an impulse existing in our minds at the moment of decision. George Katona was writing about impulsive and capricious behaviour in his 1951 book *Psychological Analysis of Human Behavior*.

'The first datum for the study of knowledge and behaviour is the fact of consciousness itself' (Knight, 1921, p. 200). Knight tells us the difference between vegetables (unconscious) and humans (conscious). The latter 'react to a situation before that situation materialises; it can see things coming . . . the farther ahead the organism can "see," the more adequately it can adapt itself, the more fully and competently it can live' (p. 200). The role of consciousness is to give us 'knowledge of the future' (p. 201).

The Ordinary Decisions in Life

The mental operations leading to these decisions are 'very obscure' (Knight, 1921, p. 211). Knight says that it is not 'reasoned knowledge'. It may be a form of analysis, but it is a 'crude' form involving inferences we make from 'our experience of the past as a whole' (Knight, 1921, p. 211). We do a lot of 'mental rambling' and then somehow and from somewhere the answer just appears, as if effortlessly. Knight adds that the 'striking feature of the judging faculty is the liability to error' (p. 230).

Our estimates (of the value of things) are of a 'crude and superficial character' (p. 210). At times we have accurate and exhaustive knowledge, or something reasonably close, but only when the characteristics of the things we are dealing with are physical characteristics such as size, mass and strength. Otherwise, it is mostly 'common sense', 'judgement' or my own personal favourite, intuition.

> The mental processes are entirely different in the two cases. In everyday life they are mostly subconscious. We know as little why we expect certain things to happen as we do the mechanism by which we recall a forgotten name . . . The real logic or psychology of ordinary conduct is rather a neglected branch of inquiry, logicians having devoted their attention more to the structure of demonstrative reasoning. This is in a way inevitable, since the processes of intuition or judgment, being unconscious, are inaccessible to study.
>
> (Knight, 1921, p. 230)

Reasoned knowledge has little to do with it. It is judgement, common sense or intuition. Alfred Marshall called it 'trained instinct'.

REFERENCES

Akerlof, George (2002). Behavioral macroeconomics and macroeconomic behavior. *American Economic Review*, 92 (3): 411–433.
Akerlof, George, & Shiller, Robert (2009). *Animal spirits*. Princeton, NJ: Princeton University Press.
Boden, M. (1990). *The creative mind. Myths and mechanisms*. London: Weidenfeld & Nicolson.
Emmett, Ross (2009). *Frank Knight and the Chicago school in American economics*. London: Routledge.
Feigenbaum, E. A., & Simon, H. (1989). EPAM-like models of recognition and learning. In *Models of thought* (Vol. 2, pp. 145–166). New Haven, CT: Yale University Press.
Frantz, Roger (2005). *Two minds*. New York: Springer.
Hershfield, Hal, et al. (2011). Increasing saving behavior through age-progressed renderings of the future self. *Journal of Marketing Research*, 48: S23–S37.
Hayek, F. A. (1952). *The sensory order*. London: Routledge.
Kahneman, Daniel (2011). *Thinking fast and slow*. New York: Farrar, Strauss, and Giroux.
Keynes, J. M. (1936/1965). *The general theory of employment, interest and money*. New York: Harcourt, Brace, and World.
Keynes, J.M. (2010). My early beliefs. In: *Essays in Biography* (pp. 433–450). London: Palgrave Macmillan.
Newell, A., & Simon, H. (1990). Computer science as empirical enquiry: Symbols and search. In M. Boden (Ed.), *The philosophy of artificial intelligence* (pp. 105–132). Oxford: Oxford University Press.

Knight, Frank (1921/1965). *Risk, uncertainty and profits.* New York: Harper & Row.
Knight, Frank (1923). The ethics of competition. *The Quarterly Journal of Economics,* 37 (4): 579–624.
Knight, Frank (1925). Fact and metaphysics in economic psychology. *American Economic Review,* 15 (#2): 247–266.
Knight, Frank (1939). Ethics and economic reform. I. The ethics of liberalism. *Economica,* New Series, 6 (21): 1–29
Knight, Frank (1940). What is the truth about economics. *Journal of Political Economy,* 48 (1): 1–32.
Leibenstein, Harvey (1966). Allocative efficiency vs. 'X-Efficiency'. *American Economic Review,* 56: 392–415.
Lewis, Michael (2017). *The undoing project.* New York: W.W. Norton and Co.
McKenzie, R. B. (1983). *The limits of economic science. Essays on methodology.* Amsterdam: Kluwer-Nijhoff Studies in Human Issues.
Newell, A., & Simon, H. (1990). Computer science as empirical enquiry: Symbols and search. In M. Boden (Ed.), *The philosophy of artificial intelligence* (pp. 105–132). Oxford: Oxford University Press.
Simon, Herbert (1965). *Administrative behavior* (2nd ed.). New York: Free Press.
Simon, Herbert (1966a). Scientific discovery and the psychology of problem solving. In G. C. Robert (Ed.), *Mind and cosmos essays in contemporary science and philosophy* (pp. 22–40). Latham, MD: Center for the Philosophy of Science.
Simon, Herbert (1966b). Thinking by computers. In G. C. Robert (Ed.), *Mind and cosmos. Essays in contemporary science and philosophy* (pp. 3–21). Latham, MD: Center for the Philosophy of Science.
Simon, Herbert (1982a). A behavioral model of rational choice. In Herbert Simon (Ed.), *Models of bounded rationality. Behavioral economics and business organization* (Vol. 2, pp. 239–258). Cambridge, MA: MIT Press.
Simon, Herbert (1982b). Decision making as an economic resource. In Herbert Simon (Ed.), *Models of bounded rationality. Behavioral economics and business organization* (Vol. 2, pp. 84–108). Cambridge, MA: MIT Press.
Simon, Herbert (1982c). Economics and psychology. In Herbert Simon (Ed.), *Models of bounded rationality. Behavioral economics and business organization* (Vol. 2, pp. 318–355). Cambridge, MA: MIT Press.
Simon, Herbert (1982d). From substantive to procedural rationality. In Herbert Simon (Ed.), *Models of bounded rationality. Behavioral economics and business organization* (Vol. 2, pp. 424–443). Cambridge, MA: MIT Press.
Simon, Herbert (1982e). New developments in the theory of the firm. In Herbert Simon (Ed.), *Models of bounded rationality. Behavioral economics and business organization* (Vol. 2, pp. 56–70). Cambridge, MA: MIT Press.
Simon, Herbert (1982f). *The sciences of the artificial* (2nd ed.). Cambridge, MA: MIT Press.
Simon, Herbert (1982g). Theories of bounded rationality. In Herbert Simon (Ed.), *Models of bounded rationality. Behavioral economics and business organization* (Vol. 2, pp. 408–423). Cambridge, MA: MIT Press.
Simon, Herbert (1983). *Reason in human affairs.* Stanford, CA: Stanford University Press.
Simon, Herbert (1987). Making management decisions: The role of intuition and emotion. In W. Agor (Ed.), *Intuition in organizations* (pp. 23–39). London: Sage.
Simon, Herbert (1989). The information-processing explanation of Gestalt phenomena. In H. Simon (Ed.), *Models of thought* (Vol. 2, pp. 481–493). New Haven, CT: Yale University Press.
Simon, Herbert (1996). *Models of my life.* Cambridge, MA: MIT Press.
Simon, Herbert (1997). *Administrative behavior* (4th ed.). New York: Free Press.
Simon, Herbert, Newell, A., & Shaw, J. C. (1989). Elements of a theory of human problem solving. In H. Simon (Ed.), *Models of thought* (Vol. 2, pp. 6–19). New Haven, CT: Yale University Press.
Simon, Herbert, & Simon, D. (1989). Individual differences in solving physics problems. In H. Simon (Ed.), Models of thought (Vol. 2, pp. 215–231). New Haven, CT: Yale University Press.
Smith, Adam (1759/1969). *The theory of moral sentiments.* London: Henry G. Bohn.
Smith, Vernon L., & Wilson, Bart J. (2019). *Humanomics.* Cambridge: Cambridge University Press.
Whitehead, Alfred North, & Russell, Bertrand (1962). *Principia Mathematica.* Cambridge: Cambridge University Press.

19. Conserve the planet, not empathy! Revising the empathy conservation framework

Natalia V. Czap and Hans J. Czap

INTRODUCTION

The COVID-19 pandemic drastically changed our lives. Even though a large proportion of the population stopped commuting for months due to stay-at-home orders, this resulted only 'in a tiny drop in the overall concentration of CO_2 in the atmosphere because of how long the gas effectively lingers' (Borunda 2020). This serves as an indicator of how much work needs to be done to combat climate change and other global environmental problems faced by humanity. In this chapter, we will discuss the four main areas of environmental economics – *air, energy, waste* and *water* – with a focus on conservation. For each area, we will summarise the key insights learned for conservation behaviour from studies on behavioural biases, social norms and other-regarding preferences. We will use the lessons learned to revise the empathy conservation framework (Czap et al. 2018).

The empathy conservation framework (Czap et al. 2018) is based on metaeconomics and dual interest (Lynne 2020) and argues that individual behaviour is guided by self-interest and empathy-based other-interest including in the context of environmental conservation. This implies that policies encouraging pro-environmental behaviour (PEB) should combine traditional financial incentives (such as subsidies/rewards and taxes/fees) with non-pecuniary behavioural interventions appealing to empathy.

Traditionally, subsidies have been used to incentivise conservation by covering some of the associated costs, while taxes have been imposed to discourage environmentally damaging behaviour. In addition to offering a financial (dis)incentive, taxes can also be viewed as a statement rather than just a control device and as such can provide extrinsic and intrinsic motivation (Carlsson & Johanson-Stenman 2012). Even more, they alter relative prices making it cheaper to have a self-image of an environmentally conscious person, decrease cognitive dissonance and lead to peer effects as they encourage more people towards PEB (Carlsson & Johanson-Stenman 2012).

On the other hand, financial incentives may interfere with viewing the PEB as 'morally ideal' or the 'right thing to do' and shift the responsibility for PEB from individuals to the government (Brekke et al. 2003). This may lead to the underprovision of the environmental public good through the crowding-out of voluntary PEB (Shogren 2012a) and reduced image motivation (Ariely et al. 2009) – some individuals use pro-environmental actions as a means to buy a good reputation and, thus, providing financial incentives may make them appear greedy instead of generous (Shogren 2012a). This implies that financial incentives are likely to be more effective for publicly invisible behaviour when image/reputation is less of a concern (Ariely et al. 2009) such as installing a high-efficiency water heater in the basement compared to solar panels on the roof.

Despite these potential negative effects, financial incentives can also be very effective if they are used to reward cooperation between individuals to protect the environment (Shogren

2012a) and to encourage people to pre-commit to substitute their environmentally damaging behaviour with PEB (Shogren 2012b).

The effectiveness of incentives and policy more generally depends on the *behavioural biases* at play. Shogren et al. (2010) argue that we have to account for bounded rationality, bounded self-interest and bounded willpower (Mullainathan & Thaler 2000). People use rules-of-thumb, 'systematically misjudge the impact of low-probability, high-severity events' (Shogren 2012b, p. 5), and are influenced by context (Shogren et al. 2010). Researchers now assume that 'people are averse to more than just risk: averse to loss, ambiguity, inequality, lying, myopic loss, guilt, regret, disappointment, inflation, and so on' (Shogren 2012a, p. 357). Moreover, the risk judgement also depends on the context: for instance, people severely overestimate risks associated with outdoor air pollution compared with risks associated with indoor pollution (Breyer 1993; Margolis 1996). The same holds true for framing effects: gain frames are more effective in improving environmental attitudes while loss frames work better to change behaviour and intentions (Homar & Cvelbar 2021). Loss framing, however, may be less effective in the long run (Michalek et al. 2015).

Self-identity is an important predictor of PEB (Whitmarsh & O'Neill 2010). Also while PEB positively affects life satisfaction, people underrate the additional utility they are getting from it (Welsch & Kuehlung 2010). Moreover, on average there is limited awareness of the contribution of different activities to climate change and a 'value-action gap': people care about the problem but are not willing to make a change (Whitmarsh et al. 2011). Present bias and hyperbolic discounting are also interfering with individual conservation behaviour suggesting the need for pre-commitment devices (Hepburn et al. 2010). Similarly, affect heuristic and rapid, automatic judgement towards a particular activity or product (such as nuclear or coal-fired power plants or GMO products) influence pro-environmental behaviour (Sunstein & Reisch 2014). Hence, Sunstein & Reisch (2014, p. 131) suggest that green defaults which harness the power of suggestion, inertia, and loss aversion 'may well have major effects on environmental outcomes – in some contexts comparable to the effects of mandates and bans, and potentially far larger than the effects of information, education, moral exhortation, and even significant economic incentives'. As such, green defaults should be considered especially when the standard tools (mandates, bans, economic incentives) are expensive and face political obstacles (Sunstein & Reisch 2014). In addition to green defaults, Schubert (2017) suggests that policymakers capitalise on people's desire to maintain a self-image through green behaviour and exploit herd behaviour. However, Schubert (2017) also cautions that the effectiveness of many nudges depends on the exact framing and the individual's predisposition to nudges. Further, as people are learning, the effect of nudges which harness biases can disappear, underlining the need to use behavioural nudges as complements to traditional incentives.

Nudges can harness not only biases but also the power of *social norms* as will be explored more in the subsequent sections on air, energy, waste and water. Prevailing social norms often serve as an important influencer of individual behaviour (Sunstein & Reisch 2014). However, the effectiveness depends on how these norms are communicated. For instance, stressing the pervasiveness of undesirable behaviour can aggravate an environmental problem by drawing attention to it and inadvertently encourage people to further contribute to the problem (Cialdini et al. 2006) instead of focusing attention on pro-environmental actions. Social norms are often based on environmental knowledge and '[w]hat people know about environmental impacts is likely to affect which behavioural options they take into consideration and which they consider to be environmentally friendly or harmful' (Artinger et al. 2016, p. 208).

Closely related to social norms are *social and other-regarding preferences*, including signalling and reputation effects. List et al. (2004) show that individuals are much more willing to vote in favour of a costly environmental project if others are informed about their choice. Sunstein and Reisch (2014, p. 130) argue that '"buying green" is often done for status reasons, while "behaving green" is usually less visible and status-laden'. As already mentioned previously, individuals may want to display a certain image to others (Ariely et al. 2009) and thus engage in socially visible actions like driving electric sports cars rather than less visible actions like paying to switch to green electricity or car sharing (Sunstein & Reisch 2014). These actions can also be used as a status symbol among peer groups (Welsch & Kühling 2009).

In addition to reputational effects, individual environmental behaviour is affected by altruistic and fairness concerns, warm glow, inequality aversion, reciprocation and intrinsic motivation (Shogren et al. 2010). While this often leads to cooperation, free-riding also happens (Carlsson & Johansson-Stenman 2012), but people are willing to make sacrifices to punish non-cooperators (Shogren 2012b). Collaboration is more likely to happen if people have an opportunity to communicate. Moreover, non-binding communication and cheap talk help to establish trust in collaboration (Shogren 2012) and facilitate coordination. This is important, because environmental actions require a great deal of collaboration, not just in small groups, but in a larger community as well. However, so far there is little evidence for civic and community engagement in environmental causes (Whitmarsh et al. 2011). This underlines the complexity of human motivations when it comes to pro-environmental behaviour and conservation and the need to consider all behavioural aspects in a consolidated manner.

With that in mind, the remainder of the chapter is structured as follows. In the next four sections we will discuss behavioural biases, social norms and social preferences as they apply to each of the four areas of environmental concern: air, energy, waste and water. After that, we will turn to revising the empathy conservation framework, which will be followed by the conclusions.

AIR

The US, Japan, Sweden and the UK started to put in place modern environmental policies in the 1960s (Weidner & Mez 2008), followed by Germany and other countries. In the US these regulations established criteria pollutants and enhanced the role of the federal government in enforcing air quality measures. More recently, global attention has shifted to carbon dioxide as one of the main drivers of global warming.

Behavioural Biases

Despite the clear scientific evidence regarding the role of greenhouse gases in global warming, people are unwilling to commit to a significant reduction in carbon emissions. Part of the reason is that people suffer from behavioural biases that need to be better understood.

For one, people are often reluctant to pay the steep upfront cost for natural resource-efficient investments, due to *time inconsistency* issues (Leicester et al. 2012) and *present bias*. The costs of reductions in carbon emissions are tangible and timewise close, whereas the benefits are much less tangible and in the distant future. In some contexts, future benefits are also underestimated due to less-intuitive measures of efficiency, for example, miles-per-gallon as used in the US, compared to the easier to understand gallons per mile measure prevalent in other countries (Larrick & Soll 2008 as cited in Croson & Treich 2014, p. 339). Regardless, consumers use *hyperbolic discounting* and thus tend to heavily discount the future and hence will be less likely to pay more right now in order to reduce future costs or increase future benefits. Because of the heavy discounting involved, carbon taxes or subsidies on future green energy consumption are likely to have little impact on the decisions of consumers in the present. Due to *loss aversion*, a carbon tax is likely more effective in encouraging PEB than a comparable subsidy. It is important to consider the salience of the loss, as people who use autopay, for instance, may not readily notice the higher energy costs or new taxes imposed.

If corrective action is the goal rather than raising revenue, then attention needs to be paid to the *framing effect*. For example, people dislike taxes and react more strongly to an increase in costs termed a tax (Leicester et al. 2012; Hardisty et al. 2010). However, one issue with taxation that has to be taken into consideration is that it potentially legitimises behaviour and thus crowds out intrinsic motivation (Leicester et al. 2012).

Behavioural biases also affect the efficiency of environmental regulations. For example, the textbook response to the question of who should get the initial permits in an emissions trading scheme is that it doesn't matter for efficiency, as those who have low abatement costs will sell their permits and those with high abatement costs are better off purchasing additional ones (e.g., Field & Field 2021). This disregards the existence of the *endowment effect*. Once the initial permits are distributed, trading isn't likely to lead to a fully efficient outcome because those who have the permits will value them more than those without. One way to counter this is to auction off the initial permits instead of distributing them for free (Leicester et al. 2012). In order for countries to agree to put in place emission trading schemes, they need to acknowledge that climate change is a serious issue that humans are partially responsible for. To avoid cognitive dissonance, the large emitters (i.e., Western countries) tend to believe that climate change and its associated problems are exaggerated (Stoll-Kleemann et al. 2001)

To decrease carbon emissions we may consider harnessing the *default bias* in carbon offset purchasing decisions or forcing people to make an active choice. For instance, Kesternich et al. (2016a) showed that forcing customers to make an active choice when considering to buy carbon offsets while purchasing bus tickets increased the purchasing of offsets by 50 per cent. This effect was persistent. Similarly, consumers are more willing to pay for carbon offsets for air travel to a conference if the default conference fee included the price of the offset (Araña & Leon 2013). However, when choosing to buy CO_2 offsets for air transport, experienced subjects do not suffer from a default bias, which calls into question the long-term impact of such an intervention (Loefgren et al. 2012).

Social Norms

Numerous papers have looked into the effect of social norms on green choices in the context of air pollution. The majority of papers in this area consider carbon offsets or the choice of efficient cars. Little has been studied about the other criteria pollutants, possibly because most of them are supply, not demand-based.

Injunctive norm messages can affect pro-environmental choices, such as the choice of the mode of transportation (Hilton et al. 2014) or the purchasing of carbon offsets (Kesternich et al. 2016b). Similarly, displaying a social norm can lead to a reduction in carbon emissions by increasing the likelihood of drivers turning off their engines when stopping (Abrams et al. 2021). Demand for offsets 'is mostly driven by internalised norms for climate change mitigation' (Blasch & Ohndorf 2015, p. 257). Social norms are particularly effective when the individual is aware of the (environmental) problems and believes that their choice matters (Lindman et al. 2013; Abrams et al. 2021). If the associated cost of PEB is not too high, a signal of an institutional norm can be effective as well (Huber et al. 2018).

The impact of descriptive and injunctive norms messages is not unequivocally positive – only in some cases do they help predict a choice (Raux et al. 2020). For instance, only a subset (25 per cent) of the Swiss population believes that purchasing carbon offsets is the social norm and it drives their behaviour (Blasch & Farsi 2014). Similarly, carbon offsets purchasing decisions of car buyers in Switzerland are not much affected by information on other people's behaviour, because this behaviour is not widespread and hence does not constitute a positive descriptive social norm (Huber et al. 2018). In the context of global warming, prosocial norms are not particularly effective, but con-social norms (i.e., 'most people *don't* do this') are (Bolsen et al. 2014). Lastly, the effect of social norms is likely to be country- and context-specific. For instance, whereas social norms are good determinants of carbon offsetting and paying a price premium for green products in the US, they are less good predictors in Germany (Schwirplies & Ziegler 2016).

Other-Regarding Preferences

Studies considering the impact of other-regarding preferences are scarce. On the individual level, Sexton and Sexton (2014) show that the willingness to pay for the 'green halo' of driving a Toyota Prius depends on neighbours' behaviour. Consumers' willingness to offset carbon emissions is predominantly determined by 'environmental awareness, warm glow motives and the desire to set a good example' (Schwirplies & Ziegler 2016, p. 756). Whether the personal carbon offset purchasing decisions should be framed as a gain or a loss depends on the relative strength of warm glow versus cold prickle (Blasch 2015 as cited in Schwirplies & Ziegler 2016).

On a more global level, Lange et al. (2010) find that climate negotiators favour fairness. However, they also have a *self-serving bias*, as they tend to view their own preferences as less self-interested than those of others. This makes efficient and equitable climate negotiations difficult.

ENERGY

Baddeley (2016, p. 216) argues that 'energy conservation decisions reflect an interaction of economic and psychological factors and principles from behavioural economics can be used to explain why people don't always "do the right thing"'. In this section, as in the rest of the chapter, we focus on behavioural economics and psychological approaches to encourage conservation behaviour either in isolation or in combination with economic factors. For a discussion of more traditional economics approaches to encourage energy conservation, including tax incentives, household liquidity constraints, demand-side management, asymmetric information and principal-agent problems, see Baddeley (2016). In some cases, however, economic factors are activating psychological responses and harnessing behavioural/cognitive biases even though they are not designed to specifically target or harness those.

The majority of individual direct energy consumption comes in the form of electricity, natural gas and vehicle fuel. People are also consuming energy indirectly – through products, including food, which can be quite energy-intensive in their production. Since most behavioural research in this context has been on electricity consumption, we will be focusing on that in this section.

Just like energy conservation in general, electricity conservation has two aspects for the consumer – environmental (through reducing their carbon emissions and switching to renewable resources) and financial (lower energy bills). Horne et al. (2017) found that people are not only cognisant of the two aspects but are also 'interested in reducing both their carbon emissions and their electricity related costs'. However, energy-saving can be costly for consumers and people tend to underestimate how challenging it is to conserve energy (Mizobuchi & Takeuchi 2013). Moreover, even if consumers are offered financial incentives to do so, these may not suffice if the marginal costs to conserve are too high (Mizobuchi & Takeuchi 2013). Furthermore, even though financial incentives increase the motivation to sign a contract to reduce energy consumption, the level of compensation does not necessarily have a significant impact on the probability of signing it – consumers may not be sensitive to the level of incentives (Golebiowska et al. 2020).

Behavioural and Cognitive Biases

In contrast to incentives (rewards and subsidies) that normally appeal to self-interest and profit maximisation, financial disincentives (taxes and higher prices) are typically harnessing *loss aversion*. For instance, Ito et al. (2018) report that higher electricity prices during peak-demand hours led to a large reduction in energy consumption and the effect was persistent over a long time period. Similarly, the introduction of time-of-use tariffs in combination with in-home displays (IHDs) providing half-hourly data on consumption was very effective in reducing energy usage during peak time and did not lead to shifting consumption to cheaper periods (Di Cosmo & O'Hora 2017). IHDs are making losses more *salient* and as a result, they work more effectively in reducing energy consumption than if consumers are provided with monthly and bi-monthly billing feedback (Di Cosmo & O'Hora 2017).

Saliency of expenses is closely connected to the *present bias* that is displayed by consumers: many are not buying energy-efficient appliances due to the high upfront costs, ignoring that they are cheaper to run in the long run (Leicester et al. 2012). For vehicles, though, some studies find that efficiency is correctly valued or even overvalued (for further discussion see Greene 2010). Another aspect of present bias and *procrastination* is that it can get in the way of energy-saving goals, underlining the importance of setting goals, using commitment devices and getting timely feedback (Baddeley 2016).

Furthermore, *status quo* and *default bias* often prevent individuals from switching to more efficient consumption and developing energy-saving habits. However, these biases can be used for good by making defaults to be environmentally friendly. For instance, if people are defaulted into green electricity, they are more likely to stick with it in contrast to those who have to opt in to use green energy sources (Pichert & Katsikopoulos 2008). Similarly, small changes in default thermostat settings lead to significant energy conservation, but moderation is the key: a large change to the default setting may lead to an active involvement to adjust the thermostat and switch away from the default, increasing overall energy consumption (Brown et al. 2013).

Social Norms

In the domain of household electricity consumption, the power of descriptive and injunctive social norms has been tested extensively. Typically the consumers are provided with reports on how their electricity usage compares to similar households. Schultz et al. (2007) and follow-up

Schultz et al. (2018) found that descriptive norms resulted in an adjustment to the norm: if the consumers were initially using more energy, they decreased consumption; if they started with lower than the 'norm' consumption, they increased it – producing a boomerang effect. However, using an emoticon to communicate an injunctive norm, eliminated the boomerang effect. Nolan et al. (2008) found that descriptive social norms had a much stronger impact on energy consumption than appeals to protecting the environment, being socially responsible and saving money.

The earlier experiments on energy conservation led to the creation of home energy reports (HERs) by Opower and other similar providers. The effect of HERs has been studied extensively (starting with Costa & Kahn 2010; Allcott & Mullainathan 2010; Allcott 2011; Ayres et al. 2013) as many interventions have been run as RCTs and such interventions have been scaled across the US. Allcott and Mullainathan (2010) argue that the Opower HER program compares very favourably to the traditional strategies to reduce carbon emissions such as plug-in hybrid vehicles, wind power and capturing carbon and adding storage to new coal power plants.

Typically the social norms/peer comparison interventions are accompanied by personalised energy-saving tips, energy usage history and injunctive emoticons. Since saving energy means that there has been some excessive/inefficient usage in the past, not surprisingly, the households with higher pretreatment energy usage per square foot of space saved more than the households with lower usage (Ayres et al. 2013). Intervention normally spurs immediate energy conservation, but efforts decay over time. However, such decay is slow and the energy savings have been shown to persist in the medium (7–12 months after beginning to receive the reports; Ayres et al. 2013) and long run (more than two years; Allcott & Rogers 2014). Allcott and Rogers (2014) found a cyclical pattern of action and backsliding, but backsliding diminishes over time. The findings that the efforts have been persistent even after two years suggest that saving electricity becomes a habit for consumers (Allcott & Rogers 2014).

This success of the HER program in the US, however, is context-dependent. Costa and Khan (2013) found that HERs are two to four times more effective with political liberals than with conservatives. Moreover, political conservatives are more likely than liberals to opt out of the report and are more likely to say that they dislike the report (Costa & Khan 2013). HER effectiveness cannot be readily generalised to other countries either. The US electricity consumption is higher than all other OECD countries (Andor et al. 2020). Given the effect sizes (reduction of 1.4–3.3 per cent) and carbon intensity of power generation, HER can be cost-effective only in the US and Australia and potentially Japan (Andor et al. 2020). The other countries may benefit only if they target a rather limited population – only the high-consumption households which are very likely to respond to the intervention. The intervention also depends on how quickly the feedback can be adjusted. For instance, in Germany the metering is annual, so a quarterly update of social comparison is not possible (Andor et al. 2020).

While HER have been the most studied method to influence household behaviour by using social norms/comparative feedback, other approaches have been applied as well. Asking households in Japan to commit to reducing energy consumption below the corresponding period of the previous year produced mixed evidence on the effectiveness of comparative feedback when it was combined with financial incentives – this combination did not work better than using financial incentives alone (Mizobuchi & Takeuchi 2013). However, since the comparative feedback alone has not been tested, it is not clear whether social norms are more powerful without the presence of financial incentives. Results of a study in Ecuador demonstrate that comparative feedback works better alone than in combination with financial incentives, suggesting the possibility of crowding out of intrinsic motivation by extrinsic financial motivation (Pellerano et al. 2017). However, in Poland Golebiowska et al. (2020) found that neither personal nor social norms affected the probability of signing a contract with an electrical company to save energy, while financial incentives did.

Electricity usage has also been studied in a non-home context. In a field experiment, administrative staff of a university received a report similar to HER but related to their organisational energy use (Wong-Parodi et al. 2019). Those who received social norms/peer comparison messages reduced electricity usage as compared to their own previous consumption while those who received a notification that their usage is simply monitored did not. Wong-Parodi et al. (2019) also found that the social norms messages made people more aware of their energy usage and, strikingly, the participants reduced the usage without realising that they had done so, suggesting an automaticity/subconsciousness in the process of conforming to a social norm.

Not surprisingly, if in an intervention a social norm is communicated in stronger terms and more directly, individuals are demonstrating high levels of compliance/conforming to it. Guests in a hotel in South Africa were more motivated by the descriptive norm that the majority of hotel guests find 20° C to be comfortable than by an environmental appeal to protect the environment (Idahosa & Akotey 2021). Similarly, users of a public restroom were more likely to turn the lights off if they were off when they entered the restroom (Dwyer et al. 2015). Personal responsibility moderated the influence of norms on behaviour – when participants were not responsible for turning the lights on, they were less likely to turn them off when leaving (Dwyer et al. 2015).

As mentioned earlier, energy conservation can also happen indirectly – when individuals are consuming goods which are more or less energy-intensive. Descriptive social norms were shown to be effective to encourage hotel guests to reuse towels (potentially saving both energy and water). Goldstein et al. (2008) found that descriptive norms were more effective than a message focusing only on environmental protection. Moreover, the normative message had a higher impact when it was describing the behaviour of people in the same setting (e.g., guests staying in the same room). Terrier and Marfaing (2015) reported that the social norms message was as effective as an invitation to commit to PEB (by hanging a card on the door to indicate support for the hotel's pro-environmental initiative). However, the authors also found that the combination of both strategies does not result in further increases in conservation behaviour. In the context of tire inflation (tire-pressure neglect leads to lower energy efficiency) Yeomans and Herberich (2014) found that the effect of social norms depended on the circumstances: it discouraged tire inflation when the tire inflation fee ($0.5) was waived but encouraged it when help to inflate tires was offered (potentially due to an increase in social pressure).

Other-Regarding Preferences

When it comes to other-regarding preferences in the context of energy conservation, the majority of the research emphasises a strong relationship between individuals' pro-environmental choices on one side and their concern for reputation, desire to send a specific signal and to be consistent with their pro-environmental self-identity on the other side.

Installation of solar systems is not driven so much by economic considerations, but it is rather considered as a status symbol and it (along with the subscription to green electricity) is significantly correlated with 'consumption patterns of reference persons' (Welsch &

Kühling 2009, p. 173). Furthermore, as argued by Sunstein and Reisch (2014, p. 130), some consumers select green energy due to 'expressive considerations', i.e., the self-perception of their identity and preferred self-understanding. Individuals are also eager to send a signal to others by reporting more efforts to reduce their emissions (Horne et al. 2017) which is suggesting that they are expecting such signals to produce positive reactions and potentially increase cooperation by the other party.

Along the same lines, when the previously unobservable electricity-saving individual behaviour is made public, it provides an additional motivation to engage in such behaviour in order to earn a green reputation (Delmas & Lessem 2014). And this, just like any prosocial behaviour, can potentially 'lead to a number of rewards such as mates, leadership opportunities and friends' (Delmas & Lessem 2014, p. 366).

Direct appeals to conserve energy have received little attention so far. Ito et al. (2018) found that an appeal to restrict electricity usage during peak-demand hours led to a reduction in energy consumption. However, the response to the appeal faded quickly during repeated interventions suggesting habituation. At the same time, when interventions restarted after a significant break, energy conservation was restored to the previous level (dishabituation), but then faded again (Ito et al. 2018). It is unclear what effect the direct conservation requests will have if they were to appeal through a specific other-regarding preference – guilt, shame, fairness, altruism or empathy.

WASTE

In 2015, each person in the US, on average, created 4.5 pounds per day of municipal waste. Of this, 52.5 per cent went to landfills, 12.8 per cent to combustion, and 34.7 per cent was recycled, with the remainder going to composting (U.S. Environmental Protection Agency, Advancing Sustainable Materials Management: 2015 Fact Sheet). Given the space constraints faced in some areas and the limited resources on earth, either decreasing waste or increasing the recycling percentage is of ever-increasing importance. Connected to the previous section, we should also stress the energy savings associated with increased recycling and reuse rates.

While the section highlights that social norms have, generally, a significant impact on recycling, those norms are partially determined by recycling laws and regulations (Viscusi et al. 2011). This implies that social norms cannot substitute for regulations but work in conjunction.

Behavioural Biases

The two main biases that have been highlighted in the context of waste are *default bias* and *framing effect*.

To reduce paper waste, a university in the US changed the default on printers from one-sided to two-sided printing. This small change led to a significant reduction in paper usage (as reported in Sunstein & Reisch 2014, p. 133). While not an experiment or scientific study, this provides some evidence that this bias can be harnessed to change behaviour with a statistically and economically significant impact. The results of an experimental study by Egebark and Ekström (2016) further support this supposition: a change in the default to double-sided printing at a large public university in Sweden led to a 15 per cent reduction in paper waste, a less significant impact than was observed at the US university, but nonetheless substantial.

Waste behaviour has been also shown to be sensitive to framing. Wernstedt et al. (2019), for instance, found that framing matters when it comes to solid waste disposal in Tanzania. In their study, they compared a negative framing, in which respondents had to choose between a guaranteed loss and a lottery with the same expected outcome, to a positive framing with the same overall expected outcomes. The results showed that the positive framing leads to a much more risk-averse choice by people.

Social Norms

In their landmark study, Cialdini et al. (1990) found that presenting people with a clean environment was interpreted as a descriptive social norm message of PEB. This led to a significant reduction in littering. The general result that social norms are important determinants of littering, recycling, and waste has been confirmed in many other studies (e.g., Berquist et al. 2021; Czajkowski et al. 2019; Keuschnigg & Kratz 2018; Tong et al. 2018; Wadehra & Mishra 2018; De Groot et al. 2013; Viscusi et al. 2011; Andersson & von Brogstede 2010; Schultz 1999; Hopper & McCarl Nielsen 1991). For instance, providing feedback to households on the food waste recycling of their street compared to other streets, i.e., providing a descriptive social norm, can lead to a significant increase in recycling (Nomura et al. 2011), especially among those that previously perceived the activity as one with low benefits and also faced low perceived barriers (Geislar 2017) Also, there is potential in combining descriptive and injunctive norms, which has been shown to significantly increase food waste collection (Linder et al. 2019).

However, the positive effects of social norms messages are neither ubiquitous nor homogeneous and depend on the specific context. For instance, while it might be possible to increase the salience, and hence impact of a non-littering social norm by introducing a single piece of garbage (Cialdini et al. 1990), this effect seems context-dependent or isn't consistent (Berquist et al. 2021). Similarly, even though a message combining an appeal to conservation and an injunctive social norm can be effective and persistent in reducing paper waste (Chakravarty & Mishra 2019), this depends on the medium for the message used. A one-time electronic message (Egebark & Ekström 2016) has not been effective, but a poster displayed at the printer (Chakravarty & Mishra 2019) was. This is an indication that the salience of the message is important.

Even if social norms messages work to encourage PEB, they aren't necessarily the most effective on their own. For example, in the context of waste segregation in India, while providing information together with a social norms message is effective in increasing recycling rates, it is less so than providing information only or information combined with financial incentives (Wadehra & Mishra 2018). Furthermore, using absolute and relative information together increases the effect of the nudge. However, nudging only works well as long as the descriptive social norm is not much higher than what people do, because otherwise, the social norm might seem unattainable, which might even lead to a boomerang effect (Czajkowski et al. 2019). Perhaps surprisingly, a geographically closer reference group is not necessarily more effective when it comes to a social norm nudge, and may even turn out to be worse in the case of a message with a social norm that is perceived to be too high (Czajkowski et al. 2019).

For social norms to be effective, they don't necessarily have to be stated directly. For instance, showing evidence of behaviour that is consistent with a particular norm, such as a clean environment (Cialdini et al. 1990) or providing smaller plates at a buffet (Kallbekken & Sælen 2013) serve as easily understood messages conveying social norms.

Other-Regarding Preferences

Various authors (e.g., Brekke et al. 2010; Brekke et al. 2003; Nyborg 2011) find that recycling reflects 'duty orientation' and implies that people want to see themselves as socially responsible. Beyond self-image or status symbol, people also care about impartiality and fairness, as seen in Oberholzer-Gee et al. (1997) in the context of the siting of nuclear waste.

WATER

Water consumption differs significantly by country, with a person in the US consuming on average about 156 gallons a day and a person in France 77 gallons a day, whereas figures for India and Mali are 38 and 3 respectively (CDC 2021). Given the water scarcity in many parts of the world and the predicted increased frequency of droughts due to global warming, it is important to consider factors that determine PEB and alternative, behavioural approaches to encourage water conservation. For a more extensive discussion of the behavioural literature see Koop et al. (2019).

Behavioural Biases

There is some sparse research in the context of water that tested the *framing effect*. For example, people are more receptive to suggestive than assertive messages (Katz et al. 2018), in particular, if households don't have strong preconceptions about water conservation (Kronrod et al. 2012). Similarly, appeals that target intrinsic instead of extrinsic motivation can reduce the frequency of showering (Tijs et al. 2017). Harnessing the *present bias* by focusing the message on present benefits leads to more positive attitudes (Zhuang et al. 2018), indicating that there also might be *hyperbolic discounting*.

Social Norms

Technical information on how to conserve water, information on the personal consumption of water (Ferraro & Price 2013; Schultz et al. 2016) or even a reminder of potential fines for violations of water restrictions (Jaeger & Schultz 2017) does not affect household behaviour to a significant degree. However, messages that contain weak social norms, appealing to the residents' environmental consciousness lead to a significant reduction in household water consumption (Ferraro & Price 2013). Even stronger results can be achieved by using strong social norms, including peer comparison, or information on the behaviour of 'most' other people (Goldstein et al. 2008; Ferraro & Price 2013; Terrier & Marfaing 2015; Schultz et al. 2016), with the effect equivalent to a price increase of 12–15 per cent (Ferraro & Price 2013). Even easier, a combination of information, descriptive and injunctive norms message has also been shown to be very effective (Jaime & Carlsson 2018; Carlsson et al. 2020). Adding a commitment option to the social norm message may further increase the effectiveness (Jaeger & Schultz 2017). Repeated messages of a descriptive social norm can increase the observed effect, highlighting the need for additional exposure (Landon et al. 2018). Not only does the type of message matter, but also the medium of communication. For instance, Schultz et al. (2016) found that web-based messages didn't work as well as posted mail.

Contrary to the above research, Fielding et al. (2013) found that providing technical information on how to conserve water was as, if not more effective in reducing water consumption than a descriptive norm treatment and a treatment in which detailed individual-level feedback was given on water consumption. The likely reason for this is that the inhabitants of Queensland, Australia (where the study was conducted) had experienced a drought during the previous years, hence making the need for water conservation salient, without the need for further messaging. This highlights the power of *context effect* and the need to consider the specifics of the situation when designing such interventions.

The effect of social norms messages decays over time but shows some persistence depending on the type of message. Ferraro and Price (2013) found that after two years there was no discernible effect of the weak social norm treatment. The effect of a strong social norm treatment can persist for longer (Schultz et al. 2019), but its impact will decrease over time (Ferraro et al. 2011). However, the effect remains detectable even after six years, making this a very cost-effective intervention (Bernedo et al. 2014). Effects may disappear more quickly if water is abundant because it decreases the perceived need for water conservation (Fielding et al. 2013).

As in other environmental contexts, there is heterogeneity in the effect of messages on households – high-consuming households reduce consumption by more than low-consuming households in response to social norms messages (Ferraro & Price 2013; Schultz et al. 2019). This can even turn into a *boomerang effect*, i.e. low-consuming households starting to consume more water than prior to the messaging (Landon et al. 2018). The existence of a boomerang effect seems to depend on the type of comparison that is used. In a neutrally framed peer comparison, i.e., 'the average of households', low water users start using more water. In a competitively framed peer rank, the effect is reversed, with low water users consuming even less water, but high water users consuming more (Bhanot 2017). Furthermore, the boomerang effect can be avoided if an injunctive message is included (Schultz et al. 2016).

Social norms messages are not only affecting the targeted household but potentially have a more wide-reaching impact through spillover effects. For instance, such messages can reduce the water consumption of households that aren't targeted (Jaime & Carlsson 2018) suggesting that the messages and associated behavioural changes create a new social norm and result in a peer effect in the neighbourhood. Moreover, the messages, even if targeted at water consumption, have been shown to also impact the use of other resources, such as electricity. This impact can be positive, when cognitive dissonance is a bigger determinant for PEB than moral licensing (Carlsson et al. 2020), or negative, when moral licensing dominates (Tiefenbeck et al. 2013).

REVISING THE EMPATHY CONSERVATION FRAMEWORK

The term *empathy conservation* refers to 'individual environmental conservation decisions that are motivated by empathy towards nature, other fellow human and non-human beings, and future generations' (Czap et al. 2018, p. 71; with a more detailed discussion in Czap et al. 2015 and Lynne et al. 2016). Empathy conservation is based on the metaeconomics framework and the dual-interest theory Lynne (2006, 2020) and Lynne et al. (2016), which argues that individuals are motivated by two inseparable yet conflicting interests: self-interest and other-/empathy-based interest.

Empathy implies imagining the struggles of others and walking in their shoes. It is through empathy that we can temper our self-interest and achieve a more balanced decision. The *empathy conservation framework* consists of four layers: societal needs and individual motives; societal expectations and public policy; individual behaviour; and societal outcome.

The societal need for environmental conservation partially overlaps with individual motives represented by dual interests, including self-interest and empathy-driven other-interest. The overlap indicates that fulfilling the societal need can be in line with either self- or other-interest. As the overlap is not perfect, it calls for interventions from society through social norms, values, and peer pressure as well as public policy interventions, including nudges and financial incentives. Here we also observe an overlap between policy and societal expectations as some nudges can work through social norms. Societal expectations and public policy are targeting individual behaviour in the form of empathy conservation which, in turn, should serve the ultimate goal of achieving the societal outcome of long-term environmental sustainability. This framework was based on the findings from our earlier experiments testing various aspects of empathy conservation (Figure 19.1).

This original empathy conservation framework includes social norms and empathy as one of the other-regarding preferences. However, it does not include the important elements discussed in the previous sections, namely behavioural biases, reputation and signalling. As it was discussed earlier in this chapter, various emotional and cognitive biases such as the endowment effect, context effect, default bias, present bias, hyperbolic discounting, self-serving bias, loss aversion and procrastination, have been shown to affect intentions and pro-environmental behaviour and as such need to be considered in the framework. In addition, it has been demonstrated that individuals want to promote their pro-environmental reputation and use certain PEB actions for the purposes of signalling to others. It should be also noted that even though conservation behaviour can be potentially motivated not only by empathy but also by other other-regarding preferences (e.g. shame, guilt), we are not considering them as part of this theoretical framework as it focuses specifically on empathy and not on all possible individual motivations of PEB.

Following this, we revise the empathy conservation framework in three ways. First, we add behavioural biases (emotional and cognitive) to the first layer (Figure 19.2). All three components, including societal needs, individual motives and biases intersect underlining their connection and interdependency. Individuals can be motivated by self-interest and/or empathy in

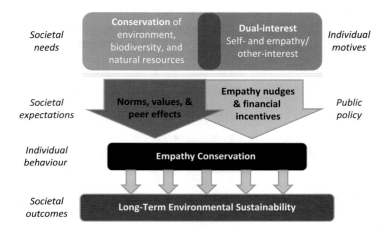

Source: Reprinted with permission from Czap et al. 2018, Fig. 1, p. 74.

Figure 19.1   *Framework of empathy conservation*

Conserve the planet, not empathy! 345

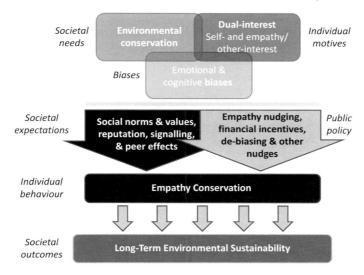

Figure 19.2   Revised empathy conservation framework

performing environmental conservation. Biases can get in the way of conservation behaviour, but they can also encourage it. Similarly, biases can promote and depress the pursuit of self-interest and/or empathy.

Second, we add de-biasing and other nudging as tools of public policy to complement empathy nudging and financial incentives on the second layer. Environmental public policy should help individuals to correct their systematic errors by de-biasing where feasible and effective and harnessing the biases for social good where appropriate and ethical (following the FORGOCD ethical framework proposed by Lades & Delaney 2020).

Third, societal expectations are changing to include reputation and signalling as local communities and society in general often expect the members to maintain a certain reputation (e.g., the one who bicycles, recycles, brings reusable bags to the stores) and to behave accordingly. Similarly, signalling (e.g., buying electrical cars, installing solar panels) is used as a strong communication and commitment device for the members to demonstrate their belonging, to reinforce their common values, as well as the local community's and society's identity.

The two wide arrows overlapping underscores that certain public policies are shaping societal expectations. Societal expectations, in turn, are influenced by public policies. Societal expectations together with public policy aim at encouraging empathy conservation (the third layer) both intrinsically and extrinsically. The pursuit of empathy conservation, in turn, leads to the desirable societal outcome of long-term environmental sustainability (the fourth layer).

This revised empathy conservation framework provides the basis for contextualising and designing environmental conservation policy appealing to dual interest and accounting for the role of behavioural biases and societal expectations in individual conservation behaviour. As the individual motivations to protect the environment are inherently multidimensional and people face external constraints and influences, environmental policymakers should consider multifaceted behaviourally based approaches when designing policies. Above all, such approaches should move away from appealing solely to self-interest or harnessing the biases or social norms (even for a greater societal good) towards a focus on voluntary behaviour motivated by empathy conservation for only then it will lead to a shift in behaviour and habits and, as such, it will become embedded into the fabric of society and will be sustainable long-term.

CONCLUSION

In this chapter, we considered the four areas of environmental economics – *air, energy, waste* and *water* – from a behavioural perspective. We found that while a lot of literature on encouraging conservation behaviour is devoted to testing the power of social norms, biases and other-regarding preferences have received relatively little attention so far.

Based on our analysis we revised our empathy conservation framework (Czap et al. 2018) to include biases, reputation and signalling. As emotional and cognitive biases can affect individual motives and the understanding of conservation, they were added to the top layer of the framework. Reputation and signalling are closely connected to social norms and peer effects which led to their inclusion into the second layer. Finally, we recognised the necessity to address behavioural biases by helping people to correct them through de-biasing and to harness some biases by ethically nudging people towards conservation.

We posit that encouraging individuals towards empathy conservation requires an understanding of the full complexity of motivations and external influences. It also demands a fundamental shift in environmental policy and societal expectations regarding conservation behaviour away from the short-run materialistic focus on consumption and automatically green/green-by-default behaviour towards the empathy-driven conscious and voluntary focus on environmental sustainability in the long run.

REFERENCES

Abrams, D., Lalot, F., Hopthrow, T., Templeton, A., Steeden, B., Ozkeçeci, H., Imada, H., Warbis, S., Sandiford, D., Meleady, R., Fell, E., Abrams, Z., Abrams, A., Qing Ngan, X., Celina, S., Tanyeri, A., Gammon, M., Abrams, B., Fischer, L., Drysdale, S., Dewi, R., Leite, A., Mills, A. & Peckham, S. (2021). Cleaning up our acts: Psychological interventions to reduce engine idling and improve air quality. *Journal of Environmental Psychology*, 74(101587): 1–10.
Allcott, H. (2011). Social norms and energy conservation. *Journal of Public Economics*, 95: 1082–1095.
Allcott, H. & Mullainathan, S. (2010). Behavior and energy policy. *Science*, 327: 1204–1205.
Allcott, H. & Rogers, T. (2014). Behavioral interventions: Experimental evidence from energy conservation. *American Economic Review*, 104(10): 3003–3037.
Andersson, M. & von Borgstede, C. (2010). Differentiation of determinants of low-cost and high-cost recycling. *Journal of Environmental Psychology*, 30: 402–408.
Araña, J.E. & León, C.J. (2013). Can defaults save the climate? Evidence from a field experiment on carbon offsetting programs. *Environmental Resource Economics*, 54: 613–626. DOI: 10.1007/s10640-012-9615-x.
Ariely, D., Anat, B. & Meier, S. (2009). Doing good or doing well? Image motivation and monetary incentives in behaving prosocially. *American Economic Review*, 99 (1): 544–55. DOI: 10.1257/aer.99.1.544.
Aronsson, T. & Schöb, R. (2018). Climate change and psychological adaptation: A behavioral environmental economics approach. *Journal of Behavioral and Experimental Economics*, 74: 79–84. https://doi.org/10.1016/j.socec.2018.03.005.
Artinger, F.M., Bortoleto, A.P. & Katsikopoulos, K.V. (2016). Environmental behavior and fast and frugal heuristics. In F. Beckenbach & W. Kahlenborn (eds.), *New Perspectives for Environmental Policies Through Behavioral Economics*, 195–211. DOI: 10.1007/978-3-319-16793-0_9.

Ayres, I., Raseman, S. & Shih, A. (2013). Evidence from two large field experiments that peer comparison feedback can reduce residential energy usage. *Journal of Law, Economics, & Organization,* 29(5): 992–1022. http://www.jstor.org/stable/43774381.

Baddeley, M. (2016). Behavioral approaches to managing household energy consumption. In F. Beckenbach & W. Kahlenborn (eds.), *New Perspectives for Environmental Policies Through Behavioral Economics,* 213–235. DOI: 10.1007/978-3-319-16793-0_9.

Belgiorno-Nettis, A. (2017). Evaluating Australian environmental taxes through behavioural economics. *Australian Tax Forum,* 32(4): 857–873. https://search.informit.org/doi/10.3316/agispt.20180905001324.

Bergquist, M., Blumenschein, P., Karinti, P., Köhler, J., Martins Silva Ramos, É., Rödström, J. & Ejelöv, E. (2021). Replicating the focus theory of normative conduct as tested by Cialdini et al. (1990). *Journal of Environmental Psychology,* 74: 1–17.

Bernedo, M., Ferraro, P.J. & Price, M. (2014). The persistent impacts of norm-based messaging and their implications for water conservation. *Journal of Consum Policy,* 37: 437–452. https://doi.org/10.1007/s10603-014-9266-0.

Bhanot, S.P. (2017). Rank and response: A field experiment on peer information and water use behavior. *Journal of Economic Psychology,* 62: 155–172. https://doi.org/10.1016/j.joep.2017.06.011.

Blasch, J. (2015). Doing good or undoing harm – Framing voluntary contributions to climate change mitigation. Conference Paper presented at EAERE21, Helsinki, June 27.

Blasch, J. & Farsi, M. (2014). Context effects and heterogeneity in voluntary carbon offsetting – A choice experiment in Switzerland. *Journal of Environmental Economics and Policy,* 3(1): 1–24. doi:10.1080/ 21606544.2013.842938.

Blasch, J. & Ohndorf, M. (2015). Altruism, moral norms and social approval: Joint determinants of individual offset behavior. *Ecological Economics,* 116: 251–260.

Bolsen, T., Leeper, T.J. & Shapiro, M.A. (2014). Doing what others do: Norms, science, and collective action on global warming. *American Politics Research,* 42(1): 65–89. DOI: 10.1177/1532673X13484173.

Borunda, A. (2020). Plunge in carbon emissions from lockdowns will not slow climate change. *National Geographic: Science,* May 20. Accessed on July 28, 2021 at https://www.nationalgeographic.com/science/article/plunge-in-carbon-emissions-lockdowns-will-not-slow-climate-change.

Brekke, K.A, Kipperberg, G. & Nyborg, K. (2010). Social interaction in responsibility ascription: the case of household recycling. *Land Econ,* 86(4): 766–767.

Brekke, K.A, Kverndokk, S. & Nyborg, K. (2003). An economic model of moral motivation. *Journal of Public Economics,* 87: 1967–1983.

Brown, G. & Hagen, D. (2010). Behavioral economics and the environment. *Environmental & Resource Economics,* 46(2): 139–146.

Brown, Z., Johnstone, N., Haščič, I., Vong, L. & Barascud, F. (2013). Testing the effect of defaults on the thermostat settings of OECD employees. *Energy Economics,* 39: 128–134. https://doi.org/10.1016/j.eneco.2013.04.011.

Carlsson, F., Jaime, M. & Villegas, C. (2020). Behavioral spillover effects from a social information campaign. *Journal of Environmental Economics & Management.* https://0-doi-org.wizard.umd.umich.edu/10.1016/j.jeem.2020.102325.

Carlsson, F. & Johansson-Stenman, O. (2012). Behavioral economics and environmental policy. *Annual Review of Resource Economics,* 4(1): 75–99.

CDC (Center for Disease Control and Prevention) (2021). *Water Use Around the World.* Accessed August 7, 2021 at https://www.cdc.gov/globalhealth/infographics/food-water/water_use.htm.

Chakravarty, S. & Mishra, R. (2019). Using social norms to reduce paper waste: Results from a field experiment in the Indian Information Technology sector. *Ecological Economics,* 164: 1–11.

Cialdini, R.B., Demaine, L.J., Sagarin, B.J., Barrett, D.W., Rhoads, K. & Winter, P.L. (2006). Managing social norms for persuasive impact. *Social Influence,* 1(1): 3–15. https://doi.org/10.1080/15534510500181459.

Cialdini, R.B., Reno, R.R. & Kallgren, C.A. (1990). A focus theory of normative conduct: Recycling the concept of norms to reduce littering in public places. *Journal of Personality and Social Psychology,* 58(6): 1015–1026.

Costa, D.L. & Kahn, M.E. (2013). Energy conservation 'nudges' and environmentalist ideology: Evidence from a randomized residential electricity field experiment. *Journal of the European Economic Association,* 11: 680–702.

Croson, R. & Treich, N. (2014). Behavioral environmental economics: Promises and challenges. *Environmental & Resource Economics*, 58: 335–351. Doi: 10.1007/s10640-014-9783-y.

Czajkowski, M., Zagórskaa, K. & Hanley, N. (2019). Social norm nudging and preferences for household recycling. *Resource and Energy Economics*, 58: 1–17.

Czap, N.V., Czap, H.J., Khachaturyan, M., Burbach, M.E. & Lynne, G.D. (2018). Experiments on empathy conservation: Implications for environmental policy. *Journal of Behavioral Economics for Policy*, 2(2): 71–77.

Czap, N.V., Czap, H.J., Lynne, G.D. & Burbach, M.E. (2015). Walk in my shoes: Nudging for empathy conservation. *Ecological Economics*, 118: 147–158.

De Groot, J.I.M., Abrahamse, W. & Jones, K. (2013). Persuasive normative messages: The influence of injunctive and personal norms on using free plastic bags. *Sustainability*, 5: 1829–1844. Doi:10.3390/su5051829.

Delmas, M. & Lessem, N. (2014). Saving power to conserve your reputation? The effectiveness of private versus public information. *Journal of Environmental Economics & Management*, 67(3): 353–370. https://doi.org/10.1016/j.jeem.2013.12.009.

Di Cosmo, V. & O'Hora, D. (2017). Nudging electricity consumption using TOU pricing and feedback: evidence from Irish households. *Journal of Economic Psychology*, 61: 1–14. https://doi.org/10.1016/j.joep.2017.03.005.

Dorner, Z. (2019). A behavioral rebound effect. *Journal of Environmental Economics & Management*, 98: 102257. https://doi.org/10.1016/j.jeem.2019.102257.

Dwyer, P., Maki, A. & Rothman, A. (2015). Promoting energy conservation behavior in public settings: The influence of social norms and personal responsibility. *Journal of Environmental Psychology*, 41: 30–34. https://doi.org/10.1016/j.jenvp.2014.11.002.

Egebark, J. & Ekström, M. (2016). Can indifference make the world greener? *Journal of Environmental Economics & Management*, 76: 1–13. https://doi.org/10.1016/j.jeem.2015.11.004.

Engler, J.O., Abson, D.J. & von Wehrden, H. (2019). Navigating cognition biases in the search of sustainability. *Ambio*, 48: 605–618. https://doi.org/10.1007/s13280-018-1100-5.

Ferraro, P.J., Miranda, J.J. & Price, M.K. (2011). The persistence of treatment effects with norm-based policy instruments: evidence from a randomized environmental policy experiment. *American Economic Review*, 101: 318–322. DOI: 10.1257/aer.101.3.318.

Ferraro, P.J. & Price, M.K. (2013). Using nonpecuniary strategies to influence behavior: Evidence from a large-scale field experiment. *Review of Economics & Statistics*, 95: 64–73. https://doi.org/10.1162/REST_a_00344.

Field, B.C. & Field, M.K. (2021). *Environmental economics: An introduction*, 8th ed.. McGraw-Hill Education, New York.

Fielding, K.S., Spinks, A., Russell, S., McCrea, R., Stewart, R. & Gardner, J. (2013). An experimental test of voluntary strategies to promote urban water demand management. *Journal of Environmental Management*, 114: 343–351.

Geislar, S. (2017). The new norms of food waste at the curb: Evidence-based policy tools to address benefits and barriers. *Waste Management*, 68: 571–580.

Goldstein, N.J., Cialdini, R.B. & Griskevicius, V. (2008). A room with a viewpoint: Using social norms to motivate environmental conservation in hotels. *Journal of Consumer Research*, 35(3): 472–482. https://www.jstor.org/stable/10.1086/58691.

Gołębiowska, B., Bartczak, A. & Czajkowski, M. (2020). Energy demand management and social norms. *Energies*, 13(15): 3779. https://doi.org/10.3390/en13153779.

Gowdy, J.M. (2008). Behavioral economics and climate change policy. *Journal of Economic Behavior & Organization*, 68: 632–644. https://doi.org/10.1016/j.jebo.2008.06.011.

Grafton, R.Q., Ward, M.B., To, H. & Kompas, T. (2011). Determinants of residential water consumption: Evidence and analysis from a 10-country household survey. *Water Resources Research*, 47: W08537.

Hardisty, D.J., Johnson, E.J. & Weber, E.U. (2010). A dirty word or a dirty world? Attribute framing, political affiliation, and query theory. *Psychological Science*, 21(1): 86–92. Doi: 10.1177/0956797609355572.

Hepburn, C., Duncan, S. & Papachristodoulou, A. (2010). Behavioural economics, hyperbolic discounting and environmental policy. *Environmental & Resource Economics*, 46: 189–206. https://doi.org/10.1007/s10640-010-9354-9.

Hilton, D., Charalambides, L., Demarque, C., Waroquier, L. & Raux, C. (2014). A tax can nudge: The impact of an environmentally motivated bonus/malus fiscal system on transport preferences. *Journal of Economic Psychology*, 42: 17–27.

Homar, A.R. & Cvelbar, L.K. (2021). The effects of framing on environmental decisions: A systematic literature review. *Ecological Economics*, 183: 106950. https://doi.org/10.1016/j.ecolecon.2021.106950.

Hopper, J.R. & McCarl Nielsen, J. (1991). Recycling as altruistic behavior: Normative and behavioral strategies to expand participation in a community recycling program. *Environment and Behavior*, 23(2): 195–220.

Horne, C. & Kennedy, E. (2017). The power of social norms for reducing and shifting electricity use. *Energy Policy*, 107: 43–52. https://doi.org/10.1016/j.enpol.2017.04.029.

Huber, R.A., Andersona, B. & Bernauer, T. (2018). Can social norm interventions promote voluntary pro environmental action? *Environmental Science & Policy*, 89: 231–246.

Idahosa, L. & Akotey, J. (2021). A social constructionist approach to managing HVAC energy consumption using social norms – A randomised field experiment. *Energy Policy*, 154: 112293. https://doi.org/10.1016/j.enpol.2021.112293.

Ito, K., Ida, T. & Tanaka, M. (2018). Moral suasion and economic incentives: Field experimental evidence from energy demand. *American Economic Journal: Economic Policy*, 10 (1): 240–267. DOI: 10.1257/pol.20160093.

Jaeger, C.M. & Schultz, P.W. (2017). Coupling social norms and commitments: Testing the under detected nature of social influence. *Journal of Environmental Psychology*, 51: 199–208.

Jaime Torres, M.M. & Carlsson, F. (2018). Direct and spillover effects of a social information campaign on residential water-savings. *Journal of Environmental Economics & Management*, 92: 222–243.

Kallbekken, S. & Sælen, H. (2013). 'Nudging' hotel guests to reduce food waste as a win–win environmental measure. *Economics Letters*, 119: 325–327.

Katz, D., Kronrod, A., Grinstein, A. & Nisan, U. (2018). Still waters run deep: Comparing assertive and suggestive language in water conservation campaigns. *Water*, 10(3): 275. https://doi.org/10.3390/w10030275.

Kesternich, M., Römer, D. & Florens, F. (2016a). The power of active choice: Field experimental evidence on repeated contribution decisions to a carbon offsetting program. *ZEW Discussion Papers*, No. 16–091: 1–20.

Kesternich, M., Löschel, A. & Römer, D. (2016b). The long-term impact of matching and rebate subsidies when public goods are impure: Field experimental evidence from the carbon offsetting market. *Journal of Public Economics*, 137: 70–78.

Kesternich, M., Reif, C. & Rübbelke, D. (2017). Recent trends in behavioral environmental economics. *Environmental & Resource Economics*, 67: 403–411. https://doi.org/10.1007/s10640-017-0162-3.

Keuschnigg, M. & Kratz, F. (2018). Thou shalt recycle: How social norms of environmental protection narrow the scope of the low-cost hypothesis. *Environment & Behavior*, 50(10): 1059–1091.

Koop, S.H.A, Van Dorssen, A.J. & Brouwer, S. (2019). Enhancing domestic water conservation behaviour: A review of empirical studies on influencing tactics. *Journal of Environmental Management*, 247: 867–876.

Kronrod, A., Grinstein, A. & Wathieu, L. (2012). Go green! Should environmental messages be so assertive? *Journal of Marketing*, 76: 95–102.

Lades, L. & Delaney, L. (2020). Nudge FORGOOD. *Behavioural Public Policy*, First View, 1–20. https://doi.org/10.1017/bpp.2019.53.

Landon, A.C., Woodward, R.T., Kyle, G.T. & Kaiser, R.A. (2018). Evaluating the efficacy of an information-based residential outdoor water conservation program. *Journal of Cleaner Production*, 195: 56–65.

Lange, A., Loschel, A. Vogt, C. & Ziegler, A. (2010). On the self-interested use of equity in international climate negotiations. *European Economic Review*, 54: 359–375.

Lanz, B., Wurlod, J.-D., Panzone, L. & Swanson, T. (2018). The behavioral effect of Pigovian regulation: Evidence from a field experiment. *Journal of Environmental Economics & Management*, 87: 190–205. https://doi.org/10.1016/j.jeem.2017.06.005.

Larrick, R.P. & Soll, J.B. (2008). The MPG illusion. *Science*, 320(5883): 1593–1594.

Leicester, A., Levell, P. & Rasul, I. (2012). Tax and benefit policy: Insights from behavioural economics. *The Institute for Fiscal Studies, IFS Commentary*, C125: 1–91.

Linder, N., Lindahl, T. & Borgström, S. (2019). Promoting behavioural insights to promote food waste recycling in urban households – Evidence from a longitudinal field experiment. *Frontiers in Psychology*, 9(352): 1–13.

Lindman, Å., Ek, K. & Söderholm, P. (2013). Voluntary citizen participation in carbon allowance markets: the role of norm-based motivation. *Climate Policy,* 13(6): 680–697. http://dx.doi.org/10.1080/14693062.2013.810436.

Löfgren, Å., Martinsson, P., Hennlock, M. & Sterner, T. (2012). Are experienced people affected by a pre-set default option—Results from a field experiment. *Journal of Environmental Economics & Management*, 63: 66–72.

Lynne, G.D. (2006). Toward a dual motive metaeconomic theory. *Journal of Socio-Economics*, 35(4): 634–651.

Lynne, G.D., Czap, N.V., Czap, H.J. and Burbach, M.E. (2016). A theoretical foundation for empathy conservation: Toward avoiding the tragedy of the commons. *Review of Behavioral Economics,* 3(3–4): 243–279.

Lynne, G.D. (2020). *Metaeconomics: Tempering excessive greed.* Palgrave Macmillan, New York.

Michalek, G., Meran, G., Schwarze, R. & Yildiz, O. (2015). Nudging as a new 'soft' tool in environmental policy–an analysis based on insights from cognitive and social psychology. *Discussion Paper Series recap15,* 21: October. https://www.europa-uni.de/de/forschung/institut/recap15/downloads/recap15_DP021.pdf.

Mizobuchi, K. & Takeuchi, K. (2013). The influences of financial and non-financial factors on energy-saving behaviour: A field experiment in Japan. *Energy Policy*, 63: 775–787. https://doi.org/10.1016/j.enpol.2013.08.064.

Nolan, J., Schultz, P.W., Cialdini, R.B., Griskevicius, V. & Goldstein, N. (2008). Normative social influence is underdetected. *Personality & Social Psychology Bulletin*, 34: 913–923.

Nomura, H., John, P.C. & Cotterill, S. (2011). The use of feedback to enhance environmental outcomes: A randomised controlled trial of a food waste scheme. *Local Environment*, 16(7): 637–653.

Nyborg, K. (2011). I don't want to hear about it: Rational ignorance among duty-oriented consumers. *Journal of Economic Behavior & Organization*, 79(3): 263–274.

Oberholzer-Gee, F., Bohnet, I. & Frey, B.S. (1997). Fairness and competence in democratic decisions. *Public Choice*, 91: 89–105.

Pellerano, J.A., Price, M.K., Puller, S.L. & Sánchez, G. (2017). Do extrinsic incentives undermine social norms? Evidence from a field experiment in energy conservation. *Environmental & Resource Economics*, 67: 413–428. https://doi.org/10.1007/s10640-016-0094-3.

Pichert, D. & Katsikopoulos, K.V. (2008). Green defaults: Information presentation and pro-environmental behaviour. *Journal of Environmental Psychology,* 28(1): 63–73. https://doi.org/10.1016/j.jenvp.2007.09.004.

Pothitou, M., Hanna, R. & Chalvatzis, K. (2016). Environmental knowledge, pro-environmental behaviour and energy savings in households: An empirical study. *Applied Energy*, 184: 1217–1229. https://doi.org/10.1016/j.apenergy.2016.06.017.

Raux, C., Chevalier, A, Bougna, E. & Hilton, D. (2020). Mobility choices and climate change: Assessing the effects of social norms, emissions information and economic incentives. *Research in Transportation Economics*, 101007: 1–18.

Schubert, C. (2017). Green nudges: Do they work? Are they ethical? *Ecological Economics*, 132: 329–342. https://doi.org/10.1016/j.ecolecon.2016.11.009.

Schultz, P.W. (1999). Changing behavior with normative feedback interventions: A field experiment on curbside recycling. *Basic and Applied Social Psychology*, 21(1): 25–36. https://doi.org/10.1207/s15324834basp2101_3.

Schultz, P.W., Javey, S. & Sorokina, A. (2019). Social comparison as a tool to promote residential water conservation. *Frontiers in Water*, 1: 2. Doi: 10.3389/frwa.2019.00002.

Schultz, P.W., Messina, A., Tronu, G., Limas, E.F., Gupta, R. & Estrada, M. (2016). Feedback and the moderating role of personal norms: A field experiment to reduce residential water consumption. *Environmental Behavior*, 48: 686–710.

Schultz, P.W., Nolan, J., Cialdini, R., Goldstein, N. & Griskevicius, V. (2007). The constructive, destructive, and reconstructive power of social norms. *Psychological Science*, 18: 429–434.

Schultz, P.W., Nolan, J., Cialdini, R., Goldstein, N. & Griskevicius, V. (2018). The constructive, destructive, and reconstructive power of social norms: Reprise. *Perspectives on Psychological Science*, 13(2): 249–254. Doi: 10.1177/1745691617693325.

Schusser S. & Bostedt, G. (2019). Green behavioral (in)consistencies: are pro-environmental behaviors in different domains substitutes or complements? *Environmental Economics*, 10(1): 23–47. doi:10.21511/ee.10(1).2019.03.

Schwirplies, C. & Ziegler, A. (2016). Offset carbon emissions or pay a price premium for avoiding them? A cross-country analysis of motives for climate protection activities. *Applied Economics*, 48(9): 746–758. DOI: 10.1080/00036846.2015.1085647.

Sexton, S.E. & Sexton, A.L. (2014). Conspicuous conservation: The Prius effect and willingness to pay for environmental bona fides. *Journal of Environmental Economics & Management*, 67(3): 303–317.

Shogren, J. (2012a). Behavioral environmental economics: Money pumps & nudges. *Journal of Agricultural and Resource Economics*, 37(3): 1–12.

Shogren, J. (2012b). Behavioural economics and environmental incentives. *OECD Environment Working Papers*, No. 49, OECD Publishing. http://dx.doi.org/10.1787/5k8zwbhqs1xn-en.

Shogren, J., Parkhurst, G. & Banerjee, P. (2010). Two cheers and a qualm for behavioral environmental economics. *Environmental & Resource Economics*, 46(2): 235–247. DOI: 10.1007/s10640-010-9376-3.

Shogren, J. & Taylor, L. (2008). On behavioral-environmental economics. *Review of Environmental Economics and Policy*, 2(1): 26–44. DOI: 10.1093/reep/rem027.

Stoll-Kleemann, S., O'Riordan, T. & Jaeger, C.C. (2001). The psychology of denial concerning climate mitigation measures: Evidence from Swiss focus groups. *Global Environmental Change* 11: 107–117.

Sunstein, C. & Reisch, L.A. (2014). Automatically green: Behavioral economics and environmental protection. *Harvard Environmental Law Review*, 38: 128–158.

Terrier, L. & Marfaing, B. (2015). Using social norms and commitment to promote pro-environmental behavior among hotel guests. *Journal of Environmental Psychology*, 44: 10–15.

Tiefenbeck, V. Staake, T., Roth, K. & Sachs, O. (2013). For better or for worse? Empirical evidence of moral licensing in a behavioral energy conservation campaign. *Energy Policy,* 57: 160–171.

Tijs, M.S., Karremans, J.C., Veling, H., de Lange, M.A., van Meegeren, P. & Lion, R. (2017). Saving water to save the environment: Contrasting the effectiveness of environmental and monetary appeals in a residential water saving intervention. *Social Influence*, 12: 69–79.

Tong, X., Nikolic, I., Dijkhuizen, B., van den Hoven, M., Minderhoud, M., Wackerlin, N., Wang, T. & Tao, D. (2018). Behaviour change in post-consumer recycling: Applying agent-based modelling in social experiment. *Journal of Cleaner Production*, 187: 1006–1013.

U.S. Environmental Protection Agency, Advancing Sustainable Materials Management: 2015 Fact Sheet.

Venkatachalam, L. (2008). Behavioral economics for environmental policy. *Ecological Economics*, 67(4): 640–645. https://doi.org/10.1016/j.ecolecon.2008.01.018.

Viscusi, W.K., Huber, J. & Bell, J. (2011). Promoting recycling: Private values, social norms, and economic incentives. *American Economic Review: Papers & Proceedings*, 101(3): 65–70.

Wadehra, S. & Mishra, A. (2018). Encouraging urban households to segregate the waste they generate: Insights from a field experiment in Delhi, India. *Resources, Conservation & Recycling*, 134: 239–247.

Weidner, H. & Mez, L. (2008). German Climate Change Policy - A Success Story With Some Flaws, The Journal of Environment and Development, 17(4): 356–378.

Welsch, H. & Kühling, J. (2009). Determinants of pro-environmental consumption: The role of reference groups and routine behavior. *Ecological Economics*, 69(1): 166–176. https://doi.org/10.1016/j.ecolecon.2009.08.009.

Welsch, H. & Kühling, J. (2010). Pro-environmental behavior and rational consumer choice: Evidence from surveys of life satisfaction. *Journal of Economic Psychology,* 31(3): 405–420. https://doi.org/10.1016/j.joep.2010.01.009.

Wernstedt, K., Kinila, J.M. & Kaseva, M. (2019). Biases and environmental risks in urban Africa: household solid waste decision-making. *Journal of Environmental Planning and Management*, 63(11): 1946–1954. https://doi.org/10.1080/09640568.2019.1691510.

Whitmarsh, L. & O'Neill, S. (2010). Green identity, green living? The role of pro-environmental self-identity in determining consistency across diverse pro-environmental behaviors. *Journal of Environmental Psychology*, 30(3): 305–314. https://doi.org/10.1016/j.jenvp.2010.01.003.

Whitmarsh, L., Seyfang, G. & O'Neill, S. (2011). Public engagement with carbon and climate change: To what extent is the public 'carbon capable'? *Global Environmental Change*, 21(1): 56–65. https://doi.org/10.1016/j.gloenvcha.2010.07.011.

Wong-Parodi, G., Krishnamurti, T., Gluck, J. & Agarwal, Y. (2019). Encouraging energy conservation at work: A field study testing social norm feedback and awareness of monitoring. *Energy Policy*, 130: 197–205. https://doi.org/10.1016/j.enpol.2019.03.028.

Yeomans, M. & Herberich, D. (2014). An experimental test of the effect of negative social norms on energy-efficient investments. *Journal of Economic Behavior & Organization*, 108: 187–197. https://doi.org/10.1016/j.jebo.2014.09.010.

Zhuang, J., Lapinski, M.K. & Peng, W. (2018). Crafting messages to promote water conservation: Using time-framed messages to boost conservation actions in the United States and China. *Journal of Applied Social Psychology,* 48: 248–256.

20. Behavioural economics of morality and sustainability
Shinji Teraji

INTRODUCTION

The standard conception of the economic agent, *Homo economicus*, driven by material self-interest has provided powerful theoretical tools in the analysis of diverse problems. However, experimental support for this concept has been fragile. Results from experiments on public goods games, ultimatum games, trust games and gift exchange games demonstrate that subjects in fact deviate from self-interest in systemic ways (e.g., Isaac and Walker, 1988; Fehr et al., 1993). Aside from being concerned with their own payoffs (self-interest), subjects appear to be concerned also with the payoffs of others (other-interest). Preferences having this property are referred to as being 'socially interdependent' or 'other-regarding'. Self-interest is not the only human motivation.

Many critics of neoclassical economics have focused on the construct of *Homo economicus*, arguing that humans often demonstrate altruism and mutual concern. The expanding behavioural economic literature supports the argument that *Homo economicus* is an inappropriate assumption about how humans take real economic decisions.[1] People are self-interested from a core hypothesis of neoclassical economics, but they are often socially minded from empirically adequate behavioural accounts.

This problem also arises about Adam Smith's conception of the human character. Are people self-interested or even selfish as they seem to be depicted in *The Wealth of Nations*, or are they socially minded as depicted in *The Theory of Moral Sentiments*? Is there a relationship between the two components, the self-regarding behaviour and the other-regarding one?

Adam Smith devoted *The Theory of Moral Sentiments* to explaining how individuals are transformed into moral beings. The moral sentiments are profoundly *endogenous*. The emergence or maturation of civic ethics is the subject of Smith's *The Theory of Moral Sentiments*. In the opening of *The Theory of Moral Sentiments*, '[h]ow selfish soever man may be supposed, there are evidently some principles in his nature, which interest him in the fortune of others, and render their happiness necessary to him, though he derives nothing from it except the pleasure of seeing it' (Smith, [1759] 1981, p. 9). People care and wonder about the feelings that fill the hearts of others. We are not capable of seeing into the hearts of others. But we can imagine what it would be like to be in the shoes of the parties who are affected and consider what to feel – what any one of us would or should feel – in their situation. Others' unhappiness somehow intrudes into us: if others are unhappy, we are also unhappy. Thus, following Smith ([1759] 1981), people are endowed with an altruistic mechanism that makes them share the fortunes of others.

Smith's ([1759] 1981) enduring contribution to moral philosophy is his theory of conscience in the form of the *impartial spectator*. The concept of the impartial spectator, also called the *man within the breast*, means an imagined third party who allows an individual to objectively judge the ethical status of one's actions. The agents in *The Theory of Moral Sentiments* are driven by an internal struggle between their passions and the impartial spectator (Ashraf et al., 2005). The essence of Smith's ethical system is the balance that must be considered in judgement. The judgement is divided into two parts. One is the degree to which the impartial spectator is in sympathy with the sentiments' response to the cause. The impartial spectator is a principle of moral self-reflection that develops over the course of our experience of exchanging places with others through the practice of imaginative sympathy. The other part of judgement is an act's merit or demerit. This refers to the passion leading to a behaviour. In Smith's analysis, proper balance is the key to moral sentiments; the standard of proper balance is the sympathy of an impartial spectator. Knowing this standard would be a first step towards virtue. Individual *self-command* (the propriety of behaviour) is another key concept in Smith's system of moral philosophy. Self-command is the power to enforce upon oneself the judgement of the impartial spectator. If an individual had the self-command necessary to maintain proper balance, the individual could achieve Smith's standard of perfect virtue.

This chapter considers why social preferences and social incentives matter in economics. A factor that might increase the performance of pro-social activities concerns people's incentives. People exhibit pro-social behaviour when they do not always make choices only based on external, economic incentives. Extrinsic monetary rewards to encourage pro-social behaviour can sometimes backfire and decrease the desired behaviour by crowding out intrinsic motivation to act pro-socially. Economic incentives can manipulate people into being more selfish. Social incentives will give prominence to the role of non-pecuniary drivers of pro-social behaviour. Further, the chapter discusses the issue of governing the commons with social incentives. It offers an explanation for the conservation of a common-pool resource, namely individuals who consider resource conservation to be a major concern are driven by social incentives. Besides material payoff, agents with pro-environmental preferences obtain psychological payoff related to resource conservation. A society can be sustainable to the degree that its members embody pro-environmental preferences.

ECONOMIC INCENTIVES AND SOCIAL INCENTIVES

A factor that might increase the performance of pro-social activities (e.g., volunteering, civic duty, charitable donations or other social contributions) concerns people's incentives. People might simply not find it worthwhile to engage in pro-social activities if the benefits fall short of the opportunity costs. Traditionally, policy interventions have tended to focus on providing economic incentives that change the consequences of behaviour, seeking to change the way people think about their behaviour. These interventions draw on the assumption that people change behaviour accordingly when extrinsic motivations are changed.

Motivation denotes a reason for an individual choice. Here, motivations can be distinguished into two types: extrinsic and intrinsic. Extrinsic motivation comes from *outside* the person in question, while intrinsic motivation comes from *within* the person. Specifically, extrinsic motivation is the desire for a reward or avoidance of a penalty, while intrinsic motivation is the inherent satisfaction of a task. Economic approach to human behaviour, due to the application of the relative price effect, is based on extrinsic motivation. Economic incentives are material rewards or penalties intended to shape individual behaviour by supplying an extrinsic motivation. An extrinsically motivated reward can be monetary (cash payment) or non-monetary (e.g., gift). It is designed to motivate a specific action and is offered before an action occurs. Economic incentives are framed in such a way as to induce self-interest as a response. Once a monetary payment is introduced, the activity is no longer performed when payment is withdrawn.[2] Economic incentives alter the costs and benefits of available options. In conventional economics, it has been widely accepted that desirable behaviour can be promoted by making economic incentives contingent on performance. The promise of economic incentives is that individuals are rationally motivated and are more likely to pursue an activity if it is externally rewarded. Therefore, economic incentives, as external rewards, for donating blood should raise the perceived value of the exchange and increase the likelihood of a person donating.

Recently, there is increasing recognition that individuals are not solely concerned with extrinsic rewards.[3] Economic incentives are not always an ideal motivator. Behavioural economics provides a wide array of sources for motivation by taking into consideration intrinsic motivation based on the gratification derived from taking part in a project with no external rewards. People behave as if they are intrinsically motivated rather than stimulated by any economic incentives as suggested by conventional economic theory. Intrinsic motivation is an important source of employee and organisational performance. In fact, the ideal intrinsic incentive lies in the work itself. In this case, intrinsic motivation is based on personal gratification gained from carrying out a specific task. Many employees are affected not only by their pay, but also by their perceptions of how the company treats them. Therefore, features like workplace flexibility, worker involvement in running the company and procedural justice in promotions could be important for increasing workers' non-pecuniary motivations.

To understand what kind of incentives might encourage pro-social behaviour, we must first have an understanding of the motivation behind such behaviour. People may undertake certain pro-social actions guided by intrinsic motivation. Under certain conditions, external rewards can inhibit intrinsic motivation. The exposure to extrinsic monetary incentives crowds out intrinsic motivation and thus reduces subsequent interest in the task. Motivational crowding-out occurs when introducing an economic incentive for a task provokes a loss of intrinsic motivation. That is, performance of intrinsically motivated tasks is harmed by pay for performance. In fact, offering extrinsic rewards to encourage pro-social behaviour can sometimes backfire and decrease the desired behaviour by crowding out intrinsic motivation to act pro-socially (Bowles, 2016). Blood donation has often been seen as an example of altruism with intrinsic motivations. Donating blood is a pro-social act in the sense that donors incur individual costs in exchange for a collective benefit and contribute by ensuring the blood supply system works well. People may respond negatively to extrinsic rewards, particularly if intrinsic motivation for the target behaviour is already high. As Titmuss (1970) famously pointed out, providing economic incentives to blood donors may crowd out blood supply. A crowding-out effect would mean that donation rates actually decrease after the introduction of payment. According to Titmuss's work, a system of paid donation decreases opportunities to behave altruistically and thus harms altruism, while a system without payment fosters altruism in society. Pure altruism is the key driver for giving blood in his research. Purely altruistic donors may feel less inclined to donate if monetary rewards are involved.[4] They may feel their altruism is no longer needed, or they may perceive the use of payments as controlling. Financial reimbursement for blood donation would reduce the intrinsic motivation behind individuals' donation behaviour, producing a decline in supply from those individuals. The introduction of economic incentives thus causes crowding out. Contrary to a common assumption implicit in standard economic theory, the effects of extrinsic motivations such as economic incentives do not necessarily complement intrinsic motivations. Therefore, under relevant circumstances, it is not advisable to use the price mechanism to elicit a higher supply, and one should rely on intrinsic motivation. Moreover, due to its altruistic foundation of voluntary behaviour, unpaid blood donation would be safer than paid donation. According to Titmuss's analysis, hepatitis rates from blood transfusions significantly decreased when the blood was donated rather than purchased. That is, donors who are not paid for blood have no incentive to hide an illness, which provides higher guarantees for blood quality. The blood donated for transfusion is free from harmful substances or infectious agents. There are concerns that economic incentives may compromise the safety of the blood supply by attracting higher risk donors who conceal information to obtain the rewards and undermine donors' intrinsic motivation to donate blood.

Individuals may care about what others think of them. Especially, individuals may not want to be seen as driven by monetary concerns. Then, image concerns are important for giving blood. If blood donations are not rewarded, those individuals with image concerns would be willing to donate. The prospect that others will find out how much effort is put into charitable donations motivates individuals to generate more donations. Individuals would sometimes try to fulfil the expectations of others that he or she should join a group going to a blood donor event. The reputation mechanism, which is a direct result of the influence of others, is then the decisive factor in the donation behaviour of a person. This implies that people tend to act less altruistically if no one observes their actions. However, we also seem to prefer to have a positive view of ourselves independent of the view of others (Akerlof and Kranton, 2000). People are motivated by their own views of themselves as well as by how others view them.

Day-care centres face the problem that parents sometimes arrive late to pick up their children, which forces teachers to stay after the official closing time. A standard economic approach would suggest introducing a fine for collecting children late. Such a punishment is expected to induce parents to reduce the occurrence of picking up their children late. In the Israeli day-care centre study, however, Gneezy and Rustichini (2000) find that the introduction of a penalty system increases undesired behaviour. In particular, small amounts of extrinsic incentives are expected to have large negative effects on observed pro-social behaviour. In the day-care centres, a small fine was imposed for each instance where a parent was ten or more minutes late picking up a child. The fine was intended, by imposing an additional cost to dysfunctional behaviour, to reduce the number of latecomer parents. Once a fine was imposed, being late was priced. The relatively small fine signalled to parents that being late was not important. Therefore, the lateness incidence increased. Furthermore, after the fine was removed, the increased frequency of lateness persisted. The message (that it was not so bad to be late) did not disappear once the fine was removed. It was difficult to revert back to the original level of arriving late. The formalisation of the rules regarding late pick-up entailed a change in the nature of the sanction, in this case, from social to material sanctions. Bowles (2016) argues that this type of behavioural failure occurs partly because such systems are based on faulty assumptions that people are just selfish and amoral.

SOCIAL PREFERENCES

David Hume's ethical theory is rooted in his account of human sentiments and of how some sentiments become specifically moral sentiments. In *A Treatise of Human Nature*, Hume ([1739–40] 1983) considered the imagination a prerequisite to feelings of sympathy.

Individuals morally evaluate the circumstances of others by imagining themselves in the observed situation. Hume emphasised the primary role of human sentiments in moral judgement. For Hume, reason is morally inert and appropriate moral action is necessarily based on human sentiments. The term sympathy originates in the works of 18th century moral philosophers such as David Hume and Adam Smith. Sympathy is characterised as an outcome of imagination simply because people do not have access to other minds. People only have access to others' observable situations. The imagination allows them to place themselves in the witnessed circumstance.

We can postulate a new taste to explain moral behaviour. Utility functions can take a variety of forms. They can combine self-directed and social or other-oriented preferences. This approach extends the assumption of the self-interested individual to include social preferences. For a two-person interaction, i and j, the specific form of altruism can be described as follows:

$$u_i = x_i + \xi x_j, \qquad (20.1)$$

where u_i describes the individual i's utility, x_i is i's payoff, and x_j is the payoff for the social partner j. Here, ξ ($0 \leq \xi \leq 1$) describes how much individual i cares for the payoff of one's partner. When $\xi=0$, i cares only for one's own payoff. This formula is a purely self-oriented utility function and induces i to ignore j's payoff. When $\xi=1$, i values the partner j's payoff as much as one's own. This may be referred to as egalitarian altruism.

People are said to have entirely self-interested preferences if and only if they always choose in such a way as to maximise their own (expected) pecuniary payoffs. A purely self-interested person refuses to contribute anything in the provision of a public good and free-rides on the contributions of others.[5] The self-interested hypothesis may be true for some, but it is certainly not true for all. Individuals exhibit pro-social behaviour when they do not always make choices that maximise their own pecuniary payoffs. They often act pro-socially, contribute to charities and engage in pro-environmental behaviour, even if this imposes costs on them. According to conventional economics, people care only about their own consumption of public goods but do not directly benefit from their own contribution, nor are they directly affected by others' consumption or contribution. Behavioural economics provides an alternative view to help explain why people make private provisions of public goods. People making voluntary contributions to public goods, such as blood donations and voluntary collection and recycling of waste, cannot be explained solely by pure self-interest. They can care about others' outcomes and place value on social goods. They value not only their own consumption but also the consumption of others: they are other-regarding.

The possibility that some individuals exhibit social preferences (i.e., fairness concerns, reciprocity and even pure altruism) has gained a more general acceptance among economists. Formal models of social preferences assume that some people may be self-interested but this need not be the case for all people. An individual exhibits social preferences if the individual cares not only about the resources allocated to him or her, but also to others. Some people do not like to think of themselves as motivated only by self-interest. They may be intrinsically motivated by social preferences. The effect of social incentives depends on the structure of social preferences. To generate social incentives, we need to augment preferences to include the outcomes of others. That is, a player's utility function not only depends on his or her material payoff but may also be a function of the allocation of resources within his or her reference group. More formally, given a group of N persons, let $x = (x_1, x_2, \ldots, x_N)$ denote an allocation of physical resources out of some set X of feasible allocations. The utility of individual i may be any function of the total allocation. The self-interested individual i's utility only depends on x_i, the monetary payoff of i. Individual i has social preferences if, for any given x_i, i's utility is affected by variations of x_j, $j \neq i$. Especially, individual i is altruistic if the first partial derivatives of $u(x_1, x_2, \ldots, x_N)$ with respect to $x_1, x_2, \ldots, x_N$ are strictly positive (individual i's utility increases with the well-being of other people).

People are averse to inequality between themselves and others, and they are thus motivated to reduce any inequality. Inequality aversion means that people resist outcomes that are perceived as inequitable. People are then willing to give up some material payoffs to move in the direction of more equitable outcomes. People are uneasy, to a certain extent, about the presence of inequality in the model of Fehr and Schmidt (1999). Their model of inequality aversion assumes that one's relative standing in the income distribution is important. Fehr and Schmidt (1999) set up a model of *self-centred* inequality aversion, in which inequality aversion means that people dislike inequitable outcomes and self-centred indicates that this aversion mainly stems from a comparison of their own and others' payoffs. It is assumed that people derive utility from their own income situation but suffer from inequality in terms of being either better or worse off in material terms than others. Inequality is *advantageous* if people are better off than others. This results in feelings of guilt. Reducing inequality is one way of reducing adverse feelings of guilt. Fehr and Schmidt's (1999) utility function, in addition to a standard neoclassical term, includes two terms: positive and negative deviations of one's own payoff, each weighted with its parameter. People, in this setting, dislike being worse off than others more than being better off. Heterogeneity is explicitly accounted for by assuming a distribution of preferences in the population. Utility is assigned based on a player's own payoff and an other-regarding component that compares his or her payoff with the payoffs of others. The social comparison function is based on the difference between player i's own payoff x_i and the payoffs of all other players in the game. Given a group of N persons, Fehr and Schmidt's (1999) utility function of player i is given by:

$$U_i(x) = x_i - \frac{\alpha_i}{N-1} \sum_{j \neq i} \max |x_j - x_i, 0| - \frac{\beta_i}{N-1} \sum_{j \neq i} \max |x_i - x_j, 0|, \qquad (20.2)$$

where α_i is a parameter that measures how much player i dislikes disadvantageous inequality (an *envy* weight) and β_i measures how much i dislikes advantageous inequality (a *guilt* weight). Player i's utility positively depends on his or her own income x_i and is negatively related to the difference between his or her income and that of other j. The second term expresses how player i dislikes being worse off than others, while the third term shows disutility from being better off than others. It is assumed that $\alpha_i \geq \beta_i \geq 0$ and $\beta_i < 1$. Here, $\alpha_i \geq \beta_i \geq 0$ indicates that player i's utility loss from disadvantageous inequality ($x_i < x_j$) is larger than from advantageous inequality ($x_i > x_j$). The disutility from being worse off than others is likely to be greater than the disadvantageous inequality. $\beta_i < 1$ indicates that player i does not suffer terrible guilt when he or she is in a relatively good position. By normalising terms 2 and 3 with $N - 1$, the impact of inequality aversion on i's utility becomes independent from the number of players N.

Charness and Rabin (2002), the successors to Fehr and Schmidt (1999), introduce a model which allows for a wide variety of *distributional preferences*. In Charness and Rabin's (2002) two-person model, a player's propensity to sacrifice for another player is characterised by parameters: the weight on the other's payoff when he or she is ahead and the weight on it when he or she is behind. Letting x_i and x_j be players i and j's payoffs, they consider the simple formulation of i's preferences as follows:

$$U_i(x_i, x_j) = (\rho r + \sigma s)x_j + (1 - \rho r - \sigma s)x_i, \quad i \neq j, \tag{20.3}$$

where

$r = 1$ if $x_j > x_i$, and $r = 0$ otherwise;
$s = 1$ if $x_j < x_i$, and $s = 0$ otherwise.

The weight that i places on j's payoff may depend on whether j is getting a higher or lower payoff than i. The parameters ρ and σ allow for a range of different distributional preferences. One form of distributional preference is simply competitive preference, which is presented to be $\sigma < \rho \leq 0$. Then, players like their payoffs to be higher relative to others' payoffs. Another form of distributional preference is inequality aversion, which corresponds to $\sigma < 0 < \rho < 1$. Then, players prefer to minimise disparities between their own payoffs and those of others.

Universal principles, such as fairness, individual rights, and justice, emphasise the welfare of all individuals equally. Fairness itself seems to matter for some individuals. On the other hand, the judgement of whether others consider one's behaviour fair is also taken into account in an individual's decision-making.

The use of fairness comes from the classical solution of the problem of the fair division of a cake between two persons, where one person cuts and the other chooses. This is generalised so that a lack of envy means that i does not prefer j's bundle of commodities (in this case, j's slice of cake) to i's own. No interpersonal utility comparisons are then made since each person compares the valuation of his or her bundle to the other's bundle, not the other's utility.

PUBLIC GOODS AND CHARITABLE GIVING

Pro-social behaviour includes voluntary contributions to public goods. Individuals share a common interest in the provision of public goods. Public good provision is costly, which implies a tension between the individual and collective interest. Pro-social behaviour is usually at odds with standard economic analysis, which predicts that, in a non-cooperative setting, individuals only make negligible contributions to public goods. Although mutual cooperation leads to the best possible collective outcome, individuals have an incentive to free-ride on the contributions of others. That is, collective welfare is maximised if every agent makes maximal contributions, while selfish rationality implies zero contributions. According to the voluntary contribution model of public good provision, as a general presumption, self-interested individuals who independently choose their contribution levels will generate a sub-optimal level of the public good (Bergstrom et al., 1986). People reduce their cooperation if others contribute less than themselves to public goods provision, which causes selection for non-cooperation that eventually undermines collective action. As the free-riding effect dominates in a population, the share of individuals making contributions to a public good tends to zero. In principle, governments can enforce the efficient provision of public goods. However, they generally lack the necessary information to do so, and the attainment of the social optimum is hampered by the selfish interest of each individual to give false signals.

Laboratory experiments have been intensively used to investigate whether individual and collective decision-making and behaviour correspond to theoretical predictions.[6] The public goods game is a suitable research tool for studying cooperative problems. Each group member receives an endowment of tokens in this game. Players have to decide how many tokens to keep for themselves and how many to contribute to a group project. According to experimental findings concerning the voluntary provision of public goods, there is much less free-riding and much higher voluntary contribution in one-shot versions of the standard public good games than theory suggests, but the public good provision is still below the efficient level. Conditional cooperators contribute more if they expect others to contribute more.[7] Individuals would be willing to contribute to public goods if they know that others do not free-ride and also contribute. They adapt their expectation of others' contributions on the basis of their experience of the average collective contribution in the previous rounds. In repeated public good games, free-riding increases and contributions decline over time. Conditional cooperators decrease their contribution accordingly, which causes the average contribution to further decline.

Individuals are often tempted to cheat in social interactions, thereby gaining a benefit at the expense of cooperative partners. To encourage partners to behave cooperatively, individuals might therefore use control mechanisms that render cooperative behaviour a more profitable option than cheating. One such mechanism is punishment. The opportunity to impose sanctions on free-riders can potentially solve the collective action problem because being punished induces free-riders to cooperate more. Rational and selfish free-riders never sanction when this is costly. However, anticipation of being sanctioned will induce them to contribute, provided that the loss due to received punishment offsets the payoff advantage of free-riding. Punishing a free-rider, in cooperative group situations, can be considered a cooperative act because all group members benefit from the resulting increase in the free-rider's level of cooperation.

Altruism has traditionally been studied in the context of helping, but punishment can also qualify as an altruistic act. An altruistic punisher is willing to punish unfair others at a personal cost. Altruistic punishment describes behaviour for which individuals are willing to incur personal costs to punish wrongdoing, even though they do not personally suffer from the misconduct and are an unrelated stranger. That is, people punish norm-violators not for what they did to the punisher but for what they did to others (third-party punishment). A strong reciprocator is defined as an individual who is both a conditional co-operator (reciprocal altruist) and an altruistic punisher (Gintis et al., 2005). If the number of altruistic punishers in a population is too small, selfish actions would become more profitable and drive out reciprocal altruism. Since it is costly to punish, no selfish third party will ever punish. When there is a sufficient proportion of strong reciprocators, high-level cooperation in a group could be attained.

People trust punishers more than non-punishers. When punishing a free-rider is good for a group, it could signal the punisher's trustworthiness, concern with fairness or commitment to that group. Others might be more willing to enter into relationships with people who have demonstrated that they will not tolerate unfairness. If punishment is a signal of trustworthiness or fairness, punishers may receive more benefits from cooperative partnerships than non-punishers.

The economic value of the resources devoted to charitable giving or volunteering is considerable. In economics, a charitable act is a voluntary transfer that is not motivated by market exchange. It is a form of economic sacrifice by the giver in exchange for the receivers' benefit for which the giver expects no return. Charitable donations are a form of indirect helping, often without any direct exposure to the beneficiary or direct knowledge of how the money will be used. There are two sources of utility that may encourage an individual to behave pro-socially and contribute to the public good. First, individuals care about the provision of the public good (*pure altruism*). Second, individuals may also gain utility from contributing, meaning that they value their own contribution more highly than that of someone else's (*impure altruism*). That is, individuals may experience a feeling of moral satisfaction derived from their contribution to the common good environment. When contributing to the public good yields some utility benefit to the individual, voluntary contributions can be consistent with standard economic models. Andreoni (1990) develops a model of donation with *warm glow*: the individual's utility is not just a function of the consumption of private and public goods, but also of the individual's contribution to the public good itself. That is, the utility of individual i is typically specified as:

$$U_i = U_i(x_i, Y, g_i), \tag{20.4}$$

where x_i is private consumption by i, $Y = \sum_i g_i$ is the total supply of charitable giving and g_i represents i's private gift, the form of a warm glow associated with charitable giving. In particular, when $U_i = U_i(x_i, Y)$, the individual i cares nothing for the private gift. Then, the individual is thought to be purely altruistic. Likewise, when $U_i = U_i(x_i, g_i)$, the individual is motivated to give only by warm glow, hence is purely egoistic. When both Y and g_i are arguments, the individual is impurely altruistic.

Donors report feeling proud or experiencing a warm glow after or during the blood donation. Warm glow may increase an individual's likelihood of engaging in charitable behaviour and can induce helping behaviour. A prominent proximal explanation for charitable giving is the warm-glow utility flow (i.e., feeling good from doing good) from the act of giving. In the warm-glow model, individuals do not donate because of pure altruism, but partly because of a utility gain from donating. The individual driven by purely altruistic motives is indifferent to the source of the increased welfare of others. Individual contribution to the cause can be substituted by the contribution of another one. Warm glow is the personal satisfaction an individual enjoys from being actively involved in an activity independent of any consideration of the outcome. Warm glow does not imply selfishness. It motivates people to help all others. Donors never know who receives their donation. Because warm glow is unrelated to the characteristics of the recipient, it can be characterised as an unconditional motivation for helping.

Combining warm glow and pure altruism results in impure altruism. The individual then donates to attain warm glow and benefit others simultaneously. When people make donations to public goods, instead of being motivated by the increase in value of the common good, they rather experience a direct, personal benefit arising from the contribution itself. That is, the individual driven by impure altruism receives a private benefit through the act of giving that cannot be substituted by the contribution of another individual.

GOVERNING THE COMMONS WITH SOCIAL INCENTIVES

The term *commons* are widely used in political discourses on how to tackle challenges such as climate change, food security, and transmission of knowledge. Climate change can be viewed as an illustration of collective action problems detrimental to the commons. The greenhouse gases that any individual emits have an imperceptible impact on climate change, while activities producing greenhouse gases (e.g., driving, heating, and air conditioning) have noticeable benefits to the individual's personal well-being. In academic writings, the commons have come to represent an alternative model of social organisation, going beyond the market–state dichotomy. Governance is about forming institutional structures: the concerns are making social priorities, resolving conflicts and facilitating coordination.

The tragedy of the commons is a thought experiment used by Hardin (1968). It is a metaphor that refers to the ultimate destruction of a common. According to Hardin (1968), users of a common are selfishly rational, and they will consequently overuse the common, resulting in the tragedy of its destruction. Imagine some herdsmen who have access to a common pasture. Each of them can increase one's herd by at least one sheep. If the herdsmen behave fully rationally and self-interestedly, they bring one more sheep to the common. This process is repeated, and the herds increase progressively, which causes exploitation from which the pasture cannot recover. Thus, the excessive search for the individual good results in the destruction of the common.

Environmental degradation and resource depletion have been globally pervasive concerns over the last few decades. The problem of the management of common-pool resources has received relatively increased attention in economics. The properties of common-pool resources lead to at least two types of collective action problems in management: those of resource appropriation and provision. An appropriation problem can result in the over-consumption of a subtractable resource, in which an individual benefits from personal consumption at the expense of the community and the conditions of the resource. Conserving common-pool resources is problematic because many individuals rely on the benefits of extraction for their livelihoods. A common-pool resource exists when multiple parties appropriate a resource, and appropriation by any one party reduces the resources available to others. It differs from a public good in that the resource units harvested by one appropriator are not available to any other appropriator. A public good has two essential attributes: non-excludability and non-rivalry in consumption. A common-pool resource is, on the other hand, non-excludable but rival.[8] Non-excludability means the difficulty to exclude non-paying consumers from consumption, which is a feature that both types of goods share. The possibility of non-rival consumption by multiple consumers is the major feature that distinguishes public goods from common-pool resources. One person's enjoyment of a sunset does not subtract from others' enjoyment of a sunset. On the other hand, if one fisherman lands a ton of fish, that ton is not available for others.

Common-pool resources are expected to suffer from collective action problems when individuals act in a self-interested manner. Individuals make independent and anonymous decisions and primarily focus on their own immediate payoffs in a common-pool resource setting. Hardin's (1968) metaphor is based on the assumption that human behaviour is driven by selfish preferences. Individual selfish users are unwilling to pay the costs of conservation because the benefits of doing so are shared collectively. Resources involving open access are much more vulnerable to over-harvesting than those with restricted access. Joint users may harvest resources without gaining prior permission. Unrestricted individualistic decision-making in relation to common-pool resources will result in tragedy: the greater the individual effort, the worse off people become. The action of one agent affects the resource stock, which in turn affects the well-being of another agent through decreased resource availability. Given their rival and non-excludable properties, common-pool resources are expected to suffer from overexploitation. The fact that consumption of the resource by one person reduces the amount available to others implies that these resource users face a typical social dilemma. Social dilemmas are group interactions in which an individual maximises one's own payoff when one does not cooperate, but attaining the social optimum requires cooperation. In order for a governance arrangement to be successful, it should stop the overuse of the resources it governs. Incentives need to be provided to users to limit their consumption levels and boost their provision levels. Several approaches have been suggested to mitigate the social dilemmas. The structure of decision-making arrangements has to be modified to enable individuals to act jointly in relation to those resources as common property.[9] Appropriators may attempt to implement governance by investing in monitoring and enforcement.

The assumption of self-enforcement is consistent with the case-study analysis by Ostrom (1990). If communities are able to design their own usage schemes, organise themselves and enforce the rules they design, then collective action and self-governance can be successful in reducing the impact of the social dilemmas. Ostrom's (1990) work finds that, in common-pool resource situations, collectively desirable outcomes arise when users are left to develop the rules and enforcement mechanisms themselves. Ostrom (1990) suggests that users are not necessarily always short-term maximisers and that they can develop self-governing institutional arrangements to regulate the commons. For Hardin (1968), there are only two solutions to the tragedy of the commons: the coercive state and privatisation. One solution is the control of natural resources by a central government agency, and the second solution is the imposition of private property. Ostrom (1990) suggests that user self-governance can be a third option to prevent tragic outcomes.[10] Community management is a system which is based on cooperation, in which individual decision units formulate both individual and common goals. Local communities often develop their own cooperative rules without enforcement from the top down and without imposing private property rights. Bottom-up processes are more appealing than authoritarian enforcement. Local spheres must have some autonomy for systems to function properly; local actors resolve problems within their own sphere. The community-based governance is self-regulating because individual interests are balanced against the collective interest for environmental sustainability.

Following Teraji (2019), this section focuses on individual's preferences as a source of selfish or pro-environmental behaviour. Consider a community which is made up of a fixed number n of individuals. Individuals have complete rights of access to a common-pool resource. They simultaneously decide the amount of resources to exploit from a common pool of renewable resources. The total stock of the resource in existence is denoted by F. Each agent is endowed with a fixed activity level, one, which he or she can allocate to harvesting the common-pool resource or to an alternative activity (resource conservation). The agent selects activity allocation between resource extraction and resource conservation. The agent chooses a degree of effort expended on the resource extraction, e, where $0 \leq e \leq 1$. That is, if the agent chooses to allocate effort e in the resource extraction, then he or she puts in the remaining $1 - e$ in the resource conservation.

The resource extraction entails a (direct) cost $c(e)$. The agent puts in effort e at a cost $c(e)$ in the resource extraction. It is assumed that $c(.)$ is strictly increasing and strictly convex in e, that is, $c'(.) > 0$ and $c''(.) > 0$. In addition, to ensure an interior solution, it is assumed that $c'(0) = 0$ and $\lim_{e \to 1} c'(e) = \infty$. Then, the marginal cost of harvesting, $c'(e)$, becomes sufficiently large as e approaches a common maximum effort level that can be exerted by each individual.

There are two types of preferences that an individual can have: selfish (S) and pro-environmental (PE). An agent with selfish or pro-environmental preferences receives material payoff related to resource extraction e. Each receives a share of the total, equal to his or her share of the total effort in the resource extraction.

The material payoff $b(e)$ is then given by:

$$b(e) = \begin{cases} e & \text{if } ne \leq F \\ (1/n)F & \text{otherwise} \end{cases} \tag{20.5}$$

If the sum of all harvesting efforts, ne, does not exceed the available amount of the resource F, then each agent receives a return equal to his or her own effort e. However, if the sum of harvesting efforts exceeds the resource stock, the resource might be exhausted. Then, it is supposed that each agent receives $(e/ne)F = (1/n)F$ if $ne > F$.

The agent with selfish preferences only cares for the material payoff U_S.

Definition 1: An agent has selfish preferences, where the utility function is given by:

$$U_S = b(e) - c(e). \tag{20.6}$$

Besides the material payoff, the agent with pro-environmental preferences also obtains a psychological payoff per unit of activity in the resource conservation defined by k, where $0 < k < 1$. It is interpreted as the degree of moral satisfaction that the agent with pro-environmental preferences derives from the resource conservation. Let U_{PE} denote the payoff for the agent with pro-environmental preferences.

Definition 2: An agent has pro-environmental preferences, where the utility function is given by:

$$U_{PE} = b(e) + k(1-e) - c(e), \tag{20.7}$$

where k reflects the degree of moral preferences for the resource conservation.

The model focuses on *intra-personal* dimensions within an individual, not on *inter-personal* ones among individuals. The timing of the situation is the following:

[Stage 1] Each agent holds either selfish preferences or pro-environmental ones.
[Stage 2] Each agent chooses an effort e in the resource extraction.

At stage 1, each agent gets an opportunity to hold either selfish preferences or pro-environmental ones. Let x be the agent's subjective belief about holding pro-environmental preferences, where $0 \leq x \leq 1$. With probability x, the agent holds pro-environmental preferences; with probability $1 - x$, he or she holds selfish preferences.

Taking into account his or her own preferences, each agent chooses the effort level at stage 2. The agent's expected utility at stage 2 is written as:

$$\begin{aligned}(1-x)U_S + xU_{PE} &= (1-x)\{b(e) - c(e)\} \\ &\quad + x\{b(e) + k(1-e) - c(e)\} \\ &= b(e) - c(e) + xk(1-e).\end{aligned} \tag{20.8}$$

Individual utility is composed as a weighted sum of two different types: selfish and pro-environmental. Each agent chooses the optimal level of effort in the resource extraction to maximise his or her utility. The problem that he or she faces at stage 2 is: $\max_e b(e) - c(e) + xk(1 - e)$. The optimal level of effort equates the marginal benefit of providing effort to its marginal cost.

Teraji (2019) shows how the equilibrium value of e varies with the parameter x. The equilibrium resource extraction depends on the probability that the individual holds pro-environmental preferences. That is, the value e decreases as x increases, where $0 \leq x \leq 1$: $de(x)/dx < 0$. The greater an individual's exposure to x, the greater his or her effort in the resource conservation. A different probability that the agent holds pro-environmental preferences prescribes a different behaviour in which a different amount of effort is selected in the resource extraction. As the probability that the agent holds pro-environmental preferences increases, he or she is expected to provide a lower activity level to the resource extraction. A significant departure from conventional models of the commons is that the amount of effort expended on the resource extraction depends on the agent's subjective belief that he or she holds pro-environmental preferences.

The model can be set in discrete time, and time is denoted by $t = 0, 1, 2, \ldots$ Resource extraction and conservation occur at discrete points in time. If $F(t+1) - F(t) \geq 0$ for all $t \geq 0$, resource sustainability can be achieved. It is assumed that the stock of the resource, $F(0)$, is exogenously given at $t = 0$. In the common-pool resource extraction problem, each individual would be better off if all would restrain their use, but it is not in the interest of the agent with selfish preferences to do so.[11] Pro-environmental preferences can be deterred from over-exploitation by moral satisfaction from resource conservation.

The conservation activity regrows the renewable resource, while effort in the extraction depletes the resource. For a fixed number n of individuals, the aggregate resource conservation (or renewal) is given by $n(1 - e(t))$ at t, while the aggregate resource extraction is given by $ne(t)$ at t. The interaction of these components governs the dynamics of the model. After the individual decisions, the resource stock is depleted by an amount equal to the sum of extraction efforts, and it regrows by an amount equal to the sum of conservation activities. The regrown stock of the resource is then available for the agents in the next period. The next period's resource stock, $F(t + 1)$, is given by:

$$F(t+1) = F(t) + n(1 - e(t)) - ne(t). \tag{20.9}$$

In the context here, $F(t)$ is given at the beginning of t. Common-pool resources are sustainable over time if $F(t+1) - F(t) \geq 0$ for any t. We consider whether a threshold value, e^*, exists such that $F(t-1) - F(t) \geq 0$ holds for any $e \leq e^*$. Thus, we can consider $e^* = e(x^*)$ such that $x \geq x^*$ holds for $e(x) \leq e(x^*)$. Teraji (2019) shows that resource sustainability can be attained by increasing the probability that he or she holds pro-environmental preferences.

Resource conservation may be seen as a burden entailing costs due to foregone resource-use opportunities. Then, economic incentives may be seen as critical to offset these costs. However, it is demonstrated that common-pool resources are successfully and sustainably governed without economic incentives. Resource users balance self-interest with conformity. Individuals who have social preferences tend to restrain their harvesting in attempts to preserve the resource. Communities composed of such individuals do not overharvest the resource even when there are benefits from over-usage and monitoring is nearly non-existent.

CONCLUSION

The problem of the management of common-pool resources has received increased attention in economics. Conventional economics has argued that people's morality is futile and people only cooperate for fear of external constraints such as punishments. Following this view, resource conservation is seen as a burden entailing costs due to foregone resource-use opportunities, and economic incentives seem to be critical to offset these costs. However, common-pool resources are often sustainably governed without economic incentives. An agent faces the tension between economic and social incentives for the sustainability of a common-pool resource. A factor that might increase the performance of pro-social activities concerns people's incentives. People exhibit pro-social behaviour when they do not always make choices only based on economic incentives. Extrinsic monetary rewards to encourage pro-social behaviour can sometimes backfire and decrease the desired behaviour by crowding out intrinsic motivation to act pro-socially. Economic incentives can manipulate people into being more selfish. On the other hand, social incentives will give prominence to the role of non-pecuniary drivers of pro-social behaviour. Individuals who consider resource conservation to be a major concern are driven by social incentives. A society can be sustainable to the degree that its members embody social or pro-environmental preferences.

NOTES

1. Especially, the ultimatum game by Güth *et al.* (1982) played an important role in weakening the exclusive reliance on the self-interest hypothesis. The ultimatum game involves two parties, the proposer and the responder, who have to agree on the division of a fixed sum of money. Subjects in the ultimatum game experiments deviate from the self-interested choice: the vast majority of the offers to the responder are between 40 and 50 per cent of the available surplus. They exhibit some form of other-regarding preferences.
2. In an example of a boy cutting the lawn for his father, once the father agrees to pay for the lawn to be cut, the boy is no longer willing to do it without payment.
3. A reward is offered after an action is completed, while an incentive is more appropriately described as a strategy employed to motivate action.
4. Payments may crowd out the pro-social attitude in certain situations where people act to support a common good without being paid to do so. In the environmental arena, for example, Frey and Oberholzer-Gee (1997) found that Swiss residents were willing to accept nuclear waste disposal in their community purely out of a sense of public spiritedness about twice as frequently as when they were offered compensation for accepting the negative externality.
5. In a public good game, players are endowed with a certain number of tokens that they can either contribute to a project that is beneficial for all or keep for themselves. All players profit equally from the public good, no matter whether they contributed or not; each player receives a lower individual profit from the tokens contributed to the public good than from the tokens kept.
6. Zelmer (2003) and Chaudhuri (2011) provide surveys on experimental findings concerning the voluntary provision of public goods.
7. Economists have assumed that each player chooses a public good contribution that maximises his or her utility, given his or her beliefs about levels of contributions by others. Sugden (1985) studies what the levels of contributions imply about individual beliefs about others' behaviour. In order to rationalise observed high levels of voluntary contributions, the beliefs that individuals must hold in order are mutually inconsistent. As Sugden (1985, p. 123) argues, '[i]t would hardly be satisfactory to claim to explain voluntary contributions to public goods by assuming individuals hold systematically false beliefs about one another's behavior'.
8. More precisely, according to Ostrom *et al.* (1999), common-pool resources are defined as natural or human-constructed resource systems in which (1) exclusion of beneficiaries through physical

and institutional means is especially costly and (2) exploitation by one user reduces resource availability for others.
9. In the voluntary contribution mechanism by Isaac and Walker (1988), each member of a group receives an endowment of money and then the members simultaneously decide to contribute some proportion of their endowment to the group account. These contributions benefit all group members. The endowment left over goes to the individual's private account. The dominant strategy is then to place all of one's endowment in the private account. However, for the social optimum to be attained, all individuals need to contribute their entire endowment to the group account. The percentage of the endowment placed in the group account is interpreted as a measure of cooperation in this mechanism.
10. Ostrom, based on her case-study analysis, identified eight design principles needed to achieve long-enduring institutions: (1) clearly defined boundaries that allow the exclusion of external resource users; (2) rules for the resource use that is adapted to local conditions; (3) collective arrangements that let most resource users take part in the decision-making process; (4) effective monitoring under responsibility of the local users; (5) a scale of graduated sanctions for users who violate the community rules; (6) cheap and easy mechanisms of conflict resolution; (7) community self-determination that is recognised by higher-level authorities; and (8) a larger common-pool resource that is organised in the form of multiple layers of nested enterprises, with small local common-pool resources at the base level.
11. Sethi and Somanathan (1996) study the evolution of three strategies, namely defecting, cooperating and enforcing, among agents interacting in a common-pool resource game. The evolutionary process is described by a replicator dynamics equation, and differential survival is proportional to the relative performance value of each strategy.

REFERENCES

Akerlof, G.A., and R.E. Kranton. 2000. "Economics and identity." *Quarterly Journal of Economics* **115**(3): 715–753.
Andreoni, J. 1990. "Impure altruism and donations to public goods: A theory of warm-glow giving." *Economic Journal* **100**(401): 464–477.
Ashraf, N., C.F. Camerer, and G. Loewenstein. 2005. "Adam Smith, behavioral economist." *Journal of Economic Perspectives* **19**(3): 131–145.
Bergstrom, T., L. Blume, and H. Varian. 1986. "On the private provision of public goods." *Journal of Public Economics* **29**(1): 25–49.
Bowles, S. 2015. *The Moral Economy: Why Good Incentives Are Not Substitutes for Good Citizens.* London: Yale University Press.
Charness, G., and M. Rabin. 2002. "Understanding social preferences with simple tests." *Quarterly Journal of Economics* **117**(3): 817–869.
Chaudhuri, A. 2011. "Sustaining cooperation in laboratory public goods experiments: A selective survey of the literature." *Experimental Economics* **14**(1): 47–83.
Fehr, E., G. Kirchsteiger, and A. Reidl. 1993. "Does fairness prevent market clearing? An experimental investigation." *Quarterly Journal of Economics* **108**(2): 437–460.
Fehr, E., and K.M. Schmidt. 1999. "A theory of fairness, competition, and cooperation." *Quarterly Journal of Economics* **114**(3): 817–868.
Frey, B.S., and F. Oberholzer-Gee. 1997. "The cost of price incentives: An empirical analysis of motivation crowding-out." *American Economic Review* **87**(4): 746–755.
Gintis, H., S. Bowles, R. Boyd, and E. Fehr (eds.), 2005. *Moral Sentiments and Material Interests: The Foundations of Cooperation in Economic Life.* Cambridge, MA: The MIT Press.
Gneezy, U., and A. Rustichini. 2000. "A fine is a price." *Journal of Legal Studies* **29**(1): 1–17.
Güth, W., R. Schmittberger, and B. Schwarze. 1982. "An experimental analysis of ultimatum bargaining." *Journal of Economic Behavior and Organization* **3**(4): 367–388.
Hardin, G. 1968. "The tragedy of the commons." *Science* **162**(3859): 1243–1248.
Hume, D. [1739–40] 1983. *A Treatise of Human Nature.* Oxford: Clarendon Press.
Isaac, R.M., and J.M. Walker. 1988. "Group size effects in public goods provision: The voluntary contribution mechanism." *Quarterly Journal of Economics* **103**(1): 179–200.

Ostrom, E. 1990. *Governing the Commons*. New York: Cambridge University Press.
Ostrom, E., J. Burger, C.B. Field, R.B. Norgaard, and D. Policansky. 1999. "Revisiting the commons: Local lessons, global challenges." *Science* **284**(5412): 278–282.
Sethi, R., and E. Somanathan. 1996. "The evolution of social norms in common property resource use." *American Economic Review* **86**(4): 766–788.
Smith, A. [1759] 1981. *The Theory of Moral Sentiments*. Indianapolis: Liberty Fund.
Sudgen, R. 1985. "Consistent conjectures, and voluntary contributions to public goods." *Journal of Public Economics* **27**(1): 117–124.
Teraji, S. 2019. "Identity switching and conservation on the commons." *International Review of Economics* **66**(2): 101–113.
Titmuss, R.M. 1970. *The Gift Relationship: From Human Blood to Social Policy*. New York: Allen and Unwin.
Zelmer, J. 2003. "Linear public goods experiments: A meta-analysis." *Experimental Economics* **6**(3): 299–310.

21. Antisocial punishment
Alexis V. Belianin

INTRODUCTION

The concept of antisocial punishment emerges in the context when the participants have an option to impose unilateral or mutual sanctions on each other. These sanctions, or punishments, are typically, though not always, costly, and constitute a deduction from the payoffs earned by the punished participant in the course of social interactions.

Putting it concisely, the practice of antisocial punishment may be defined as 'paying a cost to reduce the resources of a person whose previous cooperative behavior benefited the punisher and their group' (Sylwester et al., 2013, p. 167). Typical experiments featuring punishments are social dilemma games, such as ultimatum, dictator, trust and public goods/prisoner's dilemma. In these games, the valence of the actions of each player is unambiguously clear. Equal splits of the pie in the ultimatum or dictator game are cooperative, while an offer of 0 to the receiver is selfish. Similarly, Pareto efficient (full) contribution to the public good is cooperative, while equilibrium (zero) contribution is not. Punishments applied to such actions also have clear valences: punishment of a non-cooperative action is prosocial (or else, altruistic), but punishment of a cooperative one is termed antisocial, perversive (Cinyabuguma et al., 2006) or spiteful.[1] It should be noted that, although sometimes spiteful punishments are studied in the context of bilateral interactions (Pillutla et al., 1996; Brañas-Garza et al., 2014; Rabellino et al., 2016), this context is much less common than that of public goods. The reason is that in two-player games it is more appropriate to speak of punishment for strategic or personal, rather than social interests.

PUBLIC GOODS GAME WITH PUNISHMENT

A typical context for punishment is that of the conventional public goods game of n players each of whom (indexed by i) has an endowment of size 1 and may contribute any share of it x_i to the public good, keeping the rest on her private account. Contributions of all players are summed up, multiplied by efficiency factor $1 < k < n$, and divided equally among all n players, regardless of their contribution. The payoff to each player is then

$$u_i = 1 - x_i + k/n \sum x_i$$

Each unit contributed to the public good yields $k/n < 1$, while each unit kept on private account is worth 1. This implies that the individually rational (Nash equilibrium in dominant strategies) decision is to contribute nothing, no matter what the other players do. At the same time, full contribution of all players would have yielded $k > 1$ to each, which is Pareto optimal, but strictly dominated strategy (each player who would free-ride would deplete the public good by $k/n < 1$ units, but save 1 unit for herself).

Punishment in this context (Fehr and Gaechter, 2000) takes place upon the revelation of all individual contributions to all participants. Having observed the contribution of each other participant, each individual i has an option (not an obligation) to decrease participant j's payoff by p_{ij} and pay $0 \leq s < 1$ units per unit of this punishment. Other players have analogous options, so the total payoff of player i is

$$U_i = u_i - s \sum p_{ij} - \sum p_{ji}$$

If punishment cost $s > 0$, punishments constitute pure deductions from participants' payoffs, hence their equilibrium level is expected to be zero. However, in practice (Fehr and Gaechter, 2002) it is strictly positive on average, suggesting that the participants who apply it receive positive value from their choice.

Either kind of punishment constitutes a problem from the viewpoint of conventional theory. A rational economic individual should care about personal well-being only, which is reduced by costly punishment without any material benefits. Altruistic punishment, however, can be rationalised by prosocial motivation (Carpenter, 2007; Rand and Nowak, 2011), including retaliation for non-cooperative action and inducement of further cooperation in repeated settings (Falk et al., 2005; Egas and Riedl, 2008). But antisocial punishments are paradoxical even from that perspective: if prosocial punishments are aimed at the reduction of detrimental, antisocial actions, then antisocial punishments apparently seek to abate actions which are beneficial for everyone, including the punisher. However, this practice is regular and even quite common in some parts of the world. Figure 21.1 taken from the canonical paper by Herrmann et al. (2008) illustrates this point in the context of bilateral punishment in a repeated public goods game with voluntary contributions of up to 20 experimental tokens. Valences of punishments are coded with colours: mean sizes of punishment for prosocial comparisons, when the contribution of the punishing player is larger than that of the punished one, are coloured in green: dark green when the difference in contributions is from 11 to 20 tokens, light green for lower differences. Red colours correspond to spiteful punishment (in the narrow sense) when the contribution of the punished player is larger than that of the punisher by at least 11 tokens (maroon) or less than that (red). In yellow are marked punishments in cases when the contributions of the punisher are the same as that of the punished participant (in the aforementioned terms, instances of antisocial but not spiteful punishment). In every case, bars length represent mean punishment sizes, stacked across categories of prosocial and antisocial punishments, respectively.

While mean prosocial punishments are approximately similar across participating countries, antisocial punishments systematically differ. In Northern and Central Europe and New England, the mean sizes of these latter are quite low, and most often infrequent, never exceeding 25 per cent of all punishment instances. In other places, like the Middle East, Southern and Eastern Europe, antisocial punishments are way larger in size, and much more frequent, sometimes amounting to and exceeding 50 per cent of all punishment instances (see Figure 2S in the supplementary material to Herrmann et al., 2008). Bruhin et al. (2020), using the same data, have shown that 30 per cent of participants have been engaged in both prosocial and antisocial punishment, and over 50 per cent to prosocial punishment only. At the same time, heterogeneity across cultures is also large: in the Arab-speaking countries, represented by Oman and Saudi Arabia, mixed types of punishments take place in over 50 per cent of all punishment cases, followed by Orthodox Europe (Belarus, Ukraine and Russia), where frequencies of this pattern exceed 40 per cent. Belianin (2022), using a sample of Russian data, finds also that antisocial punishments are significantly more serial, i.e. once a person punishes antisocially,

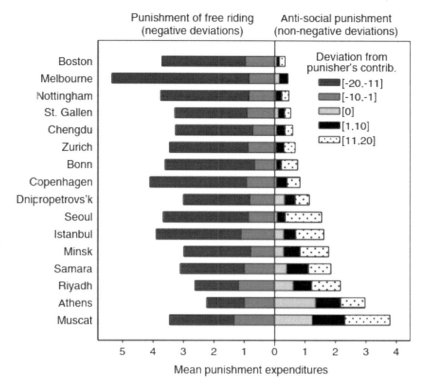

Source: Herrmann et al. (2008).

Figure 21.1 Prosocial and antisocial punishment. Mean differences in contributions are in square brackets

(s)he is more likely to punish more of her or his groupmates and spend more on that purpose per punishment instance than their prosocial counterparts. Gaechter and Herrmann (2011) in an experiment in urban and rural central Russia, have found that the share of expenditures on antisocial punishments among all punishments varies from 35 to 78 per cent, which trend seems to be stable across periods of the game, regions and age of the participants. Thus far there seems to be no published work which reports the systematic and specific effect of antisocial punishment on cooperative behaviour.

COMPARATIVE STUDIES

Substantive cross-country variance in the spread of antisocial punishments made the respective countries very attractive for comparative research of social preferences. Gaechter and Herrmann (2009) compare such punishment patterns (strong negative reciprocity) in Russia and Switzerland and find them to be systematically more common for the Russians. Rabellino et al. (2016), studying third-party punishment in dictator games in groups of Italian and Chinese participants, have found that Italians punish antisocially significantly more than Chinese. This effect is especially pronounced for punishing senders who commit unfair actions to receivers, although no systematic discrimination of either nation was found in cross-country groups. This effect of stronger punishment directed towards an outgroup, including antisocial ones, has been established in many other contexts (Bernhard et al., 2006). Finally, Grimalda et al. (2022) have shown that antisocial punishment, while present and different across the participants of the threshold public goods experiment, is smaller both in scale and in the difference between the participants from Germany and Russia (see Figure 21.2), even though independent contributions of the Germans were significantly larger than those of the Russians.

This experiment was motivated by the abatement of climate change literature, which allows attributing this result to coincident and commonly known interests among the participants on both sides. For this reason, contributions to public good in that study were rather large, and punishments were as low as 10 per cent of possible instances; no systematic discrimination between nations was observed. These experiments show, inter alia, that although the phenomenon of antisocial punishment itself is quite robust, its scale and cross-cultural attributions are sensitive to contexts.

The colour scheme in Figure 21.2 is the same as in Figure 21.1; the max contribution is 50 tokens, and the punishment allowed is zero, one or two tokens.

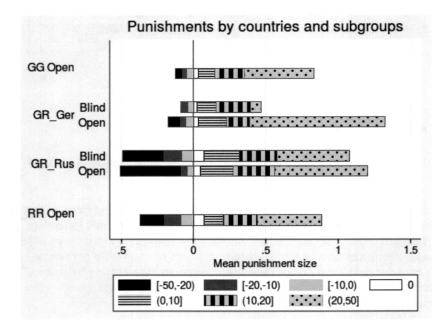

Source: Grimalda et al. (2022).

Figure 21.2 *Patterns of punishments. GG Open and RR Open: within-countries German and Russian sessions; GR_Ger and GR_Rus: punishments of Germans and Russians in mixed sessions; Open: participants aware of the nationality of partners; Blind: participants unaware of it*

MOTIVES

Altogether, although antisocial punishment seems a madness, there is a method to it. This conjecture is further confirmed by various evidence. Masclet et al. (2003) have found that antisocial punishment is almost non-existent in non-monetary games. Fatas and Mateu (2015) find antisocial punishment to be much lower in the 'weakest link' type of public goods game, i.e. when the public good produced depends on the lowest contribution. Cinyabuguma et al. (2006) report that second-order punishments (i.e. punishments after observing first-order punishments of the groupmates in the public goods game) of the non-cooperators are primarily directed to those who punish spiteful punishers. For the prosocial participants, the effect is the opposite: they second-order punish primarily those who punish antisocially. This seems to suggest that behind both types of punishment there are strategic reasons.

What might these reasons be? One simple explanation mirrors the reasons for prosocial punishment: if this latter is driven by the disapproval of the (low) contribution of the selfish participants, then antisocial punishment should reveal the dissatisfaction of greedy participants with the generosity of the cooperative ones. This logic in itself sounds highly counterintuitive: why should one punish those who did to you (and others) nothing but good? Several more compelling reasons have been raised in the literature.

One of the strongest punishment motives is revenge, which is natural to humans in many contexts, and confirmed at the neural level (de Qurevain et al., 2004). The conventional approach suggests that cooperators have every right to be angry at those who do not cooperate – yet this motive is only part of the picture. Prosocial intentions are not the only ones typical of humans – in fact, all classical economics was teaching that humans are competitive and that competition is good. Extending this logic, prosocial punishers behave 'anti-economically', while antisocial ones behave in line with this logic, wiping out inefficient altruism. Another, perhaps more compelling explanation might be that high cooperators violate tacit (or even explicit) norms that prescribe not to contribute too much. For instance, in Islamic cultures, the most generous person must be the one who is also richer. Hence participants who believe that they are richer than others may view those who contribute more than them as violators of social norms and impose sanctions on them. Similarly, in Orthodox countries of Eastern Europe, traditional values of humility, modesty and egalitarianism suggest that one should not take the initiative and 'show up' oneself as superior in anything, be it even prosocial activities. In such instances, antisocial punishment looks like rational revenge for the violation of social norms.

Another powerful motive for antisocial punishment is competition. By the structure of the game, the cost of sanctions is typically less than the damage they impose on the punished person. Hence indiscriminate punishment of one's groupmates (especially more generous ones) is a nice way to increase one's performance relative to that of the other participants. Hence, 'decisions to punish appear to be logically tied to the effectiveness of such punishment and to the ability to increase the positive difference between others' payoffs and one's own' (Sylwester et al., 2013). This competitive motive can be traced in such experiments as Houser and Xiao (2010) and is also consistent with the evidence that antisocial punishers tend to spend fewer resources on getting information about the decisions of others (Page et al., 2013; Nikiforakis, 2008, 2010).

CONCLUSION

The aforesaid considerations suggest that both prosocial and antisocial punishments are driven by natural social dynamics. This viewpoint is essentially evolutionary (Hauert et al., 2007; Traulsen et al., 2009) and is supported by the available data. Rand and Nowak (2011) study the motives for antisocial punishment in the context of the optional public goods game. In this game, each of the n players decides whether to opt in to participate in the public goods game or opt out and act as a loner. Participants decide whether to make a lump-sum contribution c to the public good, from which every participant receives the same return at a factor $r > 1$. Loners neither contribute nor gain from public goods and receive fixed exogenous payment s which is between full contribution and full defection payoff of the opt-in players. Finally, all players – contributors, defectors and loners – observe the payoff accrued to everyone and decide whether to apply a lump-sum costly punishment to the group members depending on their type.

In the long run, participants are supposed to change their strategies proportional to current earnings and subject to random mutations. Intuitively, when the number of cooperators becomes large, it makes sense to defect when there are many defectors. Public goods yield nothing and loners earn more, and when there are many loners, cooperation becomes an attractive strategy because the gains from the public goods are split among a small group of players who may concur to cooperate. Rand and Nowak show that this circular dynamic, akin to the rock-papers-scissors game, is qualitatively unchanged when the possibility of punishment is embedded in it: the limited distribution of strategies in the steady state of the dynamics of 24 strategies features both prosocial and antisocial punishments, and the conclusion remains robust to parameter changes.

NOTE

1. Sometimes in the literature distinction is drawn between antisocial punishment, when the action of the punished individual is at least as cooperative as that of the punisher, and spiteful punishment, when the action of the former is strictly more cooperative than that of the latter.

REFERENCES

Belianin A. V. (2022). Punishment without crime: A study of causes of antisocial punishment. Manuscript, Department of Economics, Higher School of Economics, Moscow, Russia.

Bernhard, H., Fischbacher, U., & Fehr, E. (2006). Parochial altruism in humans. *Nature*, 442, 912–915. Doi:10.1038/nature04981

Brañas-Garza, P., Espín, A. M., Exadaktylos, F., & Herrmann, B. (2014). Fair and unfair punishers coexist in the Ultimatum Game. *Scientific Reports*, 4, 6025. Doi:10.1038/srep06025

Bruhin, A., Janizzi, K., & Thöni, C. (2020). Uncovering the heterogeneity behind cross-cultural variation in antisocial punishment. *Journal of Economic Behavior & Organization*, 180, 291–308. ISSN 0167-2681, https://doi.org/10.1016/j.jebo.2020.10.005

Carpenter, J. P. (2007). The demand for punishment. *Journal of Economic Behavior & Organization*, 62, 522–542. Doi:10.1016/j.jebo.2005.05.004

Cinyabuguma, M., Page, T., & Putterman, L. (2006). Can second-order punishment deter perverse punishment? *Experimental Economics*, 9, 265–279. Doi:10.1007/s10683-006-9127-z

Egas, M., & Riedl, A. (2008). The economics of altruistic punishment and the maintenance of cooperation. *Proceedings of the Royal Society B: Biological Sciences*, 275, 871–878. Doi:10.1098/rspb.2007.1558

Espin, A. M., Brañas-Garza, P., Herrmann, B., & Gamella, J. F. (2012). Patient and impatient punishers of free-riders. *Proceedings of the Royal Society B: Biological Sciences*, 279, 4923–4928. Doi:10.1098/rspb.2012.2043

Falk, A., Fehr, E., & Fischbacher, U. (2005). Driving forces behind informal sanctions. *Econometrica*, 73, 2017–2030. Doi:10.1111/j.1468-0262.2005.00644.x

Fatas, E., & Mateu, G. (2015). Antisocial punishment in two social dilemmas. *Frontiers in Behavioral Neuroscience*, 9, 107. Doi:10.3389/fnbeh.2015.00107

Fehr, E., & Gächter, S. (2000). Cooperation and punishment in public goods experiments. *American Economic Review*, 90, 980–994.

Fehr, E., & Gächter, S. (2002). Altruistic punishment in humans. *Nature*, 415, 137–140. Doi:10.1038/415137a

Fowler, J. H. (2005). Altruistic punishment and the origin of cooperation. *Proceedings of the National Academy of Sciences of the USA*, 102, 7047–7049.

Gächter, S., & Herrmann, B. (2009). Reciprocity, culture, and human cooperation: Previous insights and a new cross-cultural experiment. *Philosophical Transactions of the Royal Society B – Biological Sciences*, 364, 791–806.

Gächter, S., & Herrmann, B. (2011). The limits of self-governance in the presence of spite: Experimental evidence from urban and rural Russia. *European Economic Review*, 55, 193–210. Doi:10.1016/j.euroecorev.2010.04.003

Grimalda, G., Belianin, A., Hennig-Schmidt, H., Requate, T., & Ryzhkova, M. V. (2022). Sanctions and international interaction improve cooperation to avert climate change. *Proceedings of the Royal Society B*, 289, 2021–2174. http://doi.org/10.1098/rspb.2021.2174

Hauert, C., Traulsen, A., Brandt, H., Nowak, M. A., & Sigmund, K. (2007). Via freedom to coercion: The emergence of costly punishment. *Science*, 316, 1905–1907.

Herrmann, B., Thöni, C., & Gächter, S. (2008). Antisocial punishment across societies. *Science*, 319, 1362–1367. Doi:10.1126/science.1153808

Houser, D., & Xiao, E. (2010). Inequality seeking punishment. *Economics Letters*, 109, 20–23. Doi:10.1016/j.econlet.2010.07.008

Masclet, D., Noussair, C., Tucker, S., & Villeval, M. C. (2003). Monetary and nonmonetary punishment in the voluntary contributions mechanism. *American Economic Review*, 93, 366–380. Doi:10.1257/000282803321455359

Nikiforakis, N. (2008). Punishment and counter-punishment in public good games: Can we really govern ourselves? *Journal of Public Economics*, 92, 91–112. Doi:10.1016/j.jpubeco.2007.04.008

Nikiforakis, N. (2010). Feedback, punishment and cooperation in public good experiments. *Games and Economic Behavior, Elsevier*, 68(2), 689–702.

Page, T., Putterman, L., & Garcia, B. (2013). Voluntary contributions with redistribution: The effect of costly sanctions when one person's punishment is another's reward. *Journal of Economic Behavior & Organization, Elsevier*, 95©, 34–48.

Pillutla, M., & Murnighan, K. J. (1996). Unfairness, anger, and spite: Emotional rejections of ultimatum offers. *Organizational Behavior and Human Decision Processes*, 68, 208–224. doi:10.1006/obhd.1996.0100

de Quervain, D. J.-F., Fischbacher, U., Treyer, V., Schellhammer, M., Schnyder, U., Buck, A., & Fehr, E. (2004). The neural basis of altruistic punishment. *Science*, 305, 1254–1258. doi:10.1126/science.1100735

Rabellino, D., Morese, R., Ciaramidaro, A., Bara, B. G., & Bosco, F. M. (2016). Third-party punishment: Altruistic and anti-social behaviours in in-group and out-group settings. *Journal of Cognitive Psychology*, 28(4), 486–495. doi:10.1080/20445911.2016.1138961

Rand, David G., & Nowak, M. A. (2011). The evolution of antisocial punishment in optional public goods games. *Nature Communications*, 2, Article number: 434.

Sylwester, K., Herrmann, B., & Bryson, J. J. (2013). Homo homini lupus? Explaining antisocial punishment. *Journal of Neuroscience, Psychology, and Economics,* 6(3), 167–188. https://doi.org/10.1037/npe0000009

Traulsen, A., Hauert, C., De Silva, H., Nowak, M. A., & Sigmund, K. (2009). Exploration dynamics in evolutionary games. *Proceedings of the National Academy of Sciences of the USA*, 106, 709–712.

PART VIII

EVALUATION AND FORMATION OF BELIEFS AND PREFERENCES

22. Auction methods of valuation and the endowment effect

Fang-Fang Tang

INTRODUCTION

Since the field contingent-valuation study by Hammack and Brown (1974) first uncovered a significant divergence of willingness-to-pay (WTP, to buy an object) and willingness-to-accept (WTA, to sell an object) in value measures, named as the endowment effect henceforth, a systematic body of consistent experimental evidence has been documented in the past decades as one of the most robust findings of the psychology of decision making (see, e.g., Rowe, d'Arge and Brookshire 1980; Knetsch and Sinden 1984; Kahneman, Knetsch and Thaler 1990; Knetsch, Tang and Thaler 2001; List 2003; Plott and Zeiler 2005; Knetsch and Tang 2006; Knetsch 2020).

Theoretically, Hanemann (1991) tried to explain the value divergence by substitution effects, namely, when the good in question has an imperfect substitute, value measures will diverge and the divergence will expand with the decreasing degree of substitution. Shogren et al. (1994) tried to test Hanemann's proposition with an experimental market and, in particular, they found that for two private market goods with a relatively close substitute (a candy bar and a coffee mug) the endowment effect disappeared with repeated exposure to the market through Vickrey second-price sealed-bid auctions (see also Harless 1989). Shogren et al. (1994) also experimented with a private nonmarket good with no close substitute (reduction of human health risk) and found that the divergence of WTP and WTA value measures was robust and persistent, with repeated market participation and full information on the characteristics of the good.

Contrary to these authors' claim that their experimental results provide some support for Hanemann's argument, we pointed out that there were in fact two possible interpretations: (1) the endowment effect was eliminated under 'appropriate' market settings, or (2) there was something very wrong with the demand-revealing properties of the Vickrey auction. In fact, we provided clear evidence through Vickrey auction experiments – using mugs (in Canada and Singapore) and comparably priced graduation photo albums (in China) – to support the second alternative in Knetsch, Tang and Thaler (2001) and Knetsch and Tang (2006). The WTP-versus-WTA value convergence findings of private market goods with a relatively close substitute (a candy bar) in Shogren et al. (1994) were mainly due to the fact that they auctioned only one item in their experiments through Vickrey second-price sealed-bid auctions. We found similar patterns of one auctioned item in our experiments as well. However, if the auctioned items are several (more than one), value measures of WTP versus WTA diverge even further, namely the endowment effect is strengthened rather than weakened. It is the number of items to be auctioned that plays the key role here, even in the private market goods with relatively close substitutes (mugs and comparably priced graduation photo albums), not the substitution effect as Hanemann (1991) claimed theoretically.

Nevertheless, Knetsch, Tang and Thaler (2001) and Knetsch and Tang (2006) only conducted paper-pencil experimental sessions, thus the repeated trials were unfortunately limited to only six rounds in each session. This may cause a natural curiosity about what behavioural patterns would emerge if more trials were to be run in each session. In fact, Shogren et al. (1994) conducted their first experiment in two stages: stage 1 was the market-good (a regular-size brand-name candy bar) auction repeated over five trials, followed by stage 2's nonmarket-good (reduced health risk) auction repeated over 20 trials in five separate sessions with five food-borne pathogens considered (*Campylobacter, Salmonella, Staphylococcus aureus, Trichinella spiralis* and *Clostridium perfrigens*). 'Naïve' bids were elicited in the first ten trials and then 'informed' bids in trials 11–20 (the monitor supplied three items of information after the tenth trial). They claim that: 'For most of the naïve bids (trials 7–10), the average bidding prices stay relatively constant in both the WTP and the WTA bids. This result is consistent with Coursey's (1987) observation that Vickrey auctions usually stabilise by the sixth or seventh trial' (Shogren et al. 1994, p. 263). Meanwhile, 'For the informed bids (trials 17–20), we observed that bids initially increased from the information shock. . . . Again, after six trials with information, the mean WTP bid stabilizes' (p. 264). Further, they had run an additional experiment with ten trials where the auctioned good was the Iowa State coffee mug (available from the campus bookstore), which they claim rejects the endowment proposition overall. In any sense, it seems necessary and important to conduct a long sequence of experimental trials with the basic design. We will review such an experiment in the next section.

VICKREY AUCTION EXPERIMENTS WITH 60 REPEATED TRIALS

Two sets of experiments have been run, based on the design in Knetsch, Tang and Thaler (2001), but extended to 60 rounds of repeated trials in a fully computerised laboratory in the Herbert A. Simon and Reinhard Selten Behavioral Research Center, Southwest Jiao Tong University in Chengdu, PR China (see also Pan et al. 2018).

Experiment One

This experiment follows the between-subject design in Knetsch, Tang and Thaler (2001), which in turn replicated the auction procedures used by Shogren et al. (1994) in nearly all details, except that the repeated trials in this experiment were extended to 60 rounds by the same subjects on fixed computer terminals throughout a session. Eighty participants were recruited among students of Southwest Jiao Tong University, averaging around 20 years old, from various engineering and business study backgrounds, with 43males and 37 females (1.16:1). They were randomly divided into eight groups, with two groups of ten buyers and two groups of ten sellers for the second-price version of the Vickrey auction and two groups of ten buyers and two groups of ten sellers for the ninth-price version of the auction. Since there were 24 computer terminals in this lab, two groups of the same auction method participated in their experiment simultaneously but there was no interaction between the two groups.

The subjects were not paid a fee to show up for the experiment, but all transactions were real. That means all the subjects had to earn their income or wealth through the tough competition during the experimental auctions, without any other possible income. All subjects were informed whether they would be buyers or sellers before the experiment, seated randomly in a numbered cubicle (Bonn Lab setting) and given a copy of the respective written experimental instructions. The experimental instructions described the auction method in their respective groups and the respective calculation method of their incomes. In the meantime, the auctioned good (an ADATA 4G USB flash disk – priced at RMB 43 which the experimenters purchased online) was given to every subject for a close check and physical acquaintance. For the sellers, experimental instructions specified: 'The disk is yours now; your income in this experiment is the cash income for which you can sell this disk to the experimenter at the successful auction price or the disk itself if you do not succeed in selling the disk during the auction'. For the buyers, experimental instructions specified: 'You can purchase the disk by bidding for it during the auction. If your bid for the disk is successful during the auction, you must purchase this disk at the rule-specified bidding price in cash'. When all subjects expressed that they had understood the experimental instructions, a written test with two questions was conducted with every subject to see whether the subjects truly understood the experimental instructions. Only after all the subjects passed this written test did the experimental session formally begin.

With the help of the computerised lab, 60 rounds of the same auction programmed by Z-Tree were conducted in each session, a much longer sequence than previous experiments. Each round of auction contained two stages. The first stage was the bidding process: all sellers (buyers) were required to input the lowest selling price (highest buying price) for the disk which they would accept, and the bidding price could be any integer between zero and 100 (inclusive). After all ten subjects in one group finished their biddings, this round of auction entered the second stage of transaction results exhibition: all subjects could see the transaction price of this round and whether he/she succeeded in this transaction from the computer terminal screen, with a confirmation icon to be ticked on the screen. Only after all the subjects confirmed the transaction results of this round did the experimental session enter the next round, for a repetition of 60 rounds. After the completion of 60 rounds in one experimental session, one of the 20 subjects would be randomly selected by the experimenter and this randomly chosen subject would select one round randomly from the 60 rounds as the binding round to determine the terms of the actual transactions. After the experimental session, when all subjects were paid by their identification number sequence, they were asked to give an estimation of the auctioned item's price (a price estimation of the disk).

As one can see from Table 22.1, the mean values of WTP increase from 41.75 in the first round to 71.15 in the tenth round, then fluctuate around 80 (between 76 and 83) in the next 50 rounds, ending at 81.8 in the sixtieth round. The overall mean value of WTP (buying prices) by all respective subjects is 77.89, far above the mean value of subjects' price estimation (41.3) and the actual price (43). The overall mean value of WTA (selling prices) by all respective subjects is 52.93, also significantly higher than the mean value of subjects' price estimation (42.7) and the actual price (43).

The ratio of mean WTA/WTP decreases from 1.53 in the first round to 0.78 in the tenth round, then fluctuates between 0.56 and 0.70 in the next 50 rounds, ending at 0.58 in the sixtieth round. The overall mean value of this ratio is 0.77, with a certain difference from even the results of Knetsch, Tang and Thaler (2001, p. 260) which documented this mean ratio at 1.00 for six rounds of auction. Both Shogren et al. (1994) and Knetsch, Tang and Thaler (2001) documented clear evidence of the convergence between WTP and WTA values for second-price Vickrey; however, the new evidence seems to attribute this convergence more to their limited number of auction rounds rather than the second-price Vickrey auction per se. One possible explanation is that buyers may tend to bid higher prices for a possible transaction since there is only one buyer who could succeed to reach a transaction. When the auction goes on, buyers may bid higher prices gradually and thus the transaction prices would increase

Table 22.1 Experiment one: comparison of WTA and WTP values for second-price Vickrey auction (exhibition of only seven rounds of data due to space constraint)

Values	Round 1	10	20	30	40	50	60	Means
WTA								
Mean	63.85	55.65	55.75	51.05	46.95	50.4	47.3	52.93
Median	63	58	51.50	49.5	45.5	46	47	50.30
Std. dev.	18.80	23.61	17.28	21.2	25.14	24.48	24.86	21.57
WTP								
Mean	41.75	71.15	80.2	76.2	83.2	83.2	81.8	77.89
Median	37	70	90	85	90	91.5	92	85.18
Std. dev.	27.82	17.70	19.54	23.24	17.60	16.15	19.94	20.32
Ratio of mean WTA/WTP	1.53	0.78	0.70	0.67	0.56	0.61	0.58	0.77
Ratio of median WTA/WTP	1.70	0.83	0.57	0.58	0.51	0.50	0.51	0.74

accordingly, which can be seen from the mean and median values of bidding prices at each round (mean and median WTP values increasing with auction rounds). In fact, the actual transaction prices remained at 99 and 100 (the upper limit set for the buyers) after round 20. There was a subject who constantly bid 100 at every round after round 20. Theoretically, the second-price Vickrey auction should be able to eliminate auction fever, thus preventing the winner's curse. Nevertheless, the buyer data in Table 22.1 seems to indicate that this is not the case: the second-price Vickrey auction did not well reveal the actual price estimation of the subject buyers, with the actual bidding prices of buyers quite far away from the price estimation of the subject buyers and exhibiting some auction fever.

For the sellers of the second-price Vickrey auction, as Table 22.1 shows, the mean values of WTA decreased from 63.85 in the first round to slightly above 55 in the twentieth and thirtieth rounds and then fluctuated around 46 to 51 in the rest of the rounds with 47.3 at the end. Since there could be only one seller to successfully sell his/her item, sellers seemed to offer relatively lower prices in order to make a transaction and the offer prices of sellers exhibited clear lowering trends.

Overall, it seems that both WTP and WTA values reach relatively stable trends after 20 rounds, that is, the bids of buyers and offers of sellers fluctuate around certain values. Mann-Whitney tests (two-sided) show that both the means and medians of WTP are significantly higher than those of the WTA, respectively, for the last 40 rounds of the second-price Vickrey auction (t=0.000).

As Figure 22.1 shows, the means of WTA and WTP diverge with the experimental rounds rolling out and never reach the actual value of the auctioned items or the means of price estimations of the auctioned items by the subjects. The results of both the second- and ninth-price manipulation of a Vickrey auction fail to produce a consistent revelation of values, over a long sequence of 60 trials. This finding is partially consistent with what Knetsch, Tang and Thaler (2001) found in six rounds, but completely contrary to what Shogren et al. (1994) claimed from their experiments with 10–20 trials.

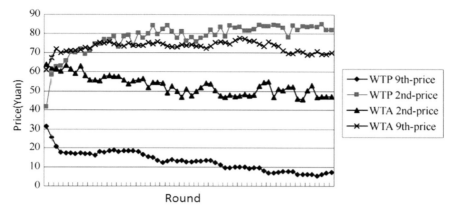

Figure 22.1 Trends of price means in experiment one

Table 22.2 Experiment one: comparison of WTA and WTP values for ninth-price Vickrey auction (exhibition of only seven rounds of data due to space constraint)

Values	Round							
	1	10	20	30	40	50	60	Means
WTA								
Mean	60.9	72.4	73.7	73.95	76.45	71	69.9	71.19
Median	54.5	78.5	77	76.5	79	70.5	69.5	72.21
Std. dev.	16.5	15.34	13.75	12.75	14.67	11.13	12.7	13.83
WTP								
Mean	31.75	17.15	18.1	12.8	10.1	7.7	7.45	15.01
Median	28	5.5	16.00	8	5.5	5.5	5.5	10.57
Std. dev.	21.82	16.41	20.53	10.52	8.03	6.06	8.35	13.1
Ratio of mean WTA/WTP	1.92	4.22	4.07	5.78	7.57	9.22	9.38	6.02
Ratio of median WTA/WTP	1.95	14.27	4.81	9.56	14.36	12.82	12.64	10.06

As one can see from Table 22.2, the mean values of WTP (buying prices) sharply decrease from 31.75 in the first round to 17.15 in the tenth round and 18.1 in the twentieth round, then from 12.8 in the thirtieth round continually falling to 7.45 in the sixtieth round. The overall mean value of WTP by all respective subjects is 15.01, far below the mean value of subjects' price estimation (40.2) and the actual price (43).

On the other hand, the mean values of WTA (selling prices) sharply increase from 60.9 in the first round to 72.4 in the tenth round, and then fluctuate around 73 (between 70 and 76) in the next 50 rounds, ending at 69.9 in the sixtieth round. The overall mean value of WTA by all respective subjects is 71.19, far above the mean value of the subjects' price estimation (45.6) and the actual price (43). The endowment effect is straightforwardly clear and strong here, consistent with the findings in Knetsch, Tang and Thaler (2001).

One possible explanation is that buyers may tend to bid lower prices because eight out of ten buyers can obtain one auctioned item at the ninth price in every round of this ninth-price Vickrey auction. Similarly, sellers ask for relatively high prices because eight out of ten sellers can sell their item at the ninth price in every round of this ninth-price Vickrey auction. The mean value of WTA in the first round (60.9) was almost double the mean value of WTA (31.75) in the first round, and the differences sharply increase with the experimental rounds rolling out. The ratio of mean WTA/WTP increases from 1.92 in the first round to slightly above 4 in the tenth and twentieth round, then 5.78 in the thirtieth and 7.57 in the fortieth round, and finally slows down to reach 9.22 in the fiftieth and 9.38 in the sixtieth round. The overall mean value of this ratio is 6.02, slightly higher than the overall mean ratio of 4.94 (14.22 over 2.88) in Knetsch and Tang (2006, p. 436, Table 21.3) while clearly higher than the overall mean ratio of 3.84 in Knetsch, Tang and Thaler (2001, p. 260, Table 22.2) for six rounds of this ninth-price auction, but tend to be close to the mean ratio of over 7 reported in Horowitz and McConnell (2002) who reviewed 45 tests of the value differences. In fact, the increase of the WTA/WTP mean ratio stabilises after 40 rounds, averaging around 9.3 in the last 20 rounds, significantly higher than even the mean ratio reported by Horowitz and McConnell (2002). Furthermore, Mann-Whitney tests (two-sided) show that both the means and medians of WTA are significantly higher than those of the WTP (t = 0.000, respectively).

Another interesting finding is that Mann-Whitney tests (two-sided) also exhibit clear significance in comparison of the mean value of WTA (71.19) versus the mean value of subjects' price estimation (45.6), and the mean value of WTP (15.01) versus that of subjects' price estimation (40.2), at t = 0.022 and t = 0.000, respectively.

Since the sequence of trials is long enough, more interesting patterns are observed during the 60 rounds, which were not so clear in previous studies such as Shogren et al. (1994) and Knetsch, Tang and Thaler (2001). In the second-price auction, WTP mean values of the buyers increase from 41.75 in the first round to 81.8 in the sixtieth round, while the WTA mean values of the sellers decrease from 63.85 in the first round to 47.3 in the sixtieth round, clearly. However, in the ninth-price auction, WTP mean values of the buyers decrease from 31.75 in the first round to 7.45 in the sixtieth round, while the WTA mean values of the sellers increase from 60.9 in the first round to 69.9 in the sixtieth round, also clearly. Apparently, it is the specific details of the auction methods, even though both are Vickrey auctions, that may have caused the different trends of the prices (WTA versus WTP) which in turn caused the differences in its value ratios. It may be due to the change in the 'competition intensity' (ratio of the number of auction participants versus the number of auctioned items; see the fourth section).

In the second-price auction, there is only one auction item, thus the intensity of competition is high. Buyers may want to obtain the only auction item and thus increase their bidding prices gradually when the experimental auction rounds roll out. Sellers may want to sell the only auction item more quickly, thus decreasing their offering prices during the auction process. In the ninth-price auction, however, there are eight auction items so the competition intensity is much lower. Buyers may think that since there are many more auction items it is thus possible to obtain an auction item at relatively lower prices, fuelled further by their learning experiences when the experimental auction trials roll out, therefore sharply lowering their bidding prices during the experimental session. Sellers may be more patient, thus they are not willing to lower their selling prices, while they may even experiment with increasing their selling prices through their learning experiences when the auction trials roll out. As we pointed out previously (Knetsch and Tang 2006, p. 423), 'The findings indicate that instead of according with the usual axioms, people's preferences commonly depend on the context, or the reference position, in which valuations are made'.

Experiment Two

This experiment follows the within-subject design in Knetsch, Tang and Thaler (2001) in nearly all details, except that the repeated trials in this experiment were extended to 60 rounds by the same subjects on fixed computer terminals throughout a session. Forty participants were recruited among students of Southwest Jiao Tong University, averaging around 20 years old, from various engineering and business study backgrounds, with 19 males and 21 females (0.9:1). They were randomly divided into four groups, with two groups of ten buyers and two groups of ten sellers, in which the *same* subjects named both a second price and a ninth price in each round Since there were 24 computer terminals in this lab, two groups of the same role (buyer or seller) participated in their experiment simultaneously but there was no interaction between the two groups.

The experimental procedure was similar to experiment one, except that the subject buyers were told:

> For each round, the auction will be conducted in one of two ways. (1) One rule is that only the person bidding the highest price will buy an ADATA 4G USB flash disk, but this person will pay the second-highest price bid.
> (2) The other rule is that the eight people bidding the highest eight prices will buy an ADATA 4G USB flash disk, but all eight will pay the ninth-highest price bid.
> The rule that will 'count' will be determined later by a random draw by computer. Therefore, you will need to make two bids in each round, the prices you are willing to pay for each rule – these can be the same or different.

Subject sellers were given analogous instructions.

For the subject buyers in the second-price auction, as one can see from Table 22.3, the mean values of WTP increase from 48.3 in the first round to 57.2 in the tenth round, then fluctuate around 56 (between 52 and 60) in the next 50 rounds, ending at 59.8 in the sixtieth round. The overall mean value of WTP (buying prices) by all respective subjects is 56.62, far *above* the mean value of subjects' price estimation (41.3) and the actual price (43). Strikingly, for the same subject buyers in the ninth-price auction, the mean values of WTP decrease from 15.1 in the first round to 10.2 in the tenth round, then stabilised from around 13 to around 12 in the next 50 rounds, ending at 12.1 in the sixtieth round. The overall mean value of WTP (buying prices) by all respective subjects is 11.7, far *below* the mean value of subjects' price estimation (41.3) and the actual price (43).

For the subject sellers in the second-price auction, as one can see from Table 22.3, the mean values of WTA decrease from 49.35 in the first round to 25.25 in the tenth round, then fluctuate around 28 (between 24 and 31) in the following 40 rounds, ending at 41.95 in the sixtieth round (close to the actual price of 43). The overall mean value of WTA (selling prices) by all respective subjects is 27.28, far *below* the mean value of subjects' price estimation (42.7) and the actual price (43). Also strikingly, for the same subject sellers in the ninth-price auction, the mean values of WTA increase from 62.3 in the first round to 82.25 in the tenth round, then stabilise there around 82 to 83 in the following 30 rounds, ending at 79.4 from the fiftieth to sixtieth rounds. The overall mean value of WTA (selling prices) by all respective subjects is 80.24, far *above* the mean value of subjects' price estimation (42.7) and the actual price (43).

Table 22.3 Experiment two: comparison of WTA and WTP values for second- and ninth-price Vickrey auction (exhibition of only seven rounds of data due to space constraint)

Values	Round 1	10	20	30	40	50	60	Means
WTA								
2nd-price								
Mean	49.35	25.25	24.35	28.25	25.45	30.8	41.95	27.28
Median	50	5	6	9	3	5	42.5	8.91
Std. dev.	26.93	29.47	30	33.13	32.18	34	38.11	30.65
9th-price								
Mean	62.3	82.25	82.3	83.25	82.7	79.4	79.4	80.24
Median	60	84	83	84.5	80.5	83.5	82.5	82.32
Std. dev.	23.21	5.44	2.65	2.88	5.22	19.39	18.4	10.34
WTP								
2nd-price								
Mean	48.3	57.2	60.85	56.25	56.25	52.25	59.8	56.62
Median	51.29	65	72.5	62.5	65	55.5	75	65.9
Std. dev.	29.02	30.13	31.1	30.89	30.29	29.52	31.26	30.31
9th-price								
Mean	15.10	10.2	13.24	12.59	11.99	11.95	12.10	11.7
Median	25.05	16.05	18.9	19	20	20	20.15	19.22
Std. dev.	20.5	13	20	23.5	24	20	18	21.28
Ratio of 2nd-price auction								
WTA/WTP	1.02	0.44	0.4	0.5	0.45	0.59	0.7	0.59
Median WTA/WTP	0.98	0.08	0.08	0.14	0.05	0.09	0.57	0.28
Ratio of 9th-price auction								
Mean WTA/WTP	4.13	8.07	6.21	6.61	6.9	6.64	6.56	6.45
Median WTA/WTP	2.4	5.23	4.39	4.45	4.03	4.18	4.09	4.11

This is highly interesting because of the experimental procedure that 'the *same* subjects named both a second price and a ninth price in each round'. The same subjects produced similar price patterns in experiment one as if they each were two different persons when they named a second price and a ninth price in each round. It seems to indicate that the competition intensity drives the bidding/offering strategies of both the buyer and seller subjects, no matter whether the experimental design is between subjects or within subjects. In fact, there is not a single subject who named the same number in both the second- and ninth-price auctions consistently throughout the 60 rounds. Among all the 2,400 pairs of data (40 subjects in 60 rounds), there are only 103 pairs of data with the same second and ninth prices, accounting

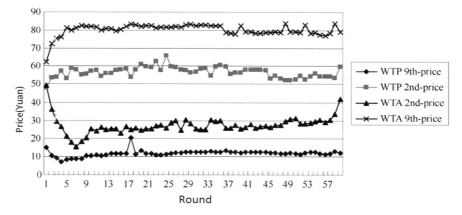

Figure 22.2   Trends of price means in experiment two

for only 4.29 per cent of the whole data set. Clearly, it is the auction method that produces such a striking difference in the price patterns of the subjects, either in the role of a buyer or seller.

For the second-price auction, the ratio of mean WTA/WTP decreases from 1.02 in the first round to 0.44 in the tenth round, then fluctuates between 0.4 and 0.7 in the next 50 rounds, with the overall mean value of this ratio at 0.59, all consistently below their counterparts in experiment one except in the sixtieth round.

For the ninth-price auction, the ratio of mean WTA/WTP increases from 4.13 in the first round to 8.07 in the tenth round, then fluctuates between 6.2 and 6.9 in the next 50 rounds, with the overall mean value of this ratio at 6.45, exhibiting an even more stable pattern than their counterparts in experiment one.

One particularly interesting observation, see Figure 22.2, is that prices in both second- and ninth-price auctions tend to stabilise after the ninth round. For the second-price auction, the mean values of WTP stably fluctuate around the overall mean value of 56.62, while for the ninth-price auction they sit at a significantly lower mean of 11.7.

ANALYSIS OF INDIVIDUAL DATA

There were four kinds of subjects in experiment one and two: the second-price buyers, the second-price sellers, the ninth-price buyers and the ninth-price sellers. We find several regularities through the analysis of individual data for the means and standard deviations of each subject at each round.

The Second-price Buyers

It is easy to observe, from Figure 22.3, that the price curves of some subjects seem to be not much different. Since the mean value of all subjects' price estimation is 41.3 and the actual price is 43, we call a subject 'realistic' if the mean value of his/her bidding prices (WTP) over 60 rounds falls between 30 to 60, otherwise, they are an 'extreme' type. In addition, we call a subject 'stable' if the standard deviation of this subject's bidding prices falls between zero to 80, otherwise they are a 'fluctuant' type.

386 *Handbook of research methods in behavioural economics*

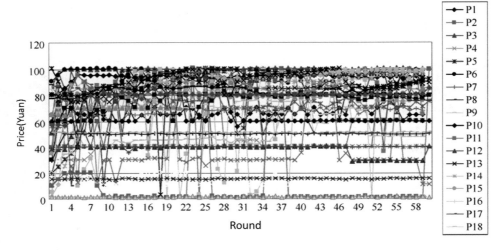

Figure 22.3   The bidding prices of all second-price buyers

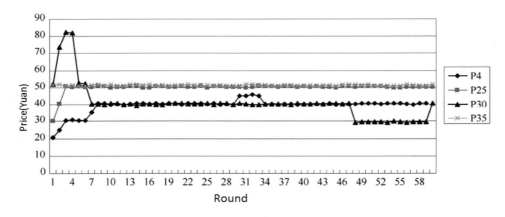

Figure 22.4   The bidding prices of 'realistic and stable' second-price buyers

(1) 'Realistic and stable': This type of subject seems to bid somehow based on their estimation of the auctioned object and their bidding prices do not seem to change too much with the auction rounds unravelling. That is, learning about the transaction prices and other market information did not seem to impose any significant impact on their bidding behaviour. There are four among the 40 second-price buyer subjects, 10 per cent, as in Figure 22.4.

(2) 'Extreme and stable': This type of subject seems to bid in order to succeed in making transactions. With the auction rounds unravelling, they gradually learned about the market with more and more information, thus they could manage to speculate what prices could be the closest for reaching a transaction. In order to obtain the auctioned object, they bid 'extreme' prices at each round, stably, far above the actual value of the auctioned

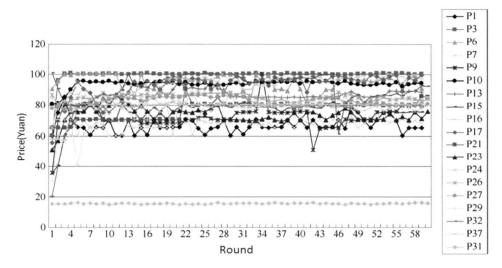

Figure 22.5   The bidding prices of 'extreme and stable' second-price buyers

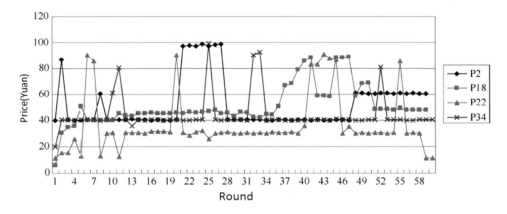

Figure 22.6   The bidding prices of 'realistic and fluctuant' second-price buyers

object. There are 19 among the 40 second-price buyer subjects, 47.5 per cent, as in Figure 22.5.

(3) 'Realistic and fluctuant': The typical feature of this type of subject is that they bid with sharp fluctuations – very large standard deviations of bidding prices – in different rounds of the auction, but the overall mean values of their bidding prices are somehow consistent with the reasonable estimation of the auctioned objects. These subjects seem to be vulnerable to the influence of market information, auction fever and whatever else is there. There are four among the 40 second-price buyer subjects, 10 per cent, as in Figure 22.6.

(4) 'Extreme and fluctuant': This type of subject bids with sharp fluctuations – very large standard deviations of bidding prices – in different rounds of the auction, and their bidding prices seem to be quite extreme rather than around their estimation of the true values

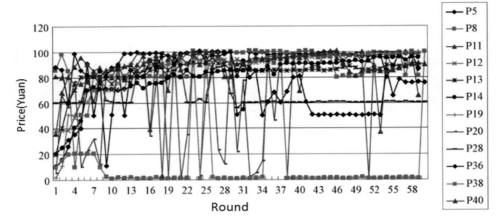

Figure 22.7 The bidding prices of 'extreme and fluctuant' second-price buyers

of the auctioned object. These subjects seemed to adjust their biddings according to the new information of transaction updates, in order to succeed in reaching a transaction while giving up their true estimation of the auctioned object's value. There are 13 among the 40 second-price buyer subjects, 32.5 per cent, as in Figure 22.7.

The Second-price Sellers

Similarly, since the mean value of all subjects' price estimation is 41.3 and the actual price is 43, we call a subject 'realistic' if the mean value of his/her selling prices (WTA) over 60 rounds falls between 30 to 60, otherwise they are an 'extreme' type. In addition, we call a subject 'stable' if the standard deviation of this subject's selling prices falls from zero to 150, otherwise they are a 'fluctuant' type. The reason for the larger number of upper limits (150 rather than 80) in standard deviation is that sellers showed much larger price differences in each round than buyers. There would be no 'stable' subjects if one kept the upper limit at 80 in standard deviation. A careful examination of the raw data led to the subjective delineation of 80 versus 150 for a tentative classification. From behavioural intuition, buyers may tend to limit their bids because they had to pay in cash of their own money, while sellers may well explore the market with higher or lower prices for their best benefits in possible transactions.

In this case, there are 13 'realistic and stable' subjects, 32.5 per cent; 14 'extreme and stable' subjects, 35 per cent; four 'realistic and fluctuant' subjects, 10 per cent; and nine 'extreme and fluctuant' subjects, 22.5 per cent. See Table 22.4 for a summary.

The Ninth-price Buyers

With similar definitions (also 80 as the upper limit in standard deviation), there are two 'realistic and stable' subjects, 5 per cent; 34 'extreme and stable' subjects, 85 per cent; zero 'realistic and fluctuant' subjects, 0 per cent; and four 'extreme and fluctuant' subjects, 10 per cent. See Table 22.4 for a summary.

The Ninth-price Sellers

With similar definitions (again 150 as the upper limit in standard deviation), there are three 'realistic and stable' subjects, 7.5 per cent; 34 'extreme and stable' subjects, 85 per cent; one

Auction methods of valuation and the endowment effect 389

Table 22.4   Types of all subjects

Role/type	Realistic and stable (%)	Extreme and stable (%)	Realistic and fluctuant (%)	Extreme and fluctuant (%)
2nd-price buyer	10	47.5	10	32.5
2nd-price seller	32.5	35	10	22.5
9th-price buyer	5	85	0	10
9th-price seller	7.5	85	2.5	5

'realistic and fluctuant' subject, 2.5 per cent; and two 'extreme and fluctuant' subjects, 5 per cent. See Table 22.4 for a summary.

Table 22.4 shows that there are few 'realistic' subjects (except for the second-price seller type) and most are the 'extreme' type: 80 per cent for the second-price buyers, 57.5 per cent for the second-price sellers, 95 per cent for the ninth-price buyers and 90 per cent for the ninth-price sellers. It is clear that the mechanism of Vickrey price auctions does not well reflect the subjects' overall estimation of the auctioned object value.

Individual Behaviour in Experiment Two

It may be particularly interesting to examine the individual data in experiment two, because subjects there must input both the second price and ninth price at each round, simultaneously. If the Vickrey auction methods can reflect the truthful valuation of the subjects, the prices of both rules should be very close.

A tentative definition of 'approximation' (approximate to the actual valuation) is proposed as the following: if a subject exhibited ten or more times using the same prices in both the second- and ninth-price auctions during the 60 rounds and the difference of the mean values of second- versus ninth-price auctions is within ten yuan, which is a very reasonable number since the mean value of all subjects' price estimation is 41.3 and the actual price is only 43 yuan. Unfortunately, even for such a loose classification, there are only three subjects (two buyers and one seller only) who can qualify for this 'approximation' definition in all the 40 subjects in experiment two. For the role of buyers, subject P13 exhibited ten times of inputting the same prices for both second- price and ninth-price auction rules, with mean values of 10.56 and 17.96, respectively, while subject P18 used the same prices 20 times, with mean values of 13.24 and 5.66, respectively. For the role of sellers, only subject P3 exhibited 17 times (more than ten) of inputting the same prices for both second-price and ninth-price auction rules, with mean values of 77.71 and 87.19, respectively.

It is also worth noting that there was only one subject who exhibited the same prices during all six rounds, in experiment two by Knetsch, Tang and Thaler (2001), while there were only three subjects who exhibited the same prices during three or more rounds in that experiment. Furthermore, only 4.29 per cent input the same prices for both the second- and ninth-price auction methods in experiment two here, out of 4,800 data, 40(subjects) × 60(rounds) × 2(rules). The ratio was 15.8 per cent in Knestch, Tang and Thaler (2001).

It is clear to see, from Figure 22.8 and Figure 22.9, that the mean values of the same subject during the 60 rounds under different auction methods (second price versus ninth price) are sharply different.

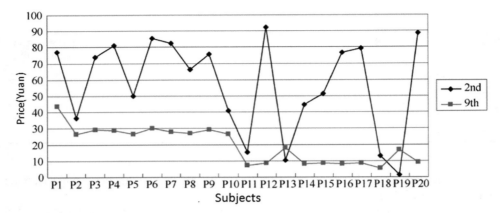

Figure 22.8   The mean values of each subject (as buyers) over 60 rounds for the second-price versus ninth-price auction method in experiment two

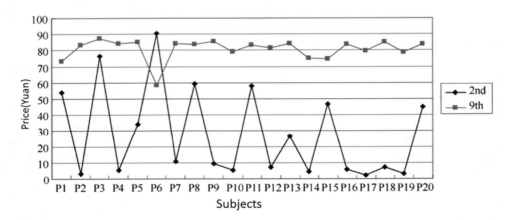

Figure 22.9   The mean values of each subject (as sellers) over 60 rounds for the second-price versus ninth-price auction method in experiment two

Knetsch, Tang and Thaler (2001) did not observe the price trend stability as what is shown here after nine rounds, probably due to the limitation of six rounds only in the experiments there. It is possible that subjects try to explore the mechanism of the Vickrey auction methods during the early rounds, based on their own valuation and other market elements from the information feedback. With the auction unravelling further with more rounds and information feedback of more 'patterns', subjects may think that they have grasped certain 'regularities' and thus identified ways for their best benefits in such auctions, although such influence might well lead them further away from their valuations on the auctioned objects.

THE IMPACT OF COMPETITION INTENSITY

The aforementioned experiments only increased the number of auction trials from six to 60, based on the designs in Knetsch, Tang and Thaler (2001), although very interesting results were obtained. In the following experiment, one concept, 'competition intensity', was introduced as the control variable, which was defined as the ratio between the number of auction participants and the number of auctioned items. One pilot set of experiments, using groups of five, ten and 20 subjects respectively for a fourth-price Vickrey auction rule (bidding/selling three identical objects), was run at Peking University (see Tang et al. 2019). The experimental procedure followed the between-subject design in Knetch, Tang and Thaler (2001) and Knetsch and Tang (2006) in almost exact manners, also six repeated trials by paper and pencil, except that the control variable of competition intensity was carefully manipulated.

Experiment Three

Seventy subjects were recruited among students of various departments in Peking University, averaged around 20 years old from various science, engineering, humanities and business study backgrounds, with 35 males and 35 females (1:1). They were randomly divided into six groups, with three groups of five, ten and 20 buyers, respectively, and three groups of five, ten and 20 sellers, respectively. The highest three bidders bought the auctioned items at the fourth highest price in the buyer groups, while the three lowest offers sold the auctioned items at the fourth lowest price in the seller groups. The auctioned items were notebooks printed with PKU letterheads and logos, which were available throughout the Peking University campus at five yuan (RMB). Six sessions in three days were conducted, one session with one group, with no subject participating in any two different sessions. All subjects were given a notebook each before the experimental session, for an inspection time to check the item carefully. For sellers: 'You will receive RMB 5 yuan for participating in this experiment. Your take-home income will consist of your initial income (RMB 5 yuan) plus the value of any good you sell. You will be asked to decide the lowest price you are willing to accept to sell a PKU notebook'. The instruction wording is equivalent for buyers, except that the subject received RMB 15 yuan for his/her participation to buy a PKU notebook.

All the raw data is in the attachment, for each subject. For the two experimental sessions of five different subjects as seller versus buyer in each group, respectively, Table 22.5 summarises the means and medians of WTPs versus WTAs. The competition intensity in this case is 1.67 (i.e. 5/3), with the ratios of overall WTAs to WTPs as 4.21 for the mean values and 4.76 for the median values, a clear and stable pattern consistent with Knetsch, Tang and

Table 22.5   Experiment three: comparison of WTA and WTP values for fourth-price Vickrey auction in the groups of five subjects

	1	2	3	4	5	6	Mean values
WTP							
Mean	1.45	1.3	1.425	1.375	1.225	1.55	1.39
Median	1	0.7	1	1.5	1.3	2	1.25
WTA							
Mean	5.6	5	4.88	6.26	6.56	6.54	5.80
Median	5	5	4.8	5.5	6.5	6	5.46
Ratio of mean WTA/WTP	3.86	3.85	3.42	4.55	5.36	4.22	4.21
Ratio of median WTA/WTP	5	7.14	4.8	3.67	5	3	4.76

Thaler (2001) and Knetsch and Tang (2006). Mann-Whitney tests (two-sided) show that both the means and medians of WTA are significantly higher than those of the WTP, respectively, for all six rounds of the fourth-price Vickrey auction in groups of five subjects (t=0.004).

For the two experimental sessions of ten different subjects as seller versus buyer in each group, respectively, Table 22.6 summarises the means and medians of WTPs versus WTAs. The competition intensity in this case is 3.33 (i.e., 10/3), with the ratios of overall WTAs to WTPs as 1.63 for the mean values and 2.0 for the median values, much less than the previous case when the competition intensity is 1.67.

For the two experimental sessions of 20 different subjects as seller versus buyer in each group, respectively, Table 22.7 summarises the means and medians of WTPs versus WTAs. The competition intensity in this case is 6.67 (i.e., 20/3), with the ratios of overall WTAs to WTPs as 1.56 for the mean values and 1.60 for the median values, again much less than the case when the competition intensity is 1.67 but only slightly lower than the case when the competition intensity is 3.33. Due to the limited sample size, it is not yet clear whether the ratios of WTA versus WTP would stabilise above 1.5 or reduce even further (see also Figure 22.10).

Table 22.6 Experiment three: comparison of WTA and WTP values for fourth-price Vickrey auction in the groups of ten subjects

	1	2	3	4	5	6	Mean values
WTP							
Mean	2.93	3.46	3.31	3.07	3.22	3.36	3.23
Median	2.4	3.7	3.45	3	3.1	3.15	3.13
WTA							
Mean	5.94	6.44	4.81	4.24	5.59	4.57	5.26
Median	8.95	6	5.5	5	6	6	6.24
Ratio of mean WTA/WTP	2.03	1.86	1.45	1.38	1.73	1.36	1.63
Ratio of median WTA/WTP	3.73	1.62	1.59	1.67	1.94	1.90	2.0

Table 22.7 Experiment three: comparison of WTA and WTP values for fourth-price Vickrey auction in the groups of 20 subjects

	1	2	3	4	5	6	Mean values
WTP							
Mean	3.30	2.84	2.99	3.21	3.38	3.46	3.20
Median	3	3	3.25	3.7	4	3.85	3.47
WTA							
Mean	6.31	4.52	5.38	4.55	4.74	4.32	4.97
Median	8	5	5	4.45	4.95	4.95	5.39
Ratio of mean WTA/WTP	1.92	1.59	1.80	1.42	1.40	1.25	1.56
Ratio of median WTA/WTP	2.67	1.67	1.54	1.20	1.24	1.29	1.60

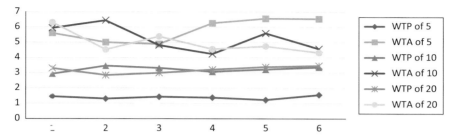

Figure 22.10 The price trends in experiment three

There could be a possibility that the gaps between WTAs and WTPs reduce even further when the numbers of auction participants increase while the auction method and auctioned items remain unchanged, that is, the competition intensity increases. More experiments are certainly needed when the pandemic gets over, with further varied competition intensities and, equally importantly, with more rounds if possible.

Individual Behaviour in Experiment Three

It is manageable to examine the individual data in experiment three for each subject, with letters A and B to represent each subject in a buyer or seller role of the five-subject groups, while C and D for the ten-subject groups, and E and F for the 20-subject groups, respectively (see Appendix 22.1). Similar behavioural patterns are categorised according to the respective features. For example, it was observed that some subjects significantly increased (or decreased) their prices in the last rounds when the prices of other subjects tended to stabilise, thus they would be able to buy (or sell) the PKU notebooks at relatively low (or high) prices through such a trading strategy, especially if one of such rounds was chosen to be the real transaction round. Therefore, we call a subject 'speculative' if the subject submitted a price 50 per cent higher (or lower) than the previous round during one or more rounds in the last three rounds of the experimental session. There are nine 'speculative' subjects in total, 12.9 per cent (9/70), including A4, A5, C6, D4, D7, D9, E12, E15 and F18. See, also, Figure 22.11.

Some subjects were observed to submit quite stable prices each round, although their prices might not reflect the actual value of the auctioned PKU notebooks. The advantage of such a trading strategy is the consistent continuity of their valuation of the auctioned items, no matter what trial was finally chosen as the real transaction round. We call a subject 'stable' if the standard deviation of a subject's submitted prices is less than 0.5 in the experimental session. There are 18 'stable' subjects in total, 25.7 per cent (18/70), including A1, A2, A5, B1, C2, C4, C9, E1, E5, E6, E8, E12, E13, E16, E19, E20, F7 and F10.

We call a subject 'transactional' if the standard deviation of a subject's submitted prices is less than 1 in the experimental session and the absolute value of the mean value of his/her submitted prices minus the mean price of the experimental session is not greater than 1 (|subject mean price – auction mean price | ≤0.5). Such subjects exhibit two features: 1) their submitted prices are relatively stable with a valuation continuity of the auctioned item, although the definition of their stability is more relaxed than the 'stable' type to accommodate more fluctuation in consideration of the market learning process by the subjects; 2) their mean prices are close to the mean transaction prices of the auction, indicating that these subjects tend to make a transaction as their goal. The typical trading strategy of such subjects is: when they obtained

394 *Handbook of research methods in behavioural economics*

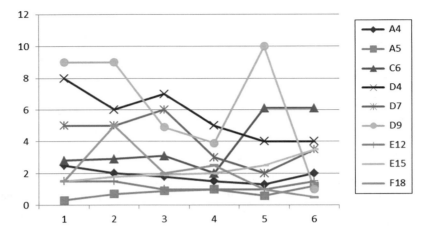

Figure 22.11 The price trends of 'speculative' subjects in experiment three

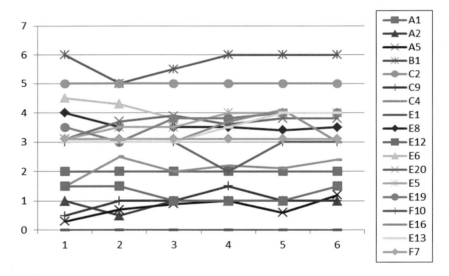

Figure 22.12 The price trends of 'stable' subjects in experiment three

sufficient market information after the first round of the auction, their submitted prices moved towards the transaction price value in the following rounds in order to make a transaction. There are 22 'transactional' subjects in total, 36.4 per cent (22/70), including: A2, A4, A5, B1, C3, C8, C10, D7, E5, E6, E8, E9, E11, E13, E14, E16, E18, E19, E20, F1, F3 and F10.

It may be particularly interesting to note that 63.6 per cent of the 'transactional' subjects belong to the largest experimental groups with 20 subjects, while only 36.4 per cent of 'transactional' subjects are in the groups of five or ten subjects. It seems that the number of 'transactional' subjects increases with the increase of competition intensity, although this observation needs to be scrutinised by further experimental evidence. It is well possible that the nth-price

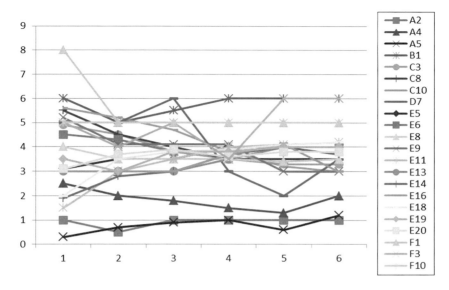

Figure 22.13 The price trends of 'transactional' subjects in experiment three

Vickrey auction may better reveal the true demand when the competition intensity becomes even larger. The group size in the experimental sessions may not be large enough to examine such an issue, although it is certainly worthwhile to try groups of 30, 50, 100 or even more subjects through more paper and pencil trials.

On the other hand, if online auctions can be designed to attract very large groups of participants, more interesting results may emerge. Another possibility is to carefully collect existing online auction data, from a field experiment perspective, although the difficulty is obvious: how to obtain clean and independent individual data? Laboratory experiments face the unfortunate limit of group sizes, while the challenge of field experiments is the quality of the data collection. Either way is highly interesting and worthy of further pursuit for future studies.

REFERENCES

Cousey, Don L. (1987). "Markets and the Measurement of Value." *Public Choice* 55(3), 291–297.
Hammack, J., & Gardner M. Brown, Jr. (1974). *Waterfowl and Wetlands: Toward Bio-Economic Analysis*. Baltimore: Johns Hopkins University Press.
Hanemann, W. M. (1991). "Willingness to Pay and Willingness to Accept: How Much Can They Differ?" *American Economic Review* 81, 635–647.
Harless, D. W. (1989). "More Laboratory Evidence on the Disparity Between Willingness To Pay and Compensation Demanded." *Journal of Economic Behavior and Organization* 11, 359–379.
Horowitz, J. K., & K. E. McConnell (2002). "A Review of WTA/WTA Studies." *Journal of Environmental Economics and Management* 44, 426–447.
Kahneman, D., & A. Tversky (1979). "Prospect Theory: An Analysis of Decision under Risk." *Econometrica* 47(2), 263–291.
Knetsch, J. L. (2020). "Behavioural Economics, Benefit-Cost Analysis, and the WTP vs. WTA Choice." *International Review of Environmental and Resource Economics* 14(2–3), 153–196.

Knetsch, J. L., & J. Sinden (1984). "Willingness To Pay and Compensation Demanded: Experimental Evidence of An Unexpected Disparity in Measures of Value." *Quarterly Journal of Economics* 99, 507–521.

Knetsch, J. L., & F.-F. Tang (2006). "The Context, or Reference, Dependence of Economic Values: Further Evidence and Some Predictable Patterns." in *Handbook of Contemporary Behavioral Economics: Foundations and Developments* (ed. Morris Altman), Chapter 21, 423–440. Routledge.

Knetsch, J. L., F.-F. Tang, & R. H. Thaler (2001). "The Endowment Effect and Repeated Market Trials: Is the Vickrey Auction Demand Revealing?" *Experimental Economics* 4, 257–269.

List, John A. (2003). "Does Market Experience Eliminate Market Anomalies?" *Quarterly Journal of Economics* 118, 41–71.

Pan, B., F.-F. Tang, D. Zheng, H. Fu, Z. Dong, & J. Zha (2018). "Can Multiple-Rounds' Vickrey Auction Eliminate the Endowment Effect in the Valuation of Goods?" *Financial Science (in Chinese)* 1(3), 18–40.

Plott, Charles R., & K. Zeiler (2005). "The Willingness To Pay/Willingness To Accept Gap, the 'Endowment Effect', Subject Misconceptions and Experimental Procedures for Eliciting Valuations." *American Economic Review* 95(3), 530–545.

Rowe, Robert D., Ralph C. d'Arge, & David S. Brookshire (1980). "An Experiment on the Economic Value of Visibility." *Journal of Environmental Economics and Management* 7(1), 1–19.

Shogren, J. F., & D. J. Hayes (1997). "Resolving Differences in Willingness to Pay and Willingness to Accept: Reply." *American Economic Review* 87, 241–244.

Shogren, J. F., S. Y. Shin, D. J. Hayes, & J. B. Kliebenstein (1994). "Resolving Differences in Willingness To Pay and Willingness To Accept." *American Economic Review* 84, 255–270.

Tang, F.-F., B. Pan, Z. Zhao, L. Wang, & L. Ye (2019). "A Study on the Endowment Effect based on the Competition Intensity Impact of Vickrey Auctions." *Financial Science (in Chinese)* 2(6), 19–35.

Vickrey, W. (1961). "Counterspeculation, Auctions, and Competitive Sealed Tenders." *Journal of Finance* 16, 8–37.

APPENDIX 22.1

Individual data in experiment three

WTP in group of five buyers

Round	1	2	3	4	5	6
A1	2	2	2	2	2	2
A2	1	0.5	1	1	1	1
A3	0.5	0.3	0.1	15	15	6
A4	2.5	2	1.8	1.5	1.3	2
A5	0.3	0.7	0.9	1	0.6	1.2

WTA in group of five sellers

Round	1	2	3	4	5	6
B1	6	5	5.5	6	6	6
B2	2	4	4.6	4.8	6.5	7.2
B3	5	5	5	10	8	6
B4	5	6	4.5	5	5.5	8
B5	10	5	4.8	5.5	6.8	5.5

WTP in group of ten buyers

Round	1	2	3	4	5	6
C1	2	5.5	5	4.5	3	3.5
C2	5	5	5	5	5	5
C3	4.9	4.5	3.8	3.5	3.3	3.3
C4	1.5	2.5	2	2.2	2.1	2.4
C5	1	2	2.5	2.5	2.5	3
C6	2.8	2.9	3.1	2	6.1	6.1
C7	0.5	1.5	2	2.2	2.5	2.8
C8	5.5	4.5	4	3.5	3.5	3.5
C9	0.5	1	1	1.5	1	1
C10	5.6	5.2	4.7	3.8	3.2	3

WTA in group of ten sellers

Round	1	2	3	4	5	6
D1	15	4.95	8	6	5	20
D2	10	5	4	6	7	8
D3	0.3	1.2	1.8	1.8	2.1	3.5
D4	8	6	7	5	4	4
D5	20	20	5	1	20	100
D6	3.5	6	6	5	4	4
D7	5	5	6	3	2	3.5
D8	20	20	30	10	15	18
D9	9.9	15	4.9	3.9	10	1
D10	4.9	6.9	4	5	10	8

WTP in group of 20 buyers

Round	1	2	3	4	5	6
E1	0	0	0	0	0	0
E2	3	2	2	2.5	2	3
E3	2	2.5	2.5	3.8	3.9	3.9
E4	0.1	1	3	3.8	4.1	4.2
E5	3.1	3.5	3.5	4	4	4
E6	4.5	4.3	3.8	3.8	4	4
E7	10	4	4	4	4.5	4.5
E8	4	3.5	3.5	3.5	3.4	3.5
E9	5.2	4.1	4.1	4.1	3	3
E10	3	3	3	2	3	3
E11	1.5	3	3.5	4	4.1	4.2
E12	1.5	1.5	1	1	1	1.5
E13	3	3	3	3.5	4	4
E14	1.9	2.8	3	3.7	4	3.7
E15	1.5	1.8	1.9	2	2.5	3.5
E16	3	3	3	3.7	4.1	3
E17	10	3.5	3.5	3.5	4	4.2
E18	2	3.5	3.8	3.9	4.1	4.2
E19	3.5	3	3.8	3.8	4	4
E20	3.1	3.7	3.9	3.6	3.8	3.8

WTA in group of 20 sellers

Round	1	2	3	4	5	6
F1	8	5	5	5	5	5
F2	10	5	5	10	10	50
F3	5	4	5	3.5	6	6
F4	12.8	8.8	8.8	4.9	5.8	4.9
F5	4	2.5	3	4	3.5	3
F6	8	6	5	4.9	4.9	4.9
F7	3.1	3.1	3.1	3.1	3.1	3.1
F8	40	41	20	20	20	20
F9	50	10	5	4	3.5	4
F10	5	5	5	5	5	5
F11	6.9	5.9	4.9	2.9	2.8	2.7
F12	5.5	8	9	10	12	5
F13	20	20	30	40	50	60
F14	10	5	5	4	3	3
F15	4.5	3.5	3	3.5	3	2.8
F16	9.5	5	4	3	4	5
F17	1	1	8	2	2.1	4
F18	1.5	5	2	2.5	1	0.5
F19	49.9	39.9	29.9	19.9	9.9	10
F20	9.9	0	9.9	9.9	9.9	9.9

23. Statistical approaches to the analysis of belief patterns
David Leiser

INTRODUCTION

Surveys are ubiquitous, as they are a convenient way to collect information about beliefs. The methods used to elicit beliefs fall into several categories, including multiple-choice questions, self-reports about the degree of support for statements, free associations to 'inducing' concepts and judgements of proximity between concepts. It is a widespread practice to present the results in raw form, showing, for example, what proportion of the public holds a certain view; it is also of interest to break down the views according to specific segments of the population.

Professional surveyors understand that this practice, centred on individual questions, can be misleading. The answer given by a respondent to any one question is affected by the topic the surveyor had in mind, but various influences related to the formulation play their part and may interact with the idiosyncratic traits of the respondent. For instance, the question might be ambiguous or be formulated in a way that strikes a particular chord in the respondent, as when examples are given that affect different people in diverse ways.

For this reason, it is good practice to include in the questionnaires several related questions intended to address the same question in alternate ways. The researcher can then analyse the resulting answers and compute the commonality they share.

Assessing the internal consistency of a set of scale items used is typically done by Cronbach's alpha measure, that has its weaknesses, but is a standard component of item reliability analysis. Cronbach's alpha is computed by correlating the score for each scale item with the total score for each respondent and then comparing that to the variance for all individual item scores. The resulting α coefficient of reliability ranges from 0 to 1. If all the scale items are entirely independent of one another (i.e., are not correlated or share no covariance, the worst possible case), then $\alpha = 0$; the higher the coefficient, the more the items have shared covariance and measure the same underlying concept. Alpha coefficients that are less than 0.5 are generally considered unacceptable, and one aims for a value above 0.70 (Taber, 2018). Bear in mind that very high levels, such as above 0.90, mean that the scale is asking the same question repeatedly, suggesting that it is too narrowly focused.

It is possible to identify the individual items that have the strongest link with the underlying topic, as judged by the correlation between the individual question and the total score. Item reliability analysis can identify items that don't behave like the others in the questionnaire. Items that have a low correlation with the total score may be removed at this stage, to obtain a good measure of the underlying trait. Alternatively, it is possible to run a confirmatory factor analysis to identify the items with the highest 'loading' on the underlying factor, when the researcher wants to identify a small set of essential questions.

With such techniques, the researcher begins with a dimension or trait in mind and develops a questionnaire to produce a scale that will reliably measure that trait. This is a top-down approach.

However, it is extremely rewarding to take the opposite route, and this is what we will illustrate in this chapter. Starting from the data, one can let the data speak, as it were, and look for *patterns* in the answers. The field of data mining evolved ways to identify such patterns. We will briefly present a few main methods that we found useful and illustrate each with one application in our work.

CONCEPTUAL CORE IDENTIFICATION

To identify what a concept, such as inflation or the central bank, means for a person, it is of course possible to ask for a definition, and this can be an informative first step. However, experience has shown that for many concepts, especially ones that were absorbed by the respondents without formal training in the relevant domain, such an approach is disappointing. People have a hard time formulating what a concept means to them, and most struggle to produce a proper definition. Another approach that works better was developed mostly by French social psychologists within the framework commonly called social representation. It starts by asking respondents simply to name the concepts that come to mind when the concept of interest is mentioned. There are various techniques to analyse the resulting responses (see Abric, 2005; deRosa, Bocci, & Dryjanska, 2018; Flament & Rouquette, 2003; Moscovici, 1988; Vergès, 1994; Vergès & Ryba, 2012). The researchers then study the neighbours of the inducing concept in the respondent's semantic map.

Amongst these neighbours, one can further distinguish between a *central core* and a peripheral system (Abric, 1993; Vergès, 1992). The central core is defined as a stable, non-transformable part of the representations, whereas the peripheral system accounts for inter-individual differences with respect to a stimulus object.

ASSOCIATIONS WITH 'INFLATION'

In Leiser and Drori (2005), participants were asked to write down a list of terms or short phrases that they considered to be related to inflation. These terms were later content-analysed and regrouped into a manageable number of concepts. Two obvious criteria for assessing the importance of a concept are the average *rank* it occupies in the respondents' lists, and how *frequently* it is mentioned across respondents. An elaborated technique was developed by Vergès (1994) and Flament and Rouquette (2003) to analyse this type of data. We will merely use the criterion used by Vergès to detect the 'central core' which is, simply enough, to identify those concepts that are both mentioned frequently and early on as forming the core.

Figure 23.1 plots frequency against mean position across all 200 participants. As is generally found, the two criteria go together in an orderly fashion, and no concept occurs early on that is not also frequent, as concepts that are strongly associated with inflation are popular and come to mind early on.

The central core, clearly identifiable in the bottom-right quadrant, includes the following concepts: money, price increases, the cost-of-living index (COL) and devaluation. To the economically naive individual, inflation is perceived as something bad that befalls prices and money: money is worth less, and prices are higher. Tellingly, whereas devaluation is salient, imports and exports are rarely mentioned and don't feature among the early associates. This is because inflation is thought of as something that happens to money. Money loses its value; devaluation only expresses that fact. There are other glaring omissions: absent from

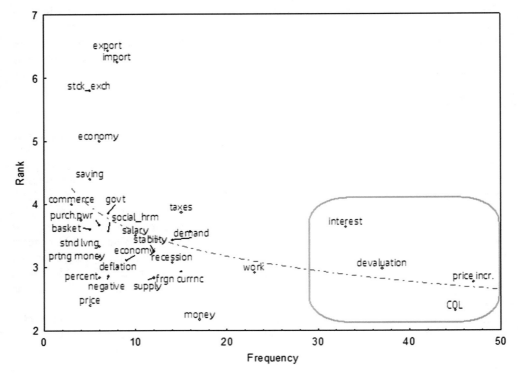

Figure 23.1 Core and peripheral concepts evoked by the prompt 'inflation'

this account are wages and salaries, unemployment, the government, the central bank, foreign trade, savings and, indeed, any reference to economics as a system (Leiser & Shemesh, 2018).

HIERARCHICAL CLUSTER ANALYSIS

Identifying the central core and the periphery of a concept is an important first step, useful when one focuses on an individual concept and tries to understand its relations to other concepts in the same general domain. The inducing concept is represented as a node, and one looks for the other nodes nearby.

But concepts are not zero-dimensional dots. They are often more akin to a skein, a set of threads that loosely cohere but can nevertheless be individualised.

Capitalism

Take for instance the concept of capitalism. Over the course of the televised debates leading up to the 2016 US presidential elections, capitalism took centre stage. Contender for the Democratic Party nomination, Bernie Sanders, was asked whether he identified as a capitalist. His reply:

> Do I consider myself part of the casino capitalist process, by which so few have so much and so many have so little, by which Wall Street's greed and recklessness wrecked this economy? No, I don't. (Democratic Debate: Hillary Clinton and Bernie Sanders Spar | Time)

To which his opponent, Hillary Clinton, retorted:

> When I think about capitalism, I think about all the small businesses that were started because we have the opportunity and the freedom in our country for people to do that and make a good living for themselves and their families. (Democratic Debate: Hillary Clinton and Bernie Sanders Spar | Time)

Casino, inequality, greed, recklessness, small businesses, opportunity, freedom, making a good living – all these are part of what capitalism means to different people. When people extol or object to capitalism, what is it that they praise or reject? To identify the main underlying dimensions of capitalism in public discourse, we proceeded as follows (Leiser & Shemesh, 2018).

We mapped out the various beliefs and attitudes pertaining to capitalism in the public mind by identifying themes and memes in public discourse. We then distilled those beliefs and attitudes into a brief questionnaire (see Table 23.1). Lastly, we looked for commonalities between responses to questionnaire items and deduced their underlying conceptual basis. This is the step that interests us here. (In our study we used this outcome to analyse how people differ in their responses and related those differences to individual and social factors.)

Our approach was to find questionnaire items for which participants tended to provide similar responses, on the assumption that items that run together represent issues that are conceptually related. To do this, we submitted our questionnaire to a hierarchical or 'joining tree' cluster analysis.

Cluster analysis is a technique used to group variables according to similarity to maximise within-group homogeneity. Hierarchical cluster analysis involves an algorithm that does this repeatedly (Hastie, Tibshirani & Friedman, 2017). A dendrogram provides a highly interpretable complete description of the hierarchical clustering in a graphical format (see Figure 23.2) and this constitutes an important aspect of its appeal.

Table 23.1   Examples of statements in the questionnaire

1. Businesspeople get rich off the backs of their workers, who don't get to enjoy the fruits of their labour
2. Inequality is natural and acceptable
3. One of the roles of the government in the economy is to make income distribution more equitable
4. Providing welfare doesn't really help poor people escape poverty
5. Regulation is essential to restrain exaggerated power concentration in the hands of the rich and to protect citizens against foreign interest
6. The government with its regulations cripples the economy
7. Capitalism is a system fuelled by greed for money and power
8. Capitalism is compatible with people's natural tendency to act in their own self-interest
9. Businesspeople arouse people's appetite for consumption of things no one really needs
10. If CEOs and entrepreneurs are taxed and regulated, they will take their business elsewhere
11. Compassion, altruism and community are important values for a healthy society
12. Entrepreneurs are not driven by greed, but by ambition
13. When the economy grows, wealth trickles down to the poor
14. The competitive free market brings out the creativity and ingenuity in people
15. The free-market system is to thank for the improved standards of living we enjoy today
16. The free market is responsible for the climate crisis and environmental degradation we face today

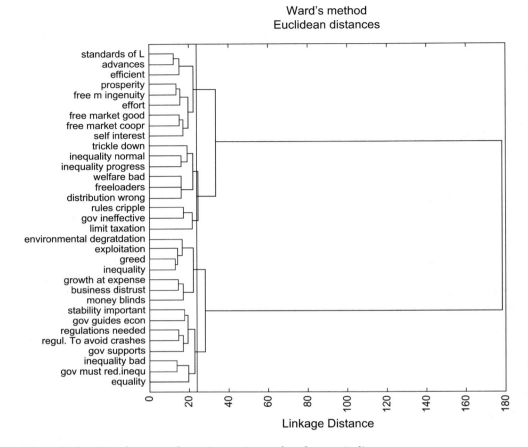

Figure 23.2   Dendrogram clustering notions related to capitalism

There are two parameters to the method of hierarchical clustering, the *distance metric* and the clustering method. There are many ways of assigning a 'distance' when comparing two statements. Suppose all participants were told to grade their agreement with the two statements A and B on a scale from 0 (strongly disagree) to 10 (endorse wholeheartedly). We are looking to quantify to what extent the participants gave similar responses to the two. We could try to simply subtract for the first respondent the score she gave to A from that she gave to B, and add those differences across all participants. This method would run into trouble, as differences in opposite directions for different participants would cancel out. The improved method, commonly used in statistics, is to take each of those differences, square it, add the squared differences, and then extract the square root of the sum of squared differences. This is the method we used in our example involving capitalism. Another commonly used method is to compute the Pearson correlation between the two vectors representing the degree of agreement with each statement. Other possibilities depend on the subject matter or the theoretical purpose of the operation. For instance, when possible answers categories cannot be ordered, it is possible to use the number of overlaps.

The second parameter is the *clustering method*. Distance of course involves two items, judgements about two statements in our example. Our goal is to organise all the statements so that statements that are close together will be clustered in increasingly larger branches, joining clusters of statements based on their proximity. But how do you measure the distance between two groups of items? If you have two clusters composed of many elements, what is the proper way to express the distance between the two? This depends on the structure of the data and on the goals of the analyst. They can be joined according to the closest pair of elements, for instance, one statement from each group. This would be appropriate when thinking of medical contagion or of potential security risks, much as a chain is as strong as its weakest link. Or one might use the most distant pair of elements in the groups, again one from each group, when the goal is to merge teams of people and the goal is to avoid putting incompatible people in the same team as much as possible.

One method deserves pride of place, Ward's method, which can be considered as a kind of reverse analysis of variance method. ANOVA analysis examines two clusters and their intra-cluster variance and compares that variance to the between-cluster variance. To the extent that the intra-cluster variance is small compared to that between clusters, the clusters may be deemed to form a natural way of grouping the elements, true to the relations they entertain with one another. Ward's method doesn't begin from existing clusters. Instead, it uses the same logic to form the best clusters. At the outset, each variable is situated in its own unique cluster. At each successive iteration, an algorithm seeks a merger between two clusters that would incur the least increase in total within-cluster variance, compared to all other possible mergers.

To illustrate, let us take three questionnaire items. One item (A) expresses the view that capitalism is responsible for the increased standards of living we enjoy today; the second (B), that capitalism is responsible for much of the environmental degradation we face today; and the third (C), that in a capitalistic system, the rich get richer and the poor get poorer. If a given participant were to rate the first item as high, the second as low, and the third as low, then the difference between our participant's A and the average of A∪B would be large, and that for B∪C would be small. If another participant rated A as low, and both B and C as high, once again, the result would be a relatively large increase in variance within A∪B and a small increase in B∪C. If that pattern would repeat across participants, then B∪C would be retained, and we would say that the two items are more alike and group them in a cluster. After the merger is implemented, another iteration is carried through and another merger is applied until all variables are ultimately unified under a single 'trunk'. The cluster structure for our data is presented in Figure 23.2.

The most accurate portrayal of a person's views would include every opinion solicited in the survey (37 in total). The next step was to determine the level at which to cleave our joining tree, which would provide an optimum on the tradeoff between accuracy and practicality, and avoid over-fitting. Surveying the contents of the clustered questionnaire items, we decided on a criterion that seemed to us to preserve the most within-cluster conceptual integrity while providing relatively few dependent variables for further analysis. The vertical line in Figure 23.4 represents the criterion we chose.

To make sure that the results from the clustering procedure were not spurious, we subjected all clusters to item reliability analysis (see earlier). We found all five clusters to be highly internally consistent (Cronbach's alphas are satisfactory):

- Cluster 1 – Capitalism works (Cronbach's alpha = 0.89).
- Cluster 2 – Capitalism is exploitive (Cronbach's alpha = 0.89).
- Cluster 3 – Government meddling is bad (0.68).
- Cluster 4 – Government regulation is essential for fairness and stability (0.89).
- Cluster 5 – Welfare is wrong (Cronbach's alpha = 0.88).

As a next step, we calculated five new scales, one for each cluster, representing the mean response values averaging across their constituent items. Taken together, the scale values represent a person's overall *response profile*, that is, they reflect where he or she stands with respect to each important dimension characterising lay views of capitalism.

The number of different underlying dimensions may be suggested by factor analysis, more specifically by running a *screen test* to check how much each additional factor adds (the usual criterion being not to add factors whose eigenvalue is < 1). Hierarchical cluster analysis is more subtle, as it displays the clustering of questions, and leaves greater latitude to the researcher in deciding how fine-grained they want their analysis to be.

The example we just presented involved clustering *questions* into columns, in the usual presentation of data in a spreadsheet. Note that the technique is equally applicable to cluster the rows, that is, the *respondents* who give the same pattern of answers, which may provide valuable insights too.

MULTI-DIMENSIONAL SCALING

Hierarchical clustering is closely related to another method, multi-dimensional scaling (MDS), and is sometimes used as a preliminary step. MDS is an attempt to present graphically in space or on a plane the relative distances of the objects of interest. 'Distance; can have widely divergent meanings, from semantic similarity to causal interdependence, but the outcome is always a map intended to facilitate the interpretation of the relevant phenomenon.

Let us begin with a concrete example. Suppose you know the distance between any two localities in a distant and unfamiliar region, say the French Jura. You know the distances from Dole to Lons-le Saunier, St Amour, St Claude and Salins les Bains are 53 km, 91 km, 115 km and 44 km, respectively. Indeed, you have the complete table with the distances between every pair of localities, in the familiar triangular matrix. However, as most readers of this chapter, you have never examined a map of the region. Would it be possible to reconstruct the map from which those measures were taken? Are there several different solutions? Our first intuition would be the latter, but that intuition would be wrong. It is in fact possible to reconstruct the map of that part of the French Jura, though, of course, such a map will not specify which direction is north, and moreover, a mirror image of that reconstructed map would also be a solution; but beyond these caveats, there can exist no other solution. Anyone who remembers triangle congruence theorems (specifically 'side-side-side') from high school geometry classes should be able to demonstrate this.

Remember now the questionnaire in the previous section, where respondents reported how much they each endorse a set of statements. We can use the following measure of distance: for

Statistical approaches to the analysis of belief patterns 407

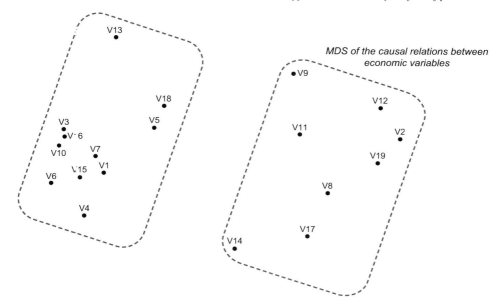

Figure 23.3   Good begets good

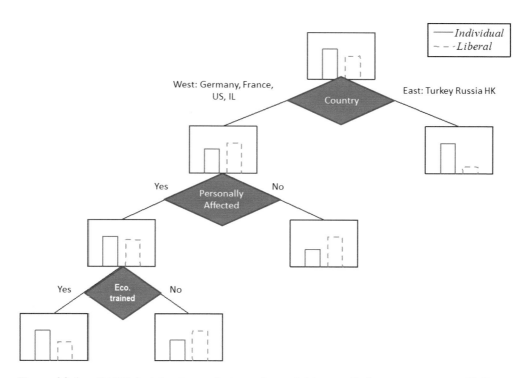

Figure 23.4   CART decision tree: what are the variables predicting a response profile?

any two statements, compute the *correlation* across respondents between the answers given to the two statements. If that correlation is high, it means that from the answer given by a participant to the first we can hope to predict the answer they provided to the other.

This puts us in a situation like that involving the distances between localities: we have a matrix describing the proximity between any two statements and from these distances it is possible to construct a map where closely correlated statements lie close together, less correlated ones are further apart, while negatively correlated ones are the furthest away. Such maps can be invaluable, as we will presently illustrate.

Note that it is not always possible to represent distances on a flat plane. Even for the Jura map we took as an example, the localities are not all at the same altitude and this may matter. This is why the algorithm that maps is called multi-dimensional scaling: it will generate a 2D or 3D map according to circumstances. In principle, it is possible to generate even higher-order maps involving four dimensions or more. This too is sometimes very useful, though in those cases visualisation of the map is impossible. In practice one mostly uses 2D maps, which involve constraining the configuration to a flat plane. The degree to which the 2D representation distorts the relation between the items is expressed by the 'alienation' or 'stress' coefficient. The larger the coefficient, the more caution is warranted when interpreting the map.

Good Begets Good

Let us consider an example of the use of MDS maps. Leiser and Aroch (2009) presented 19 macroeconomic variables to participants. These included measures of aggregate economic activity (like the GNP), the rate of economic growth, corporate profits, wages, private spending, private investments in the stock market, etc. (see Table 23.2).

For every pair of variables, participants were asked to judge whether, and how they were causally related. Specifically, they were asked, for every pair of variables A and B: *if variable A increases, how will this affect variable B?* Possible answers were: B will increase/B

Table 23.2   *'Good' and 'bad' changes in economic indicators*

Positive change	Negative change
GNP	Government expenditures
National credit rating	Rate of inflation
Corporate profits	Unemployment rate
Investment by the public in stock market	Interest rate on loans
Average net salary	Income tax rate
Consumption rate	Consumer debt
Money supply	Depth of recession
Rate of economic growth	Government welfare expenditure
Competitiveness of the market	
Preference for local products	
Personal savings rate	

will decrease/B will not be affected/I don't know. For example, *if the unemployment rate increases, how will this affect the inflation rate?*

An illuminating pattern emerges when all the variables are plotted by MDS. The distance measure that we used is straightforward: the more two variables are associated positively (A increases B), the closer together they appear on the map; conversely, the more they are negatively associated (A decreases B), the further apart they are plotted (see Figure 23.3). As can be observed, the variables cluster nicely into two groups. To interpret this pattern, one examines the contents of the two clusters. It is then seen that the clusters correspond to a distinction between positively and negatively valued change (see Table 23.2).

That clustering enables us to infer how laypeople derive economic predictions even as they understand little about macroeconomic causation (Leiser & Aroch, 2009). Changes in economic variables are judged as good or bad, and this provides the (dubious) ground for their answers: if both A and B belong to the same pole (good or bad), an increase in one is believed to raise the other; if they belong to opposite poles, a raise in one is supposed to cause the other to drop. This heuristic was called the *good-begets-good (GBG) heuristic*.

CART DECISION TREES

Our last technique is called classification and regression tree building, and we will discuss the simplest case, that of the classification tree. The purpose of the algorithm is to build an optimal tree structure to predict categorical dependent variables (see Hastie, Tibshirani & Friedman, 2017, section 9.2 for a detailed discussion). We turn directly to our illustration.

Financial Crisis

We ran a large international questionnaire about people's views of a great many aspects of the 2008 financial crisis, looked for answering patterns of answers, and identified two distinct patterns. Most respondents tended to attribute the crisis to moral, cognitive and character shortcomings of individuals, while others gave more weight to systemic features of the economic system. We will refer to the first pattern as the *individual* profile, and to the other, which put less emphasis on individual foibles, as the *liberal* profile (Leiser, Bourgeois-Gironde & Benita, 2010). Besides the questions about the crisis, we also collected demographic variables, such as education, country, gender and the extent to which they were personally affected by the crisis.

Our goal was to determine which combinations of demographic variables predict the answering pattern. We suspected that the importance of some variables depends on that of others, and this led us to adopt the classification tree approach. This is akin to the relationship of a leaf to the tree on which it grows: it can be described by the hierarchy of splits of branches (starting from the trunk) leading to the last branch from which the leaf hangs. The tree is grown by comparing all possible splits for each predictor variable at each node, to identify the split producing the largest improvement in goodness of fit (as measured by chi-squared). Note that the grouping of categories (such as Turkey, Russia and Hong Kong) was produced by the algorithm. Similarly, it might have produced a cut-off point along the age dimension and introduced a split contrasting people above and below age 35.

We return to our question: what typifies the members of the two profiles? The answer is illustrated in Figure 23.4 (see Leiser, Benita & Bourgeois-Gironde, 2016). The binary classification tree can be described by the statement:

Respondents that come from a Western country were not personally affected and benefited from economic training are likely to exhibit the liberal pattern. If they are not from a Western country, the other questions are immaterial, and they will likely endorse the individual pattern of answer. Likewise, those in the West who were personally affected, or that were themselves unaffected but have no economic training, will also endorse the individual pattern.

This tree was produced by the algorithm, and it is a very simple one. Other possible outcomes could have involved different branches depending on grouping higher up, so that for instance age or gender doesn't matter in the West, but is very informative for the East. This shows the power of the method. Consider the traditional way to proceed: discriminant regression. Doing this, one would determine the weight to be given to each independent variable. The specific combination of traits would then jointly determine the pattern predicted. The predicted classification would be made by *simultaneously* considering the patient's scores on the three variables. With CART, as we noted, a *hierarchy* of questions is asked, and the final decision depends on the answers to all the previous questions in the same branch.

Running CART analysis requires setting numerous parameters and demands a good understanding of the method. One of them is a stopping rule. It is essential to know when to stop to avoid overfitting, as it is possible to have increasingly fine analyses that can turn into an exercise in interpreting noise. But when used advisedly, the method can yield truly illuminating insights.

CONCLUSION

This chapter briefly discussed several valuable methods to analyse data: conceptual core identification, hierarchical cluster analysis, multi-dimensional scaling and CART decision trees. All these methods can be considered data-mining approaches. Rather than formulating hypotheses in advance and assessing them, they allow the data to speak on its own. Because this goal is open-ended, great caution should be exercised in the application and interpretation of the resulting findings.

REFERENCES

Abric, J.-C. (2005). La recherche du noyau central et de la zone muette des représentations sociales. In J.-C. Abric (Ed.), *Méthodes d'étude des représentations sociales* (pp. 59–80). Toulouse: ERES.

De Rosa, A. S., Bocci, E., & Dryjanska, L. (2018). The generativity and attractiveness of social representations theory from multiple paradigmatic approaches in various thematic domains. *Papers on Social Representations, 27*(1), 6.1–6.35.

Flament, C., & Rouquette, M.-L. (2003). *Anatomie des idées ordinaires- Comment etudier les représentations sociales*. Paris: Armand Colin/VUF.

Hastie, T., Tibshirani, R., & Friedman, J. H. (2017). *The elements of statistical learning: Data mining, inference, and prediction - Data Mining, Inference and Prediction* (12th ed.). New York: Springer.

Leiser, D., & Aroch, R. (2009). Lay understanding of macroeconomic causation: The good-begets-good heuristic. *Applied Psychology, 58*(3), 370–384.

Leiser, D., Benita, R., & Bourgeois-Gironde, S. (2016). Differing conceptions of the causes of the economic crisis: Effects of culture, economic training, and personal impact. *Journal of Economic Psychology, 53*, 154–163. doi:http://dx.doi.org/10.1016/j.joep.2016.02.002

Leiser, D., Bourgeois-Gironde, S., & Benita, R. (2010). Human foibles or systemic failure—Lay perceptions of the 2008–2009 financial crisis. *The Journal of Socio-Economics, 39*(2), 132–141.

Leiser, D., & Drori, S. (2005). Naïve understanding of inflation. *Journal of Socio-Economics, 34*(2), 179–198. doi:10.1016/j.socec.2004.09.006

Leiser, D., & Shemesh, Y. (2018). *How we misunderstand economics and why it matters: The Psychology of bias, distortion and conspiracy.* London: Routledge.

Moscovici, S. (1988). Notes towards a description of social representations. *European Journal of Social Psychology, 18*(3), 211–250.

Taber, K. S. (2018). The use of Cronbach's alpha when developing and reporting research instruments in science education. *Research in science education, 48*(6), 1273–1296.

Vergès, P. (1994). Approche du noyau central: Propriétés quantitatives et structurales. In C. Guimelli (Ed.), *Structures et transformations des représentations sociales* (pp. 233–253). Neuchâtel: Delachaux et Niestlé.

Vergès, P., & Ryba, R. (2012). Social representations of the economy. In A. S. de Rosa (Ed.), *Social Representations in the 'Social Arena'* (pp. 233–244). New York: Routledge.

24. Motivated preferences
Matthew G. Nagler

INTRODUCTION

While it is widely recognised that bounded rationality affects individual decision-making, a less-explored area is the influence of bounded rationality on preferences. The basic idea relates to the notion that an individual does not *know* what she wants: she must ascertain this, much as she must ascertain the relative characteristics of choice objects in relation to one another. When an individual is boundedly rational, salience influences judgements with respect to both tasks. This means framing will influence not just choices, but also the individual's perception of the very preferences she holds and which drive her choices. As Rabin (1998, p. 37) observes:

> Framing effects can often be viewed as heuristic errors – people are boundedly rational, and the presentation of a choice may draw our attention to different aspects of a problem, leading us to make mistakes in pursuing our true, underlying preferences . . . But sometimes framing effects cut more deeply to economists' model of choice: More than confusing people in pursuit of stable underlying preferences, the 'frames' may in fact partially determine a person's preferences.

But if frames affect preferences, how then does a utility-maximising boundedly rational individual behave when making choices? If one decides not only among choice objects, but also where one directs one's attention, is our traditional model of choice descriptively correct, and will predictions based on this model be accurate?

This chapter explores the notion of motivated preferences. The idea is simple: if what one prefers depends in part on what one focuses on, then the boundedly rational individual may manipulate her own preferences through the deliberate effort of focusing attention on certain aspects of her choice objects (but not others), as well as certain aspects of her predilections over choice objects (but not others). Doing so will make certain aspects of the objects and predilections salient.

In a paper on focusing and its effects on choices, Koszegi and Szeidl (2013) introduce weights into a utility function to reflect aspects of choices that are more or less salient to the individual. Their model concentrates on a specific application of this framework – to the hypothesis that individuals focus more on, hence overweight in their decisions, product attributes in which their options differ more. But their structure provides a broad basis for thinking about how the preferences of boundedly rational individuals might be influenced by what they direct their attention to – even if the model was not originally intended for use in this way.

In psychology, there is a substantial amount of experimental evidence on the complementarity of actions and cognitive processes that alter perceptions of actions. Individuals asked to re-rate alternatives following a decision or in anticipation of one increase their ratings of chosen alternatives and in some cases diminish ratings of non-chosen alternatives (Lieberman et al., 2001; Kitayama et al., 2004; Sharot et al., 2010; Wakslak, 2012). Studies using functional magnetic resonance imaging (fMRI) indicate changes in preference-related brain activity contemporaneous with the changes in subjects' subjective rating of stimuli accompanying decisions or actions (Sharot et al., 2009; Van Veen et al., 2009; Izuma et al., 2010; Jarcho et al., 2011; Qin et al., 2011; Kitayama et al., 2013; Tompson et al., 2016). These studies offer empirical support for the notion that preference adjustment is a routine ingredient in the process of choice.

In popular culture, these ideas have currency as well. We have all heard common sayings such as 'Life is what you make it', 'Love the one you're with' and 'Roll with it', which suggest a general awareness of the feasibility of altering, if one tries, one's disposition towards the things one does. And yet the conceptualisation and empirical validation of these ideas are only nascent areas in economics as of this writing.[1]

The rest of this chapter is organised as follows. The second section outlines a theoretical structure, involving complementary choices of action and cognition, made either by a forward-looking agent who maximises discounted future utility or by a 'backwards-glancing' agent who also cares about justifying past actions. The third section describes several applications of the framework. The fourth section offers concluding remarks.

THEORETICAL MODELLING

If you are going to do something, you are better off loving it. The saying embodies the logic that one should apply one's *mind* to the task of utility maximisation – getting the most out of what one chooses by, in effect, getting 'psyched up' about it – rather than merely making choices among different goods or activities. Along these lines, let us conceive of an optimising individual who has control over both choices and thoughts, employing them, in effect, as complementary inputs in a production function of satisfaction.

Thoughts might influence utility in two ways: focusing effort directed at characteristics of one's presumptive choice that are most aligned with one's preferences, and focusing effort directed at aspects of one's preferences that are most aligned with one's presumptive choice. Consider, for example, an optimising boundedly rational individual who is shopping for a car. On the one hand, he might focus his attention on the car's great gas mileage, because it is aligned with his concerns about the environment, rather than the leather detailing that comes with the car's 'standard package,' which is not particularly interesting to him. On the other hand, he may focus on how, as a middle-aged liberal, he sees himself well-suited to a compact hybrid vehicle, while not focusing on how being a father of three he might perhaps have liked something larger.

Of course, one cannot get maximally psyched up about everything one does, and thereby increase utility without bound. A modified, decision problem arises in which thinking is in essence *costly* both because cognitive resources are scarce and because good opportunities whereby cognition can effectively increase utility are limited. The individual allocates costly cognition where it will be most valuable, based on the exogenous importance or intrinsic value of the consumption activity to the individual, which we shall refer to as its *quality*. The allocation problem can be embodied in a reduced-form cost of cognition.

A bit more formally,[2] let us posit the instantaneous utility of an activity in period t for an individual as given by

$$u(\mu, x_t, y_t) \tag{24.1}$$

Here, x_t is the quantity of the activity in t, μ is its time-independent quality, and y_t is the individual's attitude, which is determined by the process

$$y_t = (1-\sigma)y_{t-1} + T_t \qquad (24.2)$$

where T_t is contemporaneous attitude-improving thought and $\sigma \in [0,1]$ is the depreciation rate of attitude. The idea behind (24.2) is that elaborative thinking about the goodness of fit of an activity with one's preferences has a lasting effect, creating an attitude that persists over time and decays slowly. That lasting attitude, in turn, complements the activity, such that it increases the marginal utility of x_t in (24.1). The marginal utilities of both x and y, in turn, are increasing in the activity quality μ. The utility function (24.1) is in essence a satisfaction production function, with x_t, y_t and μ as inputs.[3]

In this context, let us consider the possibility of an *endowment*, an exogenously determined level of initial consumption $\hat{x}_0$, or alternatively an initial level of x chosen before μ is known. In the context of endowments, we may think of T_0 as being chosen subsequent to the revelation of μ. Comparative static analysis of the optimising choices of agents in the model with respect to μ and $\hat{x}_0$ are of particular interest and form the jumping-off point for the main applications of this framework. Figure 24.1 summarises these comparative statics for a forward-looking agent – one who chooses x_t and T_t (hence y_t) in each t to maximise discounted future utility, subject to a 'budget' constraint that recognises the limits on cognitive resources.[4]

As shown in the figure, the maximising levels of both consumption and attitude for such an agent increase with quality μ. High quality results in a high-quality steady state with a high level of consumption and a high investment in attitude, while low quality results in a low-quality steady state with low consumption and low investment in attitude. This is intuitive: it is worth consuming more of and getting more psyched up about something that is really great. Meanwhile, when there is an exogenous low-quality surprise, in the case where consumption is chosen before quality is revealed, *complementary* adjustment results: the agent sets a lower attitude to account for the lower-than-expected quality. The effect of an exogenously determined excess endowment (such as a gift or windfall), occurring in the context of known low quality, also results in complementary adjustment: attitude is increased to account for the high amount of the good on hand. In the latter case, if σ is very small or x_0 very large, consumption in future periods may be higher than warranted on the basis of the good's low quality (i.e., the low-quality steady state consumption). This occurs because attitude is durable – particularly so when σ is small. We discuss this 'endowment effect' further in the next section.

Now consider a 'backwards-glancing' agent – one who makes decisions not purely with the future in mind, but in part out of concern about past choices.[5] We posit that the agent weights into his objective function a term of the form

$$u(\mu, \hat{x}_0, y) - u(\mu, x_0^*(y), y) \qquad (24.3)$$

Analysis of this term reveals that such an agent cares, in effect, about justifying his prior choice of $\hat{x}_0$; he experiences disutility (or *regret*) when $\hat{x}_0$ departs from the optimising choice x_0^*. Since the level of that optimising choice depends on his attitude y, the agent uses his elaborative thinking at least in part to manipulate his attitude towards x so as to reduce the size of (24.3). In the extreme, with maximal weight on this term, the agent will choose y so that $\hat{x}_0 = x_0^*(y)$.

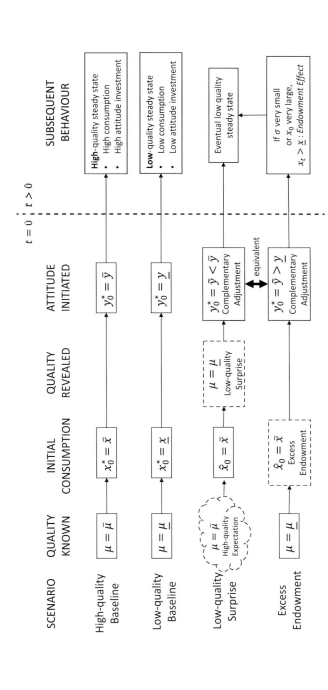

Note: Box with dashed border indicates relevant exogenous shock.

Figure 24.1   Comparative statics: forward-looking agent

Figure 24.2 summarises comparative statics for the backwards-glancing agent.[6] The first two rows of the flow chart are identical to Figure 24.1: a backwards-glancing agent behaves identically to a forward-looking agent when quality and consumption align optimally such that there is no reason for regret. The difference is where there is a low-quality surprise or excess endowment. Regret reverses the sign of the effect of exogenous quality on attitude-improving thought, so that a low-quality surprise causes the backwards-glancing agent to *increase* attitude investment relative to the no-regret case. In the extreme, attitude will actually be set higher than if quality were at its expected level. Intuitively, an unexpectedly low level of μ indicates to agents that they 'chose too much' x in period 0. Whereas the forward-looking agent takes this realisation in stride and sets a lower level of T_0 that *complements* the lower realised quality of the activity, the backwards-glancing agent *compensates*, choosing a *higher* level of T_0 in order to justify the high level of the endowment relative to the quality level.

With an excess endowment, the backwards-glancing agent engages in *hyper*-complementary adjustment, setting attitude at a higher level than the forward-looking agent would. The result is an endowment effect that is strictly larger.

Note that in Figures 24.1 and 24.2 we've considered only a low quality surprise (and, correspondingly, an excess endowment). Alternatively, the agent could face a high-quality surprise, such that complementary adjustment by the forward-looking agent would set attitude higher than in the baseline known-quality case, while compensatory adjustment by the backwards-glancing agent would potentially set attitude lower. In view of the full range of possibilities, it is indeed not clear as a general matter whether attitude-improving thought should be expected to be greater in the case of forward-looking or backwards-glancing activity. This may contradict the intuition one garners from the psychological literature on cognitive dissonance, which has emphasised the role of post-decision regrets in attitude-adjustive thought. (We will discuss cognitive dissonance further in the next section.) Indeed, our purpose here in conceiving of the broader complementarity of thought and action is to recognise that neither regret nor pure forward-looking optimisation should be expected *prima facie* to imply a greater motivation to adjust one's attitude.

Other than quality, the main factor we would expect to influence the amount of attitude-adjustive thinking in (24.1) is the perceived importance of the decision. The purchase of a house or car would likely elicit a substantial amount of complementary thinking, whereas the purchase of a bar of soap would not; and the purchase of 1,000 bars of soap would elicit more complementary thinking than just one bar of soap.

APPLICATIONS AND EVIDENCE

A number of familiar behavioural phenomena may be conceived of as somehow involving optimising individuals altering their attitudes towards activities through complementary or compensatory focusing effort. The value of the motivated preferences model arises from the ways in which explicit recognition of a cognitive layer that accompanies behaviour provides a better understanding of the behaviour and associated outcomes. In what follows, I describe several applications. I discuss existing models of the phenomena identified, and I characterise the ways in which accounting for the cognitive layer provides a more accurate description and improves predictions.

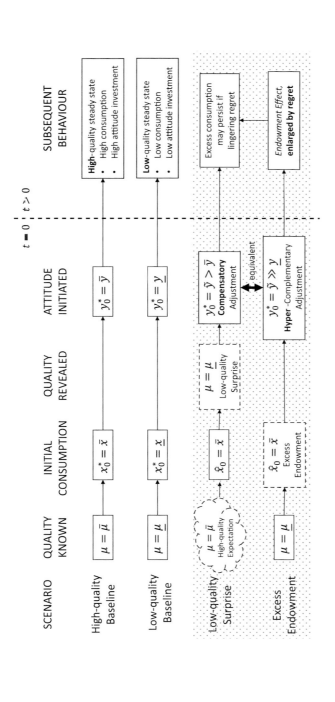

Note: Box with dashed border indicates relevant exogenous shock.

Figure 24.2 Comparative statics: backwards-glancing agent

The Endowment Effect

Motivated preferences offer an advance in explaining the endowment effect – the finding that people demand greater compensation to relinquish an owned item (typically) than they would be willing to pay to acquire an identical item if they did not own it (Kahneman et al. 1990, 1991). The widely replicated effect is rightly held up as conclusively indicating that reference points matter to how people value goods; however, its standard attribution to loss aversion fails adequately to explain some key observations. If one supposes the super-normal valuations of endowments accrue simply to losses looming larger than gains, then those who are selling their own possessions should invariably require more in trade than what buyers, regardless of what they currently own, are willing to pay. And yet, Morewedge et al. (2009) find that traders – whether buyers or sellers, and whether what they are trading is their own or not – value objects *more* when they own an identical item. The loss aversion account of the endowment effect similarly fails to explain why owners' valuations of objects in experimental settings are vulnerable to treatments aimed at affecting subjects' cognitive basis for caring about the things they own (Chatterjee et al. 2013; Dommer et al. 2013).

The motivated preference model tells us that increased valuation accrues to endowments because endowments entail complementary attitude adjustment, as per Figure 24.1. Moreover, endowments may increase consumption of the same good at the margin in future periods because the adjustment of attitude is durable. This simple mechanism is able to explain the pure effect of ownership on valuation, consistent with Morewedge et al. (2009); and, because the mechanism is *cognitive*, it can explain the effects that cognitive treatments have in tweaking the super-normal valuations that accrue to owning things. Because rational expectations impact the perceived value of attitude change just as they do the undesirable prospect of loss, the motivated preference theory explains on par with the loss aversion account the dependence of object valuations on individuals' rational expectations of ongoing ownership (Ericson et al. 2011), the absence of an endowment effect for experienced traders (List 2003, 2004) and the absence of an endowment effect with respect to money (Kahneman et al. 1990; Svirsky 2014).

Sunk-Cost Effects and Habit Formation

The motivated preference theory provides a more robust account of so-called 'sunk-cost bias' – that is, cases in which people make economic decisions with a dependence on past history – than prior accounts that ignore the role of cognition. Existing rationality-based explanations of autoregressive behaviours rely generally on some form of strategic complementarity of past and present actions. For example, Eyster (2002) posits agents who look to what they did in the past when deciding what to do in the present because they have a taste for consistency of action. This approach is able to explain Thaler's (1980) classic example of a family that decides to go to a basketball game during a snowstorm, the family noting that they would not have gone had they received the tickets for free rather than purchasing them. Taste-driven complementarity of the initial action (deciding to purchase the tickets) and a subsequent action that justifies the initial one (attending the game) propels the observed sunk-cost behaviour. Thaler's scenario may alternatively be viewed through the lens of expectations-based reference dependence, in that, one may suppose, the family's purchase of basketball tickets creates a rational expectation of attendance that receiving the tickets for free does not. A reference point – that ticket buyers go to the games they paid for – is the means by which the past matters in deciding the best present course of action in this particular scenario: not attending would be perceived as a loss.

But action-based complementarities run into trouble as an explanation of sunk-cost bias in cases where a cognitive layer is essential to understanding the mechanism of post hoc justification. For example, consider the scenario described by Akerlof and Dickens (1982) in which individuals face a cognitive dissonance-producing decision of whether to work in a hazardous industry and, subsequently, are given the opportunity to purchase safety equipment. Based purely on the complementarity of actions, one would expect the workers to purchase the safety equipment in some cases when the benefits to improved safety do not exceed equipment costs: the adoption of the equipment renders more prudent in retrospect one's decision to work in the industry. Yet, consistent with the anecdotal evidence on safety-related behaviour in a range of situations (e.g., motorcycle helmet adoption, hockey headgear use, AIDS testing), workers in such situations typically *avoid* the equipment even when its isolated net benefit is positive. Reference points framed by rational expectations are unhelpful in understanding why this happens.

In positing a role for cognition, the motivated preference approach can provide an explanation. The behaviour occurs because the initial action is out of line with the level dictated by the individual's preferences – in the model's parlance, $\hat{x}_0 \neq x_0^*(y)$, for the initial level of attitude y. The resultant regret precipitates compensatory adjustment of y to bring x_0^* more in line with $\hat{x}_0$. The adjustment is durable, whence it leads to a reduction in the adoption of future behaviours that might have been rational *but for* the adjustment. Critically, then, it is *cognition* that, in compensating for the initial problematic action in retrospect, sets in motion the observed behavioural dynamic.

Along similar lines, the motivated preference model recognises the phenomenon of *escalation of commitment* – continuing or even expanding a course of action to justify a prior decision to act – as driven by attitude adjustment that is invoked to reduce ongoing regret. The low-quality surprise in Figure 24.2 represents this scenario: the agent realises his initial consumption decision was 'too high', but reacts by doubling down with compensatory thinking that builds a committed attitude around the initial action. If regret persists over time, then excess consumption of the 'low-quality' activity persists, such that the agent compounds his error. The model's predictions in this regard are consistent with experimental evidence that regret fosters repeat purchase behaviour by consumers (Mittelstaedt 1969) and, more broadly, fit with descriptive accounts of escalation of commitment from the literature (e.g., Staw 1976).

A prominent special case of past history mattering for future consumption is presented by habit formation, according to which willingness to pay for a good is determined by one's past pattern of consumption for the same good (Wathieu 2004). Habit formation has been framed variously on the basis of endogenously determined reference points (Rozen 2010), the tendency of consumption to create a capital stock that complements future consumption (Becker and Murphy 1988), and consumption adjustment costs (Chetty and Szeidl 2016). Common to all these models – and quite consistent with Eyster's (2002) approach – is a presumption of *per se* complementarity of present and future actions. As such, the scope for habit formation is properly either specific to an intrinsic habit-forming quality of the good (e.g., addictive goods, such as heroin) or to how the good is transacted (e.g., involving commitments, as per Chetty and Szeidl 2016), whence not every form of consumption would be predicted to be habit-forming. As such, the theory is not effective at explaining persistent behaviour outside its limited purview.

Moreover, factors that exist specifically on a psycho-cognitive level are necessary to fully explain observable habit-forming tendencies in all events. Consider a hypothetical experiment in which two groups of human subjects who do not have extensive familiarity with classical music are exposed over time to pieces of music that are particularly challenging to approach – say, the symphonies of Gustav Mahler – and so constitute what might be called an 'acquired taste'. One group is tasked with performing math problems, or perhaps a tedious letter-finding task such as proposed by Azar (2019), while listening to the music; while the other (control) group is just allowed to listen undisturbed. The treatment group, by virtue of the cognitive load imposed by the side task, would likely fail to develop a complementary stock of 'music appreciation' at the same rate as the control group. This group might be expected to exhibit a decreased propensity to listen to the Mahler symphonies voluntarily following the conclusion of the treatment as compared to the control. Thus, the habit formation tendencies of the two groups with respect to the same action differ in a way that the traditional habit formation models cannot explain. Put another way: if one conceives of habit formation models that propose complementarity of current and future actions as a shorthand for underlying cognitive processes that might play a role in such complementarity, it is clear that the primitives are insufficiently specified.

The contribution of motivated preference theory is that it allows for an accounting of variations that relate to the degree of complementary cognition an individual will engage in support of a potentially habituated consumption activity. Further, it identifies a mechanism according to which the broader class of *all* activities demonstrates qualities of habit formation. Thus the theory is able to offer a more robust characterisation of persistent behaviour.

Classic Cognitive Dissonance

The concept of 'motivated preferences' naturally brings to mind cognitive dissonance, the aversive psychological condition that occurs when an individual takes actions that are inconsistent with her attitudes. To be sure, individuals who experience cognitive dissonance may alter their attitudes to align them with their actions so as to reduce their cognitive discomfort (Festinger 1962; Aronson 2004). The approach of the motivated preferences model, however, is to posit attitude adjustment as a routine part of the consumer decision process, including in situations in which dissonance is not being experienced. Reaction to cognitive dissonance, then, is placed into the context of a broader set of phenomena involving complementary action and cognition.

What is helpful about this general approach is that it offers an advance in identifying key aspects of the action and cognition that are common to all cognitive dissonance phenomena observed in application. Specifically, what characterises a cognitive dissonance reaction is the adaptation of flexible attitude to a restriction of the choice set experienced by a backwards-glancing agent.

Considering our setup from the second section, suppose the domain for choice is the unit interval [0, 1] and that quality μ known at the outset is such that the individual's preferred initial action is interior to the interval, to wit, $x_0^* \in (0,1)$. Define the set $\mathbb{C} \subseteq [0,1]$ of choice options actually available to the individual. In the unrestricted case where $\mathbb{C} = [0,1]$, the individual chooses x_0^* and sets T_0 to optimally adjust to x_0^*. In such a situation, she experiences no regret. But if instead $\mathbb{C} = [\underline{x},1]$, where $1 \geq \underline{x} \geq x_0^*$, then the individual is compelled to take a greater quantity of action than she would have chosen given its quality level μ. This scenario precisely describes forced compliance, as per the classic cognitive dissonance experiments of Festinger and Carlsmith (1959). The situation creates the potential for regret: the quantity $\underline{x}$ is 'too high' and must be rationalised. To reduce her misgivings, the individual adjusts her attitude with greater intensity to support the endowed action. Given the durability of the adjustment, her initial adjustive thinking may decrease misgivings about taking the action in the future, increasing her tendency to engage in it again. Both the hypothesised attitudinal adjustment to the endowed action and the increased propensity to take that action again are consistent with outcomes observed by Festinger and Carlsmith (1959).

Another example is provided by the scenario discussed previously in the third section of the workers in the hazardous industry. Suppose a particular worker judges the dangers of the industry a priori as neither extreme nor non-existent, such that he would like to participate in the industry workforce but only tentatively or partially (i.e., $x_0 \in (0,1)$). Of course, life does not normally permit a worker to be tentative: you have to take a job, or else pass it up. Here, then, $\mathbb{C} = \{0,1\}$. If the worker judges that taking the job is his best option of the two available and he takes it, he experiences dissonance: the job is more dangerous than he is comfortable with for a full-time commitment, which is to say his self-perception as an intelligent and rational person is at odds with his beliefs about the hazards of the job he has taken. His response is to engage in attitude adjustment to convince himself the job is not as hazardous as people say; in doing so, he causes his actual action and preferred action to converge. Such beliefs tend to persist, whence the dynamic problem arises. If, in the future, the individual is given the opportunity to purchase safety equipment, the option to do so does not look as attractive as it might have before he started the job.

Prices in Markets with Differentiated Products

If consumers do not just choose products, but also their attitudes towards the products they consume, then failing to account for a cognitive layer in the choice process can result in the misprediction of equilibrium price outcomes in competitive markets.

The standard approach used in the industrial organisation literature to analyse prices in markets with differentiated products is the spatial competition model developed by Hotelling (1929). In its most basic form, the model conceives of two products, each produced by an independent firm. Along these lines, let us posit two firms that are located at either end of a unit segment [0,1] representing the product space. Suppose consumers are continuously and uniformly distributed along the segment. A consumer's location $x \in [0,1]$ identifies his relative preference between the two products. The consumer buys at most one unit of a single product, whence his utility from purchasing product j is given by

$$\tilde{U}_x = V - p_j - t|x - j| \tag{24.4}$$

where V is the common reservation price for the product, p_j is the price of product j and t parameterises the utility loss due to j's not being the consumer's ideal choice.

The model in (24.4) presumes the consumer's disutility from consuming a non-ideal product is linear in his distance from the product, which seems innocuous enough. But implicit in this formulation is the assumption that utility losses from the imperfect matching of choices and preferences are completely unavoidable, and that the consumer's acceptance of these losses is optimising behaviour.

Suppose instead[7] that the consumer can, subject to a convex cost, improve his attitude towards a chosen product, in essence relocating to be closer to it on the segment. (The cost of relocation may be convex if, say, self-persuasion is easy at first, but assembling arguments

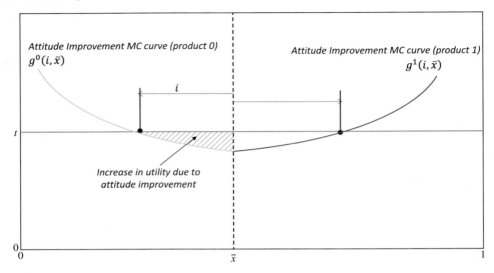

Figure 24.3   Product choice with attitude improvement

becomes increasingly difficult as one struggles to see a non-ideal product as increasingly aligned with one's ideal.) Figure 24.3 illustrates the analysis. A consumer will relocate up to the point that the benefit of doing so exceeds the cost, as indicated by the point of intersection of the convex 'attitude improvement marginal cost curve' with the linear incremental disutility cost t. As the figure shows, consumers who engage in attitude improvement towards their chosen product are better off: the consumer located initially at $\bar{x}$, if he were to choose product 0 and optimally adjust to it, would reduce his disutility by the shaded region.

Now suppose that this cost of attitude improvement differs for consumers with differing intensities of initial preference for the product – that is, the marginal cost g, as shown in the figure, is a function both of the individual's accumulated attitude improvement i and his initial location x. It turns out that the price that obtains in the market in equilibrium depends on the pattern of variation of g with x in the vicinity of the marginal (i.e., just indifferent) consumer. If the attitude improvement cost curves grow flatter as one moves in the direction of more brand-loyal consumers (i.e., nearer to 0 and 1), the equilibrium price will be higher. If instead the curves grow steeper in the direction of 0 and 1, the equilibrium price will be lower.

From a purely geometric standpoint, the price differences accrue to the introduction of nonlinearity into the Hotelling (1929) framework, and so they are predictable on the basis of that traditional model. If the disutility costs decline as one moves from marginal towards inframarginal consumers, then price increases result in reduced switching; consequently, prices will be higher. Correspondingly, if the disutility costs rise as one moves from marginal towards inframarginal consumers, then price increases result in increased switching, leading to lower prices in equilibrium.

Various measurable factors likely affect the pattern of attitude improvement relative to the strength of initial preference. Among consumers who do not have a strong initial liking for a product, those who are more intelligent, more open to experience, or less bandwidth-constrained may find adjustment easier than other people similarly situated. Products that are free from complicated, technical features invite easier adjustment by those without strong initial preferences relative to other products. In both cases, prices are predicted to be lower.

To the extent that such factors are demonstrated empirically to have the predicted effects, and to the extent that these effects can be distinguished from other possible causes, accounting for motivated preferences can be shown to be empirically relevant to the determination of prices.

Advertising and Motivated Preferences

In a model of differentiated product competition in which consumers are able to discretionarily improve their attitudes towards products, a natural extension is to envision the role of advertising as facilitating this otherwise costly process of self-persuasion. This conception, while novel, has precursors. The elaboration likelihood model posits the effectiveness of a stimulus at persuading consumers to be a function of the degree to which a consumer engages in thinking about information relevant to a persuasive issue (Petty and Cacioppo 1986; O'Keefe 2013). Such engagement, in turn, is influenced by a number of factors, including characteristics of the stimulus itself (e.g., an advertisement). A literature on the uses and gratifications more directly addresses advertising as a tool that consumers engage with for their own benefit (O'Donohoe 1994; Ko et al. 2005; Aitken et al. 2008; Phillips and McQuarrie 2010; Kim et al. 2015).

Examining advertising's role in consumers' attitude improvement serves two essential functions on the applied side. First, it points the way to the empirical validation of the predictions of a motivated preferences model of differentiated product pricing, as discussed in the previous subsection. Second, taking a motivated preferences perspective on advertising resolves important questions as concerns advertising's functional role that have remained unresolved in the economics and marketing literatures.

The model of differentiated products articulated in the previous subsection anticipates price effects that depend on the relationship of ease of self-persuasion (in essence) to strength of initial product preference. In the context of this model, advertising presents as a potential source of exogenous variation in the ease of self-persuasion for different consumers. One might therefore conceive of field experiments involving targeted advertising as an approach for empirically measuring predicted price effects. Specifically, advertising targeted at inframarginal consumers would be predicted to raise prices, while advertising targeted at marginal consumers should lower prices. Evaluating these hypotheses could provide validation of the price mechanism posited by the motivated preferences theory.

Advertising has been described in the literature as variously serving some combination of a persuasive role and an informative role (Bagwell 2007). Yet both the persuasive and informative theories of advertising face significant limitations. The notion of persuasion is at odds with the prevailing economic view that consumers' preferences are fixed; given this, traditional economics affords no basis for explaining why putative persuasive advertising should elicit a response from a rational consumer. Meanwhile, the notion that advertising can be informative is incontrovertible to a large extent – for example, advertising advises consumers on product features, price and availability. But advertising theorists have gone so far as to propose that even non-substantive advertisements – such as those projecting gauzy images of consumers and products, or attaching products to celebrities – convey, as valuable information, that *the product is advertised*. This, in turn, signals that the product must be of sufficiently high quality to have been worth the expenditure (Nelson 1974). But this theory fails to explain efforts devoted to the crafting of messages and images in ads otherwise devoid of informational content. If the purpose of such ads is just to show that money is being spent on the product, then such details should not matter.

Advertising's empirically observed effects on prices are likewise complex, resulting in a range of complex explanations in the literature. Often, the ideas boil down to the notion that observed outcomes – whether consumer price sensitivity is increased or decreased – depend upon which of multiple purposes in product marketing advertising happens to be serving in the observed instance. Popkowski Leszcyc and Rao (1990), for example, theorise that national advertising's purpose is to affect product preference, whence this form of advertising reduces price sensitivity; whereas local advertising's intent, to deliver immediate sales, explains why it engenders increased price sensitivity. Meanwhile, discussions in the literature of connections between observed price effects and psychological primitives have been limited, and to my knowledge, no one has offered a unifying primitive that can explain differing price effects across differing situations.

The theory that advertising facilitates self-persuasion offers such a unifying primitive. The same experimental designs that may be used to validate the motivated preference theory of prices in differentiated product markets also provide an approach to confirming the differing price effects of advertising on the basis of this theory. Meanwhile, the theory resolves the conceptual problem of advertising's role – proposing a basis according to which a rational individual might be productively influenced by non-informative advertising.

CONCLUDING REMARKS

This chapter has discussed a new theoretical framework of consumer choice according to which bounded rationality gives rise to the malleability of preferences. We pointed to the empirical relevance of this construct as an explanation of several phenomena superior to existing explanations. We also pointed to ways in which the predictions that arise based on the motivated preferences theory may be taken to data.

Other enticing possibilities for ways in which motivated preferences might play out exist beyond the scope of what was covered here. For example, individuals often make choices between risky options and riskless alternatives. It is quite conceivable that thinking focused on the match between one's risk preferences and the relative riskiness inherent in a particular choice could be complementary to making that choice, such one might observe adjustments in measured risk preferences concurrent with the adoption of choices. (For example, an individual who goes bungee jumping may become more risk-loving concurrent with electing to bungee jump.)

The further empirical and experimental examination of phenomena in which cognitive processes play a role in determining actions and market outcomes remains a largely unexplored area. As economists grow more accustomed to measuring psychological phenomena that play a role in markets and exchanges, the scope for more precise models of behaviour, supported or supportable by evidence, will continue to grow.

NOTES

1. In a very recent paper, Bernheim et al. (2021) conceive of individuals who choose among 'worldviews' that, in turn, influence the utility levels the individual obtains from experiences. The mechanism they posit for preference adjustment differs from that proposed by motivated preferences; their approach offers explanations of many of the same phenomena.

2. Nagler (2022) develops a full formal model of choice and complementary attitude adjustment.
3. The notion of a production function for satisfaction derives from Becker (1965), as more fully exposited in Michael and Becker (1973). Becker and his collaborators have used this approach to explain diverse behaviours that appear *prima facie* to represent changing tastes, including addiction and effect stemming from the accumulation of human capital (Stigler and Becker 1977; Becker and Murphy 1988). However, Becker's function does not admit discretionary cognition as an input, nor has he explicitly incorporated personal efforts at attitude improvement as a part of his theory.
4. Results summarised in the figure are more fully developed in Nagler (2022).
5. Through this construct, we may incorporate inter alia agents who engage in motivated reasoning (e.g., Kunda 1990).
6. See Nagler (2022) for a full development of the results presented in this figure.
7. For a complete analysis, see Nagler (2021).

REFERENCES

Aitken, R., Gray, B., Lawson, R., 2008. Advertising effectiveness from a consumer perspective. *International Journal of Advertising, 27*(2), 279–297.

Akerlof, G. A., Dickens, W. T., 1982. The economic consequences of cognitive dissonance. *American Economic Review, 72*(3), 307–319.

Aronson, E., 2004. *The social animal*, 9th Edition. Worth Publishers.

Azar, Ofer H., 2019. Do fixed payments affect effort? Examining relative thinking in mixed compensation schemes. *Journal of Economic Psychology, 70*, 52–66.

Bagwell, K., 2007. The economic analysis of advertising. *Handbook of industrial organization, 3*, 1701–1844.

Becker, G. S., 1965. A theory of the allocation of time. *Economic Journal, 75*(299), 493–517.

Becker, G. S., Murphy, K. M., 1988. A theory of rational addiction. *Journal of Political Economy, 96*(4), 675–700.

Bernheim, B. D., Braghieri, L., Martínez-Marquina, A., Zuckerman, D., 2021. A theory of chosen preferences. *American Economic Review, 111*(2), 720–754.

Chatterjee, P., Irmak, C., Rose, R. L., 2013. The endowment effect as self-enhancement in response to threat. *Journal of Consumer Research, 40*(3), 460–476.

Chetty, R., Szeidl, A., 2016. Consumption commitments and habit formation. *Econometrica, 84*(2), 855–890.

Dommer, S. L., Swaminathan, V., 2013. Explaining the endowment effect through ownership: The role of identity, gender, and self-threat. *Journal of Consumer Research, 39*(5), 1034–1050.

Ericson, K. M. M., Fuster, A., 2011. Expectations as endowments: Evidence on reference-dependent preferences from exchange and valuation experiments. *Quarterly Journal of Economics, 126*(4), 1879–1907.

Eyster, E., 2002. Rationalizing the past: A taste for consistency. Nuffield College Mimeograph.

Festinger, L., 1962. *A theory of cognitive dissonance*. Vol. 2. Stanford, CA: Stanford University Press.

Festinger, L., Carlsmith, J. M., 1959. Cognitive consequences of forced compliance. *Journal of Abnormal and Social Psychology, 58*(2), 203.

Hotelling, H., 1929. Stability in competition. *Economic Journal, 39*(153), 41–57.

Izuma, K., Matsumoto, M., Murayama, K., Samejima, K., Sadato, N., Matsumoto, K., 2010. Neural correlates of cognitive dissonance and choice-induced preference change. *Proceedings of the National Academy of Sciences, 107*(51), 22014–22019.

Jarcho, J. M., Berkman, E. T., Lieberman, M. D., 2011. The neural basis of rationalization: Cognitive dissonance reduction during decision-making. *Social Cognitive and Affective Neuroscience, 6*(4), 460–467.

Kahneman, D., Knetsch, J. L., Thaler, R. H., 1990. Experimental tests of the endowment effect and the coase theorem. *Journal of Political Economy, 98* (6), 1325–1348.

Kahneman, D., Knetsch, J. L., Thaler, R. H., 1991. Anomalies: The endowment effect, loss aversion, and status quo bias. *Journal of Economic Perspectives, 5*(1), 193–206.

Kim, J., Lee, J., Jo, S., Jung, J., Kang, J., 2015. Magazine reading experience and advertising engagement: A uses and gratifications perspective. *Journalism & Mass Communication Quarterly, 92*(1), 179–198.

Kitayama, S., Chua, H. F., Tompson, S., Han, S., 2013. Neural mechanisms of dissonance: An fMRI investigation of choice justification. *NeuroImage, 69*, 206–212.

Kitayama, S., Snibbe, A. C., Markus, H. R., Suzuki, T., 2004. Is there any 'free' choice? Self and dissonance in two cultures. *Psychological Science, 15*(8), 527–533.

Ko, H., Cho, C.-H., Roberts, M. S., 2005. Internet uses and gratifications: A structural equation model of interactive advertising. *Journal of Advertising, 34*(2), 57–70.

Kőszegi, B., Szeidl, A., 2013. A model of focusing in economic choice. *The Quarterly Journal of Economics, 128*(1), 53–104.

Kunda, Z., 1990. The case for motivated reasoning. *Psychological Bulletin, 108*(3), 480–498.

Lieberman, M. D., Ochsner, K. N., Gilbert, D. T., Schacter, D. L., 2001. Do amnesics exhibit cognitive dissonance reduction? The role of explicit memory and attention in attitude change. *Psychological Science, 12*(2), 135–140.

List, J. A., 2003. Does market experience eliminate market anomalies? *Quarterly Journal of Economics, 118*(1), 41–71.

List, J. A., 2004. Neoclassical theory versus prospect theory: Evidence from the market-place. *Econometrica, 72*(2), 615–625.

Michael, Robert T., Gary S. Becker, 1973. On the new theory of consumer behavior. *Swedish Journal of Economics, 75*, 378–396.

Mittelstaedt, R., 1969. A dissonance approach to repeat purchasing behavior. *Journal of Marketing Research, 6*(4), 444–446.

Morewedge, C. K., Shu, L. L., Gilbert, D. T., Wilson, T. D., 2009. Bad riddance or good rubbish? Ownership and not loss aversion causes the endowment effect. *Journal of Experimental Social Psychology, 45*(4), 947–951.

Nagler, M. G., 2021. Loving what you get: The price effects of consumer self-persuasion. *Review of Industrial Organization, 59*, no. 3 (November), 529–560.

Nagler, M. G., 2022. Thoughts matter: A theory of motivated preference. *Theory and Decision*, forthcoming.

Nelson, P., 1974. Advertising as information. *Journal of Political Economy, 82*(4), 729–754.

O'Donohoe, S., 1994. Advertising uses and gratifications. *European Journal of Marketing, 28*(8/9), 52–75.

O'Keefe, Daniel J., 2013. The elaboration likelihood model. *The Sage Handbook of Persuasion: Developments in Theory and Practice*, 137–149.

Petty, R. E., Cacioppo, J. T., 1986. The elaboration likelihood model of persuasion. In *Communication and persuasion* (pp. 1–24). New York: Springer.

Phillips, B. J., McQuarrie, E. F., 2010. Narrative and persuasion in fashion advertising. *Journal of Consumer Research, 37*(3), 368–392.

Popkowski Leszczyc, P. T., Rao, R. C., 1990. An empirical analysis of national and local advertising effect on price elasticity. *Marketing Letters, 1*(2), 149–160.

Qin, J., Kimel, S., Kitayama, S., Wang, X., Yang, X., Han, S., 2011. How choice modifies preference: Neural correlates of choice justification. *NeuroImage, 55*(1), 240–246.

Rabin, M., 1998. Psychology and economics. *Journal of Economic Literature, 36*(1), 11–46.

Rozen, K., 2010. Foundations of intrinsic habit formation. *Econometrica, 78*(4), 1341–1373.

Sharot, T., De Martino, B., Dolan, R. J., 2009. How choice reveals and shapes expected hedonic outcome. *Journal of Neuroscience, 29*(12), 3760–3765.

Sharot, T., Velasquez, C. M., Dolan, R. J., 2010. Do decisions shape preference? Evidence from blind choice. *Psychological Science, 21*(9), 1231–1235.

Staw, B. M., 1976. Knee-deep in the big muddy: A study of escalating commitment to a chosen course of action. *Organizational Behavior and Human Performance, 16*(1), 27–44.

Stigler, George J., Becker, Gary S., 1977. De gustibus non est disputandum. *The American Economic Review, 67*(2), 76–90.

Svirsky, D., 2014. Money is no object: Testing the endowment effect in exchange goods. *Journal of Economic Behavior and Organization, 106*, 227–234.

Thaler, R., 1980. Toward a positive theory of consumer choice. *Journal of Economic Behavior and Organization, 1*(1), 39–60.

Tompson, S., Chua, H. F., Kitayama, S., 2016. Connectivity between mpfc and pcc predicts post-choice attitude change: The self-referential processing hypothesis of choice justification. *Human Brain Mapping, 37*(11), 3810–3820.

Van Veen, V., Krug, M. K., Schooler, J. W., Carter, C. S., 2009. Neural activity predicts attitude change in cognitive dissonance. *Nature Neuroscience, 12*(11), 1469–1474.

Wakslak, C. J., 2012. The experience of cognitive dissonance in important and trivial domains: A construal-level theory approach. *Journal of Experimental Social Psychology, 48*(6), 1361–1364.

Wathieu, L., 2004. Consumer habituation. *Management Science, 50*(5), 587–596.

25. Might ambiguity exist when none seems to exist?

Mina Mahmoudi, Mark Pingle and Rattaphon Wuthisatian

INTRODUCTION

Because risk preferences tend to influence choices under uncertainty and because choices under uncertainty are ubiquitous, many scholars have worked on developing methods for eliciting and characterising risk preferences. (See Charness, Gneezy and Imas (2013) and Holt and Laury (2014) for good reviews). Common to all the methods is the assumption that human subjects experience no ambiguity when the administrators of the experiments present probabilities to subjects in a transparent manner. This chapter considers the possibility that we humans may experience ambiguity, or effectively experience it because of our bounded rationality, even when we know the probabilities of uncertain events.

Gilboa and Schmeidler (1989) provide a general model of ambiguity known as the maxmin expected utility model. The logic underlying this model is that the decision maker recognises that many different probability distributions may apply to a given set of possible outcomes. Applying a different distribution will tend to yield a different expected utility. Not knowing which probability distribution applies, the maxmin criterion proposes that the decision maker is pessimistic to the extreme. For each possible choice, the decision maker assumes the probability distribution that applies is the one that will minimise the expected utility for that choice. The decision maker then makes the choice that maximises this minimal utility. The pessimism built into this maxmin model can explain ambiguity aversion, which Ellsberg (1961) identified by looking at data from his seminal experiment.

While ambiguity aversion is common, it is not universal. Among others, Trautmann and van de Kuilen (2015) present experimental evidence indicating people may be ambiguity seeking as well as ambiguity averse. For this reason, the alpha-maxmin expected utility model (α-$MMEU$) is of interest (Frick, Iijima and Le Yaouanq, 2020). The α-$MMEU$ model generalises the maxmin expected utility model in the same way the Hurwicz (1951) criterion generalises the minimax criterion. There is a parameter, α, that can shift weight from the extremely pessimistic maxmin criterion to the extremely optimistic maxmax criterion. By admitting different values for α, the α-$MMEU$ model allows different decision makers to have preferences toward ambiguity expressed as varying degrees of optimism.

If there is no ambiguity, as we normally assume when experiment administrators transparently present human subjects with probabilities for uncertain outcomes, then a subject's degree of optimism is of no consequence. However, the degree of optimism (or pessimism) becomes increasingly consequential as the level of ambiguity increases. As we illustrate in the following, when we admit ambiguity as a possibility so the degree of optimism can play a role, it is possible to explain anomalous decision behaviour that we cannot readily explain when we assume there is no ambiguity.

We examine data from an experiment where the same subject makes corresponding choices under total ambiguity and 'no ambiguity'. We place no ambiguity in quotes here because the hypothesis we explore is that subjects experience ambiguity even when there apparently is none. Under total ambiguity, subjects receive no information about probabilities; they only observe possible outcomes. By examining the behaviour of subjects under total ambiguity, we have a baseline in terms of how subjects cope with ambiguity. When we then examine behaviour under 'no ambiguity', where subjects transparently observe both probabilities and possible outcomes, we can examine whether the behaviour exhibited under total ambiguity spills over to the 'no ambiguity' case.

We find we cannot readily explain choice behaviour in our No Ambiguity Treatment using risk aversion alone. Specifically, as the variance of a prospect increases while holding the expected value constant, we find the level of relative risk aversion of the average subject not only does not stay constant but also fluctuates down, up and down, without a discernable pattern. Under constant relative risk aversion, with the expected value held constant, a subject would find a higher variance prospect less attractive. This is not the case for our average subject. Indeed, we have two anomalous behaviours in our No Ambiguity Treatment to explain: (1) the most preferred prospect is not the prospect with the lowest variance but one with an intermediate variance level, and (2) the attractiveness of the prospect does not decrease, as the variance increases, as fast as constant relative risk aversion predicts.

We find that admitting the possibility of ambiguity helps explain these two anomalies. When facing total ambiguity, we find that subjects reduce their optimism as the size of the largest possible outcome increases, but the reduction of the optimism does not occur at a rate sufficient to hold the 'implicit expected value' of the prospect constant. Put differently, the average subject facing ambiguity believes a larger possible outcome will be less likely, but the increase in the size of the outcome weighs heavier in the mind of the subject. When we humans observe probabilities transparently, we may nonetheless effectively experience ambiguity because we may not have the cognitive capacity to apply the probabilities to outcomes precisely enough to make decisions with the precision predicted by expected utility theory. Because we need to apply some method when we make a decision, it is reasonable to think that the method we use under total ambiguity might spill over. If the size of the largest outcome especially motivates us, which it clearly did with our human subjects when they faced total ambiguity, then it could explain why we might find an increase in the variance of a prospect more attractive rather than less when we know the probabilities. Risk aversion will eventually make a prospect less attractive when the variance is high enough. However, an affinity for larger possible outcomes not only can explain why the attractiveness of higher variance prospects does not decrease like constant relative risk aversion predicts, but also it can explain why a prospect of intermediate variance may be most attractive, as is the case for our average subject.

Our chapter proceeds as follows. In the next section, we present a version of the alpha-maxmin expected utility model and relate it to the lottery pricing task subjects perform in our experiment. We then present our experiment. Next, we report bidding behaviour in our 'No Ambiguity Treatment', where subjects know probabilities. We then present theory and review some previous research that indicates subjects may experience ambiguity, even when they know probabilities, because of bounded rationality. Next, we demonstrate that the alpha-maxmin model can capture the behaviour of our subjects. We first fit the model to the choices made by subjects in our 'Total Ambiguity Treatment'. Then, we fit the model to the choices made by subjects in our No Ambiguity Treatment, illustrating we can better explain the data in this No Ambiguity Treatment by recognising the possibility of ambiguity than by assuming it does not exist. We conclude with a discussion of the implications of these findings for future research.

THE ALPHA-MAXMIN EXPECTED UTILITY MODEL

To have a framework where ambiguity may be present to varying degrees, we use a version of the α-*MMEU* model presented by Melkonyan and Pingle (2010). We examine the simplest case, where there are only two possible outcomes, X_{max} and X_{min}. In this case, the decision maker DM perceives the value of a prospect $(X_{max}, p; X_{min}, 1-p)$ to be

$$V = [1-\lambda]\left[pU(X_{max})+[1-p]U(X_{min})\right] \\ + \lambda\left[\alpha U(X_{max})+[1-\alpha]U(X_{min})\right]. \quad (25.1)$$

The parameter λ measures the degree of ambiguity; α measures the degree of optimism (or equivalently the degree of ambiguity tolerance); p is the probability of obtaining the larger X_{max} outcome when there is no ambiguity; and $1-p$ is the probability of obtaining the smaller X_{min} outcome when there is no ambiguity.

Let X denote the subject's bid on the lottery. In the experiment described in the following, the Becker, DeGroot and Marschak (1964) process was used to simulate competition and motivation subjects to bid their maximum willingness to pay for the lottery. Theoretically, the maximum willingness to pay is the bid level that makes the net value of the prospect just equal to the value of the subject's endowment. That is, the bid X that maximises the willingness to pay will satisfy the equation.

$$U(W) = [1-\lambda]\left[pU(W-X+X_{max})+[1-p]U(W-X+X_{min})\right] \\ + \lambda\left[\alpha U(W-X+X_{max})+[1-\alpha]U(W-X+X_{min})\right]. \quad (25.2)$$

Assuming subjects exhibit constant relative risk aversion, the isoelastic utility function uniquely captures subject risk preferences. Applying the isoelastic function $U(c)=\dfrac{c^{1-\rho}-1}{1-\rho}$ for $\rho \neq 0$, condition (2) becomes[1]

$$\frac{W^{1-\rho}-1}{1-\rho} = [1-\lambda]\left[p\frac{[W-X+X_{max}]^{1-\rho}-1}{1-\rho}+[1-p]\frac{[W-X+X_{min}]^{1-\rho}-1}{1-\rho}\right] \\ + \lambda\left[\alpha\frac{[W-X+X_{max}]^{1-\rho}-1}{1-\rho}+[1-\alpha]\frac{[W-X+X_{min}]^{1-\rho}-1}{1-\rho}\right] \quad (25.3)$$

AN EXPERIMENT DESIGNED TO COMPARE BEHAVIOUR: NO AMBIGUITY VERSUS TOTAL AMBIGUITY

We are interested in estimating model (25.3) under different assumptions, and we can do so using data obtained from an experiment described fully in Mahmoudi and Pingle (2018). In

Table 25.1   Experimental design: no ambiguity

Outcome		Probability		Expected value
High	Low	p (high)	$1-p$ (low)	
5	1	0.500	0.500	3.00
9	1	0.250	0.750	3.00
21	1	0.100	0.900	3.00
201	1	0.010	0.990	3.00

the experiment, human subjects competitively bid for an investment opportunity that is a simple lottery. Becker, DeGroot and Marschak's (1964) competition motivates each subject to bid up to their personal maximum that satisfies the models (25.2) and (25.3). All 50 subjects played this investment game multiple times in two treatments: a No Ambiguity Treatment and a Total Ambiguity Treatment.

Table 25.1 presents the experimental design for the No Ambiguity Treatment. Each subject plays four different games. In a given game, the subject competes for the opportunity to play the lottery prospect by offering a bid. Each prospect offers a low outcome gain of one dollar, while the high outcome gain varies across the prospects: 5, 9, 21 or 201. The subject is informed that the high outcome will occur with probability p and that the low outcome occurs with probability $1-p$. To make probability information transparent, the experiment administrator shows the subjects a clear plastic bag that contains blue and red beads. By examining the bag, any subject could count the number of beads in total and the number of each colour, allowing each subject to readily see that the proportion of blue beads was p and the proportion of red beads was $1 - p$. As shown in Table 25.1, the experimental design was such that the probability p decreases as the high outcome increases, so the expected value of each prospect is $3.00.

As in the No Ambiguity Treatment, subjects competitively bid for a given prospect in the Total Ambiguity Treatment, and subjects received information on the possible prospect outcomes for the four prospects shown in Table 25.1. However, subjects in the Total Ambiguity Treatment received no information on the likelihoods. Specifically, the administrator informed subjects of the true total number of red and blue beads in an opaque urn, but not the number of blue versus red beds.

BEHAVIOUR ASSUMING NO AMBIGUITY

If a subject perceives no ambiguity and has preferences that exhibit constant relative risk aversion, then the optimal bid obtained from model (25.3) is precisely determined by the subject's degree of risk aversion ρ. Table 25.2 reports the mean bid of the 50 subjects in the No Ambiguity Treatment, for each of the four lottery prospects, along with the optimal bid obtained from model (25.3) for various risk aversion levels. If the subject is risk neutral (i.e., $\rho=0.00$), then the optimal bid obtained from model (25.3) is $X = \$3$ for each prospect, as shown in the fourth column of Table 25.2. Alternatively, if the subject is risk averse (i.e., $\rho>0$), the optimal bid decreases as the variance of the prospect increases, as shown in columns 5–8 in Table 25.2. Column 3 in Table 25.2 is included to present an example of the optimal bid

Table 25.2   Actual mean bids versus optimal bids assuming constant relative risk aversion

Stake	Actual mean bid	Optimal bids by risk aversion level					
		$\rho=(.30)$	$\rho=0.00$	$\rho=0.18$	$\rho=0.47$	$\rho=0.70$	$\rho=1.86$
5	2.64	3.06	3.00	2.96	2.91	2.86	2.64
9	3.00	3.17	3.00	2.90	2.76	2.66	2.23
21	2.50	3.43	3.00	2.78	2.50	2.31	1.73
201	2.34	5.18	3.00	2.34	1.75	1.49	1.11

pattern when the subject is risk seeking (i.e., $\rho<0$); the bid increases as the variance of the prospect increases.

Examining the actual mean bids, we find that the average subject is risk averse, as we might expect, but there are two aspects of the mean bid pattern we cannot explain using the assumption that subjects exhibit constant relative risk aversion. The primary problem is that the peak mean bid occurs at the intermediate level stake 9, rather than at the minimum stake 5. A second problem is the bid patterns in columns 5–8 indicate the mean bid does not decrease as fast as constant relative risk aversion indicates.

We chose the parameter value $\rho=1.86$ in column 8 so the optimal value was 2.64 for the stake 5 prospect, equal to the actual mean value. The other optimal bids shown in column 8 indicate that the average bid should have decreased much faster than it actually did if the relative risk aversion level for the average subject remained constant as the stake increased. Keeping $\rho=1.86$, the average subject mean should be 1.11 for stake 201, but the actual mean was 2.34.

To produce column 6, we chose $\rho=0.47$, which produces an optimal bid for stake 21 of 2.50, equal to the mean actually bid. Examining the other optimal bids, we find that the actual mean for stake 201 is much greater than the optimal bid (i.e., 2.34 > 1.75), while the actual mean bid for stake 5 is less than the optimal bid (i.e., 2.64 < 2.91). If we reduce the level of risk aversion to $\rho=0.18$, as shown in column 5, the optimal bid is equal to the actual mean of 2.34 for the 201 stake. Examining the other stakes for this risk aversion level, we find that the optimal bids tend to be much higher than the actual bids for stake levels 5 and 21.

If subjects neither experience nor perceive ambiguity, then the mean bids presented in Table 25.2 indicate the relative risk aversion of the average subject changes non-monotonically as the variance of the prospect increases while holding the expected value constant. When the variance increases from the 5 stake prospect to the 9 stake prospect, the risk aversion parameter decreases substantially from $\rho=1.86$ to $\rho=0.00$. When the variance increases further from the 9 stake prospect to the 21 stake prospect, the estimate of the risk aversion parameter increases from $\rho=0.00$ to $\rho=0.47$. Finally, when the variance increases still further from the 21 stake to the 201 stake prospect, the estimate of the risk aversion parameter decreases from $\rho=0.47$ to $\rho=0.18$.

Because each subject plays each of the four games shown in Table 25.1, we can use those four games to estimate the best fit value for ρ for each of the 50 subjects. Of course, the evidence just presented indicates the value of or ρ tends to vary for the average subject as the stake changes. However, as long as the variation is relatively consistent across subjects, then the distribution of estimates we obtain should still roughly capture the variation in risk aversion across the subjects.

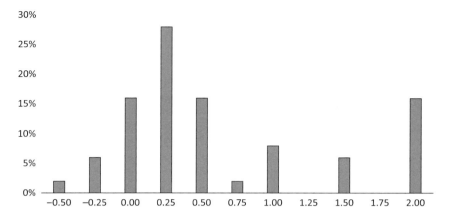

Figure 25.1   Distribution of relative risk aversion

Figure 25.1 presents the distribution of relative risk aversion we obtain by estimating the best fit value of ρ for each subject. The median for this distribution is 0.18, indicating the median person is slightly risk averse. Twelve of the 50 subjects, or 24 per cent, had an estimate $\rho<0$, indicating risk-seeking preferences on average rather than risk-averse preferences. Eight, or 16 per cent, had an estimate $\rho=0$, indicating risk-neutral preferences. Nineteen, or 38 per cent, had an estimate $0<\rho<0.9$, which we might label slight to moderate risk aversion. Eleven, or 2 per cent, had an estimate $\rho>1$, which we might label substantial risk aversion.

If a subject has a constant relative risk aversion level, then the choices will decrease monotonically as the variance of the prospect increases. A total of 32 subjects, or 64 per cent, made choices consistent with constant relative risk aversion. Of these, two exhibited pure risk neutrality, bidding 3 on each of the prospects; nine exhibited risk-seeking preferences by bidding 4 or more on a prospect and not decreasing a bid as the variance increased; and 21 exhibited risk aversion by bidding 2 or less on a prospect and not increasing the bid as the variance increased. Thus, our experiment provides evidence that a large share of people makes choices consistent with constant relative risk aversion.

While it is possible that the exceptionally high bid for the 9 stake prospect is an aberrant, non-replicable result, we are interested in the possibility that is a replicable result caused by ambiguity. Of course, there are subjects who make inexplicable choices, and this reduces the systematic nature of the data. However, nine of the 50 subjects, or 22 per cent, made a higher bid for the 9 stake prospect than for any other prospect. Such a high proportion indicates there was something especially attractive about the 9 stake prospect compared to the other prospects.

As we proceed, we seek to examine the degree to which ambiguity as presented in the alpha-maxmin model can explain the choice behaviour we observe in our data that risk aversion alone does not well explain. To explain our data, we need to explain why subjects might find a prospect more attractive that has an intermediate level variance rather than a small or large variance. We also need to explain why, as the variance increases, the average bid does not decrease as fast as constant relative risk aversion predicts. One explanation could be that there is no ambiguity, and risk aversion changes as the variance increases, but the alternative we seek to explore is that ambiguity is playing a role.

A THEORY RELATING BOUNDED RATIONALITY TO AMBIGUITY

As Mahmoudi and Pingle (2018) note, there are reasons to think bounds to rationality create ambiguity. People do not have the cognitive capacity to perceive numeric magnitudes precisely, though training can improve this capacity (Peters and Par, 2015). Experimental studies indicate understanding probability requires higher-level cognition, something young children often cannot manage (Falk and Wilkening, 1998). A probability is useful because it characterises the degree of uncertainty in a specific way, but it is nonetheless a heuristic (Mulligan, 2013 and Crovelli, 2012). Karelitz and Budescu (2004, p. 26) conclude, 'Except in very special cases, all representations of uncertainties are vague to some degree in the minds of the originators and in the minds of the receivers'.

Heiner (1983) proposes that people use heuristics, or imperfect behavioural rules, to address what he calls the 'competence-difficulty gap', or C-D gap. Comparing two uncertain prospects is not an entirely simple task, so there will tend to be a C-D gap, and it is sensible to think the C-D gap will vary across decision makers. For example, those trained in statistics might be able to use that training to compare different uncertain prospects more effectively. Nonetheless, it is reasonable to think we all will have a C-D as they are uncertain prospects that are more complex.

How might people cope with a C-D gap when facing uncertainty? Heiner's (1983) general answer is people cope by using heuristics. In terms of finding a more specific answer, the work of Jeske and Ute (2008) is particularly applicable. Jeske and Ute present neurological evidence that people distinguish outcomes from probabilities when they make decisions under risk. Outcomes and probabilities activate different areas of the brain. Important for our work, they find, 'the brain is much more responsive to changes in gain size than to equivalent changes in probability' (Jeske and Ute, 2008, p. 52). That is, it appears that we humans cope with the difficulty of evaluating uncertain prospects by disproportionately focusing on outcomes, even when probabilities are transparently available.

The ubiquitous presence of ambiguity may explain why our minds focus more on changes in outcomes than on changes in probabilities. Under total ambiguity, no information is available on outcomes. To be able to make a decision in this situation, we must have some method for making a choice only using the possible outcomes. The minmax, maxmin and the more general Hurwicz criterion are examples of heuristics people might use under total ambiguity. If information is available on probabilities, would people entirely abandon the heuristics they find effective under ambiguity? Perhaps, but it is also reasonable to at least a remnant would remain, and a strong candidate is a heuristic that gives disproportionate attention to outcomes.

When Jeske and Ute (2008, p. 62) found people disproportionately focus on outcomes, they had presented subjects with full information on probabilities. To explain their result, they first note, 'information about probability might be useless without the corresponding information on outcome, but not necessarily vice versa'. Given this fact, they provide the following theory: 'This inherent asymmetry alone might explain the overall finding that participants spent more time looking at outcomes' when probabilities are available.

To summarise, there is theory and evidence that the ubiquitous presence of ambiguity trains us to use heuristics that spill over into situations where probabilities are transparently available. Moreover, there is specific evidence that the average person will give disproportionate attention to changes in outcomes compared to the attention given to changes in probabilities.

WHY MIGHT THE ALPHA-MAXMIN MODEL CAPTURE HOW DECISION MAKERS COPE WITH AMBIGUITY?

When people have full information on probabilities and outcomes, they may apply decision heuristics that expected utility theory captures effectively, but perceived ambiguity or bounded rationality may lead people to use heuristics that bias decision making away from expected utility theory. The alpha-maxmin model (1) has the capability of capturing particular types of systematic bias.

If people cope with ambiguity or their bounded rationality by giving weights to outcomes that are distinct and independent from the probability weights that expected utility theory gives, then the alpha-maxmin model may capture it. If $\lambda=0$ in model (1), then there is no bias, and expected utility theory applies. If $\lambda>0$, then there will be a bias that depends upon the relationship between the probability level p and the degree of optimism α.

If $\alpha<p$, then the decision maker is biased toward placing more weight on the smaller outcome X_{min} than expected utility theory indicates. Thus, in this case, the decision maker is more pessimistic, or seemingly more risk averse, than expected utility alone would predict. Formally, this is ambiguity aversion. Alternatively, if $\alpha<p$, then the decision maker is biased towards placing more weight on the larger outcome X_{max} than expected utility theory indicates. In this case, the decision maker is more optimistic, or seemingly more risk seeking, than expected utility alone would predict. Formally, this is ambiguity-seeking behaviour. Importantly, when there is some ambiguity (i.e., $\lambda>0$), anomalous behaviours under uncertainty need not be explained by variations in the degree of risk aversion, but they can also be explained by variations in the degree of optimism parameter α.

BEHAVIOUR UNDER TOTAL AMBIGUITY

Under total ambiguity, a decision maker has no opportunity to apply expected utility theory. In this case, where $\lambda=1$, the alpha-maxmin model (1) reduces to the Hurwicz criterion. The Hurwicz criterion reduces to the maxmax criterion when $\alpha=1$. In this case, the decision maker is as optimistic as possible. The Hurwicz criterion reduces to the maxmin criterion when $\alpha=0$. In this case, the decision maker is as pessimistic as possible. The general Hurwicz model admits a varying degree of optimism.

Using data collected on subjects in the total ambiguity condition, we can estimate model (3) under the assumption of total ambiguity. In particular, if we assume a particular level of risk aversion ρ, then a given bid choice X for a given prospect will imply there will be a specific optimism level α that supports the choice (i.e., satisfies model (3)). A higher bid implies more optimism or a larger α value. Mahmoudi and Pingle (2018) found $\rho=0.69$ was the constant level of risk aversion that best fit the pattern of average bids in the No Ambiguity Treatment. Assuming this level of risk aversion applies to each subject, we can find the value of α for each subject and prospect in the Total Ambiguity Treatment.

Table 25.3 presents estimates of the mean level of optimism for each stake level for the subjects in the Total Ambiguity Treatment,[2] along with some other useful data. For purposes of comparison, we show the probabilities of the large outcome for each stake level for the No Ambiguity Treatment and the associated expected value of 3 for each stake level. As will be explained further below, the optimism estimates imply an expected value under total ambiguity, so we also show the implicit expected values the Total Ambiguity Treatment in Table 25.3.

Table 25.3   Estimated mean level of optimism by stake level

	No ambiguity		Total ambiguity	
Stake level	Probability of large outcome	Expected value of the prospect	Mean estimate for optimism parameter α under total ambiguity	Implicit expected value of the prospect
5 stake	0.50	3.00	0.37	2.46
9 stake	0.25	3.00	0.28	3.22
21 stake	0.10	3.00	0.17	4.40
201 stake	0.01	3.00	0.05	10.02

Examining the optimism level estimates in Table 25.3, the key finding is that subjects decrease their level of optimism as the stake size increases. The principle of insufficient reason, also known as the principle of indifference, hypothesises that subjects in total ambiguity facing two possible outcomes will allocate a 0.5 probability to each because there is no information available to indicate that one outcome is more likely. The observed decreasing estimate for α in Table 25.3 clearly rejects the hypothesis that people apply the principle of insufficient reason. The parameter α under total ambiguity is comparable to the probability parameter p under no ambiguity because α, like the probability p, is the weight the decision maker places on the larger outcome. Rather than allocate equal weight to each outcome, as the principle of insufficient reason suggests, subjects allocate less weight to the large outcome as it gets larger relative to the small outcome.

If we compare the estimated values of α in Table 25.3 to the probability values of p for the prospects in the No Ambiguity Treatment, we observe an interesting pattern: the probability p decreases faster than the degree of optimism α. Remember, the No Ambiguity Treatment is designed to keep the expected value equal as the stake and variance increased, as shown in Table 25.3. To accomplish this, the probability of the large outcome decreases in a manner roughly proportionate to the increase in the large outcome. The data in Table 25.3 indicates when subjects observe the same change in prospect outcomes without any information about likelihoods, they decrease the weight they put on the larger outcome as it increases, but the rate of decrease in the weight is not sufficient to keep the expected outcome constant.

In particular, if we apply the parameter α weights shown in Table 25.3 to the outcomes, so we get a valuation comparable to the expected value, we find the values for the stake levels 5, 9, 21 and 201 are 2.46, 3.22, 4.40 and 10.02 as shown in the table. That is, in valuation terms, subjects in total ambiguity are increasingly optimistic about the value of the prospect as the variance of the prospect increases. If this behaviour spills over into uncertain situations where there is no apparent ambiguity, then the optimism generating the higher valuation of more risky prospects can override the subject's risk aversion. In that case, a risk-averse subject may find a higher stake, higher variance prospect more attractive.

When we examine the behaviour of individual subjects, most individuals had an optimism estimate pattern similar to the pattern for the average shown in Table 25.3. In particular, 29 of the 50 subjects had a monotonically decreasing pattern for the level of optimism estimates, becoming less optimistic as the variance of the stake increased. Only three of these 29 subjects had an estimate for α that was less than or equal to the $p=.01$ probability for the 201 stake large outcome. Thus, the 29 subjects nearly all decreased their rate of optimism more slowly than the probability decreased. The only other evident pattern among the 50 subjects was the fact that nine of 50 subjects exhibited a level of optimism with 'a hump'. These nine were most optimistic on the 9 stake prospect, less optimistic on the 21 stake prospect and then even less optimistic on the 201 stake prospect. The remaining 12 subjects did not have a discernable pattern to their estimated level of optimism.

ILLUSTRATING AND ESTIMATING THE ROLE AMBIGUITY MAY PLAY IN EXPLAINING RISKY CHOICE BEHAVIOUR

When we observe the mean bid choices of the 50 subjects in the No Ambiguity Treatment presented in Table 25.2, there are two patterns that correlate with two results in the previous section that indicate ambiguity may be affecting choice behaviour even when the probability information is transparently available. First, there is a hump in the mean level of choices in Table 25.2 at the intermediate 9 stake level. Correspondingly, when those same subjects made choices under total ambiguity a sizeable share, nine of 50 or 18 per cent, exhibited the highest level of optimism under total ambiguity at the intermediate 9 stake level. Second, as the variance increases with the stake, the mean bid choices in Table 25.2 do not decrease as fast as constant relative risk aversion predicts. Correspondingly, the implicit valuations of prospects with the identical outcomes increased as the stake increased under total ambiguity.

Observing this evidence that ambiguity is influencing choice behaviour in a systematic way in the No Ambiguity set of games, we seek to fit the general alpha-maxmin model (25.1) to our data using the specific model (25.3). To fit the model, we must make some assumptions. The standard approach is to assume no ambiguity is present because subjects transparently observe the probabilities. This simplifies the estimation because assuming no ambiguity for all subjects (i.e., $\lambda=0$) implies any subject's degree of optimism α also can be ignored for it can have no impact on choice. The cost of the strict assumption is any deviations in average choice behaviour from constant relative risk aversion must be explained by changes in the average estimate for the constant relative risk aversion parameter ρ.

We will be less restrictive by admitting the possibility of ambiguity (i.e., $\lambda>0$), which implies a subject's degree of optimism α will impact choice. To comparably maintain a set of relatively restrictive assumptions, we will see what we can explain by assuming both a constant relative risk aversion level ρ and constant degree of ambiguity λ.

The way we choose to fit the data is to take the average values for α by stake level shown in Table 25.3 and ask the question, 'What average levels of risk aversion ρ and degree of perceived ambiguity λ best fit the average bid data?' Table 25.4 presents the results we obtain. The second column presents the mean degree of optimism obtained for each stake level. The estimates $\rho=0.63$ and $\lambda=0.31$ were the best fit levels obtained by minimising a loss function, where the loss for a given stake is the difference between the optimal bid shown in Table 25.4 and the actual mean bid. The optimal bid is obtained from the alpha-maxmin model (25.3) given the parameters shown. Notice that the best fit optimal bid pattern we obtained does not perfectly fit the actual mean data. However, it does have the qualitative characteristics. First, like the actual mean bid, the optimal bid peaks for the intermediate 9 stake prospect. Second, like the actual mean bid, the 5 stake optimal bid is larger than the 21 stake optimal bid, and the 201 optimal bid is the smallest.

Table 25.4 Estimated optimal bid pattern versus actual mean bid pattern

Stake level	Mean estimated α from total ambiguity treatment	Estimated ρ	Estimated λ	Optimal bid	Actual mean bid from the No Ambiguity Treatment
5 stake	0.37	0.63	0.31	2.70	2.64
9 stake	0.28	0.63	0.31	2.74	3.00
21 stake	0.17	0.63	0.31	2.66	2.50
201 stake	0.05	0.63	0.31	2.15	2.34

Why is ambiguity able to help explain the 'hump' in the preferences exhibited by the average subject, where the 9 stake was found to be most attractive? Examining model (25.1), it is evident that additional ambiguity will reduce the valuation of the prospect when $\alpha<p$ but increase the valuation when $\alpha>p$. Examining Table 25.3, we find, therefore, $\alpha<p$ for the 5 stake prospect. Thus, if subjects perceive some ambiguity even when there appears to be none, or if the coping mechanisms for bounded rationality are effectively captured by the ambiguity placed into model (25.1), then additional ambiguity will reduce the attractiveness of the 5 stake prospect relative to the others. This is one explanation for the hump at the 9 stake in our data.

The fact that $\alpha>p$ for the 9 stake prospect also explains the hump to some degree, but risk aversion also helps explain it. The probability p is 0.25 for the 9 stake prospect, and α is slightly greater at 0.28. Thus, as ambiguity increases, the ambiguity makes the 9 stake relatively more attractive. However, $\alpha>p$ for both the 21 stake and 201 stake prospects and by much larger multiples. Therefore, an increase in ambiguity more significantly enhances the valuation of those prospects than it increases the valuation of the 9 stake prospect. Given this fact, in order for the 9 stake prospect to be valued more than the 21 stake and 201 stake prospects, there must be some significant risk aversion. As the level of risk aversion increases, a higher stake prospect is devalued more than a lower stake prospect. We found that a risk aversion level of $\rho=0.63$ was high enough to bring the optimal bids for 21 stake and 201 stake prospects down below the 9 stake prospect and close to the actual mean levels. At the same time, we found that the relatively significant level of ambiguity $\lambda=0.31$ was necessary to place the valuation of the 9 stake prospect above the lowest-risk 5 stake prospect.

To summarise, we have shown admitting the possibility that subjects effectively experience ambiguity in situations where there seems to be none allows one to restore the possibility that subjects maintain a constant level of relative risk aversion as they uncertain consider prospects. As noted in the discussion surrounding Table 25.2, if we do not admit the possibility of ambiguity, the estimated value for risk aversion parameter ρ ranges from 1.86 to 0 and the estimated level of risk aversion bounces down and up unsystematically as the variance and stake size increase, while holding the expected value constant. In contrast, when we admit the possibility of ambiguity, we can explain the behaviour of the average subject relatively well with a constant moderate level of risk aversion of $\rho=0.63$. The driving force of the explanatory power is our finding that, under ambiguity, subjects tend to discount higher stake outcomes, but they do not do so at a rate that keeps the expected value constant. Rather, as a stake size increases, ambiguity makes subjects biased toward thinking the expected value of the prospect is increasing. Consequently, subjects perceiving some ambiguity may not find a higher variance prospect less valuable, as constant relative risk aversion predicts.

INDIVIDUAL VARIATION

Because each subject makes four choices in the No Ambuity Treatment, we can estimate an average level of optimism α for each subject. To do so, we need an assumed level of risk aversion ρ and an assumed level of ambiguity λ. For our estimation, we choose to use the best fit $\rho=0.63$ and $\lambda=0.31$ we estimated as fitting the average bid data. Of course, we know from our previous observations that the level of optimism α will vary with the stake for the average subject. It is reasonable to think that the level of risk aversion and perceived ambiguity would also vary by subject. If we had much more data for each subject, we could estimate ρ, λ and α for each subject. However, with only four observations per subject, we can only estimate one parameter and only do so by making some strong assumptions.

While our approach surely does not provide a complete picture of how individuals vary as they make choices under uncertainty, there is value in finding rough individual estimates for the level of optimism. We can compare the individual estimates we obtain from the No Ambiguity Treatment to the individual estimates we obtain from the Total Ambiguity Treatment. By doing so, we can see whether we have evidence that the level of optimism exhibited in the Total Ambiguity Treatment transfers over to the No Ambiguity Treatment. We also can compare the estimates for optimism to the estimated levels of risk aversion in the No Ambiguity Treatment. By doing so, we can see the extent to which individual variation in risk aversion might actually be individual variation in the degree of optimism.

Figure 25.2 presents the distribution of the degree of optimism estimated for the 50 subjects from both the No Ambiguity Treatment, as just described, and from the Total Ambiguity Treatment, as described earlier (fitting the choices to the Hurwicz criterion). The median degree of optimism is 0.12 in the No Ambiguity Treatment and 0.22 in the Total Ambiguity Treatment. The correlation between the two optimism measures is 0.74. This high positive correlation is an indication that the decision behaviours subjects use under total ambiguity do spill over and help explain choices when probabilities are transparently available.

From our data for the No Ambiguity Treatment, if we assume no ambiguity, we obtain individual subject estimates for the risk aversion parameter ρ that are distributed as shown in Figure 25.1. When we take the same data and assume subjects experienced ambiguity

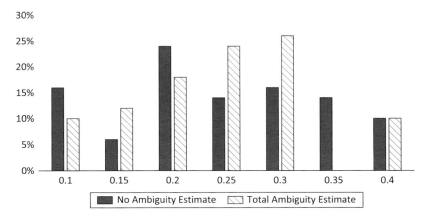

Figure 25.2   Distribution of degree of optimism

$\lambda = 0.31$ and risk aversion level $\rho = 0.63$, we obtain individual subject estimates for the degree of optimism parameter α that are distributed as shown in Figure 25.2. Our interest is in the possibility that what we estimated as variations in risk aversion are actually variations in the degree of optimism. For our 50 subjects, we find the correlation between risk aversion and degree of optimism to be −0.65. This finding, that a higher risk aversion estimate is associated with a lower level of optimism estimate, does suggest that what we might typically perceive as differences in risk aversion may not be such. Rather, the dree of risk aversion may vary less across people than we think. Differences in risk aversion may well remain, but perceived or effective ambiguity together with differences in the degree of optimism might be explaining a good portion of the behavioural differences we observe across individuals making the same uncertain decisions.

CONCLUSION

Because uncertainty is so prevalent, understanding how people make choices under uncertainty is exceptionally important. The work we present here is far from definitive, but we have provided theory and evidence that suggest it is too simplistic to assume people do not experience ambiguity in risky situations where they know the relevant probabilities. Our work suggests the average person effectively experiences ambiguity, even when the probabilities are transparently presented, and the ambiguity biases the decision behaviour.

Our particular experimental setting is valuable relative to others. We know of no other experimental framework examining risk preferences where the expected value remains constant as the riskiness of the choice is increased. Changing the expected value and variance of the prospect at the same time seems to introduce a confound. Our experimental framework allows us to examine how a change in the variance alone influences the choice.

As the variance increases, while holding the expected value constant, a subject with a constant degree of relative risk aversion will find the prospect less attractive. Using 50 subjects, which provides us with substantial statistical power, we do not find this predicted monotonic decrease in attractiveness. As the variance increases, the average subject finds the prospect more attractive up to a point and then less attractive. While we can explain this decision pattern by assuming the relative risk aversion of the average subject changes as the prospect changes, the resulting explanation is not very satisfying. Economists normally do not like to explain behaviour using changes in preferences, and in this case, the preference for risk of the average subject must decrease, increase and then decrease again to explain the behaviour of the average subject.

If we admit the possibility that subjects experience ambiguity and assume the decision behaviours that subjects use under total ambiguity spill over, then we can explain the behaviour of the average subject more readily. The most sensible explanation seems to be as follows. The presence of ambiguity, most prevalently caused by the bounded rationality relative to being able to evaluate lottery prospects, makes the subject's degree of optimism relevant. Under total ambiguity, the degree of optimism decreases as there is an increase in the gap between the highest possible outcome and the lowest possible outcome. However, for the average subject, the degree of optimism will not decrease as fast as the highest possible outcome increases, which will tend to increase the perceived attractiveness of prospects with larger possible outcomes. It is this role optimism can play under ambiguity which can make a more risky prospect more attractive and can explain why an increase in the variance of a prospect does not discourage chance taking to the degree constant relative risk aversion would predict.

We have not yet been able to identify an experimental design that can clearly measure the degree to which a subject experiences ambiguity when information on probabilities is transparently available. This presents a challenge for future research. Until such an experimental framework is available, the hypothesis that subjects experience no ambiguity when they fully know the probabilities must compete against the alternative hypothesis that they do effectively experience ambiguity. To the extent that these alternative hypotheses predict different outcomes in an experimental setting, we can test the two against each other. Our work here indicates we should pursue more such experimental work: may the theory that better predicts behaviour win!

NOTES

1. For the special case $\rho = 0$, the isolastic utility function is $U(c) = \ln(c)$.
2. Mahmound and Pingle (2018) test for an order effect by having another set of subjects play the total ambiguity treatment prior to the No Ambiguity Treatment. The mean levels for the 30 subjects in this group were very similar. In particular, the mean levels in the second experiment for the 5, 9, 21 and 201 stake levels were 0.41, 0.27, 0.19 and 0.08. That is, there was no order effect. Thus, we focus on the 50 subjects here who did the No Ambiguity Treatment prior to doing the total ambiguity treatment.

REFERENCES

Becker, Gordon M., Morris H. DeGroot and Jacob Marschak, 1964. "Measuring utility by a single-response sequential method," *Systems Research and Behavioral Science* **9**(3): 226–32.

Charness, Gary, Uri Gneezy and Alex Imas, 2013. "Experimental methods: Eliciting risk preferences," *Journal of Economic Behavior & Organization* **87**: 43–51.

Crovelli, Mark, 2012. "All probabilistic methods assume a subjective definition for probability," *Libertarian Papers* **4**(1): 163–74.

Ellsberg, Daniel, 1961. "Risk, ambiguity, and the savage axioms," *Quarterly Journal of Economics* **75**(4): 643–69.

Falk, Ruma and Friedrich Wilkening, 1998. "Children's construction of fair chances: Adjusting probabilities" *Developmental Psychology* **34**(6): 1340–57.

Frick, Mira, Ryota Iijima and Yves Le Yaouanq, 2020. "Objective rationality foundations for (Dynamic) α – MEU," *Cowles Foundation Discussion Paper* No. 2244.

Gilboa, Itzhak and David Schmeidler, 1989. "Maxmin expected utility with non-unique prior," *Journal of Mathematical Economics* **18**(2):141–53.

Holt, Charles and Susan Laury, 2014. "Assessment and estimation of risk preferences." In Mark Machina and William Kip Viscusi (eds), *Handbook of the Economics of Risk and Uncertainty* (pp. 135–201). Oxford: North Holland.

Heiner, Ronald A., 1983. "The origin of predictable behavior," *American Economic Review* **73**(4): 560–95.

Hurwicz, Leonid, 1951. "The generalized Bayes minimax principle: A criterion for decision making under uncertainty," *Cowles Commission Discussion Paper*, Statistics 335.

Jeske, Klaus-Jürgen and Werner Ute, 2008. "Impacts on decision making of executives - Probabilities versus outcomes," *Journal of Neuroscience, Psychology, and Economics* **1**(1): 49–65.

Karelitz, Tzur and David Budescu, 2004. "You say 'probable' and I say 'likely': Improving interpersonal communication with verbal probability phrases," *Journal of Experimental Psychology* **10**(1): 25–41.

Mahmoudi, Mina and Mark Pingle, 2018. "Bounded rationality, ambiguity, and choice," *Journal of Behavioral and Experimental Economics* **75**: 141–53.

Melkonyan, Tigran and Mark Pingle, 2010. "Ambiguity, pessimism, and rational religious choice," *Theory and Decision* **69**(3): 417–38.

Mulligan, Robert F., 2013. "The enduring allure of objective probability," *Review of Austrian Economics* **26**: 311–27.
Peters, Ellen and Bjalkebring Par, 2015. "Multiple numeric competencies: When a number is not just a number," *Journal of Personality and Social Psychology* **108**(5): 802–22.
Trautmann, Stefan T. and Gijs van de Kuilen, 2015. "Ambiguity attitudes." In Gideon Keren and George Wu (eds), *The Wiley Blackwell Handbook of Judgment and Decision Making* (pp. 89–116.). Chichester: John Wiley & Sons Ltd.

PART IX

BEHAVIOURAL APPROACHES TO POLICY

26. Norms, networks, nudges: Non-traditional approaches to improve healthy behaviours
Irene Mussio and Angela C.M. De Oliveira

INTRODUCTION

Second-hand smoke. Herd immunity. Sexually transmitted diseases. From a public health perspective, many health-related behaviours involve externalities. These externalities create a divergence between privately optimal and socially optimal behaviour. The good news is that appropriately designed policy can improve social welfare by decreasing the divergence. In addition to externalities, behaviours may diverge from welfare-maximising due to information failures or deviations from the assumptions of 'rationality', as people systematically misestimate risk and sometimes impose internal costs to decision-making – internalities (Tversky and Kahneman 1974; Allcott and Sunstein 2015). More specifically, the risk of death from unhealthy behaviours is typically underestimated, resulting in an undervaluing of the utility gains from making healthier choices and a higher probability of taking up unhealthy behaviours (Hersch and Viscusi 1998).

Thus, encouraging healthy behaviours has the potential to increase both individual and social welfare. In this chapter, we discuss some of the key research advances focused on achieving this goal.

Smoking, alcohol consumption, physical inactivity and a poor diet are leading causes of mortality in the United States (US) (Mokdad et al. 2000) and put pressure on the health care system, both through the costs associated with the prevention and treatment of the unhealthy behaviour and through the costs associates with secondary risks for cancer, heart disease and diabetes. In the US, almost 15 per cent of the US adult population smokes (Centers for Disease Control and Prevention 2017), 6.3 per cent of adults have an alcohol use disorder (National Institutes of Health 2015) and more than one-third of American adults are classified as obese (with a Body Mass Index > 30; Ogden et al. 2014). The cost of vaccine hesitancy in the US is also significant, with small declines in vaccination having consequences not only in monetary terms but also in health and mortality – affecting not only individuals but also communities due to disease outbreaks (Lo and Hotez 2017; Mesa et al. 2021).

Many interventions to encourage and sustain healthier behaviours have short-term but not long-term results. This is particularly evident in those interventions that include financial incentives, where few studies find persistent effects once the incentives are removed (Charness and Gneezy 2009; Loewenstein et al. 2016; Hussam et al. 2017; Mochon et al. 2017; Carrera et al. 2020). Financial incentives can sometimes reduce or crowd out other motives for undertaking healthy behaviours even in the short-run (Gneezy et al. 2011). Further, the cost of financial incentives is an additional burden to the already existing pressure on the health care system in terms of care provision, human resources and overall treatment costs.

Given the costs of financial incentive programs and the short-lived effects of behaviour changes under these interventions, there is potential to examine whether and when other interventions that operate through reducing cognitive errors or through social, rather than financial, incentives are successful at changing behaviour. In this chapter, we focus on examining how norms, peer effects, interactions in social networks and nudges (both traditional nudges and normative nudges) have been used as non-financial instruments to encourage healthier decision-making. Non-financial, low-cost interventions have been used to tackle key public health issues such as smoking, alcohol over-consumption, physical inactivity, poor diet and vaccine hesitancy. We explore some of the findings in the next sections.

In this review, we also discuss the implications for improving healthy decision-making and welfare in terms of both policy-making and research. We begin by analysing how altering either the perception of a health-related social norm or the norm itself has the potential to improve individual and social welfare (through the provision of direct health benefits; Charness and Gneezy 2009; Zimmerman 2009; Galizzi and Wiesen 2018). We then discuss the impact of social interactions on preference formation and information diffusion through networks in the third section. In the fourth section, we examine how low-cost interventions that change the setting in which individuals make decisions can successfully affect individual healthy decision-making. At the individual level, nudges often operate either through social norms or by decreasing the influence of cognitive biases. Therefore, we also focus on understanding how nudges based on norms can impact individual decisions (the fifth section). We discuss joint implications and directions for future work in the sixth section.

NORMS AND THE IMPLICATIONS FOR HEALTHY BEHAVIOUR

A significant and growing literature demonstrates that behaviour is influenced by the individual's perception of what others do, approve and disapprove of (Van Bavel et al. 2020; Cialdini and Goldstein 2004). Social norms can affect behaviour in ways that are similar to financial interventions: while financial incentives imply material rewards, social norms imply social rewards, which in many cases are greater when compared to monetary outcomes (Lindbeck 1997; Jaime Torres and Carlsson 2018).

Background

Social norms usually refer to common standards for behaviour, set by and for members of a group (Cialdini and Trost 1998). These norms may be either descriptive, involving perceptions of *what is*, or injunctive, involving perceptions of what *ought to be* (Reid et al. 2010). While both types of norms affect behaviour, one can think of descriptive norms as providing information to individuals about how to act in a certain situation while injunctive norms provide information about behaviours that a majority of individuals approve or disapprove of (Cialdini et al. 1990; Mollen et al. 2013; Cialdini and Goldstein 2004).[2] An example of a descriptive norm would be perceiving that school friends get vaccinated against the flu every year. Injunctive norms could include the perception that the same school friends approve of vaccinating every year against the flu. Norms can also be static or dynamic (Sparkman and Waltman 2017), where dynamic norms draw attention to a norm over time and how that norm might change (such as how people are eating less meat – static – versus how people are trying to reduce the amount of meat they consume – dynamic). Dynamic norms have been shown to promote reduced meat consumption (Sparkman and Waltman 2017) and pro-environmental behaviours such as water consumption and the use of reusable cups (Loschelder et al. 2019; Mortensen et al. 2019).

Norms are more likely to affect behaviour when they are salient at the time a decision is made – that is, when people's attention can be drawn to the norms (Lawrence 2015). A significant amount of research has focused on how norms can be used to modify risky decision-making (Rivis and Sheeran 2003; Reid et al. 2010), including health risks. Norms are also most influential when they are common to social groups, especially for health-related behaviours (Abrams et al. 1990; Centola 2011; Van Bavel et al. 2020).

There is extensive applied research showing that social norms are one of the key determinants of health-related behaviours. Theories of health behaviour, such as the theory of planned behaviour (Ajzen 1985) and the social cognitive theory (Bandura 2001) have also incorporated normative concepts into their explanations for health-based decisions, with the aim of understanding how norms, intentions, behaviour and views and opinions about the group and the behaviour of others are linked.

Using Norms to Affect Behaviour

People systematically over and underestimate risks of death and health decline, as perceived risks are influenced by available and incomplete information and heuristics (Tversky and Kahneman 1974). Normative influence can be defined as a form of influence that uses perceived behavioural patterns as well as approval and disapproval of social norms as a way of modifying behaviour (Cialdini et al. 1990).

Normative influence has been used to increase levels of physical activity (Burger and Shelton 2011), influence healthier food consumption (Burger et al. 2010; Lally et al. 2011; Yun and Silk 2011; Smith-McLallen and Fishbein 2008), reduce alcohol consumption (Clapp et al. 2008) and increase take-up of vaccinations (Mussio and de Oliveira 2018), handwashing and infection control (Lapinski et al. 2013; Dickie et al. 2018) and the use of sun protection (Reid and Aiken 2013). In the following we present four main areas of healthy behaviours in which norms have been used: vaccines, alcohol consumption, exercise and food intake.

Vaccinations

Because the decision to vaccinate in many countries is voluntary, a significant focus of the literature has been on the individual decision-making process, given that the benefits of getting and being protected by the vaccine usually outweigh the costs (of going to get the vaccine and minimal side effects). Research on the topic includes how individuals respond to information about the personal and social benefits of disease protection (Verelst et al. 2019) and perceptions of social norms (Larson et al. 2014). For example, individuals are more willing to vaccinate when uptake among the general population, family and friends is high, highlighting the relevance of the descriptive norm (Hooglink et al. 2020; Bruine de Bruin et al. 2019; Schmid et al. 2017; Oraby et al. 2014).

Key determinants of vaccine uptake include perceptions of the social norms, beliefs about vaccine effectiveness and misperceptions of vaccine safety. Several studies observe a positive effect of norms on vaccination decisions and vaccination intentions.[3] These studies focus on correcting misinformation and using norms to tackle vaccine hesitancy (Verelst et al. 2018, 2019; Thorpe et al. 2012; Gidengil et al. 2012). As an example, Daley et al. (2007) show that parents' decisions regarding children's influenza vaccination depend on perceptions of both the descriptive and injunctive norms, in particular focusing on 'what other parents do' and whether the people who are 'most important' to them think that the child needs to be vaccinated. Harmsen et al. (2013) find similar results for the case of child vaccination against hepatitis B.

With the current coronavirus disease (COVID-19) pandemic underway, vaccine hesitancy (including delay in getting vaccines, lack of convenience and trust and complacency) has become an increasingly prevalent, polarising and complex issue. Correcting misperceptions about the vaccine and providing information on what others do has been a powerful motivator for vaccination decisions. The SAGE group on immunisations has highlighted individual and social group influence as one of the three determinants of vaccine hesitancy (MacDonald and SAGE group 2014). This suggests that robustly designed interventions that focus on normative concepts could be one of the ways to highlight the behaviour and attitudes of peers, increasing vaccination uptake. The use of normative interventions could be especially relevant for minority groups, who are disproportionally affected by hesitancy (Graupensperger et al. 2021; Razai et al. 2021; Xiao and Wong 2020).

Alcohol over-consumption

Individuals' perception of the social norms within their peer group is a key factor explaining engagement in risky behaviours affecting health, especially with younger populations (Berkowitz 2005). Key risky behaviours where overestimating peer norms has negative consequences include needle sharing among injection drug users (Davey-Rothwell et al. 2009), tobacco consumption (Etcheverry and Agnew 2008) and alcohol and drug use in adolescents (Vallentin-Holbech et al. 2017).

Consider alcohol consumption and over-consumption among youth. Norms influence alcohol consumption through a two-step process. First, personal alcohol consumption is compared to the perceived norms. Exaggerated norms are then applied as the standard for one's own behaviours (Perkins and Berkowitz 1986; Borsari and Carey 2001) – that is, if the perceived norm is two to four drinks, this cognitive process would apply four to five drinks as the personal standard. Exaggerating the norm of peers' risky behaviour thus further exacerbates individual levels of risk-taking through the exaggeration because, in these settings, individuals typically conform to the perceived peer norm (Vallentin-Holbech et al. 2017).

The perception of peers' drinking behaviour is among the best predictors of college student drinking (Neighbors et al. 2007, 2010; Perkins and Berkowitz 1986). Students reporting higher perceived descriptive norms for peer alcohol use also report being heavy drinkers (Baer et al. 1991; Borsari and Carey 2000; Lewis and Neighbors 2004). This relationship holds for younger adults as well as middle and high school students (Linkenbach and Perkins 2003; Perkins and Craig 2003). Stronger identification of students with reference groups of the same sex, race and Greek status is translated into a stronger association between their perceived group and one's drinking norms (Neighbors et al. 2010).

Focusing on over-consumption, perceptions about peer approval of heavy episodic drinking (more than five/more than four drinks for men/women in a short period of time) are positively related to an individual's intent to have alcohol-induced blackouts (Ward and Guo 2020). This is consistent with prior findings by Neighbors et al. (2007), who show that descriptive and injunctive norms (measured using scales and perception indexes) were among the best predictors of college student drinking. The authors come up with social norm proxies, using the average drinking of each individual's reference group to construct a descriptive norm and an average perception drinking index for the injunctive norm. The study finds a large, significant effect of the descriptive norm in predicting alcohol consumption and a smaller effect of injunctive norms.

As students tend to overestimate peers' drinking when making comparisons, tailored normative feedback is an attractive method to change perceptions (Nye et al. 1999; Neighbors et al. 2007). That is, correcting misperceptions has been identified as a promising strategy to reduce alcohol use (Borsari and Carey 2000; Larimer and Cronce 2002; Lewis and Neighbors 2004; Neighbors et al. 2004). Given the limited resources campuses have to plan health-related programs, identifying factors that could be directly targeted would have the greatest impact on drinking. Thus, tailored but broadly reaching, low-cost interventions that target norms, coupled with directed health support for those who need it could provide effective solutions for alcohol consumption.

Physical activity and food consumption in childhood and adolescence

Social influence also plays a significant role in the decisions to be physically active and establish healthy eating patterns. Obesity is a particularly significant health concern, as rates of non-communicable diseases are on the rise. This is partly due to physical inactivity and unhealthy diets (WHO 2018; other key drivers are tobacco use and alcohol over-consumption). With health patterns and behaviours usually being learned during childhood and adolescence and carried into adulthood, it is essential that the risk factors for non-communicable diseases – such as obesity and unhealthy diets – are addressed early on (Draper et al. 2015; Murray et al. 2012).

Children and adolescents frequently eat in social contexts (e.g., school lunches and family dinners), and many of their learnt behaviours are social norms that are passed on from parents. In the case of children and adolescents, parenting styles have been found to influence dietary intake (Pearson et al. 2009; Krølner et al. 2011; Sleddens et al. 2011) as well as sedentary behaviour (Sleddens et al. 2011) and obesity (Gerards et al. 2011).

Parents significantly determine their child's lifestyle, and results have shown that involving parents in the prevention of their child's obesity by being active participants in their diet and physical activity has positive and long-term results (Campbell and Hesketh 2007; Epstein et al. 1994). An authoritative parenting style (imposing their own social norms and boundaries on the diet and physical activity of their children) combined with health-conscious preferences can have a positive effect on the child's healthy behaviours and result in healthier eating (Draper et al. 2015) and less sedentary behaviour (Sleddens et al. 2011). Interventions to change physical activity patterns in adolescents have also been successful when involving communities such as families or schools (van Grieken et al. 2012). Lastly, Pedersen et al. (2015) argue that interventions may be most effective in early childhood, reinforcing parents' influence on their children's healthy eating while strengthening positive outcome norms and expectations.

Summary

In sum, social norms and the perception of normative cues are one of the key determinants of lifestyle choices. Yet, changing behaviours is challenging. Normative influence has been found to be one of the pathways to promote health behaviours in a positive manner, by highlighting the relevant social norms, correcting misperceptions of perceived norms and comparing oneself to peers, family and friends. But making social norms salient for the individual at the time of behaviour and correcting misperceptions about social norms is not as easy as it seems, as individuals are not independent entities but are part of various overlapping groups.

NETWORKS, INTERACTIONS, PEER EFFECTS AND HEALTH

Social networks encompass an individual and all of the other individuals with whom they interact. For these networks, the relevant 'nodes' are individuals and the 'ties' that join them represent some form of interaction – such as friendship, kinship, work relations, exchange of money, communication patterns or even sexual relationships (Newman 2010). Network analysis in a social context can be used to study the process of change within a group over time, to describe regularities and social interactions and understand the features of individuals in a social context (Wasserman and Faust 1994).

The potential for economic outcomes to depend on network structure has been widely discussed. In economics, social networks are used to explain patterns of diffusion of resources, information, learning and social capital (Currarini et al. 2014; Kirchkamp and Nagel 2007), team production (Fatas et al. 2010), job search (Holzer 1987; Montgomery 1992) as well as cooperation among different networks (Bramoullé and Kranton 2007; Carpenter 2007; Choi and Lee 2015. Leibbrandt et al. 2015).

When it comes to health, social interactions can shape preferences for healthy behaviours, such as physical activity, eating habits and vaccination decisions. These social interactions serve to identify and reinforce the relevant social norms. Risky behaviours affecting health – choices that can lead to sexually transmitted diseases (STDs), obesity and even mental health issues like depression, self-esteem or anxiety (which can result in behaviours which further increase health risks; Blanco et al. 2013; Cobb et al. 2022) – are of particular interest to those examining social influence and health. Studies have shown that peers can influence risky behaviours, such as smoking, drinking and doing drugs, especially for adolescents and college students (Lundborg 2006).

A significant amount of the health-related literature has focused on understanding peer and network effects, both in correlational studies and attempts to achieve causal inference. This is what we describe here.

Background

Friends and peers have been shown to be a determinant of social, cognitive and emotional development, especially during childhood and adolescence (Duncan et al. 2001; Maxwell 2002). Some studies argue that the degree of social connection between partners in an experiment – taken for example, as the number of friends in common and how much time they spend with them per week, or how long they have been friends – has both positive and negative impacts on decision-making in topics such as exercising and alcohol consumption (Leider et al. 2010). Peers can affect others' endowment or choice sets, including the exposure and transmission of information (Duflo and Saez 2002) and even teen pregnancy (Evans et al. 2001).

Peer effects are also important when it comes to policy interventions and the possibility of amplifying these effects throughout the network (the social multiplier). If the social multiplier is large, policies such as changing the minimum age to drink and smoke, legalising drugs or even campaigns to get vaccinated, donate blood or exercise might have larger effects when the interventions are small. However, the relevant peer group for an individual is sometimes difficult to determine (Halliday and Kwak 2012).

Peer effects can diffuse not just to one additional person but through a broader social network. Social networks can amplify the spread of behaviours that are both harmful and beneficial (for example, breaking lockdown rules and deciding not to vaccinate), and these effects may spread through the network to family, friends, acquaintances and friends of friends (Van Bavel et al. 2020; Aral et al. 2009). How social networks influence contagion is perhaps more obvious for infectious diseases, like the spread of severe acute respiratory syndrome (SARS; Colizza et al. 2006, 2007). However, other behaviours, such as obesity or smoking have also been shown to percolate through the network in a similar manner (Gwozdz et al. 2015; Christakis and Fowler 2007, 2008).

Applications

As individuals are connected, their health is connected as well (Smith and Christakis 2008; Valente and Vega Yon 2020). Social relationships affect the cognitive development of an individual, altering self-perception as well as how individuals interpret rewards, threats, reciprocation and sensitivity to others' decisions (Pachucki et al. 2015). Next we present four examples of how social networks affect health-related decisions.

Smoking

From a public policy point of view, smoking is one of the leading causes of death around the world, killing around eight million people a year (WHO 2020). Although it is a preventable cause of mortality, 12 per cent of deaths worldwide are related to smoking (WHO 2019). The WHO has determined that tobacco is a public health threat as it is addictive and given that smoking affects both smokers and people exposed to second-hand smoke.

A wide number of studies have determined that adolescent smoking can be predicted by peer influence, although the magnitude of the effect varies (Conrad et al. 1992; De Vries et al. 2003; Leventhal and Cleary 1980). At the school level, peers who smoke, especially popular students increase the likelihood of someone starting smoking, and the impact is larger in those schools with high smoking prevalence (Alexander et al. 2001). So, there is potential to target those individuals who are more central to a network, as transmission through the networks has to go through these specific and more popular students. For adolescents, the peer effect on smoking and drinking behaviours is not only significant in that stage, but it also transitions into adulthood (Ali and Dwyer 2009; Kremer and Levy 2008). Interaction with substance-using friends predicts increasing substance use for oneself, and this effect is larger when looking at close friendships (Bauman and Ennett 1996; Ennett and Bauman 1996; Ennett et al. 2008; Knecht et al. 2011; Kobus and Henry 2010).

Vaccinations

There are several avenues through which social networks relate to vaccinations. First, the people with whom we physically interact are the ones most likely to infect (or be infected by) us – disease transmission and direct vaccine value are thus directly affected by the social network. Second, because of social norms and influence, discussed in the second section, an individual's decision to vaccinate affects, and is affected by, the vaccination decisions of others in their network, generating herd immunity (Adams et al. 2013; Neaigus et al. 2006; Havens et al. 2013). This is especially important in the current pandemic context, with COVID-19 vaccines being rolled out. Third, vaccinations are often presented as a social dilemma, as the decision to vaccinate contributes to herd immunity, protecting those who cannot get vaccinated, but free-riding leads to lower rates of vaccination, usually below what is socially optimal (Fu et al. 2011).

Vaccinations are one of the health-related decisions that can spread through a network, but not many studies take a network approach towards this social dilemma, as it is costly to fully map a network to optimise public policy. An alternative approach taken by Banerjee et al. (2021) to increase vaccination rates includes identifying the 'best' people to spread information about children's vaccination clinics, focusing on individuals in a sample of Indian villages. The focus is on those who are trusted and at the same time who would quickly share the information, which usually translates into choosing individuals with central characteristics. The authors find that those villages where information was spread through those nominated by the village as the best people to pass on information experienced an increase of 22 per cent in vaccinated children every month.

Physical activity, nutrition and obesity

Obesity is a derivate of unhealthy behaviours that puts substantial pressure on the health care system, affecting people of all ages. Obesity comes with comorbidities which include coronary heart disease, hypertension, stroke and pulmonary diseases, which increase the risk of death and hospitalisation. Although obesity is derived from individual characteristics and behaviours, Christakis and Fowler (2007) found that social contact influences obesity levels. Several studies suggest that food consumption patterns and weight loss can be influenced by peers, both positively and negatively (Gwozdz et al. 2019; Feunekes et al. 1998; Monge-Rojas et al. 2002; Pachucki and Goodman 2015). Social support from friends (such as being part of a sports team or exercising with a friend) has been shown to influence the levels of physical activity (Duncan et al. 2005; Voorhees et al. 2005). Other studies have shown that in school-based friendship networks friends have similar measures of physical activity and food consumption (de la Haye et al. 2010; Feunekes et al. 1998; Monge-Rojas et al. 2002; Unger et al. 2004).

In Christakis and Fowler (2007), an individual's chance of becoming obese increased by almost 60 per cent if she had a friend or a sibling who became obese in the timeframe of the study. The authors conclude that obesity could spread as a disease through social ties, so policies and support that targets not only the individual, but his peers would be more successful than those who do not. Similar results have been found by a wide range of research, including Gwozdz et al. (2019), Mora and Gil (2013) and Fortin and Yazbeck (2015).

Peers also further alter the perception of how acceptable weight is defined, especially among females and adolescents with higher body mass index (Crawford and Campbell 1999; Trogdon et al. 2008; Unger et al. 2004). Weight has further been shown to be a predictor of marginalisation and social stigma, which directly affects network position and composition in addition to increasing mental health risks (Strauss and Pollack 2003). Yakusheva et al. (2011) analyse college students' weight gain and show that weight gain is negatively correlated with their roommate's initial weight. In addition, females were more likely to adopt weight-loss behaviours (in terms of both eating and exercising) from roommates.

Obesity both affects, and is affected by, an individual's position in their social network. Overweight adolescents have been found to be more isolated and peripheral (Strauss and Pollack 2003), while adolescents with similar body weight and weight-related behaviours are more likely to share a tie (Zhang et al. 2018). Njeru et al. (2020) and Smith et al. (2020) find similar results, where participants who were overweight or obese had more network members who were also overweight or obese. From a global network perspective, some behaviours, such as the decision to get vaccinated or what to eat can have a bigger impact than just in the individual's closest social circle, as it involves the transmission of an illness or behavioural patterns from one person to another throughout the network. This means, for example, that the position of the individual in their network can influence their obesity levels.

For adults, there are contradictory findings in terms of social capital. For some studies, the higher the network social capital (position of the individual and prestige of the job), the higher the chance of being obese (Moore et al. 2009). For others, high network social capital and trust reduce the likelihood of obesity but having more kinship ties had the opposite effect (Wu et al. 2018). Cohen-Cole and Fletcher (2008) argue that there is also an environmental component to the spread of obesity, related to the place in which individuals live, and what is near them, such as restaurants or gyms.

Mental well-being
Network studies have not only focused on the physical transmission of diseases but also on mental issues and health-related emotional states, such as depression (Rosenquist et al. 2011), self-esteem (Pachucki et al. 2015), happiness (Fowler and Christakis 2008; Hill et al. 2010), social isolation (Mc Pherson et al. 2001) and suicide (Bearman and Moody 2004; Mueller and Abrutyn 2015). From an individual perspective, 'emotional contagion' (Hatfield et al. 1992) has been shown to happen between people with close contact, such as family or roommates (Larson and Almeida 1999). Emotional contagion also happens in experimental settings (Fowler and Christakis 2010). Hill et al. (2010) show that emotional contagion can percolate throughout a network over time like an infectious disease, not only by direct contact but also by media exposure (Joiner and Katz 1999).

Depression has been found to be contagious through interactions with friends, family and strangers (Joiner and Katz 1999). There is a gender differential, however, as women seem to respond to depressive symptoms and low self-esteem by reducing their social interactions when compared to men (Pachucki et al. 2015). Female friends are more influential in spreading depressive symptoms from one person to another (Rosenquist et al. 2011). Bearman and Moody (2004) find that females who were socially isolated were more likely to have suicidal thoughts.

Although there is extensive research on the impact of networks on mental health, the potential for interventions to improve mental health is still untapped, particularly using the tools of behavioural economics. Mental health network interventions should use existing social support and the existing network structure to diffuse behaviour change (Latkin and Knowlton 2015; Wölfer and Scheithauer 2014; Terzian et al. 2013). In the case of serious illnesses, members of the individuals' network of peers, friends and family are often emotionally, economically and socially affected (Latkin and Knowlton 2015). Interventions should consider potential spillover effects on mental health and the potential changes in economic behaviour that these spillovers can bring, particularly when it comes to changes in individual preferences.

Summary
Prior research has shown that individual decisions such as food choices and alcohol consumption could be affected by peers and could percolate through a network. However, the analysis

of individual interactions is not enough from a policy point of view. Although other methods have been successful to run interventions to improve healthy behaviours, such as finding central or optimal individuals to pass on information, the use of complete networks has its advantages when it comes to determining whether solutions to the problem should be targeted to a specific group of individuals or specific parts of the network (clusters). Thus, there is not a one-size-fits-all solution to the diffusion of (un)healthy behaviours: it depends on the problem, the type of network, the health issue and who the relevant individuals are.

Separating the influence of different peer groups and tackling the biases encountered in peer selection are two of the main research questions on this topic. There is some degree of endogeneity when analysing peers, as individuals in most cases decide who to associate with and individual characteristics tend to be similar to their peers (homophily[4]). One of the ways to overcome this issue is to draw a sample of individuals for whom ties are randomly assigned, such as the assignment of college students' roommates or the assignment of school students to different classrooms (Kremer and Levy 2008; Sacerdote 2001; Yakusheva et al. 2011). Disentangling the influence of the correct peer group and reducing the impact of peer selection is important when trying to assess policy impacts, as otherwise, estimates could be biased (as well as policy guidelines).

Another potential avenue for research involves the type of network individuals have and how this may interact with or affect the effectiveness of an intervention. For example, an individual who has only very close friends (or strong ties) might not be the most beneficial network structure for an individual to choose for themself. In a classic paper, Granovetter (1973) argued that weak ties (such as colleagues, contacts or friends of friends) and not strong ties increase the chances of, for example, someone getting a job. The argument behind this is that weak ties tend to expand the network of an individual, thus playing important roles in disseminating information, increasing mobility and reducing the fragmentation of a network. A network only composed of strong ties would be relatively small and highly fragmented. Thus, the ability to use a network-targeted policy to improve health, education or even cooperation towards a common goal may be less effective in networks with few weak ties.

Targeting well-connected individuals and making their behaviour change visible and salient may leverage behaviour change in other parts of the network, such as getting a vaccine or socially distancing could be successful low-cost and straightforward policies (Bond et al. 2012). As an example, disease transmission among drug users is one of the riskiest aspects of networks composed of only weak ties. Neaigus et al. (1995) show that people displaying high-risk behaviours are more likely to be infected with HIV: networks of drug injectors are unstable as they are formed by weak ties (usually short-term relationships).

HEALTH-BASED NUDGES AND CHOICE ARCHITECTURE

Due to biases and cognitive errors, individuals do not always make the 'best' (utility-maximising) choices for themselves. Motivation, or wanting to be healthy, is not always sufficient for behavioural change (Gollwitzer 1993), especially when addiction or impulsivity affects decisions. Nudges are easy and low-cost interventions to indirectly guide individuals to make better choices, such as following through with their intentions to do something for their health (such as getting a vaccine), eating better or using the stairs instead of the elevator.

Background

Health-related decisions tend to deviate from the principles of utility maximisation due to biases, cognitive errors, incomplete information or non-standard discounting of future costs and benefits (Li and Chapman 2013; Baron 2000, 2004). Some of the reasons for unhealthy choices that are not a result of utility maximisation include cognitive load, rules of thumb, copying someone else's behaviour, subconscious cues or emotions.

Attempts to understand decision-making in these settings tend to draw insights from the psychological 'model of dual-system', used to explain unexpected choices which are usually driven by cues such as emotions (Bernheim and Rangel 2004; Fudenberg and Levine 2006; Loewenstein and O'Donoghue 2004, 2007; Metcalfe and Mischel 1999; Thaler and Shefrin 1981). This model argues that individuals make most of their decisions in an intuitive, automatic or fast manner (the so-called 'System 1') instead of doing it in a comprehensive, systematic and slow manner ('System 2'; Kahneman 2003). One potential method of inducing health-focused behavioural change is to identify some of the psychological factors contributing to non-optimal health choices, specifically through System 1, and alter the decision-making environment to steer individuals away from those decisions. This is where nudges come in.

Nudging, which could be broadly translated into 'gently helping people to make better choices' (Vallgårda 2012), is an approach used to change individual behaviour in both psychology and economics (Thaler and Sunstein 2021). A clear definition of a nudge is provided by Thaler and Sunstein (2008, p. 6): a nudge is

> any aspect of the choice architecture that alters people's behavior in a predictable way without forbidding any options or significantly changing their economic incentives. To count as a mere nudge, the intervention must be easy and cheap to avoid. Nudges are not mandates. Putting the fruit at eye level counts as a nudge. Banning junk food does not.

Health nudges are therefore designed to facilitate healthy options through decision architecture and include positive reinforcements and small suggestions. Nudges should increase welfare: anyone who is already optimising will not be affected and those who are not optimising will make decisions that improve their welfare (Galizzi 2012).

Types of Nudges

Nudging towards healthier decisions has been studied by economics and used in public policy to steer individuals towards healthier choices. There are two main forms of nudging used in health interventions: implementation intentions and defaults. A third type of nudge, called a normative nudge, will be described in more in the next section.

Implementation intentions

Many people want to improve their health, but when the time comes they fail to follow through. Implementation intentions are a planning exercise where an individual sets a time and date when an action will take place. More specifically, implementation intentions are an inexpensive way of generating concrete plans towards the fulfilment of a goal, for example, to get a flu vaccine. When individuals are required to make concrete and detailed plans, the probability that they are able to successfully follow through with their plan increases significantly (Locke and Latham 2002; Gollwitzer and Sheeran 2006).

Nudging by using implementation intentions targets the individual's forgetfulness and procrastination (Milkman et al. 2011) with the aim of encouraging healthier decision-making. As an example, implementation intentions have been used to help individuals get their flu vaccinations. In Milkman et al. (2011), individuals generate concrete plans to get their flu vaccine by writing down the date and time. The authors find that people who received specific prompts to write down a date and time to get their vaccines had a 4.2-point higher vaccination rate than the control group (who only received information about the vaccination clinic dates and times). People who just had to write a date had a 1.5-point higher vaccination rate than the control group.

In a follow-up study, Milkman et al. (2021) run a large-scale study where they test a variety of planning prompts using text messages to tackle flu vaccination during the COVID-19 pandemic. The most successful messages include texts where a flu shot is assigned to the individual (a modified implementation intention setting where the time and date are assigned exogenously), and messages that include a combination of an individual prompt, an altruistic prompt or priming to reduce COVID-19 exposure.

Making plans also helps with behaviours affected by procrastination, such as eating healthy, exercising and scheduling physical exams or cancer screening appointments (Loewenstein et al. 2007; Armitage 2007; Milkman et al. 2013; Dai et al. 2012; Prestwich et al. 2003; Milne et al. 2002). Implementation intentions are particularly effective when paired with social pressure or accountability. For example, Rogers et al. (2014) argue that a potential low-cost intervention to increase exercise is to schedule workouts with an exercise partner. If the person does not show up, it will cause disappointment to the partner. If the person shows up, it will increase individual exercise.

Exercising is one of the areas in which implementation intentions have been successful, as many individuals tend to be time-inconsistent (Laibson 1997). Individuals usually do not properly weigh the long-term benefits of physical activity, which can ultimately affect goal setting (Ebrahim and Rowland 1996; Etkin et al. 2015). For example, planning where more steps could be added to a weekly routine to reach the exercise goals was successful in increasing physical activity (Robinson et al. 2019). Bhattacharya et al. (2015) show that individuals prefer and choose longer contracts (20 weeks) over short contracts (eight weeks) as exercise commitments, indicating that individuals recognise the usefulness of the commitment mechanism. This type of intervention could help develop longer-term exercise habits, as individuals were more likely to choose the longer contract again after it expired.

Defaults

Modifying how options are presented is another form of choice architecture. Default options are pre-specified choices used by the decision-maker (Thaler and Sunstein 2008). People are more likely to choose the default option as it is a fast and intuitive decision (under System 1 of decision-making). Effectively designing defaults may provide an inexpensive yet effecting method of changing behaviour, not only in the health domain but in other domains as well (such as pro-environmental choices and charitable donations; see Ghesla et al. 2019; Ebeling and Lotz 2015; Altmann et al. 2014).

A well-known example of the power of defaults is the organ donor registry (Johnson and Goldstein 2003). Johnson and Goldstein examine individual decision-making in the US when the default for organ donation is opting in (people are not donors by default), opting out (people are donors by default) or no default. The authors find that 'donation rates' (the decision to be an organ donor) are twice as high when opting out compared to opting in. Defaults in this case make a significant difference and could change the number of lives saved through organ donations by thousands every year.

Defaults have been also successfully used to influence flu vaccination decisions. Chapman et al. (2010) find that individuals who can opt out of the vaccine (by giving individuals a set time and date to get their vaccine) have a vaccination take-up rate of 45 per cent, while those who are assigned to an opting-in intervention (asking individuals to set up their appointment) only have a 33 per cent take-up rate. Similar results in terms of the likelihood of being vaccinated were found by Lehmann et al. (2016).

The creation of a default choice in menus is another common case of nudging (e.g. offering a medium-sized meal versus paying a bit more to get the large one or offering fries instead of a salad as the standard option), as people tend to exhibit inertia and stick with the default or first option (Rogers et al. 2014). Evidence suggests that in the case of repeated choices such as food consumption, individuals do not always use all the information available (Köster 2003; Samek 2019), thus defaults could be an efficient tool to help improve nutrition and calorie intake, which in the end reduces the incidence of non-communicable diseases.

As an example, Friis et al. (2017) show that defaults successfully increased vegetable consumption by providing pre-measured salad bowls instead of a buffet, lowering the calorie intake among the study participants (124 kcal versus 90 kcal in control). How the choice is presented at the point of purchase can nudge people towards healthier options while simultaneously reducing the cognitive load associated with eating-related decision-making. Other healthier defaults such as the positioning of desserts, food in supermarkets or default bread choices have also shown positive effects on healthy eating (Hansen et al. 2019; van Kleef et al. 2018; Bergeron et al. 2019; Kroese et al. 2016; Carroll and Samek 2018). Meat-free days and vegetarian defaults are increasingly common defaults to induce healthier decisions. Research shows that vegetable options increase the percentage of patrons choosing this alternative when determined as the default (Hansen et al. 2021). Meat-free days have been found to be supported in a variety of countries ranging from Canada to South Africa (Sunstein et al. 2018).

Prior research also shows that parents prefer healthier food defaults for their children (Loeb et al. 2017). Mothers especially, prefer healthier defaults in restaurants to reduce conflict with children and increase efficiency (Henry and Borzekowski 2015).

Summary

Nudges have been a successful tool in a variety of situations, as they are interventions that are low-cost and relatively easy to implement. A variety of countries support the use of nudges for public-policy purposes and in a broad range of health behaviours, including smoking, drinking, childhood obesity and food labels (Reisch et al. 2021; Sunstein et al. 2019 Reisch and Sunstein 2016; Sunstein 2017a).

However, there is a continuous debate on the ethics of nudges, and how they affect freedom of choice, individual autonomy and the degree of control institutions can have over populations (Schmidt and Engelen 2020). Moreover, nudges still present all the available information to individuals and individuals still have the freedom to make the same decision as before. Nudges do not deprive people of choices or information but aim to stimulate the choice that is in the best interest of their own health (Li and Chapman 2013; van Kleef et al. 2018) while keeping up with the complexities of intuitive decision-making.

For some public health decisions, especially those with large negative externalities, nudges may be too weak of an intervention: nudges will not result in fully internalising the externalities and more formal regulations may be needed to induce change (for example, requiring masks during a pandemic, soda taxes).

A word of caution is warranted: poorly designed nudges can also backfire. In settings ranging from food packaging to food warnings and informational campaigns, poorly designed nudges have been demonstrated to either not affect behaviour or to induce behaviour that is less socially desirable than what was observed prior to the intervention (Osman et al. 2020; Pham et al. 2016; Berman and Johnson 2015; Fairchild 2013). Nudges are not a panacea – it is important for researchers and policy makers to fully understand the motives of individuals for the behaviour they are attempting to change (Sunstein 2017).

MAKING HEALTH NORMS SALIENT: THE USE OF NORM NUDGES

Nudges have gained attention as a method for improving health-related decisions without regulation. In addition to the nudges that operate through reducing cognitive bias or time inconsistency, another type of nudge operates through either emphasising or trying to change social norms. These nudges are known as normative nudges.

Background

Normative nudges are defined as nudges whose mechanism of action relies on social norms, eliciting or changing social expectations (Bicchieri and Dimant 2019). Norm nudges also influence behaviour through the modification of choice architecture and the context in which people make decisions (Van Babel et al. 2020; Thaler and Sunstein 2008).

Nudges can lead individuals and groups to behave in beneficial ways, by drawing on additional information, beliefs and cognitive biases to change behaviour. In short, a normative nudge provides information about a social norm and makes the norm more salient (and thus more likely to affect choices). Nudges with information about what others do or (dis)approve of can be used to induce both individual and collective change, particularly when nudges focus on social comparisons (Bicchieri and Dimant 2019; Alcott 2011).

Normative nudges have been used most extensively to induce more environmentally conscious behaviour, including saving water in hotels by reusing towels (Goldstein et al. 2008) or reducing water (Jaime Torres and Carlsson 2018) or electricity (Carlsson et al. 2020) consumption at home. In these studies, information about the social norm is provided with the intent of inducing behavioural change. For example, in Carlsson et al. (2020), an information campaign that compared electricity use with neighbours showed a 6 per cent decrease in water consumption compared to a control who did not receive electricity use comparisons. Generally, these messages have been found to effectively alter behaviour for a short time after the intervention.

We discuss the literature on health-related norm nudges next.

The Use of Normative Nudges in Health

In the case of health, information-based nudges are designed to change the perception of health-based behaviours and to provide correct information to individuals (for example to correct the belief that flu vaccines give you the flu). This includes conveying truthful information, motivating individuals to be healthier and leveraging the individual's peer group as a way to change decisions. Social norm-nudging to induce pro-social behaviours, such as vaccinating to build herd immunity is especially important when behaviour depends on both empirical and normative expectations (Bicchieri and Dimant 2019).

Informational interventions

Normative influence could happen through social interactions or by providing tailored feedback but also by using signs, posters, printed messages or electronic communications. These informational interventions are either direct (e.g., comparing an individual's choices to the norm) or indirect (e.g., providing information that either makes the norm salient or changes an individual's perception of what the norm is).

Direct methods use a comparison between an individual's behaviour and that of a relevant reference group. Using these comparisons to nudge behaviour has resulted in less drinking (when using comparisons of drinking norms for excessive drinkers; Taylor et al. 2015), healthier food consumption (Aldrovandi et al. 2015; Emrich et al. 2017) and more appropriate sunscreen use (using homophilic norms related to ethnic and racial groups regarding sunscreen use; Hoffner and Ye 2009).

As an example, consider Taylor et al. (2015) who show participants information about how they ranked in their reference group in terms of alcohol consumption. This intervention resulted in a greater behavioural change (probability of asking for help and seeking treatment) than just providing information about average drinking.

Information may be direct to an individual but less personalised. Emrich et al. (2017) use a traffic light labelling system for food, including sodium and sugar levels. The authors find that calorie intake was reduced by 5 per cent, total fat by 13 per cent, saturated fat by 14 per cent and sodium by 6 per cent compared to no labelling (no impact on sugar intake).

In order to effectively induce change, direct interventions need to be properly tailored as providing information about the 'average' has not been shown to consistently affect choices. The literature on these directed normative nudges is still rather limited and potential future directions include identifying the most effective type of information/feedback and feedback delivery system and examining how to leverage homophilic social norms to improve decision-making.

Indirect methods are particularly useful when the target audience is large, harder to reach and involves repeat interactions. For example, Burger and Shelton (2011), use posters to highlight descriptive norms and analyse the choice between taking the elevator and using the stairs. Making the norm salient at the time of the decision (when facing the elevator) has a positive effect on exercise, with more people taking the stairs rather than using the elevator.

Indirect methods have been also widely used to help individuals make healthier eating choices. Mollen et al. (2013) use descriptive and injunctive normative messages to indirectly incentivise healthy food choices at an on-campus food court. They find that healthy descriptive messages (poster-based) resulted in more healthy food choices compared to no message, unhealthy descriptive or injunctive messages.

Using photographs and images to emphasise norms also has a positive impact on healthy decisions. Reicks et al. (2012) conduct a field study in a school cafeteria where they place photographs of vegetables in their lunch tray, conveying the perceived norm that vegetables should be part of the meal. The authors find a significant increase in the percentage of children eating green beans (from 6.3 per cent to 14.8 per cent) and carrots (11.6 per cent to 36.8 per cent). Similar results were found by Collins et al. (2019) when eliciting social eating and health norms at a student canteen and by Vermote et al. (2020) when emphasising social norms on fruit consumption and healthy eating in a visual manner (poster charts and poster messages).

Another common method to signal expected social norms in food consumption is the order in which the food in a restaurant is placed or made salient (Dayan and Bar-Hillel 2011; Wisdom et al. 2010; Thorndike et al. 2012), as well as recommended calorie intake in a menu (Wisdom et al. 2010; Roberto et al. 2010).

Nudging with social preferences: the case of vaccinations

As discussed in the second section, the decision to vaccinate can bring about large improvements in long-term health and social welfare through both the direct protection of the vaccine and herd immunity. Normative nudges may be especially valuable to a choice architect where mandates for some types of vaccinations cannot be put into place for ethical reasons (Dubov and Phung 2015).

Flu vaccines can be considered a joint product, as vaccines have both individual and social benefits. However, when it comes to getting vaccinated, individuals have an incentive to free-ride, avoiding the cost of the vaccine and indirectly benefiting from others getting vaccinated. Normative nudges for vaccines have been found to be effective if they emphasise both individual and social benefits (Mussio and de Oliveira 2022). Normative nudges may also emphasise other aspects of the social norm by providing information about who gets vaccinated, why they get vaccinated and the level of protection provided by vaccines.

Due to the positive social benefits of vaccination, there may also be a pro-social or altruistic component of individual vaccination decisions. Mussio and de Oliveira (2022) use posters to run a nudge-based influenza vaccination campaign among college students. They find that including normative messages highlighting both the individual and societal benefits of the vaccine has the largest impact on actual vaccinations compared to only one of the benefits or no message at all.

Normative interventions that highlight the benefits of vaccinations for parents are commonplace, particularly when vaccinating is framed as a preventive, healthy behaviour. Several studies find that parents who believe that their children do not need a vaccine argue that this is because other children already received the vaccine (Benin et al. 2006; Meszaros et al. 1996). Abhyankar et al. (2008) study how positive (gains: vaccinating protects your children) and negative (losses: not vaccinating fails to protect your children) framing of vaccination normative messages impact parents' intentions to vaccinate their child and show that a loss ('failing to vaccinate') rather than a gain ('vaccinate') framed message has a stronger positive impact on parent vaccination intentions. That is, positive reinforcement of vaccination social norms through nudges that highlight the benefits of the vaccine and the benefits to the community have been shown to be successful in steering vaccination decisions.

Summary

Normative nudges have been successful at changing healthy behaviours, from vaccinations to alcohol consumption. However, although straightforward and potentially low-cost, normative nudges do not take into account several key issues. Nudges do not usually consider issues of equity or distribution. That is, nudges are usually successful at disentangling the complexities between behaviour, emotions and cognition, but these broad-based nudges do not account for income disparities that might render the nudge ineffective (for example, nudging towards healthier eating in a poor neighbourhood in the middle of a food desert; Van Den Broucke 2014).

In addition, nudges do not usually consider what happens when the nudge disappears: individuals could become less responsive after the intervention compared to prior to the intervention. Thus, normative nudges need to be carefully designed to be effective at inducing both individual socially beneficial change. Although nudges can prime behaviour in the short-term, the behaviour change might not be sustainable in the long-term. This is especially relevant in the case of health, where some behaviours, such as healthy eating and exercising have to be done on a regular basis to see positive long-term effects.

DISCUSSION

The range of low-cost, easy-to-implement behavioural tools that are available nowadays best affect one-shot decisions with lasting consequences (such as vaccines or what to eat for lunch). Unfortunately, repeated decisions are harder to positively affect as reinforcement needs to come consistently from multiple avenues and, even then, behaviour may be subject to boomerang effects and moral licensing. More research is needed to understand when interventions will be most effective based on the characteristics of the population and the relevant decision.

One avenue for long-lasting change is to focus interventions on changing the norms themselves instead of highlighting existing norms. Researchers have the tools to understand and measure norms (e.g., Krupka and Weber 2009), and these tools can be adapted to run low-cost interventions that focus on correcting norms and beliefs about norms. In more context-free environments, researchers are examining norm formation and transmission (e.g., Chaudhuri et al. 2006), thus, extending this work to interventions that not only leverage current social norms but also establish healthier norms is an exciting avenue for future work.

Perhaps one of the most exciting components of work in this area is the interconnectedness of the social system. We affect others through our network ties, just as they affect us. This interconnectedness leads to both the potential for leveraging social networks to improve decision-making (reducing cognitive errors, improving information transmission, etc.) and social welfare. It also leads to one of the more interesting challenges: how do we establish causality when it is unethical to force individuals into different social networks or network structures? An avenue of research would involve interventions which have both peer effects (at least getting instruments or only treating part of an established dyad) and transmission through the network, but that do not account for the formation of the network itself (an intervention that is exogenous to the network).

While interventions can be used to improve welfare, the reverse can occur as well. The anti-vaccination movement is a current example of misinformation at the group level. Social networks are a strong predictor of vaccination uptake, as vaccine refusers are likely to be surrounded by refusers (and accepters by accepters; Oraby et al. 2014; Brunson 2013). Thus, in this case, social norm change and the communication of alternative norms have to happen at the group level, which makes designing and rolling out interventions a more complex and refined process (Brondolo et al. 2009).

Health-related nudges have shown high levels of acceptance in various worldwide studies, particularly when there is high trust in the authorities (Sunstein et al. 2019, 2018). Behavioural policies with public acceptance have a higher chance of being effective, and taking into consideration public opinion and engaging citizens is a way of open and transparent policy-making (Sunstein et al. 2019). In addition, new ways of incorporating reflection, self-awareness and participation in nudges, such as 'nudge plus', are currently being proposed and developed to answer health-related and other economic questions (John and Stoker 2019; Banerjee and John 2021; Mühlböck et al., 2020).

Two final considerations: first, known in addition to the already existing health disparities by wealth and race (Kawachi et al. 2005), interventions making use of social ties need to be mindful that in some communities financial resource constraints are paired with already poor neighbourhoods, low social capital and high income inequality (Fuller et al. 2005; Latkin et al. 1995), which can affect access to health care, misinformation about health and health behaviours. This means that interventions need to account not only for the financial and time constraints of the population but also understand who they trust to deliver information.

Finally, many of the health-focused decisions discussed here may be related to mental health issues (e.g., obesity, alcohol over-consumption). Ignoring, or failing to de-stigmatise, the mental health component of these decisions will make lasting individual and social change more difficult to achieve. Changing the norms around mental health care is perhaps one of the most important avenues for long-lasting social change and welfare. Interventions which only attend to multiple aspects of mental and physical health at the same time (for example, psychological therapy for eating disorders and medical treatment for the eating disorder itself, medical support for weight loss with a mental health group support programme) are likely to be potential, integral avenues to tackle health issues and have longer-term positive effects on individuals and their peers.

NOTES

1. Some behavioural researchers have focused on relating preferences to health decisions (e.g., Anderson and Mellor 2008; de Oliveira et al. 2016; Sadoff et al. 2020 among many others) or to understand physician decision making (e.g., Green 2014; Leeds et al. 2017). This is not the focus of this review.
2. Note that among norms scholars, these definitions and applications are subject to debate. We use these definitions for clarity.
3. In the case where medical records include individual vaccinations, the decision to vaccinate is used. When medical records are not available or vaccination records cannot be matched to individual medical histories, vaccination intentions are used as a proxy for the decision to vaccinate.
4. Homophily is a preference for being around individuals similar to oneself (Lazarsfeld and Merton 1954).

REFERENCES

Abhyankar, P., O'Connor, D. B., & Lawton, R. (2008). The role of message framing in promoting MMR vaccination: Evidence of a loss-frame advantage. *Psychology, Health and Medicine*, *13*(1), 1–16.

Abrams, D., Wetherell, M., Cochrane, S., Hogg, M. A., & Turner, J. C. (1990). Knowing what to think by knowing who you are: Self-categorization and the nature of norm formation, conformity and group polarization. *British Journal of Social Psychology*, *29*(2), 97–119.

Adams, J., Moody, J., & Morris, M. (2013). Sex, drugs, and race: How behaviors differentially contribute to the sexually transmitted infection risk network structure. *American Journal of Public Health*, *103*(2), 322–329.

Ajzen, I. (1985). From intentions to actions: A theory of planned behavior. In J. Kuhl and J. Beckmann (Eds.), *Action control* (pp. 11–39). Berlin, Heidelberg: Springer.

Aldrovandi, S., Brown, G. D., & Wood, A. M. (2015). Social norms and rank-based nudging: Changing willingness to pay for healthy food. *Journal of Experimental Psychology: Applied*, *21*(3), 242.

Alexander, C., Piazza, M., Mekos, D., & Valente, T. (2001). Peers, schools, and adolescent cigarette smoking. *Journal of Adolescent Health*, *29*(1), 22–30.

Ali, M. M., & Dwyer, D. S. (2009). Estimating peer effects in adolescent smoking behavior: A longitudinal analysis. *Journal of Adolescent Health*, *45*(4), 402–408.

Allcott, H. (2011). Social norms and energy conservation. *Journal of Public Economics*, *95*(9–10), 1082–1095.

Allcott, H., & Sunstein, C. R. (2015). Regulating internalities. *Journal of Policy Analysis and Management*, 34, 698–705.

Altmann, S., Falk, A., Heidhues, P., Jayaraman, R., & Teirlinck, M. (2019). Defaults and donations: Evidence from a field experiment. *Review of Economics and Statistics*, *101*(5), 808–826.

Anderson, L. R., & Mellor, J. M. (2008). Predicting health behaviors with an experimental measure of risk preference. *Journal of Health Economics*, *27*(5), 1260–1274.

Aral, S., Muchnik, L., & Sundararajan, A. (2009). Distinguishing influence-based contagion from homophily-driven diffusion in dynamic networks. *Proceedings of the National Academy of Sciences*, *106*(51), 21544–21549.

Armitage, C. J. (2007). Effects of an implementation intention-based intervention on fruit consumption. *Psychology and Health*, *22*(8), 917–928.

Baer, J. S., Stacy, A., & Larimer, M. (1991). Biases in the perception of drinking norms among college students. *Journal of Studies on Alcohol*, *52*(6), 580–586.

Bandura, A. (2001). Social cognitive theory of mass communication. *Media Psychology*, *3*(3), 265–299.

Banerjee, A., Chandrasekhar, A. G., Duflo, E., & Jackson, M. O. (2019). Using gossips to spread information: Theory and evidence from two randomized controlled trials. *Review of Economic Studies*, *86*(6), 2453–2490.

Banerjee, S., & John, P. (2020). Nudge plus: Incorporating reflection into behavioral public policy. *Behavioural Public Policy*, 1–16. https://doi.org/10.1017/bpp.2021.6

Baron, J. (2000). *Thinking and deciding* (3rd edn). Cambridge: Cambridge University Press.

Baron, J. (2004). Normative models of judgment and decision making. In D. J. Koehler & N. Harvey (Eds.), *Blackwell handbook of judgment and decision making* (pp. 19–36). London: Blackwell.

Bauman, K. E., & Ennett, S. T. (1996). On the importance of peer influence for adolescent drug use: Commonly neglected considerations. *Addiction*, *91*(2), 185–198.

Bearman, P. S., Moody, J., & Stovel, K. (2004). Chains of affection: The structure of adolescent romantic and sexual networks. *American Journal of Sociology*, *110*(1), 44–91.

Benin, A. L., Wisler-Scher, D. J., Colson, E., Shapiro, E. D., & Holmboe, E. S. (2006). Qualitative analysis of mothers' decision-making about vaccines for infants: The importance of trust. *Pediatrics*, *117*(5), 1532–1541.

Bergeron, S., Doyon, M., Saulais, L., & Labrecque, J. (2019). Using insights from behavioral economics to nudge individuals towards healthier choices when eating out: A restaurant experiment. *Food Quality and Preference*, *73*, 56–64.

Berkowitz, A. D. (2005). An overview of the social norms approach. *Changing the culture of college drinking: A socially situated health communication campaign*, *1*, 193–214.

Berman, E. R., & Johnson, R. K. (2015). The unintended consequences of changes in beverage options and the removal of bottled water on a university campus. *American Journal of Public Health*, *105*(7), 1404–1408.

Bernheim, B. D., & Rangel, A. (2004). Addiction and cue-triggered decision processes. *American Economic Review*, *94*(5), 1558–1590.

Bhattacharya, J., Garber, A. M., & Goldhaber-Fiebert, J. D. (2015). *Nudges in exercise commitment contracts: A randomized trial* (No. w21406). National Bureau of Economic Research.

Bicchieri, C., & Dimant, E. (2019). Nudging with care: The risks and benefits of social information. *Public Choice*, *191*(3), 1–22. https://link.springer.com/article/10.1007/s11127-019-00684-6

Blanco, N. J., Otto, A. R., Maddox, W. T., Beevers, C. G., & Love, B. C. (2013). The influence of depression symptoms on exploratory decision-making. *Cognition*, *129*(3), 563-568.

Bond, R. M., Fariss, C. J., Jones, J. J., Kramer, A. D., Marlow, C., Settle, J. E., & Fowler, J. H. (2012). A 61-million-person experiment in social influence and political mobilization. *Nature*, *489*(7415), 295–298.

Borsari, B., & Carey, K. B. (2000). Effects of a brief motivational intervention with college student drinkers. *Journal of Consulting and Clinical Psychology*, *68*(4), 728.

Borsari, B., & Carey, K. B. (2001). Peer influences on college drinking: A review of the research. *Journal of Substance Abuse*, *13*(4), 391–424.

Bramoullé, Y., & Kranton, R. (2007). Public goods in networks. *Journal of Economic Theory*, *135*(1), 478–494.

Brondolo, E., Gallo, L. C., & Myers, H. F. (2009). Race, racism and health: Disparities, mechanisms, and interventions. *Journal of Behavioral Medicine*, *32*(1), 1.

Bruine de Bruin, W., Parker, A. M., Galesic, M., & Vardavas, R. (2019). Reports of social circles' and own vaccination behavior: A national longitudinal survey. *Health Psychology*, *38*(11), 975.

Brunson, E. K. (2013). How parents make decisions about their children's vaccinations. *Vaccine*, *31*(46), 5466–5470.

Burger, J. M., Bell, H., Harvey, K., Johnson, J., Stewart, C., Dorian, K., & Swedroe, M. (2010). Nutritious or delicious? The effect of descriptive norm information on food choice. *Journal of Social and Clinical Psychology*, *29*(2), 228–242.

Burger, J. M., & Shelton, M. (2011). Changing everyday health behaviors through descriptive norm manipulations. *Social Influence*, *6*(2), 69–77.

Campbell, K. J., & Hesketh, K. D. (2007). Strategies which aim to positively impact on weight, physical activity, diet and sedentary behaviours in children from zero to five years. A systematic review of the literature. *Obesity Reviews*, *8*(4), 327–338.

Carlsson, F., Jaime, M., & Villegas, C. (2020). Behavioral spillover effects from a social information campaign. *Journal of Environmental Economics and Management*, *109*, 102325. https://doi.org/10.1016/j.jeem.2020.102325

Carpenter, J. P. (2007). Punishing free-riders: How group size affects mutual monitoring and the provision of public goods. *Games and Economic Behavior*, *60*(1), 31–51.

Carrera, M., Royer, H., Stehr, M., & Sydnor, J. (2020). The structure of health incentives: Evidence from a field experiment. *Management Science*, *66*(5), 1890–1908.

Carroll, K. A., & Samek, A. (2018). Field experiments on food choice in grocery stores: A 'how-to' guide. *Food Policy*, *79*, 331–340.

Centers for Disease Control and Prevention (2017). Smoking & tobacco use. https://www.cdc.gov/tobacco/index.htm

Centola, D. (2011). An experimental study of homophily in the adoption of health behavior. *Science*, *334*(6060), 1269–1272.

Chapman, G. B., Li, M., Colby, H., & Yoon, H. (2010). Opting in vs opting out of influenza vaccination. *Jama*, *304*(1), 43–44.

Charness, G., & Gneezy, U. (2009). Incentives to exercise. *Econometrica*, *77*(3), 909–931.

Chaudhuri, A., Graziano, S., & Maitra, P. (2006). Social learning and norms in a public goods experiment with inter-generational advice. *Review of Economic Studies*, *73*(2), 357–380.

Choi, J., & Lee, J. K. (2015). Investigating the effects of news sharing and political interest on social media network heterogeneity. *Computers in Human Behavior*, *44*, 258–266.

Christakis, N. A., & Fowler, J. H. (2007). The spread of obesity in a large social network over 32 years. *New England Journal of Medicine*, *357*(4), 370–379.

Christakis, N. A., & Fowler, J. H. (2008). The collective dynamics of smoking in a large social network. *New England Journal of Medicine*, *358*(21), 2249–2258.

Cialdini, R. B., & Goldstein, N. J. (2004). Social influence: Compliance and conformity. *Annual Review of Psychology*, *55*, 591–621.

Cialdini, R. B., Reno, R. R., & Kallgren, C. A. (1990). A focus theory of normative conduct: Recycling the concept of norms to reduce littering in public places. *Journal of Personality and Social Psychology*, *58*(6), 1015.

Cialdini, R. B., & Trost, M. R. (1998). Social influence: Social norms, conformity and compliance. In D. T. Gilbert, S. T. Fiske & G. Lindzey (Eds.), *The handbook of social psychology* (pp. 151–192). New York: McGraw-Hill.

Clapp, J. D., Min, J. W., Shillington, A. M., Reed, M. B., & Ketchie Croff, J. (2008). Person and environment predictors of blood alcohol concentrations: A multi-level study of college parties. *Alcoholism: Clinical and Experimental Research*, *32*(1), 100–107.

Cobb-Clark, D. A., Dahmann, S. C., & Kettlewell, N. (2022). Depression, risk preferences, and risk-taking behavior. *Journal of Human Resources*, *57*(5), 1566–1604.

Cohen-Cole, E., & Fletcher, J. M. (2008). Is obesity contagious? Social networks vs. environmental factors in the obesity epidemic. *Journal of Health Economics, 27*(5), 1382–1387.

Colizza, V., Barrat, A., Barthelemy, M., Valleron, A. J., & Vespignani, A. (2007). Modeling the worldwide spread of pandemic influenza: Baseline case and containment interventions. *PLoS Med, 4*(1), e13.

Colizza, V., Barrat, A., Barthélemy, M., & Vespignani, A. (2006). The role of the airline transportation network in the prediction and predictability of global epidemics. *Proceedings of the National Academy of Sciences, 103*(7), 2015–2020.

Collins, E. I., Thomas, J. M., Robinson, E., Aveyard, P., Jebb, S. A., Herman, C. P., & Higgs, S. (2019). Two observational studies examining the effect of a social norm and a health message on the purchase of vegetables in student canteen settings. *Appetite, 132*, 122–130.

Conrad, K. M., Flay, B. R., & Hill, D. (1992). Why children start smoking cigarettes: Predictors of onset. *British Journal of Addiction, 87*(12), 1711–1724.

Crawford, D., & Campbell, K. (1999). Lay definitions of ideal weight and overweight. *International Journal of Obesity, 23*(7), 738–745.

Currarini, S., Feri, F., & Meléndez-Jiménez, M. (2014). An experimental study on information sharing networks. Unpublished manuscript. https://sites.fas. harvard. edu/~ histecon/informationtransmissi on/papers/CurrariniFeriMelendez_January15. pdf.

Dai, H., Milkman, K. L., Beshears, J., Choi, J. J., Laibson, D., & Madrian, B. C. (2012). Planning prompts as a means of increasing rates of immunization and preventive screening. *Public Policy and Aging Report, 22*(4), 16–19.

Daley, M. F., Crane, L. A., Chandramouli, V., Beaty, B. L., Barrow, J., Allred, N., ... & Kempe, A. (2007). Misperceptions about influenza vaccination among parents of healthy young children. *Clinical Pediatrics, 46*(5), 408–417.

Davey-Rothwell, M. A., Siconolfi, D. E., Tobin, K. E., & Latkin, C. A. (2015). The role of neighborhoods in shaping perceived norms: An exploration of neighborhood disorder and norms among injection drug users in Baltimore, MD. *Health & Place, 33*, 181–186.

Dayan, E., & Bar-Hillel, M. (2011). Nudge to nobesity II: Menu positions influence food orders. *Judgment and Decision Making, 6*(4), 333–342.

De la Haye, K., Robins, G., Mohr, P., & Wilson, C. (2010). Obesity-related behaviors in adolescent friendship networks. *Social Networks, 32*(3), 161–167.

de Oliveira, A. C., Leonard, T. C., Shuval, K., Skinner, C. S., Eckel, C., & Murdoch, J. C. (2016). Economic preferences and obesity among a low-income African American community. *Journal of Economic Behavior & Organization, 131*, 196–208.

De Vries, H., Engels, R., Kremers, S., Wetzels, J., & Mudde, A. (2003). Parents' and friends' smoking status as predictors of smoking onset: Findings from six European countries. *Health Education Research, 18*(5), 627–636.

Dickie, R., Rasmussen, S., Cain, R., Williams, L., & MacKay, W. (2018). The effects of perceived social norms on handwashing behaviour in students. *Psychology, Health & Medicine, 23*(2), 154–159.

Draper, C. E., Grobler, L., Micklesfield, L. K., & Norris, S. A. (2015). Impact of social norms and social support on diet, physical activity and sedentary behaviour of adolescents: A scoping review. *Child: Care, health and development, 41*(5), 654–667.

Dubov, A., & Phung, C. (2015). Nudges or mandates? The ethics of mandatory flu vaccination. *Vaccine, 33*(22), 2530–2535.

Duflo, E., & Saez, E. (2002). Participation and investment decisions in a retirement plan: The influence of colleagues' choices. *Journal of Public Economics, 85*(1), 121–148.

Duncan, G. E., Anton, S. D., Sydeman, S. J., Newton, R. L., Corsica, J. A., Durning, P. E., ... & Perri, M. G. (2005). Prescribing exercise at varied levels of intensity and frequency: A randomized trial. *Archives of internal medicine, 165*(20), 2362–2369.

Duncan, G. J., Boisjoly, J., & Harris, K. M. (2001). Sibling, peer, neighbor, and schoolmate correlations as indicators of the importance of context for adolescent development. *Demography, 38*(3), 437–447.

Ebeling, F., & Lotz, S. (2015). Domestic uptake of green energy promoted by opt-out tariffs. *Nature Climate Change, 5*(9), 868–871.

Ebrahim, S., & Rowland, L. (1996). Towards a new strategy for health promotion for older women: Determinants of physical activity. *Psychology, Health & Medicine, 1*(1), 29–40.

Emrich, T. E., Qi, Y., Lou, W. Y., & L'Abbe, M. R. (2017). Traffic-light labels could reduce population intakes of calories, total fat, saturated fat, and sodium. *PloS one, 12*(2), e0171188.

Ennett, S. T., & Bauman, K. E. (1996). Adolescent social networks: School, demographic, and longitudinal considerations. *Journal of Adolescent Research, 11*(2), 194–215.

Ennett, S. T., Foshee, V. A., Bauman, K. E., Hussong, A., Cai, L., Reyes, H. L. M., ... & DuRant, R. (2008). The social ecology of adolescent alcohol misuse. *Child Development, 79*(6), 1777–1791.

Epstein, L. H., Klein, K. R., & Wisniewski, L. (1994). Child and parent factors that influence psychological problems in obese children. *International Journal of Eating Disorders, 15*(2), 151–158.

Etcheverry, P. E., & Agnew, C. R. (2008). Romantic partner and friend influences on young adult cigarette smoking: Comparing close others' smoking and injunctive norms over time. *Psychology of Addictive Behaviors, 22*(3), 313.

Etkin, J., Evangelidis, I., & Aaker, J. (2015). Pressed for time? Goal conflict shapes how time is perceived, spent, and valued. *Journal of Marketing Research, 52*(3), 394–406.

Evans, J., Heron, J., Francomb, H., Oke, S., & Golding, J. (2001). Cohort study of depressed mood during pregnancy and after childbirth. *BMJ, 323*(7307), 257–260.

Evans, W. N., Oates, W. E., & Schwab, R. M. (1992). Measuring peer group effects: A study of teenage behavior. *Journal of Political Economy, 100*(5), 966–991.

Fairchild, A. L. (2013). Half empty or half full? New York's soda rule in historical perspective. *New England Journal of Medicine, 368*(19), 1765–1767.

Fatas, E., Meléndez-Jiménez, M. A., & Solaz, H. (2010). An experimental analysis of team production in networks. *Experimental Economics, 13*(4), 399–411.

Feunekes, G. I., de Graaf, C., Meyboom, S., & van Staveren, W. A. (1998). Food choice and fat intake of adolescents and adults: Associations of intakes within social networks. *Preventive Medicine, 27*(5), 645–656.

Fortin, B., & Yazbeck, M. (2015). Peer effects, fast food consumption and adolescent weight gain. *Journal of Health Economics, 42*, 125–138.

Fowler, J. H., & Christakis, N. A. (2008). Dynamic spread of happiness in a large social network: Longitudinal analysis over 20 years in the Framingham Heart Study. *Bmj, 337.* https://www.bmj.com/content/337/bmj.a2338

Fowler, J. H., & Christakis, N. A. (2010). Cooperative behavior cascades in human social networks. *Proceedings of the National Academy of Sciences, 107*(12), 5334–5338.

Friis, R., Skov, L. R., Olsen, A., Appleton, K. M., Saulais, L., Dinnella, C., ... & Perez-Cueto, F. J. (2017). Comparison of three nudge interventions (priming, default option, and perceived variety) to promote vegetable consumption in a self-service buffet setting. *PloS One, 12*(5), e0176028.

Fu, F., Rosenbloom, D. I., Wang, L., & Nowak, M. A. (2011). Imitation dynamics of vaccination behaviour on social networks. *Proceedings of the Royal Society B: Biological Sciences, 278*(1702), 42–49.

Fudenberg, D., & Levine, D. K. (2006). A dual-self model of impulse control. *American Economic Review, 96*(5), 1449–1476.

Fuller, C. M., Borrell, L. N., Latkin, C. A., Galea, S., Ompad, D. C., Strathdee, S. A., & Vlahov, D. (2005). Effects of race, neighborhood, and social network on age at initiation of injection drug use. *American Journal of Public Health, 95*(4), 689–695.

Galizzi, M. M. (2012). Label, nudge or tax? A review of health policies for risky behaviours. *Journal of Public Health Research, 1*(1), 14.

Galizzi, M. M., & Wiesen, D. (2018). Behavioral experiments in health economics. In Jonathan H. Hamilton, Avinash Dixit, Sebastian Edwards and Kenneth Judd (Eds.), *Oxford research encyclopedia of economics and finance. Oxford research encyclopedias.* Oxford: Oxford University Press.

Gerards, S. M., Sleddens, E. F., Dagnelie, P. C., De Vries, N. K., & Kremers, S. P. (2011). Interventions addressing general parenting to prevent or treat childhood obesity. *International Journal of Pediatric Obesity, 6*(2Part2), e28–e45.

Ghesla, C., Grieder, M., & Schmitz, J. (2019). Nudge for good? Choice defaults and spillover effects. *Frontiers in Psychology, 10*, 178.

Gidengil, C. A., Parker, A. M., & Zikmund-Fisher, B. J. (2012). Trends in risk perceptions and vaccination intentions: A longitudinal study of the first year of the H1N1 pandemic. *American Journal of Public Health, 102*(4), 672–679.

Gneezy, U., Meier, S., & Rey-Biel, P. (2011). When and why incentives (don't) work to modify behavior. *Journal of Economic Perspectives*, *25*(4), 191–210.

Goldstein, N. J., Cialdini, R. B., & Griskevicius, V. (2008). A room with a viewpoint: Using social norms to motivate environmental conservation in hotels. *Journal of Consumer Research*, *35*(3), 472–482.

Gollwitzer, P. M. (1993). Goal achievement: The role of intentions. *European Review of Social Psychology*, *4*(1), 141–185.

Gollwitzer, P. M., & Sheeran, P. (2006). Implementation intentions and goal achievement: A meta-analysis of effects and processes. *Advances in Experimental Social Psychology*, *38*, 69–119.

Granovetter, M. S. (1973). The strength of weak ties. *American Journal of Sociology*, *78*(6), 1360–1380.

Green, E. P. (2014). Payment systems in the healthcare industry: An experimental study of physician incentives. *Journal of Economic Behavior & Organization*, *106*, 367–378.

Gwozdz, W., Nie, P., Sousa-Poza, A., DeHenauw, S., Felső, R., Hebestreit, A., ... & Family Consortium, I. (2019). Peer effects on weight status, dietary behaviour and physical activity among adolescents in Europe: Findings from the I. Family Study. *Kyklos*, *72*(2), 270–296.

Gwozdz, W., Sousa-Poza, A., Reisch, L. A., Bammann, K., Eiben, G., Kourides, Y., ... & Pigeot, I. (2015). Peer effects on obesity in a sample of European children. *Economics & Human Biology*, *18*, 139–152.

Halliday, T. J., & Kwak, S. (2012). What is a peer? The role of network definitions in estimation of endogenous peer effects. *Applied Economics*, *44*(3), 289–302.

Hansen, P. G., Schilling, M., & Malthesen, M. S. (2021). Nudging healthy and sustainable food choices: Three randomized controlled field experiments using a vegetarian lunch-default as a normative signal. *Journal of Public Health*, *43*(2), 392–397.

Harmsen, I. A., Mollema, L., Ruiter, R. A., Paulussen, T. G., de Melker, H. E., & Kok, G. (2013). Why parents refuse childhood vaccination: A qualitative study using online focus groups. *BMC Public Health*, *13*(1), 1–8.

Hatfield, E., Cacioppo, J. T., & Rapson, R. L. (1992). Primitive emotional contagion. *Review of Personality and Social Psychology*, *14*, 151–177.

Havens, J. R., Lofwall, M. R., Frost, S. D., Oser, C. B., Leukefeld, C. G., & Crosby, R. A. (2013). Individual and network factors associated with prevalent hepatitis C infection among rural Appalachian injection drug users. *American Journal of Public Health*, *103*(1), e44–e52.

Henry, H. K., & Borzekowski, D. L. (2015). Well, that's what came with it. A qualitative study of US mothers' perceptions of healthier default options for children's meals at fast-food restaurants. *Appetite*, *87*, 108–115.

Hersch, J., & Viscusi, W. K. (1998). Smoking and other risky behaviors. *Journal of Drug Issues*, *28*(3), 645–661.

Hill, A. L., Rand, D. G., Nowak, M. A., & Christakis, N. A. (2010). Emotions as infectious diseases in a large social network: The SISa model. *Proceedings of the Royal Society B: Biological Sciences*, *277*(1701), 3827–3835.

Hoffner, C., & Ye, J. (2009). Young adults' responses to news about sunscreen and skin cancer: The role of framing and social comparison. *Health Communication*, *24*(3), 189–198.

Holzer, H. J. (1987). Job search by employed and unemployed youth. *ILR Review*, *40*(4), 601–611.

Hoogink, J., Verelst, F., Kessels, R., Van Hoek, A. J., Timen, A., Willem, L., ... & De Wit, G. A. (2020). Preferential differences in vaccination decision-making for oneself or one's child in The Netherlands: A discrete choice experiment. *BMC public health*, *20*, 1–14.

Hussam, R. N., Rabbani, A., Reggiani, G., & Rigol, N. (2017). Habit formation and rational addiction: A field experiment in handwashing. *Harvard Business School working paper series# 18-030*.

Jaime Torres, M. M., & Carlsson, F. (2018). Direct and spillover effects of a social information campaign on residential water-savings. *Journal of Environmental Economics and Management*, *92*, 222–243.

John, P., & Stoker, G. (2019). Rethinking the role of experts and expertise in behavioural public policy. *Policy & Politics*, *47*(2), 209–226.

Johnson, E. J., & Goldstein, D. (2003). Do defaults save lives?. *Science*, *302*(5649), 1338–1339.

Joiner Jr, T. E., & Katz, J. (1999). Contagion of depressive symptoms and mood: Meta-analytic review and explanations from cognitive, behavioral, and interpersonal viewpoints. *Clinical Psychology: Science and Practice*, *6*(2), 149–164.

Kahneman, D. (2003). Maps of bounded rationality: Psychology for behavioral economics. *American Economic Review*, *93*(5), 1449–1475.

Kawachi, I., Daniels, N., & Robinson, D. E. (2005). Health disparities by race and class: Why both matter. *Health Affairs*, *24*(2), 343–352.

Kirchkamp, O., & Nagel, R. (2007). Naive learning and cooperation in network experiments. *Games and Economic Behavior*, *58*(2), 269–292.

Knecht, A. B., Burk, W. J., Weesie, J., & Steglich, C. (2011). Friendship and alcohol use in early adolescence: A multilevel social network approach. *Journal of Research on Adolescence*, *21*(2), 475–487.

Kobus, K., & Henry, D. B. (2010). Interplay of network position and peer substance use in early adolescent cigarette, alcohol, and marijuana use. *The Journal of Early Adolescence*, *30*(2), 225–245.

Köster, E. P. (2003). The psychology of food choice: Some often encountered fallacies. *Food Quality and Preference*, *14*(5–6), 359–373.

Kremer, M., & Levy, D. (2008). Peer effects and alcohol use among college students. *Journal of Economic Perspectives*, *22*(3), 189–206.

Kroese, F. M., Marchiori, D. R., & de Ridder, D. T. (2016). Nudging healthy food choices: A field experiment at the train station. *Journal of Public Health*, *38*(2), e133–e137.

Krølner, R., Rasmussen, M., Brug, J., Klepp, K. I., Wind, M., & Due, P. (2011). Determinants of fruit and vegetable consumption among children and adolescents: A review of the literature. Part II: Qualitative studies. *International Journal of Behavioral Nutrition and Physical Activity*, *8*(1), 1–38.

Krupka, E., & Weber, R. A. (2009). The focusing and informational effects of norms on pro-social behavior. *Journal of Economic Psychology*, *30*(3), 307–320.

Laibson, D. (1997). Golden eggs and hyperbolic discounting. *The Quarterly Journal of Economics*, *112*(2), 443–478.

Lally, P., Bartle, N., & Wardle, J. (2011). Social norms and diet in adolescents. *Appetite*, *57*(3), 623–627.

Lapinski, M. K., Maloney, E. K., Braz, M., & Shulman, H. C. (2013). Testing the effects of social norms and behavioral privacy on hand washing: A field experiment. *Human Communication Research*, *39*(1), 21–46.

Larimer, M. E., & Cronce, J. M. (2002). Identification, prevention and treatment: A review of individual-focused strategies to reduce problematic alcohol consumption by college students. *Journal of Studies on Alcohol, Supplement*, (14), 148–163. https://www.jsad.com/doi/abs/10.15288/jsas.2002.s14.148

Larson, H. J., Jarrett, C., Eckersberger, E., Smith, D. M., & Paterson, P. (2014). Understanding vaccine hesitancy around vaccines and vaccination from a global perspective: A systematic review of published literature, 2007–2012. *Vaccine*, *32*(19), 2150–2159.

Larson, R. W., & Almeida, D. M. (1999). Emotional transmission in the daily lives of families: A new paradigm for studying family process. *Journal of Marriage and the Family*, *6*(1), 5–20.

Latkin, C., Mandell, W., Oziemkowska, M., Celentano, D., Vlahov, D., Ensminger, M., & Knowlton, A. (1995). Using social network analysis to study patterns of drug use among urban drug users at high risk for HIV/AIDS. *Drug and Alcohol Dependence*, *38*(1), 1–9.

Latkin, C. A., & Knowlton, A. R. (2015). Social network assessments and interventions for health behavior change: A critical review. *Behavioral Medicine*, *41*(3), 90–97.

Lawrence, N. K. (2015). Highlighting the injunctive norm to reduce phone-related distracted driving. *Social Influence*, *10*(2), 109–118.

Lazarsfeld, P. F., & Merton, R. K. (1954). Friendship as social process: A substantive and methodological inquiry. In M. Berger, T. Abel and H. Charles (Eds.), *Freedom and control in modern society*. New York: Van Nostrand.

Leeds, I. L., Sadiraj, V., Cox, J. C., Gao, X. S., Pawlik, T. M., Schnier, K. E., & Sweeney, J. F. (2017). Discharge decision-making after complex surgery: Surgeon behaviors compared to predictive modeling to reduce surgical readmissions. *The American Journal of Surgery*, *213*(1), 112–119.

Lehmann, B. A., Chapman, G. B., Franssen, F. M., Kok, G., & Ruiter, R. A. (2016). Changing the default to promote influenza vaccination among health care workers. *Vaccine*, *34*(11), 1389–1392.

Leibbrandt, A., Ramalingam, A., Sääksvuori, L., & Walker, J. M. (2015). Incomplete punishment networks in public goods games: Experimental evidence. *Experimental Economics*, *18*(1), 15–37.

Leider, S., Rosenblat, T., Möbius, M. M., & Do, Q. A. (2010). What do we expect from our friends?. *Journal of the European Economic Association*, *8*(1), 120–138.

Leventhal, H., & Cleary, P. D. (1980). The smoking problem: A review of the research and theory in behavioral risk modification. *Psychological Bulletin*, *88*(2), 370.

Lewis, M. A., & Neighbors, C. (2004). Gender-specific misperceptions of college student drinking norms. *Psychology of Addictive Behaviors, 18*(4), 334.

Li, M., & Chapman, G. B. (2013). Nudge to health: Harnessing decision research to promote health behavior. *Social and Personality Psychology Compass, 7*(3), 187–198.

Lindbeck, A. (1997). Incentives and social norms in household behavior. *American Economic Review, 87*(2), 370–377.

Linkenbach, J. W., & Perkins, H. (2003). MOST of us are tobacco free: An eight-month social norms campaign reducing youth initiation of smoking in Montana. In H. W. Perkins (Ed.), *The social norms approach to preventing school and college age substance abuse: A handbook for educators, counselors, and clinicians* (pp. 224–234). San Francisco: Jossey-Bass/Wiley.

Lo, N. C., & Hotez, P. J. (2017). Public health and economic consequences of vaccine hesitancy for measles in the United States. *JAMA Pediatrics, 171*(9), 887–892.

Locke, E. A., & Latham, G. P. (2002). Building a practically useful theory of goal setting and task motivation: A 35-year odyssey. *American Psychologist, 57*(9), 705.

Loeb, K. L., Radnitz, C., Keller, K., Schwartz, M. B., Marcus, S., Pierson, R. N., ... & DeLaurentis, D. (2017). The application of defaults to optimize parents' health-based choices for children. *Appetite, 113*, 368–375.

Loewenstein, G., & O'Donoghue, T. (2004). Animal spirits: Affective and deliberative processes in economic behavior. *Available at SSRN 539843*.

Loewenstein, G., & O'Donoghue, T. (2007). The heat of the moment: Modeling interactions between affect and deliberation. *Unpublished Manuscript*, 1–69.

Loewenstein, G., Price, J., & Volpp, K. (2016). Habit formation in children: Evidence from incentives for healthy eating. *Journal of Health Economics, 45*, 47–54.

Loschelder, D. D., Siepelmeyer, H., Fischer, D., & Rubel, J. A. (2019). Dynamic norms drive sustainable consumption: Norm-based nudging helps café customers to avoid disposable to-go-cups. *Journal of Economic Psychology, 75*, 102–146.

Lundborg, P. (2006). Having the wrong friends? Peer effects in adolescent substance use. *Journal of Health Economics, 25*(2), 214–233.

MacDonald, N. E., SAGE Working Group on Vaccine Hesitancy (2015). Vaccine hesitancy: Definition, scope and determinants. *Vaccine, 33*(34), 4161–4164.

Maxwell, K. A. (2002). Friends: The role of peer influence across adolescent risk behaviors. *Journal of Youth and Adolescence, 31*(4), 267–277.

McPherson, M., Smith-Lovin, L., & Cook, J. M. (2001). Birds of a feather: Homophily in social networks. *Annual Review of Sociology, 27*(1), 415–444.

Mesa, D. O., Hogan, A., Watson, O., Charles, G., Hauck, K., Ghani, A. C., & Winskill, P. (2021). Quantifying the impact of vaccine hesitancy in prolonging the need for Non-Pharmaceutical Interventions to control the COVID-19 pandemic. WHO Collaborating Centre for Infectious Disease Modelling, MRC Centre for Global Infectious Disease Analysis, Jameel Institute (J-IDEA), Imperial College London. https://www.imperial.ac.uk/mrc-global-infectious-disease-analysis/covid-19/report-43-vaccine-hesitancy/

Meszaros, J. R., Asch, D. A., Baron, J., Hershey, J. C., Kunreuther, H., & Schwartz-Buzaglo, J. (1996). Cognitive processes and the decisions of some parents to forego pertussis vaccination for their children. *Journal of Clinical Epidemiology, 49*(6), 697–703.

Metcalfe, J., & Mischel, W. (1999). A hot/cool-system analysis of delay of gratification: Dynamics of willpower. *Psychological Review, 106*(1), 3.

Milkman, K. L., Beshears, J., Choi, J. J., Laibson, D., & Madrian, B. C. (2011). Using implementation intentions prompts to enhance influenza vaccination rates. *Proceedings of the National Academy of Sciences, 108*(26), 10415–10420.

Milkman, K. L., Beshears, J., Choi, J. J., Laibson, D., & Madrian, B. C. (2013). Planning prompts as a means of increasing preventive screening rates. *Preventive Medicine, 56*(1), 92–93.

Milkman, K. L., Patel, M. S., Gandhi, L., Graci, H. N., Gromet, D. M., Ho, H., ... & Duckworth, A. L. (2021). A megastudy of text-based nudges encouraging patients to get vaccinated at an upcoming doctor's appointment. *Proceedings of the National Academy of Sciences, 118*(20). https://www.pnas.org/doi/10.1073/pnas.2101165118

Milne, S., Orbell, S., & Sheeran, P. (2002). Combining motivational and volitional interventions to promote exercise participation: Protection motivation theory and implementation intentions. *British Journal of Health Psychology*, 7(2), 163–184.

Mochon, D., Schwartz, J., Maroba, J., Patel, D., & Ariely, D. (2017). Gain without pain: The extended effects of a behavioral health intervention. *Management Science*, 63(1), 58–72.

Mokdad, A. H., Serdula, M. K., Dietz, W. H., Bowman, B. A., Marks, J. S., & Koplan, J. P. (2000). The continuing epidemic of obesity in the United States. *JAMA*, 284(13), 1650–1651.

Mollen, S., Rimal, R. N., Ruiter, R. A., & Kok, G. (2013). Healthy and unhealthy social norms and food selection. Findings from a field-experiment. *Appetite*, 65, 83–89.

Monge-Rojas, R., Nunez, H. P., Garita, C., & Chen-Mok, M. (2002). Psychosocial aspects of Costa Rican adolescents' eating and physical activity patterns. *Journal of Adolescent Health*, 31(2), 212–219.

Montgomery, J. D. (1992). Job search and network composition: Implications of the strength-of-weak-ties hypothesis. *American Sociological Review*, 57(5), 586–596.

Moore, S., Daniel, M., Paquet, C., Dubé, L., & Gauvin, L. (2009). Association of individual network social capital with abdominal adiposity, overweight and obesity. *Journal of Public Health*, 31(1), 175–183.

Mora, T., & Gil, J. (2013). Peer effects in adolescent BMI: Evidence from Spain. *Health Economics*, 22(5), 501–516.

Mortensen, C. R., Neel, R., Cialdini, R. B., Jaeger, C. M., Jacobson, R. P., & Ringel, M. M. (2019). Trending norms: A lever for encouraging behaviors performed by the minority. *Social Psychological and Personality Science*, 10(2), 201–210.

Mueller, A. S., Abrutyn, S., & Stockton, C. (2015). Can social ties be harmful? Examining the spread of suicide in early adulthood. *Sociological Perspectives*, 58(2), 204–222.

Mühlböck, M., Kalleitner, F., Steiber, N., & Kittel, B. (2020). Information, reflection, and successful job search: A nudging experiment. *Reflection, and Successful Job Search: A Nudging Experiment* (April 15, 2020). Available at SSRN: https://ssrn.com/abstract=3576740

Murray, C. J., Vos, T., Lozano, R., Naghavi, M., Flaxman, A. D., Michaud, C., ... & Haring, D. (2012). Disability-adjusted life years (DALYs) for 291 diseases and injuries in 21 regions, 1990–2010: A systematic analysis for the Global Burden of Disease Study 2010. *The Lancet*, 380(9859), 2197–2223.

Mussio, I. & de Oliveira, A. (2022). An (un)healthy social dilemma: Using normative messaging to increase flu vaccinations. Department of Resource Economics, University of Massachusetts Amherst.

National Institute on Alcohol Abuse and Alcoholism (2020). Alcohol facts and statistics, alcohol use in the United States. https://www.niaaa.nih.gov/publications/brochures-and-fact-sheets/alcohol-facts-and-statistics

Neaigus, A., Friedman, S. R., Goldstein, M., Ildefonso, G., Curtis, R., & Jose, B. (1995). Using dyadic data for a network analysis of HIV infection and risk behaviors among injecting drug users. *NIDA Research Monograph*, 151, 20–37.

Neaigus, A., Gyarmathy, V. A., Miller, M., Frajzyngier, V. M., Friedman, S. R., & Des Jarlais, D. C. (2006). Transitions to injecting drug use among noninjecting heroin users: Social network influence and individual susceptibility. *JAIDS Journal of Acquired Immune Deficiency Syndromes*, 41(4), 493–503.

Neighbors, C., LaBrie, J. W., Hummer, J. F., Lewis, M. A., Lee, C. M., Desai, S., ... & Larimer, M. E. (2010). Group identification as a moderator of the relationship between perceived social norms and alcohol consumption. *Psychology of Addictive Behaviors*, 24(3), 522.

Neighbors, C., Larimer, M. E., & Lewis, M. A. (2004). Targeting misperceptions of descriptive drinking norms: Efficacy of a computer-delivered personalized normative feedback intervention. *Journal of Consulting and Clinical Psychology*, 72(3), 434.

Neighbors, C., Lee, C. M., Lewis, M. A., Fossos, N., & Larimer, M. E. (2007). Are social norms the best predictor of outcomes among heavy-drinking college students?. *Journal of Studies on Alcohol and Drugs*, 68(4), 556–565.

Newman, M. E. J. (2010). *Networks: An introduction*. Oxford; New York: Oxford University Press. ISBN: 9780199206650 0199206651

Njeru, J. W., Wieland, M. L., Okamoto, J. M., Novotny, P. J., Breen-Lyles, M. K., Osman, A., ... & Sia, I. G. (2020). Social networks and obesity among Somali immigrants and refugees. *BMC Public Health*, 20(1), 1–10.

Nye, E. C., Agostinelli, G., & Smith, J. E. (1999). Enhancing alcohol problem recognition: A self-regulation model for the effects of self-focusing and normative information. *Journal of Studies on Alcohol, 60*(5), 685–693.

Ogden, C. L., Carroll, M. D., Kit, B. K., & Flegal, K. M. (2014). Prevalence of childhood and adult obesity in the United States, 2011-2012. *JAMA, 311*(8), 806–814.

Oraby, T., Thampi, V., & Bauch, C. T. (2014). The influence of social norms on the dynamics of vaccinating behaviour for paediatric infectious diseases. *Proceedings of the Royal Society B: Biological Sciences, 281*(1780), 20133172.

Osman, M., McLachlan, S., Fenton, N., Neil, M., Löfstedt, R., & Meder, B. (2020). Learning from behavioural changes that fail. *Trends in Cognitive Sciences, 24*(12), 969–980.

Pachucki, M. C., & Goodman, E. (2015). Social relationships and obesity: Benefits of incorporating a lifecourse perspective. *Current Obesity Reports, 4*(2), 217–223.

Pachucki, M. C., Ozer, E. J., Barrat, A., & Cattuto, C. (2015). Mental health and social networks in early adolescence: A dynamic study of objectively-measured social interaction behaviors. *Social Science & Medicine, 125*, 40–50.

Pearson, N., Biddle, S. J., & Gorely, T. (2009). Family correlates of fruit and vegetable consumption in children and adolescents: A systematic review. *Public Health Nutrition, 12*(2), 267–283.

Pedersen, S., Grønhøj, A., & Thøgersen, J. (2015). Following family or friends. Social norms in adolescent healthy eating. *Appetite, 86*, 54–60.

Perkins, H. W., & Berkowitz, A. D. (1986). Perceiving the community norms of alcohol use among students: Some research implications for campus alcohol education programming. *International Journal of the Addictions, 21*(9–10), 961–976.

Perkins, H. W., & Craig, D. W. (2003). The Hobart and William Smith Colleges experiment: A synergistic social norms approach using print, electronic media, and curriculum infusion to reduce collegiate problem drinking. In H. W. Perkins (Ed.), *The social norms approach to preventing school and college age substance abuse: A handbook for educators, counselors, and clinicians* (pp. 35–64). San Francisco: Jossey-Bass/Wiley.

Prestwich, A., Lawton, R., & Conner, M. (2003). The use of implementation intentions and the decision balance sheet in promoting exercise behaviour. *Psychology and Health, 18*(6), 707–721.

Razai, M. S., Osama, T., McKechnie, D. G., & Majeed, A. (2021). Covid-19 vaccine hesitancy among ethnic minority groups. *BMJ: British Medical Journal (Online), 372*.

Reicks, M., Redden, J. P., Mann, T., Mykerezi, E., & Vickers, Z. (2012). Photographs in lunch tray compartments and vegetable consumption among children in elementary school cafeterias. *Jama, 307*(8), 784–785.

Reid, A. E., & Aiken, L. S. (2013). Correcting injunctive norm misperceptions motivates behavior change: A randomized controlled sun protection intervention. *Health Psychology, 32*(5), 551.

Reid, A. E., Cialdini, R. B., & Aiken, L. S. (2011). Social norms and health behavior. In A. Steptoe, K. Freedland, J. R. Jennings, M. M. Llabre, S. B. Manuck, & E. J. Susman (Eds.), *Handbook of behavioral medicine: Methods and applications* (pp. 263–274). New York: Springer.

Reisch, L. A., & Sunstein, C. R. (2016). Do Europeans like nudges?. *Judgment and Decision Making, 11*(4), 310–325.

Reisch, L. A., Sunstein, C. R., & Kaiser, M. (2021). Most people like nudges: And why that matters. In S. Grundmann & P. Hacker (Eds.), *Theories of choice: The social science and the law of decision making* (pp. 73–86). Oxford: Oxford University Press.

Rivis, A., & Sheeran, P. (2003). Social influences and the theory of planned behaviour: Evidence for a direct relationship between prototypes and young people's exercise behaviour. *Psychology and Health, 18*(5), 567–583.

Roberto, C. A., Larsen, P. D., Agnew, H., Baik, J., & Brownell, K. D. (2010). Evaluating the impact of menu labeling on food choices and intake. *American Journal of Public Health, 100*(2), 312–318.

Robinson, S. A., Bisson, A. N., Hughes, M. L., Ebert, J., & Lachman, M. E. (2019). Time for change: Using implementation intentions to promote physical activity in a randomised pilot trial. *Psychology & Health, 34*(2), 232–254.

Rogers, T., Milkman, K. L., & Volpp, K. G. (2014). Commitment devices: Using initiatives to change behavior. *JAMA, 311*(20), 2065–2066.

Rosenquist, J. N., Fowler, J. H., & Christakis, N. A. (2011). Social network determinants of depression. *Molecular Psychiatry, 16*(3), 273–281.

Sacerdote, B. (2001). Peer effects with random assignment: Results for Dartmouth roommates. *The Quarterly Journal of Economics, 116*(2), 681–704.

Sadoff, S., Samek, A., & Sprenger, C. (2020). Dynamic inconsistency in food choice: Experimental evidence from two food deserts. *Review of Economic Studies, 87*(4), 1954–1988.

Samek, A. (2019). Gifts and goals: Behavioral nudges to improve child food choice at school. *Journal of Economic Behavior & Organization, 164*, 1–12.

Schmid, P., Rauber, D., Betsch, C., Lidolt, G., & Denker, M. L. (2017). Barriers of influenza vaccination intention and behavior–a systematic review of influenza vaccine hesitancy, 2005–2016. *PloS One, 12*(1), e0170550.

Schmidt, A. T., & Engelen, B. (2020). The ethics of nudging: An overview. *Philosophy Compass, 15*(4), e12658.

Sleddens, E. F., Gerards, S. M., Thijs, C., De Vries, N. K., & Kremers, S. P. (2011). General parenting, childhood overweight and obesity-inducing behaviors: A review. *International Journal of Pediatric Obesity, 6*(2Part2), e12–e27.

Smith, K. P., & Christakis, N. A. (2008). Social networks and health. *Annual Review of Sociology, 34*, 405–429.

Smith, N. R., Zivich, P. N., & Frerichs, L. (2020). Social influences on obesity: Current knowledge, emerging methods, and directions for future research and practice. *Current Nutrition Reports, 9*(1), 31–41.

Smith-McLallen, A., & Fishbein, M. (2008). Predictors of intentions to perform six cancer-related behaviours: Roles for injunctive and descriptive norms. *Psychology, Health and Medicine, 13*(4), 389–401.

Sparkman, G., & Walton, G. M. (2017). Dynamic norms promote sustainable behavior, even if it is counternormative. *Psychological Science, 28*(11), 1663–1674.

Strauss, R. S., & Pollack, H. A. (2003). Social marginalization of overweight children. *Archives of Pediatrics & Adolescent Medicine, 157*(8), 746–752.

Sunstein, C. R. (2017a). Nudges that fail. *Behavioral Public Policy, 1*(1), 4–25.

Sunstein, C. R. (2017b). People like nudges (mostly). In *Human agency and behavioral economics* (pp. 17–39). Cham: Palgrave Macmillan.

Sunstein, C. R., Reisch, L. A., & Kaiser, M. (2019). Trusting nudges? Lessons from an international survey. *Journal of European Public Policy, 26*(10), 1417–1443.

Sunstein, C. R., Reisch, L. A., & Rauber, J. (2018). A worldwide consensus on nudging? Not quite, but almost. *Regulation & Governance, 12*(1), 3–22.

Taylor, M. J., Vlaev, I., Maltby, J., Brown, G. D., & Wood, A. M. (2015). Improving social norms interventions: Rank-framing increases excessive alcohol drinkers' information-seeking. *Health Psychology, 34*(12), 1200.

Terzian, E., Tognoni, G., Bracco, R., De Ruggieri, E., Ficociello, R. A., Mezzina, R., & Pillo, G. (2013). Social network intervention in patients with schizophrenia and marked social withdrawal: A randomized controlled study. *The Canadian Journal of Psychiatry, 58*(11), 622–631.

Thaler, R. H., & Shefrin, H. M. (1981). An economic theory of self-control. *Journal of Political Economy, 89*(2), 392–406.

Thaler, R. H., & Sunstein, C. R. (2008). *Nudge: Improving decisions about health, wealth, and happiness.* Yale University Press.

Thaler, R. H., & Sunstein, C. R. (2021). *Nudge: The final edition.* London: Penguin.

Thorndike, A. N., Sonnenberg, L., Riis, J., Barraclough, S., & Levy, D. E. (2012). A 2-phase labeling and choice architecture intervention to improve healthy food and beverage choices. *American Journal of Public Health, 102*(3), 527–533.

Thorpe, E. L., Zimmerman, R. K., Steinhart, J. D., Lewis, K. N., & Michaels, M. G. (2012). Homeschooling parents' practices and beliefs about childhood immunizations. *Vaccine, 30*(6), 1149–1153.

Trogdon, J. G., Nonnemaker, J., & Pais, J. (2008). Peer effects in adolescent overweight. *Journal of health economics, 27*(5), 1388–1399.

Tversky, A., & Kahneman, D. (1974). Judgment under uncertainty: Heuristics and biases. *Science, 185*(4157), 1124–1131.

Unger, J. B., Reynolds, K., Shakib, S., Spruijt-Metz, D., Sun, P., & Johnson, C. A. (2004). Acculturation, physical activity, and fast-food consumption among Asian-American and Hispanic adolescents. *Journal of Community Health*, 29(6), 467–481.

Valente, T. W., & Vega Yon, G. G. (2020). Diffusion/contagion processes on social networks. *Health Education & Behavior*, 47(2), 235–248.

Vallentin-Holbech, L., Rasmussen, B. M., & Stock, C. (2017). Are perceptions of social norms regarding peer alcohol and other drug use associated with personal use in Danish adolescents?. *Scandinavian Journal of Public Health*, 45(8), 757–764.

Vallgårda, S. (2012). Nudge—A new and better way to improve health?. *Health Policy*, 104(2), 200–203.

Van Bavel, J. J., Baicker, K., Boggio, P. S., Capraro, V., Cichocka, A., Cikara, M., ... & Willer, R. (2020). Using social and behavioural science to support COVID-19 pandemic response. *Nature Human Behaviour*, 4(5), 460–471.

Van den Broucke S. (2014). Health literacy: A critical concept for public health. *Archives of public health = Archives Belges de sante publique*, 72(1), 10. https://doi.org/10.1186/2049-3258-72-10

van Grieken, A., Ezendam, N. P., Paulis, W. D., van der Wouden, J. C., & Raat, H. (2012). Primary prevention of overweight in children and adolescents: A meta-analysis of the effectiveness of interventions aiming to decrease sedentary behaviour. *International Journal of Behavioral Nutrition and Physical Activity*, 9(1), 1–11.

van Kleef, E., Seijdell, K., Vingerhoeds, M. H., de Wijk, R. A., & van Trijp, H. C. (2018). The effect of a default-based nudge on the choice of whole wheat bread. *Appetite*, 121, 179–185.

Verelst, F., Kessels, R., Delva, W., Beutels, P., & Willem, L. (2019). Drivers of vaccine decision-making in South Africa: A discrete choice experiment. *Vaccine*, 37(15), 2079–2089.

Verelst, F., Willem, L., Kessels, R., & Beutels, P. (2018). Individual decisions to vaccinate one's child or oneself: A discrete choice experiment rejecting free-riding motives. *Social Science & Medicine*, 207, 106–116.

Vermote, M., Nys, J., Versele, V., D'Hondt, E., Deforche, B., Clarys, P., & Deliens, T. (2020). The effect of nudges aligned with the renewed Flemish Food Triangle on the purchase of fresh fruits: An on-campus restaurant experiment. *Appetite*, 144, 104479.

Voorhees, C. C., Murray, D., Welk, G., Birnbaum, A., Ribisl, K. M., Johnson, C. C., ... & Jobe, J. B. (2005). The role of peer social network factors and physical activity in adolescent girls. *American Journal of Health Behavior*, 29(2), 183–190.

Ward, R. M., & Guo, Y. (2020). Examining the relationship between social norms, alcohol-induced blackouts, and intentions to blackout among college students. *Alcohol*, 86, 35–41.

Wasserman, S., & Faust, K. (1994). *Structural analysis in the social sciences. Social network analysis: Methods and applications.* Cambridge University Press. https://doi.org/10.1017/CBO9780511815478

Wisdom, J., Downs, J. S., & Loewenstein, G. (2010). Promoting healthy choices: Information versus convenience. *American Economic Journal: Applied Economics*, 2(2), 164–178.

Wölfer, R., & Scheithauer, H. (2014). Social influence and bullying behavior: Intervention-based network dynamics of the fairplayer manual bullying prevention program. *Aggressive Behavior*, 40(4), 309–319.

World Health Organization (2018). Obesity. https://www.who.int/health-topics/obesity.

World Health Organization (2019). Tobacco: Data and statistics. https://www.euro.who.int/en/health-topics/disease-prevention/tobacco/data-and-statistics

World Health Organization (2020). Tobacco. https://www.who.int/news-room/fact-sheets/detail/tobacco

Wu, Y. H., Moore, S., & Dube, L. (2018). Social capital and obesity among adults: Longitudinal findings from the Montreal neighborhood networks and healthy aging panel. *Preventive Medicine*, 111, 366–370.

Xiao, X., & Wong, R. M. (2020). Vaccine hesitancy and perceived behavioral control: A meta-analysis. *Vaccine*, 38(33), 5131–5138.

Yakusheva, O., Kapinos, K., & Weiss, M. (2011). Peer effects and the freshman 15: Evidence from a natural experiment. *Economics & Human Biology*, 9(2), 119–132.

Yun, D., & Silk, K. J. (2011). Social norms, self-identity, and attention to social comparison information in the context of exercise and healthy diet behavior. *Health Communication*, 26(3), 275–285.

Zhang, S., De La Haye, K., Ji, M., & An, R. (2018). Applications of social network analysis to obesity: A systematic review. *Obesity Reviews*, 19(7), 976–988.

Zimmerman, F. J. (2009). Using behavioral economics to promote physical activity. *Preventive Medicine*, 49(4), 289–291.

27. Bridging psychology and sociology: Towards a socio-ecological perspective in behavioural economics and policy

Noah V. Peters and Lucia A. Reisch

INTRODUCTION

Behavioural economics (BE) refutes standard economic axioms of rationality and utility maximisation. As Thaler (2016, p. 1578) summarises, BE 'replaces Econs with *Homo sapiens*, otherwise known as Humans'. In this vein, BE has provided new micro-foundations for macroeconomic behaviour (Akerlof, 2002). Those micro-foundations are chiefly informed by psychology. Social and macro-determinants of individual behaviour – as studied in sociology, anthropology or geography – feature less prominently in BE.

Indeed, numerous scholars claim there is a lack of interdisciplinary perspectives in BE and behavioural public policy (BPP), the application of behavioural insights to policymaking. Feitsma and Whitehead (2022) argue that behavioural economists pride themselves on interdisciplinarity whilst not sufficiently delivering on this promise. Frerichs (2019, p. 243) laments BE's emphasis on psychology and 'a truncated understanding of the social'. Harbers et al. (2020), in a recent review, find that nudging studies rarely explore the moderating impact of socioeconomic variables. Ewert (2020), Ewert and Loer (2020), and Ewert et al. (2020) develop a research agenda for a more diverse BPP. Specifically, Ewert (2020, p. 352) argues that 'advanced BPP' can move beyond nudge theory by deploying interdisciplinary concepts, contextual insights, mixed methods and a policy blend. Underpinning this argument, Ewert and Loer (2020, p. 28) 'identify so far underrepresented intellectual foundations and practices of BPP that utilise insights from other disciplines than behavioural economics and psychology'.

In principle, we agree with these propositions; BE can benefit from more interdisciplinarity, and we seek to contribute with a sociological perspective. Nonetheless, we maintain that BPP proponents in general (Oliver, 2017; Ruggeri, 2019) and the tenets of choice architecture (Thaler et al., 2013) have always emphasised the crucial roles of context, social norms and ecological determinants of decision-making. To this end, psychology itself can provide novel perspectives that have not yet been fully leveraged.

In this chapter, we identify *blind spots* surrounding the social and environmental determinants of individual choice. Based on this, we aim to extend the conceptual and analytical toolkit of BPP whilst balancing complexity and practical applicability.

First, we outline how socio-ecological psychology can enrich choice architecture/nudge theory (second section). Adopting a sociological perspective, we then argue that Bourdieusian sociology and a social-practice lens enable behavioural economists to capture contingent human behaviour (third section). To close, we describe how these new pathways can be reconciled with established research paradigms and policy practices (fourth section), and how a diverse methodological toolkit contributes to this endeavour (fifth section).

INCORPORATING SOCIO-ECOLOGICAL DETERMINANTS MORE EXPLICITLY

Our first inquiry line examines how situational factors impact the interplay between behavioural interventions, individual choice, and underlying psychological processes. One particular stream in psychology that has experienced highs and lows in popularity (Oishi & Graham, 2010) offers a fruitful perspective: Socio-ecological psychology 'investigates how mind and behavior are shaped in part by their natural and social habitats (social ecology) and how natural and social habitats are in turn shaped partly by mind and behavior' (Oishi, 2014, p. 582). This research stream relaxes the emphasis on individual psychological processes detached from social and ecological contexts (Gurven, 2018; Oishi, 2014). Oishi (2014, p. 583) differentiates three types of analysis: *association studies* investigate how features of the social ecology are connected to specific psychological processes like 'cognition, emotion, or behavior'. *Process studies* discern psychological mediators' role in the interplay of social ecology and individual-level outcomes. *Niche construction studies* reverse the direction of inquiry by examining how psychological phenomena contribute to the development of social ecology structures (*niche*) (Oishi, 2014).

By illuminating the links between ecological variables and individual behaviour, socio-ecological psychology resembles choice architecture (Thaler et al., 2013). Both approaches are informed by Bronfenbrenner's (1977) ecological theory, and choice architecture is fundamentally concerned with individuals' decision environment: '[C]onsumers do not decide in a vacuum, but always in a choice context. Conscious design of choice architecture is ubiquitous, and there is no setting or situation without a choice architecture' (Reisch & Zhao, 2017, p. 201). These decision constraints include environmental characteristics like neighbourhoods, foodscapes and the built environment. According to Thaler et al. (2013, p. 429), '[a] good rule of thumb is to assume that "everything matters"'. To spell this out explicitly in a macro-context, findings from socio-ecological psychology can supplement choice architecture.

Choice architecture itself is closely related to nudge theory (Thaler & Sunstein, 2008, 2021), which describes *modifications* in the choice environment. Socio-ecological psychology, however, has a more analytical purview by discerning the *interrelatedness* between social ecology and psychological processes. Variables of interest like residential mobility or the weather often lie beyond the immediate scope of interventions but still alter their effectiveness. Socio-ecological psychology can help specify and operationalise what choice architects already highlight, albeit rather generally: context. We propose to integrate both streams more explicitly.

Linking Social Ecology and Behavioural Public Policy

We now present some examples of nudge interventions affected by socio-ecological determinants. Afterwards, we outline, in a more theoretical manner, the potential causal pathways linking behavioural interventions, psychological processes and features of social ecology.

Self-control interventions and physical environments

Psychological research has repeatedly shown that individuals' ability to exert self-control is limited (Baumeister et al., 1998; Hagger et al., 2010). This insight influenced BE (Cohen et al., 2020; Frederick et al., 2002) and stimulated research on behavioural interventions enhancing discipline and willpower (for example, Fishbach & Hofmann, 2015). Even a small reminder can suffice to steer people towards their original intentions (Sunstein, 2014).

Going beyond this intrapsychic perspective, research in socio-ecological psychology has found that natural environments can enhance mental resources (Kaplan & Berman, 2010). Conversely, urban environments tend to induce stress and cognitive load (Lederbogen et al., 2011; Oishi, 2014). Combining both threads, we hypothesise that self-control nudges implemented in natural vis-à-vis urban realms can trigger varying outcomes as the salience of the underlying bias is influenced by social ecology. A nudge, such as a reminder, might be a godsend for stressed-out urbanites, who notoriously miss their cancer screenings. In contrast, relaxed villagers might not derive significant benefits from this intervention.

Features of social ecology influence individuals' mental capacities. Likewise, mental restrictions and ill-considered choices are fertile ground for choice architects. Linking both lines of inquiry can augment the effectiveness of behaviourally informed policies.

Social-norm interventions and geographic characteristics

Social-norm nudges (Sunstein, 2014) further illustrate this point because prosocial attitudes and collectivist values are associated with a host of macro-characteristics (Oishi, 2014). Areas strained by high rates of pathogens have been shown to develop a robust set of collectivist virtues like family and in-group ties (Fincher et al., 2008; Fincher & Thornhill, 2012; Morand & Walther, 2018). Interventions drawing on social norms to, for example, boost tax-return rates ('Nine out of ten people in the UK pay their tax on time. You are currently in the very small minority of people who have not paid us yet' [Hallsworth et al., 2017, p. 17]) might strike home in those regions.

This prospect might also apply to stable and low-density neighbourhoods. In areas with low residential mobility (stable), individuals were shown to contribute more to community activities than those living in more mobile areas (Kang & Kwak, 2003; see also Choi & Oishi, 2020). Interventions targeted accordingly might be particularly effective in stable neighbourhoods. Torgler (2004, p. 240, emphasis original) reports on an intervention that could be interpreted along these lines: '*If the taxpayers did not contribute their share, our commune with its 6226 inhabitants would suffer greatly. With your taxes you help keep Trimbach attractive for its inhabitants*'.

Also, Oishi (2014) reviews the association between weather and pro- or antisocial engagement. Repeatedly, people have been found to be more likely to perform prosocial behaviour on pleasant days (Cunningham, 1979; Rind, 1996). This might, in turn, influence the effectiveness of social-norm nudges, especially those targeting more context-driven, one-off behaviour like opting for reusable mugs (Loschelder et al., 2019) or climbing the stairs (Burger & Shelton, 2011).

Of course, there is a substantive difference between explicitly altruistic behaviour and mere cues from other people's actions (social-norm nudges). In any case, social prompts are an influential behaviour-change tool, and the underlying signals – actual behaviour or internalised collective values – are shaped by diverse features of social ecology.

Present bias, overconfidence and politico-economic environments

Another essential feature of social ecology is the politico-economic environment. Oishi (2014) reviews the association between wealth, (in)equality and wellbeing. Potentially, a booming macroeconomic climate contributes to higher levels of overconfidence, risk-seeking or present bias. Conversely, economic downturns might induce loss aversion and status-quo bias. These effects are of central importance in BPP (Reisch & Zhao, 2017), and the effectiveness of interventions drawing on these mechanisms might be co-determined by broader economic sentiment. Economic narratives like frugality or conspicuous consumption likely affect individuals' psychological states (Shiller, 2019).

How Socio-ecological Psychology can Supplement Behavioural Public Policy

Having contemplated exemplary links amongst social ecology, psychological processes and behaviourally informed interventions, we now formalise these mechanisms by outlining potential causal directions (Figure 27.1).

Process study

The first conceptualisation (panel I in Figure 27.1) draws on a central method of socio-ecological psychology: the process study (Oishi, 2014). A characteristic of social ecology gives rise to a psychological process (heuristic/bias), which is likewise targeted by a choice-architecture intervention to help individuals opt for a specific choice. People living in stable neighbourhoods, for example, might be more susceptible to status-quo bias so a

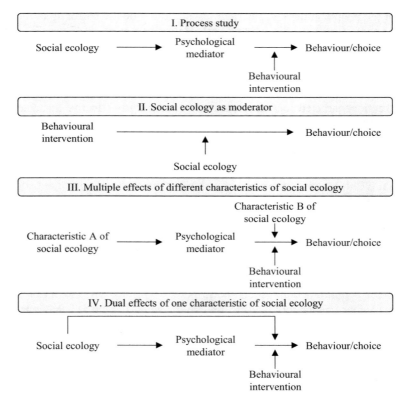

Figure 27.1 Socio-ecological and behavioural interventions

default (opt-out) nudge targeting organ donation rates might be particularly effective in these areas.

Social ecology as moderator

The first conceptualisation extends our understanding of psychological processes addressed by interventions. In the second step (panel II in Figure 27.1), we examine how social ecology affects the policy outcome. Specifically, a feature of social ecology moderates the impact of a nudge on actual behaviour. In this case, the social ecology does not affect the underlying heuristic/bias but stimulates a different mechanism that moderates the intervention.

Imagine a reminder nudge seeking to increase charitable giving. The intervention is rolled out in a sparsely populated area where people tend to be more prosocial. This phenomenon of social ecology contributes favourably to the intervention. Yet the relationship between population density and pro-sociality does not (directly) affect the underlying bias targeted by the reminder (procrastination, forgetfulness).

Multiple effects of different characteristics of social ecology

To extend this example, we assume that the underlying psychological process is likewise affected by a distinct characteristic of social ecology, different from the previous determinant (panel III in Figure 27.1). For instance, the area where an intervention is rolled out is both sparsely populated (characteristic A) and features a mundane environment (characteristic B). Characteristic A benefits the intervention by making individuals susceptible to social norms (psychological mediator). Conversely, characteristic B contributes to a lack of self-control and fosters procrastination; this mechanism could undermine charitable giving. Characteristic A amplifies the intervention's influence, whereas characteristic B co-explains why the policy was required in the first place. Both effects could also act upon each other, and more features of social ecology can be included in the analysis.

Dual effects of one characteristic of social ecology

The last panel in our schematic (panel IV in Figure 27.1) builds on the previous process. Precisely, the effects formerly exerted by two different social ecology features are now induced by one characteristic. This aspect gives rise to the psychological process subject to intervention and similarly shapes the policy's impact via a second, moderating channel. As previously, the two effects can either reinforce or confound each other.

For instance, a salience nudge seeking to increase contraception rates to fend off sexually transmittable infections could be effective in areas with high levels of pathogens because disease-related experiences are prevalent (availability heuristic). However, collectivist and religious values also tend to be more pervasive in such areas (Fincher et al., 2008; Fincher & Thornhill, 2012), which might trigger aversion towards contraceptives. Related associations between the salience of disease and cultural phenomena have recently been deployed in the context of the SARS-CoV-2 pandemic (Van Bavel et al., 2020) and might influence the effectiveness of behavioural interventions (Soofi et al., 2020).

Relevance

Why should policymakers grapple with the effect of social ecology? They could simply examine their target groups' psychological characteristics to fine-tune interventions and not jostle with macro-variables. However, a socio-ecological perspective can help practitioners comprehend the broader and diverse environment in which interventions are implemented. The Organisation for Economic Co-operation and Development (OECD) (2019, p. 60) recommended that policymakers '[p]rovide context to the set of options where the behavioural pattern unfolds (the "when-and-where")' when designing behavioural interventions. This can contribute to both efficient and effective policymaking.

First, applying mid-range theories of socio-ecological psychology can be more *efficient* than measuring individual-level phenomena. Testing an intervention based on the well-reasoned assumption that people living in stable communities are susceptible to social norms can be more efficient than measuring actual levels of pro-sociality. Second, interventions can be tailored to real contexts, rendering them more *effective* than policies drawing on general intrapsychic lessons. In our example, the observation that residents in stable localities are fonder of prosocial values than peers in mobile neighbourhoods is a more precise guide for effective policy than the general insight that people respond to social norms.

INTEGRATING PRACTICE THEORIES

Having examined how objective macro-variables impact psychological processes, and hence, behavioural interventions, we now explore how social interaction predisposes people to the common heuristics and biases that matter so much in BE.

The Social Determinants of Rationality

Sociologists have long argued that rationality and utility maximisation are positivist constructs providing the normative basis for standard economics (Bourdieu, 2005; Parsons, 1940). Hayes (2020) applies this perspective to BE: he argues that rationality has been established as the self-evident maxim of economic interaction. Financially literate individuals comfortable with calculus, cost-benefit analysis and expected utility theory can meet this benchmark. However, less privileged individuals may not be able to reach this yardstick: they struggle between automatic and deliberate thinking, exhibit loss aversion and fall prey to present bias (Hayes, 2020). Drawing on Beckert and Lutter's (2013) lottery study, Hayes (2020, p. 23) gives a simple illustration: '[A] working-class mother may think it natural to play the lottery to get ahead (Beckert and Lutter 2013), whereas a businesswoman would never waste her money on such a bad bet'.

This scenario is based on Pierre Bourdieu's oeuvre. Put very simply: people assume differing power relations in social interaction. Dominant actors determine the '*rules* of the game' such as rationality, whereas dominated participants comply or become marginalised (Bourdieu, 2005, p. 76, emphasis original). This imbalance is steeped in *habitus*, people's unique social dispositions comprising subjective experiences in relation to objective social structure (Bourdieu, 1984). In the above example, the working-class mother has a different habitus than the businesswoman, which shapes her economic behaviour. Capturing divergent decision-making, habitus is an analytically richer concept than generic notions like socioeconomic status or poverty. While the latter two feature in contemporary BE (Bertrand et al., 2004; Mani et al., 2013), habitus can further enrich the behavioural economist's compendium.

Another illustration is societies and cultures that are not permeated by market logic. Here, Hayes (2020, p. 23) draws from Bourdieu's (1979) work on Algeria and the indigenous Kabyle people, a Berber group:

Bourdieu (1979) documented contradictory logics between the Kabyle's precapitalist society and the sudden integration of market institutions brought by colonialism prior to the Algerian War. The pursuit of monetary profits and the newfound need for applied calculation created practical mismatches between the existing set of dispositions socialized into the Kabyle and those demanded by the free market.

Polanyi (1944/2001) outlines a similar argument by showing that market institutions are only a modern mode of governance. Before that, 'order in production and distribution' (Polanyi, 1944/2001, p. 49) was embedded in institutions like reciprocity, redistribution, and householding. Heterodox behavioural economists embrace this view and examine the contemporary roles of altruism (Fehr & Fischbacher, 2003), reciprocity, fairness and cooperation (Fehr & Gächter, 2000; Fehr & Schmidt, 1999; Gintis et al., 2008; Oliver, 2019).

A more orthodox strand in BE, grounded in experimental economics and game theory, still applies (relaxed) assumptions like exogenous and ordered preferences or susceptibility to incentives. Furthermore, experimental and behavioural approaches to development policy (Duflo et al., 2008, 2011) tend to neglect idiosyncratic cultural contexts and focus on generic market structures (Kvangraven, 2020).

Broadly speaking, the sociocultural context – including past experiences, education, profession and taste – informs individuals' decision-making processes and how they deviate from rational benchmarks. Behavioural anomalies are not necessarily generalisable across populations. Instead, social dispositions and individuals' relative position in social interaction affect how patterns of (ir)rationality play out. This sociological lens can enrich burgeoning discourses in heterodox BE.

Behaviour and Social Practice

To move in this direction, conceiving choice and behaviour as social practice rather than unrelated, one-off decisions can be instructive. According to Reckwitz (2002, p. 249), '[a] "practice" (*Praktik*) is a routinized type of behaviour which consists of several elements, interconnected to one other: forms of bodily activities, forms of mental activities, "things" and their use, a background knowledge in the form of understanding, know-how, states of emotion and motivational knowledge'. Accordingly, three elements constitute social practices: 'meanings', 'competences' and 'materials' (Shove et al., 2012, p. 14).

Some proponents of social practice theory castigate behavioural approaches. Shove (2010b, p. 1274) argues that 'policy – as currently configured – is incapable of moving beyond the ABC – this being an account of social change in which "A" stands for attitude, "B" for behaviour, and "C" for choice'. In this vein, Strengers and Maller (2014) differentiate social practice theory and 'behaviour change'. Reid and Ellsworth-Krebs (2018) contrast the theoretical underpinnings of nudge and practice theory.

We argue that dichotomies are neither accurate nor helpful. First, behavioural science is not primarily a normative instrument for 'change', but an analytical lens on human behaviour. Reducing behavioural science to 'behaviour change' (Strengers & Maller, 2014) is too simplistic. Second, practice theorists disguise the fact that their agenda is concerned with change or, reframed in a more compatible way, 'transition'. A plethora of texts, and indeed the core literature, apply theoretical insights to topical fields such as sustainability (Shove, 2010a, 2010b; Strengers & Maller, 2014) or transport (Larsen, 2016). There is nothing wrong with that. However, stigmatising behavioural scientists as avid interventionists whilst stylising oneself as a superior theorist is unconstructive. Instead, harnessing the strengths of both approaches bears excellent potential.

Whitmarsh et al. (2011) endorse interdisciplinarity instead of theoretical isolation and lament that Shove (2010b) pits social science disciplines against each other. Wilson and Chatterton (2011, p. 2781) link behaviour and practice by arguing that behaviours are 'physical manifestations of practices'. The authors provide a pragmatic approach maintaining that policymakers choose from a range of models best suited to a given context (Chatterton & Wilson, 2014; Wilson & Chatterton, 2011). Boldero and Binder (2013) build a model linking psychological and sociological theories.

Adding to this literature, we argue that psychological processes can be considered *mental practices*. Reckwitz (2002, p. 256) repeatedly points out that practices include 'not only bodily, but also mental routines'. Heuristics, for example, rely on internalisation (Gigerenzer & Gaissmaier, 2010), and cognitive biases are systematic distortions. Furthermore, several behavioural economic concepts relate to objects, another component of practice theory: self-control problems are steeped in the consumption of items conveying specific meanings; mental accounting attaches symbolism to money (Thaler, 1999; Zelizer, 1989). Both BE and practice theory seek to reassess common perceptions of human conduct: '[P]ractice theory revises the hyperrational and intellectualized picture of human agency and the social offered by classical and high-modern social theories' (Reckwitz, 2002, p. 259). Scholars categorically discriminating between the social and the psychic unduly dismiss that emotion, the mind, and feelings are central components of practices (Wacquant, 2015). BE has great potential to draw on practice theory but focuses on the vocabulary of 'behaviour' and 'choice'. This narrow conception invites economics and psychology critics to cast doubt on BE and its policy applications. Proponents of BE and BPP are well-advised to harness the full potential of the discipline's theoretical underpinnings and empirical findings.

But why is it desirable to bridge BE and practice theory? Shove (2011) argues that different paradigms can coexist without any need to merge them. Strengers et al. (2014, p. 66) are concerned that 'the "mixing" of theories places [researchers] in a theoretically compromised position'. We are not advocating for incorporating or 'mixing' BE and social practice theory. Rather, we show how BE can be reinterpreted and extended from a practice perspective. This endeavour takes seriously Reckwitz's (2002) and Wacquant's (2015) pleas not to discredit mental mechanisms, which are central to (some) social theory. Bruch and Feinberg's (2017) review shows that mental and social models of decision-making can inform each other. Writing on sociological insights in BE, Daminger (2017) argues along the same lines, summarising that 'some of the questions each discipline already asks could be better answered via a collaborative approach, or one that integrates conceptual or methodological elements from multiple fields'.

Towards a behavioural public policy of practice

To move towards a BPP of practice, we now sketch five domains fusing behavioural insights and social practice concepts.

Materials
Conventional choice-architecture interventions alter the material by modifying various aspects of the choice environment (Thaler & Sunstein, 2008). Default rules, position, interfaces or

portion sizes draw on the materials people interact with (see Hollands et al., 2013, 2017). Thus, discovering the potential of materials in the context of a practice approach to BPP is not novel. We advocate that practitioners rigorously analyse how materials give rise to practices rather than one-off behaviour. For instance, food consumption can be considered a social practice (Delormier et al., 2009), and nudge interventions addressing this routine often target the materials involved (for reviews see Cadario & Chandon, 2019; Reisch et al., 2021).

Meanings

Interventions based on framing strategies affect practices via changes in meaning. This pertains in particular to social-norm interventions, a broadly applied element of the nudge toolkit (for a review see Yamin et al., 2019). Social norms are established in social psychology (Bicchieri, 2006), and behavioural economists highlight their influence to fend off critiques raised by sociologists. However, merely incorporating social norms does not qualify as an inherently sociological approach. 'When economists talk about institutions, norms, and the like, their vocabulary is identical to that of sociologists, but they often mean something quite different' (Smelser & Swedberg, 2010, p. 5). Reckwitz (2002) outlines the simplistic notion of *Homo sociologicus* associated with an emphasis on norm-based structure. Social practice theory goes beyond this perspective (Reckwitz, 2002). Only relying on social-norm interventions – as useful as they are – does not account for the depth of practice theory. Sophisticated sociological explanations of behaviour and agency are mostly missing in the choice-architecture literature (Brown, 2012).

Thus, choice architects should go beyond merely deploying general concepts like reciprocity, altruism, or social pressure to investigate the *idiosyncratic* meanings of practices. Larsen (2016), investigating cycling culture in Copenhagen, uncovers concrete notions associated with cycling, for example, internalisation or harmony. These could be harnessed in transport interventions, a critical domain of choice architecture (Forberger et al., 2019). Furthermore, Gauri et al. (2020) report on social-norm measurements and policies targeting open defecation in rural India. Open defecation is embedded in cultural meanings, and addressing them requires a reassessment of norms and materials, especially latrines. The social-norm interventions are grounded in the local context, seek to enhance people's knowledge of local latrine use rates, and alter toilets' meaning (Gauri et al., 2020). More conceptually, Yamin et al. (2019) develop a framework of social-norm interventions accounting for contextual factors and various mechanisms of norms. Not all of these approaches might convince practice theorists, but they contribute to a more rigorous take on norms and meaning in the context of choice architecture.

Competences and knowledge

In the domain of competence and knowledge building, a host of behavioural interventions are instructive. For instance, so-called 'boost policies' seek to '[empower] people by expanding (boosting) their competences and thus helping them to reach their objectives (without making undue assumptions about what those objectives are)' (Grüne-Yanoff & Hertwig, 2016, p. 156). According to the inventors of the concept of boosts, these policies are not akin to formal education or informational campaigns (Hertwig & Grüne-Yanoff, 2017). Grounded in the *Fast and Frugal Heuristics* programme (Gigerenzer et al., 1999), boosts leverage heuristics as sources for learning and internalisation (Grüne-Yanoff et al., 2018; Grüne-Yanoff & Hertwig, 2016). This comprises *risk literacy boosts*, *uncertainty management boosts* and *motivational boosts* (Hertwig & Grüne-Yanoff, 2017). As an illustration, boosts can take the form of decision trees that help identify medical conditions like depression or cardiovascular attacks (Grüne-Yanoff & Hertwig, 2016).

Whilst some researchers see a conceptual difference between nudge and boost (Grüne-Yanoff & Hertwig, 2016), frameworks merging both approaches have been proposed (Banerjee & Peter, 2021). We endorse this latter perspective and concur that capacity-building system-2 nudges and boosts should go hand in hand in facilitating human agency (Sunstein, 2016). Various instruments have their place in the policy toolkit, and they should complement each other rather than instigate intellectual divides. By providing the cognitive elements for competence building (Reckwitz, 2002), a range of behaviourally informed interventions take a central position in a BPP of practice.

Long-term evaluation

Choice architects are advised to extend the lifecycle of interventions. Investigating long-term effects of interventions in longitudinal designs can help illuminate (change in) practices. This broader scope is central to moving from singular behaviours and choices to practices.

Linking nudge and social practice theories, Kaljonen et al. (2020) investigate long-term effects of labelling and default interventions on customers and the practices of the kitchen staff in a Finnish cafeteria. By employing a long-term approach, mixed methods, and focus on multiple target groups, the authors successfully close the gap between choice architecture and practice theory. Similar studies are needed. In a recent review of 174 articles, Beshears and Kosowsky (2020, p. 14) also advocate for exploring long-term effects, as they find that 'at most 21% of articles attempt to assess the long-run effect of a nudge'. Related to our social-practice approach, they argue that long-term assessments can examine habit formation induced by nudges (Beshears & Kosowsky, 2020).

Target groups

Considering the needs of specific target groups when designing practice-oriented interventions complements the components sketched so far. It enables the operationalisation of the habitus, positions in social interaction, and lived realities of individuals targeted by interventions (see third section). For example, the particular circumstances of disadvantaged and marginalised groups can be incorporated by choice architects in the design of interventions that reflect actual behavioural patterns.

Ruggeri et al. (2020) review personalisation strategies aiding disadvantaged groups in accessing public health services. '[A] personalized approach begins with calibration based on individual circumstances (e.g., age, income, living in an urban or rural area), seeking an equitable result in spite of initial inequities' (Ruggeri et al., 2020, p. 3). Implicitly, the authors touch upon aspects linked to subjective experiences (habitus) and more objective social structure: 'Drivers of behavior are multifaceted, involving individual factors such as dispositions, abilities, and preferences, as well as external factors that are more or less stable over time' (Ruggeri et al., 2020, p. 6). In addition to mere 'calibration', personalisation seeks to address substantial barriers faced by disadvantaged groups (Ruggeri et al., 2020). Yet compensating for such obstacles is not straightforward, as they are often rooted in social structure; policy-makers would need to address systemic inequities. This agenda exceeds the scope of mere behavioural interventions. Hence, identifying and addressing proxies – such as providing transportation, childcare or language services (Ruggeri et al., 2020) – aligns with the purview of small-scale interventions.

Lastly, the nascent discourse about *sludge* – overt and costly administrative burden (Sunstein, 2022; Thaler, 2018) – can benefit from sociological inquiry. For instance, Sunstein's (2022, pp. 654–655) sludge examples feature multiple groups of negatively affected individuals – immigrants, a professor, poor students and students with mental health issues – whose distinct social dispositions certainly influence how they navigate red tape.

Emerging Ethical Challenges

A BPP of practice taps into perennial ethical debates about behavioural insights in general and nudging in particular (Grüne-Yanoff, 2012; Mitchell, 2004; Sunstein & Thaler, 2003). For instance, avid interventionists could level the criticism that target group personalisation is too tentative and ignores structural deficits. More liberal regulators might steer clear of this approach altogether to avoid redistribution debates. Ruggeri et al. (2020, p. 10) are probably aware of this tension, as they assert that 'personalized approaches take nothing away from anyone, and only seek to offer policy equity to diverse populations'. Evading strict regulation, BPP is grounded in a middle course between free choice and government intervention (Thaler & Sunstein, 2003). This stance is at stake when addressing the needs of disadvantaged groups, an arguably more partisan policy goal. Thus, choice architects are encouraged to grapple with and reassess the normative underpinnings of policymaking.

This need becomes even more urgent in light of the sociological perspective outlined in the third section. Assuming that irrational behaviour is tied to a particular social milieu, interventions mitigating behavioural anomalies tacitly judge social structure: Irrational agents are literally nudged towards the dogma of rationality. Consequently, policymakers must carefully reflect if they discriminate or even try to transform habitus when circumventing associated patterns of irrationality (Brown, 2012).

This difficulty is increased in the ongoing debate about choice architects' ability to anticipate the choices that maximise welfare. Adverse behaviours like smoking or eating junk food are deeply embedded in some people's practices and constitute humble antidotes to an otherwise mundane life. Those individuals might wish to give up their vices (and would welcome a simple nudge), but the deeper desire is a craving for a life void of the daily depression that makes them indulge in the first place. Given an overall challenging life, a health regimen would constitute a relatively minor improvement in welfare, if any. It is imperative that choice architects consider how lifestyles are embedded in social structure and humans' non-economic motives. The practice lens critically assesses the established notion of exogenous preferences sealed off against social influences (Altman, 2018; Frerichs, 2019). Likewise, behavioural economists can hardly be accused of castigating irrationality and animal spirits (Akerlof & Shiller, 2009), for the discipline has contributed significantly to the rediscovery of a human factor in economics.

THE BALANCE BETWEEN SIMPLIFICATION AND COMPLEXITY

In this chapter, we make a point for *complementing* current BE and its psychological foundations with sociological and socio-ecological perspectives. Juxtaposing psychology and economics has occupied scholars for centuries (Adam Smith, John Maynard Keynes and Friedrich Hayek, to name but a few). The prominence of contemporary BE has been established against the resistance of neoclassical traditions. Integrating sociology and psychology is destined to be an equally tedious endeavour. So far, BE and (economic) sociology have largely neglected each other (Hayes, 2020; Weber & Dawes, 2010), owing to opposing epistemological and methodological traditions. While the former discipline strives for causal inference afforded by laboratory experiments, the latter investigates structural and contingent phenomena best explored qualitatively. The widespread use of randomised controlled trials (RCTs) in BPP further exacerbates this opposition. While the disparities between BE and sociology are exemplified in the use of different methods, the core conflict is rooted in the dispute between a (post-)positivist paradigm (economics and psychology) and a social constructivist, interpretive philosophy (sociology).

This disparity has practical consequences: '[S]ociologists often find themselves both effectively marginalized *and* shying away from direct policy involvement' (Fourcade et al., 2015, p. 109, emphasis original). Their research often jostles with complex theoretical arguments, whereas many behavioural economic findings are intuitive and relatable – a discrepancy also lamented by UK public servants (Hampton & Adams, 2018). Consequently, it was BE that established itself as a treasure trove of inspiration for policymakers (Holmes, 2018; OECD, 2017). Behavioural insights teams and consultants have translated the scholarly study of BE into handy concepts like MINDSPACE (Dolan et al., 2012), EAST (Service et al., 2014) or the BASIC toolkit (OECD, 2019). There is a business case and potential for real-world impact. Yet polished, practitioner-oriented frameworks encapsulate the peril of overt simplification: the fallacy that every heuristic, every bias can be mitigated or leveraged by a specific intervention. Avoiding buzzwords is especially necessary when integrating complex socio-ecological concepts. Otherwise, one falls prey to 'a blaze of amateur sociology' (Solow, 1970, p. 103). It is a central commitment of this chapter to curb this impression and encourage more nuance.

However, sociology has been criticised for this emphasis on nuance: 'By calling for a theory to be more comprehensive, or for an explanation to include additional dimensions, or for a concept to become more flexible and multifaceted, we paradoxically end up with less clarity' (Healy, 2017, p. 122). This claim could be raised against the present chapter's framework. Yet we maintain that our approach retains a practical angle. The socio-ecological perspective proposed in the second section introduces additional but concrete variables, which can be modelled (see Figure 27.1) and examined empirically (notably quantitatively). At the heart of our BPP of practice lies an applied aim: to develop more effective interventions tailored to specific socioeconomic contexts, with the overall aim of improving people's welfare (in many forms). Our extended frameworks seek to boost explanatory power and shed light on omitted variables (see Altman, 2018), rather than inflating BE as an end-in-itself.

LEVERAGING DIVERSE METHODS

To move in this direction, we now briefly sketch new methodological pathways that enable a rigorous integration of seemingly opposing disciplines.

Ewert and Loer (2020) espouse the use of diverse methods, including canonical qualitative tools. From our perspective, this requires a more lenient (realist) approach to causality. The dictum of external validity and isolated causal pathways cherished by experimental scholars should be relaxed when integrating more complex, dynamic variables (for an example on social equity and urban walkability, see Oishi et al., 2019).

Researchers have discussed at length the drawbacks of experiments and RCTs in particular (see Deaton, 2020; Deaton & Cartwright, 2018; Hortal, 2020). We do not amend or review this literature, but merely welcome the debate in light of more interdisciplinary ventures. In particular, Bonell et al. (2018) argue that sociological theory can elucidate moderators to explain, and potentially generalise, the outcomes of RCTs. Socio-ecological psychology can contribute similarly.

Although experimental methods remain helpful to trace causality in socio-ecological studies, it is questionable to what extent social ecologies can be replicated in the lab. In this vein, field experiments have been advocated and applied repeatedly in BE. The *Behavioural Public Policy* journal devoted a special issue to field experiments, discussing the potentials and shortcomings of the method (see also Al-Ubaydli et al., 2021).

In addition to semi- and field experiments, a range of methods is readily available to include socio-ecological attributes in the study of BPP. For instance, multilevel modelling techniques are essential for investigating higher-level determinants (see Reisch et al., 2017; Sunstein et al., 2018).

Lastly, advocating a sociological perspective would be incomplete without recourse to qualitative methods. The target-group approach discussed in the third section requires in-depth exploration through interviews and focus-group studies. Moreover, many pertinent intervention sites like cafeterias, fast-food restaurants and public transport lend themselves to participant observation. This way, researchers can observe first-hand *how* individuals engage with behavioural interventions. Uncovering those mechanisms of engagement goes beyond merely analysing the quantitative outcomes of trials and provides valuable contextual information. In a practitioner-oriented report, van Bavel and Dessart (2018) stress the merits of qualitative inquiry and argue that methods like in-depth interviews, focus groups and ethnography can inform behavioural policymaking. The authors emphasise the potential of multi-strategy designs (see Bryman, 2006) for harnessing the complementary virtues of quantitative and qualitative methods. This approach provides the link between exploratory qualitative tools and the confirmatory approaches already established in BE and BPP.

Irrespective of the inquiry method, samples need to become more diverse for researchers to capture multiple social dispositions (Hayes, 2020). This is a long- standing debate in psychology and should be intensified in light of the interdisciplinary forays advocated in this chapter (Gurven, 2018).

CONCLUSION

This chapter has attempted to extend the lively discourse about interdisciplinary perspectives in BE and BPP. We have argued that advances in socio-ecological psychology can supplement the analytical purview of behavioural interventions. Also, we have advocated a more nuanced understanding of economic (ir)rationality in the context of Bourdieu's habitus. We have discussed how social practice theory – seemingly detached from economics and psychology – can be integrated with the theoretical underpinnings and practical applications in BPP. Lastly, we have espoused a constant reassessment of the trade-off between reasonable simplification and theoretical complexity inherent in interdisciplinary BPP. This perspective warrants new methodological pathways beyond quantitative approaches and the canonical experimental methods. We hope that the present chapter contributes to the ongoing theoretical and methodological debate in the field and stimulates original research emancipated from the implicit paradigms already established in BE.

REFERENCES

Akerlof, G. A. (2002). Behavioral macroeconomics and macroeconomic behavior. *American Economic Review*, 92(3), 411–433. https://doi.org/10.1257/00028280260136192

Akerlof, G. A., & Shiller, R. J. (2009). *Animal spirits: How human psychology drives the economy, and why it matters for global capitalism*. Princeton University Press.

Altman, M. (2018). Extending the theoretical lenses of behavioral economics through the sociological prisms of Gary Becker. *Journal of Behavioral Economics for Policy*, 2(1), 45–51.

Al-Ubaydli, O., Lee, M. S., List, J. A., Mackevicius, C. L., & Suskind, D. (2021). How can experiments play a greater role in public policy? Twelve proposals from an economic model of scaling. *Behavioural Public Policy*, 5(1), 2–49. https://doi.org/10.1017/bpp.2020.17

Banerjee, S., & Peter, J. (2021). Nudge plus: Incorporating reflection into behavioural public policy. *Behavioural Public Policy*, Advance online publication. https://doi.org/10.1017/bpp.2021.6

Baumeister, R. F., Bratslavsky, E., Muraven, M., & Tice, D. M. (1998). Ego depletion: Is the active self a limited resource? *Journal of Personality and Social Psychology*, 74(5), 1252–1265. https://doi.org/10.1037/0022-3514.74.5.1252

Beckert, J., & Lutter, M. (2013). Why the poor play the lottery: Sociological approaches to explaining class-based lottery play. *Sociology*, 47(6), 1152–1170. https://doi.org/10.1177/0038038512457854

Bertrand, M., Mullainathan, S., & Shafir, E. (2004). A behavioral-economics view of poverty. *American Economic Review*, 94(2), 419–423. https://doi.org/10.1257/0002828041302019

Beshears, J., & Kosowsky, H. (2020). Nudging: Progress to date and future directions. *Organizational Behavior and Human Decision Processes*, 161, 3–19. https://doi.org/10.1016/j.obhdp.2020.09.001

Bicchieri, C. (2006). *The grammar of society: The nature and dynamics of social norms*. Cambridge University Press.

Boldero, J. M., & Binder, G. (2013). Can psychological and practice theory approaches to environmental sustainability be integrated? *Environment and Planning A: Economy and Space*, 45(11), 2535–2538. https://doi.org/10.1068/a130196c

Bonell, C., Melendez-Torres, G. J., & Quilley, S. (2018). The potential role for sociologists in designing RCTs and of RCTs in refining sociological theory: A commentary on Deaton and Cartwright. *Social Science & Medicine*, 210, 29–31. https://doi.org/10.1016/j.socscimed.2018.04.045

Bourdieu, P. (1979). *Algeria 1960: Essays*. Cambridge University Press.

Bourdieu, P. (1984). *Distinction: A social critique of the judgement of taste*. Harvard University Press.

Bourdieu, P. (2005). Principles of an economic anthropology. In *The social structures of the economy* (pp. 75–89). Polity Press.

Bronfenbrenner, U. (1977). Toward an experimental ecology of human development. *American Psychologist*, 32(7), 513–531. https://doi.org/10.1037/0003-066X.32.7.513

Brown, P. (2012). A nudge in the right direction? Towards a sociological engagement with libertarian paternalism. *Social Policy and Society*, 11(3), 305–317. https://doi.org/10.1017/S1474746412000061

Bruch, E., & Feinberg, F. (2017). Decision-making processes in social contexts. *Annual Review of Sociology*, 43(1), 207–227. https://doi.org/10.1146/annurev-soc-060116-053622

Bryman, A. (2006). Integrating quantitative and qualitative research: How is it done? *Qualitative Research*, 6(1), 97–113. https://doi.org/10.1177/1468794106058877

Burger, J. M., & Shelton, M. (2011). Changing everyday health behaviors through descriptive norm manipulations. *Social Influence*, 6(2), 69–77. https://doi.org/10.1080/15534510.2010.542305

Cadario, R., & Chandon, P. (2019). Which healthy eating nudges work best? A meta-analysis of field experiments. *Marketing Science*, 39(3), 465–486. https://doi.org/10.1287/mksc.2018.1128

Chatterton, T., & Wilson, C. (2014). The 'Four Dimensions of Behaviour' framework: A tool for characterising behaviours to help design better interventions. *Transportation Planning and Technology*, 37(1), 38–61. https://doi.org/10.1080/03081060.2013.850257

Choi, H., & Oishi, S. (2020). The psychology of residential mobility: A decade of progress. *Current Opinion in Psychology*, 32, 72–75. https://doi.org/10.1016/j.copsyc.2019.07.008

Cohen, J., Ericson, K. M., Laibson, D., & White, J. M. (2020). Measuring time preferences. *Journal of Economic Literature*, 58(2), 299–347. https://doi.org/10.1257/jel.20191074

Cunningham, M. R. (1979). Weather, mood, and helping behavior: Quasi experiments with the sunshine samaritan. *Journal of Personality and Social Psychology*, *37*(11), 1947–1956. https://doi.org/10.1037/0022-3514.37.11.1947

Daminger, A. (2017, May 22). Bringing sociology back. *Behavioral Scientist*. https://behavioralscientist.org/bringing-sociology-back/

Deaton, A. (2020). *Randomisation in the tropics revisited: A theme and eleven variations* (NBER Working Paper No. 27600; NBER Working Paper Series). National Bureau of Economic Research. https://doi.org/10.3386/w27600

Deaton, A., & Cartwright, N. (2018). Understanding and misunderstanding randomised controlled trials. *Social Science & Medicine*, *210*, 2–21. https://doi.org/10.1016/j.socscimed.2017.12.005

Delormier, T., Frohlich, K. L., & Potvin, L. (2009). Food and eating as social practice – understanding eating patterns as social phenomena and implications for public health. *Sociology of Health & Illness*, *31*(2), 215–228. https://doi.org/10.1111/j.1467-9566.2008.01128.x

Dolan, P., Hallsworth, M., Halpern, D., King, D., Metcalfe, R., & Vlaev, I. (2012). Influencing behaviour: The mindspace way. *Journal of Economic Psychology*, *33*(1), 264–277. https://doi.org/10.1016/j.joep.2011.10.009

Duflo, E., Kremer, M., & Robinson, J. (2008). How high are rates of return to fertiliser? Evidence from field experiments in Kenya. *American Economic Review*, *98*(2), 482–488. https://doi.org/10.1257/aer.98.2.482

Duflo, E., Kremer, M., & Robinson, J. (2011). Nudging farmers to use fertiliser: Theory and experimental evidence from Kenya. *American Economic Review*, *101*(6), 2350–2390. https://doi.org/10.1257/aer.101.6.2350

Ewert, B. (2020). Moving beyond the obsession with nudging individual behaviour: Towards a broader understanding of Behavioural Public Policy. *Public Policy and Administration*, *35*(3), 337–360. https://doi.org/10.1177/0952076719889090

Ewert, B., & Loer, K. (2020). Advancing behavioural public policies: In pursuit of a more comprehensive concept. *Policy & Politics*, *49*(1), 25–47. https://doi.org/10.1332/030557320X15907721287475

Ewert, B., Loer, K., & Thomann, E. (2020). Beyond nudge: Advancing the state-of-the-art of behavioural public policy and administration. *Policy & Politics*, *49*(1), 3–23. https://doi.org/10.1332/030557320X15987279194319

Fehr, E., & Fischbacher, U. (2003). The nature of human altruism. *Nature*, *425*, 785–791. https://doi.org/10.1038/nature02043

Fehr, E., & Gächter, S. (2000). Fairness and retaliation: The economics of reciprocity. *Journal of Economic Perspectives*, *14*(3), 159–181. https://doi.org/10.1257/jep.14.3.159

Fehr, E., & Schmidt, K. M. (1999). A theory of fairness, competition, and cooperation. *Quarterly Journal of Economics*, *114*(3), 817–868. https://doi.org/10.1162/003355399556151

Feitsma, J., & Whitehead, M. (2022). Bounded interdisciplinarity: Critical interdisciplinary perspectives on context and evidence in behavioural public policies. *Behavioural Public Policy*, *6*(3), 358–384. https://doi.org/10.1017/bpp.2019.30

Fincher, C. L., & Thornhill, R. (2012). Parasite-stress promotes in-group assortative sociality: The cases of strong family ties and heightened religiosity. *Behavioral and Brain Sciences*, *35*(2), 61–79. https://doi.org/10.1017/S0140525X11000021

Fincher, C. L., Thornhill, R., Murray, D. R., & Schaller, M. (2008). Pathogen prevalence predicts human cross-cultural variability in individualism/collectivism. *Proceedings of the Royal Society B: Biological Sciences*, *275*(1640), 1279–1285. https://doi.org/10.1098/rspb.2008.0094

Fishbach, A., & Hofmann, W. (2015). Nudging self-control: A smartphone intervention of temptation anticipation and goal resolution improves everyday goal progress. *Motivation Science*, *1*(3), 137–150. https://doi.org/10.1037/mot0000022

Forberger, S., Reisch, L., Kampfmann, T., & Zeeb, H. (2019). Nudging to move: A scoping review of the use of choice architecture interventions to promote physical activity in the general population. *International Journal of Behavioral Nutrition and Physical Activity*, *16*(1), Article 77. https://doi.org/10.1186/s12966-019-0844-z

Fourcade, M., Ollion, E., & Algan, Y. (2015). The superiority of economists. *Journal of Economic Perspectives*, *29*(1), 89–114. https://doi.org/10.1257/jep.29.1.89

Frederick, S., Loewenstein, G., & O'Donoghue, T. (2002). Time discounting and time preference: A critical review. *Journal of Economic Literature*, *40*(2), 351–401. https://doi.org/10.1257/002205102320161311

Frerichs, S. (2019). Bounded sociality: Behavioural economists' truncated understanding of the social and its implications for politics. *Journal of Economic Methodology*, *26*(3), 243–258. https://doi.org/10.1080/1350178X.2019.1625217

Gauri, V., Rahman, T., & Sen, I. K. (2020). Shifting social norms to reduce open defecation in rural India. *Behavioural Public Policy*. Advance online publication. https://doi.org/10.1017/bpp.2020.46

Gigerenzer, G., & Gaissmaier, W. (2010). Heuristic decision making. *Annual Review of Psychology*, *62*(1), 451–482. https://doi.org/10.1146/annurev-psych-120709-145346

Gigerenzer, G., Todd, P. M., & ABC Research Group. (1999). *Simple heuristics that make us smart*. Oxford University Press.

Gintis, H., Henrich, J., Bowles, S., Boyd, R., & Fehr, E. (2008). Strong reciprocity and the roots of human morality. *Social Justice Research*, *21*(2), 241–253. https://doi.org/10.1007/s11211-008-0067-y

Grüne-Yanoff, T. (2012). Old wine in new casks: Libertarian paternalism still violates liberal principles. *Social Choice and Welfare*, *38*(4), 635–645. https://doi.org/10.1007/s00355-011-0636-0

Grüne-Yanoff, T., & Hertwig, R. (2016). Nudge versus boost: How coherent are policy and theory? *Minds and Machines*, *26*, 149–183. https://doi.org/10.1007/s11023-015-9367-9

Grüne-Yanoff, T., Marchionni, C., & Feufel, M. A. (2018). Toward a framework for selecting behavioural policies: How to choose between boosts and nudges. *Economics and Philosophy*, *34*(2), 243–266. https://doi.org/10.1017/S0266267118000032

Gurven, M. D. (2018). Broadening horizons: Sample diversity and socio-ecological theory are essential to the future of psychological science. *Proceedings of the National Academy of Sciences*, *115*(45), Article 11420. https://doi.org/10.1073/pnas.1720433115

Hagger, M. S., Wood, C., Stiff, C., & Chatzisarantis, N. L. (2010). Ego depletion and the strength model of self-control: A meta-analysis. *Psychological Bulletin*, *136*(4), 495–525. https://doi.org/10.1037/a0019486

Hallsworth, M., List, J. A., Metcalfe, R. D., & Vlaev, I. (2017). The behavioralist as tax collector: Using natural field experiments to enhance tax compliance. *Journal of Public Economics*, *148*, 14–31. https://doi.org/10.1016/j.jpubeco.2017.02.003

Hampton, S., & Adams, R. (2018). Behavioural economics vs social practice theory: Perspectives from inside the United Kingdom government. *Energy Research & Social Science*, *46*, 214–224. https://doi.org/10.1016/j.erss.2018.07.023

Hayes, A. S. (2020). The behavioral economics of Pierre Bourdieu. *Sociological Theory*, *38*(1), 16–35. https://doi.org/10.1177/0735275120902170

Healy, K. (2017). Fuck nuance. *Sociological Theory*, *35*(2), 118–127. https://doi.org/10.1177/0735275117709046

Hertwig, R., & Grüne-Yanoff, T. (2017). Nudging and boosting: Steering or empowering good decisions. *Perspectives on Psychological Science*, *12*(6), 973–986. https://doi.org/10.1177/1745691617702496

Hollands, G. J., Bignardi, G., Johnston, M., Kelly, M. P., Ogilvie, D., Petticrew, M., Prestwich, A., Shemilt, I., Sutton, S., & Marteau, T. M. (2017). The TIPPME intervention typology for changing environments to change behaviour. *Nature Human Behaviour*, *1*, Article 0140. https://doi.org/10.1038/s41562-017-0140

Hollands, G. J., Shemilt, I., Marteau, T. M., Jebb, S. A., Kelly, M. P., Nakamura, R., Suhrcke, M., & Ogilvie, D. (2013). Altering micro-environments to change population health behaviour: Towards an evidence base for choice architecture interventions. *BMC Public Health*, *13*(1), Article 1218. https://doi.org/10.1186/1471-2458-13-1218

Holmes, B. (2018). Nudging grows up (and now has a government job). *Knowable Magazine | Annual Reviews*. https://doi.org/10.1146/knowable-020518-122501

Hortal, A. (2020). Evidence-based policies, nudge theory and Nancy Cartwright: A search for causal principles. *Behavioural Public Policy*. Advance online publication. https://doi.org/10.1017/bpp.2020.55

Kaljonen, M., Salo, M., Lyytimäki, J., & Furman, E. (2020). From isolated labels and nudges to sustained tinkering: Assessing long-term changes in sustainable eating at a lunch restaurant. *British Food Journal*, *122*(11), 3313–3329. https://doi.org/10.1108/BFJ-10-2019-0816

Kang, N., & Kwak, N. (2003). A multilevel approach to civic participation: Individual length of residence, neighborhood residential stability, and their interactive effects with media use. *Communication Research*, *30*(1), 80–106. https://doi.org/10.1177/0093650202239028

Kaplan, S., & Berman, M. G. (2010). Directed attention as a common resource for executive functioning and self-regulation. *Perspectives on Psychological Science*, *5*(1), 43–57. https://doi.org/10.1177/1745691609356784

Kvangraven, I. H. (2020). Nobel rebels in disguise—Assessing the rise and rule of the randomistas. *Review of Political Economy*, *32*(3), 305–341. https://doi.org/10.1080/09538259.2020.1810886

Larsen, J. (2016). The making of a pro-cycling city: Social practices and bicycle mobilities. *Environment and Planning A: Economy and Space*, *49*(4), 876–892. https://doi.org/10.1177/0308518X16682732

Lederbogen, F., Kirsch, P., Haddad, L., Streit, F., Tost, H., Schuch, P., Wüst, S., Pruessner, J. C., Rietschel, M., Deuschle, M., & Meyer-Lindenberg, A. (2011). City living and urban upbringing affect neural social stress processing in humans. *Nature*, *474*(7352), 498–501. https://doi.org/10.1038/nature10190

Loschelder, D. D., Siepelmeyer, H., Fischer, D., & Rubel, J. A. (2019). Dynamic norms drive sustainable consumption: Norm-based nudging helps café customers to avoid disposable to-go-cups. *Journal of Economic Psychology*, *75*(Part A), Article 102146. https://doi.org/10.1016/j.joep.2019.02.002

Mani, A., Mullainathan, S., Shafir, E., & Zhao, J. (2013). Poverty impedes cognitive function. *Science*, *341*(6149), 976–980. https://doi.org/10.1126/science.1238041

Mitchell, G. (2004). Libertarian paternalism is an oxymoron. *Northwestern University Law Review*, *99*(3), 1245–1277.

Morand, S., & Walther, B. A. (2018). Individualistic values are related to an increase in the outbreaks of infectious diseases and zoonotic diseases. *Scientific Reports*, *8*(1), Article 3866. https://doi.org/10.1038/s41598-018-22014-4

OECD. (2017). *Behavioural insights and public policy. Lessons from around the world*. OECD Publishing. https://doi.org/10.1787/9789264270480-en

OECD. (2019). *Tools and ethics for applied behavioural insights: The BASIC Toolkit*. OECD Publishing. https://doi.org/10.1787/9ea76a8f-en

Oishi, S. (2014). Socio-ecological psychology. *Annual Review of Psychology*, *65*(1), 581–609. https://doi.org/10.1146/annurev-psych-030413-152156

Oishi, S., & Graham, J. (2010). Social ecology: Lost and found in psychological science. *Perspectives on Psychological Science*, *5*(4), 356–377. https://doi.org/10.1177/1745691610374588

Oishi, S., Koo, M., & Buttrick, N. R. (2019). The socio-ecological psychology of upward social mobility. *American Psychologist*, *74*(7), 751–763. https://doi.org/10.1037/amp0000422

Oliver, A. (2017). *The origins of behavioural public policy*. Cambridge University Press. https://doi.org/10.1017/9781108225120

Oliver, A. (2019). *Reciprocity and the art of behavioural public policy*. Cambridge University Press. https://doi.org/10.1017/9781108647755

Parsons, T. (1940). The motivation of economic activities. *Canadian Journal of Economics and Political Science*, *6*(2), 187–202. https://doi.org/10.2307/137203

Polanyi, K. (2001). *Great transformation: The political and economic origins of our time* (2nd ed.). Beacon Press. (Original work published 1944)

Reckwitz, A. (2002). Toward a theory of social practices: A development in culturalist theorising. *European Journal of Social Theory*, *5*(2), 243–263. https://doi.org/10.1177/13684310222225432

Reid, L., & Ellsworth-Krebs, K. (2018). Nudge(ography) and practice theories: Contemporary sites of behavioural science and post-structuralist approaches in geography? *Progress in Human Geography*, *43*(2), 295–313. https://doi.org/10.1177/0309132517750773

Reisch, L. A., Sunstein, C. R., Andor, M. A., Doebbe, F. C., Meier, J., & Haddaway, N. R. (2021). Mitigating climate change via food consumption and food waste: A systematic map of behavioral interventions. *Journal of Cleaner Production*, *279*, Article 123717. https://doi.org/10.1016/j.jclepro.2020.123717

Reisch, L. A., Sunstein, C. R., & Gwozdz, W. (2017). Viewpoint: Beyond carrots and sticks: Europeans support health nudges. *Food Policy*, *69*, 1–10. https://doi.org/10.1016/j.foodpol.2017.01.007

Reisch, L. A., & Zhao, M. (2017). Behavioural economics, consumer behaviour and consumer policy: State of the art. *Behavioural Public Policy*, *1*(2), 190–206. https://doi.org/10.1017/bpp.2017.1

Rind, B. (1996). Effect of beliefs about weather conditions on tipping. *Journal of Applied Social Psychology*, 26(2), 137–147. https://doi.org/10.1111/j.1559-1816.1996.tb01842.x

Ruggeri, K. (Ed.). (2019). *Behavioral insights for public policy. Concepts and cases*. Routledge.

Ruggeri, K., Benzerga, A., Verra, S., & Folke, T. (2020). A behavioral approach to personalizing public health. *Behavioural Public Policy*. Advance online publication. https://doi.org/10.1017/bpp.2020.31

Service, O., Hallsworth, M., Halpern, D., Algate, F., Gallagher, R., Nguyen, S., Ruda, S., Sanders, M., Pelenur, M., Gyani, A., Harper, H., Reinhard, J., & Kirkman, E. (2014). *EAST: Four simple ways to apply behavioural insights*. Behavioural Insights Team. https://www.bi.team/wp-content/uploads/2015/07/BIT-Publication-EAST_FA_WEB.pdf

Shiller, R. J. (2019). *Narrative economics. How stories go viral & drive major economic events*. Princeton University Press.

Shove, E. (2010a). Social theory and climate change. Questions often, sometimes and not yet asked. *Theory, Culture & Society*, 27(2–3), 277–288. https://doi.org/10.1177/0263276410361498

Shove, E. (2010b). Beyond the ABC: Climate change policy and theories of social change. *Environment and Planning A: Economy and Space*, 42(6), 1273–1285. https://doi.org/10.1068/a42282

Shove, E. (2011). On the difference between Chalk and Cheese—A response to Whitmarsh et al.'s comments on "Beyond the ABC: Climate Change Policy and Theories of Social Change". *Environment and Planning A: Economy and Space*, 43(2), 262–264. https://doi.org/10.1068/a43484

Shove, E., Pantzar, M., & Watson, M. (2012). *The dynamics of social practice: Everyday life and how it changes*. Sage Publications. https://doi.org/10.4135/9781446250655

Smelser, N. J., & Swedberg, R. (2010). Introducing economic sociology. In N. J. Smelser & R. Swedberg (Eds.), *The handbook of economic sociology* (2nd ed., pp. 3–25). Princeton University Press.

Solow, R. M. (1970). Science and ideology in economics. *Public Interest*, 21, 94–107.

Soofi, M., Najafi, F., & Karami-Matin, B. (2020). Using insights from behavioral economics to mitigate the spread of COVID-19. *Applied Health Economics and Health Policy*, 18(3), 345–350. https://doi.org/10.1007/s40258-020-00595-4

Strengers, Y., & Maller, C. (Eds.). (2014). *Social practices, intervention and sustainability. Beyond behaviour change*. Routledge. https://doi.org/10.4324/9781315816494

Strengers, Y., Moloney, S., Maller, C., & Horne, R. (2014). Beyond behaviour change. Practical applications of social practice theory in behaviour change programmes. In Y. Strengers, & C. Maller (Eds.), *Social practices, intervention and sustainability. Beyond behaviour change* (pp. 64–77). Routledge. https://doi.org/10.4324/9781315816494

Sunstein, C. R. (2014). Nudging: A very short guide. *Journal of Consumer Policy*, 37(4), 583–588. https://doi.org/10.1007/s10603-014-9273-1

Sunstein, C. R. (2016). Choice and its architecture. In *The ethics of influence: Government in the age of behavioral science* (pp. 18–42). Cambridge University Press. https://doi.org/10.1017/CBO9781316493021

Sunstein, C. R. (2022). Sludge audits. *Behavioural Public Policy*, 6(4), 654–673. https://doi.org/10.1017/bpp.2019.32

Sunstein, C. R., Reisch, L. A., & Rauber, J. (2018). A worldwide consensus on nudging? Not quite, but almost. *Regulation & Governance*, 12(1), 3–22. https://doi.org/10.1111/rego.12161

Sunstein, C. R., & Thaler, R. H. (2003). Libertarian paternalism is not an oxymoron. *University of Chicago Law Review*, 70(4), 1159–1202. https://doi.org/10.2307/1600573

Thaler, R. H. (1999). Mental accounting matters. *Journal of Behavioral Decision Making*, 12(3), 183–206. https://doi.org/10.1002/(SICI)1099-0771(199909)12:3<183::AID-BDM318>3.0.CO;2-F

Thaler, R. H. (2016). Behavioral economics: Past, present, and future. *American Economic Review*, 106(7), 1577–1600. https://doi.org/10.1257/aer.106.7.1577

Thaler, R. H. (2018). Nudge, not sludge. *Science*, 361(6401), 431. https://doi.org/10.1126/science.aau9241

Thaler, R. H., & Sunstein, C. R. (2003). Libertarian paternalism. *American Economic Review*, 93(2), 175–179. https://doi.org/10.1257/000282803321947001

Thaler, R. H., & Sunstein, C. R. (2008). *Nudge. Improving decisions about health, wealth and happiness*. Yale University Press.

Thaler, R. H., & Sunstein, C. R. (2021). *Nudge. The final edition*. Yale University Press.

Thaler, R. H., Sunstein, C. R., & Balz, J. P. (2013). Choice architecture. In E. Shafir (Ed.), *The behavioral foundations of public policy* (pp. 428–439). Princeton University Press. https://doi.org/10.2307/j.ctv550cbm.31

Torgler, B. (2004). Moral suasion: An alternative tax policy strategy? Evidence from a controlled field experiment in Switzerland. *Economics of Governance*, 5(3), 235–253. https://doi.org/10.1007/s10101-004-0077-7

Van Bavel, J. J., Baicker, K., Boggio, P. S., Capraro, V., Cichocka, A., Cikara, M., Crockett, M. J., Crum, A. J., Douglas, K. M., Druckman, J. N., Drury, J., Dube, O., Ellemers, N., Finkel, E. J., Fowler, J. H., Gelfand, M., Han, S., Haslam, S. A., Jetten, J., ... Willer, R. (2020). Using social and behavioural science to support COVID-19 pandemic response. *Nature Human Behaviour*, 4(5), 460–471. https://doi.org/10.1038/s41562-020-0884-z

van Bavel, R., & Dessart, F. J. (2018). *The case for qualitative methods in behavioural studies for EU policy-making* (JRC Science for Policy Report EUR 29061 EN). Publications Office of the European Union. https://doi.org/10.2760/861402, JRC109920

Wacquant, L. (2015). For a sociology of flesh and blood. *Qualitative Sociology*, 38(1), 1–11. https://doi.org/10.1007/s11133-014-9291-y

Weber, R., & Dawes, R. (2010). Behavioral economics. In N. J. Smelser & R. Swedberg (Eds.), *The handbook of economic sociology* (2nd ed., pp. 90–108). Princeton University Press.

Whitmarsh, L., O'Neill, S., & Lorenzoni, I. (2011). Climate change or social change? Debate within, amongst, and beyond disciplines. *Environment and Planning A: Economy and Space*, 43(2), 258–261. https://doi.org/10.1068/a43359

Wilson, C., & Chatterton, T. (2011). Multiple models to inform climate change policy: A pragmatic response to the "Beyond the ABC" Debate. *Environment and Planning A: Economy and Space*, 43(12), 2781–2787. https://doi.org/10.1068/a44404

Yamin, P., Fei, M., Lahlou, S., & Levy, S. (2019). Using social norms to change behavior and increase sustainability in the real world: A systematic review of the literature. *Sustainability*, 11(20), Article 5847. https://doi.org/10.3390/su11205847

Zelizer, V. A. (1989). The social meaning of money: "Special monies". *American Journal of Sociology*, 95(2), 342–377. https://doi.org/10.1086/229272

Index

2SLS 275, 276
9/11 attacks on the World Trade Center 294
18-item verbal questionnaire 18
1987 William James Lectures 37
2008 economic crisis 109–10

Abar, S. 52
abduction (or retroduction) 65
Abhyankar, P. 459
Abric, J.-C. 107, 113
academic quality 86
accountability theatre 96, 97
accounting rates of return (ARR) 130–131
Acemoglu D. 126
Ackermann, K.A. 21
'acting humanly' approach 46
'acting rationally' approach 40, 46
action logics 52
act of trusting 303–9
adaptive preference formation 17
advanced BPP 473
advertising and motivated preferences 423–4
'advice against' condition 233
'advice for' condition 233
advice quality 226, 231, 235
agent-based models (ABM) 33, 47
　action logics 52
　agent granularity 51
　goal-oriented action planning (GOAP) and 52
　tools and software programs 52
　use of 43–4
agent granularity 51
aggregate complexity 45
Ainslie G. 126
air, empathy conservation framework
　behavioural biases 334–5
　carbon offset purchasing decisions 336
　default bias 335
　endowment effect 335
　global warming 334
　hyperbolic discounting 335
　social norms 335–6
　time inconsistency issues and present bias 334
Akerlof, G.A. 25, 87, 88, 145, 191, 192, 203, 255, 257, 293, 324, 327, 419
alcohol over-consumption 445, 447–8, 461
algorithm, description 124
Ali, D.A. 25
Allcott, H. 338

alpha-maxmin expected utility model (α-MMEU model) *see* ambiguity
Alter, A.L. 217, 218
altruism 21–2, 360
altruistic preferences 21–2, 24, 89
ambiguity
　actual mean bids *vs.* optimal bids 432
　alpha-maxmin expected utility model (α-MMEU model) 430
　ambiguity aversion 428
　behaviour
　　assuming no ambiguity 431–3
　　under total ambiguity 435–7
　bounded rationality and ambiguity 434
　and decision makers 435
　degree of optimism, distribution of 439
　estimated mean level of optimism by stake level 436
　estimated optimal bid pattern *vs.* actual mean bid pattern 438
　individual variation 439–40
　maxmin expected utility model 428
　no ambiguity
　　experimental design 431
　　vs. total ambiguity, experiment to compare behaviour 430–431
　　treatment 429
　relative risk aversion, distribution of 433
　in risky choice behaviour 437–8
　total ambiguity treatment 429
anchoring 106–7
Andreoni, J. 88, 89, 361
Angeletos G.M. 24
Angner, E. 14
animal spirits 72, 123, 125, 131–3, 143, 145–6, 160, 164, 326–7, 483
anomalies 15–16, 25
　and biases 85
　detection 47
anti-chaos theory 45
anti-reductionism and holism 46
antisocial punishment
　comparative studies 371–2
　motives 373
　optional public goods game 374
　Pareto efficient (full) contribution 369
　patterns of punishments 372
　public goods game with punishment 369
　　altruistic punishment 370

prosocial and antisocial, mean differences
   in contributions 370–371
revelation of all individual contributions
   370
valences of punishments 370
third-party punishment in dictator games 372
Antonides, G. 7, 16, 19, 20, 25
anxiety-driven supermarket runs 295
appropriate spending 215
approximately rational 32–4
aquatic product export volume prediction 47
Arapoc, J. 9
Arkes, H.R. 214
Aroch, R. 110, 408
artificial intelligence (AI) 39–40, 52–3, 300
   approaches to AI studies 39
   and big data 50
   CBE and human-centred approaches 40
   data analysis in statistics and econometrics 52
   data manipulation tools and techniques 52
   hardware side of computation, advances in 52–3
   machine learning and deep learning 40
   MBE and Olympian rationality 40
   methods
      acting humanly approach 46
      acting rationally approach 46
      AI and quantum computing methods 47
      ML methods applied in economics-related fields 47
      narrative economics and 46–7
      technological innovations 47
      text/semantic analysis using AI methods 46–7
      thinking humanly approach 46
      thinking rationally approach 46
   mixed and integrated approach to AI methods 40
   ML and econometrics 52
   problem-solving methods 41
   and quantum computing methods 47
   rational-agent or *acting rationally* approach 40
   studies, approaches to 39
   text/semantic analysis using 46–7
Asea, P.K. 144
'as if' method 63
   assumptions 82
   behavioural and non-behavioural variables 2
   methodological leanings of Friedman 2
assumption on utility 69–70
assumptions, economic modelling
   2008 GFC 73
   behavioural applications 68–76
   behavioural economics as meta- and meso-economic foundations 74
behaviour-related confidence crisis 73
causal holism *see* causal holism
constructive empiricism *see* constructive empiricism and realism
deregulation 73–4
description 60
homosapiens 61, 62
impact of 68
instrumentalism and logical positivism 62–4
with philosophical foundations 61–8
rationality assumptions and bounded rationality 68–9
realism of assumptions 60–61
risk *vs.* uncertainty and financial modelling with time factors 74–6
social, cultural and emotive dimensions and outcomes 71–2
subprime mortgage lending 73
utility maximisation and the expected utility theory 69–71
assumptions, microeconomic 82–5
   anomalies and biases 85
   certainty illusion 85
   composite social goods or self-affirming goods 83
   expected utility formula 84
   fixed preference maps, notion of 82
   fixity of perception and preference 84
   just-in-time preference construction 82–3
   motivations 84
   present bias and framing bias 85
   social behaviour and motivators 83
   utility functions, types of 83–4
   zero costs to mental effort 84–5
auction methods of valuation and endowment effect
   appropriate market settings 377
   bidding prices
      of all second-price buyers 386
      of extreme and fluctuant second-price buyers 388
      of extreme and stable second-price buyers 387
      of realistic and fluctuant second-price buyers 387
      of realistic and stable second-price buyers 386
   demand-revealing properties of Vickrey auction 377
   impact of competition intensity 390–395
   individual data analysis 385–90
   'naïve' bids 378
   second-price buyers 385–8
   Vickrey auction experiments *see* Vickrey auction experiments with 60 repeated trials

Index 495

Vickrey second-price sealed-bid auctions 377
willingness-to-accept (WTA) 377
willingness-to-pay (WTP) 377
authoritative parenting style 448
Azar, O.H. 420

Bach, J. 40, 44
backwards-bending labour supply curve 155
Baddeley, M. 8, 336
Baddeley, M.C. 131
bad heuristics 249
Bandelj, N. 215
Banerjee, S. 451
Bartel, R.D. 147
Baumol, W.J. 175
Bearman, P.S. 452
Becker, E. 209
Becker, G.S. 88
Becker, G.M. 430, 431
Beckert, J. 478
Behavioral Economics: Moving Forward (Ghisellini and Chang) 69
Behavioral Theory of the Firm (Cyert and March) 190
behavioural and non-behavioural variables 2
behavioural applications 68–76
behavioural biases, description 125
behavioural economics (BE) 473
　as-if behavioural economics methodology 2
　assumptions, predictions and causality 2–3
　behavioural economists analytical toolbox 7
　bounded rationality approach 6
　causal model and causal analysis 2
　fast and frugal heuristics 4–5
　good or excellent analytical prediction 2
　and health, fitness and sports industries 263
　individuals and choice making 3
　measures 23
　as meta- and meso-economic foundations 74
　satisficing 3
　smart decision-making 5–6
behavioural economic methods
　anomalies 15–16, 25
　application of psychological insights 14
　behaviourism 14
　cognitive revolution 14
　definition 14
　history of 14
　integration of economic and psychological models and insights 23–5
　integration of psychological insights 25
　introspection 14
　limitations 14
　measures of economically relevant concepts 17–23

psychoanalysis 14
rise of contemporary behavioural economics 14
types of utility *see* utility
behavioural economics and obesity 248–53
　accurate knowledge on sports and physical activity 252
　bad heuristics 249
　biased decision-making 252
　Body Mass Index (BMI) 252–3
　demand for gym memberships 251
　determinants of overweight and obesity rates 253
　environmental constraints 251
　error-prone choices 249
　error-prone decisions 249–50
　food-related education 249
　information on calories 250
　institutional variables 250
　psychological and other non-economic variables 252
　socio-institutional constraints 249
　sports facilities 251
　sub-optimal consumption behaviour 248
　sufficient and appropriate physical activity 251
　utility- or welfare-maximising choices 248
behavioural economics methodologies 2, 6
behavioural economists analytical toolbox 7
behavioural life-cycle models 127
behavioural macroeconomics 120
　and aggregation problem 121–2
　constraints on expectations formation 122
　ex-post and *ex-ante* rate of profit 122
　methods for
　　aggregation and uncertainty 120
　　and aggregation problem 121–2
　　behavioural approaches to risk, uncertainty and expectations 122–4
　　dynamic stochastic general equilibrium 120
　　ex-ante and *ex-post* consumption 121
　　heuristics, algorithms and behavioural bias 124–32
　　micro-founded approach 121
　　rational expectations hypothesis 122
　　variants of DSGE models 121
behavioural public policy (BPP) 473
　of practice 480–483
　　boost policies 481
　　choice architects ability, debates on 483
　　competences and knowledge 481–2
　　emerging ethical challenges 483
　　Fast and Frugal Heuristics programme 481
　　idiosyncratic meanings of practices 481
　　long-term evaluation 482
　　materials 480–481

496 *Handbook of research methods in behavioural economics*

    meanings 481
    nudge and social practice theories 482
    personalisation strategies to disadvantaged groups 482
    risk literacy boosts, uncertainty management boosts and motivational boosts 481–2
behavioural theories of firm and x-efficiency/effort discretion
    efficiency wage and x-efficiency theory 191–2
    effort discretion-related behavioural theory of the firm 203–4
    implications of x-inefficiency plus employment 201–3
        efforts to reduce wage rates 202
        equilibrium employment 201
        labour demand, effort variability and x-efficiency 202
        well-being of workers 203
    managerial x-efficiency theory of the firm 193–5
    neoclassical-type behaviour 190
    quality of management and x-efficiency 200–201
    x-efficiency *see also* x-efficiency plus theory of the firm
        plus theory of the firm 195–8
        theories of the firm 192–3
    x-efficient and technical change 199
    x-inefficiency 199–200
behaviour and decision-making in pandemic 289–92
    emotions, experience, identity and preferences 290
    factors, influencing decision-making of individuals 289
    long periods of high stress 290
    mass panic 291
    probability of risk 291
    prospect theory 291
    risk, perception and uncertainty 290
    risk attitudes 290–291
    risk-averse and risk-taking 291–2
behaviour and social practice
    behaviour change 479
    meanings, competencies and materials 479
    mental practices 480
    physical manifestations of practices 480
behaviour change 444, 452, 453, 460, 475, 479
behaviourism 14
behaviour-related confidence crisis 73
Belianin, A.V. 9, 370
belief patterns analysis, statistical approaches
    capitalism 402–7
    cart analysis *see* cart decision trees

    cluster method 403–5
    conceptual core identification 401
    core and peripheral concepts 401–2
    cost-of-living index (COL) 401
    Cronbach's alpha measure 400
    Dendrogram clustering notions 404
    distance metric 404
    good-begets-good (GBG) heuristic 409
    hierarchical cluster *see* hierarchical cluster analysis
    inflation *see* inflation, associations with
    multi-dimensional scaling *see* multi-dimensional scaling (MDS)
    professional surveyors 400
    reliability analysis of clusters 406
    statements in the questionnaire, examples 403
    Ward's method 405
Bénabou, R. 88
Bentham, J. 14
Benz, M. 16
Berg, J. 311
Berger, A.N. 144
Beshears, J. 482
Besomi, D. 138
best practice behaviour 3
Betz, N.E. 19
Bhattacharya, J. 455
bias blind spot 236
biased decision-making 5, 165, 166, 252, 263
biased thinking to the advisor 236
biases and irrationality 72, 76
'a bias for the whole' 217
Bickley, S.J. 7
big data 50, 300
Binder, G. 480
Blais, A.-R. 19
Blomberg, B.S. 144
Bloom, N. 172, 175
Boden, M.A. 44
Body Mass Index (BMI) 252–3
Boldero, J.M. 480
Bonaccio, S. 227
Bonell, C. 485
boost policies 481
Bordalo, P. 146
bounded rationality 3, 6, 68, 154, 166, 243
    and ambiguity 434
    assumptions and bounded rationality 68–9
    optimal heuristics in 255
    sports and health and fitness industries 243
    vs. heuristics and biases modelling 3–4, 434
    see also labour, behavioural economics
Bourdieu, P. 478, 479, 485
Bourgeois-Gironde, S. 114
Bowles, S. 356

Boylan, T.A. 65–7
brand switching 17
Brechot, M. 276
Brickman, P. 22
Brighton, H. 124
Bronfenbrenner, U. 474
Brown, G.M. Jr. 377
Bruhin, A. 370
Brunello, G. 275
bubble 145
Budescu, D. 434
Burger, J.M. 458
business cycle and cycles of behavioural economics
  animal spirits, concept of 145–6
  bubbles 144–6
  characteristic of the (trade) cycle 137–8
  classic Industrial Fluctuations 138
  credit booms 144–6
  debt-deflation theory of depression 140
  early 20th-century contributions 138–40
  first round of mathematical expectations modelling 140–141
  macroeconometrics 141
  Markov switching model of the business cycle 145
  overly restrictive models 141
  return of cycle 144–6
  second round of expectations modelling
    rational expectations 142
    challenges and criticism 143
    concept of sunspots 143
    multiple macroeconomic equilibria 143–4
    systematic errors 142
  surveys, measuring expectations through 141–2
  tech boom of the 1990s 144
  tendencies towards mania and panic 138
  third round of expectations modeling 146
business investment heuristics 128–31
  accounting rates of return (ARR) 130
  Cobb-Douglas production function (CDPF) 128
  complexities 130
  discounted cash flow (DCF) 128
  expected discounted cash flow (DCF) 128
  impact of uncertainty on business decision-making 129
  Knightian uncertainty 130
  mathematical constrained optimisation techniques 130
  neoclassical model of fixed asset investment 128
  NPV and DCF algorithms 130–131
  NPV/DCF algorithm/techniques 130–131
  payback periods (PBP) 130
  PBP and ARR techniques 130–131
  rational expectations theory 129
  stock markets and fixed asset investments, connection 129
  trigger rate of return 130

Cagan, P. 141
capitalism 402–7
Carlsmith, J.M. 420, 421
Carlsson, F. 457
Carrier, J.G. 14
Carroll, C.D. 146
Carruthers, B.G. 215
cart decision trees 406, 409–10
  combinations of demographic variables 409
  discriminant regression 410
  financial crisis 409–10
  limitations in running CART analysis 410
Cartwright, E. 15
case studies 7, 44
cash usage 217
catastrophe theory 45
causal analysis 2, 244, 245
causal-effect relation 66
causal holism 66–8
  causal-effect relation 66
  causal holism 66–7
  description 66–7
  market mechanisms with human interactions 67
  meta-economics 67
  transcendental realism 66
causalities simplification 110–111
causal model and causal analysis 2
Cawley, J. 275
CBE see classical behavioural economics (CBE)
CBE and MBE 34–5
  concepts
    approximately rational 32–34
    concepts 34–5
    endogenous and exogenous activity 34
    maladaptation 34
    use of heuristics 34–5
  methods 42–4
    heterogeneity in ABM framework 44
    MBE, theories in 42
    narratives for policymakers and the community 43
    qualitative/quantitative understanding 43
    use of ABM 43–4
    use of softer empirical approaches 43
Ceddia, M.G. 38
cellular automata 46
certainty illusion 85

Chang, B.Y. 7, 69
Chang, T.Y. 228
chaos theory 45
Chapman, G.B. 456
Charness, G. 21, 24, 358
Chater, N. 226
Chatterton, T. 480
Chrisley, R.L. 37
Christakis, N.A. 451
Cialdini, R.B. 341
Cinyabuguma, M. 373
classical behavioural economics (CBE) 32
   agent-based models (ABM) 51–2
   artificial intelligence 39–41, 52–3
   big data 50
   CMM (constrained methods matrix) 33, 41, 42
   cognitive models and architectures 48–9
   cognitive psychology 35–7
   complexity theory 37–9
   future directions 47–53
   and human-centred approaches 40
   informational complexity, measures of 41
   and MBE *see* CBE and MBE
   methods 40–47
   micro, meso and macro foundations 49–50
   neuroscience 50–51
   tools and methods of investigation 33
classic 'Industrial Fluctuations' 138
Clinton, H. 403
cluster method 403–4, 405
Coase, R.H. 1
Coates, D. 22
Cobb-Douglas production function (CDPF) 25, 128
coercive state and privatisation 363
cognitive ability and trust 314
cognitive elements 105, 107, 482
cognitive models and architectures 48–9
   CMM (constrained methods matrix) 48–9
   massive parallel information integration 48
   situated, distributed and embodied (SDE) cognition 48
cognitive (optical) illusions 322–3
cognitive psychology 35–7
   computer science, effect of 35
   concepts
      decision problems 35–6
      General Problem Solver (GPS) 35
      H-Cogaff 36
      higher-order design of bootstrapping mechanisms 37
      K-line and elaboration tolerance 36
      meta-cognition 36
      thinking fast and slow 36
      use of the computer 35
   methods
      case studies 44
      correlational studies 44
      experimental studies 44
      K-lines 45
      'Mind as Machine' approach 44
      network science 45
      use of neuroscience techniques 44–5
cognitive revolution 14, 45
Cohen-Cole, E. 452
coin and note, subjective value of 218
Colander, D. 39
collective action problems 362
Collins, E.I. 458
commercial society of strangers 321
common-pool resources 362–3, 365, 366
common-sense economy *see* social representation
community management 363
competences and knowledge 481–2
complex adaptive systems (CAS) 287–8
complexities 130
   concepts
      complexity policy frame 39
      description 37
      in economics 37
      formation of hierarchical structures 38
      heterogeneous human agents in humans 37
      levels, nested feedback loops of a hierarchical system 38
   environment 105
   methods
      aggregate complexity 45
      anti-reductionism and holism 46
      cellular automata 46
      cybernetics 46
      deterministic complexity 45
      neural networks, study of 46
   policy frame 39
   theory 37–9
complex systems and pandemic behaviour 286–8
   CAS and various aspects 287–8
   more self-interested type of actions 286
   one-size-fits-all solutions 286
   other-regarding unselfish-type behaviours 286
composite social goods or self-affirming goods 83
computer, use of 35
computer science, effect of 35
conditional cooperators 360
confidence heuristic 231
confirmation effect in evaluating advisors authority 233–6
   'advice against' condition 233
   'advice for' condition 233

bias blind spot 236
biased thinking to the advisor 236
expert advice 234
naïve realism phenomenon 236
'positive opinion' condition 233
psychological motivations 235–6
self-serving attributional bias 236
valence of social norm 234
conscience, theory of 353
constrained methods matrix (CMM) 33, 41–4, 46, 48
constructive empiricism and realism 65
constructive rationality 69
consumer behaviour during pandemic 292–3
consumer-driven change, rate of 296–7
consumer sentiment, analyses of 128
contemporary experimental economics 4, 6
content-blind norms 75
conventional economics 1, 49
conventions and herding 125–6
cooperative strategy 114
correlational studies 44, 449
Costa, D.L. 338
Costello, T. 47
cost inefficiency 172
cost-of-living index (COL) 401
counterfactual thinking 36, 237
country- and context-specific social norms 336
COVID-19 pandemic 447
    economic problem 285
    'panic buying' and stockouts 286
    supply chain problem 285–6
Cowles Commission 120
credit card fraud detection 47
cultural beliefs and traditions 72
current assets 213
current spendable income 213
Curtin, R.T. 126, 142
customer behaviour and recommender systems 47
Cutting, J.C. 44
cybernetics 46, 47
Cyert, R.M. 190
Czap, H.J. 9
Czap, N.V. 9, 343

Dalal, R.S. 227
Daley, M.F. 446
Damjan, P. 114
Darriet, E. 114
Darwin, C. 90–93, 95
data manipulation tools and techniques 52
Day Reconstruction Method (DRM) 22
Deaton, A. 22
debt-deflation theory of the depression 140

decision makers and ambiguity 435
decision-making capabilities 3, 5–7, 9, 35, 71, 190, 243–6, 254–6, 258–63
decision problems 34–6
decisions, affecting elements 153
decision utility 16
deep learning (DL) 40
De Grauwe, P. 145
De Groot, M.H. 18, 430, 431
de Hoog, A.N. 16
Del Bono, E. 279
demand-driven supply problems and stockouts in pandemic 294–5
Dendrogram clustering notions 404
denomination and physical attributes 216, 217
de Oliveira, A.C.M. 10, 459
depression and low self-esteem 452
deregulation 60, 73–4
descriptive norm 338, 339, 342, 445–8, 458
Dessart, F.J. 485
deterministic complexity 45
devaluation 218, 401
d'Hombres, B. 275
Dickens, W.T. 419
difference-in-differences regression (DID) approach 277–80
    DID in labour economics 278–9
    DID method 277–8, 280
    identification of the policy effect 278
    impact of intervention 279
    impact of smoking ban policies 279
    impact of the pay for performance (P4P) programme 279
    overview of 277–8
    propensity score (PS) matching strategy 279–80
    selected applications of 278–80
differentiated products, model of 423
direct and indirect methods of information 458
dirty money or bloody money, concepts of 216
discouraged worker effect 160, 164
discriminant regression 410
disparities across disciplines 307–8
dispersion of information 106
dissipative structures 45
distance metric 404
distributional preferences 358–9
distributive fairness 314, 315
Ditto, P.H. 232
'divine inspiration' view of research 96
Dixit A.K. 129
Dolansky, E. 218
domain-specific risk-attitude scale (DOSPERT) 19
downward causation 47

Dräger, L. 114
Drori, S. 401
dual processing, intuition and analysis 322
dynamic stochastic general equilibrium (DSGE) models 120, 121, 127

early beliefs 325
Easterlin, R.A. 22
e-banking failures 47
Ecken, P. 233
ecological rationality
　applications 69
　principle of 4
economic actors 114, 115
economically relevant concepts, measures of 17–23
　loss aversion 17
　mental accounting 23
　other behavioural economic measures 23
　positive and negative reciprocity and trust 23
　risk aversion 18–19
　scarcity and financial stress 23
　social preference 21–2
　time, concept of 20
　well-being 22–3
economic and psychological models, integration of 23–5
　characteristics 24–5
　concept of psychological attitude 25
　identity or self-image factor 25
　loss aversion 23
　power law and power function 25
　risk preference 24
　social preference 24
　theory of motivated preference 25
　theory of planned behaviour 24–5
　time preference 23–4
economic assumptions 15, 16, 82–5
The Economic Consequences of the Peace (Keynes) 324
economic events and market behaviour set foundations 62
economic man, assumption of 328–9
economic modelling, impact of assumptions in 68
Economic Possibilities for Our Grandchildren (Keynes) 324
economics, teaching of 114–15
An Economic Theory of Greed, Love, Groups, and Networks 94
Edwards, K. 232
efficiency wage theory 8, 163, 191–2, 196
effort discretion-related behavioural theory 203–4
Egebark, J. 340

egocentric discounting of expert advice 231–3
　interpersonal cognitive consistency 232
　my-side thinking in social cognition 232
　overweight advice 233
　prior belief effect 232
Eichengreen, B. 144
Ekström, M. 340
elaboration likelihood model 230
Ellsberg, D. 428
Ellsworth-Krebs, K. 479
El-Sehity, T. 110
Elster, J. 17
emotional accounting studies 215
emotional influences on macroeconomy 128
emotions 71–2
　and decision making 243–4
empathy conservation framework
　air *see* air, empathy conservation framework
　empathy, importance of 80
　energy *see* energy, empathy conservation framework
　financial incentives 332–3
　FORGOOD ethical framework 345
　framework of empathy conservation 344
　nudges 333
　PEB actions 344
　pro-environmental behaviour (PEB) 332
　revising 343–6
　self-identity 333
　self-interest and empathy-driven other-interest 344
　social and other-regarding preferences 334
　societal expectations 345
　waste *see* waste, empathy conservation framework
　water *see* water, empathy conservation framework
empirical economics 86, 87, 95
employment, x-inefficiency plus theory for 201–3
　efforts to reduce wage rates 202
　equilibrium employment 201
　labour demand, effort variability and x-efficiency 202
　well-being of workers 203
Emrich, T.E. 458
The End of Laissez-Faire (Keynes) 324
endogenous and exogenous activity 34
endowment effect 9, 18, 335, 344, 377–95, 416, 418
energy, empathy conservation framework
　behavioural and cognitive biases 337
　individual direct energy consumption 336
　other-regarding preferences 339–40
　　direct appeals to conserve energy 340
　　installation of solar systems 339–40
　　self-perception of their identity 340

social norms 337–9
  descriptive social norms 339
  electricity usage 339
  home energy reports (HERs) program 338–9
  Opower HER program 338
  social norms/peer comparison interventions 338
Engelmann, J.B. 230
environment (al)
  conscious behaviour 457
  constraints 251
  degradation and resource depletion 362
  factors 5
  for physical activity 276
epistemic authority (EA) 229–30
epistemic schemes as themata 108
Epstein, J.M. 287
equilibrium resource extraction 365
error-prone decisions 167, 249–50
errors/biases, in labour market decision-making 163–6
errors in decision-making 5, 6, 165, 166, 243, 246, 249, 250, 253, 260, 321
errors in judgement 329
  conception of the goal 329
  reaching a goal 329
Espeland, W.N. 215
An Essay on the Principle of Population (Malthus) 91
Essays in Biography (Keynes) 324
Essays in Persuasion (Keynes) 324
ethical challenges 483
ethical professional relationships 93
euro illusion 212–13
EUT modelling of a rational agent 70
Ewert, B. 473, 484
exercising 129, 449, 451, 455, 460
expansion and contraction 140
expectations
  about future 324
  measuring through surveys 141–2
  of prices of consumer products rising in euros 213
expected discounted cash flow (DCF) 128, 130, 131
expected utility formula 84
experienced utility 16
experiences, notion of 146
experimental evidence 83, 123, 127, 377, 394, 412, 419, 428
experimental studies 17, 44, 273, 434
expert advice 227, 231, 234–6, 243
extrapolation bias 144
extrapolative expectations 146

extrinsic motivations 354–5
  effects of 355–6
Eyster, E. 418, 419

face value effect 212
fairness 324, 359
Falk, A. 19–22
fast and frugal heuristics 4–5
  methodological approach 253–4
  optimal and sub-optimal outcomes 5
  optimal norms 4
  principle of ecological rationality 4
Fast and Frugal Heuristics programme 481
Fatas, E. 373
fear and risk aversion 294
Fehr, E. 14, 358
Feitsma, J. 473
Ferraro, P.J. 343
Festinger, L. 420, 421
field approaches, examples 112
Fielding, K.S. 342
financial advice
  advice quality 226
  confirmation effect in evaluating advisors authority 233–6
    'advice against' condition 233
    'advice for' condition 233
    bias blind spot 236
    biased thinking to the advisor 236
    expert advice 234
    naïve realism phenomenon 236
    'positive opinion' condition 233
    psychological motivations 235–6
    self-serving attributional bias 236
    valence of social norm 234
  counterfactual thinking 237
  egocentric discounting of expert advice 231–3
    egocentric discounting of advice 232–3
    my-side thinking in social cognition 232
  laypeople's evaluations of expert authority
    confidence heuristic 231
    elaboration likelihood model 230
    epistemic authority (EA) 229–30
    overconfidence effect 231
    white-coat effect 231
  potential bias in advice taking 227
  psychological motivations in 227–9
    mutual funds 228, 229
    prior research 229
    protecting against cognitive dissonance 227, 228
    regret 227–8
  recognition-primed decision model 226
financial crisis 409–10
financial incentives 332–3

firm survival 5–6
Fisher, I. 140, 146
fixed asset investments, impact of 131
fixed preference maps, notion of 82
Flament, C. 401
Fletcher, J.M. 452
focus phenomenon 106
Fontaine, P. 89
food expenditure and per capita GDP 247
food-related education 249
forecasts 295, 325–6
FORGOOD ethical framework 345
formal and informal institutions, impact of 293
Fortin, B. 451
Foss, N.J. 85
Foster, G. 7
Fowler, J.H. 451
framing bias 85
Frank, R. 15
Frantz, R. 9
Frederick, S. 15
Frerichs, S. 473
Frey, B.S. 16
Friday, D. 9
Friedman, M. 2, 3, 62, 65–7, 244
Friis, R. 456
Frijters, P. 7, 23
Frisch, R. 138
functional magnetic resonance imaging (fMRI) 413
fundamental scientific creation 92
fundamental uncertainty, treatment of 76
Furnham, A. 219
Fuster, A. 146
future time orientation 20

Gächter, S. 18, 371
Galbraith, J.K. 1
game, trust 311
game theory 42, 287, 295, 308, 309, 479
Gandelman, N. 24
Gasiorowska, A. 8
Gauri, V. 481
Gelman, S.A. 216
gender-based obesity effect on labour market outcomes 275–6
generalised trust 310, 316
General Problem Solver (GPS) 35
general social survey (GSS) 310–312
The General Theory (Keynes) 324
genetic information 275
Gennaioli, N. 146
George, H. 93
Ghisellini, F. 69
Gigerenzer, G. 4, 69, 75, 124, 254, 255
Gigerenzer, G.E. 131

Gil, J. 451
Gilboa, I. 428
Glimcher, P.W. 14
Global Financial Crisis (GFC) 60, 63, 66, 72, 73, 75, 87, 286
Gneezy, U. 356
goal-oriented action planning (GOAP) 52
Goldstein, D. 455
Goldstein, N.J. 339
Gomes, O. 37
good-begets-good (GBG) 10, 110, 409
Google's AI system Alpha Go 300
Granato, J. 313
Granovetter, M.S. 453
Great Depression 138, 140, 144
Grimalda, G. 372
group
  behaviour, aspects of 292
  dynamics 88
  identity, notion of 87–8
groupthink 144
Gruen, N. 96
Guadalupe-Lanas, J. 15
Gubareva, M. 37
Gwozdz, W. 451

Haberler, G. 140
habit formation tendencies 419–20
Hammack, J. 377
Han, E. 275, 276
Handgraaf, M.J.J. 20, 21
Hardin, G. 362, 363
hardware side of computation, advances in 52–3
Harmsen, I.A. 447
Hayek, F.A. 287, 327
Hayes, A.S. 478
H-Cogaff 36
health and health behavior
  difference-in-differences regression approach 277–80
  instrumental variable methods 273–7
  policies using financial incentives 268
  RCTs 269–73, 280
  see also individual entries
health-based nudges and choice architecture 453–7
  defaults 455–6
  implementation intentions 454–5
  nudging, description 454
  psychological model of dual-system 454
  types of nudges 454
healthy behaviours, non-traditional approaches for improvement
  health-based nudges and choice architecture 453–7
  interventions on changing the norms 460

networks, interactions, peer effects and health 449–53
norm nudges, use of 457–60
norms and the implications for healthy behaviour 445–9
nudge plus 460–461
see also individual entries
Heerink, N. 25
Heiner R.A. 434
Hellmich, S.N. 14
Herberich, D. 339
Herbert Simon 1
herding 257
    behaviour in financial market 72
    and conventions in financial markets 126
Hernández-Murillo, R. 24
Herrmann, A. 18
Herrmann, B. 370, 371
Hershfield, H.E. 323
Hertwig, R. 75
heterogeneity 358
    in ABM framework 44
    human agents in humans 37
heuristics, algorithms and behavioural bias 124–32
    and biases methodological approach 4
    business investment heuristics 128–31
    description 124
    optimism bias and animal spirits 131–2
    shifting risk and time preferences 126–8
    SMEs' investment activity 125
    status quo bias, conventions and herding 125–6
    use of 34–5
Hidalgo, M. 113, 114
hierarchical cluster analysis 402–7
    capitalism 402–7
    cluster method 403–5
    Dendrogram clustering notions 404
    distance metric 404
    reliability analysis of clusters 406
    statements in the questionnaire, examples 403
    Ward's method 405
Higgins, J.P. 179
higher-order design of bootstrapping mechanisms 37
higher-order thinking and reasoning processes 50–51
Hilario, M. 46
Hill, A.L. 452
Holton, G. 108
Homo economicus 63, 64, 67, 68, 71, 111, 287, 329, 353
Homo sapiens 61, 62, 64, 66, 67, 473
Homo sociologicus 481
Horne, C. 337

Horowitz, J.K. 382
Hotelling, H. 85, 421, 422
Houser, D. 373
humans' computational capabilities, limitations of 1
Hume, D. 80, 81, 87, 89, 356, 357
Hurwicz, L. 428, 434, 435
hyperbolic discounting 165, 333, 335, 342, 344

identity or self-image factor 25
impartial spectator (IS) 321–5, 353–4
inaccurate perceptions 163
incentives 81
    economic and social 354–6, 366
        effects of extrinsic motivations 355–6
        extrinsic motivation 354–5
        intrinsic motivation 355
        motivations 354–5
        penalty system 356
        pro-social activities 354
        pro-social behaviour 355, 366
        pure altruism 355
        reputation mechanism 356
    in economic research 85–7
        academic quality 86
        empirical economics 86
        policy-irrelevant trade models 86
        self-referential peer review system 86
    and pro-social behavior 88
income 214
    evaluation 23
    nonmarket time trade-off 159
    and scores on (global) happiness, relationship 22
incomplete and stockout markets in pandemic 297–9
    demand exceeding its ability to resupply the market, illustration 298
    demand shock quickly overcomes resupply ability, illustration 299
    incomplete at point (C) and zero 297
    increase in demand 297
    markets response to changes in demand by regulating prices, illustration 297
incrementalism
    on groups and power 87–8
        group dynamics 88
        incentives and pro-social behavior 88
        notion of group identity 87–8
        preferences and information and intrinsic valuations 88
        social norms 87–8
    on love 88–9
        notion of pure altruism 89
        social virtues 89
        split-screen approach 89

Inderst, R. 227
individuals and choice making 3
individual self-command 354
inequality 314–15
inequality aversion 334, 358–9
inflation, associations with 401
information, lack of 5
informational complexity, measures of 41
information on calories 250
inheritance 127, 215
in-home displays (IHDs) 337
institutional trust 315–16
instrumentalism and logical positivism 62–4
　'as if' method 63
　auxiliary and generative forms of assumptions 64
　economic events and market behaviour set foundations 62
　unobservables in hard data 63
instrumental variable methods and selected applications 273–7
　2SLS regression method 275–6
　applications of 275–7
　built environment to influence healthy lifestyles 276–7
　environment for physical activity 276
　gender-based obesity effect on labour market outcomes 275–6
　genetic information 275
　IV approach 274–5
　overview of 273–5
　regression model 273–4
　selection bias 273
　sources in observational studies 274
intercommunications between and among minds 327
intergroup representations 113
interpersonal trust 309–10, 316
intervention
　impact of 271–2, 279
　for intervention 269
intransitive preferences 15
intrinsic motivation 9, 219, 332, 334–5, 339, 354–6, 366
intrinsic valuations 88
introspection 14, 46, 80
intuition
　economic man, assumption of 328–9
　Keynes see Keynes, J.M.
　Knight see Knight, F.
　risk, uncertainty and profit 329–30
　　conception of goal 329
　　errors in judgement 329
　　limitations of theoretical economics 329–30
　　mental rambling 330

　　ordinary decisions in life 330
　　practical omniscience 329
　　reaching a goal 329
　Smith see Smith, A.
involuntary unemployment 164, 191, 192
Ito, K. 337, 340

James, W. 37
Janoff-Bulman, R. 22
Jeske, K.-J. 434
Jiang, H. 182
Johnson, E.J. 18
Jöhr, W.A. 140
Joireman, J.A. 24
Jorgenson D.W. 125, 128–31
Juglar, C. 138
'just-in-time' preference construction 82–3

Kahn, M.E. 338
Kahneman, D. 4, 6, 16–19, 22, 36, 48, 69, 85, 127, 143, 146, 153, 165, 228, 243, 245, 290, 321, 322, 325, 326
Kaljonen, M. 482
Kamas, L. 315
Kao, Y.-F. 32, 42
Karelitz, T. 434
Katona, G. 123, 128, 141, 142, 329
Kauffman, S.A. 44
Kesternich, M. 335
Keynes, J.M. 93, 123–6, 128, 132, 137, 140, 141, 145, 257, 321
　early beliefs 325
　expectations about the future 324
　forecasts 325–6
　long-term expectations and investment 325–6
　orthodox economics 326–7
　time gap in making forecasts 325
Keynesian principles 125–6
Kirchler, E. 110
Klein, G.A. 226
Klein, L.R. 141
K-lines 36, 45
Knetsch, J.L. 17, 377–83, 389–92
Knight F.H. 65, 123, 321, 327–30
Knightian risk, definition 123
Knightian uncertainty 123–4, 130
knowledge
　of maximisation 327
　of self and others 327–8
　on sports and physical activity 252
Koop, S.H.A. 342
Kosowsky, H. 482
Kőszegi, B. 412
Kranton, R.E. 25, 87, 88, 293
Krishnamurthi, L. 23

Kruglanski, A.W. 230
Krugman, P. 86, 87
Kuhn, T.S. 147
Kunda, Z. 48
Kupers, R. 39

labour, behavioural economics 153–4
  bounded rationality approach 154
  errors or biases in labour market decision-making 163–6
  neoclassical approach 154–6
  non-labour market income and 161–2
  sub-optimal decisions 153–4
  target approach 156–61
  unemployment insurance and 162–3
  see also labour supply
labour-leisure choice, model of 154
labour market
  discrimination 161
  indifference curves 158
labour supply
  curve 154, 160
  determinants of 166
  model of labour-leisure choice 154
  neoclassical approach 154–6
    backwards-bending labour supply curve 155
    labour supply curve 154
    minimal acceptable wage, increase in 154
    model of labour-leisure choice 154
    problem in neoclassical model 155
    s-shaped labour supply curve 155–6
    substitution effect 154
  and non-labour market income 161–2
  s-shaped curve 155–6
  target approach 156–61
    discouraged worker effect 160
    income-nonmarket time trade-off 159
    increasing nonmarket time 159
    labour market discrimination 161
    labour market indifference curves 158
    labour supply curve and target income 160
    political-legal environment, effect of 160
    real target income 156–7
    s-shaped labour curves 156
    target theory 156
    trade-off between market income and nonmarket activities 158
  target income 160
  unemployment insurance and 162–3
Laibson, D. 23, 24, 126
Lamla, M. 114
Lancaster, K.J. 25
Lange, A. 336
Lawson, T. 65

laypeople's evaluations of expert authority
  confidence heuristic 231
  elaboration likelihood model 230
  epistemic authority (EA) 229–30
  overconfidence effect 231
  white-coat effect 231
Legardez, A. 114
Lehmann, B.A. 456
Leibenstein, H. 5, 8, 172–4, 178, 190–197, 200, 201, 258, 261, 262, 326
Leiser, D. 9, 110, 401, 408
Levav, J. 215
Li, J. 279
Liberman, V. 232
life expectancy 164, 246
Lindsey, C. 23
List, J.A. 17, 334
Liu, C. 215
Lo, A.W. 34
localised trust 310
Loer, K. 473, 484
Loewenstein, G. 14–16, 74
logical positivism 62, 64
  see also instrumentalism and logical positivism
long periods of high stress 290
long-term
  changes 17
  evaluation 482
  expectations and investment 325–6
  savings 213–14
  unemployment, effects 164
Lopez, D.L. 232
loss aversion 17, 23, 165, 323
  18-item verbal questionnaire 18
  endowment effect 18
  willingness to accept the loss of object in possession (WTA) 18
  willingness to pay to acquire the object (WTP) 18
lottery task for use in large surveys 19
love as additional data points 95
love principle 94
lower subjective value of money 211
Lutter, M. 478
Lynne, G.D. 343

machine learning (ML) 40, 300
  and econometrics 52
  methods applied in economics-related fields 47
Mahmoudi, M. 10, 430, 434, 435
Maki, U. 63, 65
maladaptation 34
Maller, C. 479
Malthus, T. 91–3

managerial quality
  effect on firm productivity 184
  stochastic frontier modelling 184
  technical efficiency in NZ 184–5
  and TFP of firms 185
managerial x-efficiency theory of firm 193–5
  competitive pressures 194
  co-operation and trust 195
  Golder Rule solution 195
  managerial output and average cost 194
  x-inefficient preferences 193
managerial x-inefficiency 172
Manevska-Tasevska, G. 175
Manson, S.M. 45
March, J.C. 190
Marfaing, B. 339
market forces 63, 172, 182, 221, 258, 260
market logic 478
market mechanisms with human interactions 67
Markov switching model, business cycle 145
Marschak, J. 18, 430, 431
Marx, K. 93
Masclet, D. 373
massive parallel information integration 48
mass panic 291
materials 96, 297, 480–481
Mateu, G. 373
mathematical constrained optimisation
    techniques 130
mathematical expectations modelling 140–141
Maynard, J. 93
Maynard, L. 23
Mazumdar, T. 23
MBE see modern behavioural economics (MBE)
McBride, D.M. 44
McCarthy, J. 34, 47
McConnell, K.E. 382
McGraw, A.P. 215
media and stock markets 104
Mehnert, T. 22
Meier-Pesti, K., E. 110
Melkonyan, T. 430
mental accounting 23, 213–16
  appropriate spending 215
  current assets 213
  current spendable income 213
  definition 213
  emotional accounting studies 215
  income 214
  inheritance 215
  long-term savings 213–14
  pride-tagged money 214
  relational earmarking 215
  surprised-tagged money 215
  unhappy money 215
  windfall money 214

mental practices 480
mental rambling 330
mental well-being 452
meta-cognition 36
meta-economics 67, 72, 332, 343
micro, meso and macro foundations 49–50
  conventional economic and financial
    modelling methods 49
  quasi-micro foundations 49–50
Milkman, K.L. 455
Miller, G.F. 35, 272
'Mind as Machine' approach 44
mind reading 327, 328
MINDSPACE 484
minimal acceptable wage, increase in 154
Minsky, M. 33, 36, 41, 44, 46, 48
Minson, J.A. 232
Mishra, A. 217
misinterpretation 93
missing data problem 270
Mitchener, K. 144
mobile social commerce 47
mobility data 50
Models of My Life (Simon, H.) 35
modern behavioural economics (MBE) 32
  interpretation of bounded rationality 53
  and Olympian rationality 40
  theories in 42
modern-day research culture
  accountability theatre 96
  divine inspiration view of research 96
  need for a realeconomik approach 99
  notion of pre-registration plans 97
  prior hypotheses 96
  randomista culture 97
  scientific articles 98
  second-guessing 98
Mojzisch, A. 232
Moliner, P. 8
Mollen, S. 458
money
  associated with achievement 219
  attitudes 219–20
  'a bias for the whole' 217
  cash usage 217
  coin and a note, subjective value of 218
  decreasing marginal utility 210
  definition 209
  denomination and physical attributes 217
  desire for money 219
  dichotomy between instrumental and symbolic
    meaning 210
  difficulties in money valuations 211
  dirty money or bloody money, concepts of 216
  factors affecting subjective value of money
    210–219

fluency effect on subjective valuations 217
interpersonal and intrapersonal regulation 209
lower subjective value of money 211
moral history 216
objective *vs.* subjective 210–211
petty cash or loose change 217
physical features of 216–18
preference of non-stolen over stolen money 216
priming 220–221
purchasing power 210
relational earmarking 216
relative disutility of coins 218
subjective valuation 210–219
symbolic meaning of money 219–21
symbol or sign 210
see also money, value of
money, value of
  decreasing marginal utility 210
  difficulties in money valuations 211
  factors affecting subjective value of money 210–219
  lower subjective value of money 211
  objective *vs.* subjective 210–211
  purchasing power 210
  subjective valuation 210–219
  symbol or sign 210
money attitudes 220–221
  Love of Money Scale 220
  Money Attitude Scale (MAS) 219
  Money Attitudes Questionnaire (MAQ) 220
  Money Beliefs and Behaviour Scale (MBBS) 219
  Money Ethics Scale (MES) 219
money illusion 212–13
money priming 220–221
money valuations, difficulties in 211
Moody, J. 452
Moore, G.E. 325
Mora, T. 451
morality and sustainability
  coercive state and privatisation 363
  collective action problems 362
  common-pool resources 362–3
  community management 363
  concept of the impartial spectator 353
  economic and social incentives 354–6
    effects of extrinsic motivations 355–6
    extrinsic motivation 354–5
    intrinsic motivation 355
    motivations 354–5
    penalty system 356
    pro-social activities 354
    pro-social behaviour 355, 366
    pure altruism 355
    reputation mechanism 356

environmental degradation and resource depletion 362
equilibrium resource extraction 365
governing the commons 361–5
individual self-command 354
and pro-environmental preference 364–5
public goods and charitable giving 359–61
  altruism 360
  conditional cooperators 360
  pro-social behaviour 359
  provision and contribution 361
  punishment 360
  rational and selfish free-riders 360
  volunteering 360–361
  warm glow 361
resource extraction and conservation 363–5
self-enforcement 363
self-interest 353
selfish or pro-environmental behaviour 363
selfish preferences 364–5
social preferences 356–9
  distributional preferences 358–9
  fairness 359
  heterogeneity 358
  inequality aversion 358
  self-centred inequality aversion 358
  self-interested hypothesis 357
  social incentives and 357
  sympathy 357
theory of conscience 353
tragedy of commons 362
Morewedge, C.K. 418
Moscovici, S. 106, 108
motivated preferences
  advertising *see* advertising and motivated preferences
  applications and evidence 416–24
  classic cognitive dissonance 420–421
  comparative statics
    backwards-glancing agent 417
    forward-looking agent 415
  complementary adjustment 414
  endowment effect 418
  habit formation 418–20
  hyper-complementary adjustment 416
  intensities of initial preference for the product 422
  loss aversion account of endowment 418
  possibility of endowment 414
  prices in markets with differentiated products 421–3
  quality 413–14
  self-persuasion 423–4
  spatial competition model 421
  sunk-cost effects *see* sunk-cost effects and habit formation

theoretical modelling 413–16
theory of 25
utility 413
motivation 84, 354–5
   assumptions, microeconomic 84
   financial advice 235–6
   incentives *see* incentives
motivational boosts 481–2
Mullainathan, S. 14, 52, 115, 338
multi-dimensional scaling (MDS) 406–9
   2D or 3D map 408
   good and bad changes in economic indicators 408
   good-begets-good (GBG) heuristic 409
multiple macroeconomic equilibria 143–4
multiplier-accelerator models 126
Murphy, R.O. 21
Mussio, I. 10, 459
Muth, J.F. 142
mutual funds 19, 112, 228, 229
'my-side thinking' in social cognition 232

Nagler, M.G. 10, 25
naïve realism phenomenon 236
narrative economics 46–7, 257
National School Lunch Program, in Florida school 272
Neaigus, A. 453
Neighbors, C. 447
neoclassical behavioural norms 3–4
neoclassical model of fixed asset investment 128
neoclassical-type behaviour 190
Nerlove, M. 141
networks, social 449–53
   application 450
   depression and low self-esteem 452
   determinant of social, cognitive and emotional development 449
   mental well-being 452
   network social capital 452
   overweight adolescents 451–2
   peer effects 449
   peer groups influence 453
   physical activity, nutrition and obesity 451–2
   smoking 450
   social networks 449–50
   visible behaviour change 453
network science 45
network social capital 452
neural networks, study of 46
neuroscience 33, 50–51
   higher-order thinking and reasoning processes 50–51
   pro-social behaviours 51
   techniques, use of 44–5

Newell, A. 35, 37, 44
Newton, I. 95, 325
Newtonian-style mathematics 47
next-generation quantum computing 300
Nietzsche, F. 72
nine-item triple-dominance measure 21
Njeru, J.W. 452
no ambiguity
   experimental design 431
   treatment 429
   vs. total ambiguity, experiment to compare behaviour 430–431
Nofsinger, J.R. 144
Nolan, J. 338
non-economic variables and errors/biases in labour market decision-making 163–6
   biased decision-making 165
   bounded rationality approach 166
   errors and biases approach 165–6
   hyperbolic discounting 165
   inaccurate perceptions 163
   involuntary unemployment 164
   long-term unemployment, effects 164
   loss aversion 165
   present or status quo bias 165
   psychological variables 164
non-equilibrium thermodynamics 45
non-linear dynamic systems theory 45
nonlinear science 47
normative influence and physical activity 446
normative nudges use of 457–60
   direct and indirect methods of information 458
   environmentally conscious behaviour 457
   in health 457–8
   informational interventions 458–9
   photographs and images, use of 458–9
   pro-social behaviours 458
   social preferences 459
   vaccinations, benefits of 459
norm nudges, use of 457–60
norms and implications, for healthy behaviour 445–9
   alcohol over-consumption 447–8
   authoritative parenting style 448
   COVID-19 pandemic and 447
   descriptive norm 445
   determinants of health-related behaviours 446
   effect on behaviour 446
   exaggerating the norm of peers' risky behaviour 447
   normative influence and physical activity 446
   obesity 448
   peers' drinking 447–8

physical activity and food consumption in childhood and adolescence 448
SAGE group on immunisations 447
social influence 448
social norms 445
static or dynamic 445
vaccinations 446–7
North, D.C. 1, 72
Norton, E.C. 275, 276
Norvig, P. 39, 46
Nowak, M.A. 374
NPV/DCF algorithm/techniques 130–131
nudges 333
    description 454
    narrative 4
    plus 460–461
    and social practice theories 482
nutrition-based intervention, in daycare settings 272

Oberholzer-Gee, F. 342
obesity 448
    and overweight 246–8
        food expenditure and per capita GDP 247
        life expectancy 246
        obesity-related death rates 247
        preference formation 247
        price theory and obesity 247–8, 262
    related death rates 247
objectification 106, 113
objective *vs.* subjective value of money 210–211
objects, representation of 108–9
    causalities simplification 110–111
    concept of *homo oeconomicus* 111
    good-begets-good 110
    scale for measuring or evaluating 111
    simplification
        by anchoring 109
        by categorisation 109
        of globalisation 109
        of objects 109–10
        by trivialisation 109
    thema of good and evil 111
O'Donoghue, T. 15, 16, 24
OECD Corporate Governance Factbook 2015, 181
O'Gorman, P.F. 67
Oishi, S. 475
one-size-fits-all solutions 286
On the Origin of Species by Means of Natural Selection (Darwin) 91
ontological realism 65
Oppenheimer, D.M. 217, 218
optimal heuristics in bounded rationality 255
optimal norms 4

optimal outcomes 5, 255
optimism bias
    and animal spirits 131–2
    and overconfidence effect 323–4
Organisation for Economic Co-operation and Development (OECD) 172–3, 175, 179, 181–2, 185, 217, 338, 478, 484
orthodox economics 326–7
Osman, B.A. 276
Osman, M. 279
Ostrom, E. 363
other-regarding unselfish-type behaviours 286
Ottaviani, M. 227
outcome utility 16
overconfidence 475–6
overconfidence effect 231, 323–4
overly restrictive models 141
over-optimism 138–9, 147
overweight
    adolescents 451–2
    and obesity rates, determinants of 253

pandemics, behavioural impact of
    anxiety-driven supermarket runs 295
    CAS and various aspects 287–8
    complex systems *see* complex systems and pandemic behaviour
    consumer behaviour *see* consumer behaviour during pandemic
    decision-making 289–92
    demand-driven supply problems and stockouts 294–5
    fear and risk aversion 294
    incomplete and stockout markets 297–9
    one-size-fits-all solutions 286
    other-regarding unselfish-type behaviours 286
    panic buying 294–5
    supply chains *see* supply chains and economics during pandemic
panic buying 285–6, 294–5, 299
particularised trust *see* localised trust
passions 80, 322, 354
pattern-based expectations 146
payback periods (PBP) 130–131
pay for performance (P4P) programme, impact of 279
peak-and-end rule 16
Pedersen, S. 448
peer effects 10, 163, 272, 332, 343, 346, 445, 449–50, 460
peer groups influence 453
peer pressure 1, 5, 252, 344
peers drinking 447–8
penalty system 356
Penrose, E.T. 190

perfect knowledge and information 68
performance outcomes 259, 261
performance x-efficiency, level of 260–261
personalisation strategies to disadvantaged groups 482
Peters, N.V. 10
petty cash or loose change 217
photographs and images, use of 458–9
physical activity 254
   and diet programmes, impact of 271
   and food consumption in childhood and adolescence 448
   nutrition and obesity 451–2
physical manifestations of practices 480
Pibernik, R. 233
Pigou, A.C. 138–40, 325
Pindyck, R.S. 129
Pingle, M. 10, 430, 434, 435
Pittman, T.S. 215
planned behaviour, theory of 24–5, 446
Plato 308
playfulness 80, 91–3, 95
Polanyi, K. 479
policies using financial incentives 268
policy effect, identification 278
policy-irrelevant trade models 86
policymakers and community, narratives for 43
political-legal environment, effect of 160
politico-economic environments 475–6
Popkowski Leszczyc, P.T. 424
population density and pro-sociality 477
positive and negative reciprocity and trust 23
positive opinion condition 233
potential bias in advice taking 227
power law and power function 25
practical omniscience 329
practice theories, integrating 478
predicted utility 16
preferences
   dynamic inconsistency of 15
   formation 247
   and information 88
   of non-stolen over stolen money 216
   pro-environmental 364–5
   risk *see* risk preferences
   social *see* social preferences
pre-registration plans, notion of 97
present bias 85, 165, 342, 475–6
Preston, A. 315
Price, M.K. 343
Price, P.C. 231, 247–61
price increase 23, 211, 342, 401, 422
price theory and obesity 247–9, 262
pride-tagged money 214–15
Prigogine, I. 38

prior hypotheses 96
prior research 81, 227, 229–31, 452, 456
procedurally rational process 124
procedural utility 16
procrastination 337, 455
pro-environmental behaviour (PEB) 332–6, 341–4, 357, 363, 445
professional forecasters, survey of 142
professional surveyors 400
profit maximisation 1, 3, 64, 124, 172, 191, 203, 337
profit maximisers or satisficers 255–6
Pronin, E. 236
pro- or antisocial engagement 475
propensity score (PS) matching strategy 279–80
pro-social activities 354, 366
pro-social behaviours 51, 355, 359, 366, 458
prosocial punishments 370–371, 373
prospect theory 18, 70, 291
psychoanalysis 14
Psychological Analysis of Human Behavior (Katona) 329
psychological and non-economic variables 252
psychological and sociological obstacles 257–8
psychological attitude 25
psychological insights
   application of 14
   integration of 25
psychological model of dual-system 454
psychological motivations 235–6
   in financial advice taking 227–9
   mutual funds 228, 229
   prior research 229
   protecting against cognitive dissonance 227, 228
   regret 227–8
psychological variables 141, 159, 163–4, 245, 252, 261
public goods and charitable giving 359–61
   altruism 360
   conditional cooperators 360
   pro-social behaviour 359
   provision and contribution 361
   punishment 360
   rational and selfish free-riders 360
   volunteering 360–361
   warm glow 361
punishments 360
   antisocial *see* antisocial punishment
   prosocial 370–371, 373
   public goods and charitable giving 360
purchasing power 8, 210–212, 217–19, 221, 252, 254
pure altruism 88–9, 355, 357, 361
Putler, Daniel S. 23

Qian, C. 25
quadriplegics, adaptation in 22
qualitative inquiry 485
qualitative/quantitative understanding 43
quality of management and x-efficiency 200–201
quasi-micro foundations 49–50

Rabellino, D. 371
Rabin, M. 21, 24, 358, 412
Rad, S.A. 182
Raghubir, P. 212, 217
Raj, S.P. 23
Rand, D.G. 374
RAND Health Insurance Experiment (HIE) 269
randomisation, purpose of 270
randomised controlled trials (RCTs) 269–73, 280
   applications and limitations 271–3
   in BPP 484
   effect 269
   estimation issues 270
   impact of interventions 271–2
   impact of physical activity and diet programmes 271
   intervention for intervention 269
   missing data problem 270
   National School Lunch Program, in Florida school 272
   nutrition-based intervention in daycare settings 272
   purpose of the randomisation 270
   regression-based methods 273
randomista culture 97
random search 91
Rao, R.C. 424
Ratchford, B.T. 25
Rateau, P. 8
rational-agent or *acting rationally* approach 40
rational and selfish free-riders 360
rational errors 5–6
rational expectations 142–4
   challenges and criticism 143
   concept of sunspots 143
   models 123
   multiple macroeconomic equilibria 143–4
   systematic, errors 142
   theory 129
rationality 328
   assumptions and bounded rationality 68–9
rational x-inefficiency 199–200
Rattaphon, W. 10
Read, D. 16, 20
Read, N.L. 20
realeconomik
   anomalies and biases 85
   'as-if' assumptions 82

   certainty illusion 85
   composite social goods or self-affirming goods 83
   dichotomy between strategies of dominance and submission 94
   elements in Darwin's approach 91
   ethical professional relationships 93
   expected utility formula 84
   fixed preference maps, notion of 82
   fixity of perception and preference 84
   fundamental microeconomic assumptions 82–5
   fundamental scientific creation 92
   incentives in economic research 85–7
   incrementalism
      on groups and power 87–8
      on love 88–9
   'just-in-time' preference construction 82–3
   love as additional data points 95
   love principle 94
   misinterpretation 93
   modern-day research culture 96
   motivations 84
   notion of fixed preference maps 82
   notion of utility function 83
   playfulness 91, 93
   present bias and framing bias 85
   random search 91
   reams of data 94
   research culture *see* modern-day research culture
   social behaviour and motivators 83
   use of 'to-and-fro sieving' of data 93–4
   utility functions, types of 83–4
   zero costs to mental effort 84–5
realism of assumptions 60–61
real target income 156–7
   definition 156–7
   increase in 157
   wants and desires of individuals 157
reciprocal charity, model of 21
reciprocal fairness 315
Reckwitz, A. 479–81
recognition-primed decision model 226
regression-based methods 269, 273
regression model 270, 273–5, 278
regret 227–8
Reicks, M. 458
Reid, L. 479
Reinhart, C.M. 144
Reisch, L.A. 10, 333, 334, 340
relational earmarking 215, 216
relative disutility of coins 218
reliability analysis of clusters 406
remembered utility 16

Repetto, A. 24
representation, phenomenology of 107–8
representational realism 65
reputation mechanism 356
resource conservation 9, 354, 363–6
resource extraction 363–5
risk 122–4
  attitudes 290–291
  averse and risk-taking 291–2
  constrained optimisation techniques 124
  Knightian risk
  negative impacts of uncertainty 123–4
  perception and uncertainty 290
  probability of 291
  procedurally rational process 124
  rational expectations models 123
Risk, Uncertainty, and Profit (Knight) 329
risk, uncertainty and profit 329–30
risk and time preferences 126–8
  behavioural life-cycle models 127
  consumer sentiment, analyses of 128
  emotional influences on the macroeconomy 128
  experimental evidence 127
  Thaler's mental accounting model 127
risk and uncertainty
  content-blind norms 75
  and financial modelling with time factors 74–6
  fundamental uncertainty, treatment of 76
  rules of probability 75
  zero-risk and turkey illusions 75
risk aversion
  and ambiguity 433
  domain-specific risk-attitude scale (DOSPERT) 19
  lottery task for use in large surveys 19
  risk-perception scale 19
  risk preferences and outcomes 18
risk literacy boosts 481–2
risk-perception scale 19
risk preferences
  asymmetric value function 24
  and outcomes 18
risky choice behaviour and ambiguity 437–8
Rogers, T. 338, 455
Rogoff, K. 144
Ross, W.T. 16
Rötheli, T.F. 8, 120, 144–6
Rouquette, M.-L. 401
Rousseau, J.J. 80, 81
Ruggeri, K. 483
rules of probability 75
Ruseski, J.E. 276

Russell, S.J. 39, 46
Rustichini, A. 356

SAGE group on immunisations 447
Sari, N. 9, 276, 279
SARS-CoV-2 pandemic 477
satisficing 3, 34–5, 48, 174, 248, 253
Savage, D.A. 9, 286, 287
scarcity and financial stress 23
Schelling, T.C. 43
Schmeidler, D. 428
Schubert, C. 333
Schultz, P.W. 337, 338, 342
Schultze, T. 233
Schumpeter, J.A. 140
scientific articles 97–8
second-guessing 98
selection bias 272–3
self-centred inequality aversion 358
self-control interventions and physical environments 474–5
self-enforcement 363
self-identity 333, 339
self-interested hypothesis 357
selfish or pro-environmental behaviour 363
selfish preferences 80, 362, 364–5
self-organisation theory 45
self-organised criticality 45
self-persuasion 421, 423–4
self-referential peer review system 86
self-serving attributional bias 236
Sent, E.-M. 32
Sexton, A.L. 336
Sexton, S.E. 336
sexually transmitted diseases (STDs) 449
Shafir, E. 115, 212
Shakespeare, W. 45, 94
Shefrin, H.M. 190, 213
Shelton, M. 458
Shiller, R.J. 44, 145, 256, 327
Shogren, J.F. 333, 377–80, 382
short-term job searches 163
Shove, E. 479, 480
Simon, H.A. 1–4, 6, 32, 35, 39, 44, 46, 64, 68, 69, 90, 99, 124, 143, 147, 153, 154, 190, 243–5, 261, 321, 326, 378
Simonson, I. 16
simplification
  by anchoring 109
  by categorisation 109
  and complexity, balance between 483–4
    MINDSPACE 484
    randomised controlled trials (RCTs) in BPP 484
  of globalisation 109

of objects 109–10
by trivialisation 109
Sims, C.A. 146
situated, distributed and embodied (SDE) cognition 48
Sloman, A. 36, 37, 41, 44, 48
slow thinking 36
smart decision-making 5–6
 environmental factors 5
 firm survival 5–6
 lack of decision-making capabilities 5
 lack of information 5
 lack of power in decision-making process 5
 peer pressure 5
 preferred choices of individuals 5
 rational errors 5
 sociological variables 5
 sub-optimal outcomes 5
 x-inefficiency 5
SMEs' investment activity 125
Smith, A. 14, 80, 81, 87, 321–6, 353, 354, 357
 and intuition
  cognitive (optical) illusions 322–3
  commercial society of strangers 321
  dual processing, intuition and analysis 322
  fairness 324
  impartial spectator (IS) 322
  loss aversion 323
  optimism bias and overconfidence effect 323–4
  spatial intelligence 323
  sympathy 321–2
  valuing out-of-pocket costs 323
Smith, E.E. 232
Smith, N.R. 452
Smith, V.L. 4, 6, 69, 70, 190
smoking 450
 ban policies, impact of 279
Snell, J.S. 16
social, cultural and emotive dimensions and economic outcomes 71–2
 biases and irrationality 72
 cultural beliefs and traditions 72
 emotion 71–2
 herd behaviour in financial market 72
social and other-regarding preferences 334
social behaviour and motivators 83
social classes, role of 115–16
social determinants of rationality 478–9
 market logic 478
 order in production and distribution 479
 Pierre Bourdieu's oeuvre 478
social distance and trust 314
social distancing and isolation protocol 293

social ecology
 and behavioural public policy 474
 as moderator 477
 multiple effects of characteristics of 477
social heritage 105
social ills 80
social incentives, governing commons with 361–5
 coercive state and privatisation 363
 collective action problems 362
 common-pool resources 362–3
 community management 363
 environmental degradation and resource depletion 362
 equilibrium resource extraction 365
 and pro-environmental preference 364–5
 resource extraction 363–4
 resource extraction and conservation 365
 self-enforcement 363
 selfish or pro-environmental behaviour 363
 selfish preferences 364–5
 tragedy of the commons 362
social influence 121, 126, 448–9, 483
social isolation and travel bans 293
social networks 449–50
social norms 87–8, 293, 445
 interventions and geographic characteristics 475
social preferences 21–2, 24, 356–9, 459
 altruism and public good contributions 21
 altruistic preferences 21–2
 distributional preferences 358–9
 fairness 359
 heterogeneity 358
 household utility function 24
 inequality aversion 358
 model of reciprocal charity 21
 nine-item triple-dominance measure 21
 self-centred inequality aversion 358
 self-interested hypothesis 357
 social incentives and 357
 sympathy 357
 utility function of two-player outcomes 24
social representation 104–5
 anchoring 106–7
 and behaviour, links between 112
 causalities simplification 110–111
 cognitive elements 107
 collectively produced 108
 complexity environment 105
 concept of *homo economicus* 111
 cooperative strategy 114
 definition 105
 development of 106–7
 dispersion of information 106

epistemic schemes as themata 108
field approaches, examples 112
focus phenomenon 106
good-begets-good 110
intergroup representations 113
links between social representations and behaviour 112
objectification 106
of objects or economic phenomena 108–9
organised 107
phenomenology of 107–8
role in economic behaviour 112–14
scale for measuring or evaluating 111
shared within the social group 107
simplification by anchoring 109
simplification by categorisation 109
simplification by trivialisation 109
simplification of globalisation 109
simplification of objects 109–10
socially useful 108
thema of good and evil 111
social virtues 89
social welfare payments/unemployment insurance 161
socio-ecological and behavioural interventions 476
socio-ecological perspectives
 advanced BPP 473
 BE and BPP 473
 behavioural public policy *see* behavioural public policy (BPP)
 behaviour change 479
 diverse methods, use of 484–5
 dual effects of characteristic of social ecology 477
 linking social ecology and behavioural public policy 474
 market logic 478
 meanings, competencies and materials 479
 mental practices 480
 modifications in the choice environment 474
 multiple effects of characteristics of social ecology 477
 natural environments, to enhance mental resources 475
 order in production and distribution 479
 physical manifestations of practices 480
 population density and pro-sociality 477
 practice theories, integrating 478
 present bias, overconfidence and politico-economic environments 475–6
 process studies 474
 pro- or antisocial engagement 475
 qualitative inquiry 485

 relevance 477–80
 self-control interventions and physical environments 474–5
 simplification and complexity, balance between 483–4
 social determinants of rationality 478–9
 social ecology as moderator 477
 social-norm interventions and geographic characteristics 475
 socio-ecological and behavioural interventions 476
 socio-ecological psychology 473, 476–7
 stable and low-density neighbourhoods 475
 target-group approach 485
socio-institutional constraints 249
sociological variables 5, 256, 259–60, 262
Sodany, T. 8
softer empirical approaches, use of 43
soft/non-coercive nudging 6
Solow, R.M. 153
Soman, D. 217
Somerville, J. 24
Spanish Flu (H1N1) pandemic of 1918, 296
spatial competition model 421
spatial intelligence 323
Spiess, J. 52
split-screen approach 89
sports and health and fitness industries
 basic methodological underpinnings 244–6
 and behavioural economics *see* behavioural economics and obesity
 behavioural economics and health, fitness and sports industries 263
 bounded rationality approach 243
 causal analysis 245
 decision-making capabilities 245, 262
 emotions and decision making 243–4
 food expenditure and per capita GDP 247
 life expectancy 246
 obesity and overweight 246–8
 obesity-related death rates 247
 preference formation 247
 price theory and obesity 247–8, 262
 sub-optimal choices *see* sub-optimal choices in health and fitness industry
 sub-optimal outcomes 244
 systemic biases 246
 unrealistic assumptions 244
 x-efficiency theory and 257–61
Srivastava, J. 212, 217
s-shaped labour curves 155
stable and low-density neighbourhoods 475
standard economic model 14–17, 20, 22–5, 361
status quo bias 165
 conventions and herding 125–6

herding and conventions in financial markets 126
  Keynesian principles 125–6
  multiplier-accelerator models 126
stay-at-home moms and disabled 162
Sternberg, K. 35
Sternberg, R.J. 35
stock markets and fixed asset investments, connection 129
stock price prediction 47
Stone, E.R. 231
Strengers, Y. 479, 480
Strotz R.H. 126
Stutzer, A. 16
subjective valuation 210–219
subjective value of money, factors affecting 212–19
  mental accounting 213–16
  money illusion 212–13
  moral history of money 216
  physical features of money 216–18
  see also individual terms
sub-optimal choices in health and fitness industry 253–7, 262
  fast and frugal methodological approach 253–4
  herding 257
  optimal heuristics in bounded rationality 255
  physical activity 254
  profit maximisers/satisficers 255–6
  sub-optimal information environment 256–7
  sub-optimal outcomes for clients 255
sub-optimal consumption behaviour 248
sub-optimal decisions 153–4, 243–4, 246, 261
sub-optimal information environment 256–7
sub-optimal outcomes 5, 244
  for clients 255
subprime mortgage lending 60, 73
Subramaniam, V. 23
substitution effect 154–5, 157–9, 162, 166, 247, 377
sufficient and appropriate physical activity 251
sunk-cost bias 418–19
sunk-cost effects and habit formation 418–20
  action-based complementarities 419
  escalation of commitment, phenomenon of 419
  habit formation tendencies 419–20
  sunk-cost bias 418
sunspots, concept of 143
Sunstein, C.R. 4, 246, 333, 334, 340, 454, 483
supply chains and economics during pandemic 295–7
  forecasts 295
  as inward-looking 295
  rate of consumer-driven change 296–7

surprised-tagged money 215
survey data, drawback of 142
Sustainable Development Goals 50
sympathy 321–2, 324–5, 354, 356, 357
systematic errors 142, 345
systemic biases 245–6, 251, 262
systems theory 45–7
Szeidl, A. 412

Tajfel, H. 115
Talukdar, D. 23
Tang, F.-F. 9, 377–83, 389–92
Tang, T.L. P. 219
target approach 156–61
target-group approach 485
target theory 156
Tasimi, A. 216
tax rate, restructuring of 161–2
Taylor, M.J. 458
tech boom of the 1990s 139, 144
Templer, D.J. 219
Teraji, S. 9, 363, 365
Terrier, L. 339
Thagard, P. 48
Thaler, R.H. 4, 14, 15, 17, 127, 213, 214, 246, 321, 377–83, 389–92, 418, 454, 473, 474
thema of good and evil 111
The Theory of Moral Sentiments (Smith) 322–3, 353
theory of the firm, Coase's 1
'thinking fast and slow' 36
thinking humanly approach 39, 46
thinking rationally approach 39, 46
time 20
time gap in making forecasts 325
time preference 20, 23–4
  future time orientation 20
  quasi-hyperbolic discount function 23–4
  time orientation scale 20
  time-tradeoff questions 20
  willingness to delay gratification 20
Tinbergen, J. 141
Titmuss, R.M. 355, 356
'to-and-fro sieving' of data, use of 93–4
Tobacman J. 24
Todd, P.M. 131
Torgler, B. 7, 475
total ambiguity treatment 429, 431, 435, 439
total factor productivity (TFP) 173, 175–9, 184–5, 192
A Tract on Monetary Reform (Keynes) 324
trade cycle, characteristics 137–8
transcendental realism 65–6
Trautmann, S.T. 428
A Treatise of Human Nature (Hume) 356

A Treatise on Money (Keynes) 324
Treatise on the Family (Becker) 88
trigger rate of return 130
trust
   act of trusting 308–9
   categorisation 309–10
   cognitive ability and 314
   in context of societies 315–16
   definition 307–8
   dependent trades 312
   determinants 313–14
   determinants of 313–14
   disparities across disciplines 307–8
   and economic development 312–13
   in economics 308–9
   economic transactions 309
   game theory 309, 311
   generalised trust 310
   general social survey (GSS) 310–311
   and inequality 314–15
   institutional trust 315–16
   interpersonal trust 310
   localised trust 310
   measuring trust 310–312
   socio-demographic characteristics 313
   WVS 310–312
Tversky, A. 4, 6, 15, 18, 19, 69, 124, 127, 153, 165, 228, 243, 245, 321, 322, 325, 326
Tykocinski, O.E. 215

Udell, G.F. 145
Ulanowicz, R.E. 38
uncertainty management boosts 481–2
unemployment insurance and labour supply 162–3
unhappy money 215
unobservables, in hard data 63
unrealistic assumptions 49, 77, 202, 244, 308
Ute, W. 434
utility
   functions 83
   maximisation and expected utility theory 69–71
      assumption on utility 69–70
      EUT modelling of rational agent 70
      gains or losses relating to utility 70
   or welfare-maximising choices 248
   types of 83–4
      adaptive preference formation 17
      decision utility 16
      experienced utility 16
      long-term changes 17
      outcome utility 16
      peak-and-end rule 16
      predicted utility 16
      procedural utility 16
      remembered utility 16

vaccinations
   benefits of 459
   norms and implications for healthy behaviour 446–7
   social networks 450–451
valence of social norm 234
valuing out-of-pocket costs 323
van Bavel, R. 485
Van Beek, J. 20
van de Kuilen, G. 428
Van de Stadt, H. 19
Vandoros, S. 218
van Fraassen, B. 64, 66
Van Praag, B.M.S. 19, 23
Van Reenen, J. 172
Veblen, T.B. 81, 126
Velupillai, K.V. 32, 42
Vergès, P. 401
Verhoef, P.C. 16
veristic realism 64
Vermote, M. 459
Vickrey auction experiments with 60 repeated trials 378–85
   experiment one 378–83
      60 rounds programmed by Z-Tree 379
      comparison of WTA and WTP values 379–80
      earn tough competition 378
      Mann-Whitney test 382
      second-price auction 382–3
      trends of price means 381
      WTA and WTP values for ninth-price 381
   experiment three 391–3
      individual behaviour 393
      individual data 397–9
      price trends 393
      trading strategy 393
      transactional subject 393
      WTA and WTP values for fourth-price, comparisons 391–2
   experiment two 383–5
      individual behaviour in experiment two 389–90
      mean values of each subject 390
      overall mean value of WTP 383
      trends of price means 385
      WTA and WTP values for second- and ninth-price 384
Vignaux, G. 108
visible behaviour change 453
Voirin bow, F.N. 70

volunteering 360–361
Volz, K.G. 75
Vuri, D. 279

Wallace, J. 92
Ward, D.S. 272
Ward's method 405
warm glow 88–9, 334, 336, 361
Wärneryd, K.E 126
waste, empathy conservation framework
   behavioural biases 340–341
   impartiality and fairness 342
   other-regarding preferences 342
   social norms 341
water, empathy conservation framework
   behavioural biases 342
   social norms 342–3
      boomerang effect 343
      effect of social norms messages 343
      messages of a descriptive norm 342
      technical information 342–3
The Wealth of Nations (Smith) 353
Weber, E.U. 19
well-being 22–3
   adaptation in quadriplegics 22
   Day Reconstruction Method (DRM) 22
   income and scores on (global) happiness, relationship 22
   income evaluation 23
   utility and 22
Wernstedt, K. 341
white-coat effect 231
Whitehead, M. 473
Whitmarsh, L. 480
Williamson, O.E. 1
willingness to accept the loss of an object in possession (WTA) 18
willingness-to-accept (WTA) 18, 377–85, 388, 391–3
willingness to delay gratification 20
willingness-to-pay (WTP) 18, 211, 377–85, 391–3, 397–8
Wilson, C. 480
windfall money 214
Wong-Parodi, G. 339
WVS 310–312

x-efficiency plus theory of the firm 195–8
   behavioural narrative, curve BM 198
   effort-related modelling of the firm 197
   firm decision-makers and the power relationships 197
   labour and related costs 196
   labour costs, average costs and effort variability 198

   preferences for more own-efforts 196
   preferences of managers and owners 197
   wages and overall labour compensation 195–6
x-efficiency theories 163, 191–2
   of the firm 192–3
      perfect product market competition 192–3
      variability 192
   and sub-optimal sports performance 257–61
      demand and supply for quality health and fitness professionals 259
      errors in decision-making 260
      level of performance x-efficiency 260–261
      market forces 258
      performance outcomes 259, 261
      psychological and sociological factors 257
      psychological and sociological obstacles 257–8
x-efficiency theory for managerial quality
   behavioural perspectives
      firm ownership and performance 175
      firm technical inefficiencies 175
      flexibilities of x-efficiency 174
      managerial inefficiency 175
      optimal profit-maximising 174
      variations in managerial quality 175
   effect on firm productivity 184
   empirical model
      ownership structure and firm performance 176
      technical efficiency and firm productivity 176–9
   entrenchment and expropriation effects 181–3
      firms financial needs 181
      in Germany 182–3
      in NZ 182
      in Spain 182
      in Turkey 182
   high-yield work cultures and practices 185
   incentive and monitoring effects 183
   neoclassical perspectives
      cost minimisation 174
      performance variations 174
      productivity growth gaps 174
      TFP growth decomposition 179
   OECD countries, managerial quality, ownership and performance 179–81
      meta-regression analysis of ownership-performance relationship 179–80
      substantial effect size variations 181
   ownership-performance/productivity 173
   quality of managerial practices across firms 172–3
x-efficient and technical change 199
Xiao, E. 373

x-inefficiency 5
  managerial 172
  plus theory for employment 201–3
  rational 199–200
  smart decision-making 5

Yakusheva, O. 451
Yamagishi, T. 310
Yamauchi, K.T. 219
Yamin, P. 481

Yan, Ji 23
Yaniv, I. 232, 233, 235
Yazbeck, M. 451
Yeomans, M. 339

Zaleskiewicz, T. 8
Z-commodities 17
zero costs to mental effort 84–5
zero-risk and turkey illusions 75
Z-production technologies 17